ASPEN PUBLISHERS

Roth IRA Answer Book
Sixth Edition

by Gary S. Lesser, Esq., Michelle L. Ward, Esq., and Gregory Kolojeski, Esq.

Roth IRA Answer Book provides in-depth coverage of the administration and operation of Roth IRAs. A team of practicing experts analyzes the most recent developments in practice, as well as legislation, regulation, and law. It is the one resource that takes pension professionals step by step through all aspects of plan administration and compliance.

Highlights of the Sixth Edition

The *Roth IRA Answer Book, Sixth Edition*, includes:

- A fully revised chapter 3 on conversions, contribution recharacterization, and rollovers, and chapter 4 on voluntary distributions.

- Expanded coverage and more examples of the distribution ordering rules.

- Discussion of why a Roth IRA conversion after 2009 may or may not make sense and the mathematical and financial planning aspects of converting to a Roth IRA.

- An examination of how the removal of the $100,000 modified adjusted gross income (MAGI) limit for Roth conversions from an eligible retirement plan beginning after 2009 will effectively eliminate the income limit for contributing to a Roth IRA.

- Expanded coverage of special purposes distributions and repayments, including qualified recovery assistance distributions and qualified disaster recovery distributions.

- An examination of the circumstances that allow special-purpose distributions to be recontributed (i.e., repaid by being rolled over) to an eligible retirement plan, including a Roth IRA.

- Expanded coverage of the rollover rules applicable to certain airline payments, military death gratuities, Exxon Valdez settlements, and Servicemembers' Group Life Insurance (SGLI) to a Roth IRA.

Wolters Kluwer
Law & Business

- Expanded coverage of the qualified rollover rules that allow a direct "conversion" from an eligible retirement plan to a Roth IRA.

- Coverage of same-sex marriages, civil unions, domestic partnerships, and similar relationships in California, Connecticut, Hawaii, Maine, Massachusetts, New Hampshire, New Jersey, Oregon, Vermont, Washington, and the District of Columbia and how they affect an owner's or participant's beneficiary designation.

10/09

For questions concerning this shipment, billing, or other customer service matters, call our Customer Service Department at 1-800-234-1660.

For toll-free ordering, please call 1-800-638-8437.

ASPEN PUBLISHERS

Roth IRA Answer Book

Sixth Edition

Gary S. Lesser, Esq.
Michelle L. Ward, Esq.
Gregory Kolojeski, Esq.

Wolters Kluwer
Law & Business

AUSTIN   BOSTON   CHICAGO   NEW YORK   THE NETHERLANDS

© 2010 Aspen Publishers. All Rights Reserved.

No part of this publication may be reproduced or transmitted in any form or by any means, electronic or mechanical, including photocopy, recording, or any information storage and retrieval system, without permission in writing from the publisher. Requests for permission to reproduce content should be directed to the Aspen Publishers website at *www.aspenpublishers.com*, or a letter of intent should be faxed to the permissions department at 212-771-0803.

Printed in the United States of America

ISBN 978-0-7355-8455-6

1 2 3 4 5 6 7 8 9 0

About Wolters Kluwer Law & Business

Wolters Kluwer Law & Business is a leading provider of research information and workflow solutions in key specialty areas. The strengths of the individual brands of Aspen Publishers, CCH, Kluwer Law International and Loislaw are aligned within Wolters Kluwer Law & Business to provide comprehensive, in-depth solutions and expert-authored content for the legal, professional and education markets.

CCH was founded in 1913 and has served more than four generations of business professionals and their clients. The CCH products in the Wolters Kluwer Law & Business group are highly regarded electronic and print resources for legal, securities, antitrust and trade regulation, government contracting, banking, pension, payroll, employment and labor, and healthcare reimbursement and compliance professionals.

Aspen Publishers is a leading information provider for attorneys, business professionals and law students. Written by preeminent authorities, Aspen products offer analytical and practical information in a range of specialty practice areas from securities law and intellectual property to mergers and acquisitions and pension/benefits. Aspen's trusted legal education resources provide professors and students with high-quality, up-to-date and effective resources for successful instruction and study in all areas of the law.

Kluwer Law International supplies the global business community with comprehensive English-language international legal information. Legal practitioners, corporate counsel and business executives around the world rely on the Kluwer Law International journals, loose-leafs, books and electronic products for authoritative information in many areas of international legal practice.

Loislaw is a premier provider of digitized legal content to small law firm practitioners of various specializations. Loislaw provides attorneys with the ability to quickly and efficiently find the necessary legal information they need, when and where they need it, by facilitating access to primary law as well as state-specific law, records, forms and treatises.

Wolters Kluwer Law & Business, a unit of Wolters Kluwer, is headquartered in New York and Riverwoods, Illinois. Wolters Kluwer is a leading multinational publisher and information services company.

ASPEN PUBLISHERS SUBSCRIPTION NOTICE

This Aspen Publishers product is updated on a periodic basis with supplements to reflect important changes in the subject matter. If you purchased this product directly from Aspen Publishers, we have already recorded your subscription for the update service.

If, however, you purchased this product from a bookstore and wish to receive future updates and revised or related volumes billed separately with a 30-day examination review, please contact our Customer Service Department at 1-800-234-1660 or send your name, company name (if applicable), address, and the title of the product to:

ASPEN PUBLISHERS
7201 McKinney Circle
Frederick, MD 21704

Important Aspen Publishers Contact Information

- To order any Aspen Publishers title, go to *www.aspenpublishers.com* or call 1-800-638-8437.

- To reinstate your manual update service, call 1-800-638-8437.

- To contact Customer Care, e-mail *customer.care@aspenpublishers .com*, call 1-800-234-1660, fax 1-800-901-9075, or mail correspondence to Order Department, Aspen Publishers, PO Box 990, Frederick, MD 21705.

- To review your account history or pay an invoice online, visit *www.aspenpublishers.com/payinvoices*.

For Evelyn and Alvin
GSL

In memory of my father, Keith Prechter
MLW

For Lynn
GK

Preface

Aspen Publishers' *Roth IRA Answer Book, Sixth Edition*, provides an up-to-the-minute tutorial on this subject for a wide variety of professional markets, including pension consultants, insurance agents, financial planners and investment advisors, plan administrators, lawyers, and accountants, as well as businesses that promote, market, service, or provide technical support to retirement plans, products, and related services. The subscriber will find in-depth coverage of the administration and operation of a Roth IRA, as mandated by the Internal Revenue Code, Treasury regulations, and other IRS guidance.

Written by a team of practicing experts preeminent in their fields, *Roth IRA Answer Book, Sixth Edition*, takes the reader, step by step, through the creation, operation, and extinction of a Roth IRA. Topics covered include the following:

- How a Roth IRA is established, how documents are designated, and how a Roth IRA may be revoked

- Trustee and custodian disclosure requirements and governmental form reporting requirements—Forms 1099-R, 5329, and 8606

- Limits on contributions, including the contribution phase-out rules, and the definition of modified adjusted gross income (MAGI)

- How the taxation of a Roth IRA distribution depends upon the source of funding for the amount distributed

- How abusive transactions having the effect of shifting value from a pre-existing business into a Roth IRA for less than fair market value may be challenged

- How the contribution recovery rules under the ordering rules determine whether a Roth IRA distribution consists of annual contributions, conversions from an eligible retirement plan, other rollover contributions, or earnings

- How to make and treat a rollover (conversion) from an eligible retirement plan to a Roth IRA

- Which taxpayers will benefit most from a conversion, and when (especially in a declining investment environment) can a conversion be undone in a recharacterization

- How a 2010 conversion is spread out over two years, but accelerated into income if received before 2013

- How the elimination of the $100,000 MAGI requirement and, if married, the joint filing requirement for rollover conversions to Roth IRAs will accelerate conversions after 2009

- Income and estate tax benefits of establishing a Roth IRA, and of converting a traditional IRA to a Roth IRA

- How Roth IRAs may be used to enhance overall wealth-transfer planning

- The treatment of penalty-free distributions from an eligible retirement plan for special purposes, such as hurricane distributions, qualified recovery assistance distributions, qualified disaster recovery distributions, and qualified reservist distributions

- How the suspension of the 2009 RMD rules affect Roth IRA owners and beneficiaries

- How and when special-purpose distributions may be repaid (rolled over) to an eligible retirement plan, including a Roth IRA

- How certain airline payments, military death gratuities, Exxon Valdez settlements, and Servicemembers' Group Life Insurance (SGLI) that are rolled over to a Roth IRA are treated

- When additional Roth IRA contributions may be made for participants in a 401(k) plan of certain employers in bankruptcy

- Explanation of why a participant naming his or her beneficiary, even if providing a benefit upon death, is *not* important

- The benefits of naming a Roth IRA trust as the beneficiary of a Roth IRA, as well as the considerations in drafting and the generation-skipping aspects of a Roth IRA trust

- How to create and transfer distributions into a separate-share trust to use each beneficiary's life expectancy

- How sample provisions, documents, and forms can provide for the efficient operation of a Roth IRA arrangement

- Discussion of the final regulations on the tax treatment of distributions from designated Roth accounts (DRAs), including the guidance on how a 60-day rollover or a direct-transfer rollover of a designated Roth account under an employer's 401(k) or 403(b) plan to a Roth IRA is treated

- Analysis of the Roth IRA List of Required Modifications and Information Package (LRMs)

- How to value an annuity contract that is converted to a Roth IRA

- A "top-ten" list of common mistakes that people make when designating beneficiaries and how a practitioner might help clients avoid those mistakes

- The opportunities and restrictions in making a beneficiary designation, including marriage and family rights that restrain a beneficiary designation.

Format. The question-and-answer format breaks down complex subject areas into concise units. Introductory text provides an overview of the subject. Extensive cross-referencing facilitates locating information.

List of Questions. The detailed List of Questions that follows the Table of Contents helps the subscriber locate areas of immediate interest. A series of sub-headings organizes questions by topic within each chapter.

Examples. Questions contain numerous examples that illustrate specific points. Where relevant, sample calculations are provided.

Practice Pointers and Cautions. Many answers direct a reader to a "Caution" that describes a problem that many people might miss, or to a "Practice Pointer" that illustrates how a financial planner or tax-planning professional might help a client optimize his or her use of Roth accounts and other retirement plans.

Appendices. For the subscriber's convenience, supplementary reference materials relevant to Roth IRAs are provided.

Index. A subject index is provided as a further aid to locating specific information. All references in the index are to question numbers.

Abbreviations and Acronyms. A number of the terms and statutory references that appear repeatedly in this book are referred to by their abbreviations and/or acronyms after the first mention. The most common of the abbreviations and acronyms are:

- Ann.—IRS Announcement

- BAPCPA—Bankruptcy Abuse Prevention and Consumer Protection Act of 2005

- C.B.—Cumulative Bulletin of the IRS

- CCM—Chief Counsel Memorandum

- Code; I.R.C.—Internal Revenue Code

- DOL—the U.S. Department of Labor, which regulates non-tax aspects of employment-based retirement plans
- DRA—Designated Roth Account (see chapter 10)
- DRCP—designated Roth contribution programs
- EBSA—the Employee Benefits Security Administration, a division of the U.S. Department of Labor
- EGTRRA—Economic Growth and Tax Relief Reconciliation Act of 2001
- ERISA—Employee Retirement Income Security Act of 1974
- GOZA—Gulf Opportunity Zone Act of 2005
- HEART—Heroes Earnings Assistance and Relief Tax Act of 2008
- IRA—Individual retirement arrangement (account and annuity)
- I.R.B.—Internal Revenue Bulletin
- I.R.C.—Internal Revenue Code
- IRS—Internal Revenue Service
- LRM—Listing of Required Modifications
- Ltr. Rul.—Letter Ruling
- OBRA '89—Omnibus Budget Reconciliation Act of 1989
- PPA—Pension Protection Act of 2006
- Prop. Treas. Reg.—Proposed Treasury Regulation
- Pub. L.—Public Law
- QDOT—qualified domestic trust (see chapter 8)
- QJSA—qualified joint and survivor annuity (see chapter 8)
- QOSA—qualified optional survivor annuity (see chapter 8)
- QPSA—qualified preretirement survivor annuity (see chapter 8)
- QRCP—qualified Roth contribution program
- QTIP—qualified terminable interest property (see chapter 8)
- Rev. Proc.—Revenue Procedure
- Rev. Rul.—Revenue Ruling
- TCA '98—Technical Corrections Act of 1998
- Temp. Treas. Reg.—Temporary Treasury Regulation
- TIPRA—Tax Increase Prevention and Reconciliation Act of 2005

- TRA '97—Taxpayer Relief Act of 1997
- Treas. Reg.—Treasury Regulation

Gary S. Lesser
Michelle L. Ward
Gregory Kolojeski
September 2009

About the Authors

Gary S. Lesser, Esq., is the principal of GSL Galactic Consulting, located in Indianapolis, Indiana. Mr. Lesser maintains a telephone-based consulting practice providing services and plan illustrations to other professionals and business owners. He is a nationally known author, educator, and speaker on retirement plans for individuals and smaller businesses, and has broad technical and practical knowledge of both qualified and nonqualified retirement plans.

Mr. Lesser is the technical editor and co-author of Aspen Publishers' *SIMPLE, SEP, and SARSEP Answer Book, Health Savings Account Answer Book, 457 Answer Book,* and *Quick Reference to IRAs.* Mr. Lesser is also the principal author and technical editor of *The CPA's Guide to Retirement Plans for Small Businesses* and *The Adviser's Guide to Health Savings Accounts,* publications of the American Institute of Certified Public Accountants (AICPA). He has developed several software programs that are used by financial planners, accountants, and other pension practitioners to design and market retirement plans for smaller businesses. His two software programs—*QP-SEP Illustrator* and *SIMPLE Illustrator*—are marketed and distributed nationally. He has also been published in the *EP/EO Digest, Journal of Taxation of Employee Benefits, Journal of Compensation and Benefits, Journal of Pension Benefits, Life Insurance Selling, Rough Notes,* the *Planner,* and the *NAPFA Advisor.* Mr. Lesser is an associated professional member of the American Society of Pension Professionals & Actuaries (ASPPA).

Mr. Lesser started his employee benefits career with the Internal Revenue Service, as a Tax Law Specialist/Attorney in the Employee Plans/ Exempt Organizations (EP/EO) Division. He later managed and operated a pension administration and actuarial service organization, was an ERISA marketing attorney for a national brokerage firm, and was a senior vice president/director of retirement plans for several nationally known families of mutual funds and variable annuity products. Mr. Lesser graduated from New York Law School and received his B.A. in accounting from Fairleigh Dickinson University. He is admitted to the bars of the state of New York and the United States Tax Court. Comments and suggestions can be forwarded to Mr. Lesser at GSL Galactic Consulting, 944 Stockton St., Indianapolis, IN 46260-4925, (317) 254-0385, or to *QPSEP@aol.com.* Information is also available on his Web site at *www.GaryLesser.com.*

Michelle L. Ward, Esq., is a senior consultant with the Financial and Estate Planning Group of Baker Tilly Virchow Krause, LLP, located in Appleton, Wisconsin. Ms. Ward's emphasis is in estate planning with primary focus on retirement distribution planning. Ms. Ward is a Certified Specialist in Estate Planning through the National Institute for Excellence in Professional Education, LLC. She has had articles published in *Trusts and Estates*, *Tax Management Compensation Planning Journal*, *Journal of Retirement Planning*, and is a contributing author to Aspen Publishers' *Quick Reference to IRAs*. Ms. Ward also assisted in the writing of the *Big IRA Book* by Robert Keebler, Cecil Smith, and Carol Gonnella.

Ms. Ward received her B.S. from the University of Wisconsin–Madison and her J.D. from the University of Wisconsin Law School. She is licensed to practice in Wisconsin and is a member of the State Bar of Wisconsin's Real Property, Probate & Trust Law Section and the American Bar Association's Taxation Section.

Gregory Kolojeski, Esq., is the president of Brentmark Software, Inc., which he founded in 1985. Brentmark specializes in developing estate, financial, and retirement planning software for professionals. Mr. Kolojeski directs the design of Brentmark products, including its popular retirement distributions planning program—the *Retirement Plan Analyzer* (which was used to check all of the calculation examples in chapter 5). Before founding Brentmark, Mr. Kolojeski was employed by Coopers & Lybrand, Aardvark Software, and the Internal Revenue Service.

Mr. Kolojeski has numerous published articles on estate, financial, and retirement planning topics. He is also the founder and editor of the leading source of information on Roth IRAs on the Internet at *www.rothira.com*. Since the enactment of the Roth IRA legislation, Mr. Kolojeski has been frequently quoted on Roth IRA topics in numerous published articles. Mr. Kolojeski's e-mail address is *greg@brentmark.com*.

Mr. Kolojeski received a J.D. from the Syracuse University College of Law and an M.S. in Accounting from the Syracuse University School of Management. He received a B.A. from the University of Pennsylvania.

Contributing Authors

Denise Appleby, CISP, CRC, CRPS, CRSP, APA, is a retirement plans consultant, trainer, freelance writer, editor, and owner of Appleby Retirement Plans Consulting, located on the Internet at *http://www.applebyconsultinginc.com* and *http://www.RetirementDictionary.com*. Ms. Appleby's retirement-plans-related experiences include working as a retirement plans product manager, training manager, compliance consultant, technical help desk manager, and writer. She has written over 200 articles for many financial newsletters including http://*www.Investopedia.com*, Pershing LLC's "Sixty Something," "The Pershing Press," and "Ed Slott's IRA Advisor."

Ms. Appleby is a frequent speaker at seminars, where she explains the importance of saving for retirement, and how to prevent paying avoidable taxes and penalties on distributions from retirement plans.

Ms. Appleby has appeared on CNBC's "Business News," where she gave insights on saving and planning for retirement. She has earned the following professional designations: The Accredited Pension Administrator (APA) from the National Institute of Pension Administrators, the Certified IRA Services Professional (CISP) designation from the Institute of Certified Bankers; the Chartered Retirement Plans Specialist (CRPS) designation from the College for Financial Planning; Certified Retirement Services Professional (CRSP) designation from the Institute of Certified Bankers; and the Certified Retirement Counselor (CRC) designation from the International Foundation for Retirement Education (InFRE).

Peter Gulia, Esq., is shareholder of Fiduciary Guidance Counsel, a Philadelphia, Pennsylvania, law firm that advises retirement plans' fiduciaries located in any of the United States.

After more than 21 years of experience with one of America's largest retirement services businesses, Mr. Gulia now counsels the people who manage retirement plans. In addition, he offers advice about employers' and executives' smart use of plan designs permitted under Code Sections 125, 401(k), 403(b), 409A, and 457(b) or (f).

Although Mr. Gulia concentrates his practice on advising a retirement plan's lead fiduciary, he also counsels investment advisers about their fiduciary duties and compliance procedures under the Investment Advisers Act, the Employee Retirement Income Security Act, and other laws. Likewise, he advises lawyers and certified public accountants about their professional conduct.

Since 1984, Mr. Gulia has focused on the design, governance, fiduciary investment procedures, and administration of retirement plans. His firsts to resolve then-novel ERISA, tax, and securities issues for asset-allocation investment advice and other retirement plan services remain models that practitioners use today. Beyond ERISA-governed plans, Mr. Gulia has wide experience with church plans and governmental plans, and with how securities law and other laws beyond ERISA and the Internal Revenue Code affect retirement plans.

He is a widely published expert on plan investments (including qualified default investment alternatives), beneficiary designations, and domestic relations orders. Mr. Gulia has published primarily with Wolters Kluwer Law & Business. He is a contributing author of six books in its Answer Book series. He is an author of *The CPA's Guide to Retirement Plans for Small Businesses* (AICPA), and recently expanded the book's coverage of fiduciary issues. His other recent topics include the Pension Protection Act of 2006 generally, and using a managed account as a default investment option. ALI-ABA and Westlaw published his explanation of the Economic Growth and Tax Relief Reconciliation Act of 2001.

Mr. Gulia teaches a broad range of professional education programs, including for the National Association of Personal Financial Advisors (NAPFA), *Pensions & Investments* magazine, Financial Research Associates, and ALI-ABA, a collaboration of the American Law Institute and the American Bar Association. He is a member of the American Society of Pension Professionals and Actuaries (ASPPA), the ASPPA Benefits Council of the Delaware Valley, the American Bar Association, the Philadelphia Bar Association, and the Philadelphia Compliance Roundtable.

Further information is available at *http://www.FiduciaryGuidance Counsel.com.*

Acknowledgments

Roth IRA Answer Book, Sixth Edition, is the product of the hard work, insight, and dedication of many people.

Special thanks to William F. Sweetnam Jr., Groom Law Group, Washington, D.C., for taking the time to explain various aspects of the Roth IRA legislation as it was being written and released. Before joining the Groom Law Group, Mr. Sweetnam was the Benefits Tax Counsel at the U.S. Department of the Treasury from April 2001 to February 2005 and was Tax Counsel on the majority staff of the U.S. Senate Committee on Finance from January 1998 to February 2001.

We wish to express our appreciation and deep gratitude to Alex DiMuro, Richard Epstein, Michael S. Flintoff, Peter Gulia, Barry Kozak, Barry C. Picker, David W. Powell, David Pratt, and Larry Starr for their assistance and contributions whenever called upon. Many thanks to John VanDuzer for reviewing the manuscript and for his thoughtful comments and suggestions.

With this edition, the very talented and highly credentialed Denise Appleby joins our team as a contributing author. Her training and expertise, coupled with her diverse practical experience with financial organizations involving retirement and financial planning matters, were very helpful with applying rules and regulations to operational practices.

Special thanks to Bruce J. Temkin for sharing his keen insight. His practical approach to both problems and their solutions has always been helpful. His latest book, *How the Internet and Longevity Revolution Will Transform Retirement*, examines how medical science and technological advancements have changed the landscape of financial planning. His thought-provoking findings convincingly illustrate why we need to approach retirement—and our working lives—strategically and comprehensively.

Thanks also go to Lisa Yi Hamond and the rest of the professional staff at Aspen Publishers for making this book a reality. Although they hide behind firewalls and routers, I would also like to thank the individuals involved in the maintenance of the electronic version of this book on *IntelliConnect*.

Over the years, numerous people have made contributions to this book, portions of which remain. We thank Robert S. Keebler for his keen insight and the knowledge he so graciously provided, as well as Susan D. Diehl for her expertise and assistance.

In addition, thanks are due to Butch the Beast Slayer, Amber the Twerp, and Hi-Ho Silver Zorro for their astute conversation, companionship, warmth, and for their occasional assistance in typing and editing. Thanks, too, to Gracie for her relentless canine security services in protecting the manuscript for as long as she could.

Contents

CHAPTER **3**
Conversion, Contribution Recharacterization, and Rollovers 3-1

CHAPTER **4**

Voluntary Distributions 4-1

Contents

CHAPTER 8

Beneficiary Designations and Estate Planning 8-1

CHAPTER 9

Required Reporting for Roth IRAs 9-1

Contents

Contents

List of Questions

Records Retention

Revoking a Roth IRA

Prototype Roth IRA Documents

Prohibited Transactions and Related Definitions

Chapter 2 Annual Contributions to a Roth IRA

Age and Plan Participant Status

Annual Contribution Deadline

Excess Contributions

Chapter 3 Conversion, Contribution Recharacterization, and Rollovers

Conversion of Traditional IRA to Roth IRA

Eligibility

Taxation

Rollover of Military Death Gratuities and SGLI Payments

Chapter 4 Voluntary Distributions

Chapter 6 Financial Planning

Chapter 7 Roth IRA Trusts

Roth IRA Trust Distribution Rules

In-Kind Distributions upon Termination of Trust

Generation-Skipping Trust

Taxation

Permissible Transfer

QTIPing a Roth IRA

Chapter 8 Beneficiary Designations and Estate Planning

Making a Beneficiary Designation

Using Trusts

Family Rights That Restrain a Beneficiary Designation

Failing to Provide for a Child

Charitable Gifts

Simultaneous Death; Absentees

Marriage

Ceremonial Marriage

Common-Law Marriage

Same-Sex Marriage

Spouse's Rights

ERISA Survivor Benefits or Spouse's-Consent Rights

Chapter 9   Required Reporting for Roth IRAs

Deceased IRA Owner

Recharacterization Contributions

Revoked Roth IRAs

Penalties

Records Retention

Reporting Roth IRA Distributions on Form 1099-R

Chapter 10 Designated Roth Contribution Programs

Chapter 1

Introduction to Roth IRAs

This chapter examines the rules that apply to the establishment of Roth individual retirement accounts and annuities (IRAs), including documentation requirements and restrictions. Requirements pertaining to disclosure, designation, and revocation are also reviewed. Prohibited transaction issues include borrowing from a health savings account (HSA), loans from a trustee to an HSA, pledging HSA assets as security for a loan, and the consequences for entering into a prohibited transaction.

The final DOL regulations and a proposed class exemption relating to the provision of fee-level or computer model investment advice arrangements that were published on August 22, 2008, are also discussed in this chapter.

Overview

Q 1:1   What is a *Roth IRA*?

A *Roth IRA* is an individual retirement account (trust, custodial account, or annuity contract) that is designated (see Q 1:13) at the time of establishment as a Roth IRA. A Roth IRA must meet the requirements of Code Section 408A (see Q 1:20). [I.R.C. § 408A(b); Treas. Reg. § 1.408A-8, Q&A 1(a)(5), 1(a)(10)]

> **Note.** A simplified employee pension plan (SEP) IRA or savings incentive match plan for employees (SIMPLE) IRA may not be designated as a Roth IRA. [I.R.C. § 408A(f)]

A qualifying individual and his or her spouse may make a *nondeductible* contribution each year to a Roth IRA or convert a traditional IRA into a Roth IRA (see Qs 1:10, 3:1). The Roth IRA rules allow for adjustments in the case of unwanted contributions and provide a way to undo a conversion that is either erroneous or unwanted (see Q 3:29). Beginning in 2007, a 60-day rollover conversion, or a direct rollover conversion from a qualified plan, 403(b) plan, or eligible governmental 403(b) plan, generally is permitted to be made to a Roth IRA (see Q 3:52). Thus, establishment of a traditional IRA before converting that IRA to a Roth IRA is no longer required. Furthermore, a beneficiary, including a nonspouse beneficiary, may make a direct rollover conversion (no 60-day rollover conversion allowed) to a Roth IRA from an employer's plan. Except for a surviving spouse beneficiary, no rollovers to a Roth IRA are permitted to be made from an "inherited" traditional IRA.

> **Note.** Beginning in 2006, Roth-type contributions may be made to an employer's 401(k) or 403(b) plan (see chapter 10) that permits such contributions to be made. The required minimum distribution rules that apply to designated Roth contribution accounts can be avoided by transferring an eligible rollover distribution from such a plan to a Roth IRA (see chapter 5).

Q 1:2   When did legislation creating the Roth IRA become effective?

The Taxpayer Relief Act of 1997 (TRA '97) [Pub. L. No. 105-34] contained many provisions affecting the retirement plans industry, including provisions that created the Roth IRA. Nearly all the Roth IRA provisions, including subsequent changes (see Q 1:3), are effective for taxable years beginning after 1997.

Q 1:3   How has the Roth IRA been altered since it was originally created?

Shortcomings in the original Roth IRA legislation (TRA '97) were almost immediately addressed by both the House and the Senate. In the end, it was primarily the Senate's version of changes to the Roth IRA that was enacted as part of the technical corrections to several tax and revenue acts, that is, as part of the IRS Restructuring and Reform Act of 1998, which included the Technical Corrections Act of 1998. The changes added to the complexity of the Roth IRA rules but, in the authors' opinion, were necessary, logical, and consistent with existing tax law.

Among the added rules are rules that apply to converted amounts that are withdrawn prematurely or within five years of a Roth IRA's establishment. In such cases, the amounts may be taxable or subject to a 10 percent penalty (or both). An exception was added to the old rule that the 10 percent penalty applied only if the amounts were currently includible in income (see Q 4:2). Furthermore, after age 59½ *and* after the five-year period, all distributions are generally received free of any federal income tax or penalty (see Qs 4:2, 4:3, 4:14). Within the five-year period, complicated rules are used to determine whether any part of the distribution includes gain (earnings) or an amount that was converted and whether that portion may be taxed or penalized, or both (see Q 4:9). Because *annual* Roth IRA contributions are always treated as being removed first—and are received free of federal income tax—such contributions (to the extent made, but not including gain) reduce or eliminate any potential tax or penalty caused by a taxed or penalized distribution (see Q 4:1).

In 1999 the Internal Revenue Service (IRS) released final regulations and other guidance that clarified many issues with regard to the Roth IRA; it also released several announcements extending the deadline for changing a contribution to a Roth IRA or a conversion to a Roth IRA back to a traditional IRA (see Qs 3:38, 3:39).

> **Note.** All the changes just referred to (except a provision regarding the computation of adjusted gross income (AGI), which became effective in 2005) became effective retroactively to the beginning of 1998.

On December 21, 2000, President Clinton signed the Consolidated Appropriations Act [Pub. L. No. 106-554], which contained several changes to the Roth IRA. The most significant change is that, basically, only the taxable portion of a distribution of gain in a nonqualified distribution (see Q 4:12) or in a corrective distribution (see Q 4:25) is subject to tax withholding, effective retroactively to January 1, 1998.

On January 12, 2001, the IRS released proposed regulations for determining required minimum distributions (RMDs) from, inter alia, Roth IRAs. The IRS anticipated that those regulations would become final in 2002 and apply for determining minimum distributions beginning in the 2002 calendar year. Regardless, proposed regulations could have been used to calculate minimum distributions for the 2001 calendar year; alternatively, the 1987 proposed regulations could have been used for 2001. The final regulations, issued on April 17, 2002, applied for determining RMDs for calendar years beginning on or after January 1, 2003. For calendar year 2002, a taxpayer may use the final regulations, the 2001 proposed regulations, or the regulations proposed in 1987.

On June 7, 2001, President Bush signed the Economic Growth and Tax Relief Reconciliation Act of 2001 (EGTRRA). EGTRRA made several changes to the Internal Revenue Code (Code) affecting Roth IRAs. The changes were effective beginning January 1, 2002.

With lower federal income tax rates under EGTRRA, some individuals may want to consider a recharacterization from the Roth IRA back to a traditional IRA and reconversion, especially if the value of their Roth IRA has declined. The tax rate changes also provide a number of tax planning strategies for upcoming years. In many cases, individuals will be able to ensure the most positive application of the new rules only with professional advice because EGTRRA is very complex and fraught with uncertainty. The EGTRRA provisions affecting

Roth IRAs, which are more fully discussed in other questions, include the following:

- Increase in the annual Roth IRA (and traditional IRA) contribution limits (see Q 2:1)
- Catch-up contributions for individuals age 50 or older (see Q 2:1)
- Tax credit for certain low-income taxpayers (see Q 2:36)
- Deemed Roth IRAs under most types of employer plans (see Qs 2:46, 3:81)
- Creation of designated Roth contribution program (DRCP) accounts that allow designated Roth 401(k) contributions or designated Roth 403(b) contributions to be made by participants in certain employer plans (see Qs 3:81–3:103) effective for taxable years beginning after 2005
- Guidance on updating Roth IRA (and traditional IRA) documents (see Q 1:20)
- Special rule for demutualization distributions made to Roth IRA (and traditional IRA) owners (see Q 4:37)
- Mandate for the IRS to modify the life expectancy tables under regulations governing RMDs during lifetime (see chapter 4) to reflect "current" life expectancy [EGTRRA § 634], which may impact the decision to convert a traditional IRA to a Roth IRA, which is not subject to the lifetime distribution rules (see Qs 5:1, 5:19)

On October 26, 2001, Congress passed the USA Patriot Act in response to the terrorist attacks of September 11, 2001. Certain provisions of the USA Patriot Act require financial institutions to develop a Customer Identification Program (CIP) that implements reasonable procedures (see Q 1:19).

On April 17, 2002, the IRS finalized re-proposed regulations issued in 2001 (the 2001 Proposed Regulations) under Code Section 401(a)(9) regarding RMDs. Numerous changes and clarifications were made (see Preamble to final regulations in appendix D). These changes and clarifications, which are more fully discussed in other chapters in this book, include the following:

1. *New mortality table.* The final RMD regulations contain new mortality tables. Single life divisors used by Roth IRA beneficiaries have changed slightly (see Q 5:19). [Treas. Reg. § 1.401(a)(9)-9, Q&A-1]

2. *Determining the designated beneficiary.* The designated beneficiary of the account will be determined as of September 30 of the year after the year of the account holder's death, rather than December 31 as stated in the 2001 proposed regulations (see Q 5:23, 5:27). [Treas. Reg. § 1.401(a)(9)-4, Q&A 4(a)]

3. *Death of designated beneficiary.* If the designated beneficiary dies between the account holder's date of death and the September 30 determination date, then that beneficiary will still be the measuring life for post-death RMDs, regardless of who the successor beneficiary may be (see Q 5:28). [Treas. Reg. § 1.409(a)(9)-4, Q&A-4(c)] While this provision solves the problem (i.e., a measuring life) it also eliminates the possibility that the death of the beneficiary could have resulted in a new beneficiary

having a longer life expectancy than the deceased beneficiary. [Barry Picker, letter to editor (May 24, 2002)]

4. *Life expectancy of beneficiary.* All beneficiaries of the trust are generally considered in determining the beneficiary with the shortest life expectancy (i.e., the oldest trust beneficiary by age). An individual whose benefit is contingent upon another beneficiary dying prior to the payout of the entire plan balance is ignored. However, a beneficiary whose benefit is merely postponed until the death of another beneficiary is not ignored. An example is the remainder beneficiary of a trust where another individual is only entitled to the income from the trust. [Treas. Reg. § 1.401(a)(9)-5, Q&A 7] However, if a trust meets the requirement for being qualified, distributions may possibly be made over the life expectancy of each beneficiary if separate trust shares are in existence on the date that the owner dies. In addition, the Beneficiary Designation Form must specifically name each separate share as beneficiary (see Q 7:17). [*See* Ltr. Rul. 200537044 (Mar. 29, 2005)]

5. *Disclaimer rules revised.* An individual can disclaim an interest to move a contingent beneficiary into a designated beneficiary position and use that new designated beneficiary's life expectancy as the measuring life. However, the disclaimer must be valid under Code Section 2518. The final regulations clarify that beneficiaries can be removed by disclaimer or payout, but they cannot be added (see Q 5:27). [Treas. Reg. § 1.409(a)(9)-4, Q&A-4(a)]

6. *Correction in life expectancy divisor.* The life expectancy divisor after the death of the spouse beneficiary has been corrected. The final RMD regulations clarify that, in the following year, the year of death divisor is reduced by one (see Q 5:42). [Treas. Reg. § 1.401(a)(9)-5, Q&A 5(c)(2)]

7. *Reporting requirements for trustees, custodians, and issuers.* The rules for having the custodians compute the annual minimum must take into account outstanding rollovers and recharacterized Roth conversions. Otherwise, an individual can avoid having the custodian report a required distribution by converting his or her IRA to a Roth every December, and recharacterizing it back to the traditional IRA by the following April 15. [Barry Picker, letter to editor (May 24, 2002)] The final RMD regulations do not require the custodian to report the minimum required distribution to the IRS. For 2003, the custodian had to notify the IRA holder of the amount of the minimum required distribution or that the custodian would compute the minimum required distribution for the IRA holder on request. As of 2004, however, the custodians merely have to note on Form 5498 that the IRA holder must take a minimum required distribution. There are no reporting requirements for Roth IRAs or IRAs of deceased IRA holders. The reporting requirements are listed in IRS Notice 2002-27. [2002-18 I.R.B. 1] (*See also* I.R.S. Notice 2003-3 [2003-2 I.R.B. 258] providing further guidance on methods of reporting required minimum distributions.) See chapter 9.

8. *Separate beneficiary accounts after participant's death and before RBD.* If separate accounts for each beneficiary are not established until the

calendar year following the year during which the participant died, a new special rule applies. Single life expectancies of the multiple beneficiaries may only be used the year after the separate accounts are established (see Q 5:46). [Treas. Reg. §§ 1.401(a)(9)-8, Q&A 2&3; 1.401(a)(9)-3, Q&A 3(a); 1.401(a)(9)-4, Q&A 3; 1.401(a)(9)-5, Q&A 7(a)(2)]

In August 2005, the IRS issued temporary regulations under Code Section 404A providing guidance concerning the tax consequences of converting a non-Roth annuity to a Roth IRA (see Q 3:15). In the case of a conversion involving property, the conversion amount is generally the fair market value (FMV) of the annuity contract on the date of distribution (see Q 3:20). However, the regulations did not apply to a conversion that is accomplished by the complete surrender of an annuity contract because the contract is not being converted. Instead, the cash from the surrendered contract is reinvested. The regulations also provided a rather difficult method for determining FMV.

In December 2005, the Gulf Opportunity Zone Act of 2005 (GOZA) [Pub. L. No. 109-135] attempted to clarify that the special $15,000 catch-up limit for long-term employees (15 years) is reduced by the employee's catch-up contributions that were not included in gross income for prior tax years, plus the aggregate amount of an individual's designated Roth contributions (see chapter 10) for prior years. In the author's opinion designated Roth contributions should only be counted against the $15,000 limit to the extent that the amount exceeds the normal limit on contributions for the prior years; the statute, however, does not read that way. [I.R.C. § 402(g)(7)(A)(ii); GOZA § 407(a)]

On January 17, 2006, the IRS released Revenue Procedure 2006-13 [2006-3 I.R.B. 315 (Jan. 17, 2006)], which provides safe-harbor methods that may be used in determining the FMV of an annuity contract for purposes of determining the amount includible in gross income as the result of the conversion of a non-Roth IRA to a Roth IRA (see Q 3:20).

On January 3, 2006, and not a moment too soon, final regulations were issued containing amendments to the 401(k) and 401(m) regulations that provide guidance concerning the requirements for designated Roth contributions under a qualified 401(k) plan (see chapter 10).

Practice Pointer. Taxation can no longer be avoided on undervalued non-Roth IRA annuity contracts that are surrendered and the proceeds reinvested in a rollover conversion (see Q 3:21).

On May 17, 2006, the Tax Increase Prevention and Reconciliation Act of 2005 (TIPRA) [Pub. L. No. 109-58] was enacted. It eliminated the $100,000 MAGI conversion limit and, if married, the joint filing requirement after 2009. Thus, more individuals will be able to convert taxable retirement savings into Roth IRAs starting in 2010 (see Q 3:16). The TIPRA provision eliminating the $100,000 MAGI conversion limit and, if married, joint filing requirement, was scored as revenue raisers. [See, Burman, Leonard E., "Roth Conversions as Revenue Raisers: Smoke and Mirrors," Tax Notes (May 22, 2008), available at http://taxpolicycenter.org/UploadedPDF/1000990_Tax_Break_05-22-06.pdf (visited Aug. 23, 2009).]

On August 17, 2006, the Pension Protection Act of 2006 (PPA) [Pub. L. No. 109-280, 120 Stat. 780] was enacted into law. The PPA contains a number of significant tax incentives to enhance retirement savings. EGTRRA (2001) substantially increased pension and IRA contribution limits through 2010. The PPA makes these EGTRRA changes (see discussion above) permanent and also provides for the indexing of the income limits for traditional, spousal, and Roth IRA phaseout rules to prevent these benefits from being eroded by inflation (see Q 2:7). Significant changes that affect Roth IRAs and/or designated Roth contribution programs (DRCPs, see chapter 10) under the PPA include:

1. Investment advice

The PPA adds a new category of prohibited transaction exemption under ERISA and the Code in connection with the provision of investment advice through an "eligible investment advice arrangement" to beneficiaries of Roth IRA (and other IRA) accounts and to participants and beneficiaries of a defined contribution plan who direct the investment of their accounts under the plan (e.g., DRCP, see Q 10:1). If the requirements of the exemption are met, the following are exempt from prohibited transaction treatment (see Q 1:54):

1. The provision of investment advice;
2. An investment transaction (i.e., a sale, acquisition, or holding of a security or other property) pursuant to the advice;
3. The direct or indirect receipt of fees or other compensation in connection with the provision of the advice or an investment transaction pursuant to the advice.

2. Permanency of EGTRRA pension and IRA/Roth provisions

In order to comply with reconciliation procedures, EGTRRA included a "sunset" provision, pursuant to which many of the provisions of EGTRRA expire at the end of 2010. The PPA makes permanent the EGTRRA pension and IRA provisions (e.g., catch-up contributions, designated Roth contribution programs (DRCP), deemed Roth IRAs). [EGTRRA § 901(a); PPA § 811] The saver's credit for certain low income individuals, set to expire after 2006, was also made permanent (see Q 2:35).

3. Improvements in portability, distribution, and contribution rules

- *Allow direct and indirect (60-day) rollovers (conversions) from retirement plans to Roth IRAs.* Distributions from tax-qualified retirement plans, tax-sheltered annuities, and governmental 457 plans may be rolled over directly from such plan into a Roth IRA, subject to the present law rules that apply to rollovers from a traditional IRA into a Roth IRA (see Qs 3:50, 3:52). For example, a rollover from a tax-qualified retirement plan into a Roth IRA is includible in gross income (except to the extent it represents a return of after-tax contributions), and the 10-percent early distribution tax does not apply. Similarly, an individual with AGI of $100,000 or more could not roll over amounts from a tax-qualified retirement plan directly into a Roth IRA before 2010.

Effective date. The rule is effective for distributions made after December 31, 2007. [PPA § 825(c); I.R.C. § 408A(e), as amended by PPA § 824]

- *Treatment of distributions to individuals called to active duty for at least 180 days (or an indefinite period).* Under the PPA, the 10-percent early withdrawal tax does not apply to a qualified reservist distribution. An individual who receives a qualified reservist distribution may, at any time during the two-year period beginning on the day after the end of the active duty period, make one or more contributions to an IRA (see Qs 3:19–3:124, 4:22).

- *Inflation indexing of gross income limitations on certain retirement savings incentives.*

  Saver's credit—PPA provides for indexing of the income limits applicable to the saver's credit beginning in 2007, which was also permanently extended by the PPA (see Q 2:37). Indexed amounts are rounded to the nearest multiple of $500. Under the indexed income limits, as under present law, the income limits for single taxpayers is one-half that for married taxpayers filing a joint return and the limits for heads of household are three-fourths that for married taxpayers filing a joint return.

  IRA and Roth IRA contribution income limits—The PPA indexes the income limits for IRA and Roth IRA contributions beginning in 2007. Indexed amounts are rounded to the nearest multiple of $1,000. The indexing applies to the income limits for deductible contributions for active participants in an employer-sponsored plan, the income limits for deductible contributions if the individual is not an active participant but the individual's spouse is, and the income limits for Roth IRA contributions (see Q 2:6). The provision does not affect the phaseout ranges under present law. Thus, for example, in the case of an active participant in an employer-sponsored plan, the phaseout range is $20,000 in the case of a married taxpayer filing a joint return and $10,000 in the case of an individual taxpayer.

  Effective date. The provision relating to indexing and contribution income limits are effective for taxable years beginning after December 31, 2006. [PPA § 833(d); I.R.C. §§ 25B, 219(g)(8), 408A(c)(3)(C)]

- *No reduction in unemployment compensation as a result of a rollover.* Under present law, unemployment compensation payable by a state to an individual generally is reduced by the amount of retirement benefits received by the individual. Distributions from certain employer-sponsored retirement plans or IRAs that are transferred to a similar retirement plan or IRA ("rollover distributions") generally are not includible in income. Some states currently reduce the amount of an individual's unemployment compensation by the amount of a rollover distribution. The PPA amends the Code so that the reduction of unemployment compensation payable to an individual by reason of the receipt of retirement benefits does not apply in the case of a rollover distribution.

  Effective date. The provision is effective for weeks beginning on or after the date of enactment. [I.R.C. § 3304(a), as amended by PPA § 1105]

4. *Charitable giving incentives*

Tax-free distributions from individual retirement plans for charitable purposes. The PPA provides an exclusion from gross income for otherwise taxable IRA distributions from a traditional or a Roth IRA in the case of qualified charitable distributions (see Q 4:1). Unless extended, the provision for qualified charitable distributions will expire as of December 31, 2009.

5. *Other prohibited transaction exemptions*

- *Transactions with service providers.* The PPA offers relief in that a transaction between a plan and a party-in-interest (e.g., service provider), who is not a fiduciary, is not a prohibited transaction (i.e., sale, exchange, lease, loan, or use of plan assets) under ERISA Section 406 so long as the plan receives no less than adequate consideration, or pays no more than, adequate consideration for the transaction (see Qs 1:48–1:56).

- *Block trades.* Additional relief is provided for "block trades" (any trade of at least 10,000 shares or a FMV of at least $200,000), which will be allocated among two or more client accounts of a fiduciary (see Q 1:56). [PPA § 611]

- *Electronic communication networks.* An exemption is provided for certain transactions on electronic communication networks (see Q 1:56). [PPA § 611(c)]

- *Foreign exchange transactions.* An exemption is provided for certain foreign exchange transactions (see Q 1:56). [PPA § 611(e)]

- *Cross-trading.* An exemption for certain cross-trading transactions is provided (see Q 1:56). [PPA § 611(g)]

  Effective date. The new exemptions would be effective for transactions occurring after the enactment date, August 17, 2006. The correction period exemption applies to prohibited transactions that the fiduciary discovers (or should have discovered) after the date of enactment.

On April 30, 2007, the IRS released final regulations on the taxation of distributions from designated Roth accounts under Code Section 402A. The final regulations include guidance on how both a 60-day rollover and a direct transfer of a designated Roth account under an employer's 401(k) or 403(b) plan to a Roth IRA are treated (see Q 10:48). [Treas. Reg. § 1.401A-1, Q&A-5, 72 Fed. Reg. 21103 (Apr. 30, 2007)]

In May 2007, the IRS revised its List of Required Modifications and Information Package (LRMs) for Roth IRAs, intending to satisfy the requirements of Code Sections 408A and 408(a) or (b). The LRM is reproduced in appendix G, and changes from the May 2006 LRM are underlined. The 2007 version contains new information relating to the following:

- *Repayment of qualified reservist distributions.* Repayment of qualified reservist distributions during the two-year period beginning on the day after the end of the active duty period or by August 17, 2008, if later (see Q 3:19).

- *Qualified rollover contributions.* For taxable years beginning after 2005, a qualified rollover contribution includes a rollover from a designated Roth account (see Q 10:48); and for taxable years beginning after 2007, a qualified rollover contribution also includes a rollover "conversion" from an eligible retirement plan (as described in Code Section 402(c)(8)(B)). (See Q 3:52.)

- Cost-of-living increases to the maximum regular contribution limit made permanent by the PPA (see Q 2:1).

- Removal of the $100,000 AGI limit for conversions from an eligible retirement plan beginning after 2009 (see Q 3:7). The removal of the income limit for converting to a Roth IRA also effectively eliminates the income limit for contributing to a Roth IRA.

- Special limits allowing an additional $3,000 to be contributed to a Roth IRA for participants in a 401(k) plan of certain employers in bankruptcy. If this special limit is used, the catch-up limit cannot be used for the year (see Q 2:1).

Although the procedures for obtaining opinion letters from the IRS for a Roth IRA are contained in Revenue Procedure 98-59 [1998-2 C.B. 727], a checklist for Roth IRAs was included in the IRS's update of its procedures for obtaining ruling requests (see Q 1:38). [*See* Rev. Proc. 2008-4, Appendix C, 2008-1 I.R.B. 121]

On March 24, 2008, in Notice 2008-30 [2008-12 I.R.B. 1), the IRS issued guidance on rollovers to a Roth IRA from a qualified plan, 403(b) plan, or governmental 403(b) plan. Prior to the PPA, Code Section 408A provided that a Roth IRA could only accept a rollover contribution of amounts distributed from another Roth IRA, from a non-Roth IRA (i.e., a traditional or SIMPLE IRA), or from a designated Roth account (see Qs 3:52–3:53, 10:48). These rollover contributions to Roth IRAs are called "qualified rollover contributions." A qualified rollover contribution from a non-Roth IRA to a Roth IRA is called a "rollover conversion" or, when made between trustees or custodians (no participant receipt), a "direct conversion" or "direct rollover conversion." An individual who rolls over an amount from a non-Roth IRA to a Roth IRA must include in gross income any portion of the conversion amount that would be includible in gross income if the amount were distributed without being rolled over. For distributions before 2010, a conversion contribution to a Roth IRA is permitted only if the Roth IRA owner's adjusted gross income does not exceed certain limits and, if married, files a joint return. Section 824 of PPA amended the definition of qualified rollover contribution in Code Section 408A to include additional plans. Under this expansion, in addition to the rollovers described above, a Roth IRA can accept rollovers from other eligible retirement plans (see Q 3:52). In general, such rollovers are permitted to be made by a participant, a spouse of a participant, or a nonspouse designated beneficiary. The provision allowing qualified rollover contributions to a Roth IRAs from an employer's plan applies to distributions made after December 31, 2007. It should be noted that a nonspouse beneficiary may not convert an inherited traditional IRA to a Roth IRA, but can make a direct conversion from an employer's plan to a Roth IRA if permitted. (See Qs 3:52–3:64.) The provision allowing qualified rollover contributions to a Roth IRA from an employer's plan applies to distributions made after December 31, 2007.

On December 23, 2008, the Worker, Retiree, and Employer Recovery Act of 2008 (WRERA) [Pub. L. No. 110-458] waived the requirement for a beneficiary to take a required minimum distribution (RMD) for 2009 (see Q 5:1). As a result, any distribution taken from an IRA-based plan, such as a Roth IRA, will not be treated as an RMD, unless the payment or payments are distributions necessary to satisfy RMD rules for the 2008 tax year. The RMD rules do not apply before the Roth IRA owner's death (or the death of the owner's spouse if the spouse is designated as the sole beneficiary or transfers, or rolls over, to his or her own Roth IRA, his or her interest as beneficiary of the inherited Roth IRA). A 2009 RMD would have normally been required in cases where the Roth IRA owner died in the years 2004 through 2008 with no designated beneficiary (see Q 5:12).

The taxation of voluntary contributions is discussed in chapter 4. Although the 10 percent tax penalty (see Q 4:22) would not apply to a "waived" distribution to a Roth IRA beneficiary after the death of the Roth IRA owner, any gains distributed—after all contributions are recovered in a voluntary distribution—are includible in gross income unless they are qualified distributions (not distributed within the five-taxable-year period beginning with the first year for which a contribution is made, see Qs 4:9, 4:12).

Q 1:4   Is a Roth IRA treated in the same manner as a traditional IRA?

Except as provided in Code Section 408A and the regulations thereunder, a Roth IRA is treated for all purposes under the Code in the same manner as a traditional IRA. [I.R.C. § 408A(a); Treas. Reg. § 1.408A-1, Q&A 1(a); Rev. Proc. 98-59, § 2, 1998-2 C.B. 727] For example:

1. Aggregate contributions (other than by a conversion (see chapter 3) or other rollover) to all of an individual's Roth IRAs are generally not permitted to exceed $5,000, plus catch-up contributions of $1,000 for taxpayers age 50 or older, for 2009 (see chapter 2). [I.R.C. §§ 219(b)(5), 408A(c)(2)]

2. Income earned on funds held in a Roth IRA is generally not taxable (see chapter 4). [I.R.C. §§ 408(e)(1), 408A(a)(6)]

3. The rules of Code Section 408(e)(2) (e.g., the loss of an account's tax exemption when its owner engages in a prohibited transaction) apply to a Roth IRA just as they apply to a traditional IRA.

[Treas. Reg. § 1.408A-1, Q&A 1(b)]

On the other hand, there are several significant differences between a traditional IRA and a Roth IRA, including the following:

1. Roth IRA contribution eligibility is subject to special modified adjusted gross income (MAGI) limits (see Q 2:8).

2. Code Section 219(f)(6), which provides for the deductibility of excess traditional IRA contributions in subsequent taxable years, does not apply

to the Roth IRA because contributions to a Roth IRA are never deductible (see Qs 2:24, 2:31).

3. Qualified distributions from a Roth IRA are not includible in gross income (see Q 4:9).

4. The RMD rules do not apply to a Roth IRA during the lifetime of the owner (see Q 5:1).

5. Contributions to a Roth IRA may be made after the owner has attained age 70½ (see Q 2:10).

6. Direct rollover conversions from an eligible employer's plan (but not from an "inherited" traditional IRA) are permitted to be made to a Roth IRA by a nonspouse beneficiary (see Q 3:52).

Q 1:5   What features of the Roth IRA may appeal to many taxpayers?

The tax-free withdrawal of contributions and all earnings at retirement may make the Roth IRA a more appealing choice than a traditional (deductible or nondeductible) IRA. A number of features, including the following, make a Roth IRA desirable for many taxpayers:

1. Qualified distributions are not includible in gross income (see Q 4:9). [I.R.C. § 408A(d)(1)]

2. Deductible and nondeductible IRAs remain available (see Q 2:11), although in no event may annual contributions to all IRAs (including Roth IRAs) exceed $5,000 ($6,000 with catch-up contributions) for 2009 (see Qs 2:1, 1:6, 2:6). [I.R.C. §§ 219(b)(5), 408A(c)(2)]

3. No maximum age restrictions apply to contributions (see Q 1:17). [I.R.C. § 408A(c)(2)(A)]

4. The RMD rules do not apply before the Roth IRA owner's death (or the death of the owner's spouse if the spouse is designated as the sole beneficiary or transfers, or rolls over, to his or her own Roth IRA, his or her interest as beneficiary of the inherited Roth IRA); see chapter 5. [I.R.C. § 408A(c)(5)]

5. If a taxpayer's MAGI is not more than $100,000 in the year an amount is distributed from a traditional IRA, the following advantages may be gained by converting (by transfer or rollover) the traditional IRA into a Roth IRA (see chapter 5):

    a. The ability to defer distributions beyond age 70½ (see Q 1:16),

    b. After-death tax-free growth (see Q 2:10), although certain minimum distributions must be made (see Q 5:1),

    c. Maximum accumulation of IRA value by paying conversion taxes from other assets (see Q 6:30), and

    d. A two-year spread of the income resulting from a conversion is available for conversions that occur in 2010 (and not distributed before 2012) (see Q 3:17). Thus, the conversion income on a conversion made in 2011 or 2013 cannot be spread out over two years. If the conversion occurs in 2010, the income is generally spread over two years (2011 and 2012). These rules are similar to the four-year spread that applied to a 1998 conversion (see Q 3:15).

Note. The $100,000 MAGI limit, and if married, joint filing requirement, was eliminated for taxable years beginning after 2009 (see Qs 3:7, 3:16).

Q 1:6 What is the maximum amount that may be contributed annually to a Roth IRA?

Annual contributions to a Roth IRA are normally limited to $5,000 for 2009. An individual who has attained the age of 50 by the close of the 2009 taxable year, and meets the other eligibility requirements, may make an additional, or catch-up, contribution of up to $1,000 (the 2009 limit), for a total contribution limit of $5,000 for 2009. Contributions may not generally exceed an individual's compensation (see Qs 2:1, 2:5; an exception is made for spouses (see Q 2:2).

Annual contribution limits are more fully discussed in chapter 2. Phaseout rules based on MAGI may limit the amount an eligible individual may contribute to a Roth IRA each year (see Q 2:6). [I.R.C. §§ 219(b)(1), 219(b)(5), 408A(c)(2)(A)] See Q 2:1 and appendix H for contribution limits for earlier years.

There is no limit on the amount of a rollover contribution. [Treas. Reg. § 1.408A-4, Q&A 1]

Q 1:7 Is the total annual limit on contributions to a Roth IRA reduced by rollover contributions?

No. A rollover contribution is not considered in computing the limit on total annual (normal plus catch-up) contributions to a Roth IRA. [I.R.C. § 408A(c)(6)(B)]

Example. In 2009, Lola, age 35, makes a rollover contribution to a Roth IRA in the amount of $9,000. Lola can still contribute $5,000, her contribution limit to the Roth IRA. If Lola were age 50 or older in 2009, she could contribute $6,000. [I.R.C. § 408A(c)(2)]

Q 1:8 Are the annual limits on contributions and catch-up contributions to a Roth IRA indexed for inflation?

Yes and no. After 2008, the $5,000 Roth IRA (and traditional IRA) annual contribution limits are subject to cost-of-living adjustments (COLAs), rounded to the next lower $500 increment (see Q 2:1; appendix A). Before EGTRRA, the contribution limit of $2,000 was not subject to COLAs. EGTRRA increased the annual contribution limit for Roth IRAs (and traditional IRAs) from $2,000 to $5,000 over a seven-year period (2002 through 2008). [I.R.C. § 219(b)(5)(D)]

The catch-up amount for Roth IRAs (and traditional IRAs) is not subject to COLAs. Therefore, after 2009, when the $5,000 normal annual limit increases to $5,500 as a result of COLAs, the catch-up amount will remain $1,000.

Q 1:9   Do the limits on annual contributions and catch-up contributions to a Roth IRA apply to conversions?

No. There is no limit on the amount that may be converted from a traditional IRA or other eligible plan (see Q 3:52) to a Roth IRA. [Treas. Reg. § 1.408A-1, Q&A 1]

Q 1:10   Are contributions made to a Roth IRA deductible?

No. All contributions made to a Roth IRA are nondeductible and represent basis in the Roth IRA (see Qs 1:11, 3:14, 4:1). [I.R.C. § 408A(c)(1)]

Q 1:11   What is meant by the term *basis* with regard to a Roth IRA?

With regard to a Roth IRA, *basis* refers to the sum of the taxed contributions made to the account. All contributions to a Roth IRA are fully taxed. If there is *basis* in the Roth IRA account, and the distribution is not a qualified distribution, special ordering rules apply, but contributions are recovered first—before earnings are distributed). Earnings on annual contributions and conversion contributions create basis in a Roth IRA (see chapter 5).

> **Note.** In a traditional IRA, the term *basis* refers to the sum of the nondeductible contributions, that is, to the sum of the contributions that have been subject to federal income tax. In determining basis in a traditional IRA, the calculation includes the balance in all of the taxpayer's non-Roth IRAs (e.g., SEP IRAs, SIMPLE IRAs, rollover IRAs). In a traditional IRA, a distribution of an amount considered to be basis is never subject to federal income tax or the 10 percent premature distribution penalty. [I.R.C. §§ 72(b)(2), 72(e)(8), 72(t)(1), 408(d)]

Establishing a Roth IRA

Q 1:12   When were taxpayers first permitted to establish a Roth IRA?

Taxpayers were first permitted to establish a Roth IRA for taxable years beginning after 1997. It follows, then, that a Roth IRA could not have been established before January 1, 1998 (see Q 1:2).

Q 1:13   How does a taxpayer establish a Roth IRA?

A Roth IRA is a trust, custodial account, or annuity contract created for the benefit of an individual. [I.R.C. §§ 408A(b), 7701(a)(37)] Such a trust, custodial account, or annuity contract must be "designated (in such manner as the Secretary [of the Treasury] may prescribe)" at the time of establishment as a Roth IRA. [I.R.C. § 408A(b)] A Roth IRA can be established with any bank, insurance company, or other person authorized in accordance with procedures established under treasury regulations to serve as a trustee with respect to an IRA. It should be noted that an individual would not qualify as a person under those procedures. [Treas. Reg. § 1.408-2(e)] The designation cannot be changed at a later date. [Treas. Reg. § 1.408A-2, Q&A 2] Designation may be effected by adopting a document that is approved for use only as a Roth IRA document (e.g., the IRS model documents; see Q 1:21) or by selecting the "Roth IRA" checkbox on a Roth IRA document that is combined with a traditional IRA document. Prototype documents may also be used (see Qs 1:14, 1:39).

When IRS model documents, which may be adopted at a financial institution, are used, the taxpayer's Social Security number serves as an identification number. If the taxpayer is a nonresident alien and does not have an identification number, he or she should apply for an individual taxpayer identification number. An employer identification number is required only for a Roth IRA for which a return is filed to report unrelated business income.

Note. Contributions to a Roth IRA and contributions to a traditional IRA must be maintained in separate trusts, custodial accounts, or annuities. Separate accounting within a single trust, custodial account, or annuity is not permitted (but see Q 1:39 relating to group trusts under I.R.C. § 408(c)). [I.R.S. Ann. 97-122, 1997-50 I.R.B. 63; see Rev. Rul. 81-100 (1981-1 C.B. 326), modified by Rev. Rul. 2004-67 (2004-48 I.R.B. 28), regarding group trust asset pooling]

Note. In general a Roth IRA will be treated as a domestic trust for purposes of determining whether a U.S. court may exercise primary supervision over a trusts administration ("the court test"). A second test, called the "control test," is automatically satisfied in the case of a Roth IRA. [See Treas. Reg. § 301.7701-7(a)(1), (c), (d)(1)]

Q 1:14 What are the eligibility requirements for establishing a Roth IRA?

To make an annual contribution to a Roth IRA, a taxpayer (or the taxpayer's spouse if a joint federal tax return is filed) must have compensation that is includible in his or her gross income for the taxable year. To make the maximum contribution of $5,000 (or $6,000 for taxpayers age 50 or older) for 2009, the taxpayer must have compensation equal to at least $5,000 (or $6,000 for taxpayers age 50 or older) (see Qs 2:1, 2:2). [I.R.C. §§ 219(b)(1)(A)-(B), 408A(c)(2)(A)]

Example 1. Punch and Judy are married and are under the age of 50. They file separate federal income tax returns for 2009. Judy has W-2 compensation of $6,000; Punch received a $15,000 taxable distribution from a large trust fund established by his father. Both Judy and Punch each contribute $5,000 to their Roth IRAs. No other contributions are made. Punch's contribution is an excess contribution (see Q 2:24). The income from the trust fund is not compensation. Because Punch files a separate return, Judy's compensation cannot be considered.

Example 2. Same facts as Example 1, except that Punch and Judy file a joint federal income tax return. Judy's compensation of $6,000 (reduced by her own contribution of $5,000) may be considered as compensation. Punch's excess contribution is $4,000. That is, the amount he contributed ($5,000) is reduced by the amount of considered compensation—$1,000 ($5,000 less Judy's contribution of $4,000).

Q 1:15   Does a minimum age restriction apply to the establishment of a Roth IRA?

No. No minimum age restriction applies to the establishment of a Roth IRA. Nevertheless, some financial institutions will not allow a minor to establish a Roth IRA. Others will allow a Roth IRA to be established for the benefit of a minor only if the account registration includes an adult who will make decisions with respect to the account until the minor attains the age of majority under applicable state law.

In the case of any contribution to a Roth IRA established for a minor child, the child's compensation for the taxable year for which the contribution is made must satisfy the compensation requirements (see Qs 2:1, 2:2).

Note. Bank-type organizations that restrict purchases in a minor's account to FDIC-insured products are generally more willing to risk the possibility that the owner will exercise his or her right of rescission upon the minor's reaching the age of majority.

Q 1:16   Does a maximum age restriction apply to the establishment of a Roth IRA?

No. No maximum age restriction applies to the establishment of a Roth IRA. [I.R.C. § 408A(c)(4)] Thus, if an individual (or his or her spouse) has compensation (see Qs 2:1, 2:2) and the individual is over age 70½, such individual is not precluded from making an annual Roth IRA contribution or from converting a traditional IRA into a Roth IRA (see chapter 3).

Q 1:17   Must Roth IRA contributions be made in cash?

Except in the case of a qualified rollover contribution, annual Roth IRA contributions must be made in cash [I.R.C. §§ 408(a)(1), 408(b), 408A(b), 408A(c)(1)] or by direct deposit contributions through payroll deductions (see Q 2:48). [I.R.S. Ann. 99-2, 1999-2 I.R.B. 44; *see also* D.O.L. Reg. § 2510.3-2; D.O.L. Adv. Op. 81-80A]

Note. Where the individual receives a distribution of property, the identical property received in the distribution must be rolled over.

Q 1:18   Is life insurance permitted as an investment in a Roth IRA?

No. Life insurance is not permitted as an investment in a Roth IRA. [I.R.C. § 408(a)(3); *see* Ltr. Rul. 8439026 (June 26, 1984) (regarding annuity contracts)]

Q 1:19   Does the customer identification under the USA Patriot Act affect Roth IRAs?

Yes. On October 26, 2001, Congress passed the USA Patriot Act in response to the terrorist attacks of September 11, 2001. Certain provisions of the USA

Patriot Act require financial institutions to develop a Customer Identification Program (CIP) that implements reasonable procedures for:

1. Verifying the identity of any person seeking to open an account, to the extent reasonable and practicable;

2. Maintaining records of the information used to verify the person's identity, including name, address, and other identifying information; and

3. Determining whether the person appears on any lists of known or suspected terrorists or terrorist organizations provided to the financial institution by any government agency.

Final CIP regulations were published on April 30, 2003. The definition of "account" for these purposes includes any type of retirement account, except for ERISA plans (employee benefit plans that cover at least one common-law employee). Therefore these rules apply to all types of IRAs.

Model Roth IRA Documents

Q 1:20 What types of model plan documents may be used to establish a Roth IRA?

Model Roth IRA agreements—Form 5305-R, Roth Individual Retirement Trust Account (for trustees), and Form 5305-RA, Individual Retirement Custodial Account (for custodians)—may be used to establish a Roth IRA. [I.R.S. Ann. 97-122, 1997-50 I.R.B. 63] These forms were first published in January 1998 and reissued in January 2000. In March 2002, Forms 5305-R, 5305-RA, and 5305-RB were revised to incorporate changes made by EGTRRA and the final RMD regulations. These forms are available at *http://www.irs.gov* (visited on June 18, 2009).

So far, users of Forms 5305-R, 5305-RA, and 5305-RB have not been required to use the revised version of the forms.

A model Roth IRA annuity agreement, Form 5305-RB, Roth Individual Retirement Annuity Endorsement, which is similar to Forms 5305-R and 5305-RA, may be used by insurance companies as issuers. This form was reissued in January 2000. Users of the 1998 version of Form 5305-RB were not required to use the revised 2000 form.

On January 3, 2002, the IRS released guidance on amending Roth IRA plan documents and disclosure statements (see Qs 1:29, 1:30). [Rev. Proc. 2002-10, 2002-1 C.B. 401; *see also* Rev. Proc. 2008-50, § 1.03, 2008-35 I.R.B. 464 regarding designated Roth contributions]

Q 1:21 How do the three IRS model Roth IRA agreements differ?

All three model Roth IRA agreements issued by the IRS are identical, except for the term used to identify the Roth IRA owner. In the Form 5305-R trust agreement the owner is called the "grantor"; in the Form 5305-RA custodial agreement the owner is called the "depositor"; and in the Form 5305-RB annuity endorsement the owner is called the "annuitant."

Q 1:22   May a taxpayer use a traditional model IRA agreement (Form 5305 or 5305-A) to make a Roth IRA contribution?

No. The IRS requires that the trustee or custodian of a Roth IRA maintain a separate Roth IRA document for the benefit of the Roth IRA owner. [I.R.S. Ann. 97-122, 1997-50 I.R.B. 63] Furthermore, the account must be designated as a Roth IRA at the time of establishment. [I.R.C. § 408A(b)]

Q 1:23   May a trustee or custodian change the language contained in IRS model Form 5305-R or 5305-RA?

No; however, information may be added. In addition to eight articles containing specific IRS language, Forms 5305-R and 5305-RA include an Article IX, which is blank. The purpose of Article IX is to allow the trustee or custodian of a Roth IRA to add language to provide greater flexibility, guidance, authority, and protection than Articles I through VIII provide. The IRS merely indicates that a trustee or custodian may not modify the provisions in Articles I through VIII (see Q 1:40).

Practice Pointer. A trustee or custodian should consult legal counsel with respect to any provisions to be added to Article IX. An organization should consider including provisions relating to administrative fees, available investment selections, the unilateral right to amend the plan document without obtaining the Roth IRA owner's signature (generally referred to as the negative consent), and the right to resign as trustee or custodian and appoint a successor trustee or custodian. Additional provisions that may be agreed to by the Roth IRA owner and the Roth IRA trustee, custodian, or issuer include definitions, voting rights, investment powers, exculpatory provisions, amendments and terminations, fees, state law requirements, beginning date of distributions, accepting only cash, treatment of excess distributions, prohibited transactions with the owner, and revocations and investments within the seven-day revocation period (see Qs 1:35, 1:36). Additional pages may be used if necessary and attached to the model form.

Disclosure Statement

Q 1:24   Must a disclosure statement accompany a Roth IRA agreement?

Yes. In addition to a Roth IRA agreement, Treasury regulations provide that a Roth IRA trustee or custodian must provide to an individual seeking to establish a Roth IRA an adequate disclosure statement that describes the technical rules applicable to a Roth IRA (see Q 1:26) and a financial disclosure (see Qs 1:26–1:29). [Treas. Reg. § 1.408-6; Prop. Treas. Reg. § 1.408-6(b)]

Q 1:25   What must the technical portion of the disclosure statement accompanying a Roth IRA agreement contain?

The technical portion of the disclosure statement that must accompany a Roth IRA agreement is basically a discussion of all the rules governing participation in the plan—eligibility requirements, contribution limits, taxation of distributions, treatment of excess contributions, and so on. Treasury Regulations Section 1.408-6 contains a complete list of each matter that should be described in nontechnical language in the technical disclosure statement.

In lieu of or in addition to an organization's own technical disclosure statement, IRS Publication 590, *Individual Retirement Arrangements (IRAs)*, may be used. [Treas. Reg. § 1.408-6(d)(4)(iii)(B)(15)] The IRS updates Publication 590 each year (the new version for the prior year is normally available in January) and a few complimentary copies may be obtained by calling the IRS at (800) TAX-FORM (829-3676). Publication 590 is available at *http://www.ustreas.gov* (visited on June 18, 2009).

> **Practice Pointer.** Even though a Roth IRA trustee or custodian may have either developed its own technical disclosure statement or adopted a technical disclosure statement designed by a forms vendor, it is always a good idea to make IRS Publication 590 available to customers.

Q 1:26   What must the financial portion of the disclosure statement accompanying a Roth IRA agreement contain?

The financial disclosure requirements for the disclosure statement that must accompany a Roth IRA agreement will vary depending on the type of organization and the type of investments allowed under the governing Roth IRA plan document. For example, Treasury regulations prescribe one format for investments whose return is guaranteed; another format for investments whose return is not guaranteed but can be reasonably projected; and yet another format for investments whose return can be neither guaranteed nor reasonably projected.

An organization must generally provide projections of the amounts that would be available to the Roth IRA owner at the end of the first five years and at the end of the years in which the owner attains ages 60, 65, and 70 by using certain assumptions. Those projections must take into consideration any action that would reduce the amount available at the end of each stated year, such as the imposition of fees or certificate of deposit (CD) early withdrawal penalties. In all cases, the organization must disclose any fees, commissions, or other amounts that will be charged against the Roth IRA. [Rev. Rul. 86-78, 1986-1 C.B. 208]

Q 1:27   What assumptions must be used when preparing projections for the financial disclosure that is part of the disclosure statement that must accompany a Roth IRA agreement?

With regard to the financial disclosure that is part of the disclosure statement that must accompany a Roth IRA agreement, Treasury regulations require a projection of growth of the value of the account based on "an earnings rate no greater than, and terms no different from, those currently in effect, that would be available to the benefited individual if certain assumptions are made." [Treas. Reg. § 1.408-6(d)(4)(v)(B)(1); Prop. Treas. Reg. § 1.408-6(b)]

In the case of a contributory Roth IRA, the trustee or custodian assumes that annual contributions of $1,000 are made on the first day of each year. For a rollover Roth IRA, the trustee or custodian assumes that a one-time deposit of $1,000 is made on the first day of the year.

According to Revenue Ruling 86-78 [1986-1 C.B. 208], institutions may comply with the foregoing requirements by providing a table that shows the values available at the end of each stated period of time based on various ages at the time the IRA is established.

In addition, Revenue Ruling 86-78 permits an institution to use an earnings rate that is lower than the rate being paid at the time the IRA is established. In fact, the ruling states:

> [I]f the trustee or issuer uses the greatest earnings rate allowable in the disclosure statement projections, and the actual earnings rate then falls below that rate, the disclosure statement must be revised before the IRA is offered to other individuals. Thus, trustees and issuers of Roth IRAs may prefer to use more conservative earnings rates than the greatest rate allowable so that small decreases in the earnings rate being paid will not require immediate modification of their disclosure statements.

Practice Pointer. Although an organization may use a financial disclosure designed by its own forms vendor, the organization's legal counsel should conduct a review of both the Treasury regulations and Revenue Ruling 86-78 to avoid, as best it can, having penalties assessed by the IRS.

Q 1:28   What information must the financial disclosure portion of the disclosure statement that must accompany a Roth IRA agreement contain if a reasonable projection or guarantee cannot be made?

If the financial disclosure portion of the disclosure statement that must accompany a Roth IRA agreement cannot include a reasonable projection or guarantee—for example, where mutual fund investments or annuities are at issue—the disclosure must contain the following information:

1. A description (in nontechnical language) with respect to the Roth IRA owner's or the Roth IRA owner's beneficiary's interest in the account of

    a. Each type of charge, and the amount thereof, that may be made against a contribution,

    b. The method for computing and allocating annual earnings, and

    c. Each charge that may be applied to the interest in determining the net amount of money available to the benefited individual and the method for computing each such charge;

2. A statement that the growth in the account is neither guaranteed nor projectable; and

3. The portion of each $1,000 contribution attributable to the cost of life insurance, which would not be deductible, for every year during which contributions are to be made. [I.R.C. § 408(i); Treas. Reg. §§ 1.408-6(d)(4), 1.408-6(d)(4)(vi)] Note that life insurance is not a permitted IRA investment (see Q 1:18).

Q 1:29 Is there a penalty for not providing a disclosure statement in conjunction with a Roth IRA agreement?

Yes. The Code provides for a noncompliance penalty equal to $50 for each failure to provide an accurate disclosure statement in conjunction with a Roth IRA agreement. Failure to supply a valid Roth IRA plan document invokes the same penalty. [I.R.C. § 6693; Treas. Reg. § 1.408-6(d)(ix)]

Amendment

Q 1:30 When must Roth IRA plan documents and disclosure statements be amended for EGTRRA?

On January 3, 2002, the IRS released initial guidance on amending Roth IRA plan documents and disclosure statements for EGTRRA and the RMD regulations. Similar rules apply to traditional IRA, SEP IRA, and SIMPLE IRA plan documents and disclosure statements; however, adoption, submission, and notification dates may differ from those applicable to a Roth IRA. [Rev. Proc. 2002-10, 2002-4 I.R.B. 1, *modifying* Rev. Proc. 87-50, 1987-2 C.B. 647]

Existing Model Roth IRA Documents. Sponsors that used any of the IRS model Roth IRA documents must have amended documents for EGTRRA and the RMD regulations, and existing Roth IRA owners must have adopted those amended documents by December 31, 2002. [Rev. Proc. 2002-10, §§ 3.01, 4.01, 2002-4 I.R.B. 1]

Roth IRAs Established Using Model Documents After Tuesday, October 1, 2002. Model documents that have been amended for EGTRRA and the RMD regulations must be used to establish new Roth IRAs after October 1, 2002. [Rev. Proc. 2002-10, § 4.01, 2002-4 I.R.B. 1; I.R.S. Ann. 2002-49, 2002-19 I.R.B. 919, extended the June 1, 2002, date cited in Rev. Proc. 2002-10 to October 1, 2002, for which existing instead of revised model forms may be used to establish *new* Roth IRAs] The model Roth IRAs (Forms 5305-R, 5305-RA, and 5305-RB) already contain language permitting the acceptance of rollovers from designated Roth accounts (DRAs) (see chapter 10); thus, users of such forms do not need to amend their IRA document to permit such rollovers. [I.R.S. Ann. 2007-55 (June 4, 2007)]

Prototype Roth IRAs. Approved prototype Roth IRA documents must have been submitted for a new IRS opinion letter generally no later than December 31,

2002. Roth IRA owners that had an existing approved prototype Roth IRA must have adopted the sponsoring financial organization's amended prototype document within 180 days after the date the IRS issues a favorable EGTRRA opinion letter. Alternatively, the Roth IRA owner could have adopted an appropriate model document by December 31, 2002. [Rev. Proc. 2002-10, §§ 3.01, 4.02, 2002-4 I.R.B. 1] A prototype Roth IRA must be amended in order to allow the rollover of amounts from designated Roth accounts or more simply "DRAs" (see chapter 10). In general, the amendment must be made before the DRA distribution can be rolled over. [I.R.S. Ann. 2007-55, 2007 I.R.B. 1384 (June 4, 2007)]

> **Note.** The model Roth IRA (Form 5305-R, 5305-RA, and 5305-RB) already contains language permitting the acceptance of rollovers from designated Roth accounts (see Q 1:38).

Section 408(c) IRAs. Drafters of a currently approved employer or association Roth IRA (a group Roth IRA trust, custodial account, or annuity) under Code Section 408(c) must have amended their documents and submit an application for an opinion letter no later than October 1, 2002. An employer or employee association that used an approved Section 408(c) Roth IRA must adopt the amended Roth IRA within 30 days after the date the IRS issued a favorable EGTRRA opinion letter on the amended document. [Rev. Proc. 2002-10, §§ 3.01, 4.03, 2002-4 I.R.B. 1; Rev. Proc. 98-59, § 3.05, 1998-2 C.B. 729]

Roth IRA Annuities. The issuer of a Roth IRA annuity contract must generally apply to one or more state insurance departments for state approval of amended documents. The IRS provided expedited review of such documents if

1. The IRS-approved EGTRRA document is submitted to the state insurance department within 90 days of the date the IRS issues a favorable EGTRRA opinion letter; and

2. The prototype sponsor resubmits the document as amended by the state insurance department to the IRS within 90 days after it is approved by the state insurance department.

[Rev. Proc. 2002-10, §§ 3.01, 4.03, 2002-4 I.R.B. 1]

Form 5306, Application for Approval of Prototype or Employer Sponsored Individual Retirement Arrangement (IRA) (revised October 2006), is used for submitting a prototype traditional or Roth IRA, as well as an employer-sponsored prototype traditional or Roth IRA under Code Section 408(c). To receive a favorable opinion letter (see appendix G), prototype documents must address every point in the Roth IRA Listing of Required Modifications (Roth IRA LRM) unless an item is clearly inapplicable. Form 5306 may be filed by a sponsoring organization that is:

- A bank (including savings and loan associations that qualify as banks and federally insured credit unions),
- An insurance company,
- A regulated investment company, or

- A trade or professional society or association (other than employee associations).

Employers or employee associations who want a ruling under Code Section 408(c) for a trust which will be used for individual retirement accounts may file this form. The term *employee association* means any organization composed of two or more employees, including, but not limited to, an employee association exempt from tax under Code Section 501(c)(4).

If a sponsor uses a prototype Roth IRA designed by a mass submitter, the mass submitter files Form 5306 on the sponsor's behalf.

The rules and deadlines for updating Roth IRA documents are summarized in Table 1-1.

Table 1-1. Roth IRA Document Rules and Deadlines

Document Type	Adopted By	Use for New Accounts	Adoption by Existing Accounts
Form 5305-R	Participant	After Oct. 1, 2002	By Dec. 31, 2002
Form 5305-A	Participant	After Oct. 1, 2002	By Dec. 31, 2002
Form 5305-RB	Participant	After June 1, 2002	By Dec. 31, 2002
		Submitted to IRS	*Adopt By*
Currently approved Roth IRA prototype	Participant	By Dec. 31, 2002	180 days after EGTRRA opinion letter issued
Currently approved employer or association Roth IRA	Participant	By Oct. 31, 2002	30 days after EGTRRA opinion letter issued
Roth IRA opened in 2002 using non-IRS approved prototype	Participant	By Dec. 31, 2002	180 days after EGTRRA opinion letter issued
	Submitted to IRS	*Submitted to State Insurance Dept.*	*Resubmitted to IRS*
Roth IRA documents that use annuity contracts	Dec. 31, 2002	Within 90 days of IRS opinion letter	With changes made by state insurance dept. within 90 days of state approval

Trustees, custodians, and issuers must revise each related disclosure statement associated with the EGTRRA-approved documents and distribute the revised disclosure statement to each benefited individual at the time the updated document is provided (see Q 1:29). [Rev. Proc. 2002-10, § 4.04, 2002-4 I.R.B. 1]

Q 1:31   When are mass mailings of a new Roth IRA plan document or disclosure statement required?

A mass mailing to individuals who are party to a Roth IRA agreement is required when the "written governing instrument" (Form 5305-R, 5305-RA, or 5305-RB or a prototype) is amended (see Q 1:21). A mass mailing is not required, however, when only the disclosure statement changes. [Treas. Reg. § 1.408-6(d)(4)(ii)(C)]

If the Roth IRA plan document is amended after the account is no longer subject to revocation (see Q 1:37), the trustee or custodian must, not later than the 30th day after the later of the date on which the amendment is adopted or becomes effective, deliver or mail to the last known address of the Roth IRA owner or the owner's beneficiary a copy of such amendment, and if such amendment affects a matter described in the disclosure statement, a revised disclosure statement.

When the Treasury regulations were amended, many IRA trustees and custodians used this process to amend Article IX of the IRS model forms (see Q 1:23) to permit the following amendments:

1. An amendment to allow a surviving spouse beneficiary to retain the option of not treating the Roth IRA, on the death of the owner, as his or her own. [I.R.S. Notice 98-49, Q&A A-2, 1998-38 I.R.B. 5]

2. An amendment to permit annual (normal and catch-up) Roth IRA contributions to be made to the same Roth IRA that receives conversion contributions. (When the IRS originally released its model Roth IRA agreements, it was anticipated that Congress would require annual contributions and conversion contributions to be held in separate plans; however, the final technical corrections permit an individual to make annual contributions and conversion contributions to the same account.) The version of the IRS model forms issued after 2001 (see Q 1:21) permits the acceptance of annual and conversion contributions in the same Roth IRA.

The IRS guidance on amending Roth IRA plan documents and disclosure statements that was announced on January 3, 2002 (see Q 1:30), required mass mailings of new Roth IRA plan documents and disclosure statements. [Rev. Proc. 2002-10, § 4.04, 2002-4 I.R.B. 1]

Q 1:32   How does a trustee or custodian organization make certain that amendments to its Roth IRA agreement are effective?

On making the decision to amend its Roth IRA agreement, a trustee or custodian organization should select a date from which it will begin to use the updated plan agreement. For all Roth accounts that were opened before that date, a mass mailing should be made of the amendment piece only. Such action ensures that existing clients have the amendments made to the agreement for their files. As long as the original Roth IRA agreement allowed for unilateral amendments to be made by the trustee or custodian and state law does not say otherwise, no signatures are required on the amendment. [*See* I.R.S. Ann. 93-8, 1993-3 I.R.B. 61] In other words, a mass mailing is sufficient. A revised disclosure statement may also be required (see Qs 1:29, 1:30).

Q 1:33   Is there a penalty for not informing Roth IRA owners of an amendment to their Roth IRA agreement?

Yes. There is a $50-per-failure noncompliance penalty (see Q 1:31) for failure to provide amendments to a Roth IRA agreement to Roth IRA owners as required by the Treasury regulations. [I.R.C. § 6693]

Records Retention

Q 1:34   How long should a trustee or custodian retain records with respect to Roth IRAs?

The requirements for retaining records with respect to transactions between a Roth IRA owner or beneficiary and the IRA's trustee or custodian vary among government agencies, regulatory authorities, and states. In general, IRA transaction and documentation records should be retained for a minimum of five years after the IRA is closed or five years after the last report or documentation was generated, whichever is later. A five-year retention period is usually sufficient under the different authorities that require such records to be retained. An organization should review the state law specific to its state, however, to ensure compliance with that law.

Revoking a Roth IRA

Q 1:35   May a Roth IRA be revoked?

Yes. Any individual who enters into a Roth IRA agreement must be given the opportunity to revoke the establishment of the Roth IRA. The Treasury regulations prescribe two methods for satisfying this requirement (see Q 1:37).

If a timely revocation is received by the trustee or custodian, the individual is entitled to receive the entire amount contributed without any adjustments for such items as sales commissions, administrative fees (including CD early withdrawal penalties), or fluctuation in market value.

Q 1:36   How long does an individual have to revoke a Roth IRA?

Generally, the following circumstances determine how long an individual has to revoke a Roth IRA:

1. If the individual is given the disclosure statement on the same day the Roth IRA is established, he or she has seven days after the establishment date to exercise his or her right of revocation.

2. If the individual is given the disclosure statement at least seven days before the Roth IRA is established, no additional period for revocation is required.

In either event, an organization must establish its own procedures for accepting the revocation of a Roth IRA. It may require that the notice be in writing or that it be oral, or it can require both a written and an oral notice. If a written notice is required, and that is generally the case, the trustee or custodian must accept the postmark date as evidence of a timely delivery of the revocation. Most important, a Roth IRA trustee or custodian must prominently display at the beginning of its disclosure statement the circumstances under which an individual may revoke the Roth IRA, including the name, address, and telephone number of the person designated to receive notice of the revocation. [Treas. Reg. § 1.408-6(d)(4)]

Q 1:37   How must the revocation of a Roth IRA be reported?

Beginning with IRA contributions made and revoked in 1992, trustees and custodians must report such contributions (except transfers) on Form 5498, IRA Contribution Information. The same type of procedure applies to Roth IRAs (see Q 9:22). In addition, distributions that occur as a result of the revocation must be reported on Form 1099-R, Distributions From Pensions, Annuities, Retirement or Profit-Sharing Plans, IRAs, Insurance Contracts, etc. In general, code J is used to report a revocation distribution from a Roth IRA. Code J8 is used if the revocation is of a regular contribution with earnings, regardless of age. Code J is used for all other revocations of a Roth (i.e., a revocation of a conversion, rollover, or a regular contribution without earnings). If the revocation is of a regular contribution with earnings, a rollover or transfer from another Roth IRA, or a conversion with earnings, the taxpayer must file Form 5329, Additional Taxes on Qualified Plans (Including IRAs) and Other Tax-Favored Accounts, to show that the taxable amount of the distribution (if any) is not subject to the 10-percent early distribution penalty under Code Section 72(t). Form 8606, Nondeductible IRAs, may also need to be filed.

> **Note.** Before the release of Revenue Procedure 91-70 [1991-2 C.B. 899], which is still current, the revocation of an IRA was not required to be reported.

Prototype Roth IRA Documents

Q 1:38 Has the IRS issued any guidance on obtaining an opinion letter for a prototype Roth IRA?

Yes. Revenue Procedure 87-50 [1987-2 C.B. 647] provides the procedures for a sponsoring organization or a mass submitter (a "prototype sponsor") to apply to the IRS for an opinion letter on whether a prototype traditional IRA meets the requirements of the Code. Revenue Procedure 98-59 [1998-2 C.B. 727] modifies Revenue Procedure 87-50 to permit prototype sponsors to apply to the IRS for an opinion letter on whether a prototype Roth IRA meets the requirements of Code Section 408A. Revenue Procedure 87-50 also contains procedures for employers and employee associations to apply for a ruling on a Section 408(c) employer- or association-sponsored IRA (see Q 1:30).

Although the procedures for obtaining opinion letters from the IRS for a Roth IRA are contained in Revenue Procedure 98-59 [1998-2 C.B. 727], a checklist for Roth IRAs was included in the IRS's annual update of its procedures for obtaining ruling requests (see Q 1:38). [*See* Rev. Proc. 2008-4, Appendix C, 2008-1 I.R.B. 121]

A sponsor of a prototype Roth IRA who wishes to accept rollovers from designated Roth accounts (DRAs) (see chapter 10) must amend their IRA documents to reflect the acceptance of such rollovers. After 2007, a sponsor of a prototype Roth IRA may not accept an eligible rollover contribution from a designated Roth account prior to an amendment permitting such rollovers. No application to the IRS is required for continued reliance on an opinion letter. However, other changes may require a sponsor to amend its prototype. Such changes include:

1. The repayment of qualified reservist distributions (see Qs 3:19–3:124);
2. Rollovers to Roth IRAs from an employer's plan (see Q 6:5);
3. The elimination of the $100,000 MAGI conversion limit after 2009 (see Q 3:16);
4. Applicability of the cost-of-living adjustments to the contribution phase-out rules (see Q 2:7); and
5. Additional Roth IRA contributions by employees of certain employers in bankruptcy (see Q 2:1).

These changes are included in the most recent List of Required Modifications for Roth IRAs (see appendix G).

On January 3, 2002, the IRS released guidance on amending Roth IRA plan documents and disclosure statements (see Q 1:30). Similar rules apply to traditional IRA, SEP IRA, and SIMPLE IRA plan documents and disclosure statements; however, adoption, submission, and notification dates may differ from those applicable to a Roth IRA. [Rev. Proc. 2002-10, 2002-4 I.R.B. 1]

Revenue Procedure 2009-8 [2009-1 I.R.B. 229] provides guidance for complying with the user fee program (see Q 1:43). Special user-fee rules apply in the case of requests involving multiple entities, offices, fee categories, issues, or transactions. Typical user fees for Roth IRA plan documents are as follows:

- Mass submission of a prototype Roth IRA, per plan document (new or amended)—$3,000
- Sponsoring organization's word-for-word identical adoption of a mass submitter's prototype Roth IRA, per plan document or an amendment thereof—$200
- Sponsoring organization's minor modification of a mass submitter's prototype Roth IRA, per plan document—$750
- Sponsoring organization's nonmass submission of a prototype Roth IRA, per plan document—$3,000
- Opinion letters on employer- or association-sponsored Section 408(c) Roth IRAs—$3,000
- Opinion letters on dual-purpose (combined traditional and Roth) IRAs—
  - Mass submission of a prototype dual-purpose IRA, per plan document, new or amended—$4,500
  - Sponsoring organization's word-for-word identical adoption of a mass submitter's prototype dual-purpose IRA, per plan document or an amendment thereof—$200
  - Sponsoring organization's minor modification of a mass submitter's prototype dual-purpose IRA, per plan document—$750
  - Sponsoring organization's nonmass submission of prototype dual-purpose IRA, per plan document—$4,500
- Approval to become a nonbank trustee under Treasury Regulations Section 1.408-2(e)—$14,500
- Letter rulings—generally $9,000

If a mass submitter submits, in any 12-month period ending January 31, more than 300 applications on behalf of word-for-word adopters of prototype IRAs with respect to a particular plan document, only the first 300 such applications will be subject to the fee; no fee will apply to those in excess of the first 300 such applications submitted within the 12-month period. [Rev. Proc. 2009-8, §§ 6. 02–6.03, 2009-1 I.R.B. 229]

Q 1:39   May an employer or an association of employees establish a Roth IRA for the benefit of its employees or members?

Yes. A trust established by an employer or an association of employees for the benefit of employees or members, respectively, is frequently called a "Section 408(c) IRA." Such an arrangement must provide separate accounting for each employee or member and must otherwise satisfy the requirements for a Roth IRA under Code Section 408A. [I.R.C. § 408(c)(2)]

An employer or employee association may apply to the IRS for an opinion letter on a Section 408(c) IRA that is a Roth IRA using the procedures that apply to a prototype Roth IRA (see Qs 1:38, 1:43). [*See* Rev. Proc. 87-50, 1987-2 C.B. 647 (*as modified by* Rev. Proc. 91-44, 1991-2 C.B. 733 (*as modified by* Rev. Proc. 2008-8, 2008-1 I.R.B. 233)), and Rev. Proc. 92-38, 1992-1 C.B. 859]

Q 1:40   May an IRS model Roth IRA form be submitted to the IRS as a prototype?

No. IRS model forms (see Q 1:20), including those used to create a Roth IRA agreement, should not be submitted to the IRS for consideration as a prototype. [Rev. Proc. 98-59, § 3.05, 1998-2 C.B. 729]

Q 1:41   May an IRS model Roth IRA form be submitted to the IRS as a prototype if additional provisions are included?

Yes. An IRS model Roth IRA form may not be submitted to the IRS for approval as a prototype if additional provisions are added to Article IX of the model form. Of course, the additional provisions must comply with the instructions for Article IX (see Qs 1:20, 1:23). [Rev. Proc. 98-59, §§2.04, 3.05, 1998-2 C.B. 727]

Q 1:42   May an opinion letter be obtained for a document whose language is identical to the language contained in an IRS model Roth IRA form?

No. The IRS will not issue an opinion letter on a document whose provisions match word-for-word the operative provisions of one of its model Roth IRA forms (other than any provisions that may be added to the form in Article IX; see Qs 1:24, 1:41). Such a document is deemed to meet the statutory requirements for a Roth IRA. The document should, however, indicate which model form it is identical to and the revision date of the form. [Rev. Proc. 98-59, § 3.05, 1998-2 C.B. 727]

Q 1:43   How is an opinion letter on a prototype Roth IRA requested from the IRS?

A prototype sponsor may apply to the IRS for an opinion letter on a Roth IRA by using the procedures (Form 5306) and paying the user fees that apply to a submission for an opinion letter on a traditional IRA. Form 5306 must be accompanied by a user fee that varies according to the user's intentions (see Q 1:38). [*See* Rev. Proc. 2009-8, 2009-1 I.R.B. 229]

Q 1:44   May a prototype document be used to establish more than one type of IRA?

No. Although a prototype document may be used only for one type of IRA (traditional, SIMPLE, or Roth), a prototype document may be designed for either a traditional IRA or a Roth IRA (dual-purpose prototype) if the following requirements are met:

1. On execution of the document, the IRA owner explicitly and unambiguously indicates whether the IRA is to be a Roth IRA or a traditional IRA, and it is clear that designation as one type precludes designation as the other type.

2. Contributions to a Roth IRA and contributions to a traditional IRA are maintained in separate trusts, custodial accounts, or annuities. [Treas. Reg. §§ 1.408-2(c)(3), 1.408A-2]

Q 1:45   Do any special requirements apply to the submission of a document that can be used as a dual-purpose prototype?

Yes. Application for approval of a dual-purpose prototype document (see Q 1:43) must be submitted on Form 5306, with the words "Dual-purpose IRA" written in the upper margin of the form. Except in the case of certain word-for-word identical adoptions, the user fee is $4,500 ($1,500 more than which applies to a prototype IRA or Roth IRA). [Rev. Proc. 2009-9, § 6.02, 2009-1 I.R.B. 229; Rev. Proc. 98-59, 1998-2 C.B. 727]

Q 1:46   Has the IRS issued any sample language for use by prototype sponsors?

Yes. The IRS has issued sample language (also known as an LRM) that it finds acceptable for use by prototype sponsors (see appendix G).

Prohibited Transactions and Related Definitions

Q 1:47   What is a plan for purposes of the prohibited transaction rules?

For purposes of the prohibited transaction rules, the term *plan* means (1) a trust described in Code Section 401(a) that forms a part of a plan, or a plan described in Code Section 403(a) exempt from tax under Code Section 501(a), and (2) an IRA. [I.R.C. § 4975(e)(1); ERISA § 3]

Q 1:48   Is a Roth IRA subject to the prohibited transaction provisions of the Code?

Yes. Notwithstanding whether a Roth IRA is a plan within the meaning of Title I of ERISA, the prohibited transaction provisions of Code Section 4975 are applicable to transactions by a Roth IRA. [I.R.C. §§408A(a), 4975(e)(1)]

Q 1:49   What is a *prohibited transaction*?

A *prohibited transaction* includes any direct or indirect

- Sale, exchange, or lease of any property between a plan (defined in Code Section 4975(e)(1) to include a Roth IRA) and a disqualified person (see Q 1:51);

- Loan of money or other extension of credit between a plan and a disqualified person;

- Provision of goods, services, or facilities between a plan and a disqualified person;

- Transfer to, or use by or for the benefit of, a disqualified person of the income or assets of the plan;

- Act by a disqualified person who is a fiduciary whereby he or she deals with the income or assets of a plan in his or her own interest or for his or her own account; or

- Receipt of any consideration for his or her own personal account by any disqualified person who is a fiduciary from any party dealing with the plan in connection with a transaction involving the income or assets of the plan.

[I.R.C. § 4975(c); ERISA § 406; *see* D.O.L. Interpretive Bulletin 94-3, 59 Fed. Reg. 66735 (1994) (in-kind contributions to satisfy statutory or contractual funding obligations); Marshall v. Snyder, 430 F. Supp. 1224 (E.D.N.Y. 1977), *aff'd in part and remanded in part*, 572 F.2d 894 (2d Cir. 1978) (furnishing of goods, services, or facilities); Leigh v. Engle, 727 F.2d 113 (7th Cir. 1984) (self-dealing); New York State Teamsters Council Health & Hosp. Fund v. Estate of De Perno, 816 F. Supp. 138 (N.D.N.Y. 1993), *aff'd in part and remanded*, 18 F.3d 179 (2d Cir. 1994) (self-dealing, financial loss to trust fund not necessary); *see also* D.O.L. Adv. Ops. 86-01A, 88-03A, 89-089A, 93-06A (direct expenses of salary and related cost of employees that work on plans)]

In a recent DOL Advisory Opinion, the DOL concluded that a self-directed IRA's investment in notes of a corporation, a majority of whose stock is owned by the son-in-law of the IRA owner, would be a prohibited transaction under the Code. [D.O.L. Adv. Op. 2006-09A (Dec. 19, 2006); I.R.C. § 4975(c)(1)(A)–(B)]

Example. Damian Corporation established a payroll deduction Roth IRA and makes contributions into a group (employer) Roth IRA trust under Code Section 408(c). Damian, a fiduciary, retains his daughter Miriam to provide much-needed administrative services to the plan's trust for a fee. Miriam's provision of services to the trust is a prohibited transaction. The prohibited transaction may, however, be exempt from the excise tax if it meets certain conditions. As a fiduciary, Damian's action causing the plan to pay a fee to his daughter is a separate prohibited transaction, which would not be exempt. [I.R.C. § 4975(d)(2); I.R.M. 4.72.11.3.5, Fiduciary Self-Dealing; *see* David A. Pratt, "Focus on Prohibited Transactions—Part I," 10 *J. Pension Benefits* 2 (Winter 2003), which outlines transactions that are prohibited and the transactions that are exempt from prohibitions]

Note. The penalty for initial violations is 15 percent of the amount involved for prohibited transactions occurring after August 5, 1997. If the transaction is not corrected, there is a second-tier excise tax of 100 percent of the amount involved. [I.R.C. § 4975(a); SBJPA § 1 453(a); TRA '97 § 1074(a);

Ralf Zacky v. Comm'r, T.C. Memo. 2004-130 (May 27, 2004), sole-shareholder liable for the first- and second-tier I.R.C. § 4975 excise tax on prohibited loan transactions]

Q 1:50   May the prohibited transaction rules be waived?

Yes. The Secretary of the Treasury has established a procedure under which a conditional or unconditional exemption from all or part of the prohibited transaction rules may be granted to any disqualified person or transaction or to any class of disqualified persons or transactions. [D.O.L. Reg. §§ 2570.30–2570.52] The Secretary of Labor generally may not grant an exemption unless he or she finds that such an exemption is

1. Administratively feasible;
2. In the interests of the plan and its participants and beneficiaries; and
3. Protective of the rights of participants and beneficiaries of the plan.

Although the IRS has the final authority to determine whether a Roth IRA is disqualified under Code Section 408(e)(2), the DOL has the authority to issue waivers that are binding under ERISA Section 408 and Code Section 4975. In a Field Service Advice, the IRS explained that authority to define prohibited transactions has been transferred to the DOL, although the IRS retains enforcement authority along with the DOL. [F.S.A. 1999-524]

[I.R.C. § 4975(c)(2); Reorg. Plan No. 4 of 1978, 43 Fed. Reg. 47713 (Oct. 17, 1978) (transferring the authority of the Secretary of the Treasury to issue rulings under Code Section 4975 to the Secretary of Labor)] The Secretary of Labor has delegated this authority, along with most other responsibilities under ERISA, to the Assistant Secretary for the EBSA. [Sec. of Labor's Order 1-87, 52 Fed. Reg. 13139 (Apr. 28, 1987)] This transfer of jurisdiction clarified the Reorganization Plan No. 4 of 1978 and was accomplished in meetings held between the two agencies on August 4, 1987, which were memorialized by a letter dated October 6, 1987, from the Assistant Commissioner (Employee Plans and Exempt Organizations) to the DOL.

Q 1:51   Who is a disqualified person under the Code, and who is a party in interest under ERISA?

For purposes of the Code, the term *disqualified person* refers to any of the following:

1. A fiduciary (see Q 1:52);
2. A person providing services to a plan;
3. An employer any of whose employees are covered by a plan;
4. An employee organization any of whose members are covered by a plan;
5. An owner, direct or indirect, of 50 percent or more of the combined voting power of all classes of stock entitled to vote or the total value of shares of all classes of stock of a corporation, the capital interest or the profits

interest of a partnership, or the beneficial interest of a trust or unincorporated enterprise that is an employer or an employee organization described in item 3 or 4;

6. A member of the family (spouse, ancestor, lineal descendant, or any spouse of a lineal descendant) of a person described in item 1, 2, 3, or 5;

7. A corporation, partnership, or trust or estate of which (or in which) 50 percent or more of the combined voting power of all classes of stock entitled to vote or the total value of shares of all classes of stock of such corporation, the capital interest or profits interest of such partnership, or the beneficial interest of such trust or estate is owned directly or indirectly or held by a person described in item 1, 2, 3, 4, or 5;

8. An officer or a director (or an individual having powers or responsibilities similar to those of an officer or a director), a 10 percent or more shareholder, or a highly compensated employee (earning 10 percent or more of the yearly wages of an employer) of a person described in item 3, 4, 5, or 7; or

9. A 10 percent or more (in capital or profits) partner or joint venturer of a person described in item 3, 4, 5, or 7.

Note. ERISA prohibits certain transactions between a plan and a *party in interest*. Under the Code, the term *disqualified person* is used instead of *party in interest* and it is defined slightly differently.

[I.R.C. § 4975(e)(2)]

For purposes of ERISA, the term *party in interest* refers to the following:

1. Any fiduciary (including, but not limited to, any administrator, officer, trustee, or custodian), counsel, or employee of an employee benefit plan;

2. A person providing services to a plan; [*See* Harris Trust and Savings Bank v. Solomon Smith Barney, 530 U.S. 238 (2000) (broker-dealer providing nondiscretionary equity trades to plan automatically classified as party in interest)]

3. An employer any of whose employees are covered by a plan;

4. An employee organization any of whose members are covered by a plan;

5. An owner, direct or indirect, of 50 percent or more of the combined voting power of all classes of stock entitled to vote or the total value of shares of all classes of stock of a corporation, the capital interest or the profits interest of a partnership, or the beneficial interest of a trust or unincorporated enterprise that is an employer or an employee organization described in item 3 or 4;

6. A relative (spouse, ancestor, lineal descendant, or any spouse of a lineal descendant) of any person described in item 1, 2, 3, or 5;

7. A corporation, partnership, or trust or estate of which (or in which) 50 percent or more of the combined voting power of all classes of stock entitled to vote or the total value of shares of all classes of stock of such corporation, the capital interest or profits interest of such partnership, or

the beneficial interest of such trust or estate is owned directly or indirectly or held by persons described in item 1, 2, 3, 4, or 5;

8. An employee, an officer, or a director (or an individual having powers or responsibilities similar to those of an officer or a director), a 10 percent or more shareholder, or a highly compensated employee (earning 10 percent or more of the yearly wages of an employer) of a person described in item 2, 3, 4, or 5; or

9. A 10 percent or more (in capital or profits) partner or joint venturer of a person described in item 2, 3, 4, 5, or 7.

[ERISA § 3(14)]

Example 1. George is the general partner and owner of a 6.5 percent interest in an investment club partnership formed by various family members. The partnership is managed by an outside brokerage firm and George receives no compensation. George instructs his Roth IRA trustee to purchase an interest in the partnership. Is this a prohibited transaction? No. Because of George's status in the partnership and his control over the investment of his assets, George is a disqualified person; but because he owns less than a 10 percent interest in the partnership, the partnership itself is not a disqualified person. Therefore, transactions between it and the partnership would not be prohibited. [D.O.L. Op. Ltr. 2000-10A (July 27, 2000)]

Caution. In the preceding example, George does not and will not receive any compensation from the partnership and will not receive any compensation by virtue of the Roth IRA's investment in the partnership. However, if a Roth IRA fiduciary causes the Roth IRA to enter into a transaction where, by the terms or nature of that transaction, a conflict of interest between the Roth IRA and the fiduciary (or persons in which the fiduciary has an interest) exists or will arise in the future, that transaction may violate either Code Section 4975(c)(1)(D) or (E). "Moreover, the fiduciary must not rely upon and cannot be otherwise dependent upon the participation of the IRA in order for the fiduciary (or persons in which the fiduciary has an interest) to undertake or to continue his or her share of the investment. Furthermore, even if at its inception the transaction did not involve a violation, if a divergence of interests develops between the IRA and the fiduciary (or persons in which the fiduciary has an interest), the fiduciary must take steps to eliminate the conflict of interest in order to avoid engaging in a prohibited transaction." Nonetheless, a violation of Code Section 4975(c)(1)(D) or (E) will not occur merely because the fiduciary derives some incidental benefit from a transaction involving Roth IRA assets. [D.O.L. Op. Ltr. 2000-10A (July 27, 2000)]

Example 2. Gretta established a Roth IRA. She instructs her Roth IRA custodian to execute a subscription agreement to purchase newly issued shares of a corporation that she recently formed. The Roth IRA became the sole-shareholder of the corporation of which Gretta was and remains the director. The payment of dividends by the corporation to the Roth IRA did not constitute a prohibited transaction. The corporation is not a disqualified person. A corporation without shares or shareholders does not fit the definition of a disqualified person under Code Section 4975(e)(2)(G). The newly issued shares were not owned by anyone at the time of sale; thus, their sale to the Roth IRA was not a sale or exchange of property between the plan (Roth IRA) and a disqualified person. [I.R.C. § 4975(c)(1)(A)] The dividends did not become income of the Roth IRA until unqualifiedly made subject to the demand of the Roth IRA; thus, there was no use of the Roth IRA assets for the benefit of a disqualified person. [I.R.C. § 4975(c)(1)(D); Treas. Reg. § 1.301-1(b); Swanson v. Comm'r, 106 T.C. 76 (1996); *see also* F.S.A. 1994-524 conceding *Swanson*]

Note. The *Swanson* court addressed the actions of arranging for IRA ownership of stock and for the subsequent payment of dividends by the corporation to the IRA by stating: "considered together, [the actions] did not constitute an act whereby a fiduciary directly or indirectly 'deals with income or assets of a plan in his own interest or for his own account,'" within the meaning of Code Section 4975(c)(1)(E). The court noted that the Commissioner had not alleged that the taxpayer had ever dealt with the corpus of the IRA for his own benefit, but stated that the "receipt by a disqualified person of any benefit to which he may be entitled as a participant or beneficiary in the plan, so long as the benefit is computed and paid on a basis which is consistent with the terms of the plan as applied to all other participants and beneficiaries" does not violate Code Section 4975(c). [*See exception at* I.R.C. § 4975(d)(9)]

Example 3. Same facts as in Example 2. Gretta instructs her Roth IRA trustee to loan funds to the new corporation. Although the acquisition by the Roth IRA of the shares was not a prohibited transaction, a prohibited use of plan assets or an act of self-dealing is likely to result if Gretta directs her Roth trustee to loan funds to the corporation. Code Section 4975(c)(1)(D) prohibits any direct or indirect transfer to, or use by or for the benefit of, a disqualified person of the income or assets of a plan. Code Section 4975(c)(1)(E) prohibits a fiduciary from dealing with the income or assets of a plan in his or her own interest or for his or her own account. The pension excise tax regulations characterizes transactions described in Code Section 4975(c)(1)(E) as involving the use of authority by fiduciaries to cause plans to enter into transactions when those fiduciaries have interests that may affect the exercise of their best judgment as fiduciaries. Gretta is a fiduciary with respect to the Roth IRA. In addition, she has a substantial interest in the corporation. Therefore, the corporation is a party in whom Gretta has an interest that might affect her best judgment as a fiduciary. Accordingly, a prohibited use of plan assets for the benefit of a disqualified person under Code Section 4975(c)(1)(D) or an act of self-dealing under Code Section 4975(c)(1)(E) is likely to result if Gretta directs the Roth IRA to loan funds to the corporation.

[PWBA Advisory Opinion letter issued to Joseph E. Hurst Jr., (F-3819A, dated Dec. 23, 1988); Rollins v. Comm'r, T.C. Memo 2004-260 (Nov. 14, 2004); Lowen v. Tower Asset Mgmt., Inc., 289 F.2d 1209 (2d Cir. 1987); Treas. Reg. § 54.4975-6(a)(5); *see also* Matta, Richard K., "Self-Directed IRA

Myths," Groom Law Group, Chartered (May 12, 2009), available at *http://www.groom.com/media/publication/441_IRA%20Myth%20Article%205.12.09.pdf* (visited on June 18, 2009)]

In Field Service Advice 200128011 a father owns the majority of the shares of a U.S. corporation. His three children own the remaining shares in equal amounts. The father and each of the children own separate IRAs. Each acquired a 25 percent interest in a new foreign sales corporation (FSC). The U.S. corporation then entered into service and commission agreements with the FSC and the FSC made cash distributions to the IRAs out of earnings and profits from foreign trade income from exports of the U.S. corporation. The IRS concluded that neither the original issuance of the stock of the FSC to the IRAs nor the payment of dividends is a prohibited transaction under Code Section 4975(c)(1)(D). In light of *Swanson v. Comm'r* [106 T.C. 76 (1996)], the IRS determined that the IRAs' ownership of FSC stock was not considered to be a prohibited transaction under Code Section 4975(c)(1)(E). However, the father's arrangement to have 75 percent of the FSC owned by his children, and for the FSC to earn profits under agreements with the U.S. corporation, results in a taxable gift to the children because the father did not receive any consideration for the arrangement. The IRS stated that the value of the gift is the difference between the children's combined beneficial interest in the amount of earnings and profits realized by the FSC and distributed to the IRAs, and the children's combined interest in the profits the U.S. corporation would have earned on the sales had the corporation not used the FSC. [F.S.A. 200128011 (July 13, 2001)]

> **Example 4.** Jerry and Fay set up a corporation, opened Roth IRA accounts, and then each directed their Roth IRA accounts to purchase 50 percent of the stock of the corporation. The transaction constituted a reportable transaction. Jerry and Fay must disclose the transaction on Form 8886 and include all the information required by the form. [Ltr. Rul. 200917030 (May 24, 2009); Treas. Reg. § 1.6011-4-(d)]

Q 1:52   Who is a fiduciary for purposes of ERISA?

The term *fiduciary* refers to any person who

1. Exercises any discretionary authority or discretionary control respecting management of a plan or exercises any authority or control respecting management or disposition of its assets;
2. Renders investment advice for a fee or other compensation, direct or indirect, with respect to any monies or other property of a plan, or has any authority or responsibility to do so; or
3. Has any discretionary authority or discretionary responsibility in the administration of a plan.

The ERISA statute, however, is not the only source of law in this area. The DOL, acting pursuant to a statutory grant of authority, has adopted regulations defining when a person is deemed to be providing investment advice for purposes of ERISA Section 3(21)(A)(ii). The regulations significantly narrow the class of stockbrokers who might otherwise fall within the statutory definition. The regulation's definition of the term *fiduciary*, as applied to stockbrokers, therefore, includes two classes. The regulation includes stockbrokers who actually have discretionary authority with regard to buying and selling securities, a situation not present in this case. The second alternative, however, does not require that the stockbroker have discretion or control. It merely requires rendering of investment advice pursuant to a mutual agreement that the stockbroker's advice will serve as a primary basis for investment decisions and that the broker will render "individualized investment advice" as defined by the regulations.

The law, as implemented by the regulation, requires only that the stockbroker (1) render investment advice to the plan on a regular basis, (2) pursuant to a mutual agreement, arrangement, or understanding, written or otherwise between the broker and a plan fiduciary, (3) that such services will serve as a primary basis for investment decisions with respect to plan assets, and (4) that the broker will render "individualized investment advice" to the plan based on the particular needs of the plan. [Ellis v. Rycenga Homes, Inc., 484 F. Supp. 2d 694 (W.D. Mich. 2007); 29 C.F.R. § 2510.3-21(c)(1)(ii)(B)] Thus, to be "individualized" within the meaning of the regulation, advice must pertain to investment policies or strategy or portfolio composition or diversification. [29 C.F.R. § 2510.3-21(c)(1)(ii)(B)] In other words, the advice must address the individual needs of the plan.

Note 1. A person who is designated by a named fiduciary to carry out fiduciary responsibilities (other than trustee responsibilities under the plan) is treated as a fiduciary.

Note 2. An individual who does not have discretionary authority may still be a fiduciary by providing individualized investment advice with the expectation that the account owner will act on it. This is because ERISA defines *fiduciary* to include someone who provides investment advice for a fee (see Q 1:53, but see Q 1:54).

Accountants, attorneys, actuaries, insurance agents, and consultants who provide services to a plan are not considered fiduciaries unless they exercise discretionary authority or control over the management or administration of the plan or the assets of the plan, even if such activities are unauthorized. [ERISA § 3(21)(A); P.W.B.A. Interpretive Bulletin 75-5, Q&A D-1; D.O.L. Reg. § 2509.75-5, Q&A D-1; John Hancock Mut. Life Ins. Co. v. Harris Trust & Sav. Bank, 510 U.S. 86 (1993); Kaniewski v. Equitable Life Assurance Socy., No. 88-01296, 1993 WL 88200 (6th Cir. Mar. 26, 1993) (unpublished opinion); Kyle Rys Inc. v. Pacific Admin. Servs. Inc., 990 F.2d 513 (9th Cir. 1993) (third-party administrator); Nieto v. Ecker, 845 F.2d 868 (9th Cir. 1988) (attorneys); Olson v. E.F. Hutton & Co., 957 F.2d 622 (8th Cir. 1992); Procacci v. Drexel Burnham Lambert, No. 89-0555 (E.D. Pa. 1989); Painters of Phila. Dist. Council No. 21 Welfare Fund v. Price Waterhouse, 879 F.2d 1146 (3d Cir. 1989) (accountants); Pappas v. Buck Consultants Inc., 923 F.2d 531 (7th Cir. 1991) (actuaries); Schloegel v. Boswell, 994 F.2d 266 (7th Cir. 1993) (insurance agent)]

Note 3. Although not fiduciaries, accountants, attorneys, actuaries, insurance agents, and consultants may be liable to a plan under traditional theories of malpractice.

Note 4. The Pension Protection Act of 2006 (PPA) adds a new category of prohibited transaction exemption under ERISA and the Code in connection with the provision of investment advice through an "eligible investment advice arrangement" to beneficiaries of Roth IRAs (and other IRAs) and to participants and beneficiaries of a defined contribution plan who direct the investment of their accounts under the plan (e.g., DRCP, see Q 10:1). (See Q 1.54.)

Note 5. The PPA offers relief in that a transaction between a plan and a party-in-interest (e.g., service provider), who is not a fiduciary, is not a prohibited transaction (i.e., sale, exchange, lease, loan, or use of plan assets) under ERISA Section 406 so long as the plan receives no less than adequate consideration, or pays no more than, adequate consideration for the transaction (see Qs 1:48–1:52). [I.R.C. § 4975(d)(20); ERISA §§ 406(a)(1)(A), (B) and (D), 408(b)(17); *see* PPA § 611(j)]

Q 1:53 **Is an individual who advises a participant, in exchange for a fee, on how to invest the assets in the participant's Roth IRA account, or who manages the investment of the participant's Roth IRA account, a fiduciary with respect to the Roth IRA within the meaning of ERISA Section 3(21)(A)?**

Yes. Directing the investment of a plan constitutes the exercise of authority and control over the management or disposition of plan assets and means the person directing the investments is a fiduciary, even if the person is chosen by the participant and has no other connection to the plan. Under D.O.L. Regulations Section 2510.3-21(c), "a person will be deemed to be rendering investment advice if such person renders advice to the plan as to the value of securities or other property, or makes a recommendation as to the advisability of investing in, purchasing, or selling securities or other property and such person either directly or indirectly has discretionary authority or control, whether or not pursuant to an agreement, arrangement or understanding, with respect to purchasing or selling securities or other property for the plan; or renders any such advice on a regular basis to the plan pursuant to a mutual agreement, arrangement or understanding, written or otherwise, between such person and the plan or a fiduciary with respect to the plan, that such services will serve as a primary basis for investment decisions with respect to plan assets, and that such person will render individualized investment advice to the plan based on the particular needs of the plan regarding such matters as, among other things, investment policies or strategy, overall portfolio composition, or diversification of plan investments." [D.O.L. Adv. Op. 2005-23A (Dec. 7, 2005)] The DOL has taken the position that this definition of fiduciary also applies to investment advice provided to a participant or beneficiary in an individual account plan that allows participants or beneficiaries to direct the investment of their accounts. [D.O.L. Reg. § 2509.96-1(c)]

The other fiduciaries of the plan would not be liable as fiduciaries for either the selection of the investment manager or investment adviser or the results of the investment manager's decisions or investment adviser's recommendations. Other fiduciaries of the plan may have co-fiduciary liability with regard to the plan if, for example, they knowingly participate in a breach committed by the participant's fiduciary. [ERISA § 405(a)] Other plan fiduciaries would not have any obligation to advise the participant about the investment manager or investment adviser or their investment decisions or recommendations. [D.O.L. Reg. § 2550.404c-1(f), ex. (9); *see also* D.O.L. Adv. Op. 84-04A (Jan. 4, 1984), which states that if a person is deemed to be giving investment advice within the meaning of D.O.L. Reg. § 2510.3-21(c)(1)(ii)(B), the presence of an unrelated second fiduciary acting on the investment adviser's recommendations on behalf of the plan is not sufficient to insulate the investment adviser from fiduciary liability under ERISA Section 406(b). Note that the regulation (D.O.L. Reg. § 2510.3-21(c)(1)(B)) presupposes the existence of a second fiduciary who by agreement or conduct manifests a mutual understanding to rely on the investment adviser's recommendations as a primary basis for the investment of plan assets. In the presence of such an agreement or understanding, the rendering of investment advice involving self-dealing will subject the investment adviser to liability under ERISA Section 406(b). The DOL believes that the same principles enunciated in Advisory Opinion 84-04A apply in the context of a financial planner or investment adviser who renders investment advice to a participant in a participant-directed plan.]

Q 1:54 Are there any exemptions from the prohibited transaction rules for providing individualized investment advice?

Yes. On August 17, 2006, the PPA was enacted into law. The PPA contains a number of significant tax incentives to enhance retirement savings and to relax some of the prohibited transaction rules as they apply to providing individualized investment advice.

ERISA and the Code prohibit certain transactions between an employer-sponsored retirement plan and a disqualified person, referred to as a "party-in-interest" under ERISA. [ERISA § 406; I.R.C. § 4975] Under ERISA, the prohibited transaction rules apply to employer-sponsored retirement plans and to welfare benefit plans. Under the Code, the prohibited transaction rules apply to qualified retirement plans and qualified retirement annuities, as well as to IRAs, HSAs, Archer MSAs, and to Coverdell education savings accounts.

The PPA adds a new category of prohibited transaction exemption under ERISA and the Code in connection with the provision of investment advice through an "eligible investment advice arrangement" to beneficiaries of Roth IRAs (and other IRAs) and to participants and beneficiaries of a defined contribution plan who direct the investment of their accounts under the plan (e.g., DRCP, see Q 10:1). The statutory exemption permits investment advice to be given either on a level-fee basis or via a computer model certified as unbiased by a fiduciary adviser. If the requirements of the exemption are met, the restrictions under ERISA Sections 406(a) and (b), relating to prohibited trans-actions, and the sanctions resulting from the application of the prohibited transaction rules under Code Sections 4975(c)(1)(A) through (F), do not apply, and the following are exempt from prohibited transaction treatment:

- The provision of investment advice;
- An investment transaction (i.e., a sale, acquisition, or holding of a security or other property) pursuant to the advice;
- The direct or indirect receipt of fees or other compensation in connection with the provision of the advice or an investment transaction pursuant to the advice.

[PPA § 601, adding ERISA §§ 408(b)(14), 408(g) and I.R.C. §§ 4975(d)(17), 4975(f)(8)]

Note 1. The prohibited transaction exemptions provided under the provision do not in any manner alter existing individual or class exemptions provided by statute or administrative action.

Note 2. Generally, an affiliate of a person affiliated with funds offered under a plan may not give investment advice under the prohibited transaction rules. Although the DOL had carved out administrative exceptions, the PPA's exemption added a "flat-fee" rule where any fees for the advice do not vary depending upon the option selected (see example in Q 1:55), and for model-driven advice similar to the DOL's administrative exception (but now also applicable to IRAs, including Roth IRAs, and HSAs). The PPA's statutory exemption and proposed class exemption for eligible investment advice arrangements apply to parties affiliated with the funds offered under the plan.

The determination regarding a computer model was to be made by December 31, 2007. If the Secretary of Labor determines that there is such a program (which it has), the statutory exemption described above applies to the use of the program with respect to Roth IRA beneficiaries. The DOL and Treasury Depart-ments concluded that there are computer model investment advice programs that meet the PPA criteria. As a result, the PPA restriction on the availability of the statutory exemption was lifted as of August 21, 2008, the date the DOL submitted its report to Congress. [*See* U.S. D.O.L. Report to Congress (Aug. 21, 2008), available at *http://www.dol.gov/ebsa/publications/reporttocongress.html* (visited on June 18, 2009)]

On August 21, 2008, the DOL also released a proposed regulation (which has since been finalized), implementing the statutory exemption under the PPA for the provision of investment advice to participants in participant-directed individual account plans and IRAs (including a Roth IRA), and providing for the provision of investment advice through a computer model. [RIN 1210-AB13, 73 Fed. Reg. 49896–49923 (Aug. 22, 2008); Prop. D.O.L. Reg. § 2550.408g-1(j)(2)] The proposed DOL regulations (as do the final regulations) adopt mostly procedural standards for the certification of computer models under the PPA's exemptive relief and the obligations of providers. [Prop. D.O.L. Reg.

§§ 2550.408g-1, 2550.408g-2] In addition, a proposed class exemption from the prohibited transaction rules was issued for the provision of individualized investment advice to individuals following the furnishing of recommendations generated by a computer model (or, in the case of an IRA (or Roth IRA) with respect to which modeling is not feasible, the furnishing of certain investment educational material). Additional conditions apply. [*See* Prop. PTE (RIN 1210-ZA14), 73 Fed. Reg. 49924 (Aug. 22, 2008)]

> **Note.** Unlike the statutory exemption and DOL regulations, the class exemption provides relief for individualized investment advice to individuals following the furnishing of recommendations generated by a computer model or, in the case of an IRA or Roth IRA with respect to which modeling is not feasible, the furnishing of certain investment education material. The computer-generated advice recommendations and investment education materials are intended to provide individual account plan participants and beneficiaries and IRA beneficiaries with a context for assessing and evaluating the individualized investment advice contemplated by the exemption.

On January 21, 2009, the DOL finalized the investment advice regulations and the class exemption. [74 Fed. Reg. 3822–3851 (Jan. 21, 2009)] The final regulations make clear that:

1. A plan or plan sponsor is not under any obligation to provide investment advice. [D.O.L. Reg. § 2550-408g-1(a)(2)]

2. Neither the statutory exemption under ERISA Section 408(g)(1) nor the regulations issued thereunder invalidate or otherwise affect prior guidance concerning the circumstances under which the provision of investment advice would not constitute a prohibited transaction. [D.O.L. Reg. § 2550-408g-1(a)(3)]

3. Investment advice provided to plan sponsors is not covered by the exemption.

4. ERISA Section 404(c) does not limit the liability of fiduciary advisers that, pursuant to the exemptions, specifically assume and acknowledge fiduciary responsibility for the provision of investment advice. This is because the investment advice (and related transactions) covered by the exemption and furnished to participants and beneficiaries are not the result of a participant's or beneficiary's exercise of control, and, accordingly, the fiduciary adviser would not be relieved of liability for such advice.

5. A fiduciary adviser may provide advice to its own employees (or employees of an affiliate) pursuant to an arrangement, provided that the fiduciary adviser or affiliate offers the same arrangement to participants and beneficiaries of unaffiliated plans in the ordinary course of its business. [D.O.L. Reg. §§ 2550-498g-1(b)(5)(ii) and (d)(5)(ii)]

Note. Neither the statutory exemption nor the class exemption provides relief for the selection of the fiduciary adviser or the arrangement pursuant to which advice will be provided. Accordingly, plan fiduciaries must nonetheless be prudent in their selection and may not, in contravention of ERISA Section 406(b), use their positions to benefit themselves. If a fiduciary provides services to a plan without the receipt of compensation or other consideration (other than reimbursement of direct expenses properly and actually incurred in the performance of such services) the provision of such services does not, in and of itself, constitute a prohibited act. [Preamble, D.O.L. Reg. § 2550-408g-1, 74 Fed. Reg. 3828; *see also* D.O.L. Reg. § 2550-408b-2(e)(3)]

Q 1:55   What is an "eligible investment advice arrangement?"

The exemptions discussed in Q 1:54 apply in connection with the provision of investment advice by a fiduciary adviser under an "eligible investment advice arrangement." An eligible investment advice arrangement is an arrangement:

1. That meets certain requirements (discussed below) and
2. That either
   a. Provides that any fees (including any commission or compensation) received by the fiduciary adviser for investment advice or with respect to an investment transaction involving plan assets do not vary depending on the basis of any investment option selected (sometimes referred to as fee-leveling) or
   b. Uses a computer model under an investment advice program as described below in connection with the provision of investment advice to a participant or beneficiary.

Note. Unlike the statutory exemption and final regulations, the class exemption (finalized on January 21, 2009) applies the fee-leveling limits solely to the compensation received by the employee, agent, or registered representative providing the advice on behalf of the fiduciary adviser. The fee-leveling limits under the class exemption do not consider compensation received by the fiduciary adviser on whose behalf the employee, agent, or registered representative is providing such advice. [*See also* D.O.L. Field Assistance Bulletin (Feb. 2, 2007), providing preliminary advice on the PPA's advice rules.]

Example. The Fine Family of Funds (a money management company) has an affiliate, Fine Advisors and Distributors, which provides advice to John, the owner of a Roth IRA. Sarah, a registered representative with Fine Advisors and Distributors, suggests that John exchange his fund shares in Fund Y for shares in Fund Z, which have higher expense ratios than Fund Y. Under the regulations, the additional compensation that is received by the Fine Family of Funds because of Sarah's redemption of Fund Y and exchange into Fund Z does not violate the flat fee rule. The effective date of the final rules has been delayed (see below).

In the case of an eligible investment advice arrangement, the arrangement must be expressly authorized by a plan fiduciary other than the person offering the investment advice program, or any person providing investment options under the plan, including an affiliate of either person. [D.O.L. Reg. § 2550-408g-1(b)(5); Prop. D.O.L. Reg. § 2550.408g-1(e)] An eligible investment advice arrangement does not include "brokerage windows," "self-directed brokerage accounts," or similar plan arrangements that enable participants and beneficiaries to select investments beyond those designated by the plan. [Preamble, D.O.L. Reg. § 2550-408g-1, 74 Fed. Reg. 3826 (Jan. 21, 2009)]

Investment advice program using a computer model. In general, if an eligible investment advice arrangement provides investment advice pursuant to a computer model, the model must satisfy all of the following requirements:

1. Applies generally accepted investment theories that takes into account the historic returns of different asset classes over defined periods of time. The regulations do not preclude investment advice under a computer model from also taking into account generally accepted investment theories that take into account additional considerations. [D.O.L. Reg. §§ 2550.408g-1(b)(4)(i)(A), 2550.408g-1(b)(4)(i)(C); Prop. D.O.L. Reg. § 2550.408g-1(c)(1)(i)]

2. Uses relevant information about the participant or beneficiary, such as age, time horizons (such as life expectancy and retirement age), risk tolerance, current investments in designated investment options, other assets or sources of income and investment preferences. A computer model may take into account additional information that a plan or a participant or beneficiary may provide. [D.O.L. Reg. § 2550.408g-1(b)(4)(i)(C); Prop. D.O.L. Reg. § 2550.408g-1(d)(1)(ii)]

3. Uses prescribed objective criteria to provide asset allocation portfolios comprised of investment options under the plan. [D.O.L. Reg. § 2550.408g-1(B)(4)(i)(D); Prop. D.O.L. Reg. § 2550.408g-1(d)(1)(iii)]

4. Operates in a manner that is not biased in favor of any investment options offered by the fiduciary adviser or related person. [D.O.L. Reg. § 2550.408g-1(b)(4)(i)(E); Prop. D.O.L. Reg. § 2550.408g-1(d)(iv)(B)]

5. Takes into account all the investment options under the plan in specifying how a participant's or beneficiary's account should be invested without the inappropriate weighting of any investment option. Investment options that constitute an investment in primarily employer securities or retirement annuities do not have to be included under the computer model. [D.O.L. Reg. § 2550.408g-1(b)(4)(i)(F)(1) and (2); Prop. D.O.L. Reg. § 2550.408g-1(d)(1)(v)] Where an investment fund, product, or service is itself designed to maintain a particular asset allocation taking into account the time horizons (retirement age, life expectancy) or risk level of a participant, such fund is not required to be included in the computer modeled investment advice. [Preamble, D.O.L. Reg. § 2550-408g-1, 74 Fed. Reg. 3826 (Jan. 21, 2009)]

6. An eligible investment expert must certify in writing, before the model is used and in accordance with rules prescribed by the Secretary of Labor, that the model meets these requirements. The certification must be renewed if there are material changes to the model as determined under regulations. For this purpose, an eligible investment expert is a person that, through employees or otherwise, has the appropriate technical training or experience and proficiency to analyze, determine, and certify,

in a manner consistent with the DOL regulations, whether a computer model meets the requirements of the regulations. However, the term "eligible investment expert" does not include any person who has any material affiliation or material contractual relationship with the fiduciary adviser, with a person with a material affiliation or material contractual relationship with the fiduciary adviser, or with any employee, agent, or registered representative of the foregoing. [D.O.L. Reg. § 2550.408g-1(b)(4)(ii)–(iv); Prop. D.O.L. Reg. § 2550.408g-1(d)(2)–1(d)(4)]

The fiduciary adviser (and not, for example, the plan sponsor) is responsible for determining whether a person meets these criteria. [D.O.L. Reg. § 2550.408g-1(b)(5); Prop. D.O.L. Reg. § 2550.408g-1(a) and (e)] A fiduciary adviser may not be the person (or organization) who offers the arrangement, provides designated investment options under the plan, or any affiliate of either (other than an IRA beneficiary who is an employee of such person or organization).

Note. In the case of an IRA, Roth IRA, or HSA, the beneficiary (owner) of the account owner is the fiduciary adviser. [D.O.L. Reg. § 2550.408g-1(b)(5); Prop. D.O.L. Reg. § 2550.408g-1(e)]

The certification must be signed by the eligible investment expert and contain the following:

(a) An identification of the methodology or methodologies applied in determining whether the computer model meets applicable requirements

(b) An explanation of how the applied methodology or methodologies demonstrated that the computer model met those requirements

(c) A description of any limitations that were imposed by any person on the eligible investment expert's selection or application of methodologies

(d) A representation that the methodology or methodologies were applied by a person or persons with appropriate educational background, technical training or experience

7. In the event that the report of the auditor identifies noncompliance, the DOL regulations require that the fiduciary adviser forward a copy of the report to the DOL within 30 days following the receipt of the report from the auditor. [D.O.L. Reg. § 2550.408g-1(b)(6)(ii)(A); Prop. D.O.L. Reg. § 2550.408g-1(f)(2)]

In addition, if a computer model is used, the only investment advice that may be provided under the arrangement is the advice generated by the computer model, and any investment transaction pursuant to the advice must occur solely at the direction of the participant or beneficiary. This requirement does not preclude the participant or beneficiary from requesting other investment advice, but only if the request has not been solicited by any person connected with carrying out the investment advice arrangement.

Audit requirements. In the case of an eligible investment advice arrangement with respect to an IRA-based plan, an audit is required at such times and in the manner prescribed by the Secretary of Labor. The regulations require the fiduciary adviser to, at least annually, engage an independent auditor who has appropriate technical training or experience and proficiency. [D.O.L. Reg. § 2550-408g-1(b)(6)(i); Prop. D.O.L. Reg. § 2550.408g-1(f)]

Notice requirements. Before the initial provision of investment advice, the fiduciary adviser must provide written notice (which may be in electronic form) that contains a variety of information to the recipient of the advice, including information relating to:

   (i) The role of any party affiliated with the fiduciary adviser in the development of the investment advice program

  (ii) The past performance and historical rates of return of the designated investment options available under the plan (if not otherwise provided)

 (iii) All fees or other compensation relating to the advice that the fiduciary adviser or any affiliate is to receive

 (iv) Any material affiliation or material contractual relationship of the fiduciary adviser or affiliates in the security or other property as to which advice is provided

  (v) The manner, and under what circumstances, any participant information provided under the arrangement will be used or disclosed

 (vi) The types of services provided by the fiduciary adviser in connection with the provision of investment advice (and for computer models, any limitations on the ability of the model to take into account an investment primarily in qualifying employer securities)

 (vii) The fact that the adviser is acting as a fiduciary of the plan in connection with the provision of the advice

(viii) The fact that a recipient of the advice may separately arrange for the provision of advice by another adviser who could have no material affiliation with and receive no fees or other compensation in connection with the security or other property as to which advice is provided, and

 (ix) The fact this information must be maintained in accurate form and must be provided to the recipient of the investment advice, without charge, on an annual basis, upon request, or in the case of any material change.

[D.O.L. Reg. § 2550.408g-1(b)(7); Prop. D.O.L. Reg. § 2550.408g-1(d)(3), 2550. 408g-1(g)] Any notification must be written in a clear and conspicuous manner, calculated to be understood by the average plan participant, and sufficiently accurate and comprehensive so as to reasonably apprise participants and beneficiaries of the required information. [D.O.L. Reg. § 2550.408g-1(b)(7)(ii); Prop. D.O.L. Reg. § 2550.408g-1(g)(2)] The Secretary of Labor has issued a model form for the disclosure of fees and other compensation as required by the PPA. [D.O.L. Reg. § 2550-408g-1, Appendix; Prop. D.O.L. Reg. § 2550.408g-1, Appendix] The fiduciary adviser must maintain for at least six years any records necessary for determining whether the requirements for the prohibited transaction exemption were met. A prohibited transaction will not be considered to have occurred solely because records were lost or destroyed before the end of six years due to circumstances beyond the adviser's control. [D.O.L. Reg. § 2550.408g-1(e); Prop. D.O.L. Reg. § 2550.408g-1(g)(2)]

Additional requirements. In order for the exemption to apply, the following additional requirements must be satisfied: [D.O.L. Reg. § 2550.408g-1(b)(8); Prop. D.O.L. Reg. § 2550.408g-1(h)]

1. The fiduciary adviser must provide disclosures applicable under securities laws;
2. An investment transaction must occur solely at the direction of the recipient of the advice;
3. Compensation received by the fiduciary adviser or affiliates in connection with an investment transaction must be reasonable; and
4. The terms of the investment transaction must be at least as favorable to the plan as an arm's length transaction would be.

Fiduciary adviser. For purposes of the exemption, a fiduciary adviser is defined as a person who is a fiduciary of the plan by reason of the provision of investment advice to a participant or beneficiary and who is also

1. a registered investment adviser under the Investment Advisers Act of 1940 or under state laws;
2. a bank, a similar financial institution supervised by the United States or a state, or a savings association (as defined under the Federal Deposit Insurance Act), but only if the advice is provided through a trust department that is subject to periodic examination and review by federal or state banking authorities;
3. an insurance company qualified to do business under state law;
4. a registered broker or dealer under the Securities Exchange Act of 1934;
5. an affiliate of any of the preceding; or
6. an employee, agent, or registered representative of any of the preceding who satisfies the requirements of applicable insurance, banking, and securities laws relating to the provision of advice.

A person who develops the computer model or markets the investment advice program or computer model is treated as a person who is a plan fiduciary by reason of the provision of investment advice and is treated as a fiduciary adviser, except that the Secretary of Labor may prescribe rules under which only one fiduciary adviser may elect treatment as a plan fiduciary. Affiliate means an affiliated person as defined under Section 2(a)(3) of the Investment Company Act of 1940. Registered representative means a person described in Section 3(a)(18) of the Securities Exchange Act of 1934 or a person described in Section 202(a)(17) of the Investment Advisers Act of 1940. [D.O.L. Reg. § 2550.408g-1(c)(2)(i); Prop. D.O.L. Reg. § 2550.408g-1(j)(2)]

Fiduciary rules. Subject to certain requirements, an employer or other person who is a plan fiduciary, other than a fiduciary adviser, is not treated as failing to meet the fiduciary requirements of ERISA, solely by reason of the provision of investment advice as permitted under this exemption or of contracting for or otherwise arranging for the provision of the advice. This rule applies if (1) the advice is provided under an arrangement—between the employer or plan fiduciary and the fiduciary adviser—whereby the fiduciary adviser provides investment advice as permitted under the exemption; (2) the terms of the arrangement require compliance by the fiduciary adviser with the requirements of the exemption; and (3) the terms of the arrangement include a written acknowledgement by the fiduciary adviser that the fiduciary adviser is a plan fiduciary with respect to the provision of the advice. [D.O.L. Reg. § 2550.408g-2; Prop. D.O.L. Reg. §§ 2550.408g-1(d)(4), 2550.408g-1(e), 2550.408g-2(b)(2)(C)]

> **Practice Pointer.** The employer or a plan fiduciary retains responsibility under ERISA for the prudent selection and periodic review of a fiduciary adviser with whom the employer or plan fiduciary has arranged for the provision of investment advice. However, the employer or plan fiduciary does not have the duty to monitor the specific investment advice given by a fiduciary adviser. The exemption also provides that nothing in the fiduciary responsibility provisions of ERISA is to be construed to preclude the use of plan assets to pay for reasonable expenses in providing investment advice.

> **Practice Pointer.** The person who develops a computer model or who markets a computer model or investment advice program used in an "eligible investment advice arrangement" shall be treated as a fiduciary of a plan by reason of the provision of investment advice referred to in ERISA Section 3(21)(A)(ii) to the plan participant or beneficiary, and shall be treated as a "fiduciary adviser" for purposes of ERISA Section 408(b)(14) and (g). [ERISA § 408(g)(11)(A)] Code Section 4975(f)(8) contains a parallel provision to ERISA Section 408(g)(11). This section sets forth requirements that must be satisfied in order for one such fiduciary adviser to elect to be treated as a fiduciary with respect to a plan under an eligible investment advice arrangement. In general, that identified person is the sole fiduciary adviser to be treated as a fiduciary by reason of developing or marketing the computer model, or marketing the investment advice program, used in an eligible investment advice arrangement. An eligible investment expert, in performing the computer model certification described previously, would neither be acting as a fiduciary under ERISA, nor be "handling" plan assets such that the bonding requirements would be applicable to the eligible investment expert. [Preamble, D.O.L. Reg. § 2550-408g-1, 74 Fed. Reg. 3827–3828 (Jan. 21, 2009)]

> **Note.** Any person may request the Secretary of Labor to make a determination with respect to any computer model investment advice program as to whether it can be used by IRAs, Roth IRAs, and HSAs, and the Secretary must make such determination within 90 days of the request.

Effective date. The investment adviser provisions are effective with respect to investment advice provided on or after January 1, 2007. The provision relating to the study by the Secretary of Labor is effective on the date of enactment. [ERISA §§ 408(b)(14), 408(g), 4975(d)(17), 4975(f)(8), as amended by PPA § 601] The proposed DOL regulations became effective on October 21, 2008 (which is 60 days after the publication of the proposed regulations in the Federal Register). The proposed class exemption is effective on November 20, 2008 (which is 90 days after the publication of the proposed regulations in the Federal Register). The final regulations that were issued on January 21, 2009 were to be applicable to transactions occurring on or after March 23, 2009. [D.O.L. Reg. § 2550.408g-1(g)] However, on January 20, 2009, Rahm Emanuel, chief of staff for President Obama, issued a memorandum that stopped all Federal agencies from issuing new regulations before they were first approved by the Obama Administration. This memo requires the DOL to consider delaying the March 29, 2009, effective date and reopen the regulations to public comment. On February 4, 2009, the DOL reopened the comment period until February 18, 2009. On May 22, 2009, the DOL released a document that delayed the effective and applicability dates of final rules under ERISA and parallel provisions of the Code relating to the provision of investment advice to participants and beneficiaries in individual account plans, such as 401(k) plans, and beneficiaries of individual retirement accounts (and certain similar plans). These rules were to have become effective and applicable on March 23, 2009, but were delayed until May 22, 2009 (see above). The document further delays the effective and applicability dates of these final rules from May 22, 2009, until November 18, 2009, to allow additional time for the DOL to evaluate questions of law and policy concerning the rules. [RIN 1210-AB13, 74 Fed. Reg. 23951 (May 22, 2009)]

> **Author's Note.** By allowing related parties to provide investment advice to participants, as discussed above, conflict-of-interest issues are likely to arise. On April 22, 2009, a bill was introduced that would (if enacted) significantly restrict the kinds of advice programs that providers and sponsors could offer to a 401(k) plan participant. [*See* Conflicted Investment Advice Prohibition Act of 2009 (H.R. 1988)]

Q 1:56   Did the PPA provide for any other exemptions from the prohibited transaction rules?

Yes. The PPA offers relief in that a transaction between a plan and a party-in-interest (e.g., service provider), who is not a fiduciary, is not a prohibited transaction (i.e., sale, exchange, lease, loan, or use of plan assets) under ERISA Section 406 so long as the plan receives no less than adequate consideration, or pays no more than adequate consideration for the transaction (see Qs 1:48–1:52). [I.R.C. § 4975(d)(20); ERISA §§ 406(a)(1)(A), (B) and (D), 408(b)(17); *see* PPA § 611] In addition, the PPA provided the following additional relief and other exemptions:

- *Block trades.* Additional relief is provided for "block trades" (any trade of at least 10,000 shares or an FMV of at least $200,000), between a plan and a disqualified person, which will be allocated among two or more client accounts of a fiduciary. At the time of the transaction, the interest of the plan (together with the interests of any other plans maintained by the same plan sponsor) may not exceed 10 percent of the aggregate size of the block trade. [PPA § 611(a); ERISA § 408(b)(15)(A); I.R.C. §§ 4975(d)(18), 4975(f)(9)]

- *Electronic communication networks.* An exemption is provided for certain transactions on electronic communication networks. [PPA § 611(c); I.R.C. § 4975(d)(18); ERISA § 408(b)(16)]

- *Foreign exchange transactions.* An exemption is provided for certain foreign exchange transactions. [PPA § 611(e); I.R.C. § 4975(d)(21); ERISA § 408(b)(18)]

- *Cross-trading.* An exemption for certain cross-trading transactions that allows cross-trades between accounts managed by the same investment manager is provided. [PPA § 611(g); ERISA § 408(b)(19); I.R.C. § 4975(d)(22); D.O.L. Reg. § 2550.408(b)-19, 73 Fed. Reg. 58450 (Oct. 7, 2008)]

- *Special correction period.* A prohibited transaction involving securities or commodities would be exempt if the correction is completed within 14 days after the fiduciary discovers (or should have discovered) that the transaction was prohibited. This prohibited transaction exemption does not apply to transactions involving employer securities. It also does not apply if, at the time of the transaction, the fiduciary or other party-in-interest (or any person knowingly participating in the transaction) knew (or should have known) that the transaction was prohibited. [PPA § 612]*Effective date.* The new exemptions would be effective for transactions occurring after the enactment date, August 17, 2006. The correction period exemption applies to prohibited transactions that the fiduciary discovers (or should have discovered), after the date of enactment.

Q 1:57   **Does a recommendation that a participant roll over his or her retirement plan account balance to a traditional IRA or to then convert that IRA to a Roth IRA to take advantage of investment options not available under an employer's plan constitute investment advice with respect to plan assets?**

No. Merely advising a plan participant to take an otherwise permissible plan distribution, even when that advice is combined with a recommendation as to how the distribution should be invested, does not constitute "investment advice" within the meaning of D.O.L. Regulations Section 2510.3-21(c). The investment advice regulation defines when a person is a fiduciary by virtue of providing investment advice with respect to the assets of an employee benefit plan. The DOL does not view a recommendation to take a distribution as advice or a recommendation concerning a particular investment (i.e., purchasing or selling securities or other property) as contemplated by the regulations. [D.O.L. Reg. § 2510.3-21(c)(1)(i)] However, a person recommending that a participant take a distribution may be subject to federal or state securities, banking, or insurance regulation. [D.O.L. Adv. Op. 2005-23A (Dec. 7, 2005)] Any investment recommendation regarding the proceeds of a distribution would be advice with respect to funds that are no longer assets of the plan.

On the other hand, where a plan officer or someone who is already a plan fiduciary responds to participant questions concerning the advisability of taking a distribution or the investment of amounts withdrawn from the plan, that fiduciary is exercising discretionary authority respecting management of the plan and must act prudently and solely in the interest of the participant. [*See* Varity Corp. v. Howe, 516 U.S. 489, 502–503 (1996)] Moreover, if, for example, a fiduciary exercises control over plan assets to cause the participant to take a distribution and then to invest the proceeds in an IRA account managed by the fiduciary, the fiduciary may be using plan assets in his or her own interest, in violation of ERISA Section 406(b)(1). [*See* Young v. Principal Fin. Group, Inc., 547 F. Supp. 2d 965 (S.D. Iowa 2008)]

Q 1:58 Would an adviser who is not otherwise a retirement plan fiduciary and who recommends that a participant withdraw funds from a retirement plan and invest the funds in an IRA or Roth IRA engage in a prohibited transaction if the adviser will earn management or other investment fees related to the IRA?

No. A recommendation by someone who is not connected with the plan that a participant take an otherwise permissible distribution, even when combined with a recommendation as to how to invest distributed funds, is not investment advice within the meaning of D.O.L. Regulations Section 2510.3-21(c), nor is such a recommendation, in and of itself, an exercise of authority or control over plan assets that would make a person a fiduciary within the meaning of ERISA Section 3(21)(A) (see Q 1:53). Accordingly, a person making such recommendations would not be a fiduciary solely on the basis of making such recommendations and would not engage in an act of self-dealing if he or she advises the participant to roll over his or her account balance from the plan to an IRA (or Roth IRA in a subsequent conversion) that will pay management or other investment fees to such person. On the other hand, this position applies only to advice provided by a person who is not a plan fiduciary on some other basis. Advice of this nature given by someone who is already a fiduciary of the plan would be subject to ERISA's fiduciary duties. Moreover, if the person exercised control over the participant's account in making the distribution and reinvestment outside the plan, the person would be a fiduciary and would be subject to the ERISA's fiduciary obligations. [D.O.L. Adv. Op. 2005-23A (Dec. 7, 2005)]

Miscellaneous Rules

Q 1:59 Has the Federal Deposit Insurance Corporation (FDIC) raised the coverage limit for a Roth IRA?

Yes. The FDIC raised the coverage threshold from $100,000 to $250,000 for most types of retirement plans. There also are strategies for insuring greater amounts in other accounts. On February 8, 2006, Congress passed legislation and President Bush signed it into law. Any changes in the insurance rules and their effective dates will be noted on the FDIC Web site at *http://www.fdic.gov* (visited on June 18, 2009). Strategies to increase coverage above $250,000 for most retirement accounts are available. In March 2006, the FDIC's Board of Directors approved final rules that raised the deposit insurance coverage on certain retirement accounts at a bank or savings institution from $100,000 to $250,000. The increase became effective on April 1, 2006. [*See* Federal Deposit Insurance Act (12 U.S.C. § 1811 *et seq.*) and the FDIC's regulations relating to insurance coverage (12 C.F.R. Part 330); *see also http://www.fdic.gov/deposit/ deposits/insured/yid.pdf* (visited on June 18, 2009)]

Deposits owned by one person and titled in the name of that person's retirement account qualify for coverage up to $250,000. The following types of retirement accounts which are owned by the same person in the same FDIC-insured bank are added together and the total is insured to $250,000:

- All types of traditional IRAs (including Roth IRAs and SIMPLE IRAs)
- 457(b) deferred compensation plan accounts (regardless of whether they are self-directed)
- Self-directed qualified defined contribution plan accounts, including self-directed Keogh plan accounts (or H.R. 10 plan accounts) designed for self-employed individuals

Chapter 2

Annual Contributions to a Roth IRA

This chapter explains the limits on annual contributions to a Roth IRA, including the contribution phaseout rules and the definition of modified adjusted gross income. Excess contributions are also discussed in detail.

For taxable years beginning after 2001, new limits apply to annual Roth IRA contributions and individuals age 50 or older may make catch-up contributions to their Roth IRAs. In addition, tax credits are available for certain low-income individuals and new types of Roth-like vehicles have been and will be created. The changes made by the Pension Protection Act of 2006 (PPA) regarding the extension of the saver's credit, inflation indexing of the saver's credit adjusted gross income limits, and the Roth contribution phaseout limitations are discussed in this chapter. Deemed IRAs and the additional contribution limits for participants in a 401(k) plan of certain employers in bankruptcy are more fully discussed in Chapter 3.

Certain types of contributions are treated as rollovers. The annual contribution rules do not apply to the rollover of hurricane distributions, airline payments, qualified recovery assistance distributions, qualified disaster recovery distributions, military death gratuities, Servicemembers' Group Life Insurance (SGLI), and Exxon Valdez settlements, all of which are discussed in chapter 3. Designated Roth contribution programs are discussed in chapter 10.

Limits on Annual Contributions

Q 2:1   What are the limits on annual contributions to a Roth IRA?

Annual contributions to a Roth IRA may not exceed 100 percent of the compensation includible in gross income for the taxable year (see Qs 2:2, 2:5) nor the annual limit on contributions for such year, whichever is less, reduced by the qualified retirement contribution made to all other IRAs, traditional or Roth, maintained for the benefit of the individual (see Q 2:6). The annual contribution limit per individual is phased out based on the individual's modified adjusted gross income (MAGI; see Q 2:8) and filing status (see Qs 2:2, 2:6). With regard to the 100 percent of compensation limit, there is an exception for a Roth IRA established by a spouse with insufficient compensation (see Q 2:2) who files a joint federal income tax return. Special rules apply to a deemed Roth IRA (see Qs 3:81–3:103) and to a designated contribution under a qualified Roth contribution program (see Qs 10:3–10:22).

The Economic Growth and Tax Relief Reconciliation Act of 2001 (EGTRRA) set new limits on annual Roth IRA contributions for taxable years beginning after 2001. The annual limit on contributions is now the sum of the normal contribution limit ($5,000 for 2009), and if an individual is age 50 or older by the last day of the taxable year and meets the other eligibility requirements, a catch-up amount ($1,000 for 2009). The catch-up amount will remain at $1,000 for taxable years beginning after 2005 (see Table 2-1).

The limits on annual contributions—normal and catch-up contributions—over several years are shown in Table 2-1.

[I.R.C. §§ 219(b)(1), 219(b)(5), 408A(c)(2)(A); EGTRRA § 601(a)(2); IRS News Release IR-2008-118 (Oct. 16, 2009); I.R.S. Notice 2008-102 (2008-45 I.R.B 1106)]

Special rules apply to the repayment of qualified reservists distributions (see Qs 3:19–3:24), the repayment of qualified hurricane distributions (see Q 3:125), and for participants in a 401(k) of certain employers in bankruptcy (discussed later).

After 2008, the $5,000 Roth IRA (and traditional IRA) annual contribution limit will be subject to cost-of-living adjustments (COLAs), rounded to the next lower $500 increment (see appendix A). The catch-up amount for Roth IRAs (and traditional IRAs) is not subject to COLAs. Therefore, after 2008, when the $5,000 normal limit increases to $5,500 as a result of COLAs, the catch-up amount will remain $1,000. [I.R.C. § 219(b)(5)(C)] The PPA makes the catch-up contribution rules permanent (see Q 1:37).

Note. An individual who is projected to attain age 50 before the end of a calendar year is deemed to be age 50 as of January 1 of that year regardless of whether the individual survives to his or her 50th birthday. [Treas. Reg. § 1.414(v)-1(g)(3)(ii)]

Example 1. Hubert will attain age 50 on December 31, 2009. If Hubert is otherwise eligible, he may contribute $6,000 to his Roth IRA on January 1, 2009.

Table 2-1. Roth IRA Annual Contribution Limits for Taxable Years 2001–2009

Taxable year	Normal Limit	Catch-up Amount	Total Contribution
2001	$2,000	None	$2,000
2002	$3,000	$ 500	$3,500
2003	$3,000	$ 500	$3,500
2004	$3,000	$ 500	$3,500
2005	$4,000	$ 500	$4,500
2006	$4,000	$1,000	$5,000
2007	$4,000	$1,000	$5,000
2008	$5,000	$1,000	$6,000
2009	$5,000	$1,000	$6,000

Example 2. Claudia's grandmother, age 80, wants to make a contribution to Claudia's Roth IRA for 2009. Since Claudia will not be age 50 by December 31, 2009, she is not eligible for the catch-up contribution. Therefore, the trustee, custodian, or issuer of Claudia's Roth IRA may not accept more than $5,000 as a Roth IRA contribution on Claudia's behalf.

Note 1. Annual contributions do not include amounts contributed to a Coverdell Education Savings Account (formerly called an Education IRA), a simplified employee pension (SEP), a savings incentive match plan for employees (SIMPLE), a salary reduction SEP (SARSEP), or amounts converted to a Roth IRA from a traditional IRA. [I.R.C. §§ 219(a), 219(b)(2), 219(b)(4), 219(e), 530(b), 7701(a)(37)]

Note 2. The rules allowing direct deposits of federal tax refunds under the PPA into traditional IRAs as defined in Code Section 7701, also apply to Roth IRAs. Form 8888—Direct Deposit of Refund to More Than One Account, may be used to direct an individual's tax refund to either two or three financial accounts (a Roth IRA may be selected under this option). Refunds may be deposited with a U.S. financial institution so long as the taxpayer provides a valid routing and account numbers. Form 8888 contains detailed instructions. Taxpayers who want their entire refund deposited directly into one financial institution can still use the appropriate line on their Form 1040 series. [I.R.C. § 7701(a)(37) includes IRAs defined in I.R.C. §§ 401(a) and 408(b); PPA § 830; *see* IRS News Release IR-2006-85 (May 31, 2006)]

Additional contribution amount for participants in a 401(k) plan of certain employers in bankruptcy. For taxable years beginning after 2006 and before 2010, an individual who has been a participant in a plan of a bankrupt company for more than six months before the bankruptcy may generally make additional IRA contributions to his or her traditional IRA in an amount that does not exceed three times the amount of the catch-up contribution for the year. For the additional contribution limit to apply, however, in the year preceding the year of contribution, the employer (or a controlling company of the employer) must have been a debtor in bankruptcy, or the employer or any other person was subject to indictment or conviction resulting from a business transaction related to the employer or a controlling employer. To be eligible for the additional IRA contribution, the participant's plan must contain a matching contribution program that provides for a 50 percent or greater matching contribution in employer securities. The maximum amount of the additional yearly contribution (for 2007 through 2009) is equal to the applicable year's catch-up limit multiplied by three. The deadline for making the additional contribution is the normal deadline for making traditional IRA contributions for such year. If an additional contribution is made by such an individual, the individual cannot also make a catch-up contribution for the year. [I.R.C. § 219(b)(5)(C)]

Example. Daniel has been a participant in a 401(k) plan with a 50 percent matching contribution for several years. In 2008, Daniel's employer goes bankrupt. For 2009, the regular Roth IRA limit is $5,000, and the normal catch-up limit is $1,000. For 2009, Daniel may contribute $8,000 ($5,000 + 3($1,000)) to his Roth IRA.

Q 2:2   Are there special limits on annual contributions for spousal Roth IRAs?

Yes. In the case of a married couple with compensation filing a joint income tax return, the couple may establish two separate Roth IRAs. The total annual contribution for both Roth IRAs may not exceed the lesser of 100 percent of the combined compensation for both spouses or, for 2009, $10,000, with $5,000 being the limit for each individual ($12,000, with $6,000 being the limit for each individual, if they have both attained age 50) (see Q 2:1).

The maximum annual contribution to a Roth IRA for each spouse (for 2009, generally $5,000; $6,000 with catch-up contribution) is reduced by the following amounts:

1. Regular contributions made to a traditional IRA (deductible or nondeductible) on behalf of the individual and

2. Roth IRA contributions made on behalf of the individual.

A husband and wife do not have to contribute to the same type of IRA. For example, the husband may contribute to a Roth IRA and the wife may contribute to a traditional IRA, or vice versa. Excess contributions may also have to be considered (see Q 2:24).

Each spouse may establish both a Roth IRA and a traditional IRA, as long as the aggregate contributions do not exceed the annual contribution limit per individual, which is $5,000 ($6,000 with a catch-up contribution) for 2009.

Practice Pointer. Nothing in EGTRRA changed the requirements for spousal IRAs, except for the increased contribution limits.

[I.R.C. § 219(c)(1)]

Q 2:3   What is the responsibility of a Roth IRA trustee or custodian when accepting annual contributions?

The trustee or custodian of a Roth IRA has the responsibility not to accept more than the dollar limit allowed for a regular contribution, which is $5,000 ($6,000 if the owner is age 50 or older) per individual for 2009. [I.R.C. § 408A(c)(2)] Furthermore, the trustee or custodian must ensure that annual contributions are made in cash (see Q 1:18). Certain abusive transactions having the effect of shifting value from a pre-existing business into a Roth IRA for less than fair market value may be challenged on several grounds and treated as contributions. Excess contributions are discussed in Q 2:24.

Restorative payments. The determination of whether a payment is treated as a restorative payment, rather than as a contribution, is based on all of the relevant facts and circumstances. As a general rule, payments to a Roth IRA are restorative payments, only if the payments are made in order to restore some or all of the plan's losses due to an action (or a failure to act) that creates a reasonable risk of liability for breach of fiduciary duty. In contrast, payments made to a plan to make up for losses due to market fluctuations and that are not attributable to a fiduciary breach are generally treated as contributions and not as restorative payments. In no case will amounts paid in excess of the amount lost (including appropriate adjustments to reflect lost earnings) be considered restorative payments. [Rev. Rul. 2002-45, 2002-2 CB 116; Ltr. Rul. 200921039 (Feb. 25, 2009)]

Q 2:4   Can a transaction involving a Roth IRA be treated as a contribution?

Yes, and the transaction could also disqualify the Roth IRA (see Q 1:47). Certain abusive transactions having the effect of shifting value from a pre-existing business into a Roth IRA for less than fair market value may be challenged on several grounds and treated as a contribution subject to the overall annual contribution limit of $5,000/$6,000 for 2009. The IRS may recharacterize a transaction for tax purposes and may assert that it is a prohibited transaction causing the assets in the Roth IRA to become taxable as of the first day of the year in which the prohibited transaction occurred. [I.R.C. §§ 408A(e) (2)(A), 408A(a)]

Abusive transactions. An abusive transaction generally involves the following parties: (1) an individual (the Taxpayer) who owns a pre-existing business such as a corporation or a sole proprietorship (the Business), (2) a Roth IRA maintained for the Taxpayer, and (3) a corporation (the Roth IRA Corporation), substantially all the shares of which are owned or acquired by the Roth IRA. The Business and the Roth IRA Corporation enter into a transaction that has the effect of shifting value into the Roth IRA. For example,

- A transaction in which the Roth IRA Corporation acquires property, such as accounts receivable, from the Business for less than fair market value.

- Contributions of property, including intangible property, by a person other than the Roth IRA, without a commensurate receipt of stock ownership.

- Any "other arrangement between the Roth IRA Corporation and the Taxpayer, a related party described in Code Sections 267(b) or 707(b), or the Business that has the effect of transferring value to the Roth IRA Corporation comparable to a contribution to the Roth IRA." [I.R.S. Notice 2004-8, 2004-4 I.R.B. 333; see also, IRS New Release IR-2009-41 (Apr. 13, 2009), containing the "dirty dozen" tax scams for 2009.]

In such a situation, the acquisition of shares, the transactions, or both are not fairly valued and thus have the effect of shifting value into the Roth IRA. Furthermore, these transactions are tax avoidance transactions and the IRS identifies these transactions, as well as substantially similar transactions, as listed transactions. [Treas. Reg. §§ 1.6011-4(b)(2), 301.6111-2(b)(2), 301.6112-1(b)(2). Under section 102 of Reorganization Plan No. 4 of 1978 (43 Fed. Reg. 47713), the Secretary of Labor has interpretive jurisdiction over I.R.C. § 4975]

Substantially similar transactions include transactions that attempt to use a single structure with the intent of achieving the same, or substantially same, tax effect for multiple taxpayers. For example, if the Roth IRA Corporation is owned by multiple taxpayers' Roth IRAs, a substantially similar transaction occurs whenever that Roth IRA Corporation enters into a transaction with a business of any of the taxpayers if distributions from the Roth IRA Corporation are made to that taxpayer's Roth IRA based on the purported business transactions done with that taxpayer's business or otherwise based on the value shifted from that taxpayer's business to the Roth IRA Corporation.

The IRS intends to challenge the purported tax benefits claimed for these arrangements on a number of grounds. In an appropriate case, the IRS will assert that the substance of the transaction is that the amount of the value shifted from the Business to the Roth IRA Corporation is a payment to the Taxpayer, followed by a contribution by the Taxpayer to the Roth IRA and a contribution by the Roth IRA to the Roth IRA Corporation. In such cases, the deduction to the Business will be reduced or eliminated. If the Business is a corporation, it will have to recognize gain on the transfer; and the transaction may require inclusion of the payment in the income of the Taxpayer (for example, as a taxable dividend if the Business is a C corporation). [I.R.C. § 311(b); Sammons v. United States, 433 F.2d 728 (5th Cir. 1970); Worcester v. Comm'r, 370 F.2d 713 (1st Cir. 1966); Ltr. Rul. 200917030 (Dec. 2, 2008); *see also* Memorandum for the Director of Employee Plans Examination and for the Director of Employee Plans Rulings and Agreements, from Michael D. Julianelle, director of employee plans (Oct. 1, 2008) regarding rollovers as business startups (ROBS)] The IRS announced procedures under which eligible taxpayers may resolve the tax treatment of eligible abusive Roth transactions. [I.R.S. Ann. 2005-80, § 3.9, 2005-2 C.B. 967; see also, Ltr. Rul. 200929005 (July 17, 2009)

Example. In December 2009, Edger and his spouse Mildred, both over the age of 50, set up the Roth IRA Corporation, into which they would direct payments for consulting, accounting, and bookkeeping services they provided to other individuals and businesses. Also in December 2009, Edger and Mildred both established a Roth account at the Self-Directed Bank. After contributing $6,000 to their respective Roth IRA accounts, Edger and Mildred each directed their Roth IRA account to purchase 50 percent of the stock of the Roth IRA Corporation for $6,000. Consequently, following the transactions, the two Roth IRA accounts were the sole shareholders of the Roth IRA Corporation.

Before the formation of the Roth IRA Corporation, Edger worked as general manager for and received consulting fees from an unrelated company, and Mildred received income for bookkeeping services she provided to unrelated clients. After the formation of the Roth IRA Corporation, Edger and Mildred provided services to these entities and other various clients, through the Roth IRA Corporation as employees of the Roth IRA Corporation. The total value of services provided by Edger and Mildred to clients of the Roth IRA Corporation was not received by Edger and Mildred in the form of salary or other compensation from the Roth IRA Corporation. Instead, in each of its first two fiscal years, the Roth IRA Corporation made dividend distributions of $4,600 to each of the Roth IRA accounts.

The transactions are listed transactions with respect to Edger and Mildred (for whom the Roth IRAs are maintained), the business (if not a sole proprietorship) that is a party to the transaction, and the corporation where substantially all the shares of which are owned by the Roth IRAs.

In this case, similar to the transaction described in Notice 2004-8, the structure of the transaction at issue purportedly allows the taxpayers to create a Roth IRA investment that avoids the contribution limits by transferring value to the Roth IRA Corporation comparable to a contribution to the Roth IRA, thereby yielding tax benefits that are not contemplated by a reasonable interpretation of the language and purpose of Code Section 408A. [*See* ILM 200917030 (Dec. 2, 2008, *rel.* Apr. 24, 2009)]

Note. The IRS may invoke Code Section 482, regarding the allocation of income and deductions among taxpayers, to allocate income from the Roth IRA Corporation to the Taxpayer, Business, or other entities under the control of the Taxpayer, if such allocation is necessary to prevent evasion of taxes or clearly to reflect income. The standard to be applied is that of a person dealing at arm's length with an uncontrolled person. [Treas. Reg. § 1.482-1(b)] In the event of a Code Section 482 allocation between the Roth IRA Corporation and the Business or other parties, correlative allocations and other conforming adjustments may be necessary. [Treas. Reg. § 1.482-1(g); Rev. Rul. 78-83, 1978-1 C.B. 79] To the extent of any excess contribution, that amount is subject to a 6 percent penalty tax until the excess amount is eliminated.

Caution. To the extent that the Roth IRA Corporation constitutes a plan asset under the Department of Labor's (DOL) plan asset regulation, the provision of services by the Roth IRA Corporation to the Taxpayer's Business (which is a disqualified person) with respect to the Roth IRA under

Code Section 4975(e)(2)) would constitute a prohibited transaction. [I.R.C. §§ 4975(c)(1)(C), 4975(e)(2); D.O.L. Reg. § 2510.3-101] For the Roth IRA Corporation to be considered as holding plan assets under the DOL's plan asset regulation, the Roth IRA's investment in the Roth IRA Corporation must be an equity interest, the Roth IRA Corporation's securities must not be publicly offered securities, and the Roth IRA's investment in the Roth IRA Corporation must be significant. [D.O.L. Reg. §§ 2510.3-101(a)(2), 2510.3-101(b)(1), 2510.3-101(b)(2), 2510.3-101(f)] Although not likely in the above examples, the Roth IRA Corporation would not be treated as holding plan assets if the Roth IRA Corporation constituted an operating company. [D.O.L. Reg. § 2510.3-101(c)] Furthermore, if a transaction between a disqualified person and the Roth IRA would be a prohibited transaction, then a transaction between that disqualified person and the Roth IRA Corporation would be a prohibited transaction if the Roth IRA may, by itself, require the Roth IRA Corporation to enter into the transaction. [D.O.L. Reg. § 2509.75-2(c)]

Caution. Independent of their classification as "listed transactions," these transactions may already be subject to the disclosure (on tax return) requirements of Code Section 6011 [Treas. Reg. § 1.6011-4], the tax shelter registration requirements of Code Section 6111 [Treas. Reg. § 301.6111-1T, 301.6111-2], or the customer list maintenance requirements of Code Section 6112. [Treas. Reg. § 301.6112-1]

Q 2:5   What is meant by *compensation* for purposes of annual contributions to a Roth IRA?

An annual contribution to a Roth IRA may not exceed a taxpayer's compensation or a self-employed taxpayer's earned income regardless of MAGI (see Q 2:8), which is used for purposes of the contribution phaseout rules (see Q 2:6). For annual contribution purposes, the term *compensation* means wages, salary, professional fees, and other amounts derived from or received for personal services actually rendered (including but not limited to commissions paid salespersons, compensation for services on the basis of a percentage of profits, commissions on insurance premiums, tips, and bonuses) and includes earned income as defined in Code Section 401(c)(2) (which is reduced by the deduction the self-employed individual takes for contributions made to a self-employed retirement plan and half of the individual's self-employment tax). [*See* I.R.C. §§ 219(g)(3), 408A(c)(2)] The earned income of a partner in an organization established as a limited liability partnership (LLP) or limited liability company (LLC) is also treated as his or her compensation. [*See* Prop. Treas. Reg. § 1.1402(a)-2(h)(6) (REG-209824-96), examples] Keep in mind that amounts earned by partners and shareholder-partners of an LLC are not wages subject to Federal Insurance Contribution Act (FICA), Federal Unemployment Tax Act (FUTA), or federal income tax withholding. [I.R.S. Legal Memo 200117003 (Apr. 27, 2001)] The term *compensation* also includes any amount includible in an individual's gross income under Code Section 71 with respect to a divorce or separation instrument described in Code Section 71(b)(2)(A). [I.R.C. §§ 219(f), 408A(c)(2)(A)] In the years beginning after 2007, compensation also includes differential pay (voluntary wage continuation by an employer to maintain level of compensation) paid to an employee who is called to active military duty. [I.R.C. §§ 414(u)(12)(A)(ii), 3401(h)]

Note. Compensation includes the net income from operating oil, gas, or mineral interests or the net earnings of a self-employed writer, inventor, or artist; however, a royalty paid for the right to use a copyright or patent or an oil, gas, or mineral property is taxable, although it is not generally treated as earned income.

The term *compensation* does not encompass the following:

- Amounts derived from or received as earnings or profits from property (including but not limited to rental income, interest income, and dividend income)
- Amounts not includible in gross income
- Any amount received as a pension or annuity or as deferred compensation [Treas. Reg. § 1.408A-3, Q&A 4]
- Dividend income (from an S corporation or otherwise) (see the following paragraph)
- Deferred compensation received (compensation payments postponed from a prior year) [Treas. Reg. § 1.408A-3, Q&A 4]
- Income from a partnership in which services were not a material income-producing factor
- Amounts (other than combat pay) excluded from income (e.g., housing costs and foreign earned income)

Dividend income (S corporation or otherwise) is a return on invested capital, not a return on labor (wages). It does not count for plan establishment or plan contribution purposes. If a taxpayer (improperly, in the view of the IRS) either inflates his or her S corporation dividend and correspondingly reduces his or her earned income to, for example, reduce Social Security or Medicare taxes or deflates his or her S corporation dividend and correspondingly increases his or her earned income in order to get a higher pension contribution (not likely to be challenged by the IRS, but it is possible), the IRS maintains that it has the right to recharacterize the split between the two to reflect what it says is the "economic reality." If the filed return reflects economic reality, dividends do not count toward compensation for plan purposes. [Durando v. United States, 70 F.3d 589 (9th Cir. 1995)] In *Grey's Public Accountant*, the owner of a Sub S treated himself as an independent contractor and reported payments for services on Form 1099. The Tax Court held that the owner was an employee and that the wages were subject to employment taxes FICA and FUTA (i.e., not Self-Employment Contributions Act (SECA)). [Grey Public Accountant, P.C. v. Comm'r, 119 T.C. 121 (2002)]; see also Water-Pure System, Inc., TC Memo 2003-53. aff'd, 3d Cir. (2004); Nu-Look Design, Inc., TC Memo 2003-52, aff'd, 356 F3d 290 (3d Cir., 2004); Specialty Transport & Delivery Services, Inc., TC Memo 2003-51, aff'd, 3d Cir., (2004); Superior Proside, Inc., TC Memo 2003-50, aff'd, 86 Fed. Appx. 510 (3d Cir., 2004); Mike J. Graham Trucking, Inc., TC

Memo 2003-49, aff'd, 3d Cir., 2004; and Veterinary Surgical Consultants, P.C., TC Memo 2003-48, aff'd, 3d Cir., 2004]

Depending on the facts, an individual could be an independent contractor for and the sole shareholder of his or her S corporation. In *Veterinary Surgical Consultants, P.C.*, the facts worked against the taxpayer. [*Veterinary Surgical Consultants*, P.C., 117 T.C. No. 14 (Oct. 15, 2001)] The corporation did veterinary consulting and had only one employee who was a veterinarian, the president and sole shareholder, and his services were essential to the business. He claimed to be an independent contractor. The Tax Court held that he was an employee. The Court also held, as in *Grey*, that the corporation could not avail itself of the benefits of Section 530 of the Revenue Act of 1978 (which provides for reduced penalties) because the corporation did not have a reasonable basis for treating the worker as an independent contractor. The taxpayer was the only employee and his services were essential to the operation of the business. Arguably, an individual might be considered an independent contractor if his or her services are not essential to the business and he or she has another business. For example, an individual could be a 25 percent owner in a building contractor, but also do business as a lawyer. That individual could do legal work for the contractor and bill them through his law firm. (*See also* Yeagle Drywall , T.C. Memo 2001-284, where a taxpayer's services were essential and a 99 percent stockholder was treated as an employee and not an independent contractor.) Some tax court cases have adopted more narrow interpretations of what constitutes self-employment income for self-employment tax purposes. [I.R.C. §1402(a)–(b)] Whether a payment is derived from a trade or business carried on by an individual for purposes of Code Section 1402 depends on whether, under all the facts and circumstances, a nexus exists between the payment and the carrying on of the trade or business. The Tax Court articulated this "nexus" requirement in *Newberry v. Comm'r* (76 T.C. 441, 444 (1981)), where it observed that, under Code Section 1402,

> there must be a nexus between the income received and a trade or business that is, or was, actually carried on. Put another way, the construction of the statute can be gleaned by reading the relevant language all in one breath: the income must be derived from a trade or business carried on.

Thus, the trade or business must be "carried on" by the individual, either personally or through agents or employees, in order for the income to be included in the individual's "net earnings from self-employment." [S. Rep. 1669, 81st Cong., 2d Sess. (1950), 1950-2 C.B. 302, 354] Generally, the required nexus exists if it is clear that a payment would not have been made but for an individual's conduct of a trade or business. [Newberry v. Comm'r, 76 T.C. 441, 444 (1981)]

Although the IRS agreed with the Tax Court in *Newberry* that a nexus must exist, it did not agree with the court's conclusion in that case that such a nexus cannot exist if an individual is not currently engaged in the day-to-day conduct of a trade or business. Therefore, the IRS declared that it will not follow the decision in *Newberry*. [Rev. Rul. 91-19, 1991-1 C.B. 186; *see also* Ltr. Ruls. 9235040 (June 2, 1992), 200111044 (Jan. 25, 2001)]

In the case of a partnership or a limited liability company, earned income may include guaranteed payments to members. [Ltr. Ruls. 9525058 (Mar. 28, 1995), 9452024 (Sept. 29, 1994), 9432018 (May 16, 1994)l; *see* Form 1065, Schedule K-1, line 4] Code Section 1402 defines the term "self-employment income" as net earnings from self-employment derived by an individual during any taxable year. Code Section 1402(a) provides that the term "net earnings from self-employment" includes an individual's distributive share (whether or not distributed) of income or loss described in Code Section 702(a)(8) from any trade or business carried on by a partnership of which the individual is a member. Code Section 1402(a)(13) provides that the distributive share of any item of income or loss of a limited partner is not included under the definition of net earnings from self-employment unless the distributive share is a guaranteed payment to that partner for services actually rendered to or on behalf of the partnership to the extent that such payment is established to be in the nature of remuneration for those services. In the view of the IRS, it is generally not essential that an individual currently be engaged in the day-to-day conduct of a trade or business in order to be carrying on a trade or business. A taxpayer can still be engaged in a trade or business even if there is a temporary hiatus in the conduct of the activities of that trade or business. [Newberry v. Comm' r, 76 T.C. 441, 444 (1981); *see also* Reisinger v. Comm'r, 71 T.C. 568, 572 (1979); Haft v. Comm'r, 40 T.C. 2, 6 (1963); *see also* Rev. Rul. 75-120, 1975-1 C.B. 55 (job search costs may be deductible trade or business expenses even if taxpayer is temporarily unemployed)]

> **Example.** During the years 1970 through 2009, LaToya wrote and had published 38 books, from which she has received royalties in excess of $400 for each year. During the years 1970 through 2002, LaToya performed teaching services in a private school as an employee, and the employee FICA tax was deducted from her "wages" for each such year. She retired from all activities as an employee on December 31, 2009. Whether or not LaToya is engaged in a trade or business depends upon the facts in the particular case. As a general rule, a person who is regularly engaged in an occupation or profession for profit that constitutes his or her livelihood, in whole or in part, and who is not regarded as an employee for FICA purposes, is engaged in a trade or business for self-employment tax purposes. If an individual writes only one book as a sideline and never revises it, he or she would not be considered "regularly engaged" in an occupation or profession and his or her royalties therefrom would not be considered net earnings from self-employment. However, where an individual prepares new editions of the book from time to time, and writes other books and materials, such activities reflect the conduct of a trade or business, and, if it is not one of the excluded service/professions listed in Code Section 1402(c), the income from it is includible in computing net earnings from self-employment. Because author-ship is not a listed excluded service/profession, LaToya's income is subject to SECA tax and is treated as compensation for plan purposes. If LaToya was not treated as having a trade or business, then her income would be reported

as a royalty on Schedule E of and it would be exempt from self-employment tax. [*See* Rev. Ruls. 68-498, 1968-2 C.B. 377; 68-499, 1968-2 C.B. 421; 55-385, 1955-1 C.B. 100]

Practice Pointer. Code Section 401(c)(2) provides that the sale, exchange, or licensing of property (other than a capital asset) created by an individual) is earned income, whether or not they are net earnings from self-employment. In such a case, and for plan establishment purposes, the activity generating the earned income must constitute a trade or business. Establishing a corporation and receiving wages may alleviate the problem.

Practice Pointer. Compensation includes earnings from self-employment even if the earnings are not subject to self-employment taxes because of religious beliefs.

Practice Pointer. Net losses from self-employment do not reduce compensation (wages) for purposes of the 100 percent of compensation limit. [I.R.C. §§ 219(c), 408A(c)(1)(B)]

Example 1. Emily has earned income from a trade or business that is not subject to self-employment tax because of her religious beliefs. She also has salaries and wages. Her compensation for making a Roth contribution includes both amounts.

Example 2. Robert has a loss from self-employment of $10,000 and salaries and wages of $8,000. His compensation for making a Roth contribution is $8,000 because the self-employment loss is not subtracted in determining his total compensation.

Service. The performance of service as an employee does not generally constitute a trade or business. There are several exceptions. A trade or business does not include the performance of service by an individual as an employee, except in the following situations:

- *Functions of public office.* The performance of the functions of a public office, other than the functions of a public office of a state or a political subdivision thereof with respect to fees received in any period in which the functions are performed in a position compensated solely on a fee basis and in which such functions are not covered under an agreement entered into by such state and the Commissioner of Social Security. [I.R.C. § 1402(c)(1)(d); *see also* Soc. Sec. Act § 218]

- *Newspaper and magazine vendors and carriers.* An individual is engaged in the trade or business of selling newspapers or magazines and, thus, is subject to the self-employment tax if: (1) he has attained the age of 18 and (2) the newspapers or magazines are sold to the ultimate consumers under an arrangement whereby the individual purchases the items at a fixed price and his compensation is based upon the retention of the excess of his sales price over the amount at which the items were charged to him. [I.R.C. §§ 1402(c)(2)(A), 3121(b)(16); Treas. Reg. § 1.1402(c)-3(b)]

- *Arrangement with owner or tenant of land.* Service described in Code Section 3121(b)(16), regarding service performed under an arrangement with the owner or tenant of land pursuant to which (i) such individual undertakes to produce agricultural or horticultural commodities (including livestock, bees, poultry, and fur-bearing animals and wildlife) on such land, (ii) the agricultural or horticultural commodities produced by such individual, or the proceeds there from are to be divided between such individual and such owner or tenant, and (iii) the amount of such individual's share depends on the amount of the agricultural or horticultural commodities produced. [I.R.C. §§ 1402(c)(2)(B), 3121(b)(11)]

- *Government or international organization service.* Service performed in the United States by a citizen is when the service is:
  - Performed in the employ of a foreign government (including service as a consular or other officer or employee or a non-diplomatic representative). [I.R.C. §§ 1402(c)(2)(C), 3121(b)(11)]
  - Performed in the employ of an instrumentality wholly owned by a foreign government if the service is of a character similar to that performed in foreign countries by employees of the United States Government or of an instrumentality thereof; and if the Secretary of State shall certify to the Secretary of the Treasury that the foreign government, with respect to whose instrumentality and employees thereof exemption is claimed, grants an equivalent exemption with respect to similar service performed in the foreign country by employees of the United States Government and of instrumentalities thereof. [I.R.C. §§ 1402(c)(2)(C), 3121(b)(12)]
  - Service performed in the employ of an international organization, except service that constitutes "employment" under Code Section 3121(y) relating to certain transferred Federal employees. [I.R.C. §§ 1402(c)(2)(C), 3121(b)(15)]
- *Representative of railway labor organization.* Service performed by an individual as an employee or employee representative as defined in Code Section 3231 relating to any officer or official representative of a railway labor organization (with certain exceptions, who before or after June 29, 1937, was in the service of an employer and who is duly authorized and designated to represent employees in accordance with the Railway Labor Act [45 U.S.C., chapter 8], and any individual who is regularly assigned to or regularly employed by such officer or official representative in connection with the duties of his office). [I.R.C. §§ 1402(c)(3), 3231]
- *Duly ordained, commissioned, or licensed minister.* The performance of service by a duly ordained, commissioned, or licensed minister of a church in the exercise of his ministry or by a member of a religious order in the exercise of duties required by such order. [I.R.C. §§ 1402(c)(2)(d), 1402(c)(4)]
- *Christian Science practitioners.* The performance of service by an individual in the exercise of his profession as a Christian Science practitioner, provided the individual has not received an exemption from the tax on self-employment income (e.g., has taken a vow of poverty) for such year. [I.R.C. § 1402(c)(5); Treas. Reg. § 1.1402(e)-2A]

- The performance of service by members of certain religious faiths during which time they are exempt from the tax on self-employment income. [I.R.C. §§ 1402(c)(6), 1402(g); Treas. Reg. § 1.1402(c)-7]

Married individuals. In the case of a married individual filing a joint return, the greater compensation of his or her spouse is treated as that individual's own compensation, but only to the extent that the spouse's compensation is not being used for purposes of the spouse's making a contribution to a Roth IRA or a deductible contribution to a non-Roth IRA. [I.R.C. § 219(c); Treas. Reg. § 1.408A-3, Q&A 4]

Phaseout Rules

Q 2:6 How do the phaseout rules affect the amount of an annual contribution to a Roth IRA?

The annual contribution limit (see Q 2:1) for a Roth IRA is phased out based on the filing status and MAGI of the individual (see appendix A). That is, if an individual's MAGI is more than the minimum phaseout amount but less than the maximum phaseout amount, the contribution is phased out. [I.R.C. § 408A(c)(3)(A)] In general, the phaseout is determined in a ratable manner (see Q 2:9). If an individual's MAGI is below the minimum phaseout amount, the annual limit applies ($5,000; $6,000 with catch-up contribution for 2009); if the MAGI is above the maximum phaseout amount, no contribution is permitted. Table 2-2 shows the MAGI phaseout ranges.

Q 2:7 Is there a minimum amount for an annual contribution to a Roth IRA under the phaseout rules?

No. Code Section 408A(c)(3)(A) provides that if an individual whose MAGI falls within the phaseout range is eligible to make a Roth IRA contribution of more than $0 but less than $200, the individual may make a contribution of up to $200. That rule does not require that such an individual make a $200 contribution.

Table 2-2. MAGI Phaseout Ranges for 2009

Filing Status	Minimum Phaseout Amount	Maximum Phaseout Amount
Single taxpayers or head of household	$105,000[*]	$120,000
Married taxpayers filing joint return or qualifying widow(er)	$166,000[*]	$176,000
Married filing separately	$ 0	$ 10,000

---

[*] The minimum phaseout amounts are indexed for inflation in increments of $1,000 starting in 2007. [I.R.C. § 408A(c)(3)(C)(D)]

Practice Pointer. Assume an elderly married couple with income above the $176,000 maximum contribution phaseout limit for a 2009 Roth IRA contribution. Assume further, that neither has an existing traditional IRA. The couple could contribute $12,000 ($6,000 × 2) to a nondeductible traditional IRA. Then, in 2010, the couple would be able to "roll over" the amount that had accumulated in their nondeductible IRA into a Roth IRA (paying tax only on the returns the IRA account had earned to that point), and all earnings on the Roth IRA from that point forward would be forever tax-free. Moreover, in every year after 2010, the couple could deposit $12,000 in a nondeductible IRA, roll over these funds into their Roth IRA the very next day, and pay no tax on the amount converted (because the conversion would be from a nondeductible IRA containing contributions made with after-tax dollars). This process could be repeated every year. Over time, the couple could increase their tax-protected Roth IRA to a very substantial level, with the account being sheltered from taxation. This strategy may not be beneficial if the taxpayer has IRAs containing deductible contributions. In such case, the amount of taxable conversion income that may result would have to be considered. A taxpayer may not maintain nondeductible contributions in a separate IRA, because they are aggregated for distribution purposes.

Q 2:8   What is *modified adjusted gross income* for purposes of the Roth IRA phaseout rules?

For purposes of the Roth IRA phaseout rules, *modified adjusted gross income* (MAGI) means adjusted gross income (AGI) as shown on an individual's federal income tax return, modified by the following:

1. The *subtracton of* any income resulting from:
   a. The conversion of an IRA, or
   b. A Roth IRA rollover from a qualified plan or a governmental 457(b) plan to a Roth IRA, or
   c. An RMD from an IRA (for conversions and rollovers from qualified retirement plans), and
2. The addition of the following deductions and exclusions:
   a. Traditional IRA deduction,
   b. Student loan interest deduction,
   c. Foreign earned income exclusion,
   d. Foreign housing exclusion or deduction from Form 2555 or Form 2555-EZ,
   e. Exclusion of qualified bond interest shown on Form 8815,
   f. Exclusion of employer-paid adoption expenses shown on Form 8839, and
   g. Deduction for qualified tuition and related expenses shown on Form 8917, and

Note. The deduction for qualified tuition and related expenses is scheduled to expire on December 31, 2009.

h. Domestic production activities deduction from Form 1040, line 35, or Form 1040NR, line 33. Line numbers are from the 2009 version of those forms.

AGI is determined after the deduction for retirement plan contributions made on behalf of an unincorporated business owner to a Keogh, SEP, or SIMPLE.

IRA distributions includible in income but not converted to a Roth IRA are part of AGI for the year. MAGI does not include amounts that are withdrawn from a traditional IRA and converted to a Roth IRA but that are includible in income—that is, any portion of the taxable amount caused by the conversion.

Note. To compute taxable income for purposes other than the Roth IRA phaseout rules, converted amounts are taken into account. That means that other AGI-based phaseouts may be affected by converted amounts—for example, the medical expense deduction (7.5 percent AGI floor), taxability of Social Security (based on AGI), miscellaneous deductions (2 percent AGI floor), and passive loss limitations (based on AGI).

Example. Glenda receives wages of $99,000 and has a passive activity loss credit of $10,000. Under Code Section 469(i)(3) the passive activity loss credit is reduced by 50 percent of the amount by which AGI exceeds $100,000. If Glenda converts her traditional IRA to a Roth IRA, she will have to recognize $80,000 of conversion income. In that case, the conversion income will entirely eliminate the passive activity loss credit, but the $80,000 would not be considered in computing the $100,000 AGI limit on conversions. Thus, with only $99,000 of AGI for conversion purposes, Glenda may convert her traditional IRA to a Roth IRA. If she converts, however, she will not be able to claim the deduction for her $10,000 passive activity loss because half of her adjusted gross income above $100,000 ($39,500 (.50 × ($99,000 + $80,000))) exceeds Glenda's passive activity loss of $10,000. [*See* H.R. Conf. Rep. 105-599, at 747 (1998)]

Furthermore, for purposes of determining MAGI for the contribution phaseout rules, a required minimum distribution (RMD) from an IRA or a Roth IRA will not be taken into account after 2004. [I.R.C. §§ 219(g)(3), 408A(c)(3)(C)(i)(II)] RMDs from other types of plans such as qualified plans or 403(b) plans may *not* be excluded. [Treas. Reg. § 1.408A-3, Q&A 6]

The rules defining MAGI for the contribution phaseout rules are summarized in Table 2-3. The rules for determining MAGI for purposes of the $100,000 MAGI limit for Roth IRA conversions before 2010 differ slightly (see Q 3:9 and Table 3-1) than for the Roth IRA contribution phaseout rules (see Q 2:8).

Note. MAGI takes into account taxable Social Security benefits that are included in AGI.

Table 2-3. MAGI Worksheet for 2009 Roth IRA Contribution Purposes[1]

1. *AGI (Form 1040, line 38; Form 1040A, line 22; or Form 1040NR, line 36). AGI includes any Social Security benefits that are taxable.* $_____

2. Less: Conversion income resulting from the conversion of a non-Roth IRA to a Roth IRA included on Form 1040, line 15b; Form 1040A, line11b; or Form 1040NR, line 16b[2]   − $_____

3. Less: Roth IRA rollovers from qualified retirement plans included on Form 1040, line 16; Form 1040A, line 12b; or Form 1040NR, line 17b[2]   − $_____

4. Less: Minimum required distributions from IRAs (for determining MAGI limit for conversions and rollovers from qualified retirement plans only). Otherwise enter $0.   − $_____

5. AGI for MAGI purposes (line 1 minus lines 2, 3, and 4)[2]   = $_____

6. Add: Traditional IRA deduction (Form 1040, line 32; Form 1040A, line 17; or Form 1040NR, line 31)   + $_____

7. Add: Student loan interest deduction (Form 1040, line 33; Form 1040A, line 18; or Form 1040NR, line 32)   + $_____

8. Add: Foreign earned income exclusion and/or housing exclusion (from Form 2555, line 45 or Form 2555-EZ, line 18)   + $_____

9. Add: Foreign housing deduction (Form 2555, line 50)   + $_____

10. Add: Exclusion of qualified bond interest (Form 8815, line 14)   + $_____

11. Add: Exclusion of employer-paid adoption expenses (Form 8839, line 30)   + $_____

12. Add: domestic production activities deduction from Form 1040, line 35 or Form 1040NR, line 33.   + $_____

Table 2-3. MAGI Worksheet for 2009 Roth IRA Contribution Purposes (*cont'd*)

13. Add: tuition and fees deduction from
Form 1040, line 34; or Form 1040A,
line 18.   + $_____

14. MAGI for Roth IRA purposes[2] (line 5
plus lines 6 through 13)   = $_____

---

[1] Line numbers are based on the 2009 version of the forms.

[2] Conversion income must be considered when computing other AGI-based phaseouts.

[3] **Caution.** If using this table to compute MAGI for the purposes of the $100,000 (before 2010) limit on MAGI conversions, reduce AGI by the amount of any required minimum distributions from an IRA or Roth IRA (see Q 3:9 and Table 3-1).

[4] If the amount on line 12 is more than contribution phaseout limit ($176,000 if married filing jointly or a qualified widow or widower; $10,000 if married filing separately and lived with spouse at any time during year; or $120,000 for all others) *and* the taxpayer has other income or loss items, such as Social Security income or passive activity losses that are subject to AGI-based phaseouts, AGI can be refigured solely for the purpose of figuring MAGI for Roth IRA purposes. To figure MAGI for conversion purposes, refigure AGI without taking into account any income from conversions or minimum required distributions from IRAs. (If receiving Social Security benefits, use worksheet 1 in Appendix B of Publication 590—Individual Retirement Arrangements (IRAs) to refigure AGI.) Then go to line 5 in Table 2-1 to refigure MAGI. If the taxpayer does not have other income or loss items subject to AGI-based phaseouts, MAGI for Roth IRA purposes is the amount on line 14 above.

Q 2:9   How is the maximum allowable annual contribution to a Roth IRA calculated using the phaseout rules?

EGTRRA does not modify the MAGI phaseout ranges for figuring maximum allowable annual Roth IRA contributions; however, because EGTRRA increases the annual Roth IRA contribution limit, it affects the calculation of maximum allowable annual Roth IRA contributions. The following examples illustrate how the maximum allowable annual contribution to a Roth IRA is calculated using the phaseout rules.

Example 1. Gretta, age 40, is a married taxpayer who files jointly and has MAGI for 2009 of $171,000. The maximum contribution permitted to be made to Gretta's Roth IRA for 2009 is $2,500, determined as follows:

$171,000	Gretta's MAGI (see Q 2:8)
$166,000	Phaseout range ($166,000–$176,000) lower limit
$ 5,000	Difference
.5000	Adjustment ($5,000 difference/$10,000 phaseout range, see Q 2:6)
$ 2,500	Adjustment amount ($5,000 annual limit × .50)
$ 2,500	Maximum Roth contribution ($5,000 annual limit – $2,500)

Gretta could, it should be noted, contribute another $2,500 ($5,000 – $2,500) to a traditional IRA.

Example 2. Henry is married and files a joint return. The MAGI phaseout range for a married person filing a joint tax return for 2009 is $166,000 to $176,000. Assume that Henry's MAGI for 2009 is $166,000. The following shows how to calculate Henry's Roth IRA contribution limit for 2009 if Henry is under age 50 and if he will attain age 50 at any time during 2009.

$168,000	Henry's MAGI
$166,000	Phaseout range ($166,000–$176,000) lower limit
$ 2,000	Difference
.2000	Adjustment ($2,000/$10,000 phaseout range, see Q 2:6)
$ 1,000	Adjustment amount ($5,000 × .20)
$ 4,000	Maximum Roth contribution ($5,000 – $1,000)

If eligible, Henry can contribute $1,000 ($5,000 – $4,000) to a traditional IRA for 2009. Whether the $1,000 is deductible or nondeductible depends on whether Henry is an active participant in an employer's plan and on his MAGI. If Henry is age 50 or older, his maximum Roth IRA contribution can be computed as follows:

$168,000	Henry's MAGI
$166,000	Phaseout range ($166,000–$176,000) lower limit
$ 2,000	Difference
.2000	Adjustment ($2,000/$10,000 phaseout range)
$ 1,200	Adjustment amount ($6,000 × .20)
$ 4,800	Maximum Roth contribution ($6,000 – $1,200)

If eligible, Henry can contribute $4,800 ($6,000 – $1,200) to a traditional IRA for 2009. Whether the $4,800 is deductible or nondeductible depends on whether Henry is an active participant in an employer's plan and on his MAGI.

Example 3. Sara-Lee is an unmarried person who wants to contribute to a Roth IRA. The MAGI phaseout range for an unmarried individual for 2009 is $105,000 to $120,000. Assume that Sara-Lee's MAGI for 2009 is $115,500. The following shows how to calculate Sara-Lee's Roth IRA contribution limit for 2009 if Sara-Lee is under age 50 or will attain age 50 at any time during 2009.

$115,500	Sara-Lee's MAGI
$105,000	Phaseout ($105,000–$120,000) lower limit
$ 10,500	Difference
.7000	Adjustment ($10,500/$15,000 phaseout range)
$ 3,500	Adjustment amount ($5,000 × .70)
$ 1,500	Maximum Roth Contribution ($5,000 – $3,500)

If eligible, Sara-Lee can contribute $3,500 ($5,000 – $1,500) to a traditional IRA. Whether the $3,500 is deductible or nondeductible depends on whether

Sara-Lee is an active participant in an employer's plan and on her MAGI. If Sara-Lee is age 50 or older, her maximum Roth IRA contribution can be computed as follows:

$115,500	Sara-Lee's MAGI
$105,000	Phaseout ($105,000 – $120,000) lower limit
$ 10,500	Difference
.7000	Adjustment ($10,500/$15,000 phaseout range)
$ 4,200	Adjustment amount ($6,000 × .70)
$ 1,800	Maximum Roth contribution ($6,000 – $4,200)

If eligible, Sara-Lee can contribute $1,800 ($6,000 – $4,200) to a traditional IRA. Whether the $1,800 is deductible or nondeductible depends on whether Sara-Lee is an active participant in an employer's plan and on her MAGI.

Table 2-4 combines the MAGI phaseout rules and the annual contribution limits for 2009 and can be used to calculate the maximum Roth IRA contribution for those years.

Note. If MAGI is above the maximum phaseout amount, no contribution is permitted.

Table 2-4. Maximum Roth IRA Contribution Worksheet

		2009 Filing Status[1]	
Phaseout Calculation[2]	*Single*	*Joint*	*Married Filing Separately*
Maximum phaseout amount	$ 120,000	$ 176,000	$ 10,000
1. Individual's MAGI	$_____	$_____	$_____
2. MAGI limit	$105,000[2]	$ 166,000[2]	$ 0
3. Subtract line 2 from line 1 (but not below zero)	$_____	$_____	$_____
4. Phaseout range	$ 15,000	$ 10,000	$ 10,000
5. Enter *lesser* of line 3 or line 4	$_____	$_____	$_____
6. Circle applicable multiplication factor:			
Year			
2009[4]	0.3333333	0.5000000	0.500000
2009[5] **(with catch-up)**	0.4000000	0.6000000	0.6

Table 2-4. Maximum Roth IRA Contribution Worksheet (*cont'd*)

2009 Filing Status[1]

Phaseout Calculation[2]	*Single*	*Joint*	*Married Filing Separately*
7. Line 5 multiplied by factor circled in item 6 equals contribution limit for year selected.	$_____	$_____	
8. Line 7 rounded up to the nearest $10, equals contribution amount for year selected. If result less than $200, enter $200.	$_____	$_____	

---

[1] Use "Single" if single, head of household, qualifying widower, or married filing separately and did not live with spouse at any time during year.
[2] If more than zero but less than $200 may be contributed, a contribution of up to $200 may be made (see Q 2:7).
[3] Amounts indexed for inflation starting in 2007.
[4] $5,000 ÷ $15,000 = 33%; $5,000 ÷ $10,000 = 50%.
[5] $6,000 ÷ $15,000 = 40%; $6,000 ÷ $10,000 = 60%.

Table 2-5 can also be used to determine whether the Roth IRA contribution limit is reduced. Use the table to determine how much it is reduced and the contribution limit for 2009.

Table 2-5. Reduced Roth IRA Contribution Limit Worksheet

1.	Enter modified AGI for Roth IRA purposes	1._____
2.	Enter:	
	• $166,000 if filing a joint return or qualifying widow(er)	
	• $-0- if married filing a separate return and taxpayer lived with his or her spouse at any time in 2009	
	• $105,000 for all others	2._____
3.	Subtract line 2 from line 1	3._____
4.	Enter:	
	• $10,000 if filing a joint return or qualifying widow(er) or married filing a separate return and taxpayer lived his or her spouse at any time during 2009	
	• $15,000 for all others	4._____
5.	Divide line 3 by line 4 and enter the result as a decimal (rounded to at least three places). If the result is 1.000 or more, enter 1.000	5._____

Table 2-5. Reduced Roth IRA Contribution Limit Worksheet (*cont'd*)

6. Enter the lesser of:
    - $5,000 ($6,000 if age 50 or older), or
      - Taxable compensation   6._____

7. Multiply line 5 by line 6   7._____

8. Subtract line 7 from line 6. Round the result up to the
    nearest $10. If the result is less than $200, enter $200 8._____

9. Enter contributions for the year to other IRAs   9._____

10. Subtract line 9 from line 6   10._____

11. Enter the lesser of line 8 or line 10. This is the reduced
    Roth IRA contribution limit for 2009.   11._____

Example. Leonora is a 42-year-old, single individual with taxable compensation of $117,000 for 2009. She made no contributions to an IRA for the year. Her modified adjusted gross income (MAGI) is $110,000 for the year. Leonora's maximum allowable Roth IRA contribution of $3,330 can be computed as follows.

1. Enter modified AGI for Roth IRA purposes   1. $110,000

2. Enter:
    - $166,000 if filing a joint return or qualifying   2. $105,000
      widow(er)
    - $-0- if married filing a separate return and
      taxpayer lived with his or her spouse at any
      time in 2009
    - $105,000 for all others

3. Subtract line 2 from line 1   3. $ 5,000

4. Enter:
    - $10,000 if filing a joint return or qualifying   4. $ 15,000
      widow(er) or married filing a separate return
      and taxpayer lived his or her spouse at any
      time during 2009
    - $15,000 for all others

5. Divide line 3 by line 4 and enter the result as a   5.   .333
    decimal (rounded to at least three places). If
    the result is 1.000 or more, enter 1.000

6. Enter the lesser of:
    - $5,000 ($6,000 if age 50 or older), or   6. $ 5,000
      - Taxable compensation

7. Multiply line 5 by line 6   7. $ 1,667

8. Subtract line 7 from line 6. Round the result   8. $ 3,330
    up to the nearest $10. If the result is less than
    $200, enter $200

9. Enter contributions for the year to other IRAs   9. $ 0

| 10. | Subtract line 9 from line 6 | 10. | $5,000 |
| 11. | Enter the lesser of line 8 or line 10. This is the reduced Roth IRA contribution limit for 2009 | 11. | $3,333 |

Age and Plan Participant Status

Q 2:10 May annual contributions be made to a Roth IRA after an individual attains age 70½?

Yes. Annual contributions may be made to a Roth IRA after an individual attains age 70½ (see Q 1:16). [I.R.C. § 408A(c)(4)] Furthermore, the age 70½ RMD rules applicable to a traditional IRA do not apply to a Roth IRA before the owner's death (see Q 5:61). [I.R.C. § 408A(c)(5)]

Q 2:11 May annual contributions be made to a Roth IRA by an active participant in an employer' s plan?

Yes. Annual contributions to a Roth IRA are permitted without regard to the active participation rules of Code Section 219(g). [I.R.C. § 219(c)(2)]

Annual Contribution Deadline

Q 2:12 What is the deadline for making an annual Roth IRA contribution?

An annual contribution to a Roth IRA may be made for a tax year up to the individual's tax filing deadline for that year, *not including extensions.* [I.R.C. §§ 219(f)(3), 408A(c)(7)] For example, an individual may make a contribution to a Roth IRA for 2009 up until, April 15, 2010. A qualified Roth contribution program (see Q 10:3) is treated differently.

Note. The IRS has taken the position that a trustee or custodian may (but need not) accept the postmark on the envelope that contains a contribution in determining the timeliness of an annual contribution to a Roth IRA. [Ltr. Ruls. 8536085 (June 14, 1985), 8628047 (Apr. 15, 1986)] Organizations normally set their own policies regarding the matter. Special rules apply for payments and documents sent to the IRS (see Qs 2:13–2:23).

Caution. *Farmers and fishermen.* Calendar year taxpayers with at least two-thirds of their gross income derived from farming or fishing in the current or preceding tax year are required to file their federal income tax returns by March 1 (rather than the general April 15 due date), unless estimated taxes are paid by January 15. An individual is in the business of farming if he or she cultivates, operates, or manages a farm for profit, either as owner or tenant. A farm includes stock, dairy, poultry, fish, fruit, and truck farms. It also includes plantations, ranches, ranges, and orchards. Gross income from fishing includes amounts received for catching, taking, harvesting, cultivating, or farming fish, shellfish (such as clams and mussels), crustaceans (such as lobster, crab, and shrimp), sponges, seaweed, or other aquatic form of animal or vegetable life. [*See* Pubs. 225, Farmer's Tax Guide; *see* I.R.M. § 20.1.3.2.1.6 (Sept. 12, 2006)]

Q 2:13   How is the contribution deadline met if it falls on a weekend or legal holiday?

Generally, if a specific act of compliance or the due date for filing a return falls on a Saturday, Sunday, or legal holiday (see Q 2:14), the act is considered timely if it or the filing is performed on the next succeeding day that is not a Saturday, Sunday, or legal holiday. [I.R.C. § 7503; Treas. Reg. § 301.7503-1(a)] Roth IRA contributions, and if necessary, Roth IRA documentation, must be timely mailed.

Note. Trustees, custodians, and issuers are not required to follow this rule and may consider documents received after the tax return due date as not timely made and report the contribution as made for the tax year received, rather than for the prior year. [Ltr. Ruls. 8536085 (June 14, 1985); 8551065 (Sept. 27, 1985)]

Q 2:14   What is a legal holiday?

The term *legal holiday* means the legal holidays in the District of Columbia, as follows:

- New Year's Day, January 1
- Dr. Martin Luther King Jr.'s Birthday, the third Monday in January
- Inauguration Day, January 20, when the day is Inauguration Day
- Presidents' Day, the third Monday in February
- Emancipation Day in District of Columbia, April 16, 2012
- Memorial Day, the last Monday in May
- Independence Day, July 4
- Labor Day, the first Monday in September
- Columbus Day, the second Monday in October
- Veterans Day, November 11
- Thanksgiving Day, the fourth Thursday in November
- Christmas Day, December 25

[I.R.C. § 7503; Treas. Reg. § 301.7503-1(b); D.C. Code Ann. § 28-2701]

Furthermore, for any act, return, statement, or other document required to be filed at an office of the IRS, the term *legal holiday*, in addition to the legal holidays in the District of Columbia, includes any statewide legal holiday of the state where the act is required to be performed or any legal holiday that is recognized throughout the territory or possession in which the IRS office is located (e.g., Patriot's Day in New England). [Treas. Reg. § 301.7503-1(b)]

In the case of individuals affected by a presidentially declared disaster, or involved in combat zone actions or performing certain support roles, the due dates for certain time-sensitive acts have been postponed. [I.R.C. § 7508A; Treas. Reg. § 301.7508A-1; *see* I.R.S. Notice 2001-61, 2001-2 C.B. 305; Rev. Proc. 2005-17, 2005-1 C.B. 1050; *see also* Publication 4492, Information for Taxpayers Affected by Hurricanes Katrina, Rita, and Wilma]

Q 2:15   When is a document or payment that is mailed deemed filed or paid?

Generally, a document or payment is considered to be filed or paid on the date of the postmark stamped on the cover in which it was properly mailed. Thus, if the cover containing the document or payment bears a timely postmark, the document or payment is considered timely filed or paid even if it is received after the date it is normally required to be filed or paid. [Treas. Reg. §§ 301.7502-1, 301.7502-2]

Q 2:16   What date controls if a document or payment is considered not timely filed or paid?

If a document or payment is considered not timely filed or paid, the date of the postmark stamped on the cover in which it was mailed will not be considered the filing or payment date. The date the document or payment is received will be the date of filing or payment. [I.R.C. § 7502(a)]

Q 2:17   Must a payment actually be received to be considered timely paid?

Yes. Whether made in the form of currency or another medium, a payment is not treated as paid unless it is actually received and accounted for. For example, if a check is used as the form of payment, the check does not constitute payment unless it is honored on presentation.

Q 2:18   What are the requirements for a valid mailing?

Documents or payments must be mailed in accordance with the following requirements:

- They must be contained in an envelope or other appropriate wrapper and be properly addressed to the agency, officer, or office with which the document is required to be filed or to which the payment is required to be made.
- Sufficient postage must be affixed.
- They must be deposited within the prescribed time in the mail with the domestic mail service of the U.S. Postal Service (including mail transmitted within, among, and between the United States, its possessions, and Army-Air Force (APO) and Navy (FPO) post offices) or must be sent via

IRS-approved private delivery companies (see below). [*See* 39 C.F.R. § 2.1] The mail services of other countries are not generally considered.

- [Treas. Reg. § 301.7502-1(c)(ii)]

Before the Taxpayer Bill of Rights [Pub. L. No. 104-168, § 1210] was enacted in 1996, only taxpayers who sent returns via the U.S. Postal Service had the assurance that their returns would be considered to be timely filed if they were timely mailed. The change in the law permitted the IRS to extend the timely mailing as timely filing or paying rule to certain private delivery companies, also called designated delivery services. Effective, January 1, 2005, the IRS has designated three private delivery companies that filers can use with the same assurance as those who use the U.S. Postal Service that a return mailed on time will be considered filed on time:

- DHL Express (DHL): DHL Same Day Service; DHL Next Day 10:30 a.m.; DHL Next Day 12:00 p.m.; DHL Next Day 3:00 p.m.; and DHL 2nd Day Service;

- Federal Express (FedEx): FedEx Priority Overnight, FedEx Standard Overnight, FedEx 2 Day, FedEx International Priority, and FedEx International First; and

- United Parcel Service (UPS): UPS Next Day Air, UPS Next Day Air Saver, UPS 2nd Day Air, UPS 2nd Day Air A.M., UPS Worldwide Express Plus, and UPS Worldwide Express.

[I.R.S. Notice 2004-83, 2004-2 C.B. 1030]

Note. Airborne Express, Inc. was removed from the list due to its acquisition by DHL Worldwide. [I.R.S. Notice 2004-83, 2004-52 I.R.B. 1030, superseding I.R.S. Notice 2002-62, 2002-39 I.R.B. 574]

The date on which an item given to any one of the IRS-approved private delivery companies is recorded electronically in the company's database and treated as the postmark date. The private delivery companies are required to maintain their electronic databases for only six months. [Rev. Proc. 97-19, 1997-1 C.B. 644; I.R.S. Notice 97-26, 1997-1 C.B. 413] Confirmation of the date recorded can be obtained by contacting the company in question using the following toll-free telephone numbers:

- DHL "Same Day" Service: (800) 345-2727
- DHL USA Overnight: (800) 225-5345
- FedEx: (800) 463-3339
- UPS: (800) 742-5877

Practice Pointer. Private delivery services are required to maintain their electronic database only for a period of six months. Therefore, taxpayers should obtain confirmation of the date recorded by contacting the designated private delivery services within the six-month period because any action taken by the IRS is likely to occur after that period has expired.

[I.R.C. § 7502(f); *see also* Rev. Proc. 97-19, 1997-1 C.B. 644, providing the criteria currently applicable for designation of an approved postal delivery service (PDS); I.R.S. Notice 97-26, 1997-1 C.B. 413, providing special rules to determine the date that will be treated as the postmark date for purposes of I.R.C. § 7502; I.R.S. Notice 2002-62, modifying I.R.S. Notice 97-26, provides rules for determining the postmark date for items delivered by FedEx International Priority and FedEx International First; I.R.S. Notice 97-50, 1997-2 C.B. 305, *modifying* Rev. Proc. 97-19 and I.R.S. Notice 97-26, provide that each year there will be only one application period to apply for designation, which will end on June 30; I.R.S. Notice 99-41, 1999-2 C.B. 325, provides that the IRS will publish a subsequent notice providing a new list of designated PDSs only if a designated PDS (or service) is added to, or removed from, the current list.]

Q 2:19   What is the result if the postmark date is wrong or not legible?

The person required to file the document or make the payment has the burden of proving when the postmark was made. Furthermore, if the cover containing a document or payment bearing a timely postmark made by the U.S. Postal Service is received later than the date a document or payment postmarked and mailed at that time would ordinarily be received, the sender may be required to prove that it was timely mailed. [Treas. Reg. § 301.7502-1(c)(iii)(A)]

Q 2:20   What rules apply to postmarks of foreign postal services?

Special rules apply if the postmark on an envelope or wrapper is made by a foreign postal service. When the document or payment is received later than it would have been received if it had been duly mailed and postmarked by the U.S. Postal Service, it is treated as having been received when a document or payment so mailed and so postmarked would ordinarily be received. Still, the person required to file must establish that it was actually and timely deposited in the mail before the last collection of the mail from the place of deposit. The person must also show that the delay in receipt was due to a delay in the transmission of the mail and must explain the cause of that delay. [Treas. Reg. § 301.7502-1(c)(1)(iii)(B)]

Q 2:21   How can the risk that a document or payment will not be postmarked on the day that it is posted be overcome?

The risk that a mailing will not be postmarked on the day it is posted can be overcome by use of registered, certified, or express mail (see Q 2:18). [Treas. Reg. § 301.7502-1(e)(1), 301.7502-1(g)(4) (REG-138176-02, 69 Fed. Reg. 56377-56379); *see also* Raby, Burgess J.W. and Raby, William L., "Abolishing the Mailbox Rule for Tax Documents," 44 *Tax Practice* 4 (Oct. 22, 2004)]

Q 2:22   What is the postmark date for U.S. registered mail?

If a document or payment is sent by U.S. registered mail, the date of registration of the document or payment is treated as the postmark date. [Treas. Reg. § 301.7502-1(c)(2)]

Q 2:23   What is the postmark date for U.S. certified mail?

If a document or payment is sent by U.S. certified mail and the sender's receipt is postmarked by the postal employee to whom that document or payment is presented, the date of the U.S. postmark on the receipt is treated as the postmark date of the document or payment. [Treas. Reg. § 301.7502-1(c)(2)]

Excess Contributions

Q 2:24   When does an excess contribution to a Roth IRA occur, and what penalty applies?

An *excess contribution* to a Roth IRA occurs when a contribution made to a Roth IRA exceeds the amount allowable as a contribution (see Q 2:1), when ineligible amounts are rolled over (see Qs 3:8, 3:10, 3:67), or when there is a failed conversion (see Q 3:32). In addition, an excess contribution includes any excess contribution from the prior year, reduced by the sum of any distributions from the Roth IRA for the year and the contribution limit (minus regular contributions made to an IRA) for the year. For 2009 reporting purposes, excess Roth IRA contributions from the prior year (or years) are reflected in Part IV of the 2008 Form 5329.

> **Note.** Distributions from Roth IRAs are reported in Part III of Form 8606—Nondeductible IRAs. Complete this part only if a distribution from a Roth IRA was made in 2009. For this purpose, a distribution does not include a qualified distribution, a rollover or an outstanding rollover, a qualified charitable distribution, a one-time distribution to fund a Health Savings Account (HSA), a recharacterization, or amounts transferred to a spouse's Roth IRA that are incident to a divorce. In addition, the return of an excess contribution and any earnings thereon made before the due date of the return (including extensions) or within the six-month period described in Q 2:33, are not treated as distributions.

> **Caution.** Excess contributions that are not distributed from a Roth IRA on or before the tax return due date (with extensions) for the taxable year of the contributions are "reduced as a *deemed* Roth IRA contribution for each subsequent taxable year *to the extent* that the Roth IRA owner does not actually make regular IRA contributions for such years." (Emphasis added.) [Treas. Reg. § 1.408A-2, Q&A 7 (T.D. 8816, 64 Fed. Reg. 5597–5611, Feb. 4, 1999)] Form 5329, Additional Taxes on Qualified Plans (Including IRAs) and Other Tax-Favored Accounts, requires that zero be shown on line 19 when calculating the additional tax on excess contributions carried over from a

prior year, unless the individual's Roth contributions for the year is less than the maximum allowable contribution. The amount on line 19 reduces the amount of the excess that is carried over.

A 6 percent excise tax applies to an excess contribution each year that it remains in the Roth IRA, unless the excess amount is used up or distributed. A contribution to a Roth IRA that exceeds the annual contribution limit (the excess contribution) can be applied to a later year in which there is an unused contribution limit, allowing the contribution to be "used up" and avoiding the 6 percent penalty on the amount used for that year. Although the excess contribution does not have to be withdrawn, applying it to a later year does not avoid the 6 percent excise tax on the excess contribution for the year the excess remained in the Roth IRA. [I.R.C. §§ 408(d)(4), 4973(a), 4973(f)(2)]

The 6 percent excise tax does not apply to the return of an excess Roth IRA contribution if the return is made on or before the individual's tax filing deadline (including extensions) for the year for which the excess contribution was made and the net income attributable (NIA) to the excess contribution are also withdrawn. In addition, the return of an excess contribution and earnings attributable thereto are made within the six-month period described in Q 2:33, are not subject to the 6 percent tax.

Note. If the correction is made on or before the individual's tax filing deadline (including extensions) or within the six-month period described in Q 2:33 (excluding extensions), the NIA on the excess amount during the computation period (see Q 2:26) must be determined. [Treas. Reg. § 1.408-11 (T.D. 9056)]

Earnings on the excess contribution are taxable to the individual in the year for which the contribution was made. Earnings may be subject to the 10 percent tax under Code Section 72(t) (see Q 4:21).

Furthermore, an excess contribution attributed to a failed conversion can be recharacterized as a traditional IRA contribution and the 6 percent penalty avoided (see Qs 3:17, 3:32).

Example. Georgina, age 53, is eligible to contribute $1,400 for 2008 and $4,900 for 2009 (the amounts of her taxable compensation for those years) to a Roth IRA. For 2008, she actually contributes $2,000. Therefore, $600 is subject to the 6 percent excise tax in 2008 unless she withdraws the excess (including any NIA) before the due date of her 2008 income tax return plus any extensions. If Georgina does not withdraw the $600 excess by the deadline, she owes excise tax of $36 ($600 × 0.06) for 2008. To avoid the excise tax for 2009, Georgina can apply the $600 excess amount from 2008 to 2009. Since she is eligible to contribute $4,900 for 2009, she would contribute only an additional $4,300 (the allowable contribution of $4,900 minus the $600 excess from 2008 that she wants to treat as a Roth IRA contribution for 2009).

Q 2:25   What methods may be considered when correcting an excess contribution to a Roth IRA?

Generally, four methods may be used to correct an excess contribution to a Roth IRA for 2009:

1. Withdrawing a current years' excess contribution, plus the net income attributable (NIA) to the excess, before the individual's tax filing due date, including extensions, for 2009 (see Qs 2:27, 2:28). The 6 percent excise tax for excess contributions is avoided. The amount withdrawn in a correcting distribution cannot be treated as a qualified distribution. [I.R.C. § 408A(d)(2) (C), referring to I.R.C. § 408(d)(4)]

    Note. Current year contributions that are removed, together with NIA, on or before the tax filing due date, are treated as not having been contributed.

2. Treating the prior year's excess contribution as a regular contribution made in a subsequent year in which there is an unused contribution limit. Although the excess contribution does not have to be withdrawn under Method 2, applying it to a later year does not avoid the 6 percent excise tax on the excess contribution.

3. Withdrawing a current years' excess contribution, plus the earnings attributable to the excess, within the six-month period following the return due date (not including extensions). This applies when the individual files his or her return without withdrawing the excess contribution. The 6 percent excise tax for excess contributions is avoided, but amended returns are required (see Q 2:33) to be filed by the owner.

    Note. The amount of an excess contribution withdrawn in a correcting distribution that is accompanied by attributable earnings (Methods 1 and 3) cannot be treated as a qualified distribution [I.R.C. § 408A(d)(2)(C), referring to I.R.C. § 408(d)(4)]

4. Withdrawing an excess contribution after the due date of the return (including extensions) without earnings. [I.R.C. § 4973(f)] The 6 percent excise tax for excess contributions is avoided for subsequent years (2010), but not the current year (2009). Under this method, earnings are treated as distributed after all contributions (basis) have been removed (see Q 4:1). If the earnings are subsequently distributed in a qualified distribution (see Q 4:9), the earnings will not be taxable or subject to penalty.

    Under method 4, excess contributions for a prior year are treated as deemed Roth IRA contributions for the subsequent year to the extent the owner is allowed to make a Roth IRA contribution for that subsequent year (see Q 2:33).

Example. Thelma, age 40, a qualifying widow, has modified adjusted gross income (MAGI) of $200,000 for 2009, but only $30,000 for 2010. For 2009, Thelma is not eligible to make a Roth contribution or conversion contribution because her MAGI exceeds the $176,000 phaseout limit for contributions (see Q 2:7) and the $100,000 MAGI limit for conversions (see Q 3:7), but is eligible for 2010. During 2009, Thelma inadvertently converts her only IRA to a Roth

IRA. She had no basis in the IRA and the $100,000 conversion contribution to the Roth IRA was fully taxable. Thelma does not recharacterize the amount back to a traditional IRA (see Q 3:31), or correct the excess contribution (a "failed conversion") under Methods 1 or 3, and paid a 6 percent penalty of $6,000 ($100,000 × .06) for 2009. Assume the 2010 Roth contribution limit is $5,000. Because the remaining excess contribution ($100,000 from prior year) exceeds the $5,000 amount that Thelma may contribute for 2010 by $95,000 ($100,000 reduced by her $5,000 contribution limit for 2010), it cannot be entirely corrected under Method 2. Only Method 4 is available to correct the remaining $95,000 excess to avoid the 6 percent penalty for 2010. Assuming Thelma does not want to make a contribution for 2010, the deemed contribution of $5,000 could be undone by removing the $5,000 with attributable earnings before the 2010 federal return due date (assume April 15, 2011). In which case, the deemed contribution of $5,000 for 2010 would be treated as thought it was never made. The earnings on the $5,000 amount if withdrawn are taxable in 2010 (the year the contribution was deemed made), and may be subject to the 10 percent additional tax on distributions if under age 59½. Although it is not entirely clear, it would appear that the earnings attributable to the excess contribution is measured from the date the excess amount was originally contributed in 2009, rather than on April 16, 2011, the day after the 2010 return due date when the $5,000 excess was treated as a deemed Roth IRA contribution.

Had Thelma timely recharacterized (see Q 2:7) her failed 2009 conversion on or before the due date of her 2009 return (including extensions), she would have qualified to make a conversion contribution in 2010 or after 2011. [The $100,000 MAGI conversion limit does not apply after 2010 (see Q 3:16).]

It can be argued that if a Roth owner is not eligible for a Roth IRA contribution in an excess contribution carryover year, the owner should be able to remove the deemed Roth IRA contribution portion of the excess contribution (plus net income attributable) by the due date of the federal income tax return for that subsequent year (see Q 2:33). Only actual contributions can be recharacterized. If prior years' excess contributions are treated as current year's contributions, they can be recharacterized only if the recharacterization would still be timely with respect to the tax year for which the applied contribution were actually made.

Note 1. The rules under Code Section 408(d)(5) regarding corrections after the due date of a tax return for the tax-free distribution of certain excess contributions to traditional IRAs do not apply to a Roth IRA because Roth IRA contributions are always tax free on distribution (except to the extent that they accelerate income inclusion under the four-year spread (which was possible during 1998 through 2001, see Q 3:15) and under the two-year rule for amounts converted in 2010 and distributed before 2012 (see Qs 3: 12, 3:17). [Treas. Reg. § 1.408A-3, Q&A 7] Although Code Section 408(d)(5) regarding traditional IRA contributions returned before the due date of the return does not apply to a Roth IRA, Method 4 is similar to the correction of excess traditional IRA contributions under that section. [I.R.C. § 4973(f)]

Note 2. The IRS has not published any guidance regarding the correction of excess Roth contributions after the due date of the return, except as provided in Method 3. This is because of the contribution first recovery rules that apply to Roth IRAs (see Q 4:1). [The contribution first recovery rules for excess contributions to a designated Roth account (DRA) are treated differently, subject to double taxation, and with no exclusion from income for amounts attributable to basis, if not distributed (with earnings) by April 15th of the year following the year of the excess (see Q 10:68).]

Q 2:26   How are the earnings on an excess or unwanted contribution to a Roth IRA calculated?

Treasury Regulations Section 1.408-4 prescribes a rather complicated formula for determining the earnings attributable to an excess or unwanted contribution that is being corrected by withdrawing that contribution, plus the earnings attributable to the excess, before the year's tax filing due date (including extensions). It sets up a ratio comparing the unwanted contribution to the total Roth IRA (all investments held under the Roth IRA agreement) and the earnings attributable to the unwanted contribution to the total income earned by the total Roth IRA account during the computation period (see Qs 2:27, 2:29). [Treas. Reg. §§ 1.408-4(c)(2)(ii), 1.408-4(e)(2)(iii)] Earnings are deemed to be received for federal income tax purposes in the taxable year *in which* the contribution is made. [I.R.C. 408(d)(4)]

> **Note.** On May 5, 2003, the IRS finalized the proposed regulations that were issued on July 23, 2002. [T.D. 9056, 68 Fed. Reg. 23586–23590 (May 5, 2003); REG-124256-02 (67 Fed. Reg. 48067–48070), as corrected at 67 Fed. Reg. 53644 (Aug. 16, 2002)] The final regulations retain the rule that net income calculations must be based on the overall value of an IRA and the dollar amounts contributed, distributed, or recharacterized from the IRA. The regulations do not permit the calculation of net income on the basis of the return on specific assets, even when recharacterizing an amount converted to a Roth IRA.

The final regulations apply to income calculations of IRA contributions made on or after January 1, 2004. The final regulations generally utilize the "new" method announced in Notice 2000-39 [2000-30 I.R.B. 132] for calculating the net income attributable to IRA contributions that are distributed as an excess or unwanted recharacterization (see Qs 2:28, 2:29). Notice 2000-39 allows earnings to be positive or negative and does not produce irregular results for contributions made late in the year. [Treas. Reg. § 1.408A-5, A-2(c); Treas. Reg. § 1.408-11, 68 Fed. Reg. 23586–23590 (May 5, 2003)]

The *computation period* extends from January 1 of the year for which the excess contribution is made until the date of the corrective distribution.

In determining the total Roth IRA for purposes of setting up the ratio, all assets within the same Roth IRA plan are included, plus contributions made during the computation period.

For purposes of returned excess or unwanted contributions, the net income attributable to a contribution is determined by allocating to the contribution a pro rata portion of the net income on the assets in the Roth IRA (whether positive or negative) during the period the Roth IRA held the contribution. This new method can be represented by the following formula (see Q 2:32):

$$\text{Net Income} = \text{Contribution} \times \frac{\text{Adjusted Closing Balance} - \text{Adjusted Opening Balance}}{\text{Adjusted Opening Balance}}$$

[Treas. Reg. § 1.408-11(a)(1)]

The opening balance equals the fair market value (FMV) of the Roth IRA immediately before the contribution being removed was made to the account, and the closing balance is the FMV of the account immediately before the contribution is removed. The opening balance is then adjusted to include the amount of any contributions or transfers made to the Roth IRA during the computation period. In addition, the closing balance is adjusted to include the amount of any distributions or transfers made from the Roth IRA during the computation period. [Treas. Reg. § 1.408-11(b)]

If a Roth IRA that has received more than one regular contribution for a particular taxable year, the last regular contribution made to the Roth IRA for the year is deemed to be the contribution that is distributed as a returned excess or unwanted contribution, up to the amount of the contribution identified by the IRA owner as the amount distributed as a returned contribution. [Treas. Reg. § 1.408-11(c)(2)]

A transfer made in or out of an IRA during the computation period is treated in the same manner as a contribution or distribution made to or from the IRA. [Treas. Reg. §§ 1.408-11(b)(1), 1.408A, Q&A 2(c)(2)(i)] A single computation period is used if more than one contribution was made to the IRA as a regular contribution.

[Treas. Reg. §§ 1.408-11 (b)(3), 1.408A, Q&A 2(c)(2)(iii)]

Example 1. On May 1, 2009, when her Roth IRA is worth $4,800, Melissa makes a $1,600 regular contribution to her Roth IRA. Melissa requests that $400 of the May 1, 2009, contribution be returned to her pursuant to Code Section 408(d)(4). Pursuant to this request, on February 1, 2010, when the Roth IRA is worth $7,600, the Roth IRA trustee distributes the $400 plus attributable net income to Melissa. During this time, no other contributions or distributions have been made to the Roth IRA. The adjusted opening balance is $6,400 ($4,800 + $1,600) and the adjusted closing balance is $7,600. Thus, the net income attributable to the $400 May 1, 2009, contribution is $75 ($400 × ($7,600 – $6,400) ÷ $6,400). Therefore, the total to be distributed on February 1, 2010, pursuant to Code Section 408(d)(4), is $475 ($400 + $75).

Example 2. Beginning in January 2009, Fred contributes to a Roth IRA $350 on the 15th of each month in 2009, resulting in an excess regular contribution of $600 for that year (based on his 2009 AGI; see Q 2:6). Fred requests that the $600 excess regular contribution be returned to him. Pursuant to this request, on March 1, 2010, when the Roth IRA is worth $16,000, the Roth IRA trustee distributes the $600 plus attributable net income to Fred. The excess regular contributions to be returned are deemed to be the last two made in 2009: the $300 December 15 contribution and the $300 November 15 contribution. On November 15, the Roth IRA is worth $11,000 immediately before the contribution. No distributions or transfers are made from the Roth IRA and no contributions or transfers, other than the monthly contributions (including $350 in January and February 2010), are made. As of the beginning of the computation period (November 15), the adjusted opening balance is $12,200 ($11,000 + $300 + $300 + $300 + $300) and the adjusted closing balance is $16,000. Thus, the net income attributable to the excess regular contributions is $187 ($600 × ($16,000 – $12,200) ÷ $12,200). Therefore, the total to be distributed as returned contributions on March 1, 2010, to correct the excess regular contribution is $787 ($600 + $187).

[Treas. Reg. § 1.408-11(d)]

The final regulations also provide rules for calculating net income allocable to a contribution being recharacterized. Such rules are, to a large extent, similar to the rules applicable to excess and unwanted contributions being returned. However, if more than one contribution is being recharacterized, different rules apply. In the case of multiple contributions for a particular year that are eligible for recharacterization, the IRA owner chooses (by date and dollar amount, not by specific assets acquired with those dollars) which contribution is to be recharacterized. [Treas. Reg. § 1.408A-5, Q&A 2(c)(5)] In addition, if a series of regular contributions were made, and consecutive contributions in that series are being recharacterized, the computation period is determined using a single computation period, based on the first contribution in the series.

[Treas. Reg. § 1.408A-5, Q&A 2(c)(iii)]

Net income calculations must be based on the overall value of a Roth IRA and the dollar amounts contributed, distributed, or recharacterized to or from the Roth IRA. [Treas. Reg. § 1.408A-5, Q&A 2(c)(1); Treas. Reg. § 1.408-11(a)]

Example 1. On March 1, 2009, when her Roth IRA is worth $80,000, Marsha makes a $160,000 conversion contribution to the Roth IRA. Subsequently, Marsha discovers that she was ineligible to make a Roth conversion contribution in 2009, and so she requests that the $160,000 be recharacterized to a traditional IRA pursuant to Code Section 408A(d)(6). Pursuant to this request, on March 1, 2010, when the IRA is worth $225,000, the Roth IRA trustee transfers to a traditional IRA the $160,000 plus allocable net income. No other contributions have been made to the Roth IRA and no distributions have been made. The adjusted opening balance is $240,000 ($80,000 + $160,000) and the adjusted closing balance is $225,000. Thus the net income allocable to the $160,000 is a negative $10,000 ($160,000 × ($225,000 – $240,000) ÷

$240,000). Therefore, in order to recharacterize the March 1, 2009, $160,000 conversion contribution on March 1, 2010, the Roth IRA trustee must transfer from Marsha's Roth IRA to her traditional IRA $150,000 ($160,000 – $10,000).

The amount Marsha must remove can be computed and illustrated as follows:

1.	Enter amount of 2009 IRA contribution to be recharacterized.	$160,000
2.	Enter FMV of IRA immediately prior to recharacterization (include all distributions, transfers, or recharacterizations made while the contribution was in the account).	$225,000
3.	Enter FMV of IRA immediately prior to the time the contribution being recharacterized was made, including the amount of such contributions and any other contributions, transfers, or recharacterizations made while the contribution was in the account.	$240,000
4.	Subtract item 3 from item 2.	$ 15,000
5.	Divide item 4 by item 3 (enter as a decimal rounded to at least three places).	(.0625)
6.	Multiply item 1 by item 5. This is the net income attributable to the amount to be recharacterized.	($ 10,000)
7.	Add item 1 and item 6.	$150,000

Example 2. On April 1, 2009, when her traditional IRA is worth $100,000, Harriet converts the entire amount, consisting of 100 shares of stock in Moon Corp. and 100 shares of stock in Rock Corp., by transferring the shares to a Roth IRA. At the time of the conversion, the 100 shares of stock in Moon Corp. are worth $50,000 and the 100 shares of stock in Rock Corp. are also worth $50,000. Harriet decides that she would like to recharacterize the Moon Corp. shares back to a traditional IRA. However, Harriet may choose only by dollar amount the contribution or portion thereof that is to be recharacterized. On the date of transfer, November 1, 2009, the 100 shares of stock in Moon Corp. are worth $40,000 and the 100 shares of stock in Rock Corp. are worth $70,000. No other contributions have been made to the Roth IRA and no distributions have been made.

1. If Harriet requests that $50,000 (which was the value of the Moon Corp. shares at the time of conversion) be recharacterized, the net income allocable to the $50,000 is $5,000 ($50,000 × ($110,000 – $100,000) ÷ $100,000)). Therefore, to recharacterize $50,000 of the April 1, 2009, conversion contribution on November 1, 2009, the Roth IRA trustee must transfer from Harriet's Roth IRA to a traditional IRA assets with a value of $55,000 ($50,000 + $5,000).

2. If, on the other hand, Harriet requests that $40,000 (which was the value of the Moon Corp. shares on November 1) be recharacterized, the net income allocable to the $40,000 is $4,000 ($40,000 × ($110,000 –

$100,000) ÷ $100,000). Therefore, to recharacterize $40,000 of the April 1, 2009, conversion contribution on November 1, 2009, the Roth IRA trustee must transfer from Harriet's Roth IRA to a traditional IRA assets with a value of $44,000 ($40,000 + $4,000).

3. Regardless of the amount of the contribution recharacterized (as here, $50,000 and $40,000), the determination of that amount (or of the net income allocable thereto) is not affected by whether the recharacterization is accomplished by the transfer of shares of Moon Corp. or of shares of Rock Corp.

Q 2:27   How is the attributable earnings ratio used to determine earnings on an excess contribution to a Roth IRA set up?

The attributable earnings ratio under Treasury Regulations Section 1.408-4(c)(2) used to determine earnings on an excess contribution to a Roth IRA is set up as follows:

$$\frac{\text{1. Principal amount of excess or unwanted contribution}}{\text{2. January 1 Roth IRA plan balance for which excess or made plus all contributions was made plus all contributions added during computation period (as defined above)}} = \frac{\text{3. Earnings attributable } (\times) \text{ to excess or unwanted contribution}}{\text{4. Total income earned by Roth IRA plan from January 1 of unwanted contribution was year for which excess or unwanted contribution was made through date of corrective distribution (i.e., during the computation period)}}$$

- Item 1 is the principal amount of the excess contribution.
- Item 2 is the sum of the total plan balance on January 1 of the year for which the contribution was made plus all contributions (including transfers and rollovers) made by the owner to the same Roth IRA during the computation period.
- Item 3 is the earnings attributable to the excess contribution. This is the number for which the equation is solved.
- Item 4 is the total income earned by the Roth IRA during the computation period, determined as follows:
  - The FMV of the Roth IRA is determined on the day the corrective distribution is made. This amount includes all accrued but not yet credited interest. Any property in the Roth IRA, such as stock, is valued as of the date of the corrective distribution.
  - The result in Step 1 is added to any distributions from the Roth IRA plan during the computation period.
  - The result in Step 2 is reduced (but not below zero) by the sum of the FMV of the plan on January 1 of the year for which the contribution

was made and the total contributions made during the computation period.

Example 1. Leona, age 75, made a contribution to her existing Roth IRA for 2009 on May 15, 2009, in the amount of $3,500. Her compensation for the year, however, was only $3,000; thus, the $3,500 contribution created a $500 excess contribution. On March 10, 2010, Leona withdraws the $500 plus the earnings attributable to the $500, calculated in the manner shown below.

Assume that the FMV of Leona's existing Roth IRA on January 1, 2009 (the year for which the contribution was made) was $12,395 and that Leona did not take any distributions during the computation period. Assume further that the trustee of the Roth IRA does not charge an early withdrawal penalty or other fees and that the Roth IRA's FMV on March 10, 2010, is $16,545, which includes accrued but not yet credited interest. The trustee determines the four items in the attributable earnings ratio as follows:

- Item 1, principal amount of excess contribution, is $500.
- Item 2, January 1, 2009, balance ($12,395) plus all contributions ($3,500), is $15,895.
- Item 3, earnings attributable to the $500, is unknown at this time.
- Item 4, total income earned by the plan during the computation period, is determined as follows:
  - FMV on the date of the corrective distribution (March 10, 2010) is $16,545.
  - Distributions are added to the result in Step 1. No distributions occurred. Therefore, the Step 2 amount is $16,545.

The Step 2 amount, $16,545, is reduced by the sum of the FMV on January 1, 2009 ($12,395), plus all contributions made ($3,500). The result is $650 ($16,545 − $15,895).

The ratio looks like this:

$$\frac{1. \quad \$500}{2. \quad \$15,895} = \frac{3. \quad x}{4. \quad \$650}$$

To solve for the unknown (earnings attributable), Item 1 ($500) is multiplied by Item 4 ($650) and the product is divided by Item 2 ($15,895). The result is $20.45, which represents the earnings attributable to the $500 excess contribution. Leona will withdraw a total of $520.45 on March 10, 2010. The $500 is not subject either to income taxes or to the 6 percent excess contribution penalty.

The $20.45 is taxable to Leona for the year for which the contribution was made (2009) even though the corrective distribution occurs in the following year (2010). The remaining balance in Leona's Roth IRA is $16,024.55 ($16,545 − $520.45).

The amount Leona must remove can be computed and illustrated as follows:

1. Enter amount of 2009 Roth contribution. $ 3,500

2. Enter FMV of Roth IRA immediately prior to the date the excess contribution was made (include the contribution and all distributions, transfers, or recharacterizations made while the contribution was in the account). $15,895

3. Enter FM of Roth IRA immediately prior to the time the excess contribution being withdrawn was made, including the amount of such contributions and any other contributions, transfers, or recharacterizations made while the contribution was in the account. $16,545

4. Subtract item 3 from item 2. $ 650

5. Enter the excess contribution amount. $ 500

6. Divide item 5 by item 2 (enter as a decimal rounded to at least three places).   .03146

7. Multiply item 6 by item 4. This is the net income attributable to the amount to be recharacterized. $ 20.45

8. Add item 5 and item 7. $520.45

Example 2. The facts are the same as those in Example 1, except that, once Leona's earnings are calculated, the trustee organization wants to assess an early withdrawal penalty. The trustee would collect such penalty or fee of $50 from the remaining Roth IRA plan assets, not from the amount required to be distributed to Leona ($520.45). That is, although a total debit of $570.45 would apply to Leona's Roth IRA, only the $520.45 is reported as distributed. The $50 represents a cost to the Roth IRA plan.

Example 3. The facts are the same as those in Example 1, except that the trustee knows before the earnings calculation is performed that it is going to charge a $50 penalty and a $10 transaction fee. The same steps would be followed, except that in determining Item 4 in the ratio, Step 1 would be reduced by the $60 penalty and fee, and the result in Step 1 would be $16,485 ($16,545 FMV on date of distribution − $60). Therefore, Item 4 in the ratio would be $590 ($16,485 − $12,395 − $3,500), and the ratio would look like this:

$$\frac{1. \quad \$500}{2. \quad \$15,895} = \frac{3. \quad x}{4. \quad \$590}$$

As a result of reducing the FMV on the date of the corrective distribution by the fee and penalty charged by the trustee, the earnings attributable to the $500 excess contribution are $18.56. A total of $518.56 will be distributed to Leona, and $60 will be credited to the trustee's appropriate internal general ledger. The remaining balance in Leona's Roth IRA is $15,966.44 ($16,545 − $518.56 − $60).

Just as in Example 1, the $500 is not taxable or subject to the 6 percent excess contribution penalty; however, the $18.56 is taxable to Leona for the year for which the contribution was made (2009) and is subject to the 10 percent premature distribution penalty if Leona is not yet age 59½.

Q 2:28 What happens if an amount contributed to a Roth IRA is an unwanted contribution rather than an excess contribution?

A Roth IRA owner may withdraw an unwanted contribution by withdrawing that contribution plus the earnings attributable to it before the year's tax filing due date (including extensions). A Roth IRA owner who wants to withdraw an unwanted contribution must do so *only* in such fashion. [I.R.C. § 408(d)(4)]

Example. The facts are the same as those in Example 1 in Q 2:27, except that the $500 is an unwanted contribution rather than an excess contribution. In such case, all the steps would be followed in exactly the same manner, and the earnings attributable to the $500 nondeductible contribution would be $20.45.

Q 2:29 May excess contributions be recharacterized?

No. Only actual contributions may be recharacterized. [Preamble, Treas. Reg. § 1.408A-5; (T.D. 8816), 64 Fed. Reg. 5597–5611 (Feb. 4, 1999); Treas. Reg. § 1.408A-5, Q&A 1] If the prior year's excess contributions are treated as the current year's contributions, they can only be recharacterized if the recharacterization would still be timely with respect to the tax year for which the applied contribution was actually made. [I.R.C. § 408A(d)(6)]

Q 2:30 May an election to recharacterize be made on behalf of a deceased Roth IRA holder?

Yes. The preamble to the Roth regulations states that "Commentators asked for clarification regarding whether a Roth IRA may be established for the benefit of a minor child or anyone else who lacks the legal capacity to act on his or her own behalf." The final regulations provide that the election to recharacterize may be made by the executor, administrator, or other person charged with the duty of filing the decedent's final federal income tax return. [Treas. Reg. § 1.408A-6, Q&A 6; I.R.C. 6012(b)(i)] Nonetheless, it does not appear that a personal representative may make a contribution to a Roth IRA. The fiduciary (executor or executrix) of a decedent's estate will have to determine whether he or she has the option, or duty, to "recharacterize" a decedent's Roth IRA conversion.

Q 2:31   **How does the alternative method contained in Notice 2003-39 and the final regulations differ from the original method of calculation?**

The final regulations retain the method announced in Notice 2000-39 [2000-30 I.R.B. 132] and provide the following:

1. Net income may include a negative number. Therefore, losses are permitted to be allocated to an excess or recharacterized contribution.

2. The earnings calculation is determined based on the entire Roth IRA balance, and *not* on a specific investment within the Roth IRA (this was a clarification).

3. For purposes of the calculation, recharacterized contributions are taken into account for the period they are actually held in the Roth IRA. Absent this approach, the original calculation of attributable earnings often resulted in inflated amounts.

4. If there are multiple regular contributions made to the Roth IRA that need to be returned under Code Section 408(d)(4), the last contribution made is deemed to be the contribution being distributed. In other words, the last-in first-out (LIFO) method is used.

5. If a taxpayer is maintaining multiple IRAs, the earnings calculation is made only with respect to the Roth IRA *designated* by the taxpayer as the IRA holding the contribution, and the corrective distribution must be made from that Roth IRA.

6. With respect to recharacterization, a taxpayer must request a specific dollar amount. He or she may not attempt to recharacterize a specific asset, such as a specific number of shares of stock.

Q 2:32   **What is the formula for calculating earnings attributable to an excess contribution to a Roth IRA under the final regulations?**

The pro rata formula that may be used to calculate earnings (and losses) attributable to an excess contribution to a Roth IRA is as follows:

$$\text{Net Income} = \text{Contribution} \times \frac{\text{Adjusted Closing Balance} - \text{Adjusted Opening Balance}}{\text{Adjusted Opening Balance}}$$

Certain terms used in connection with the pro rata formula are defined as follows:

1. *Computation period.* The period beginning immediately before the day the contribution is made to the IRA and ending immediately before the corrective distribution.

2. *Adjusted opening balance.* The FMV of the Roth IRA at the beginning of the computation period plus contributions made to the Roth IRA during the computation period.

3. *Adjusted closing balance.* The FMV of the Roth IRA at the end of the computation period plus distributions made during the computation period.

Note. If a Roth IRA asset is not valued on a daily basis, the FMV of the asset at the beginning of the computation period is deemed to be the most recent, regularly determined FMV of the asset. That determination of the FMV will be determined as of the date that coincides with or precedes the first day of the computation period. That may in effect allow the use of the previous year-end FMV (which is required for Form 5498 reporting) if the IRA is valued only once per calendar year.

Example. On March 1, 2009, the FMV of Sandeep's Roth IRA is $100,000. Sandeep converts $120,000 from his traditional IRA to his Roth IRA. He discovers that he was not eligible to make such a conversion. He therefore requests that the $120,000 be recharacterized back to his traditional IRA. The computation period is March 1, 2009, through the date the recharacterization occurs, which is March 1, 2009. The adjusted opening balance is $220,000 ($120,000 + $100,000). The adjusted closing balance on March 1, 2010, in Sandeep' s account is $260,000.

Net income = $120,000 × ($260,000 − $220,000) ÷ 220,000

Net income = $120,000 × ($40,000) ÷ $220,000)

The net gain therefore is $21,818.

The amount to be recharacterized is $141,818 ($120,000 + 21,818).

The distribution reporting would be a 2010 Form 1099-R with a Code R.

Q 2:33   How is an excess contribution to a Roth IRA corrected after the tax filing deadline (Method 4)?

Once the tax filing deadline (including extensions) has passed, the principal amount of aggregate excess contributions to a Roth IRA is simply distributed to the owner (without earnings under Method 4, except when using the six-month exception explained below). [I.R.C. § 4973(f)] Of course, the owner is immediately subject to the 6 percent excise tax, which is applied first to the year for which the excess contribution was made and then to each subsequent year until the excess is corrected (see Q 2:24).

Note. Any distribution of an excess contribution removed on or before the due date (including extensions) for filing the federal income tax return for the year is treated as not contributed, except to the extent that a regular contribution is allowable for the subsequent year. [I.R.C. § 4973(f)(2)]

Example. Arnold, age 27, contributed a total of $5,500 to several Roth IRAs at different organizations for 2009. Inasmuch as $5,000 is his contribution limit for the year, Arnold clearly has a $500 excess contribution. Arnold's tax return is due April 15, 2010. If Arnold does not withdraw the $500 and the earnings attributable to it by April 15, 2010, he will owe excise tax of $30 ($500 × 6%) for

2009 and each year thereafter until he corrects the excess by withdrawing the $500 from his Roth IRA (or under-contributes in the following year). Under the distribution ordering rules (see Q 4:1), Arnold will not be taxed on the $500 in the year he makes the withdrawal. See exception below.

Exception. The instructions to Form 5329 concerning the deadline to timely correct an excess contribution from a Roth IRA to avoid the 6 percent excise tax provide that the normal deadline—tax filing date plus extensions—may be extended six months from the original due date (Method 3), as follows:

- If the return was timely filed without withdrawing the excess contribution, the withdrawal may be made no later than six months after the due date of the tax return, excluding extensions. This may be done by filing an amended return with "Filed pursuant to section 301.9100-2" written at the top. Related earnings should be reported on the amended return along with an explanation of the withdrawal.

- If the contribution was reported as an excess contribution on the original return, an amended Form 5329 reflecting that the withdrawal contributions are no longer treated as having been contributed should be included. [Treas. Reg. § 301.9100-2 (b) (T.D. 8742, 62 Fed. Reg. 68167-68173, Dec. 31, 1997); *see* Instructions for Form 5329 Part IV—Tax on Excess Contributions to Roth IRAs]

Practice Pointer. The exception is especially useful for a taxpayer who failed to request an automatic six-month extension in which to file federal income tax returns.

Treasury Regulations provide that aggregate excess contributions that are not distributed from a Roth IRA on or before the tax return due date (with extensions) for the taxable year of the contributions are reduced as a "deemed Roth IRA contribution" for each subsequent taxable year to the extent that the Roth IRA owner does not actually make regular traditional IRA contributions for such years. [Treas. Reg. § 1.408A-2, Q&A 7] (However, see discussion of additional extension above.) Code Section 4973 applies separately to an individual's Roth IRAs and other types of IRAs. It can be argued that if a Roth owner is not eligible for a Roth IRA contribution in an excess contribution carryover year, he/she should be able to remove the excess contribution up to the regular allowable contribution limit for the year (plus net income attributable) by the due date of the federal income tax return for that subsequent year under Code Section 408(d)(4). [*See* I.R.C. § 408A(d)(2)(C)] This argument assumes that the automatic carryover of a Roth IRA excess contribution as a subsequent year's current contribution affords the same remedies available to any current-year excess contribution. In any event, the distribution of an excess contribution (and any earning thereon) cannot be treated as a qualified distribution. [I.R.C. § 408A(d)(2)(C)]

Note 1. Only actual contributions can be recharacterized. If prior years excess contributions are treated as current years contributions, they can only be recharacterized if the recharacterization would still be timely with respect to the tax year for which the applied contribution were actually made. [I.R.C. § 408A(d)(6)]

Note 2. The rules under Code Section 408(d)(5), regarding corrections after the due date of a tax return for the tax-free distribution of certain excess contributions to traditional IRAs, do not apply to a Roth IRA, because Roth IRA contributions are always tax free on distribution (except to the extent that they accelerated income inclusion under the four-year spread, which was only possible during 1998 through 2001(see Q 3:13), or under the two-year spread, which is only possible in 2010 (see Q 3:17). [Preamble, Treas. Reg. § 1.408A (T.D. 8816)]

Q 2:34   May a Roth IRA owner treat a prior year's excess contribution as a regular Roth IRA contribution made in a subsequent year in which the owner has not reached his or her contribution limit (Method 2)?

Yes. From a trustee's point of view, treating a prior year's excess contribution as a regular Roth IRA contribution in a year in which the Roth IRA owner has not reached his or her contribution limit is the simplest method to administer and to explain to the owner. Under such an approach, no distribution occurs from the Roth IRA. The owner merely under-contributes in the first subsequent year in which he or she has not met the annual contribution limit until the excess amount is used up. [I.R.C. § 219(f)(6); Treas. Reg. § 1.408A-3, Q&A 7]

Of course, the Roth IRA owner is immediately subject to the 6 percent excess contribution penalty because a corrective distribution did not occur on a timely basis. The 6 percent penalty is applied first to the year for which the excess contribution was made and then to each subsequent year until the excess amount is used up. The 6 percent penalty may not be as bad as the results of correcting an excess contribution before the year's tax filing due date (including extensions)—a taxable distribution of the earnings attributable to the excess amount, a possible 10 percent premature distribution penalty assessed against the distribution of earnings attributable to the excess, and a possible early withdrawal penalty or other fee assessed by the trustee.

Example. Paul, age 35, makes excess contributions to several Roth IRAs at different organizations of $11,000 in 2008. He does not make a correcting distribution and pays an excise tax of $660 ($11,000 × 6%) for 2008. In 2009, he treats $5,000 of that amount as a contribution to the Roth IRA. An excess contribution of $6,000 ($11,000 − $5,000) still remains for 2009, and $600 ($10,000 × 6%) excise tax would be due for 2009. For 2010 and 2011, assume the contribution limit is $5,000. In 2010, Paul treats $5,000 (the excess from the prior) as a 2010 contribution, and an excise penalty of $360 ($6,000 × 6%) would be due for 2010. For 2011, $1,000 ($10,000 − $5,000 − $5,000) remains, and Paul treats that amount as a 2011 contribution. He would owe another $60 ($1,000 × 6%) in excise taxes for 2010.

Caution. When a Roth IRA owner uses the method discussed herein to correct a prior year's excess contribution, he or she must be eligible to make a regular Roth IRA contribution for the subsequent year. That may pose a problem if the owner has no compensation during that subsequent year or the owner's contribution is phased out (see Qs 2:5, 2:6). In the above example, Paul could have avoided the excess contribution penalty entirely under Methods 1 and 3 (see Q 2:25).

Q 2:35   How must an excess contribution be distributed if an individual contributes to both a traditional IRA and a Roth IRA during a single tax year?

If an individual contributes to both a traditional IRA and a Roth IRA during a single tax year and an excess contribution occurs, the excess must first be corrected from the Roth IRA. That is because contributions are applied first to a traditional IRA and then to a Roth IRA for purposes of the $5,000 contribution limit ($6,000 with catch-up contribution) for 2009. [I.R.C. § 408A (c)(2)]

Example. Walter, age 65, contributes $2,000 to a Roth IRA for 2009 and inadvertently contributes $4,200 to a traditional IRA for 2009. Walter must correct the excess contribution of $200 (contribution limit is $6,000) from his Roth IRA.

Tax Credits for Contributions

Q 2:36   May a taxpayer claim a credit for a Roth IRA contribution?

Possibly. An eligible individual (see Q 2:37) may receive a nonrefundable tax credit for a percentage of his or her Roth IRA that does not exceed $2,000. [I.R.C. § 25B(a)] A contribution is voluntary if it is not required as a condition of employment. [*See* I.R.S. Ann. 2001-106, 2001-44 I.R.B. 416] Individuals claiming the credit must attach Form 8880—Credit for Qualified Retirement Savings Contributions to their Federal Income Tax Return (Form 1040 or 1040A). The credit applies to taxable years beginning after 2001.

Q 2:37   Who is an eligible individual?

To be eligible for the contribution tax credit, the taxpayer must be 18 years of age or older as of the close of the tax year (born before January 2, 2001, for the 2009 tax year) and must not be a full-time student or be claimed as a dependent on another taxpayer's tax return. Only low-income taxpayers will qualify (see Q 2:40). [I.R.C. § 25B(c)]

The PPA permanently extended the saver's credit and added another provision providing for indexing of the income limits. [I.R.C. § 25B(h), stricken by PPA § 812]

Q 2:38   Will a contribution made before age 18 qualify for the credit?

No. Although Roth IRA contributions may be made after the end of a taxable year for the prior taxable year (see Q 2:12), the individual must be at least age 18 by the end of the taxable year (generally December 31) for which the contribution is made to be eligible for the credit.

Q 2:39   What is the maximum credit rate?

The maximum credit rate is 50 percent of the first $2,000 contributed. Thus, $1,000 is the maximum yearly credit per individual. [I.R.C. §§ 25B(a), 25B(b)]

Q 2:40   How is the credit computed?

First, the credit rate is determined based on AGI. The credit rate is then multiplied by up to $2,000 of contributions to a Roth IRA or traditional IRA, elective deferrals to a SIMPLE, SEP, 401(k) plan, 403(b) plan, or governmental 457(b) plan, and voluntary after-tax contributions to a qualified plan or 403(b) annuity. Credit rates for 2009 are based on AGI levels as outlined below.

Adjusted Gross Income

Joint Return		Head of Household		All Other Cases[*]		Credit
Over	Not over	Over	Not over	Over	Not over	Percentage
$ 0	$33,000	$ 0	$24,750	$ 0	$16,500	50
$33,000	$36,000	$24,750	$27,000	$16,500	$18,000	20
$36,000	$55,500	$27,000	$41,625	$18,000	$27,750	10
$55,500	N/A	$41,625	N/A	$27,750	N/A	0

---

[*] This column includes single filers and married filers filing separately. When it comes to computing this credit, EGTRRA puts a surviving spouse in an adverse position compared to a head of household.

[I.R.C. § 25B(b)]

The PPA provides for indexing of the income limits applicable to the saver's credit beginning in 2007 (as reflected above), which was also permanently extended by the PPA (see Q 2:37). Indexed amounts are rounded to the nearest multiple of $500. Under the indexed income limits, as under present law, the income limits for single taxpayers is one-half that for married taxpayers filing a joint return and the limits for heads of household are three-fourths that for married taxpayers filing a joint return.

> **Example 1.** Larry, age 58, is married and files a joint tax return with his wife. Larry's AGI for 2009 is $35,000. He contributes $4,500 to a Roth IRA or as an elective deferral. His tax credit for 2009 is $400 ($2,000 × 0.20). If Larry's contribution for 2009 is only $1,500, his tax credit for 2009 would be $300 ($1,500 × 0.20).

Example 2. Saundra, age 30, is not married. Her AGI for 2009 is $24,000. She contributes $1,000 to a Roth IRA or as an elective deferral. Saundra's tax credit for 2009 is $100 ($1,000 × 0.10).

Although the contribution tax credit could be an incentive to contribute to a Roth IRA rather than to a traditional IRA, particularly if the credit would eliminate any income tax entirely, there are situations in which the IRS is paying for the traditional IRA contribution, because the traditional IRA contribution is deducted in the calculation of AGI.

Example 3. Sal and Mandy file a joint tax return. For 2009, their AGI is $33,100 and each contributes $4,950 to a Roth IRA. Since Sal and Mandy are under age 50, their contribution limit for 2009 is $5,000 each. They are entitled to a credit of $800 (($2,000 + $2,000) × 0.20). If Sal and Mandy contribute an additional $50 each to traditional IRAs, their AGI will become $33,000 and the credit percentage will jump from 20 percent to 50 percent. Their combined credit will increase from $800 to $2,000 (($2,000 + $2,000) × 0.50), giving them a $1,200 reduction in tax for the additional IRA contribution.

Note. The maximum saver's credit is $1,000 ($2,000 for married couples). However, the credit amount is often much less, and due to the impact of other deductions and credits, may be zero.

Practice Pointer. The fact that the credit is available to spouses who file separate returns means that a lower-income spouse can qualify for the credit even if the couple's joint income is too high. For example, if the husband has AGI of $30,000 and the wife has AGI of $24,000, the wife qualifies for a credit of 10 percent of any qualified contribution on a separate return, even though the couple cannot obtain credit for the contribution on a joint return.

AGI for purposes of the contribution tax credit is generally the amount labeled *adjusted gross income* at the bottom of page one of Form 1040 or Form 1040A, increased for any exclusion or deduction for the year for

1. Foreign earned income;
2. Foreign housing costs;
3. Income for residents of American Samoa; and
4. Income from Puerto Rico.

Note. The Obama Administration's tax proposal would expand the existing Saver's Credit to match 50 percent of the first $1,000 of savings for families that earn under $75,000 and makes the tax credit refundable. To help ensure that this proposal actually strengthens retirement investments, the savings match will be automatically deposited into designated personal accounts specified on the taxpayer's tax return. [Treasury Department, General Explanations of the Administration's Fiscal Year 2010 Revenue Proposals, page 6, available at http://www.treas.gov/offices/tax-policy/library/grnbk09.pdf (visited on June 22, 2009)]

Q 2:41   Is the credit reduced by distributions?

Yes. The amount of the credit for any year is reduced by any distribution taken during the testing period. [I.R.C. § 25B(d)(2)]

Certain types of withdrawals, including the return of an excess contribution, a rollover, and a loan from an annuity contract, are not treated as distributions for this purpose. [I.R.C. § 25B(d)(2)(C)]

> **Caution.** Amounts withdrawn for first-time home purchases and for either medical or educational expenses may reduce or eliminate the credit for contributions or deferrals to retirement savings plans for the current year or future years even though they may not be subject to the 10 percent early withdrawal penalty.

Q 2:42   What is the testing period?

The testing period consists of the two preceding tax years, the tax year, and the period after the tax year and before the due date of the federal income tax return of the individual (and of the spouse of the individual if a joint return is filed) for the tax year, including extensions. [I.R.C. § 25B(c)]

> **Example 1.** Ramone requests an extension of time to file his 2009 tax return until October 15, 2010. He will be ineligible for a tax credit for 2009 if he took distributions totaling at least $2,000 at any time between January 1, 2007, and October 15, 2010.

> **Example 2.** Lolita takes a Roth IRA distribution of $2,000 on March 1, 2009. She is ineligible to claim the contribution tax credit for 2007, 2008, and 2009.

Q 2:43   Does the credit apply to other types of retirement savings accounts?

Yes. An eligible individual (see Q 2:37) may receive a nonrefundable tax credit for a percentage of his or her (1) contributions to a Roth IRA or traditional IRA, (2) elective deferrals to a SIMPLE, SEP, 401(k) plan, 403(b) plan, or governmental 457(b) plan, and (3) voluntary after-tax contributions to a tax-qualified retirement plan or 403(b) annuity that do not exceed $2,000. [I.R.C. §§ 25B(d)(1), 25B(g)]

Q 2:44   Are other tax benefits affected by the contribution tax credit?

No. The credit is in addition to any other tax benefit (i.e., the possible tax deduction) that the contribution gives the taxpayer. [I.R.C. § 25B(a), 25B(b)]

Q 2:45   Do older taxpayers qualify for the contribution tax credit?

Yes. Taxpayers qualify for the contribution tax credit even if they are over age 70½; however, distributions, including RMDs may make taxpayers ineligible for the credit (see Q 2:41).

Deemed Roth IRAs

Q 2:46   What is a deemed Roth IRA?

A *deemed Roth IRA* is a "deemed IRA" that meets the eligibility and other requirements applicable to a Roth IRA account or annuity (*see also* Q 3:81). [I.R.C. § 408(q); Treas. Reg. 1.408(q)-1] For plan years beginning after 2002, an employer's qualified plan, 403(b) plan, or governmental 457(b) plan is permitted to accept Roth IRA contributions or traditional IRA contributions, or both. [I.R.C. §§ 408(q)(1), 408(q)(3)(A), 408(q)(3)(B)] These types of contributions are called voluntary employee contributions or deemed IRA contributions. Deemed IRAs and deemed Roth IRAs are more fully discussed in Qs 3:81 through 3:103.

Q 2:47   How is a deemed Roth IRA or deemed traditional IRA treated?

If the account or annuity meets the requirements applicable to a traditional IRA, the account or annuity is deemed to be a traditional IRA, and if the account or annuity meets the requirements applicable to a Roth IRA, the account or annuity is deemed to be a Roth IRA (see Qs 3:81–3:103). [Treas. Reg. § 1.408(q)-1(b)] For practical reasons, the arrangement is sometimes referred to simply as a "deemed IRA."

Payroll Deduction Roth IRA Programs

Q 2:48   May an employer establish a payroll deduction program to enable employees to make voluntary contributions to a Roth IRA?

Yes. Although a Roth IRA is not a traditional IRA, it has been the Department of Labor's (DOL) long-held view that an employer who provides employees with the opportunity to make contributions to an IRA through payroll deductions does not thereby establish a pension plan within the meaning of ERISA Section 3(2)(A). In the authors' opinion, the DOL's view would apply equally to a payroll deduction Roth IRA program. In addition, Announcement 99-2 states that employers may permit employees to contribute to traditional IRAs or Roth IRAs by direct deposit through payroll deductions. [I.R.S. Ann. 99-2 1999-1 C.B. 305; *see also* Treasury Department, General Explanations of the Administration's Fiscal Year 2010 Revenue Proposals, page 6, available at http://www.treas.gov/offices/tax-policy/library/grnbk09.pdf (visited on June 22, 2009)]

DOL regulations provide a safe harbor under which IRAs will not be considered pension plans when the conditions of the regulation are satisfied. Thus, with few constraints, employees may be provided an additional opportunity for saving for retirement. The safe harbor rules require the following:

1. No contributions are made by the employer or employee association;
2. Participation must be completely voluntary for employees or members;

3. The sole involvement of the employer or employee organization is without endorsement to permit the sponsor to publicize the program to employees or members, to collect contributions through payroll deductions or dues checkoffs, and to remit them to the sponsor (see Qs 2:50–2:52); and

4. The employer or employee organization receives no consideration in the form of cash or otherwise, other than reasonable compensation for services actually rendered in connection with payroll deductions or dues checkoffs (see Q 2:53).

[D.O.L. Reg. § 2510.3-2(d)]

Q 2:49 May employees make pretax salary reduction contributions to a payroll deduction Roth program?

No. All contributions are made with after-tax dollars and generally treated as wages or as earned income if the individual is self-employed (see Q 1:10).

Q 2:50 When is an employer considered to "endorse" a payroll deduction Roth program?

An employer is considered to endorse a payroll deduction program when the employer does not maintain neutrality with respect to the sponsor it selects. For purposes of the regulations, if an employer maintains neutrality with respect to the sponsor in its communications with its employees, the employer will not be considered to endorse an IRA payroll deduction program (see also Q 2:51). [D.O.L. Reg. § 2509.99-1(c)(1)]

Q 2:51 May an employer encourage participation in the payroll deduction program?

Yes. An employer may encourage employee participation by providing general information on the payroll deduction program and other educational materials that explain the prudence of retirement savings, including the advantages of contributing to a Roth IRA, without thereby converting the wage contribution withholding program to an ERISA-covered plan.

Caution. The employer must make it clear that its involvement in the program is limited to collecting the deducted amounts and remitting them promptly to the sponsor and that it does not provide any additional benefit or promise any particular investment return on the employee's retirement savings.

[D.O.L. Reg. § 2509.99-1(c)(1)]

Q 2:52 How may an employer demonstrate its neutrality with respect to a sponsor?

An employer may demonstrate its neutrality with respect to a sponsor in a variety of ways, including (but not limited to) ensuring that materials distributed to employees in connection with a payroll deduction program clearly and prominently state, in language reasonably calculated to be understood by the average employee, the following:

1. The IRA payroll deduction program is completely voluntary;
2. The employer does not endorse or recommend either the sponsor or the funding media;
3. Other IRA funding media are available to employees outside of the payroll deduction program;
4. An IRA or Roth IRA may not be appropriate for all individuals; and
5. The tax consequences of contributing to an IRA or Roth IRA through the payroll deduction program are generally the same as the consequences of contributing to an IRA or Roth IRA outside of the program

The employer would not be considered neutral to the extent that either the materials distributed to the employees identified the funding medium as having as one of its purposes investing in securities of the employer or its affiliates or the funding medium has significant investments in such securities.

If the program were a result of an agreement between the employer and an employee organization, the employee organization's involvement in the program would be considered less than neutral if informational materials identified the funding medium as having one purpose to invest in an investment vehicle that is designed to benefit an employee organization by providing more jobs for its members, loans to its members, or similar direct benefits (or the funding medium's actual investments in any such investment vehicles).

[D.O.L. Reg. § 2509.99-1(c)(1), footnote 2]

Q 2:53 What is considered *reasonable compensation*?

Reasonable compensation does not include any profit to the employer. Payments an employer receives from a Roth IRA sponsor for the employer's cost of operating the IRA payroll deduction program do constitute reasonable compensation to the extent that they constitute compensation for the employer's actual program costs.

> **Example.** The Roth IRA sponsor agrees to make or permit particular investments of Roth IRA contributions in consideration for the Employer's agreement to make a payroll deduction program available to its employees. Such an arrangement exceeds reasonable compensation for the services actually rendered by the employer in connection with the program.

[D.O.L. Reg. § 2509.99-1(f)]

Q 2:54   What else may an employer do without converting the payroll deduction program into an ERISA-covered plan?

Specifically, without converting the payroll deduction program into an ERISA-covered plan, an employer may:

1. Answer employees' specific inquiries about the mechanics of the Roth IRA payroll deduction program and may refer other inquiries to the appropriate IRA sponsor;

2. Provide to employees informational materials written by the IRA sponsor describing the sponsor's IRA programs or addressing topics of general interest regarding investments and retirement savings, provided that the material does not itself suggest that the employer is other than neutral with respect to the IRA sponsor and its products; and

3. Request that the IRA sponsor prepare such informational materials and the employer may review such materials for appropriateness and completeness.

Note. A display of the employer's name or logo in the informational materials in connection with describing the payroll deduction program does not by itself suggest that the employer has endorsed the IRA sponsor or its products, provided that the specific context and surrounding facts and circumstances make clear to the employees that the employer's involvement is limited to facilitating employee contributions through payroll deductions (see Q 2:52).

[D.O.L. Reg. § 2509.99-1(c)(2)]

Q 2:55   May an employer who established a payroll deduction Roth IRA limit the number of IRA trustees/ custodians available to its employees?

Yes, an employer may limit the number of Roth IRA trustee/custodians to which its employees may make payroll deduction contributions, provided that any limitations on, or costs or assessments associated with, an employee's ability to transfer or roll over Roth IRA contributions to another Roth IRA trustee/custodian are fully disclosed before the employee's decision to participate in the program. Also, an employer may be violating the limitations of such a program if the employer negotiates with a Roth IRA trustee/custodian and thereby obtains special terms and conditions for its employees that are not generally available to similar purchasers of the Roth IRA. The employer's involvement in the Roth IRA program would also be in violation of the limitations if the employer exercises any influence over the investments made or permitted by the Roth IRA sponsor (see Q 2:48).

[D.O.L. Reg. § 2509.99-1(d)]

Q 2:56   May an employer who established a payroll deduction Roth IRA pay the fees imposed by the sponsors?

The employer may pay any fee the IRA sponsor imposes on employers for services the sponsor provides in connection with the establishment and maintenance of the payroll deduction process itself. The employer may also assume the internal costs (such as for overhead, bookkeeping, and so on) of implementing and maintaining the payroll deduction program without reimbursement from either employees or the IRA sponsor.

Caution. If an employer pays, in connection with operating an IRA payroll deduction program, any administrative, investment management, or other fee that the IRA sponsor would require employees to pay for establishing or maintaining the IRA, the employer would fall outside the safe harbor and, as a result, may be considered to have established an ERISA-covered plan.

[D.O.L. Reg. § 2509.99-1(e)]

Q 2:57   May an employer that offers Roth IRAs to the general public in the normal course of its business, or an affiliate of a Roth IRA sponsor, establish a payroll deduction Roth IRA program for its employees?

Generally, an employer that offers Roth IRAs in the normal course of its business to the general public or that is an affiliate of a Roth IRA sponsor may provide its employees with the opportunity to make contributions to Roth IRAs sponsored by the employer or the affiliate through a payroll deduction program as long as the following is true:

1) The Roth IRA products offered to the employees for investment of the payroll deduction contributions are identical to Roth IRA products the sponsor offers the general public in the ordinary course of its business; and

2) Any management fees, sales commissions, and the like charged by the Roth IRA sponsor to employees participating in the payroll deduction program are the same as those charged by the sponsor to employees of nonaffiliated employers that establish an IRA payroll deduction program.

Note. Even though the funding medium offered by an employer that is an IRA sponsor or an affiliate of an IRA sponsor might be considered an employer security when offered to its own employees, the fact that informational materials provided to employees identify the funding medium as having as one of its purposes investing in securities of the employer would not involve the employer beyond the safe harbor limits, nor would the fact that the funding medium may actually be so invested. If the informational materials that the employer provides to employees, however, suggest that the employer, in providing the IRA payroll deduction program for purposes of investing in employer securities, is acting as an employer in relation to persons who participate in the program, rather than as an IRA sponsor acting in the course of its ordinary business of making IRA products available to the public, the employer would have gone beyond the safe harbor limits (see Q 2:52).

Caution. If an employer that is a Roth IRA sponsor waives enrollment and management fees for its employees' Roth IRAs, and it normally charges those fees to members of the public who purchase Roth IRAs, the employer would be considered to be so involved in the program as to be outside the safe harbor and be deemed to have established a "pension plan" within the meaning of ERISA Section 3(2)(A) (see Q 2:48).

[D.O.L. Reg. § 2509.99-1(g); *see* ERISA § 407(d)(i) for definition of "affiliate"]

Chapter 3

Conversion, Contribution Recharacterization, and Rollovers

This chapter describes the methods by which a traditional IRA and most employer plans may be converted in a taxable movement of cash or other property to a Roth IRA. It also considers conversion of a SEP IRA and a SIMPLE IRA to a Roth IRA and explains how unwanted contributions may be transferred in a contribution recharacterization between certain types of IRAs before the due date of the IRA owner's federal income tax return for the Roth IRA contribution year. The rules applicable to rollover contributions to and from a Roth IRA are discussed in this chapter, as well as the valuation of an annuity contract that is converted to a Roth IRA. IRS and participant reporting requirements are discussed in chapter 9. Designated Roth contribution programs are discussed in chapter 10. Certain types of contributions are treated as rollovers. The rollover of hurricane distributions, airline payments, qualified recovery assistance distributions, qualified disaster recovery distributions, military death gratuities, Servicemembers' Group Life Insurance (SGLI), and Exxon Valdez settlements are discussed in this chapter.

Conversion of Traditional IRA to Roth IRA

Q 3:1   What is a *conversion*?

A qualified rollover contribution is a contribution to a Roth IRA from another Roth IRA or from a traditional IRA made through a conversion (see Qs 3:1, 3:4). The contribution must meet the general IRA rollover rules under Code Section 408(d)(3) (see Q 3:67), except that the 12-month rollover restriction does not apply to rollovers between a traditional IRA and a Roth IRA (see Q 3:8). A deemed Roth IRA (see Q 3:81) and a designated Roth contribution program (DRCP) (see Q 10:1) may also be rolled over to a Roth IRA (see Qs 3:101, 3:82). [I.R.C. §§ 402A(c)(2)(3), 408A(e)]

Effective for distributions after 2007, the Pension Protection Act of 2006 (PPA) generally will allow for direct and indirect (60-day) rollovers from a qualified plan, a tax-sheltered annuity, or a governmental plan to a Roth IRA and will treat it as a Roth conversion if all other conversion qualifications (e.g., income below the $100,000 level before 2010, see Q 3:16) are satisfied (see Q 3:64). The taxable portion of the rollover amount would be taxable at the time of the rollover. [I.R.C. §§ 408A(e)(2), 408A(c)(3)(B), 408A(d)(3)(E), as amended by PPA § 824; Notice 2008-30, 2008-12 I.R.B. 638]

Practice Pointer. It is important that the plan administrator be informed or advised of the type of IRA (traditional or Roth) into which funds are deposited, so Form 1099-R can be filled out correctly.

Practice Pointer. A distribution of an inherited traditional IRA to a nonspouse beneficiary is not a qualified distribution. [I.R.C. § 408(d)(3), 408A(e); Treas. Reg. § 1.408A-4, Q&A 1; PPA § 829, adding I.R.C. § 402(c)(11)(A), allowing for the rollover by a nonspouse beneficiary of certain retirement plan distributions starting after 2006, but only to a traditional "inherited" IRA] A nonspouse beneficiary who received an interest through a spousal disclaimer could not convert the inherited IRA to a Roth IRA. [Ltr. Rul. 200013041 (Jan. 4, 2000)]

Practice Pointer. Regardless of the means used to convert, any amount converted from a non-Roth IRA to a Roth IRA is treated as distributed from the non-Roth IRA and rolled over to the Roth IRA.

Q 3:2   May a SEP IRA or a SIMPLE IRA be converted to a Roth IRA?

Yes. Although a SEP IRA or a SIMPLE IRA may not be designated as a Roth IRA, all types of IRAs (including SEP IRAs and SIMPLE IRAs) may be converted to a Roth IRA. [I.R.C. § 408A(f)(1); Treas. Reg. § 1.408A-4, Q&A 4] Of course, a SIMPLE IRA may not be converted to any other IRA (including a Roth IRA) until the two-year holding period applicable to the SIMPLE IRA has expired. [I.R.C. §§ 72(t)(6), 408(d)(3)(G)]

Q 3:3   May a conversion be undone?

Yes. A conversion may be undone or reversed through a timely contribution recharacterization (see Q 3:29). A contribution recharacterization is a reportable event (see Q 3:43; chapter 9).

Practice Pointer. A recharacterization may be appropriate if the Roth IRA falls in value after the conversion or if the owner's financial circumstance change significantly. Furthermore, in the event of a lawsuit, a traditional IRA may offer stronger asset protection than an individual's Roth IRA.

Q 3:4   How may a traditional IRA be converted to a Roth IRA?

There are three ways to convert a traditional IRA to a Roth IRA:

1. *Rollover conversion under* Section 408A(d)(3)(B) of the Internal Revenue Code (Code). Generally, the rollover conversion of a traditional IRA to a Roth IRA is treated for federal income tax reporting purposes as a distribution from the traditional IRA and a subsequent rollover contribution to the Roth IRA if such rollover is made within 60 days (see Q 9:1). Nonreportable transfers are not permitted (see Qs 9:1, 9:30, 9:46). [I.R.C. § 408A(d)(3)(D); *see also* I.R.C. § 408(d)(3)(A)(i)]

2. *Trustee-to-trustee transfer.* An amount in a traditional IRA may be transferred in a trustee-to-trustee transfer from the trustee of the traditional IRA to the trustee of the Roth IRA. In such a case, the trustees are different institutions. Such transfers are reported.

3. *Internal conversions.* The direct transfer within the same financial institution of a traditional IRA to a Roth IRA is permitted and is generally treated as a rollover for reporting purposes. [I.R.C. §§ 408(d)(3), 408A(d)(3)(C); *see, e.g.,* Ltr. Rul. 8716058] An internal conversion is reported in the same manner as a rollover conversion [I.R.C. § 408A(d)(3)(D); Treas. Reg. § 1.408A-4, Q&A 1(c)]; that is, the amount converted is considered a distribution from the traditional IRA and a contribution to the Roth IRA. It appears that a separate written document (see Q 1:13) must be established before the conversion and a disclosure notice must be provided to the account holder (see Qs 1:24, 1:33, 4:21).

[Treas. Reg. § 1.408A-4, Q&A 1(b), 1(c)]

Of course, to convert a traditional IRA to a Roth IRA, an individual must first establish a Roth IRA. The conversion transaction must commence before the end of the taxable year to be treated as a conversion for that year.

Q 3:5   Are partial rollovers and transfers from a traditional IRA to a Roth IRA permitted?

Yes. Rollovers and transfers of less than the full amount in a traditional IRA (or an eligible rollover distribution from an employer's plan, see Q 3:52) to a Roth IRA are permitted. [I.R.C. §§ 402(c)(4), 408(d)(3)(D), 408(e); *see* Ltr. Rul. 200909074 (Dec. 2, 2008) regarding the conversion of only after-tax contributions under a 401(k) plan to a Roth IRA.]

> **Example.** Candace owns a $500,000 traditional IRA. Candace wants to rollover only $200,000 of this amount to a Roth IRA. Under Code Section 408(d)(3)(D), she is permitted to do so.

Q 3:6   May a conversion contribution and an annual Roth IRA contribution be combined in one Roth IRA?

Yes. Annual Roth IRA contributions and conversion contributions may be combined in one Roth IRA. [I.R.C. § 408A(e)]

> **Note.** If a Roth IRA owner combines conversion contributions and annual Roth IRA contributions in the same Roth IRA and is under age 59½, he or she should keep a record of the year in which each conversion to the Roth IRA was made for purposes of the five-year rule and the recapture of the 10 percent tax (see Qs 4:1, 4:14, 4:17).

Eligibility

Q 3:7   What limitations apply to an individual's eligibility to convert a traditional IRA to a Roth IRA before 2010?

In taxable years beginning before 2010, statutory requirements for eligibility to convert a traditional IRA to a Roth IRA depend on an individual's modified adjusted gross income (MAGI) (see Q 2:8) and filing status.

MAGI Limit. The MAGI limit for conversion is $100,000; that is, an individual may make a conversion to a Roth IRA from a traditional IRA if the individual's MAGI for the year in which the conversion is made does not exceed $100,000. [I.R.C. § 408A(c)(3)(B)(i)] The $100,000 limit does not apply after 2009 (see Q 3:16).

Taxable IRA distributions that are not rolled over to a Roth IRA are included in an individual's adjusted gross income (AGI) and are included in MAGI for purposes of the $100,000 MAGI limit. [*See* I.R.C. § 408A(c)(3)(C); Treas. Reg. § 1.408A-3, Q&A 6]

Example. Nancy's AGI for 2009, before she contemplates converting her traditional IRA to a Roth IRA, is $85,000. She has a traditional IRA valued at $100,000. Nancy withdraws the entire $100,000 from her traditional IRA on December 31 and rolls over the entire $100,000 to her Roth IRA within 60 days. Conversion amounts, although taxable in 2009, will not increase Nancy's MAGI for purposes of the $100,000 MAGI limit. Therefore, Nancy is eligible to convert her traditional IRA to a Roth IRA for 2009.

Filing Status. An individual is not permitted to make a conversion from a traditional IRA to a Roth IRA if that individual is a married individual filing a separate return until tax years beginning after 2009 (see Q 3:16). [I.R.C. § 408A(c)(3)(B)(ii)] For purposes of a Roth IRA, marital status is determined under Code Section 219(g)(4). [I.R.C. § 408A(c)(3)(D)] The only exception to this joint filing requirement (before 2010) is for a taxpayer who has lived apart from his or her spouse for the entire taxable year. If the married taxpayer has lived apart from his or her spouse for the entire taxable year, then such taxpayer can treat himself or herself as not married for purposes of this rule, file a separate return, and be subject to the $100,000 limit on his or her separate MAGI. [Treas. Reg. § 1.408A-4, Q&A 2(b)]

Example. Barry and Martha are married and file a joint federal income tax return. For 2009, Barry's MAGI is $30,000 and Martha's MAGI is $80,000. Neither Barry nor Martha is eligible to make a conversion contribution because their combined MAGI exceeds $100,000.

Note. Beginning in 2010, the $100,000 MAGI conversion limit and requirement for joint filing, if married, is eliminated. (See Qs 3:7, 3:16)

Q 3:8   Is a required minimum distribution from a traditional IRA eligible for conversion to a Roth IRA?

No. If an IRA owner is converting a traditional IRA to a Roth IRA and is age 70½ or older during the year of the conversion, his or her required minimum distribution (RMD) amount is not eligible to be converted. Code Section 408A(e) provides that the amount eligible to be converted from a traditional IRA to a Roth IRA must meet the requirements of Code Section 408(d)(3), except for the rule that limits rollovers (but not direct transfers) between each traditional IRA to one rollover per 12-month period. [I.R.C. § 408A(e)] Code Section 408(d)(3)(E) provides that any amount that is an RMD is not eligible for any rollover treatment. As a result, the RMD must be distributed and is includible in income in the year received.

Note. The Worker, Retiree, and Employer Recovery Act of 2008 (WRERA) suspended the requirement for a beneficiary to take RMDs in 2009 (see Q 1:32 and chapter 5).

The first amount distributed during a calendar year is treated as an RMD to the extent that the amount required to be distributed for that calendar year has not been distributed. Code Section 401(a)(9) generally requires that RMDs begin by April 1 of the calendar year following the calendar year in which the

IRA owner reaches age 70½. If the first RMD is made during the year the IRA owner reaches age 70½, it is treated as made during the preceding year and may not be rolled over. [Treas. Reg. §§ 1.401(a)(9)-1&2, 1.402(c)-2, Q&A 7(a), 1.408-8, Q&A 4]

> **Example.** Roslyn is required to receive a minimum distribution of $10,000 from her traditional IRA. Her traditional IRA currently has a value of $21,000. She converts $11,000 to a Roth IRA, leaving $10,000 in her traditional IRA, and plans to take the $10,000 later in the year to satisfy the RMD rules. Since Roslyn converted prior to receiving her RMD, $10,000 of the converted amount is treated as her RMD and is therefore ineligible for conversion. Most, if not all, of the $11,000 is an excess contribution and may be subject to penalty (see Q 2:24). Roslyn should have taken the $10,000 as her RMD first and then converted the remaining $11,000.

> **Note.** It makes no difference that a conversion from a traditional IRA to a Roth IRA is accomplished through a trustee-to-trustee transfer—a conversion is treated as a distribution regardless of how it is accomplished. The RMD amount remains ineligible for rollover and thus is also ineligible to be converted to a Roth IRA. [I.R.C. § 408A(d)(3)(C)]

Q 3:9 Is a required minimum distribution counted when determining an individual's MAGI for purposes of eligibility for conversion of a traditional IRA to a Roth IRA before 2010?

No. In taxable years beginning after 2004, an RMD from a traditional IRA is not taken into account for determining whether the $100,000 (before 2010) MAGI test has been satisfied. [I.R.C. §§ 219(g)(3), 408A(c)(3)(C)(i); Treas. Reg. § 1.408A-3, Q&A 6]

> **Example.** In 2009, Anthony must take an RMD of $20,000 from a traditional IRA. His AGI before the distribution is $90,000. The additional taxable distribution of $20,000 will not increase his MAGI over the $100,000 limit because it will not be taken into account when determining his MAGI for purposes of converting a traditional IRA to a Roth IRA.

> **Note.** The Treasury regulations exclude (after 2004) only RMDs from IRAs. RMDs from qualified plans are *not* also excluded from the MAGI limit. [I.R.C. § 408A(c)(3)(C)(i)(II); Treas. Reg. § 1.408A-3, Q&A 6]

The rules defining MAGI for conversion purposes are summarized in Table 3-1. For purposes of the Roth IRA contribution phaseout rules, AGI is not reduced by required distributions from IRAs and Roth IRAs (see Q 2:8 and Table 2-3).

> **Note.** MAGI takes into account taxable Social Security benefits that are included in AGI.

Table 3-1. MAGI Worksheet for 2009 Roth IRA Conversion Purposes

1. AGI (Form 1040, line 38; Form 1040A, line 22; or Form 1040NR, line 36). $_____

2. Less: Conversion income resulting from the conversion of a non-Roth IRA to a Roth IRA included on Form 1040, line 15b; Form 1040A, line 11b; or Form 1040NR, line 16b[1]   − $_____

3. Less: Conversion income resulting from Roth IRA rollovers from qualified retirement plans included on Form 1040, line 16; Form 1040A, line 12b; or Form 1040NR, line 17b[2]   − $_____

4. Less: Taxable portion of an RMD from an IRA or Roth IRA (included on Form 1040, line 15b; Form 1040A, line 11b; or Form 1040NR, line 16b).   − $_____

5. AGI for MAGI purposes (line 1 minus lines 2 through 4)[2]   = $_____

6. Add: Traditional IRA deduction (Form 1040, line 32; Form 1040A, line 17; or Form 1040NR, line 31)   + $_____

7. Add: Student loan interest deduction (Form 1040, line 33; Form 1040A, line 18; or Form 1040NR, line 32)   + $_____

8. Add: Foreign earned income exclusion and/ or housing exclusion (from Form 2555, line 45 or Form 2555-EZ, line 18)   + $_____

9. Add: Foreign housing deduction (Form 2555, line 50)   + $_____

10. Add: Exclusion of bond interest (Form 8815, line 14)   + $_____

11. Add: Exclusion of employer-paid adoption expenses (Form 8839, line 30)   + $_____

12. Add; Domestic production activities deduction from Form 1040, line 35 or Form 1040A, line 33.   + $_____

13. Add: tuition and fees deduction from Form 1040, line 34; or Form 1040A, line 18.   + $_____

14. MAGI for Roth IRA conversion purposes[2] (line 6 plus lines 5 through 14)   = $_____

---

[1] Conversion income must be considered when computing other AGI-based phaseouts.
[2] **Caution** If using this table to compute MAGI for the purposes of the contribution phaseout rules, *do not* reduce AGI (step 4) for required, minimum distributions from an IRA or Roth IRA (enter $0 on line 4). See Q 2:8 and Table 2-3.

Q 3:10   Is a traditional IRA from which substantially equal periodic payments are being made eligible for conversion to a Roth IRA?

Yes. The receipt of substantially equal periodic payments (SEPP) within the meaning of Code Section 72(t)(2)(A)(iv) from a traditional IRA does not prevent that IRA from being converted to a Roth IRA. The conversion amount itself not only is not subject to the early distribution tax (see Q 4:21) but also is not treated as a distribution for purposes of determining whether a modification within the meaning of Code Section 72(t)(4)(A) has occurred. To avoid a modification of the series, however, the *entire* IRA that is subject to substantially equal periodic payments should be converted, rather than only a portion of the IRA. [Rev. Rul. 2002-62, § 2.02(e); Ltr. Rul. 200720023 (Feb. 21, 2007)]

Distributions from the Roth IRA that are part of the original series of substantially equal periodic payments will be nonqualified distributions from the Roth IRA until they meet the requirements for being a qualified distribution (see Q 4:9). [Treas. Reg. § 1.408A-4, Q&A 12]

> **Note.** If the original series of substantially equal periodic payments from a traditional IRA does not continue to be distributed in substantially equal periodic payments from the Roth IRA after conversion, the series of payments will have been modified; if such modification occurs within five years of the first payment or before the IRA owner becomes disabled or attains age 59$\frac{1}{2}$, he or she will be subject to the recapture tax of Code Section 72(t)(4)(A). The modified payments may also be subject to income acceleration during the two-year spread period (see Q 3:17) and the 10 percent additional tax on early distributions (see Q 4:21). [Treas. Reg. § 1.408A-4, Q&A 12]

> **Caution.** The Tax Court determined that additional distributions used for higher education expenses that escape the 10 percent tax on early distributions did not constitute modifications to a series of substantially equal periodic payments when there was no change to the method for determining the amount of equal periodic distributions. The Tax Court reasoned that a modification does not occur when another exception—other than attaining age 59$\frac{1}{2}$ during the five-year period—under Code Section 72(t) applied. [I.R.C. § 72(t)(2)(E), last sentence; Gregory T. Benz, v. Comm'r, 132 T.C. No. 15, Docket No. 15867-07 (May 11, 2009)] It remains to be seen whether the IRS will appeal or acquiesce the decision of the Tax Court in *Benz*. From a policy prospective, it was a good decision, but in this author's opinion, the decision was a tortured technical reading of the Code. It could be argued (although not mentioned by the Tax Court) that the language excepting the higher education expense distribution (which are coordinated with other benefits) under Code Section 72(t)((2)(E), taking into account that similar (but not identical) language is used subparagraphs "(B)" relating to medical expenses (which are subject to AGI percentage limits), and "(F)" relating to first time homebuyer purchases (which are limited in amount), merely provide ordering rules for multiple distributions. In the authors' opinion, the change in substantially equal payment rules under Code Section 72(t)(4) only provide exceptions for death or disability. [I.R.C. §§ 72(t)(7)(B), 72(t)(2)(B), 72(t)(2)(E), last line, 72(t)(2)(F), 72(t)(4)(A), 72(t)(4)A)(ii);

[....; see Stecker, William, "Benz v Internal Revenue Service 132 TC 15" (May 12, 2009), available at http://www.72t.net, see Articles of Interest (visited on Aug. 28, 2009); see also, Treas. Reg. § 1.402(c), A&A 6, regarding variations in payments under the SEPP exception.]

Q 3:11   Is the transfer of a Roth IRA pursuant to a decree of divorce or a separation instrument under Code Section 408(d) treated as a modification?

No, it is not treated as a modification provided that the annual dollar amount of the substantially equal periodic payments remains unchanged. [I.R.C. § 72(t)(2)(A)(iv)]

Example. Rhoda has three Roth IRAs. The payments from each Roth IRA separately qualify as a series of substantially equal periodic payments within the meaning of Code Section 72(t)(2)(A)(iv). The amounts being distributed from each Roth IRA, computed separately, are $500, $1,000, and $2,000. Pursuant to a decree of divorce, the Roth IRA with the smallest payment was properly transferred to Rhoda's ex-husband (see Q 4:28). If Rhoda continues to remove the $1,000 and $2,000 payments from the remaining two Roth IRAs, a modification will not be deemed to occur. The Roth IRA transferred was no longer Rhoda's property. [Ltr. Rul. 200116056 (Jan. 26, 2001)]

Caution. The application of Letter Ruling 200116056 to the transfer of a partial interest in a single Roth IRA could result in unintended consequences if the remaining assets are insufficient to continue the level of contributions made before the transfer (except in case of death or disability). [I.R.C. § 72(t)(4)(A)] In several letter rulings, the IRS has allowed the taxpayers to reduce their periodic payments in proportion to the amount of the IRA that was transferred to the spouse in a divorce decree. [Ltr. Ruls. 200202074 (Jan. 11, 2002), 200202076 (Jan. 11, 2002), 200214034 (Apr. 5, 2002), 200717026 (Apr. 27, 2007)]

Taxation

Q 3:12   How is the amount included in income taxed when a qualified rollover contribution (conversion) is made from an employer's plan to a Roth IRA after 2007?

Effective for distributions after 2007, rollovers from a qualified plan, a tax-sheltered annuity, or a governmental 403(b) plan to a Roth IRA are permitted (see Qs 3:52–3:65). The rollover or direct transfer will be treated as a Roth conversion if all other conversion qualifications (e.g., income below the $100,000 level before 2010; see Q 3:16) are satisfied. In general, the taxable portion of the rollover amount would be taxable at the time of the rollover. [I.R.C. §§ 408A(e)(2), 408A(c)(3)(B), 408A(d)(3)(E), as amended by PPA § 824; Notice 2008-30, 2008-12 I.R.B. 638] However, for a qualified rollover contribution from an employer's plan made in a taxable year beginning in 2010, a special tax acceleration rule may apply (see Q 3:17).

Practice Pointer. A direct conversion avoids the aggregation rules requiring that all IRAs be treated as a single IRA. The IRA aggregation rules are particularly troublesome where an individual's retirement accounts hold substantial amounts of after-tax contributions (see examples in Q 3:13).

Q 3:13   Do the new rules allowing direct conversions from a qualified plan require that distributions be aggregated with all IRAs the individual owns?

No. In general, Code Section 408(d)(2) requires all IRAs to be considered a single IRA when determining the tax consequences of a distribution or conversion. The aggregation rules do not apply to direct rollover conversions from an employer's plan.

Before 2007, rollovers to a Roth IRA from employer-sponsored plans, such as qualified plans and 403(b) plans, were not permitted. An individual could, however, roll over the employer plan to a traditional IRA and then convert (roll over or transfer) the traditional IRA to a Roth IRA (see Q 3:52). This is no longer necessary (see Example 2). A direct conversion may be beneficial when an individual's retirement accounts hold substantial amounts of after-tax contributions (which could be recovered tax-free in a direct conversion).

Example 1. Francine is a single individual, age 60, and has an adjusted gross income of $80,000 from wages. Francine has an IRA worth $500,000. No deductions were claimed for contributions made to this account. Francine is about to retire. She has $200,000 in her 401(k), of which $40,000 consists of after-tax contributions. Francine receives a distribution of her 401(k) account ($200,000) and rolls it over into a new IRA. Francine converts the new IRA to a Roth IRA. The $200,000 Roth conversion is treated as a partial conversion of the aggregate $700,000 ($200,000 + $500,000). Because the after-tax contributions ($40,000) are recovered on a pro-rata basis, Francine will not have to include $11,428.57 ($200,000 × $40,000/$700,000, or 5.714%) of the $200,000 distribution in her gross income. She will include $188,571.43 ($200,000 – $11,428.57) as ordinary income on her tax return as a result of the indirect (60-day rollover) conversion. Special taxation rules apply to conversions made in 2010 (see Q 3:17).

Example 2. Same facts as the preceding example, except Francine transfers her 401(k) account balance ($200,000) to a Roth IRA in a direct conversion (not a 60-day rollover conversion). Because the IRA aggregation rules do not apply, $40,000 is treated as a return of principal (basis) and only $160,000 is taxable. As a result of the direct conversion, only $160,000 is taxable, compared to $188,571.43 if Francine were to receive the funds and (within 60 days) roll those funds into a Roth IRA. Thus, Francine's taxable income is $28,571.43 ($188,571.43 – $160,000) less if she directly converts her 401(k) to a Roth IRA. It should be noted that the taxable portion of subsequent distributions from Francine's $500,000 IRA will be higher than had she indirectly rolled her 401(k) to a Roth IRA within 60 days of the distribution. Special taxation rules apply to conversions made in 2010 (see Q 3:17).

Conversions After 1998

Q 3:14 How is the amount included in income taxed when a traditional IRA is converted to a Roth IRA after 1998?

For a traditional IRA converted to a Roth IRA after 1998, the taxable amount of the conversion is taxed in the year in which the conversion amount is withdrawn from the traditional IRA. [I.R.C. § 408A(d)(3)(A)(i)] Special taxation rules apply to conversions made in 2010 (see Q 3:17).

The 10 percent premature distribution penalty does not apply to the taxable amount of a traditional IRA converted to a Roth IRA. [I.R.C. § 408A(d)(3)(A)(ii)] Regardless of the means used to convert, any amount converted from a non-Roth IRA to a Roth IRA is treated as distributed from the non-Roth IRA and rolled over to the Roth IRA. In the case of a conversion involving property, the conversion amount generally is the fair market value of the property on the date of distribution or the date the property is treated as distributed from the traditional IRA. [*See* Treas. Reg. § 1.408A-4, Q&A-7, applying the traditional IRA rules of I.R.C. § 408(d)(1) and (d)(2) to Roth IRAs.]

Conversions in 1998

Q 3:15 How was the amount included in income taxed when a traditional IRA was converted to a Roth IRA in 1998?

For a traditional IRA that was converted to a Roth IRA in 1998, the amount that would have been included in income (the taxable conversion amount resulting from deductible contributions and investment gain in the account) could be included in gross income ratably over a four-tax-year period beginning in 1998 (see Qs 4:1, 4:17) if the IRA owner so elected using Form 8606. Alternatively, the owner could elect on Form 8606 to report all of the income attributable to a 1998 conversion on his or her 1998 tax return. [I.R.C. §§ 408A(d)(3)(A)(i), 408A(d)(3)(A)(iii); Treas. Reg. § 1.408A-4, Q&A 10] Either election became irrevocable after the due date (including extensions) of the IRA owner's 1998 federal income tax return. [I.R.C. §§ 408A(d)(3)(A), 408A(d)(7)] These rules were replaced by a two-year rules for conversion made in 2010, which are not withdrawn before 2012 (see Q 3:16).

If the IRA owner made no election, the default was to the four-year spread rule. [I.R.C. § 408A(d)(3)(A)(iii)]

> **Note.** An individual could not elect to have one conversion taxed under the four-year spread rule and another taxed completely in 1998. That is, the four-year spread election had to be made with respect to the taxable year. [I.R.C. § 408A(d)(3)(A)(iii)]

The four-year income spread calculation, unlike the ten-year special income averaging method used to calculate tax on certain lump-sum distributions from qualified plans, is not a calculation of a separate tax. In other words, the taxable portion of the amount converted in 1998 (not the tax itself) is included in income as ordinary income ratably over the four-year period and may affect the Roth

IRA owner's tax bracket for the years of inclusion as well as the taxability of Social Security benefits. [I.R.C. § 408A(d)(3)]

If a Roth IRA owner ratably includes the taxable conversion amount over the four-year spread period and withdraws amounts before the entire taxable conversion amount is included in gross income, then, to that extent, the amount withdrawn is also includible in income—that is, accelerated—unless there is any remaining basis attributable to annual Roth IRA contributions (which are deemed to be distributed before a conversion amount; see Q 4:1). In addition to being taxable, accelerated amounts are subject to the IRA premature distribution penalty unless one of the nine exceptions under Code Section 72(t) applies (see Q 4:22). Special rules apply when death occurs before the entire taxable conversion amount has been reported as taxable income (see Q 3:17, *Death of Distributee*).

> **Note.** A change in filing status or a divorce does not affect the application of the four-year spread rule for a 1998 conversion. Thus, if a married Roth IRA owner who is using the four-year spread files separately or divorces before the full taxable conversion amount has been included in gross income, the remainder must be included in the owner's gross income over the remaining years in the four-year period, or if applicable, in the year for which the remainder is accelerated as a result of distribution or death (see 3:17, *Death of Distributee*). [Treas. Reg. § 1.408A-4, Q&A 11(a), 11(b)]

Conversions After 2009

Q 3:16   Will the $100,000 adjusted AGI conversion limit apply after 2009?

No. For tax years beginning after 2009, the $100,000 modified AGI limit on conversions of traditional IRAs to Roth IRAs will no longer apply. In addition, married taxpayers filing a separate return will be able to convert amounts in a traditional IRA into a Roth IRA. Thus, after 2009, taxpayers may make such conversions without regard to their AGI (see Q 3:7). [Tax Increase Prevention and Reconciliation Act of 2005 (TIPRA § 512) (H.R. 4297, Pub. L. No. 109-222)]

> **Practice Pointer.** Assume an elderly married couple with income above the $176,000 maximum contribution phase-out limit for a 2009 Roth IRA contribution. Assume further, that neither has an existing traditional IRA. The couple could contribute $12,000 ($6,000 × 2) to a nondeductible traditional IRA. Then, in 2010, the couple would be able to "roll over" the amount that had accumulated in their nondeductible IRA into a Roth IRA (paying tax only on the returns the IRA account had earned to that point), and all earnings on the Roth IRA from that point forward would be forever tax free. Moreover, in every year after 2010, the couple could deposit $12,000 in a nondeductible IRA, roll over these funds into their Roth IRA the very next day, and pay no tax on the amount converted (because the conversion would be from a nondeductible IRA containing contributions made with after-tax dollars). This process could be repeated every year. Over time, the couple could increase their tax-protected Roth IRA to a very substantial level, with

the account being sheltered from taxation. This strategy may not be beneficial if the taxpayer has IRAs containing deductible contributions. In such case, the amount of taxable conversion income that may result would have to be considered. A taxpayer may not maintain nondeductible contributions in a separate IRA, because they are aggregated for distribution purposes.

Q 3:17   When are amounts converted after 2009 from an IRA to a Roth IRA included in income?

In general, an IRA-to-Roth-IRA conversion occurring after 2010 is subject to the same income inclusion rules that currently apply (that is, the income resulting from the conversion is included on the return for the tax year in which funds are transferred or withdrawn from the IRA). However, if the conversion occurs in 2010, unless a taxpayer elects otherwise, none of the gross income from the conversion is included in income in 2010; half of the income resulting from the conversion is includible in gross income in 2011 and the other half in 2012. The election is irrevocable after the due date for such taxable year. No provision was made for tax years after 2010, thus the taxable amount of a conversion contribution from an employer's plan in taxable years beginning after 2010 to a Roth IRA will have to be included in gross income in the tax year the distribution takes place. [I.R.C. §§ 408A(d)(3)(A)(iii), as amended by TIPRA (Pub. L. No. 109-222)] [I.R.C. §§ 408A(d)(3)(A)(iii), 408A(d)(3)(E)(i), as amended by TIPRA]

Note. The four-year spread rules under Code Section 408A(d)(3)(E) for 1998 conversions discussed in Q 3:15 were amended to become the two-year spread rules for conversions made in 2010.

Example. Lavern's IRA has a $50,000 balance, consisting of deductible contributions and earnings. She does not have a Roth IRA. In 2010, Lavern converts her traditional IRA to a Roth IRA. As a result of the conversion, $50,000 is includible in gross income. Unless Lavern elects otherwise (i.e., unless she elects to include the entire conversion in income for 2010), $25,000 of the income resulting from the conversion is included in income in 2011 and $25,000 in 2012. [TIPRA Conf. Rep.]

Income Acceleration for Converted Amounts Distributed Before 2012. Income inclusion is accelerated if converted amounts are distributed before 2012 (whether a distribution consists of converted amounts is determined under the pre-TIPRA-law ordering rules discussed in Q 4:1). In that case, the amount included in income in the year of the distribution is increased by the amount distributed, and the amount included in income in 2012 (or 2011 and 2012 in the case of a distribution in 2010) is the lesser of: (1) half of the amount includible in income as a result of the conversion; and (2) the remaining portion of such amount not already included in income (see Q 4:1, Example 1). [I.R.C. § 408A(d)(3)(E)(i), as amended by TIPRA Section 512; *see also* Senate Finance Committee, Summary of the Tax Increase Prevention and Reconciliation Act of 2005 (TIPRA) (Pub. L. No. 109-222)]] Unless an exception applies, the taxable amount withdrawn (accelerated into income) is also subject to the 10 percent premature distribution penalty (see Q 4:1, and Examples; see also Qs 4:10, 4:14, 4:17, 4:22).

Death of Distributee. In general, if the individual who is required to include amounts in gross income because of the income acceleration rules dies before all such amounts are included, all remaining amounts shall be included in gross income for the taxable year, which includes the date of death. [I.R.C. § 408A(d)(3)(E)(ii)(I)] A surviving spouse beneficiary may have other options, if such spouse acquires the individual's entire interest on account of death.

Special Rule for Surviving Spouse. If the individual who is required to include amounts in gross income because of the income acceleration rules dies, and his or her spouse acquires the individual's entire interest in any Roth IRA to which such qualified rollover contribution is made (or properly allocable), the spouse may elect to treat the remaining amounts as includible in the spouse's gross income in the taxable years of the spouse, ending with or within the taxable years of such individual in which such amounts would otherwise have been includible. Any such election may not be made or changed after the due date for the spouse's taxable year, which includes the date of death. [I.R.C. § 408A(d)(3)(E)(ii)(II)]

Q 3:18   Does income tax withholding apply to a distribution from a traditional IRA that is converted to a Roth IRA?

Yes. A distribution from a traditional IRA that is converted (i.e., rolled over or transferred) to a Roth IRA is subject to federal income tax withholding. [I.R.C. §§ 408A(a), 3405(e), 7701(a)(37); Treas. Reg. § 1.408A-6, Q&A 12] It is important to note, however, that the IRA owner may elect not to have federal income tax withholding apply. [I.R.C. §§ 3405(a), 3405(b)] The mandatory withholding rules applicable to a qualified rollover distribution from an employer's plan to a Roth IRA are discussed in Q 3:62.

Example. Michelle has a traditional IRA valued at $100,000. She is eligible to convert her traditional IRA to a Roth IRA and decides to do so during 2009. Knowing she will owe federal income taxes on the converted amounts for the 2009 tax year, she has the traditional IRA withhold 10 percent, or $10,000, of the distribution and converts the remaining $90,000 to her Roth IRA. The entire conversion amount is taxed on Michelle's 2009 tax return. If Michelle is under age 59½, the $10,000 not converted will be subject to the 10 percent premature distribution penalty.

Q 3:19   Are Roth IRA distributions that are part of a series of substantially equal periodic payments begun under a traditional IRA before conversion subject to the 10 percent premature distribution penalty if they are also subject to income acceleration?

No. The 10 percent premature distribution penalty under Code Section 72(t) does not apply to distributions that are part of substantially equal periodic payments within the meaning of Code Section 72(t)(2)(A)(iv), even if the distributions are not qualified distributions (see Qs 4:9, 4:21).

Caution. To the extent the periodic payments withdrawn are conversion contributions returned within five years (see Qs 4:1, 4:14), they may be subject to the 10 percent premature distribution penalty imposed by Code Section 408A even though such amounts are not taxable (see Q 4:17). [I.R.C. § 408A(d)(3)(F)]

Valuing Annuity Contracts Converted to a Roth IRA

Q 3:20 What is the amount that is includible in income as a distribution when a conversion involves an annuity contract that is an individual retirement annuity (IR-Annuity)?

In general, when part or all of a traditional IRA that is an individual retirement annuity (see Q 1:1) is converted to a Roth IRA, for purposes of determining the amount includible in gross income as a distribution, the amount that is treated as distributed is the fair market value (FMV) of the annuity contract on the date the annuity contract is distributed or treated as distributed from the traditional IRA (see Q 3:23). [I.R.C. § 408(d); Treas. Reg. §§ 1.408A-4, Q&A 7, 1.408A-4(b), 1.408-4T, Q&A 14, 70 Fed. Reg. 48868 (Aug. 18, 2005)]

Q 3:21 How may a non-Roth IRA annuity contract be converted to a Roth IRA?

A conversion may be accomplished by means of a rollover, trustee-to-trustee transfer, or account redesignation. Regardless of the means used to convert, any amount converted from a non-Roth IRA to a Roth IRA is treated as distributed from the non-Roth IRA and rolled over to the Roth IRA. In the case of a conversion involving property, the conversion amount generally is the fair market value of the property on the date of distribution or the date the property is treated as distributed from the traditional IRA. [Preamble, Treas. Reg. § 1.408A-4 (T.D. 9418, 73 Fed. Reg. 43860 (July 29, 2008))]

Q 3:22 How are amounts converted from a non-Roth IRA to a Roth IRA reported?

Any amount that is converted from a non-Roth IRA (e.g., traditional IRA, SIMPLE IRA after two years) to a Roth IRA is included in gross income for the taxable year in which the amount is distributed (or treated as distributed) from the traditional IRA. If the taxpayer has any "basis" in the traditional IRA, Form 8606, Nondeductible IRAs, must be completed by the taxpayer to determine the nontaxable return of basis in the amount converted. The trustee or custodian reports the total amount distributed or treated as distributed in Boxes 1 and 2a of Form 1099-R—Distributions from Pensions, Annuities, Retirement or Profit-Sharing Plans, IRAs, Insurance Contracts, etc.—as if the entire amount were taxable. Similarly, in a conversion involving property, Form 1099-R is used to report the FMV on the date of distribution, and the individual may have to file Form 8606 to compute the taxable portion if there is any unrecovered basis.

Q 3:23 How is FMV determined when an annuity contract is converted from a traditional IRA to a Roth IRA?

The final regulations issued in 2008 apply to any Roth IRA conversion where the annuity contract is distributed or treated as distributed on or after August 19, 2005. [Treas. Reg. § 1.408A-4, Q&A 14(c)] However, a taxpayer may instead apply the valuation methods described in the temporary regulations issued in 2005 and Revenue Procedure 2006-13 [2006-3 I.R.B. 315] for annuity contracts distributed or treated as distributed before 2009. The temporary regulations were issued in identical form as proposed regulations. [70 Fed. Reg. 48924] The interim guidance from Revenue Procedure 2006-13 (the "accumulation" method) was incorporated into the final regulations.

Valuation Under The Final Regulations

The final regulations provide for the valuation of a non-Roth IRA that is converted to a Roth IRA as follows:

- *Cost of contract or comparable contract.* If with respect to an annuity, there is a comparable contract issued by the company which sold the annuity, the fair market value of the annuity may be established by the price of the comparable contract. If the conversion occurs soon after the annuity was sold, the comparable contract may be the annuity itself, and thus, the fair market value of the annuity may be established through the sale of the particular contract by the company (that is, the actual premiums paid for such contract).

Use of reserves where no comparable contract available. If with respect to an annuity, there is no comparable contract available in order to make the comparison, the fair market value may be established through an approximation that is based on the interpolated terminal reserve at the date of the conversion, plus the proportionate part of the gross premium last paid before the date of the conversion which covers the period extending beyond that date (see below).

Accumulation method. As an alternative to the gift tax method described above where the contract has not been annuitized and there is no comparable contract, the fair market value of such an annuity contract is permitted to be determined using the methodology described in Q 3:25.

[Treas. Reg. § 1.408A-4(b)]

Note. The final regulations (only) apply where an annuity contract is distributed or treated as distributed after 2008.

Valuation Under The Temporary Regulations

When an annuity contract is deemed distributed (as in a conversion to a Roth IRA) on or after August 19, 2005, and before 2009, the proposed and temporary regulations require that the FMV is generally established as follows (and follows an approach similar to the gift tax regulations in making that valuation, see Note 2 below). [Treas. Reg. § 1.408A-4T, Q&A 14 (T.D. 9220 (Aug. 19, 2005))] The final regulations (only) apply to annuity contracts distributed or deemed distributed after 2008. The approach for "in-kind" conversions of an annuity contract under the temporary regulations generally includes the following factors (or "methods"):

- *Gift Tax Method.* If the conversion occurs "soon after" purchase of the annuity contract, and there have been no material changes in market conditions, FMV is established by the actual premiums paid for such contract;

- *Gift Tax Method.* If the conversion occurs after the contract "has been in force for some time" and no further premiums are to be paid, FMV is determined through the sale by the insurance company of comparable contracts; and

Note 1.   Under the final regulations, the comparable contract rule discussed above replaces (subsumes) both of the gift tax methods.

- *Reserve Method.* If the conversion occurs after the contract has been in force for some time and further premiums are to be paid, FMV is determined through an approximation based on the interpolated terminal reserve on the conversion date, plus the proportionate amount of the last gross premium payment reflecting the period of paid-up coverage extending beyond the conversion date; provided, however, that this approximation may not be used if it is not reasonably close to full value because of the "unusual nature" of the contract. The reserve method was retained under the final regulations where there is no comparable contract available (see Note 2). [Treas. Reg. § 1.408A-4, Q&A 14(b)(2)(ii)]

These rules were promulgated in response to the use of springing cash value annuity contracts to reduce the taxable income recognized in a Roth IRA conversion. Like the temporary regulations, the final regulations also authorize the Service to issue additional guidance regarding the fair market value of a traditional IRA annuity.

Note 2.   Treasury Regulations Section 25.2512-6 of the Gift Tax Regulations provides rules regarding the valuation of certain life insurance contracts for gift tax purposes. [*See also* Rev. Rul. 59-195, 1959-1 C.B. 18] Under these rules, the value of a life insurance contract or of a contract for the payment of an annuity issued by a company regularly engaged in the selling of contracts of that character is established through the sale of the particular contract by the company, or through the sale by the company of comparable contracts. In addition, if the value of an insurance policy through sale of comparable contracts is not readily ascertainable when the gift is of a contract that has been in force for some time and on which further premium payments are to be made, the value may be approximated by adding to the interpolated terminal reserve at the date of the gift the proportionate part of the gross premium last paid before the date of the gift that covers the period extending beyond that date. If, however, because of the unusual nature of the contract, such approximation is not reasonably close to the full value, this method may not be used. Thus, this method may not be used to determine the FMV of an insurance policy where the reserve does not reflect the value of all relevant features of the policy. These gift tax valuation rules also apply for purposes of commercial annuity contracts. [*See* Treas. Reg. § 25.2512-6, exs. 1 and 2] In addition, under Treasury Regulations Section 20.2031-8 of the Estate Tax Regulations, the same rules govern the valuation of such life insurance and commercial annuity contracts for estate tax purposes. [*See* Treas. Reg. §§ 20.2031-7(b) and 20.2039-1(c)]

Safe-Harbor Relief. On January 17, 2006, recognizing that it may be difficult to determine the fair market value of an annuity contract under the temporary regulations, the IRS and Treasury issued Revenue Procedure 2006-13 [2006-3 I.R.B. 315], expanding upon and clarifying the temporary regulations. Under Revenue Procedure 2006-13, the FMV of an annuity contract that has not yet been annuitized can be determined using the methodology in Treasury Regulations Section 1.401(a)(9)-6, Q&A 12, regarding required minimum distributions, with certain modifications (see Qs 3:24, 3:25). The final regulations add this "accumulation method" rule.

Q 3:24   What is the value of an annuity contract that has not yet been annuitized under the RMD regulations?

In general, under the RMD regulations, the value of an annuity contract that has not yet been annuitized is the sum of:

1. The dollar amount credited to the participant under the contract, not reduced to reflect any surrender charges and

2. The actuarial present value of any additional benefits, such as survivor benefits in excess of the account balance, and any charges that are expected to be refunded, rebated, or otherwise reversed at a later date.

The RMD regulations also provide that additional benefits may be disregarded if the sum of the dollar amount credited to the participant under the contract and the actuarial present value of the additional benefits is no more than 120 percent of the dollar amount credited to the participant and the additional benefits satisfy certain other requirements. [Treas. Reg. § 1.401 (a)(9)-6] However, because some benefits may be disregarded in determining the required minimum distribution, the RMD methodology does not always reflect the full value of all benefits under the contract.

Example. Homer purchases a non-Roth individual retirement variable annuity with a guaranteed minimum death benefit equal to the highest account value ever attained under the contract, adjusted for withdrawals. If an amount is withdrawn from the contract, the death benefit is reduced dollar for dollar (rather than pro rata) by the amount of the withdrawal. Prior to the date of conversion, the annuity has a death benefit far in excess of the account value and the taxpayer withdraws from the IRA annuity all but a minimum account value that will keep the IRA annuity in force. Because the withdrawal reduces the guaranteed minimum death benefit on a dollar-for-dollar basis, the remaining death benefit will be significantly greater than the current account value, and accordingly, the current account value will not reflect the fair market value of the contract. For example, suppose such an individual retirement variable annuity has a guaranteed minimum death benefit of $200,000 with an account value of $100,000. Homer withdraws $99,000, leaving a $1,000 account value and a $101,000 death benefit ($200,000 less $99,000). Homer then converts the IRA annuity into a Roth IRA and takes the position that the $1,000 account value is the conversion amount even though the account value does not reflect the fair market value of the additional $100,000 that will be paid upon the taxpayer's death. In this case, the taxpayer expects that the entire benefit payment of $101,000 will be a qualified distribution from the Roth IRA (i.e., tax-exempt), and thus expects that the $1,000 account value on the date of conversion will be the only amount ever includible in gross income. The IRS and Treasury Department have concluded that cash surrender value is not always an appropriate measure of fair market value with respect to non-Roth IRA annuities that are converted to Roth IRA annuities (see Qs 3:23, 3:25).

Q 3:25 What is the modified "safe-harbor" version of the RMD regulations that may be used in determining the fair market value of an annuity that is converted from a traditional IRA to a Roth IRA?

For purposes of determining the amount includible in gross income as a result of the conversion of a traditional IRA to a Roth IRA, the fair market value of an annuity contract that has not yet been annuitized is permitted to be determined using the methodology provided in the RMD regulations (the "accumulation" method) (see Q 3:24) with the following modifications:

1. All front-end loads and other non-recurring charges assessed in the 12 months immediately preceding the conversion must be added to the account value.

2. Future distributions are not to be assumed in the determination of the actuarial present value of additional benefits.

3. Additional benefits that are disregarded under the RMD methodology (those that meet the 120 percent rule discussed in Q 3:24) and any return of premiums on death benefits must be included in determining conversion value (e.g., the exclusions provided under paragraphs (c)(1) and (c)(2) of Treasury Regulations Section 1.401(a)(9)-6, Q&A 12, are not taken into account).

[Rev. Proc. 2006-13, 2006-3 I.R.B. 315 (Jan. 17, 2006)] Special rules are provided for the valuation of annuity contracts that were converted in 2005 (see Q 3:26).

The accumulation method (based on the RMD rules) was is included in the final regulations. [Treas. Reg. § 1.408A-4, Q&A 14(b)(3)]

Q 3:26   How was an annuity contract distributed or treated as distributed before January 1, 2006, treated for purposes of determining the amount includible in gross income as a result of the conversion of a traditional IRA to a Roth IRA?

In the case of a Roth IRA conversion where an annuity contract that has not yet been annuitized was distributed or was treated as distributed before January 1, 2006, for purposes of determining the amount includible in gross income as a result of the conversion of a traditional IRA to a Roth IRA, the fair market value of the contract was permitted to be determined using the methodology provided in the RMD regulations (see Q 3:24), except that all front-end loads and other non-recurring charges assessed in the 12 months immediately preceding the conversion must be added to the account value. [Treas. Reg. § 1.408A-4, Q&A 14(b)(3)]

Q 3:27   Do the regulations or Revenue Procedure 2006-13 apply to an annuity contract that is surrendered before a conversion to a Roth IRA?

No and yes. Neither the valuation procedures under the temporary regulations nor Revenue Procedure 2006-13 applies if an individual surrenders his or her annuity contract that is held in a traditional IRA (account or annuity), extinguishing all benefits and other characteristics of the contract, and transfers the cash proceeds to his or her Roth IRA. The annuity contract has not been converted; rather, the cash from the surrendered contract is being reinvested in the Roth IRA. In such case, the FMV will be taxable to the recipient except to the extent of any unrecovered basis in the contract. A rollover conversion (see Q 3:4) to a Roth IRA is also possible. The final regulations clarify that where a conversion is made by surrendering an annuity without retaining or transferring rights, the amount converted, and hence the amount that must be included in income as a result of the conversion, is limited to the surrendered cash value (the actual proceeds to be deposited into the Roth IRA, rather than its FMV as under the temporary regulations). Revenue Procedure 2006-13 provided that, in such a case, the valuation methods in the temporary regulations do not apply. Thus, under the final regulations, to the extent an individual retirement annuity or an annuity contract held by an individual retirement account is surrendered with no retained or transferred rights, the amount treated as a distribution is limited to the surrendered cash value (the actual proceeds available to be deposited into the Roth IRA). [Treas. Reg. § 1.408A-4, Q&A 14(a)(2)]

Q 3:28   Who is responsible for properly valuing the annuity contract that is converted to a Roth IRA for Form 1099-R reporting purposes?

The trustee or custodian is responsible for properly valuing the annuity contract that is converted to a Roth IRA for purposes of issuing Form 1099-R to the taxpayer and to the IRS (see chapter 9).

Contribution Recharacterization

Q 3:29   What is a contribution recharacterization?

A *contribution recharacterization* is (1) the "undoing" of a current year regular contribution plus earnings to a Roth IRA or (2) the "unwinding" of a conversion or failed conversion (see Q 3:32) to a Roth IRA by transferring the amount plus earnings back to a traditional IRA. [I.R.C. § 408A(d)(6); Treas. Reg. § 1.408A-5, Q&A 1] For tax purposes, upon a conversion gains and losses of the entire Roth IRA must be applied on a pro rata basis, the so called "anti-cherry picking rule," and is applied to all investments within *that* Roth IRA. By using a Roth segregation conversion strategy, it may be possible to recharacterize loss assets while leaving gain assets in a Roth IRA (see Q 3:31).

Q 3:30   For what reasons may an individual recharacterize a contribution to a Roth IRA?

An individual may recharacterize a regular contribution or a conversion contribution to a Roth IRA if the individual is ineligible to make the contribution or merely wishes to change his or her mind. All or just a portion of a regular contribution or conversion contribution may be recharacterized. [I.R.C. § 408A(d)(6); I.R.S. Notice 2008-30, 2008-12 I.R.B. 638, Q&As 1 and 2]

Q 3:31   How can a Roth segregation conversion strategy be used?

To reduce possible income taxes upon a recharacterization of a Roth IRA back to a traditional IRA, a taxpayer could maintain more than one Roth IRA. Ideally, "[a]ssets with high positive correlation coefficients would be placed in the same IRA. Assets with low positive or negative correlation coefficients would be segregated out into other IRAs. This would give the taxpayer the best chance of segregating assets from the loss account." [Keebler, Robert S., Family Tax Planning Forum, "Roth Segregation Conversion Strategy" (Taxes, June 2003)]

> **Example 1.** On January 2, 2009, when Marvin's IRA was worth $50,000, he converted the entire amount to a Roth IRA. Marvin will owe ordinary income tax on the entire $50,000. The Roth IRA consisted of 50 percent L-Fund shares ($25,000) and 50 percent G-Fund shares ($25,000). As of April 15, 2010, the L-Fund shares had declined in value to $12,500, while the G-Fund shares had

increased in value to $27,500. Thus, the total value of the Roth IRA account declined in value to $40,000. Marvin would like to re-characterize all of the L-Fund shares but none of the G-Fund shares.

Without the anti-cherry-picking rules, Marvin could reconvert only those assets that dropped in value (the L-Fund shares) and eliminate $25,000 of tax liability (the value of the L-Fund shares on the conversion date). However, these rules require that the gains and losses of the entire IRA be applied on a pro rata basis for tax purposes. The first step is to calculate the value of the L-Fund shares as a percentage of the total value of the Roth IRA as of the recharacterization date. This percentage is 31.25 ($12,500/$40,000). Then the value of the Roth IRA as of the date of conversion is multiplied by this 31.25 percent factor. Thus, if Marvin were to recharacterize the L-Fund shares, he could reduce his taxable income by only $15,625 (.3125 × $50,000). This would result in Marvin recognizing ordinary income attributable to the Roth conversion in an amount of $34,375 ($50,000 − $15,625), despite the fact that Marvin's Roth IRA is only worth $27,500.

Example 2. Assume the same facts as the preceding example, except Marvin established two Roth IRA accounts. Roth #1 holds the L-Fund shares. Roth #2 holds the G-Fund shares. Thus, if Marvin were to recharacterize the L-Fund shares in Roth #1, he would owe no income taxes on Roth #1. Marvin will only recognize $25,000 of ordinary income on Roth #2. Thus, the Roth segregation conversion strategy reduced Marvin's taxable income by $9,375 ($34,375 − $25,000). [Keebler, Robert S., Family Tax Planning Forum, "Roth Segregation Conversion Strategy" (*Taxes*, June 2003)]

Example 3. Same facts as in Example 1, except Marvin transfers all of the L-Fund shares (which he expects to decline further in value) to a separate Roth IRA. This Roth IRA is initially valued at $20,000 (half of the $40,000 value on the date of transfer). The initial conversion amount for this Roth IRA is $25,000 (half of the original $50,000 converted). If the L-Fund shares decline in value any further, Marvin might consider recharacterizing this Roth only, assuming he is eligible to do so.

Q 3:32   What is the result if a conversion contribution to a Roth IRA is determined to be ineligible and is not recharacterized?

If a conversion contribution to a Roth IRA is determined to be ineligible (a failed conversion) and it is not recharacterized in accordance with special rules (see Qs 3:38 , 3:44), the contribution amount is treated as a regular contribution to the Roth IRA and thus may be an excess contribution (see Q 2:25). [Treas. Reg. §§ 1.408A-4, Q&A 1(d), 1.408A-8, Q&A 1(b)(4)] In addition, the distribution from the traditional IRA (or an employer's plan) that was converted in error is subject to the 10 percent premature distribution penalty unless an exception applies. [Treas. Reg. § 1.408A-4, Q&A 3]

Practice Pointer. A failed conversion is treated as a distribution from the traditional IRA and a regular contribution to the Roth IRA, but it may be corrected through a timely recharacterization back to a traditional IRA (see Examples in Q 3:44).

Practice Pointer. There is no statute of limitations on a failed conversion; the IRS can make such a determination in any subsequent year. Furthermore, the statute of limitations does not run on the 6 percent excess contribution tax or the 10 percent early withdrawal penalty tax when Form 5329—Additional Taxes on Qualified Plans (Including IRAs) and other Tax-Favored Accounts—is not filed. It should be noted that once the statute of limitations runs on the tax return, a taxpayer will be unable to get permission from the IRS to correct the problem. [I.R.S. Service Center Advice (SCA 200148051) (Sept. 20, 2001)] For example, in the case of a failed 2009 conversion, it would be wise to correct the problem before the statute of limitations (for 2009) expires on Monday, April 16, 2012, for a timely filed return.

Q 3:33   Are there contributions that may not be recharacterized?

Yes. The following contributions may not be recharacterized:

1. Any amounts that were contributed to the first IRA as a rollover (such as a direct rollover from a qualified plan) or as a trustee-to-trustee transfer may not be treated as a recharacterization transfer to the second IRA. [Treas. Reg. § 1.408A-5, Q&A 4]

   Example. Zach rolls over his 401(k) plan to his traditional IRA. He may not recharacterize that amount to a Roth IRA. On the other hand, Zach could convert his traditional IRA that now holds his 401(k) assets to a Roth IRA.

2. Employer contributions (including elective deferrals) under a SEP IRA or a SIMPLE IRA may not be recharacterized to another IRA. Amounts held in a SEP IRA or a SIMPLE IRA (after the two-year holding period has expired with respect to the SIMPLE IRA) may, however, be converted to a Roth IRA. [Treas. Reg. § 1.408A-5, Q&A 5]

Q 3:34   How does an individual make a contribution recharacterization from a Roth IRA to a traditional IRA?

As originally enacted, the Roth IRA rules had no provisions for permitting a contribution made to a Roth IRA to be transferred (with earnings) to a traditional IRA. The recharacterization rules as modified by the Technical Corrections Act of 1998 (TCA '98) allow contributions plus earnings (see Qs 2:26, 2:29) to be transferred from a Roth IRA to a traditional IRA. The tax-free transfer must be made no later than the tax filing deadline for the IRA contribution year, including extensions. [I.R.C. § 408A(d)(6)(A)] (See Q 3:38 for extended deadlines available to timely filers).

An individual must make the election to recharacterize a contribution to a Roth IRA by notifying (see Q 3:38) both the trustee of the first (i.e., Roth) IRA and the trustee of the second (i.e., traditional) IRA that he or she has elected to treat the contribution as having been made to the second IRA instead of to the first IRA for federal income tax purposes. [Treas. Reg. § 1.408A-5, Q&A 6]

> **Note.** An election to recharacterize an IRA contribution may be made on behalf of a deceased IRA owner (see Q 3:35).

Q 3:35   May an executor recharacterize a Roth IRA on behalf of a deceased IRA owner?

Yes. An election to recharacterize an IRA contribution may be made on behalf of a deceased IRA owner. The final regulations provide that the election to recharacterize an IRA contribution may be made by the executor, administrator, or other person charged with the duty of filing the decedent's final federal income tax return under Code Section 6012(b)(1). [Treas. Reg. § 1.408A-5 Q&A 6(a)]

Q 3:36   May an individual take a distribution from a traditional IRA, roll it over into a Roth IRA, and call it a recharacterization?

No. The only way to accomplish a recharacterization is with a direct trustee-to-trustee transfer, rather than a distribution and subsequent rollover. A trustee-to-trustee transfer may occur between two IRAs even if those IRAs are maintained by the same trustee. [Treas. Reg. § 1.408A-5, Q&A 1(a); Form 8606 Instructions]

Q 3:37   What are the requirements for the notification of IRA trustees regarding an election to recharacterize?

Notification of IRA trustees of an election to recharacterize must include the following information:

1. The type (i.e., regular or conversion) and amount of the contribution to the first IRA that is to be recharacterized;
2. The date on which the contribution was made to the first IRA, and in the case of a regular contribution, the year for which it was made;
3. A direction to the trustee of the first IRA to transfer, in a trustee-to-trustee transfer, the amount of the contribution and earnings attributable to the trustee of the second IRA; and
4. The name of the trustee of the first IRA and of the trustee of the second IRA, plus any additional information needed to make the transfer.

[Treas. Reg. § 1.408A-5, Q&A 6(a)]

Q 3:38   What is the deadline for making an election to recharacterize a contribution to a Roth IRA?

The election to recharacterize a contribution to a Roth IRA may be made only if the transfer from the first IRA to the second IRA is made on or before the due date (including extensions) for filing the IRA owner's federal income tax return for the taxable year for which the contribution was made to the first IRA. Thus, if the owner's federal income tax return was timely filed and the individual takes timely and appropriate corrective action, an amount that had been converted from a traditional IRA to a Roth IRA can be recharacterized (as a traditional IRA contribution). [I.R.C. § 408A(d)(6); Treas. Reg. § 1.408A-3, Q&A 5]

Treasury regulations generally provide for an automatic extension of six months from the due date of a return, excluding extensions, to make elections that must otherwise be made by the due date of the return or the due date of the return plus extensions. [Treas. Reg. § 301.9100-2(b); T.D. 8742, 63 Fed. Reg. 68167–68173 (Dec. 31, 1997); I.R.S. Ann. 99-57, 1999-24 I.R.B. 50; *see* I.R. 2008-84 (June 30, 2008) reducing the extension of time to file certain business tax returns that have a tax year ending on or after Sept. 30, 2008 (i.e., Form 1065, U.S. Return of Partnership Income, Form 1041, U.S. Income Tax Return for Estates & Trusts, and Form 8804, Annual Return for Partnership Withholding Tax (Section 1446)] To change any such election, the regulations require that

1. The taxpayer's return be timely filed for the year the election should have been made and

2. The taxpayer takes appropriate corrective action within the six-month period.

Thus, a calendar-year taxpayer who has timely filed his or her federal income tax return may elect to recharacterize an IRA contribution, including a Roth IRA conversion for which the taxpayer was not eligible, provided the appropriate corrective action occurs on or before October 15 of the year following the year for which the contribution was made. [I.R.S. Ann. 99-57, 1999-24 I.R.B. 50]

Note. The types of elections to which the regulations apply should be narrowly construed. For example, the regulations may not be used to extend the due date for removing excess IRA contributions under Code Section 408(d)(4) (which must be removed before the due date, including extensions).

Note. Although it was unclear, it appears that a taxpayer who had already taken a corrective distribution of an ineligible conversion after his or her return due date (including extensions) could have applied the automatic extension under Announcement 99-57 [1999-24 I.R.B. 50] and complete the rollover, provided the amount was otherwise eligible for rollover.

Practice Pointer. The relief contained in the Treasury regulations just discussed will have little value to an individual whose tax return is under examination because most examinations will occur after the deadline for taking corrective action.

Extensions After the Deadline. A timely filer may still be granted an administrative extension if he or she was eligible for relief under either Announcement 99-57 or Announcement 99-104 but missed the deadlines stated in those announcements. Without regard to extensions, a timely filer may be granted a six-month extension to recharacterize (see the following paragraph). Code

Section 408A(d)(6) provides that a taxpayer may elect to recharacterize an IRA contribution made to one type of IRA into another type of IRA by making a trustee-to-trustee transfer of the IRA contribution, including earnings, to the other type of IRA, except as otherwise provided by the Secretary of the Treasury. [Treas. Reg. § 1.408A-5]

A recharacterization election generally must occur on or before the date prescribed by law, including extensions, for filing the taxpayer's federal income tax returns for the year of contributions. [I.R.C. § 408A(d)(6); Treas. Reg. § 1.408A-5] The IRS has the authority, however, to grant an extension of time for a taxpayer to make an election under the Code. [Treas. Reg. §§ 301.9100-1, 301.9100-3]

In Letter Ruling 200716033 (Apr. 20, 2007) the IRS granted an individual an extension to recharacterize a newly converted Roth IRA back to a traditional IRA. The individual converted a traditional IRA to a Roth IRA but was not aware that his income would exceed the $100,000 MAGI limit (see Q 3:7). [I.R.C. § 408A(c)(3)(B)] The IRS determined that the individual acted reasonably and in good faith and granted an extension of 60 days from the ruling date for the individual to recharacterize the Roth IRA.

Treasury Regulations Section 301.9100-3 states that permission to make a late election will normally be granted to a taxpayer when he or she can show that he or she acted reasonably and in good faith. The regulations list five circumstances in which a taxpayer acts in good faith:

1. The taxpayer requests relief before being contacted by the IRS and is informed that he or she is ineligible for the conversion made [Ltr. Rul. 200213030 (Mar. 29, 2002)];

2. The taxpayer failed to make the election as a result of circumstances beyond his or her control;

3. The taxpayer exercised due diligence but was unaware of the need to make the election;

4. The taxpayer relied on written advice of the IRS; or

5. The taxpayer relied on the advice of a qualified tax professional *unless* the taxpayer knew, or should have known, that the professional was not competent to render such advice.

Although the IRS found in Letter Ruling 200116058 (Apr. 23, 2001) that the taxpayers had met three of the circumstances listed in the regulation (and meeting only one would have been sufficient), the most important circumstance is that the taxpayer came forward and requested relief before the IRS contacted the taxpayer.

Practice Pointer. Once the statute of limitations has run on the taxpayer's federal income tax return, it is too late to request an extension.

Note. The tolling of the statute of limitations on the tax return of the year of the conversion is of no help because once a Roth IRA is invalid, it will always be invalid. Excess contributions are subject to a cumulative nondeductible penalty tax of 6 percent until corrected by the taxpayer (see Q 2:24).

Practice Pointer. If a taxpayer made an improper conversion and the deadline for recharacterization has passed, the taxpayer should go to the IRS for a ruling for permission to make a late recharacterization, rather than hoping the IRS will not find the taxpayer first.

In Letter Ruling 200115034 (Aug. 10, 2001) the IRS granted a six-month extension even though the taxpayer missed two regulatory extensions.

If a taxpayer's return has been timely filed without having made an election to recharacterize the contribution, the choice can still be made without penalty by filing an amended return no later than six months after the due date of the tax return, *excluding* extensions. If recharacterization occurs within this period, write "Filed pursuant to Section 301.9100-2" at the top of the amended tax return. [Treas. Reg. § 301.9100-2; Pub. 590, Individual Retirement Arrangements (IRAs), Recharacterizations, at 32 (2007)]

Note 1. In Letter Ruling 200213030, it appeared that the taxpayer was permitted to make up required minimum distributions (after late characterization was granted) without imposition of the 50-percent penalty for late distributions. In Letter Ruling 200352020, the extension was granted under Procedure and Administration Regulations Section 301.9100-3, relating to discretionary extensions of time to make a regulatory election, but required that make-up distributions under the RMD rules be made. The IRS granted the taxpayers 60 days to withdraw the missed RMDs.

Note 2. Lacking specific guidance, the IRS reasoned that TEFRA Section 242(b)(2), allowing the termination of election out of the rules relating to the RMDs and requiring that RMDs be made for prior years, was analogous. [I.R.C. § 1.401(a)(9)-8, Q&A 16]

Example. Carla, age 80, converts her traditional IRA to a Roth IRA in 2009. She timely reconverts her Roth IRA back to a traditional IRA during 2010. The resultant traditional IRA must distribute (by the end of the calendar year following the calendar year in which the recharacterization occurs) the total amount not distributed under the RMD rules.

Note 3. The IRS does not have the authority to waive estimated income tax payments. In Chief Counsel Advice 200105062 (Feb. 2, 2001) the taxpayer was found to have exceeded the $100,000 MAGI limit as a result of an adjustment on audit. The IRS stated it could not grant relief for the resulting failed conversion nor for penalty taxes owed for failing to comply with the rules for making estimated tax payments under Code Section 6654. A 6 percent penalty also applied on the excess contribution. This would seem to indicate that the IRS is concerned more with the mechanism, and not the principle, of relief.

[*See, e.g.,* Ltr. Ruls. 200921036 (Feb. 26, 2009), request made shortly after discovery of custodian's failure to recharacterize granted; 200919064 (Feb. 11, 2009), filed amended return before IRS discovered that a timely election had not been made; 200840055 (Jul. 08, 2008) failure of advisor to advise that taxpayer was ineligible; 200850052 (Sept. 10, 2008), acted reasonably and in good faith; 200850052 (Sept. 10, 2008), erroneous information from advisor; 200839039 (July 03, 2008), reliance on enrolled agent; 200826040 (Apr. 1, 2008), broker failed to follow directions; 200729037 (Apr. 27, 2007), illness]

Q 3:39   May the election to recharacterize a contribution to a Roth IRA be revoked after the transfer?

No. The election to recharacterize a contribution to a Roth IRA may not be revoked after the transfer is initiated or after it is completed; however, the amount may be transferred again. [Treas. Reg. § 1.408A-5, Q&A 6(b)] Thus, for instance, if an individual elects to recharacterize, he or she may not say to the financial institution, "I want to stop or change my recharacterization notice." Such an individual may, however, start a transaction from scratch and recharacterize again. Although there is no limit on how often an amount may be recharacterized and reconverted, special rules apply to reconversions for tax purposes (see Q 3:44).

Q 3:40   May a contribution to a Roth IRA be recharacterized only once per 12-month period?

No. Because recharacterizations are considered transfers, they are not subject to the 12-month restriction otherwise applicable to IRA rollovers (see Q 3:71). Recharacterization of a contribution is never treated as a rollover for purposes of the 12-month rule—even if the contribution would have been treated as a rollover contribution by the second IRA if it had been made directly to the second IRA, rather than as a result of a recharacterization of a contribution to the first IRA. [Treas. Reg. § 1.408A-5, Q&A 8]

Q 3:41   Must the earnings attributable to a recharacterized contribution be included in the recharacterization?

Yes. The net income attributable to a contribution that is being recharacterized must be transferred to the second IRA along with the contribution. Remember, a recharacterization is a transaction between a traditional IRA and a Roth IRA. Depending on which way the money is being moved (traditional to Roth or Roth to traditional), one IRA will be the "first IRA" and the other will be the "second IRA."

If the amount of the contribution being recharacterized represents the entire contribution and it was contributed to a separate plan and no distributions or additional contributions have been made from or to that plan at any time, the contribution is recharacterized by the trustee of the first IRA transferring the entire account balance of the first IRA to the trustee of the second IRA. In that case, the net income (or loss) attributable to the contribution being recharacterized is the difference between the amount of the original contribution and the amount transferred.

If the amount of the contribution being recharacterized represents only a portion of the contribution or was commingled with other contributions in the same first IRA, the net income (or loss) attributable to the contribution being recharacterized is calculated in the same manner as the earnings (or loss) attributable to a return of an excess contribution under Code Section 408(d)(4) and Treasury Regulations Section 1.408-4(c)(2)(ii) (see Qs 2:26, 2:29). [Treas. Reg. § 1.408A-5, Q&A 2, 9(c)]

Q 3:42   Do earnings (or losses in earnings) that are recharacterized reduce (or increase) the otherwise maximum traditional IRA contribution?

No. Any earnings that are transferred with the recharacterization of a regular contribution do not reduce the otherwise maximum regular contribution limit.

Example. Victoria contributes $1,000 to her traditional IRA as a 2009 regular contribution. She decides to recharacterize this contribution in a recharacterization transfer with earnings of $50 before the deadline for filing her 2009 federal income tax return. Therefore, $1,050 is transferred from her traditional IRA (the first IRA) to her Roth IRA (the second IRA). This transfer is treated as if Victoria had originally contributed the $1,000 to the Roth IRA (the second IRA) and not to the traditional IRA (the first IRA). If Victoria is otherwise eligible, she may contribute an additional $5,000 ($6,000 if she is age 50 or older by the end of the taxable year) to her Roth IRA or her traditional IRA for 2009. The $50 of earnings is treated as having been earned in the Roth IRA (the second IRA).

Conversely, any losses attributable to a contribution that is being recharacterized do not increase the contribution limit to the second IRA.

Example. The facts are the same as those in the example above, except that Victoria's $1,000 is now worth $900. The maximum additional contribution that Victoria may make is still $5,000 ($6,000 with a catch-up contribution). Annual contribution limits are discussed more fully in Q 2:1.

Q 3:43   What is the effect of a contribution recharacterization for tax purposes?

A contribution being recharacterized to the second IRA is treated as having originally been contributed to the second IRA on the same date (and in the case of a regular contribution, for the same taxable year) that the contribution was made to the first IRA. Consequently, no deduction is permitted for a contribution to the first IRA, and any earnings that are transferred with the recharacterized contribution are treated as earned in the second IRA, not in the first IRA. [Treas. Reg. § 1.408A-5, Q&A 3]

Q 3:44   If an IRA owner converts an amount from a traditional IRA to a Roth IRA and then transfers that amount back to a traditional IRA in a recharacterization, may the IRA owner subsequently reconvert the amount from the traditional IRA to a Roth IRA?

Conversions Made on or After January 1, 2000. Effective for conversions made on or after January 1, 2000, an IRA owner who converts an amount from a traditional IRA to a Roth IRA during any taxable year and then transfers that amount back to a traditional IRA by means of a recharacterization may not reconvert that amount from the traditional IRA to a Roth IRA before the later of

1. The beginning of the taxable year following the taxable year in which the amount was converted to a Roth IRA or
2. The end of the 30-day period beginning on the day on which the IRA owner transfers the amount from the Roth IRA back to a traditional IRA by means of a recharacterization.

[Treas. Reg. § 1.408A-5, Q&A 9(a)(1)]

If a reconversion occurs before the later of the two dates set forth above, the reconversion transaction is treated as a failed conversion (i.e., a distribution from the traditional IRA and a regular contribution to the Roth IRA) (see Q 3:32), subject to correction through a recharacterization (see Qs 3:32–3:36).

Note. A *failed conversion* is a transaction in which an individual contributes to a Roth IRA an amount transferred or distributed from a traditional IRA or SIMPLE IRA (including a transfer by redesignation) in a transaction that does not constitute a conversion under Treasury Regulations Section 1.408A-4, Q&A 1. [Treas. Reg. § 1.408A-8, Q&A 1(b)(4)]

For reconversion purposes, a failed conversion resulting from a failure to satisfy the statutory requirements for a conversion (see Q 3:7) is treated as a conversion (taken into account) for reconversion purposes after 1999. [Treas. Reg. § 1.408A-5, Q&A 9(a)(2)]

Example 1. Rhoda is a calendar-year taxpayer and satisfies all the statutory requirements for conversion. She properly converts an amount to a Roth IRA on July 10, 2009, and transfers that amount back (recharacterizes) to a traditional IRA on September 10, 2009. Rhoda may not reconvert that amount before January 1, 2010 (the beginning of the taxable year following the taxable year in which the amount was converted to the Roth IRA). Any attempt to reconvert before January 1, 2010, will result in a failed conversion.

Example 2. Holly is a calendar-year taxpayer and satisfies all the statutory requirements for converting her traditional IRA to a Roth IRA. She properly converts an amount to a Roth IRA on December 10, 2009, and transfers that amount back (recharacterizes) to a traditional IRA on December 15, 2009. Holly may not reconvert that amount before January 14, 2010 (the first day after the end of the 30-day period beginning on the day of the recharacterization transfer). Any attempt to do so before then will result in a failed conversion.

Example 3. Joseph is a calendar-year taxpayer. He converts an amount to a Roth IRA in 2009, and transfers that amount back (recharacterizes) to a traditional IRA on January 18, 2010, after realizing that his MAGI for 2009 exceeded $100,000. Joseph may not reconvert that amount until February 17, 2010 (the first day after the end of the 30-day period beginning on the day of the recharacterization transfer), because a failed conversion (resulting from a failure to satisfy the $100,000 MAGI limit for a conversion) is treated as a conversion for purposes of the post-2000 reconversion rules.

If Joseph inadvertently attempts to reconvert the failed conversion amount (again) before February 17, 2010, the attempted reconversion is a failed conversion. Therefore, if Joseph does not recharacterize the amount back to a traditional IRA, it will be deemed a regular Roth IRA contribution, and an excess Roth contribution will arise.

Example 4. The facts are the same as those in Example 3, except that Joseph satisfies all the statutory requirements for conversion. The result is the same. Joseph could transfer the amount back to a traditional IRA in a recharacterization, and if he does so timely, he could reconvert it at any time on or after February 17, 2010.

Example 5. The facts are the same as those in Example 4, except that Joseph reconverts the amount on or after February 17, 2010. If he subsequently (and timely) recharacterizes that amount, he may not reconvert that amount again until 2011. Thus, if Joseph reconverts the amount on February 18, 2010, and recharacterizes two days later, he may reconvert his traditional IRA to a Roth IRA no earlier than January 1, 2011 (the beginning of the taxable year following the taxable year in which the amount was converted to the Roth IRA). If he waits until December 15, 2010, to recharacterize, Joseph may reconvert his traditional IRA to a Roth IRA no earlier than January 14, 2011 (the first day after the end of the 30-day period beginning on the day of the recharacterization transfer). If he waits until October 15, 2010, to recharacterize (see Q 3:38 regarding the extended deadline for timely filers to recharacterize), Joseph may reconvert his traditional IRA to a Roth IRA no earlier than January 1, 2011 (the beginning of the taxable year following the taxable year in which the amount was converted).

Example 6. Stan and Marsha are both calendar-year taxpayers and unmarried. Each converts from a traditional IRA to a Roth IRA on December 1, 2009. The stock market is in a tailspin, so they both recharacterize on December 10, 2009. On December 15, 2009, they both reconvert their traditional IRAs to Roth IRAs. Failed conversions result. The following week their accountants inform them of their failed conversions.

Stan is informed that he earned in excess of the $100,000 MAGI limit in 2009 and was therefore not eligible to convert for 2009, but that he would qualify for 2010. (After 2000, a failed conversion is taken into account for the purpose of the reconversion rules.) Stan is not eligible to reconvert before January 9, 2010 (the first day after the end of the 30-day period beginning on the day of the recharacterization transfer). He may recharacterize his failed conversion and reconvert on or after January 9, 2010 (for the 2010 taxable year). His attempted December 15 conversion is a failed conversion and is not treated as a conversion for purposes of the reconversion rules (but it is a failed conversion and must be corrected). (See preamble to final regulations under Code Section 408A). [T.D. 8816, 64 Fed. Reg. 5597–5611 (Feb. 4, 1999)]

Marsha is informed that she was eligible to convert for 2009. She, too, may reconvert no earlier than January 9, 2010 (for the 2010 taxable year). Her untimely reconversion on December 15 was a failed conversion.

The same rules apply whether a recharacterization is done because the original conversion was a failed conversion or because the IRA owner changes his or her mind. When it becomes obvious that a conversion is a failed conversion, the recharacterization should be done sooner rather than later, preferably no later than December 1, to permit the owner the maximum amount of time to accomplish the following year's conversion (without running afoul of the 30-day rule).

Example 7. In 2009, Myra makes a $4,000 regular contribution for 2009 to her traditional IRA (first IRA). Before the due date (plus extensions or other deadline; see Q 3:38) for filing her federal income tax return for 2009, she decides that she would prefer to contribute to a Roth IRA instead. Myra instructs the trustee of the first IRA to transfer in a trustee-to-trustee transfer the amount of the contribution, plus attributable net income, to the trustee of a Roth IRA (second IRA). Myra notifies the trustee of the first IRA and the trustee of the second IRA that she is recharacterizing her $4,000 contribution for 2009 (and provides the other information required; see Q 3:37). On her federal income tax return for 2009, Myra treats the $4,000 as having been contributed to the Roth IRA for 2009 and not to the traditional IRA, and as a result, for federal income tax purposes, the contribution is so treated. (The result would be the same if the conversion amount had been transferred in a tax-free transfer to another traditional IRA before the recharacterization.)

Example 8. The facts are the same as those in Example 7, except that the $4,000 regular contribution is initially made to a Roth IRA and the recharacterizing transfer is made to a traditional IRA. On her federal income tax return for 2009, Myra treats the $4,000 as having been contributed to the traditional IRA for 2009 and not to the Roth IRA, and as a result, for federal tax purposes, the contribution is so treated. (The result would be the same if the contribution had been transferred in a tax-free transfer to another Roth IRA before the recharacterization, except that the only Roth IRA trustee Myra would have to notify would be the one actually making the recharacterization transfer.)

Example 9. In 2009, Jimmy receives a distribution from one traditional IRA and contributes the entire amount to a second traditional IRA in a rollover contribution described in Code Section 408(d)(3). Jimmy may not elect to recharacterize the contribution by transferring the contribution amount, plus net income, to a Roth IRA, because an amount contributed to an IRA in a tax-free transfer may not be recharacterized (see Q 3:33). Jimmy may, however, convert (other than by recharacterization) the amount in the second traditional IRA to a Roth IRA at any time, provided he satisfies all of the requirements (see Qs 3:4–3:11).

Q 3:45   May an individual make a contribution recharacterization to a traditional IRA from a Roth IRA after contributing the limit (which contains an excess) to the Roth IRA?

Probably. Code Section 408A does not specifically address the situation in which an individual attempts to make a contribution recharacterization to a traditional IRA after having contributed the limit ($5,000; $6,000 with catch-up contribution for those who are at least age 50 for 2009) to the Roth IRA.

> **Example.** Lance, age 40, contributes $5,000 to a Roth IRA during 2009. When figuring his MAGI for 2009, he determines that only $2,500 may be contributed to the Roth IRA. The $2,500 excess contribution would be subject to the 6 percent excise tax unless withdrawn with earnings before the tax filing deadline (see Q 2:24). Presumably, Lance could take the $2,500 from the Roth IRA and do a conversion rollover (a contribution crossover) to a traditional IRA, even though he has already contributed the original limit of $5,000 to the Roth IRA for 2009.

SEP IRA/SIMPLE IRA

Q 3:46   Can a SEP IRA or a SIMPLE IRA be designated as a Roth IRA?

No. A SEP IRA or a SIMPLE IRA cannot be designated as a Roth IRA. [I.R.C. § 408A(f)] Treasury regulations make it clear, however, that all types of IRAs (including SEP IRAs and SIMPLE IRAs) can be converted to a Roth IRA (see Q 3:2). [Treas. Reg. § 1.408A-4, Q&A 4]

Q 3:47   May an amount converted from a SEP IRA or a SIMPLE IRA to a Roth IRA be recharacterized back to the SEP IRA or SIMPLE IRA?

Yes. Roth IRA conversion contributions from a SEP IRA or SIMPLE IRA may be recharacterized to a SEP IRA or a SIMPLE IRA, including the original SEP IRA or SIMPLE IRA. [Treas. Reg. § 1.408A-5, Q&A 5]

Q 3:48   Must the source of assets (i.e., employer or employee contributions) converted from a SEP IRA or a SIMPLE IRA to a Roth IRA be traced for purposes of determining whether such assets may be recharacterized?

No. The prohibition on recharacterizing employer contributions to a SEP IRA or a SIMPLE IRA (see Q 3:33) applies to those contributions only at the time they are made to the SEP IRA or SIMPLE IRA by the employer. Once those contributions have been made, the SEP IRA or SIMPLE IRA may be converted to a Roth IRA and subsequently recharacterized (provided, in the case of a SIMPLE IRA, that the two-year holding period has been satisfied before the conversion). [Treas. Reg. § 1.408A-5, Q&A 5]

Rollovers

Q 3:49 May any type of rollover contribution be made to a Roth IRA?

No. The only type of rollover contribution that may be made to a Roth IRA is a qualified rollover contribution (see Qs 3:50, 3:67). [I.R.C. § 408A(c)(6)]

Q 3:50 What is a *qualified rollover contribution*?

A *qualified rollover contribution* is a contribution to a Roth IRA from another Roth IRA or from a traditional IRA made through a conversion (see Qs 3:1, 3:4). The contribution must meet the general IRA rollover rules under Code Section 408(d)(3) (see Q 3:67), except that the 12-month rollover restriction does not apply to rollovers between a traditional IRA and a Roth IRA (see Q 3:8). A deemed Roth IRA (see Q 3:81) and a DRCP (see Q 10:1) may also be rolled over to a Roth IRA (see Qs 3:101, 3:82). [I.R.C. §§ 402A(c)(2)(3), 408A(e)]

Effective for distributions after 2007, the PPA generally will allow for direct and indirect (60-day) rollovers from a qualified plan, a tax-sheltered annuity, or a governmental plan to a Roth IRA and will treat it as a Roth conversion if all other conversion qualifications (e.g., income below the $100,000 level before 2010, see Q 3:16) are satisfied (See Q 3:64). The taxable portion of the rollover amount would be taxable at the time of the rollover. [I.R.C. §§ 408A(e)(2), 408A(c)(3)(B), 408A(d)(3)(E), as amended by PPA § 824; Notice 2008-30, 2008-12 I.R.B. 638]

Practice Pointer. A distribution of an inherited traditional IRA to a non-spouse beneficiary is not a qualified distribution. [I.R.C. § 408(d)(3), 408A(e); Treas. Reg. § 1.408A-4, Q&A 1; PPA § 829, adding I.R.C. § 402(c)(11)(A) allowing for the rollover by a nonspouse beneficiary of certain retirement plan distributions starting after 2006, but only to a traditional "inherited" IRA] A nonspouse beneficiary who received an interest through a spousal disclaimer could not convert the inherited IRA to a Roth IRA. [Ltr. Rul. 200013041 (Jan. 4, 2000)]

Q 3:51 May a Roth IRA be rolled over to another Roth IRA?

Yes; however, there is a limit on how frequently a Roth IRA may be rolled over to another Roth IRA (see Q 3:73). [I.R.C. § 408A(c)(3)(B), 408A(e)] The general rollover rules, including the 60-day and 12-month rollover restriction, normally apply (see Q 3:67). The 60-day and 12-month rules (see Q 3:67) do not apply to direct transfers.

Q 3:52 Are rollovers to a Roth IRA from employer-sponsored plans such as qualified plans and 403(b) plans permitted?

Yes, beginning in 2007. Until 2007, rollovers to a Roth IRA from employer-sponsored plans such as qualified plans and 403(b) plans were not permitted.

An individual could, however, roll over the employer plan to a traditional IRA and then convert (roll over or transfer) the traditional IRA to a Roth IRA (see Q 3:12). But see Q 3:81 regarding a deemed Roth IRA, and Q 10:3 regarding qualified Roth contribution programs. The distribution must be eligible to be rolled over (see Q 3:64).

Effective for distributions after 2007, rollovers from a qualified plan, a tax-sheltered annuity, or a governmental 403(b) plan to a Roth IRA are permitted and are called "qualified rollover contributions." The rollover will be treated as a Roth conversion if all other conversion qualifications (e.g., income below the $100,000 level before 2010, see Q 3:16) are satisfied. The taxable portion of the rollover amount would be taxable at the time of the rollover. [I.R.C. §§ 408A(e)(2), 408A(c)(3)(B), 408A(d)(3)(E), as amended by PPA § 824; Notice 2008-30, 2008-12 I.R.B. 638] However, for a qualified rollover contribution (conversion) to a Roth IRA made in the taxable year beginning in 2010, the taxpayer will recognize income ratably in 2011 and 2012, unless the taxpayer elects to recognize it all in 2010. No provision was made for tax years after 2010, thus the taxable amount of a conversion contribution in taxable years beginning after 2010 to a Roth IRA will have to be included in the tax year the distribution takes place. [I.R.C. §§ 408A(d)(3)(A)(iii), as amended by TIPRA (Pub. L. No. 109-222)] The 60-day and 12-month rules (see Q 3:67) do not apply to direct transfers.

Note. Beginning in 2008, participants in the Federal Thrift Savings Plan (TSP) who are eligible to receive a distribution may transfer an eligible rollover distribution (see Q 3:64) into a Roth IRA (a direct rollover conversion), an IRA, or other eligible retirement plan. [Family Smoking Prevention and Tobacco Control Act (P.L. 111-31) § 103 (2008); see also, TSP Frequently Asked Questions (FAQ), Information about Roth IRA Transfers, available at http://www.tsp.gov/faq/faq15.html#sub2 (visited Aug. 28, 2009)]

Q 3:53 Can a beneficiary make a qualified rollover contribution to Roth IRAs from an employer-sponsored plan?

Yes. Notice 2008-30 [2008-12 I.R.B. 638] clarifies that the PPA provisions permitting rollovers from pretax accounts in qualified plans, 403(b) plans, and eligible governmental 457 plans to a Roth IRA account are available to participants, spouses, and, for direct transfers only, to nonspouse beneficiaries. [Notice 2008-30, 2008-12 I.R.B. 638, Q&As 2 and 6]

Q 3:54 Must a qualified rollover distribution be made in the form of a direct trustee-to-trustee transfer?

Generally, no. A qualified rollover distribution to a Roth IRA from an employer's plan can be directly transferred (assets not received) or indirectly transferred (within the 60-day rollover period). However, a nonspouse beneficiary rollover to a traditional IRA or rollover conversion to a Roth IRA must be in the form of a direct (trustee-to-trustee) rollover (direct conversion).

Q 3:55   How is the $100,000 MAGI conversion limit and joint filing requirement applied to a beneficiary who rolls over a distribution from an employer's plan?

In the case of a distribution from an eligible retirement plan other than a Roth IRA, the MAGI and filing status of the beneficiary are used to determine eligibility to make a qualified rollover contribution to a Roth IRA. [Notice 2008-30, 2008-12 I.R.B. 638, Q&A 6] These requirements do not apply after 2009 (see Q 3:16).

Q 3:56   What is an "eligible retirement plan?"

The term "eligible retirement plan" means—

- An individual retirement account described in Code Section 408(a)
- An individual retirement annuity described in Code Section 408(b) (other than an endowment contract)
- A qualified tax-exempt trust described in Code Section 401(a)
- An annuity plan described in Code Section 403(a)
- An eligible governmental deferred compensation plan described in Code Section 457(b)
- An annuity contract described in Code Section 403(b)

Note 1. A Roth IRA distribution may only be rolled over to another Roth IRA.

Note 2. If any portion of an eligible rollover distribution is attributable to payments or distributions from a designated Roth account (DRA), an eligible retirement plan with respect to such portion shall include only another designated Roth account and a Roth IRA (see Q 10:48).

[I.R.C. §§ 402(c)(8), 408A(e)]

Q 3:57   Must a qualified plan allow a beneficiary to make qualified rollover contributions to Roth IRAs?

Maybe. An eligible employer's plan must permit participants and spouses the option to directly roll over (convert) eligible rollover distributions, but is not (currently) required to offer a direct rollover option to a nonspouse beneficiary. [I.R.C. § 401(c)(11)]

Caution. Pending legislation may require (mandate) that nonspouse beneficiaries be permitted to directly roll over to a traditional IRA or a Roth IRA. [The U.S. House of Representatives passed a bill (H.R. 3361) on March 12, 2008, to make a series of "technical corrections" to the PPA (Pub. L. No. 109-280). The House-passed bill differs slightly from a PPA technical corrections bill (S. 1974), which the Senate approved in December 2007. If H.R. 3361 is passed in the Senate, the nonspouse beneficiary direct rollover option must be available to participants beginning in 2009.

Note. A nonspouse beneficiary of a traditional IRA may not convert that IRA to a Roth IRA. Thus, this benefit—conversion of pretax amounts to a Roth IRA—is only available to a nonspouse beneficiary (or beneficiaries) of a qualified plan, a 403(b) plan, or an eligible governmental 457 plan.

Q 3:58 May a beneficiary recharacterize a Roth IRA contribution?

Yes. A beneficiary who is ineligible to make a qualified rollover contribution to a Roth IRA may recharacterize the contribution to a traditional IRA (see Q 3:29). [I.R.C. § 408A(d)(6); Notice 2008-30, Q&As 5 and 7, 2008-12 I.R.B. 638]

Q 3:59 Can a spouse beneficiary who makes a rollover conversion from a qualified plan to a Roth IRA elect to treat the Roth IRA as his or her own Roth IRA?

Yes. A surviving spouse who makes a rollover to a Roth IRA may elect either to treat the Roth IRA as his or her own or to establish the Roth IRA in the name of the decedent with the surviving spouse as the beneficiary. [Notice 2008-30, Q&A 7, 2008-12 I.R.B. 638] By treating the Roth IRA as his or her own, a spouse beneficiary can avoid required Roth minimum distributions during his or her lifetime. If distributions are required, they are computed in accordance with Notice 2007-7, Q&As 17, 18, and 19. [2007-5 I.R.B. 395]

Q 3:60 Can a nonspouse beneficiary who makes a rollover conversion from an employer's plan to a Roth IRA elect to treat the Roth IRA as his or her own Roth IRA?

No. A nonspouse beneficiary cannot elect to treat the Roth IRA as his or her own. RMDs are computed in accordance with Notice 2007-7, Q&As 17, 18, and 19 [2007-5 I.R.B. 395]. [Notice 2008-30, Q&A 7, 2008-12 I.R.B. 638]

Q 3:61 Does the 10 percent premature distribution tax penalty apply to a qualified rollover distribution from an employer's plan?

No. The 10 percent premature distribution penalty tax does not apply. However, if the owner withdraws amounts within five years, the amount is subject to the 10 percent penalty tax as though the amount were taxable. [Notice 2008-30, Q&A 3, 2008-12 I.R.B. 638]

Q 3:62 Do the mandatory withholding rules apply to a qualified rollover distribution from an employer's plan to a Roth IRA?

Maybe. The mandatory 20-percent withholding does not apply to a direct (trustee-to-trustee) rollover conversion to a Roth IRA, including a direct rollover (conversion) by a nonspouse beneficiary. If the distribution is made to the participant, mandatory withholding rules apply. The distributee can request voluntary withholding. [I.R.C. § 3405(c); Notice 2008-30, Q&A 6, 2008-12 I.R.B. 638]

Q 3:63 Is the plan administrator responsible for determining a participant's eligibility to make a direct conversion to a Roth IRA?

No. The plan administrator is not responsible for ensuring that the participant is eligible to make a direct conversion rollover (i.e., before 2010, MAGI does not exceed $100,000, and, if married, the participant files a joint return).

Q 3:64 Must a qualified rollover contribution be an "eligible rollover distribution"?

Yes. A qualified rollover contribution must satisfy the requirements to be an "eligible rollover distribution," which is any distribution of all or any portion of the balance to the credit of the employee (including net unrealized appreciation (NUA)) from a qualified plan, an eligible governmental 457(b) plan, or a 403(b) plan except:

1. One of a series of substantially equal periodic payments made at least annually over:
   (a) The life of the employee or the joint lives of the employee and the employee's designated beneficiary;
   (b) The life expectancy of the employee or the joint life and last survivor expectancy of the employee and the employee's designated beneficiary; or
   (c) A specified period of 10 years or more.
2. An RMD under Code Section 401(a)(9). A plan administrator is permitted to assume there is no designated beneficiary for purposes of determining the minimum distribution.
3. Corrective distributions of excess contributions or excess deferrals, and any income allocable to the excess, or an excess annual addition and any allocable gains.
4. Loans treated as a distribution because it does not satisfy certain requirements when made or later (such as upon default), unless the participant's accrued benefit is reduced (offset) to repay the loan. Thus, plan loan offset amounts can be eligible rollover distributions. [See Treas. Reg. § 1.402(c)-2, Q&A-9]
5. Dividends on employer securities (Code Section 404(k) dividends).
6. Cost of current life insurance protection (P.S. 58 Costs).
7. Distributions to a payee other than the employee, the employee's surviving spouse, a spouse or former spouse who is an alternate payee under a qualified domestic relations order (QDRO).
8. Any hardship distribution.

[I.R.C. § 408A(e) referring to I.R.C. §§ 408(d)(3), 402A(c)(3)(A); Notice 2008-30, Q&A 2, 2008-12 I.R.B. 638] A contribution of a military death gratuity or an SGLI payment is treated as a qualified rollover contribution (see Qs 3:104–3:111).

Q 3:65 How is NUA treated if employer securities are transferred to a Roth IRA in a conversion?

It is unclear. NUA is the gain on employer securities in the hands of a defined contribution plan trustee as of the date of distribution. Generally, the NUA is taxable at capital gains rates at the time the employer securities are sold or disposed. Any remaining capital gain (long or short) depends on the holding period in the hands of the distributee. If the securities bearing NUA are rolled over into an IRA, the NUA is not taxable at that time, and capital gain treatment is lost forever. Any subsequent distribution of the securities from the traditional IRA will be taxable at ordinary income tax rates (and adjusted for any after-tax contributions).

Code Section 408A(d)(3)(A) regarding Roth conversions provides that gross income includes "any amount which would be includible were it not part of a qualified rollover contribution" and without regard to the rules of Code Section 72." Arguably, if employer securities bearing NUA are rolled over (or directly converted) to a Roth IRA, the NUA potentially could be distributed from the Roth IRA tax-free. That is, the NUA would not be taxable at the time of the conversion. The IRS might argue that it is a tax avoidance transaction (see Q 2:4). It seems doubtful that Congress intended such a result when it modified the rollover rules to permit rollovers and conversions directly to a Roth IRA, without having to first rollover the amount to a traditional IRA and then converting that IRA to a Roth IRA. [I.R.C. §§ 402(c)(6), 402(e)(4), 408(d)(3)(A), 402(e)(4); but see Circular 230, § 10:35 regarding the requirements for a covered opinion; PPA § 824]

Assuming the NUA is taxable at the time of the conversion, guidance is also needed to determine whether the NUA is taxable at capital gains rates (as if the stock were sold and no Roth IRA conversion occurred) or taxed as ordinary income (as if the securities were first transferred to a traditional IRA and subsequently converted to a Roth IRA). Practitioners should exercise caution when converting securities received in a lump-sum distribution containing NUA. [Compare to the known treatment of distributed designated Roth accounts (DRAs) containing NUA, see Qs 10:45, 10:46.]

Caution. NUA is not divisible. It cannot be separated from one share and transferred to another share. Thus, it is not possible to roll over, convert, or retain shares without their attributable portion of NUA. As a result, each and every share of the employer's stock will have the same cost or other basis for purposes of determining gain or loss. [*See* Rev. Rul. 57-514, 1957-2 C.B. 261]

Q 3:66   How are rollovers from an employer's plan to a Roth IRA reported by the owner?

A rollover to a Roth IRA from an employer's qualified plan, an eligible governmental 457(b) plan, or a 403(b) plan is not a tax-free distribution, other than any employee after tax contributions. Enter the total amount of the distribution before income tax or deductions were withheld on Form 1040, line 16a, Form 1040A, line 12a, or Form 1040NR, lines 17a. This amount is shown in box 1 (gross distribution) of Form 1099R, Distributions from Pensions, Annuities, Retirement or Profit-Sharing Plans, IRAs, Insurance Contracts, etc. Reduce the box 1 amount by the amount that was taxable when made (usually shown in box 5 (employee contributions)) of Form 1099R. Enter the remaining amount (even if zero) on Form 1040, line 16b, Form 1040A, line 12b, or Form 1040NR, line 17b (see also chapter 9, Required Reporting for Roth IRAs).

Q 3:67   What general IRA rollover rules apply to Roth-to-Roth rollovers?

The general IRA rollover rules that apply to Roth-to-Roth rollovers include the following:

- The 60-day rule (see Q 3:68)
- The 12-month rule (see Qs 3:73, 3:74)
- The special rules for property distributions (see Q 3:75)
- The irrevocable rollover election rule (see Q 3:76)

The 12-month rule does not apply to conversions from a traditional IRA to a Roth IRA. The 60-day and 12-month rules do not apply to direct transfers.

Q 3:68   What is the 60-day rollover rule?

Under the 60-day rollover rule, a rollover must generally be completed no later than the 60th day after the day the distribution was received by the individual. There is no provision for extending this 60-day period if the 60th day falls on a weekend or legal holiday. After 2001, the IRS was granted limited authority to extend the 60-day rollover period (see Q 3:70).

Before that grant of authority, the IRS took a very firm position on the 60-day rule in several rulings. [Ltr. Ruls. 8815032 (Jan. 19, 1988), 8824047 (Mar. 22, 1988), 9145036 (Aug. 13, 1991)] The IRS also took the position that it lacked the authority to restore funds to an IRA after the 60-day period elapsed when a taxpayer erroneously relied on the advice of a representative at a financial institution. [Ltr. Rul. 199901029 (Jan. 11, 1999)]

Note. Any rollover contribution made after the 60th day following the date of receipt from the distributing plan is treated as a regular IRA contribution, subject to the $5,000 ($6,000 with catch-up contribution) limit for 2009. Amounts in excess of the $5,000 ($6,000 with catch-up contribution) annual traditional IRA contribution limit are treated as an excess IRA contribution subject to the 6 percent excise tax unless corrected under Code Section 408(d)(4) (see Qs 2:24–2:35).

Q 3:69   Are there any exceptions to the 60-day rule?

Yes. There are two exceptions to the 60-day rule:

1. *Frozen deposits.* The 60-day rollover period is extended when an individual is unable to withdraw his or her funds because the money becomes frozen after the distribution is received but before the rollover is completed. The term *frozen deposit* means any deposit that cannot be withdrawn because of the bankruptcy or insolvency (or threat thereof) of any financial institution. The 60-day rollover period does not include any period during which the deposit is frozen and does not end earlier than 10 days after the deposit ceases to be a frozen deposit. [I.R.C. §§ 402(c)(7), 408(d)(3)(F)]

2. *First-time homebuyer.* An individual who is taking a distribution from a Roth IRA for the first-time purchase of a home must use the distribution before the close of the 120th day after the date on which the distribution is received to pay qualified acquisition costs with respect to the purchase. If the distribution from the Roth IRA fails to meet the 120-day requirement because of a delay in or cancellation of the purchase or construction of the residence, the amount of the distribution may be contributed as a rollover contribution to a Roth IRA. In such a case, the individual is allowed 120 days rather than 60 days to complete the rollover. [I.R.C. § 72(t)(8)(E); I.R.S. Notice 98-49, Q&A C-2, 1998-2 C.B. 365]

Q 3:70   May the 60-day rollover period be extended?

Yes. EGTRRA grants the IRS the authority to extend the 60-day rollover period for any eligible rollover distribution made after 2001 if the failure to do so would be "against equity or good conscience, [such as in the case of] casualty, disaster, or other events beyond the reasonable control of the individual subject to [the period]." [EGTRRA § 644(b); I.R.C. § 402(c)(3), 408(d)(3)] Procedural requirements must also be satisfied (see Q 3:72).

The IRS has released guidance for individuals to apply for a ruling waiving the 60-day rollover requirement. In making its determination, the IRS will consider facts and circumstances, including:

1. Errors committed by a financial institution;

2. The inability to complete a rollover due to death, disability, hospitalization, incarceration, restrictions imposed by a foreign country, or postal error;

3. The use of the amount distributed (e.g., in the case of payment by check, whether the check was cashed); and

4. The time elapsed since the distribution occurred.

The ruling request application fee depends upon the amount of the rollover, as follows:

For rollovers of less than $50,000, the fee is $500.

For rollovers of $50,000 but less than $100,000, the fee is $1,500.

For rollovers of $100,000 or more, the fee is $3,000.

[Rev. Proc. 2008-8, 2008-1 I.R.B. 233] An automatic extension will be granted if a financial institution receives funds on behalf of a taxpayer before the expiration of the 60-day rollover period, the taxpayer follows all procedures required by the financial institution for depositing the funds into an eligible retirement plan within the 60-day period (including giving instructions to deposit the funds into an eligible retirement plan), and solely due to an error on the part of the financial institution, the funds were not deposited into an eligible retirement plan within the 60-day rollover period. The automatic extension will be granted, however, only if the funds were deposited into an eligible retirement plan within one year from the beginning of the 60-day rollover period and, if the financial institution had deposited the funds as instructed, it would have been a valid rollover.

[Rev. Proc. 2003-16, 2003-4 I.R.B. 359; *see, e.g.*, Ltr. Ruls. 200919061 (Feb. 12, 2009), *denied*, Rev. Proc. 2003-16 factors not present; 200921039 (Feb. 25, 2009), unauthorized withdrawals; 200920061 (Feb. 19, 2009), mistake involving account numbers; 200920060 (Feb. 18, 2009), mental and physical conditions which impaired ability to manage financial affairs; 200920059 (Feb.20, 2009), settlement following unauthorized use of funds; 200920058 (Feb. 20, 2009), miscommunication, language barrier, and confusion; 200920057 (Feb. 17, 2009), joint request by couple with medical conditions; 200920056 (Feb. 18, 2009), medical treatment and condition of spouse; 200920055 (Feb. 23, 2009), settlement following unauthorized use of funds; 200920054 (Feb. 18, 2009), unauthorized use of the distributions; 200919071 (Feb. 10, 2009), *denied*, erroneous belief rollover period was 90 days; 200919070 (Feb. 10, 2009), deposit mistake by financial institution; 200919069 (Feb. 10, 2009), errors committed by financial advisor and impaired medical condition; 200919068 (Feb. 10, 2009), institution's failure to honor check; 200919067 (Feb. 09, 2009), error by financial institution; 200919066 (Feb. 13, 2009), incorrect advice provided by companies; 200919065 (Feb. 10, 2009), mistake by financial institution employee; 200919063 (Feb. 10, 2009), mistake made by financial institution; 200919062 (Feb. 11, 2009), illnesses and hospitalizations; 200919061 (Feb. 12, 2009), *denied*, deposited into co-ownership CD; 200918024 (Feb. 04, 2009), mistake made by institutions] (*See* H.R. Conf. Rep. No. 107-84 (2001) regarding authority of IRS to extend the 60-day period.)

Note. The IRS cannot waive the one-rollover-per-year rule applicable to transfers between IRAs, although there are some exceptions (see Qs 3:72, 3:74). Thus, the extension of the 60-day rule is of no use to a taxpayer who has already taken a distribution within the one-year period from that IRA that was includible in gross income.

Practice Pointer. Recently issued rulings only grant relief if the taxpayer's fact pattern falls under one of the examples outlined in Revenue Procedure 2003-16 (i.e., errors committed by a financial institution, death, disability, hospitalization, incarceration, restrictions imposed by a foreign country, or postal error). It would appear that this narrow reading of the Revenue Procedure is incorrect. The authors feel that the factors outlined in the Revenue Procedure should only be used as examples of situations the Service will consider and should not be read to be all-inclusive. The true test should be whether the failure to waive the 60-day requirement would be against equity or good conscience. The Committee Reports for Code Section 408(d)(3)(I) (House Report 107-51, H.R. 10) indicate that the inability to waive the 60-day rollover period may result in adverse tax consequences for individuals. The Committee believed that "such harsh results are inappropriate and that providing for waivers of the rule will help facilitate rollovers." In any event, the IRS's current stance is making it more difficult to get a favorable ruling, unless the Taxpayer can prove the failure was due to one of the above criteria. [See, e.g., Ltr. Rul. 200738027 (Sept. 21, 2007), IRS declined to waive the 60-day requirement where the taxpayer's failure to accomplish the timely rollover was due to mistakenly entering the wrong account number; and Ltr. Rul. 200736036 (Sept. 7, 2007), IRS denied relief to a taxpayer who made a technical error by completing the wrong form over the Internet, which resulted in a failed attempt to establish a rollover IRA.] On the other hand, in Private Letter Ruling 2009300052 [Apr. 27, 2009] the IRS waived the 60 day period, without explicitly saying so, because the 60th day was a Sunday and the taxpayer was unable to effectuate a rollover until the the next day.

Q 3:71   What special information is required to obtain a ruling request involving a recharacterization?

Revenue Procedure 2009-4 contains the general procedures for obtaining a ruling letter. The following additional information is solicited in the form of a required checklist in the case of a Roth IRA recharacterization ruling in order to assist EP Technical in processing the request. A response (yes, no, or n/a) must be indicated as well as the page on which the information can be found. The checklist questions are as follows:

1. Did you include the name(s) of the trustee and/or custodian of the traditional individual retirement account (IRA) (generally, a financial institution)?

2. Is each IRA identification number present?

3. If the ruling request involves Roth conversions of both a husband and wife, is the necessary information with respect to each IRA of each party present? Note: as long as husband and wife file a joint federal Form 1040, the IRS can issue one ruling covering both parties. Furthermore, if a joint federal income tax return has been filed for the year or years in question, the IRS requires only one user fee, even if both husband and wife had failed conversions.

4. If there were one or more attempted conversions, are the applicable dates on which the attempted IRA conversion(s) occurred included?

5. If the reason that a conversion failed is that the taxpayer or related taxpayers relied upon advice of a tax professional such as a CPA, an attorney, or an enrolled actuary, is the name and occupation of that adviser included?

6. Is certification that the taxpayer or taxpayers timely filed the relevant federal tax return(s) present?

7. Is there a short statement of facts with respect to the conversion? For example, if the ruling request involves a conversion attempted in 1998, there should be a statement of the facts that includes a representation of why the due date(s) found in Announcement 99-57 [1999-1 C.B. 1256] and Announcement 99-104 [1999-2 C.B. 555] were not met.

8. If the taxpayer recharacterized his or her Roth IRA to a traditional IRA prior to submitting a request for Section 9100 relief, are the date(s) of the recharacterization(s), name(s) of trustees and/or custodians, and the identification numbers of the traditional IRA(s) present?

9. Does the request include the type of contribution (i.e., regular or conversion) and amount of the contribution being recharacterized?

[Rev. Proc. 2009-4, Appendix C, 2009-1 I.R.B. 118]

Q 3:72   What other guidance is there concerning a request for relief?

The Procedure and Administration Regulations, in general, provide guidance concerning requests for relief submitted to the IRS. [Treas. Reg. § 301-9100-1, 301.9100-2, 301.9100-3] The regulations provide that the Commissioner of the IRS, in his or her discretion, may grant a reasonable extension of the time fixed by a regulation, a revenue ruling, a revenue procedure, a notice, or by an announcement for the making of an election or application for relief in respect of tax. [Treas. Reg. § 301.9100-11(c)] The regulations list certain elections for which automatic extensions of time to file are granted. [Treas. Reg. § 301. 9100-2] Section 301.9100-3 of the regulations generally provides guidance with respect to the granting of relief with respect to those elections that are not automatic. Under that section, the regulations provide that applications for relief will be granted when the taxpayer provides sufficient evidence (including affidavits) to establish that:

1. The taxpayer acted reasonably and in good faith and

2. Granting relief would not prejudice the interests of the government.

[Treas. Reg. § 301.9100-3(a), 301.9100-3(e)(2)]

A taxpayer will be deemed to have acted reasonably and in good faith if:

1. The request for relief is filed before the failure to make a timely election is discovered by the IRS;

2. The taxpayer inadvertently failed to make the election because of intervening events beyond the taxpayers control;

3. The taxpayer failed to make the election because, after exercising reasonable diligence, the taxpayer was unaware of the necessity for the election;

4. The taxpayer reasonably relied upon the written advice of the IRS; or

5. The taxpayer reasonably relied on a qualified tax professional, including a tax professional employed by the taxpayer, and the tax professional failed to make, or advise the taxpayer to make, the election.

[Treas. Reg. § 301.9100-3(b)(1)]

A taxpayer will be deemed to have not acted reasonably and in good faith if the taxpayer uses hindsight in requesting relief. If specific facts have changed since the due date for making the election that make the election advantageous to the taxpayer, the IRS will not ordinarily grant relief. In such a case, the IRS will grant relief only when the taxpayer provides strong proof that the taxpayer's decision to seek relief did not involve hindsight. [Treas. Reg. § 301.9100-3(b)(3)(iii)] The interests of the government are prejudiced if granting relief would result in a taxpayer having a lower tax liability in the aggregate for all taxable years affected by the election than the taxpayer would have had if the election had been timely made (taking into account the time value of money). Similarly, if facts change after the deadline for making the election, so that the election provides an advantage to the taxpayer, the IRS will not grant an extension under Section 301.9100-3. In addition, if the tax consequences of more than one taxpayer are affected by the election, the government's interests are prejudiced if extending the time for making the election may result in the affected taxpayers, in the aggregate, having a lower tax liability than if the election had been timely made. [Treas. Reg. § 301.9100-3(c)(1)(i)] Similarly, if facts change after the deadline for making the election, so that the election provides an advantage to the taxpayer, the IRS will not grant an extension under Section 301.9100-3. Ordinarily, the interests of the government will be treated as prejudiced and that ordinarily the IRS will not grant relief when tax years that would have been affected by the election had it been timely made are closed by the statute of limitations before the taxpayers receipt of a ruling granting relief under this section. [Treas. Reg. § 301.9100-3(c)(1)(ii)]

Letter Ruling 200234073 (May 28, 2002) concerns an individual who converted two traditional IRAs to Roth IRAs during 2000. The individual and her husband timely filed a joint tax return for 2000 showing adjusted gross income not in excess of the $100,000 limit for conversions. In 2001 the individual decided to recharacterize the Roth IRAs as traditional IRAs. However, due to a series of circumstances, some of which were related to the events of September 11 in New York City, she did not recharacterize the IRAs by the tax return due date including extensions (October 15, 2001). The individual subsequently contacted a CPA regarding her failure to recharacterize the IRAs, and a request for relief under Treasury Regulations Section 301.9100-3 was filed during 2001, and before the statute of limitations expired on the 2000 return. At the time of the request, the value of each IRA was *higher* than it was on the due date for making the election and the taxpayer would have to pay tax on value that was no longer there. The government's interest would not be prejudiced.

In granting an extension (60 days from the date of the letter ruling), the IRS concluded that the individual acted reasonably and in good faith. It noted that (1) she was eligible to convert her traditional IRAs; (2) the value of the Roth IRAs had increased at the time relief was requested; (3) the request for relief was filed shortly after the due date for making the election; (4) documentation submitted showed that the individual intended to recharacterize her Roth IRAs before that due date; and (5) the calendar year in question was not a closed tax year. Had the account value declined, instead, the waiver of the 60-day period would likely not have been approved.

Q 3:73   May rollovers between Roth IRAs be made only once in a 12-month period?

Superficially, yes; however, the actual rule is a little more complicated. The Code restricts rollovers between IRAs, including Roth IRAs, to once every 12 consecutive months (see Qs 3:68, 3:69). [I.R.C. § 408(d)(3)(B); Treas. Reg. § 1.408-4(b)(4)(ii)] The 12-month period is measured from the date the IRA owner received the first distribution that was rolled over to another IRA, not from the date it was rolled over. Although the literal reading of the statute seems to restrict the individual to making only one IRA-to-IRA rollover per 12-month period, the proposed regulations state that the rule applies to "each separate individual retirement account." Thus, each IRA trust is treated separately in applying the rule. Recharacterizations are treated differently (see Q 3:40).

For example, if an individual has two IRAs, IRA-1 and IRA-2, and the assets of IRA-1 are rolled over to a new IRA, IRA-3, a rollover from IRA-2 to IRA-3 or to any other IRA within one year after the rollover distribution from IRA-1 may also be made. Both rollovers are permitted because the individual has not received more than one distribution from either IRA within one year. The rule applies separately to each IRA owned. [Prop. Treas. Reg. § 1.408-4(b)(4)(ii)] According to the IRS, the assets rolled over to IRA-3 may not again be rolled over to any other IRA within the one-year period. [*See* I.R.S. Pub. 590, Individual Retirement Arrangements (2000 and earlier versions)] In the most recent Publication 590, Individual Retirement Arrangements (IRAs), for 2008, IRA-3 is subject to the 12-month restriction with respect to both existing and transferred assets.

Note. If an amount rolled over to an IRA tax free is later distributed from that IRA within a one-year period, it does not qualify as a rollover. The amount may be subject to the 10 percent premature distribution penalty (unless an exception applies). [I.R.C. §§ 72(t), 408(d)(3)(B)]

Example. Vincent has IRA Trust 1 with a savings institution and IRA Trust 2 with a brokerage firm. He takes a partial distribution of $5,000 from IRA Trust 1 at the savings institution on August 10, 2009, and rolls the amount over within 60 days to new IRA Trust 3 at a bank. Vincent may not take another distribution from IRA Trust 1 until August 10, 2010, if he wants to roll it over to another IRA. Until August 10, 2009, he must report any distributions from IRA Trust 1 as income. In addition, Vincent may not take a distribution of the same $5,000 that he rolled over to IRA Trust 3 at the bank until that same 12-month period has expired, that is, until August 10, 2010. IRA Trust 2 at the brokerage firm may, however, be rolled over to another IRA without waiting the 12 months because IRA Trust 2 has not had a distribution that has been rolled over within the last 12 months.

Note. The 12-month rule does not apply to rollovers from qualified plans, eligible governmental 457(b) plans, or 403(b) plans to traditional IRAs. [Treas. Reg. § 1.402(c)-2, Q&A 16] Therefore, an individual may roll over his or her employer's plan to a traditional IRA and immediately convert the traditional IRA to a Roth IRA. Neither does the rule apply to conversions, recharacterizations, or eligible rollovers due to the first-time homebuyer exception in the event there is a delay or cancellation of the residence. [See I.R.C. § 72(t)(8)(E)]

Practice Pointer. In part because of this rule, it is generally recommended that a transfer be completed via a direct trustee-to-trustee transfer rather than as a rollover. The one rollover per 12-month rule does not apply to direct transfers. [See Rev. Rul. 78-406, 1978-2 C.B. 157]

Q 3:74 Is there an exception to the 12-month rule?

Yes. An exception to the 12-month rule has been granted by the IRS for distributions made from a failed financial institution by the Federal Deposit Insurance Corporation (FDIC) or the Resolution Trust Corporation (RTC) as receiver for the institution. To qualify for the exception, the distribution must satisfy the following requirements:

1. The distribution must not be initiated by either the institution or the Roth IRA owner and
2. The distribution must be made because
   a. The institution is insolvent and
   b. The receiver is unable to find a buyer for the institution.

Any distribution made under the exception is eligible for rollover treatment even if the individual has already made a rollover within the previous 12 months. [I.R.S. Special Ruling Letter from James J. McGovern, Assistant Chief Counsel (Employee Benefits & Exempt Organizations), to the FDIC clarifying the rollover status of involuntary payment distributions made by the RTC from IRAs held in insolvent financial institutions (Feb. 5, 1991)]

Q 3:75 Must the same property received in a distribution be rolled over?

Yes. There is no provision under the IRA rules that allows an individual to sell any property received from an IRA and roll over the proceeds from the sale to another IRA. As a result, if an individual receives a distribution of property (e.g., stock) from one IRA, that same property must be rolled over to the next IRA. That is, property received in an IRA distribution may not be retained by the individual and replaced by cash equal to its fair market value in the rollover transaction. [Rev. Rul. 87-77, 1987-2 C.B. 115] (The rules on the sale of distributed property applicable to rollovers from qualified plans under Code Section 402 do not apply to IRAs.) [I.R.C. § 402(c)(6)]

In addition, if cash is distributed from an IRA or (employer plan) plan, there is no provision for purchasing property (e.g., stock) to place in the receiving IRA. [*See, e.g., Lemishow v. Comm'r*, 110 T.C. 346 (1998) (rollover to an IRA of stock that was purchased after a distribution of cash disqualified)]

Q 3:76 What is the irrevocable election rule for purposes of a Roth IRA rollover contribution?

The IRS requires that the receiving Roth IRA trustee obtain a written, irrevocable election from the Roth IRA owner indicating that the contribution will be treated as a rollover transaction for federal income tax purposes. That is the case even when the rollover contribution is coming from another Roth IRA (even if made by a trustee-to-trustee transfer). [Temp. Treas. Reg. § 1.402(a)(5)-1T, Q&A 3]

Q 3:77 Must an individual take a complete distribution to perform a Roth-to-Roth rollover?

No. An individual is not required to take a complete distribution from one Roth IRA in order to perform a Roth-to-Roth rollover.

Q 3:78 Must an individual roll over the entire distribution received from an IRA?

No. An individual is not required to roll over the entire amount received from the first IRA. Any taxable amount not rolled over, however, is taxed at ordinary income rates for federal income tax purposes. [I.R.C. § 408(d)(3)(D)]

Q 3:79 May an individual roll over a Roth IRA distribution back to the same Roth IRA?

Yes. As long as the other IRA-to-IRA rollover rules are met, an individual may roll over a Roth IRA distribution back to the same Roth IRA from which the distribution was originally received, even if the rollover is effected by a trustee-to-trustee transfer. In such a case, the trustee (or custodian) reports both the distribution and the rollover contribution. [Ltr. Ruls. 9010007 (Dec. 14, 1989), 8502044 (Oct. 17, 1984); *see also* Treas. Reg. § 1.408A-5, Q&A 1(a)]

> **Example.** Warren rolls over $100,000 from Roth IRA 1 into Roth IRA 2. At a later date, Warren can roll Roth IRA 2 back into Roth IRA 1 as long as the other IRA-to-IRA rollover rules are satisfied.

Q 3:80   May a required minimum distribution be rolled over to a Roth IRA?

No. A qualified rollover contribution from a traditional IRA to a Roth IRA must meet all the requirements that apply to a traditional IRA. Thus, the IRA owner may not roll over an RMD. Therefore, a Roth rollover conversion may not include an individual's RMD amount for the year. The individual should keep the RMD amount separate and roll over only the balance to the Roth IRA. [I.R.C. §§ 408(d)(3)(E), 408A(e); Treas. Reg. § 1.408A-4, Q&A 6(a)–6(c)] The Worker, Retiree, and Employer Recovery Act of 2008 (WRERA) suspended the requirement for a beneficiary to take RMDs in 2009 (see Q 1:32 and chapter 5).

> **Example.** Ted owns a traditional IRA worth $12,000. In 2009, his RMD is $2,000. Ted can roll over only $10,000 to a Roth IRA.

Deemed IRAs

Q 3:81   What is a deemed IRA?

For plan years beginning after 2002, an employer's qualified plan, 403(b) plan, or governmental 457(b) plan is permitted to accept Roth IRA contributions, traditional IRA contributions, or both (see Qs 2:46–2:60). [Treas. Reg. §§ 1.408(q)-1(a), 1.408(q)-1(b), 1.408(q)-1(h)(1)]

These types of contributions are called voluntary employee contributions (see Q 3:82) if they

1. Are separately accounted for or made into a separate account under the plan; [Treas. Reg. § 1.408(q)-1(c)]
2. Meet the eligibility and other requirements applicable to either traditional or Roth IRAs; [Treas. Reg. § 1.408(q)-1(b)] and
3. Are permitted under the employer's plan. [Treas. Reg. § 1.408(q)-1(d)(1)]

The account established under the employer's plan is called a deemed IRA. [I.R.C. § 408(q); *see* Treas. Reg. § 1.408(q)-1, Explanation of Provisions and Summary of Comments, 69 Fed. Reg. 140, 43735 (July 22, 2004)]

The plan document of the employer plan must contain the deemed IRA provisions and a deemed IRA must be in effect at the time the deemed IRA contributions are accepted. Notwithstanding the preceding sentence, employers that provided deemed IRAs for plan years beginning before January 1, 2004, (but after December 31, 2002) were not required to have such provisions in their plan documents before the end of such plan years.

> **Note.** The MAGI limitations for contributions to a Roth IRA are also applicable to a deemed Roth IRA (see Qs 2:5–2:8). [I.R.C. § 408(q)(1)(B)]

Q 3:82   What are "voluntary employee contributions" for deemed IRA purposes?

A voluntary employee contribution is any contribution (other than a mandatory contribution within the meaning of Code Section 411(c)(2)(C)), which is made by an individual as an employee under an employer plan (as described in Q 3:81) that allows employees to elect to make contributions to "deemed IRAs and with respect to which the individual has designated the contribution as a contribution to which section 408(q) applies." [Treas. Reg. § 1.408(q)-1(h)(2)]

Q 3:83   How are contributions to a deemed IRA treated?

In general, if the account or annuity meets the requirements applicable to traditional IRAs under Code Section 408, the account or annuity is deemed to be a traditional IRA, and if the account or annuity meets the requirements applicable to Roth IRAs under Code Section 408A, the account or annuity is deemed to be a Roth IRA. Under Code Section 408(q), an employer plan (described in Q 3:81) may permit employees to make voluntary employee contributions to a separate account or annuity established under the plan. If the requirements of Code Section 408(q) are met, such account or annuity is treated in the same manner as an individual retirement plan under Code Section 408 or 408A (and contributions to such an account or annuity are treated as contributions to an individual retirement plan and not to the qualified employer plan). The account or annuity is referred to as a deemed IRA.

Q 3:84   Which rules apply to the employer plan and to the deemed IRA?

In general, a qualified employer plan and a deemed IRA are treated as separate entities under the Code and each entity is subject to the rules generally applicable to that entity for purposes of the Code. Thus, a qualified employer plan (excluding the deemed IRA portion of the plan), whether it is a plan under Code Section 401(a), 403(a), or 403(b), or a governmental plan under Section 457(b), is subject to the rules applicable to that type of plan rather than to the rules applicable to IRAs under Section 408 or 408A. Similarly, the deemed IRA portion of the qualified employer plan would generally be subject to the rules applicable to traditional and Roth IRAs under Code Sections 408 and/or 408A (as the case may be), and not to the rules applicable to a plans under Code Section 401(a), 403(a), 403(b), or 457. Thus, a contribution to a deemed Roth IRA is treated as a contribution to a deemed Roth IRA rather than to the qualified employer plan or to a deemed IRA. [Treas. Reg. § 1.408(q)-1(c)] Issues regarding eligibility, participation, disclosure, nondiscrimination, contributions, distributions, investments, and plan administration are generally resolved under the separate rules (if any) applicable to each entity under the Code. [Treas. Reg. § 1.408(q)-1(c)] The availability of a deemed IRA is not a benefit, right, or feature of the qualified employer plan under Treasury Regulations Section 1.401(a)(4)-4 regarding nondiscrimination. [Treas. Reg. § 1.408(q)-1(f)(6)]

Q 3:85   May a simplified employee pension (SEP) or SIMPLE IRA be used as a deemed Roth IRA?

No. A SEP or SIMPLE plan may not contain deemed IRA provisions. [Treas. Reg. § 1.408(q)-1(b)]

Q 3:86   Must a deemed Roth IRA be designated as a Roth IRA?

Yes. A deemed Roth IRA must be clearly designated as a Roth IRA (see Q 1:13). Roth IRAs that are individual retirement accounts must be trusts separate from traditional IRAs. However, in the case of a deemed Roth IRA, the assets may be held in a single trust with deemed traditional IRAs, provided that the trustee maintains separate accounts for the deemed Roth IRAs and deemed traditional IRAs of each participant, and each of those accounts is clearly designated as such. [I.R.C. § 408(b); Treas. Reg. §§ 1.408A-2, 1.408(q)-1(f)(3)]

Q 3:87   May employer plan assets be commingled with deemed IRA and/or deemed Roth IRA assets?

Yes. Code Section 408(q) expressly provides that the requirements of Section 408(a)(5) regarding the commingling of IRA assets with other property does not apply to a deemed IRA or deemed Roth-IRA (see Q 3:88). However, the restrictions on the commingling of plan and IRA assets with other assets apply to the employer plan and deemed IRA. [I.R.C. § 408(q)(1)(B); Treas. Reg. § 1.408(q)-1(d)(2)]

Q 3:88   May a deemed IRA and a deemed Roth IRA be held in a single trust that includes the employer plan?

Yes. If deemed IRAs are held in a single trust that includes the qualified employer plan, the trustee must maintain a separate account for each deemed IRA and each deemed Roth IRA and the qualified employer plan. Similarly, separate annuities are to be established under a plan with respect to deemed individual retirement annuities. [Treas. Reg. § 1.408(q)-1(f)(2)]

In general, deemed IRAs that are individual retirement accounts may be held in separate individual trusts, a single trust separate from a trust maintained by the qualified employer plan, or in a single trust that includes the qualified employer plan. A deemed IRA trust must be created or organized in the United States for the exclusive benefit of the participants. If deemed IRAs are held in a single trust that includes the employer plan, the trustee must maintain a separate account for each deemed IRA. In addition, the written governing instrument creating the trust must satisfy additional requirements. [Treas. Reg. § 1.408(q)-1(f)(2); see requirements in I.R.C. § 408(a)(1), (2), (3), (4), and (6)]

If deemed IRAs are held in a single trust that includes the qualified employer plan, Code Section 408(a)(3) is treated as satisfied if no part of the separate accounts of any of the deemed IRAs is invested in life insurance contracts, regardless of whether the separate account for the qualified employer plan invests in life insurance contracts (see Q 3:89). [I.R.C. § 408(a)(3); Treas. Reg. 1.408(q)-1(f)(ii)]

The rules requiring each Roth IRA to be clearly designated as a Roth IRA will not fail to be satisfied solely because Roth deemed IRAs and traditional deemed IRAs are held in a single trust, provided that the trustee maintains separate accounts for the Roth deemed IRAs and traditional deemed IRAs of each participant, and each of those accounts is clearly designated as such. [I.R.C. § 408A(b), Treas. Reg. 1.408(q)-1(f)(iii)]

Deemed IRAs that are individual retirement annuities may be held under a single annuity contract or under separate annuity contracts. However, the contract must be separate from any annuity contract or annuity contracts of the employer plan. In addition, the contract must satisfy the requirements of Code Section 408(b) regarding individual retirement annuities and there must be separate accounting for the interest of each participant in those cases where the individual retirement annuities are held under a single annuity contract. [Treas. Reg. § 1.408(q)-1(f)(2)(iii)]

Q 3:89   May life insurance be purchased in a deemed IRA?

No. A life insurance contract is not permitted to be purchased or held in any type of IRA. Permitting deemed IRAs that are individual retirement accounts to be held in a single trust that includes the qualified employer plan raises the issue of whether, if the qualified employer plan portion of the trust invests in life insurance contracts, the deemed IRA would be considered to have violated Code Section 408(a)(3), which provides that "no part of the trust funds will be invested in life insurance contracts." However, in that case, Code Section 408(a)(3) is treated as satisfied if no part of the separate account of any of the deemed IRAs is invested in life insurance contracts. [I.R.C. § 408(a)(3), 408(b); Treas. Reg. § 1.408(q)-1(f)(2)(i)–(iii)]

Q 3:90   May an individual deduct his or her contributions to a deemed IRA?

It depends. The deductibility of voluntary employee contributions to a traditional deemed IRA is determined in the same manner as if they were made to any other traditional IRA. Thus, for example, taxpayers with compensation that exceeds the limits imposed by Code Section 219(g) may not be able to make contributions to deemed IRAs, or the deductibility of such contributions may be limited in accordance with Code Sections 408 and 219(g). However, Code Section 219(f)(5), regarding the taxable year in which amounts paid by an employer to an individual retirement plan are includible in the employee's income, is not applicable to deemed IRAs. [Treas. Reg. § 1.408(q)-1(f)(4)]

Q 3:91 May a trust that includes deemed IRAs and a qualified employer plan (or Roth and traditional IRAs) be segmented for other purposes?

The requirements for separate accounts within a trust are not meant to imply that a trust that includes deemed IRAs and a qualified employer plan (or Roth and traditional IRAs) can be segmented for other purposes. For example, where a qualified employer plan and deemed IRAs are included in the same trust, there cannot be separate trustees for each account, and the trustee for the trust must be either a bank or a nonbank trustee that satisfies the requirements of Code Section 408(a)(2).

Q 3:92 Would the failure of either the qualified employer plan portion or the deemed IRA portion of the plan to satisfy the applicable qualification rules of each cause the other portion to be automatically disqualified?

It depends. The failure of either the qualified employer plan portion or the deemed IRA portion of the plan to satisfy the applicable qualification rules of each will not cause the other portion to be automatically disqualified. This rule applies, however, only if the deemed IRA portion and the qualified employer plan portion are maintained as separate trusts (or separate annuity contracts, as required in the case of individual retirement annuities). If both the deemed IRA portion and the qualified plan portion are included in separate trusts and the qualified employer plan is disqualified, the IRA portion cannot be a deemed IRA under Code Section 408(q). Nevertheless, it will not fail to satisfy the applicable requirements of Sections 408 or 408A if it satisfies the applicable requirements of those sections, including, with respect to individual retirement accounts, the requirements of Section 408(a)(5) regarding commingling. However, if the IRA assets and the non-IRA assets have been commingled (except in a common trust fund or common investment fund as permitted by Code Section 408(a)(5)), the IRA portion will fail to satisfy the requirements of Code Section 408(a). Likewise, if the IRA assets and the non-IRA assets are commingled (except as permitted by Code Section 408(a)(5), and the IRA is disqualified, the plan will also be disqualified. [Treas. Reg. § 1.408(q)-1(g)(1), (2)]

Q 3:93 To what extent do the fiduciary duties under ERISA apply to deemed IRAs and deemed Roth IRAs?

The DOL "advised the IRS and Treasury that consistent with section 4(c) of the Employee Retirement Income Security Act (ERISA), accounts and annuities (and contributions thereto) established in accordance with Section 408(q) of the Code are not to be treated as part of the pension plan under which such accounts and annuities are allowed (or as a separate pension plan) for purposes of any provision of [title I of ERISA] other than Section 403(c), 404, or 405 (relating to exclusive benefit, and fiduciary and co-fiduciary responsibilities) and part 5 (relating to administration and enforcement)." Accordingly, fiduciaries need to take appropriate steps to ensure that they satisfy any fiduciary duties associated with implementation and operation of a deemed IRA feature that is related to a plan covered under title I of ERISA. These duties may include, but are not limited to, a duty to monitor the activities of holders of deemed IRAs in order to prevent disqualification of the deemed IRA feature and/or the qualified employer plan where the plan is intended to be maintained as a tax-qualified plan. [*See* Treas. Reg. § 1.408(q)-1, Explanation of Provisions and Summary of Comments, footnote 1, 69 Fed. Reg. 140, 43735 (July 22, 2004)]

Q 3:94   Who may serve as the trustee of a deemed IRA?

The trustee of the deemed IRA must be a bank or a nonbank trustee approved by the IRS. However, several requirements set forth in the regulations would be difficult for a government to satisfy. However, a governmental unit can serve as the trustee of any deemed IRA established by that governmental unit as part of its qualified employer plan if that governmental unit establishes to the satisfaction of the IRS that the manner in which it will administer the deemed IRA will be consistent with the requirements of Code Section 408 regarding IRAs. [Treas. Reg. § 1.408-2(e); Temp. Treas. Reg. § 1.408-2T(8), which also provides special rules regarding the application of Treas. Reg. § 1.408-2(e) to governmental units]

For example, Treasury Regulations Section 1.408-2(e)(5)(v), regarding IRS approval as a nonbank bank, requires that an applicant must demonstrate that, except for investments pooled in a common investment fund, the investments of each account will not be commingled with any other property. This requirement is inconsistent with the provisions of Section 408(q)(1), which provide that the requirements of Section 408(a)(5) regarding commingling do not apply to deemed IRAs. However, Treasury Regulations Section 1.408-2(e)(5)(v) provides that an applicant that intends to serve as a nonbank trustee need not satisfy this requirement with respect to any assets held in a deemed IRA. [Treas. Reg. § 1.408-2(e)(5)(v), as amended (69 Fed. Reg. 140, 43739 (July 22, 2004)]

In addition, a governmental unit need not demonstrate that it satisfies the net worth requirements if it demonstrates instead that it possesses taxing authority under applicable law. [Treas. Reg. § 1.408-2(e)(3)(ii)] The Commissioner, in his discretion, may exempt a governmental unit from certain other requirements upon a showing that the governmental unit is able to administer the deemed IRAs in the best interest of the participants. Moreover, in determining whether a governmental unit satisfies the other requirements of Treasury Regulations Section 1.408-2(e)(2) to (e)(6), the Commissioner may apply the requirements in a manner that is consistent with the applicant's status as a governmental unit. [Treas. Reg. § 1.408-2T(a)(8)(i), (iii)]

Q 3:95   Who may participate in a deemed IRA?

It depends upon the type of plan. The term employee is not defined by Section 408(q) regarding deemed IRAs. However, Code Section 408(q)(3)(B) defines a "voluntary employee contribution," in part, as a contribution by an individual "as an employee under a qualified employer plan which allows employees" to elect to make contributions to a separate account under the plan. Thus, to the extent a self-employed individual is an employee for purposes of the qualified employer plan, that individual will be treated as an employee for purposes of a deemed IRA within that plan. In the case of a qualified plan under Code Section 401(a) and a qualified annuity plan under Section 403(a), employee includes self-employed individuals as defined in Code Section 401(c). The only circumstance under which a self-employed individual may participate in a Section 403(b) plan is when a self-employed minister described in Code Section 414(e)(5) participates in a retirement income account as described in Section 403(b)(9). In contrast, Section 457(e)(2) permits independent contractors as well as employees to participate in a Section 457 plan. However, because Code Section 408(q) permits only employees to make contributions to a deemed IRA, only employees (including self-employed individuals) may be permitted to participate in a deemed IRA maintained by a governmental Code Section 457 plan. [Treas. Reg. § 1.408(q)-1(h)(3)]

Q 3:96   May an employee participate in a deemed IRA if he or she does not participate in the underlying employer plan, or even if the employee is not eligible to participate in the underlying employer plan?

There is no requirement that an employee must participate in both portions of the plan or that an employee must be eligible to participate in both portions of the plan (which are generally treated as separate entities). Accordingly, the two portions of the plan may have different eligibility requirements. [I.R.C. § 408(q)]

Q 3:97   May the automatic enrollment principles applicable to Section 401(k), 403(b), and 457 plans be applied to deemed IRAs?

Yes. The automatic enrollment principles applicable to Code Section 401(k), 403(b), and 457 plans under Revenue Rulings 2000-8 [2000-1 C.B. 617], 2000-35 [2000-2 C.B. 138], and 2000-33 [2000-2 C.B. 142] apply to deemed IRAs. These revenue rulings specify the criteria to be met in order for an employee's compensation to be automatically reduced by a certain amount where that amount is contributed as an elective deferral to these three types of plans. [*See* Treas. Reg. § 1.408(q)-1, Explanation of Provisions and Summary of Comments, Part E, 69 Fed. Reg. 140, 43735 (July 22, 2004)]

Q 3:98   May an employer take deemed IRA assets or benefits into account for other purposes under the plan?

No. Neither the assets held in the deemed IRA portion of the qualified employer plan, nor any benefits attributable thereto, are taken into account for purposes of determining the benefits of employees and their beneficiaries under the plan (within the meaning of Code Section 401(a)(2)) or determining the plan's assets or liabilities for purposes of Code Section 404 regarding deductions, or Section 412 regarding minimum funding standards.

Q 3:99   Are deemed IRAs covered or insured by the PBGC?

No. The Pension Benefit Guaranty Corporation (PBGC) has advised the IRS and Treasury that a deemed IRA feature that is related to a qualified employer plan is not covered by Title IV of ERISA. The PBGC has further advised that the deemed IRA feature is treated as a separate entity from the qualified employer plan for purposes of Title IV. For example, neither the assets in, nor the benefits attributable to, the deemed IRA are taken into account in determining the amount of the PBGC's variable-rate premium, and an individual who is a participant in the deemed IRA but who is not a participant in the qualified employer plan is not included in the PBGC's flat-rate participant count. In addition, for purposes of Title IV, the deemed IRA will be treated as separate from the qualified employer plan in the event of termination of the qualified employer plan, and the fiduciary of the deemed IRA would continue to be responsible for the continued operation, transfer, or termination of the deemed IRA. The PBGC would allocate the assets of the qualified employer plan to the priority categories under Section 4044 of ERISA without regard to any assets in, or benefits attributable to, the deemed IRA, and the PBGC would not serve as trustee of the deemed IRA. Termination of a deemed IRA would not be subject to the rules governing plan termination under Title IV of ERISA.

Q 3:100   Do the employer plan distribution rules apply to deemed IRAs?

No. Rules applicable to distributions from qualified employer plans under the Code and regulations do not apply to distributions from deemed IRAs. Instead, the rules applicable to distributions from IRAs or Roth IRAs apply to distributions from deemed IRAs. Also, any restrictions that a trustee, custodian, or insurance company is permitted to impose on distributions from traditional and Roth IRAs may be imposed on distributions from deemed IRAs (e.g., early withdrawal penalties on annuities). The required minimum distribution rules of Code Section 401(a)(9) must be met separately with respect to the qualified employer plan and the deemed IRA. The determination of whether a qualified employer plan satisfies the required minimum distribution rules of Code Section 401(a)(9) is made without regard to whether a participant satisfies the required minimum distribution requirements with respect to the deemed IRA that is established under such plan.

Q 3:101   Are deemed Roth IRAs portable?

Yes. Deemed Roth IRAs (see Q 3:81) are portable for rollover or direct rollover purposes either to another employer's plan that accepts deemed Roth 401(k) or deemed Roth 403(b) contribution accounts, or to the individual's own Roth IRA. [I.R.C. § 408(q)(1)] The same rules apply to rollovers and transfers to and from deemed IRAs as apply to rollovers and transfers to and from other

IRAs. Thus, for example, the plan may provide that an employee may request and receive a distribution of his or her deemed IRA account balance and may roll it over to an eligible retirement plan (in accordance with Code Section 408(d)(3)), regardless of whether that employee may receive a distribution of any other plan benefits. [Treas. Reg. § 1.408(q)-1(f)(5)]

> **Practice Pointer.** Distributions made after 2001 from a traditional IRA can be rolled over into the individual's qualified plan, 403(b) annuity or custodial account plan, or governmental 457(b) plan. This rule applies to all amounts in a traditional IRA (except nondeductible contributions), including a conduit IRA, SEP IRA, and a SIMPLE IRA (but only after the two-year period applicable to the SIMPLE IRA has expired). This rule does not apply to a Roth IRA unless the amount is rolled over into another Roth IRA, or if the amount is received after 2002, into a deemed Roth IRA maintained by an employer. [I.R.C. §§ 408(d)(3)(A), 408(d)(3)(D)(i)]

Q 3:102 May a governmental unit serve as the trustee of a deemed Roth IRA that is part of its qualified plan?

Yes. A governmental unit may serve as the trustee of a deemed Roth IRA (or traditional deemed IRA) established by that governmental unit as part of its qualified employer plan if that governmental unit establishes, in accordance with regulations, that the manner in which it will administer the deemed IRA (or Roth IRA) will be consistent with Code Section 408. Special rules apply regarding the application of Treasury Regulations Section 1.408-2(e) to governmental units. [Treas. Reg. § 1.408(q)-1; Temp. Treas. Reg. § 1.408-2T, regarding governmental units that seek to qualify as a nonbank trustee of a deemed Roth IRA (or a deemed traditional IRA)]

Q 3:103 Can a deemed Roth IRA be used to receive a conversion contribution?

Yes. The rules regarding the designation and redesignation (conversion and reconversion) of an IRA as a Roth IRA (see chapter 2) apply to deemed IRAs as if the separate accounts maintained for the deemed Roth IRAs and deemed traditional IRAs were separate trusts. [Treas. Reg. §§ 1.408(q)-1(f)(5), 1.408A-2, 1.408A-4]

Rollover of Military Death Gratuities and SGLI Payments

Q 3:104 What are military death gratuities?

Federal law provides for the payment of a military death gratuity to an eligible survivor of a service member. [10 U.S.C. § 1477] The full amount of the military death gratuity is excludable from gross income. [I.R.C. § 134]

Q 3:105   What are SGLI military death gratuities?

Federal law provides that certain members of the uniformed services are automatically insured against death under the SGLI program. [38 U.S.C. § 1967] In general, life insurance proceeds are excludable from gross income. [I.R.C. § 101]

Q 3:106   Are contributions of military death gratuities and SGLI to a Roth IRA treated as a rollover?

Yes. The contribution of a military death gratuity or SGLI payment to a Roth IRA is treated as a qualified rollover contribution to the Roth IRA. Similarly, the contribution of a military death gratuity or SGLI payment to a Coverdell ESA is treated as a permissible rollover to such an account. [I.R.C. § 408A(e)(2)(A)]

Q 3:107   When are the rules that permit contributions of military death gratuity and SGLI payments to be rolled over effective?

The rules that permit military death gratuity and SGLI payments to be rolled over is generally effective with respect to payments made on account of deaths from injuries occurring on or after June 17, 2008, the date of the Heroes Earnings Assistance and Relief Tax (HEART) Act's enactment. In addition, the provision permits the contribution to a Roth IRA (or a Coverdell ESA) of a military death gratuity or SGLI payment received by an individual with respect to a death from an injury occurring on or after October 7, 2001, and before June 17, 2008 (the date of enactment) if the individual makes the contribution to the account no later than June 17, 2009 (the date that is one year after the date of enactment of the provision).

[HEART Act, § 109(d) (Pub. L. No. 110-245)]

Q 3:108   Is there a limit on how much of a military death gratuity or SGLI payment can be rolled over to a Roth IRA?

Yes. In the case of an individual who receives a military death gratuity or SGLI payment, the individual may contribute an amount that is no greater than the sum of the military death gratuity and SGLI payments received by the individual to a Roth IRA, notwithstanding the contribution limits that otherwise apply to contributions to Roth IRAs (e.g., the annual contribution limit and the income phaseout of the contribution dollar limit). [I.R.C. § 408A(e)(2)(A)(i)]

In addition, the maximum amount that can be contributed to a Roth IRA or one or more Coverdell ESAs in the aggregate is limited to the sum of the military death gratuity and SGLI payments that the individual receives. [I.R.C. § 408A(e)(2)(A)(ii)]

Q 3:109   How are distributions of rolled over military death gratuity or SGLI payments treated?

In the event of a subsequent distribution from a Roth IRA that is not a qualified distribution (see Q 4:11), the amount of the distribution attributable to the contribution of the military death gratuity or SGLI payment is treated as a nontaxable investment in the contract (see Qs 4:1, 4:10). [I.R.C. § 408A(e)(2)(C)]

Q 3:110   Must a rollover of a military death gratuity or SGLI payment be made within 60 days of receipt?

No. The contribution of a military death gratuity or SGLI payment to a Roth IRA (or Coverdell ESA) must be made within a one-year period. Thus, they cannot be made later than one year after the date on which the gratuity or SGLI payment is received by the individual. [I.R.C. § 408A(e)(2)(B)]

Q 3:111   Are rollovers of military death gratuities and SGLI payments permitted to be made more than once in a 12-month period?

Yes. The annual limit on the number of rollovers does not apply to contributions of military death gratuities or SGLI payments that are treated as rollovers. [I.R.C. § 408A(e)(1), last sentence referring to I.R.C.§ 408(d)(3)(B)]

Rollover of Exxon Valdez Settlement

Q 3:112   Can an Exxon Valdez settlement be rolled over to a Roth IRA?

Yes. Section 504 of the Tax Extenders and Alternative Minimum Tax Relief Act of 2008, enacted as part of the Emergency Economic Stabilization Act of 2008, permits all or part of the amount received (up to an aggregate of $100,000) to be contributed to an eligible retirement plan that includes a Roth IRA. [I.R.C. §§ 402(c)(8)(B), 408A(e)(2)(B)]

Q 3:113   Is there a limit to how much may be contributed to an eligible retirement plan?

Yes. The amount contributed cannot exceed $100,000 (reduced by the amount of qualified settlement income contributed to an eligible retirement plan in prior tax years) or the amount of qualified settlement income received during the tax year.

Q 3:114　When must an Exxon Valdez settlement be contributed to an eligible retirement plan?

Subject to the $100,000 aggregate limit, contributions received during the year may be contributed to an eligible retirement plan until the taxpayer's return due date, not including extensions for the taxable year.

Q 3:115　When is a Roth rollover of an Exxon Valdez settlement included in gross income?

If the settlement is contributed to a retirement plan or IRA (other than a Roth IRA or designated Roth account), the amount is not taxable and is considered pretax money in the retirement account. If contributed to a Roth IRA or designated Roth account, the amount is taxable.

Q 3:116　How is a contribution of an Exxon Valdez settlement to a retirement plan treated?

The contribution is considered an eligible rollover into the receiving plan or IRA and becomes after-tax assets (e.g., basis) in the account.

Q 3:117　Do the 60-day rollover restriction and one rollover-per-12-month rules apply to a contribution of an Exxon Valdez settlement to an eligible retirement plan?

No. The 60-day rollover restriction and the one rollover-per-12-month rule for IRA rollovers do not apply to contributions of an Exxon Valdez settlement contributed to an eligible retirement plan.

Q 3:118　Is there an income or filing restriction applicable to contributions of an Exxon Valdez settlement to an eligible retirement plan?

No. The Roth IRA income and joint tax filing restrictions for conversion rollovers do not apply to an Exxon Valdez settlement that is contributed (rolled over) to a Roth IRA or other eligible retirement plan.

Qualified Reservist Distribution Repayments

Q 3:119　May an individual who receives a qualified reservist distribution from a Roth IRA or designated Roth account recontribute that distribution to a Roth IRA?

Yes. An individual who receives a qualified reservist distribution (see Q 3:122) from a Roth IRA may generally recontribute that distribution to a Roth IRA (see Q 3:124). [I.R.C. §§ 72(t)(2)(G)(i), 408A] Recontributions of qualified reservist distributions from a designated Roth contribution account under an employer's 401(k) or 403(b) plan are more fully discussed in chapter 10.

Note. A repayment of qualified reservist distributions to a Roth IRA increases the basis in the Roth IRA by the amount of the repayment (see Q 4:1).

Q 3:120   Do the Roth IRA annual contributions limits apply to qualified reservist distributions that are repaid?

No. The dollar limitations otherwise applicable to contributions to a Roth IRA (see Q 2:1) do not apply to any repayment (contribution) of a qualified reservist distribution. No deduction is allowed for any contribution of a qualified reservist distribution.

Q 3:121   Is a qualified reservist distribution taxable?

Maybe. The taxability of a qualified reservist distribution depends upon the plan type making the distribution. In the case of a Roth IRA, special ordering rules apply, and contributions previously made may be withdrawn tax-free and without penalty (see Qs 3:120, 4:1).

Q 3:122   What is a qualified reservist distribution?

A qualified reservist distribution is a distribution (1) from an IRA or Roth IRA or attributable to elective deferrals under a 401(k) plan, 403(b) annuity, (2) made to an individual who is a reservist or national guardsman (as defined in 37 U.S.C. Section 101(2)) and was ordered or called to active duty for a period in excess of 179 days or for an indefinite period, and (3) that is made during the period beginning on the date of such order or call to duty and ending at the close of the active duty period. A qualified reservist distribution cannot be made from a SARSEP, or SIMPLE IRA. [I.R.C. § 72(t)(2)(G)(iii)]

Note. This provision originally applied to individuals ordered or called to active duty after September 11, 2001, and before December 31, 2007. The HEART Act makes the rules applicable to qualified reservist distributions permanent. Thus, they now apply to individuals ordered or called to active duty after December 31, 2007. [I.R.C. § 72(t)(2)(G)(iv), as amended]

Q 3:123   Does the 10 percent early withdrawal tax apply to a qualified reservist distribution?

No. The 10 percent early withdrawal tax does not apply to a qualified reservist distribution. [I.R.C. § 72(t)(2)(G)]

Q 3:124 When must a qualified reservist distribution be repaid to a Roth IRA?

An individual who receives a qualified reservist distribution from a Roth IRA may, at any time during the two-year period beginning on the day after the end of the active duty period, make one or more contributions to a Roth IRA of such individual in an aggregate amount not to exceed the amount of such distribution. [I.R.C. § 72(t)(2)(G)(ii)]

Note. The two-year period for making recontributions of qualified reservist distributions does not end before August 17, 2008, the date that is two years after the date the PPA was enacted. If refund or credit of any overpayment of tax resulting from the provision would be prevented at any time before the close of the one-year period beginning on the date of the enactment by the operation of any law or rule of law (including res judicata), such refund or credit may nevertheless be made or allowed if claim therefor is filed before the close of such period. [PPA § 827(c); I.R.C. § 72(t)(2)(G), as amended by PPA § 827(a)]

Example 1. Alexis, a qualified reservist, was called to active duty on January 1, 2008. For personal reasons, Alexis takes an IRA distribution on September 14, 2009. The 10 percent penalty tax for early withdrawal will not apply. Assuming that Alexis is relieved of active duty on May 20, 2009, she will have until May 20, 2011 (the later of two years after the date of enactment or two years after the end of her active duty) to roll over the 2009 distribution amount and avoid having to pay federal income tax.

Example 2. Laura, age 35, made annual contributions of $12,000 to a Roth IRA over the last few years. In 2009, Laura receives a qualified reservist distribution of $6,000 which she would like to repay. She may contribute $11,000 to a Roth IRA (the regular contribution limit of $5,000, plus the $6,000 qualified reservist distribution) for 2009.

Qualified Hurricane Distribution Repayments

Q 3:125 May qualified hurricane distributions be repaid to a Roth IRA?

Possibly. Most qualified hurricane distributions (see Q 3:126) from a Roth IRA are eligible for repayment to a Roth IRA. [I.R.C. § 1400Q(a)(3)(C)] Payments received as a beneficiary are not eligible for repayment.

For distributions eligible for repayment, the owner has three years from the day after the date he or she received the distribution from the Roth IRA to repay all or part to another Roth IRA. [I.R.C. § 1400Q(a)(3)(A)] Amounts removed after 2006 do not qualify for qualified hurricane distribution treatments (see Q 3:126). Thus, a repayment of a qualified hurricane distribution must be made before 2010.

Note. A qualified hurricane distribution from a Roth IRA may only be repaid to another Roth IRA. On the other hand, a qualified hurricane distribution from a designated Roth account (DRA) may be repaid to another DRA or to a Roth IRA. [Treas. Reg. § 1.402A-10, Q&A 5]

Example. Dixie receives a qualified hurricane distribution from her IRA. The repayment would be treated as a direct rollover (see Q 3:131). If repayment is made to a Roth IRA, it would be treated as a rollover conversion (see Q 3:4) with the taxable amount (if any) treated as being rolled over first.

Q 3:126   What was a qualified hurricane distribution?

A qualified hurricane distribution was any distribution from an eligible retirement plan attributable to elective deferrals (including an IRA and Roth IRA) if all of the following conditions apply. [I.R.C. § 1400Q(a)(4)(A)]

1. The distribution was made:
   (a) After August 24, 2005, and before January 1, 2007, for Hurricane Katrina.
   (b) After September 22, 2005, and before January 1, 2007, for Hurricane Rita.
   (c) After October 22, 2005, and before January 1, 2007, for Hurricane Wilma.
2. The taxpayer's main home was located in a qualified hurricane disaster area listed below on the date shown for that area.
   (a) August 28, 2005, for the Hurricane Katrina disaster area. For this purpose, the Hurricane Katrina disaster area includes the states of Alabama, Louisiana, and Mississippi.
   (b) September 23, 2005, for the Hurricane Rita disaster area. For this purpose, the Hurricane Rita disaster area includes the states of Louisiana and Texas.
   (c) October 23, 2005, for the Hurricane Wilma disaster area. For this purpose, the Hurricane Wilma disaster area includes the state of Florida.

The taxpayer sustained an economic loss because of Hurricane Katrina, Rita, or Wilma and his or her main home was in that hurricane disaster area on the date shown in item (2) for that hurricane. Examples of an economic loss include, but are not limited to, (a) loss, damage to, or destruction of real or personal property from fire, flooding, looting, vandalism, theft, wind, or other cause; (b) loss related to displacement of main home; or (c) loss of livelihood due to temporary or permanent layoffs.

If all these conditions are met, the distribution can be designated (including periodic payments and required minimum distributions) as a qualified hurricane distribution, regardless of whether the distribution was made on account of Hurricane Katrina, Rita, or Wilma. Qualified hurricane distributions are permitted without regard to the taxpayer's need or the actual amount of economic loss.

Note. A qualified hurricane distribution is subject to the income tax withholding rules applicable to distributions which are *not* eligible rollover distributions (except for a distribution which would be treated as a qualified distribution, see Qs 4:9, 4:23). Thus, the 20-percent mandatory income tax withholding rules do not apply. [I.R.C. §§ 1400Q(a)(6)(A), 3405]

[*See also* I.R.S. Pub. 1460, Highlights of Tax Relief provided to Taxpayers in response to Hurricanes Katrina, Rita and Wilma *and* Pub. 4492, Information for Taxpayers Affected by Hurricanes Katrina, Rita, and Wilma, for additional information]

Q 3:127 Why would a taxpayer want to file an amended return following a repayment of a qualified hurricane distribution to a Roth IRA?

If, after filing the original return, a repayment was made, the repayment may reduce the amount of the qualified hurricane distributions that were previously included in income (if any). Depending on when a repayment was made, an amended tax return may have to be filed to refigure taxable income. File Form 1040X, Amended U.S. Individual Income Tax Return, to amend a return already filed. Generally, Form 1040X must be filed within three years after the date the original return was filed, or within two years after the date the tax was paid, whichever is later. [*See* I.R.S. Pub. 590, Individual Retirement Arrangements, "Hurricane-Related Relief"]

Q 3:128 How was the taxable portion of a qualified hurricane distribution from a Roth IRA treated?

If a qualified hurricane distribution was received from a Roth IRA, the taxable amount (e.g., a nonqualified distribution that includes any gain; see Q 4:12) was included in income in equal amounts over three years. For example, if $15,000 of a qualified hurricane distribution was taxable and received in 2006 (the last year for making such distributions), the owner would include $5,000 in his or her income in 2006, 2007, and 2008. However, the owner can elect to include the entire distribution in taxable income in the year it was received. [I.R.C. § 1400Q(a)(5)] Unless earnings (gain) were distributed from a Roth IRA in a qualified hurricane distribution, none of the amount distributed would be taxable.

Q 3:129 Did the 10 percent early withdrawal tax under Code Section 72(t) apply to a qualified hurricane distribution?

No. The 10 percent early withdrawal tax did not apply to a qualified hurricane distribution. [I.R.C. § 1400Q(a)(1)] Form 8915, Qualified Hurricane Retirement Plan Distributions and Repayments, was used to report hurricane distributions and repayments.

Q 3:130 How much of a qualified hurricane distribution can be repaid?

The total amount repaid cannot be more than the amount of the qualified hurricane distributions. Distributions can only be treated as qualified hurricane distributions to the extent they do not exceed $100,000. [I.R.C. § 1400Q(a)(2)(A)]

Example. In 2005, Harriet received a distribution of $50,000 from her Roth IRA. In 2006, she receives another distribution of $125,000. Both distributions meet the requirements for a qualified hurricane distribution. If Harriet decides to treat the entire $50,000 received in 2005 as a qualified hurricane distribution, only $50,000 of the 2006 distribution could be treated as a qualified hurricane distribution.

Q 3:131 How is a repayment of a qualified hurricane distribution treated?

A repayment of a qualified hurricane distribution to a Roth IRA is first considered to be a repayment of earnings. Any repayment of a qualified hurricane distribution in excess of earnings will increase the basis in the Roth IRA by the amount of the repayment in excess of earnings. No deduction is allowed. Amounts repaid are treated as a qualified rollover and are not included in the owner's income. Thus, a Roth IRA owner may have to file an amended federal income tax return if any portion of the Roth distribution treated as a qualified hurricane distribution was included in taxable income and subsequently repaid (see Q 3:127). The repayment is treated as a direct trustee-to-trustee transfer within 60 days of the distribution. [I.R.C. § 1400Q(a)(3)(C)] Unless earnings (gain) were distributed from a Roth IRA in a qualified hurricane distribution, none of the amount distributed would be taxable.

Example 1. In 2006, Lalit takes a $30,000 qualified hurricane distribution from a Roth IRA. The $30,000 is the total value of the Roth IRA. He has $20,000 in basis (contributions) and $10,000 represents earnings. He elects to include the entire distribution in income for 2006. In 2006, he reports the distribution on Form 8606, Nondeductible IRAs, and Form 8915, Qualified Hurricane Retirement Plan Distributions and Repayments, and determines that the taxable portion of the distribution is $10,000 ($30,000 − $20,000).

In 2009, Lalit makes a $15,000 repayment of the 2006 qualified hurricane distribution to his Roth IRA. He will file an amended return for 2006 for the $10,000 taxable portion of the distribution that was included in income: $5,000 of the $15,000 repayment will represent basis in his Roth IRA for future distributions, and $10,000 will be included in income when distributed in the future.

Example 2. In 2006, Annabelle takes a $30,000 qualified hurricane distribution from a deductible traditional IRA. She elects to include the entire distribution in income for 2006.

In 2009, Annabelle makes a $20,000 repayment of the 2006 qualified hurricane distribution to her Roth IRA. Annabelle's basis in her Roth IRA will be increased by $20,000.

Qualified Recovery Assistance Distributions Repayments (Kansas Disaster Area)

Retroactive rules provide for tax-favored withdrawals, repayments, and loans from certain retirement plans for taxpayers who suffered economic losses in 24 disaster-area counties as a result of the Greensboro, Kansas, storms and tornadoes that began on May 4, 2007. Included are Barton, Clay, Cloud, Comanche, Dickinson, Edwards, Ellsworth, Kiowa, Leavenworth, Lyon, McPherson, Osage, Osborne, Ottawa, Phillips, Pottawatomie, Pratt, Reno, Rice, Riley, Saline, Shawnee, Smith, and Stafford counties. These relief provisions are described in Publication 4492-A, Information for Taxpayers Affected by the May 4, 2007, Kansas Storms and Tornadoes.

[Heartland, Habitat, Harvest, and Horticulture Act of 2008 (Pub. L. 100-246), §§ 15345(a)(7), 15345(d)(5), providing relief similar to the relief provided in I.R.C. § 1400Q with respect to use of retirement plan assets (see list of "substitutions" to I.R.C. § 1400Q in amendment note to I.R.C. § 1400N(d): I.R.S. Notice KS-MO 2008-33 (July 9, 2008); *see also* I.R.S. Pub. 4492-A—Casualty and Theft Losses. For more information on additional disaster relief and current disaster relief locations, *see* IRS Notices at http://www.irs.gov/newsroom/article/0,,id = 108362,00.html (visited on June 23, 2009).]

Q 3:132   May qualified recovery assistance distributions be repaid?

Yes. In general, any portion of a qualified recovery assistance distribution (see Qs 3:137, 3:149) that is eligible for tax-free rollover treatment to an eligible retirement plan (see Q 3:141) may be repaid. A qualified recovery assistance distribution made because of a hardship from a retirement plan may also be repaid. However, the following types of distributions may not be repaid:

- Qualified disaster recovery assistance distributions received as a beneficiary (other than a surviving spouse)
- RMDs
- Periodic payments (other than from an IRA-based plan) that are for:
  - A period of 10 years or more,
  - Made over the taxpayer's life or life expectancy, or
  - Made over the joint lives or joint life expectancies of the taxpayer and his or her beneficiary.

Q 3:133   How much time does a taxpayer have to repay qualified recovery assistance distributions?

The repayment period for a qualified recovery assistance distribution is three years. The three-year period starts on the day after the date the distribution was received. Thus, the day of distribution is not counted.

Example. Donna received a qualified recovery assistance distribution on November 1, 2008. The distribution may be repaid by Donna (or her surviving spouse) on or before November 1, 2011 (the end of the third-year period that began on November 2). [*See* Minasyan v. Mukasey, No. 06-73192 (9th Cir. Jan. 20, 2009), regarding the term "after the date" (on another matter)]

Q 3:134   Are qualified recovery assistance distributions included in income?

Possibly. A qualified recovery assistance distribution (of gain only in the case of a Roth IRA, see Q 4:1) is included in income, in equal amounts, over three years, unless an election is made to include the entire distribution in income the year it was received.

Note. If a qualified recovery assistance distribution is repaid to a Roth IRA, the repayment is first considered to be a repayment of earnings. Any repayment of qualified recovery assistance distributions in excess of earnings will increase the taxpayer's basis in the Roth IRA by the amount of the repayment in excess of earnings (see Q 1.11). If repayment is made to a Roth IRA from a non-Roth account, it would be treated as a rollover conversion.

Q 3:135   Is the repayment of a qualified recovery assistance distribution taxable?

No. Amounts that are repaid are treated as a qualified rollover and are not included in income. The taxpayer may have to file an amended return (see Q 3:134).

Note 1. A repayment to an IRA or Roth IRA is not counted when figuring the one-rollover-per-year limit.

Note 2. The repayment to a Roth IRA from a non-Roth account is treated as a rollover conversion.

Q 3:136   Is a qualified recovery assistance distribution subject to the 10- or 25-percent additional tax penalty on early distributions?

No. Although possibly taxable (see Q 3:135), a qualified recovery assistance distribution is not subject to the additional 10 percent tax (or the additional 25 percent tax for certain distributions from a SIMPLE IRA) on early distributions. The taxable amount is figured in the same manner as other IRA distributions.

However, the distribution is included in income over three years unless the taxpayer elects to report the entire amount in the year of distribution.

> **Note.** If the distribution is repaid, the taxpayer is not taxed on the distributions. It may be necessary to file amended tax returns. [*See* Pub. 4492-A, Information for Taxpayers Affected by the May 4, 2007, Kansas Storms and Tornadoes]

Q 3:137 What is a "qualified recovery assistance distribution"?

A qualified recovery assistance distribution is any distribution received and designated as such from an eligible retirement plan if all of the following apply.

1. The distribution was made after May 3, 2007, and before January 1, 2009.
2. The taxpayer's main home was located in the Kansas disaster area on May 4, 2007.
3. An economic loss because of the storms and tornadoes was sustained. Examples of an economic loss include, but are not limited to:
   (a) Loss, damage to, or destruction of real or personal property from fire, flooding, looting, vandalism, theft, wind, or other cause;
   (b) Loss related to displacement from the taxpayer's home; or
   (c) Loss of livelihood due to temporary or permanent layoffs.

> **Note 1.** Generally, any distribution (including periodic payments and required minimum distributions) from an eligible retirement plan can be designated as a qualified recovery assistance distribution, regardless of whether the distribution was made on account of the storms or tornadoes.

> **Caution.** Not all qualified recovery assistance distribution can be repaid (see Q 3:132).

> **Note 2.** A qualified recovery assistance distribution is subject to the income tax withholding rules applicable to distributions which are not eligible rollover distributions (except for a distribution which would be treated as a qualified distributions, see Qs 4:9, 4:23). Thus, the 20-percent mandatory income tax withholding rules do not apply. [I.R.C. §§ 1400Q(a)(6)(A), 3405]

Q 3:138 What is a taxpayer's main home?

Generally, a taxpayer's main home for qualified recovery assistance distribution purposes is the taxpayer's main home where he or she lives most of the time. A temporary absence due to special circumstances, such as illness, education, business, military service, evacuation, or vacation, will not be considered a change in the taxpayer's main home.

Q 3:139 Are qualified recovery assistance distributions limited to need or the actual amount of loss?

No. Qualified recovery assistance distributions are permitted without regard to need or the actual amount of economic loss.

Q 3:140 Are qualified recovery assistance distributions limited in amount?

Yes. The total of all qualified recovery assistance distributions from all plans is limited to $100,000. If there are distributions in excess of $100,000 from more than one type of plan, the $100,000 limit can be allocated among the plans any way the taxpayer chooses.

Note. A reduction or offset after May 3, 2007, of an account balance in an eligible retirement plan in order to repay a loan can also be designated as a qualified recovery assistance distribution. A distribution of a plan loan offset can occur for a variety of reasons, such as when a participant terminates employment or does not comply with the terms of repayment. Plan loan offsets are treated as actual distributions and are reported in box 1 of Form 1099-R, Distributions From Pensions, Annuities, Retirement or Profit-Sharing Plans, IRAs, Insurance Contracts, etc., but are not eligible for special tax treatment (i.e., 10-year forward income averaging or the 20 percent capital gains election).

Q 3:141 What is an "eligible retirement plan?"

Qualified recovery assistance distributions can be made from and repaid to any eligible retirement plan. For this purpose, the term eligible retirement plan means any of the following:

- A qualified pension, profit-sharing, or stock bonus plan (including a 401(k) plan).
- A qualified annuity plan.
- A tax-sheltered annuity contract.
- An eligible governmental 457(b) deferred compensation plan.
- A traditional, SEP, SIMPLE, or Roth IRA.

Q 3:142 May a distribution from an eligible retirement plan be designated as a qualified recovery assistance distribution?

The reporting rules are rather complex and depend upon the year (2007 or 2008) that the qualified recovery assistance distributions was received.

2007 qualified recovery assistance distributions. If a distribution was received after May 3, 2007, from an eligible retirement plan, it may be able to be designated as a qualified recovery assistance distribution (see the following paragraph). Detailed instructions for reporting these distributions on Form

8915, Qualified Hurricane Retirement Plan Distributions and Repayments, and Form 8606, Nondeductible IRAs, are provided in Publication 4492-A, Information for Taxpayers Affected by the May 4, 2007, Kansas Storms and Tornadoes.

2008 qualified recovery assistance distributions. If a distribution was made in 2008 from an eligible retirement plan, it may be able to be designated as a qualified recovery assistance distribution (see Q 3:137). Complete and attach Form 8915, Qualified Hurricane Retirement Plan Distributions and Repayments, and Form 8606, Nondeductible IRAs (if required) to a 2008 income tax return (or amended return) for any qualified recovery assistance distributions. [*See* Form 8915 and Form 8606 in Publication 4492-A for instructions on completing the forms for this purpose]

Qualified Disaster Distributions for the Purchase or Construction of a Main Home (Kansas Disaster Area)

Q 3:143   Can a qualified disaster distribution used to purchase or construct a main home in the Kansas disaster area be repaid?

If a qualified disaster distribution to purchase or construct a main home in the Kansas disaster area is received after May 3, 2007, but no later than October 22, 2008, all or part of that distribution can be repaid to an eligible retirement plan. For this purpose, an eligible retirement plan is any plan, annuity, or IRA to which a qualified rollover can be made.

To be a qualified disaster distribution, the distribution must meet all of the following requirements.

1. The distribution is a hardship distribution from a 401(k) plan, a hardship distribution from a tax-sheltered annuity contract, or a qualified first-time homebuyer distribution from an IRA.

2. The distribution was received after November 4, 2006 and before May 5, 2007.

3. The distribution was to be used to purchase or construct a main home in the Kansas disaster area that was not purchased or constructed because of the storms and tornadoes.

   Note. A qualified disaster distribution is subject to the income tax withholding rules applicable to distributions which are not eligible rollover distributions (except for a distribution which would be treated as a qualified distributions, see Qs 4:9, 4:23). Thus, the 20-percent mandatory income tax withholding rules do not apply. [I.R.C. §§ 1400Q(a)(6)(A), 3405]

Q 3:144   How are qualified disaster distributions that are repaid treated?

Amounts that are repaid before October 23, 2008, are treated as a qualified rollover and are not included in income. Also, for purposes of the one-rollover-per-year limit for IRAs, a repayment to an IRA is not considered a qualified rollover.

Q 3:145   How are qualified disaster distributions that are not repaid treated?

A qualified disaster distribution not repaid before October 23, 2008 may be taxable for 2006 or 2007 and subject to the additional 10 percent tax (or the additional 25 percent tax for certain SIMPLE IRAs) on early distributions). See Q 3:134. The taxability of a qualified reservist distribution depends upon the plan type making the distribution. In the case of a Roth IRA, special ordering rules apply, and contributions previously made may be withdrawn tax-free and without penalty (see Qs 3:120, 4:1).

Q 3:146   How are qualified disaster distributions that are repaid reported?

Complete Form 8915, Qualified Hurricane Retirement Plan Distributions and Repayments, if a qualified disaster distribution is received that was repaid, in whole or in part, before October 23, 2008.

To report the repayment of a qualified disaster distribution for the purchase or construction of a main home that was not purchased or constructed due to the storms and tornadoes, use the 2005 Form 8915, Qualified Hurricane Retirement Plan Distributions and Repayments, Part IV. [Instructions for modifying the form for this purpose are provided in Publication 4492-A.]

Note. If all or part of a qualified disaster distribution is repaid by October 22, 2008, the taxpayer may file an amended return for that part of a distribution that was previously included in income.

Chapter Note 1. The following two Kansas-related benefits are also available to qualified individuals.

Qualified individual. To be a qualified individual, the taxpayer's main home on May 4, 2007, has to be located in the Kansas disaster area and the taxpayer had an economic loss because of the storms and tornadoes. Examples of an economic loss include, but are not limited to: loss, damage to, or destruction of real or personal property from fire, flooding, looting, vandalism, theft, wind, or other cause, loss related to displacement from the taxpayer's home, or loss of livelihood due to temporary or permanent layoffs.

1. Increases to the limits for distributions treated as loans from employer plans.

Limits on plan loans. The $50,000 limit for distributions treated as plan loans is increased to $100,000. In addition, the limit based on 50 percent of the vested accrued benefit is increased to 100 percent of that benefit. If the taxpayer's home was located in the Kansas disaster area, the higher limits apply only to loans received during the period beginning on May 22, 2008 and ending on December 31, 2008.

2. A one-year suspension for payments due on plan loans.

One-year suspension of loan payments. Payments on plan loans outstanding after May 3, 2007 may be suspended for one year by the plan administrator. To qualify for the suspension, the due date for any loan payment must occur during the period beginning on May 4, 2007 and ending on December 31, 2008.

Qualified Disaster Recovery Assistance Distribution Repayments (Midwestern Disaster Areas)

Retroactive rules provide for tax-favored withdrawals, repayments, and loans from certain retirement plans for taxpayers who suffered economic losses in 24 disaster-area counties as a result of the Midwest storms, tornadoes, and flooding that occurred in Arkansas, Illinois, Indiana, Iowa, Kansas, Michigan, Missouri, Minnesota, Nebraska, and Wisconsin (the Midwestern Disaster Area), which the federal government declared a disaster during the period beginning May 20, 2008 and ending July 31, 2008.

[Heartland Disaster Tax Relief Act of 2008 (Pub. L. No. 110-343), Division C, § 702(d), providing relief similar to the relief provided in I.R.C. § 1400Q with respect to use of retirement plan assets (see list of "substitutions" to I.R.C. § 1400Q in amendment note to I.R.C. § 1400N(a); *see also* I.R.S. Pub. 4492-B, Information for Affected Taxpayers in the Midwestern Disaster Areas. *See* I.R.S. Fact Sheet FS-2008-27 (Dec. 29, 2008). Both the IRS Fact Sheet and Publication 4492-B contain two tables, listing the counties in these states that encompass the "Midwestern Disaster Area" and applicable disaster dates. The qualified disaster recovery assistance distribution repayment provisions apply to taxpayers located in both Tables 1 and 2.]

These relief provisions are described in Publication 4492-B, Information for Affected Taxpayers in the Midwestern Disaster Areas. [For more information on additional disaster relief and current disaster relief locations, *see* IRS Notices at http://www.irs.gov/newsroom/article/0,,id = 108362,00.html (visited on June 23, 2009)]

Q 3:147   May qualified disaster recovery assistance distributions be repaid?

Yes. In general any portion of a qualified disaster recovery assistance distribution (see Q 3:152) that is eligible for tax-free rollover treatment to an eligible retirement plan (see Q 3:132) may be repaid. A qualified disaster recovery assistance distribution made because of a hardship from a retirement plan may also be repaid. However, the following types of distributions may not be repaid:

- Qualified disaster recovery assistance distributions received as a beneficiary (other than a surviving spouse)
- Required minimum distributions (RMDs)

- Periodic payments (other than from an IRA-based plan) that are for:
  — A period of 10 years or more,
  — Made over the taxpayer's life or life expectancy, or
  — Made over the joint lives or joint life expectancies of the taxpayer and his or her beneficiary.

Q 3:148 How long does a taxpayer have to repay a qualified disaster recovery distribution?

The repayment period for a qualified disaster recovery assistance distribution is three years. The three-year period starts on the day after the date the distribution was received. Thus, the day of distribution is not counted.

Example. Donna lives in Nebraska received a qualified disaster recovery assistance distribution on June 1, 2008. The distribution may be repaid by Donna (or her surviving spouse) on or before June 1, 2011 (the end of the third-year period that began on June 2). [*See* Minasyan v. Mukasey, No. 06-73192 (9th Cir. Jan. 20, 2009), regarding the term "after the date" (on another matter)]

Q 3:149 Are qualified disaster recovery assistance distributions included in income?

Yes. A qualified disaster recovery assistance distribution (of gain in the case of a Roth IRA) is included in income, in equal amounts, over three years, unless an election is made to include the entire distribution in income the year it was received. The taxability of a qualified reservist distribution depends upon the plan type making the distribution. In the case of a Roth IRA, special ordering rules apply, and contributions previously made may be withdrawn tax-free and without penalty (see Qs 3:120, 4:1).

Note. A qualified disaster recovery assistance distribution is subject to the income tax withholding rules applicable to distributions which are not eligible rollover distributions (except for a distribution that would be treated as a qualified distribution, see Qs 4:9, 4:23). Thus, the 20-percent mandatory income tax withholding rules do not apply. [I.R.C. §§ 1400Q(a)(6)(A), 3405]

Q 3:150 How is the repayment of a qualified disaster recovery assistance distribution treated?

Amounts that are repaid are treated as a qualified rollover and are not included in income. If a qualified disaster recovery assistance distribution is repaid to a Roth IRA, the repayment is first considered to be a repayment of earnings. Any repayments of qualified disaster recovery assistance will increase the taxpayer's basis in the Roth IRA by the amount of the repayment in excess of earnings (see Q 1.11). If repayment is made to a Roth IRA from a non-Roth account, it would be treated as a rollover conversion.

Note 1. A repayment to an IRA or Roth IRA is not counted when figuring the one-rollover-per-year limit.

Note 2. The repayment to a Roth IRA from a non-Roth account is treated as a conversion (see Chapter 3).

Q 3:151   Is a qualified disaster recovery assistance distribution subject to the 10- or 25-percent additional tax penalty on early distributions?

No. Although taxable (see Q 3:149), a qualified disaster recovery assistance distribution is not subject to the additional 10 percent tax (or the additional 25 percent tax for certain distributions from a SIMPLE IRA) on early distributions. The taxable amount is figured in the same manner as other IRA distributions. However, the distribution is included in income over three years unless the taxpayer elects to report the entire amount in the year of distribution.

Note. If the distribution is repaid (see Q 3:151) the taxpayer is not taxed on the distributions. Thus, it may be necessary to file amended tax returns. [*See* I.R.S. Pub. 4492-B, Information for Affected Taxpayers in the Midwestern Disaster Areas] The repayment to a Roth IRA from a non-Roth account is treated as a conversion.

Q 3:152   What is a "qualified disaster recovery assistance distribution"?

A qualified disaster recovery assistance distribution is any distribution received and designated as such from an eligible retirement plan if all of the following apply.

1. The distribution was made after the applicable disaster date and before January 1, 2010.
2. The taxpayer's main home was located in the Midwestern disaster area on the applicable disaster date (see Q 3:153).
3. An economic loss because of the severe storms, tornadoes, and flooding was sustained on the applicable disaster date. Examples of an economic loss include, but are not limited to:
   (a) Loss, damage to, or destruction of real or personal property from fire, flooding, looting, vandalism, theft, wind, or other cause;
   (b) Loss related to displacement from the taxpayer's home; or
   (c) Loss of livelihood due to temporary or permanent layoffs.

Note 1. Generally, any distribution (including periodic payments and required minimum distributions) from an eligible retirement plan can be designated as a qualified disaster recovery assistance distribution, regardless of whether the distribution was made on account of the storms, flooding, or tornadoes.

Caution. Not all qualified disaster recovery assistance distribution can be repaid (see Q 3:132).

Note 2. A qualified disaster recovery assistance distribution is subject to the income tax withholding rules applicable to distributions which are not eligible rollover distributions (except for a distribution which would be treated as a qualified distributions, see Qs 4:9, 4:23). Thus, the 20-percent mandatory income tax withholding rules do not apply. [I.R.C. §§ 1400Q(a)(6)(A), 3405]

Q 3:153 What is a taxpayer's main home?

Generally, a taxpayer's main home for qualified disaster recovery assistance distribution purposes is the taxpayer's main home where he or she lives most of the time. A temporary absence due to special circumstances, such as illness, education, business, military service, evacuation, or vacation, will not be considered a change the taxpayer's main home.

Q 3:154 What does the term *applicable disaster date* mean?

The term *applicable disaster date* refers to the date on which the severe storms, tornadoes, or flooding occurred in the Midwestern disaster areas. Different dates apply to the various affected counties.

Q 3:155 Are qualified disaster recovery assistance distributions limited to need or the actual amount of loss?

No. Qualified disaster recovery assistance distributions are permitted without regard to need or the actual amount of economic loss.

Q 3:156 Are qualified recovery assistance distributions limited in amount?

Yes. The total of all qualified disaster recovery assistance distributions from all plans is limited to $100,000. If there are distributions in excess of $100,000 from more than one type of plan, the $100,000 limit can be allocated among the plans any way the taxpayer chooses.

Note. A reduction or offset (on or after the applicable disaster date), of an account balance in an eligible retirement plan (see Q 3:157) in order to repay a loan can also be designated as a qualified disaster recovery assistance distribution. A distribution of a plan loan offset can occur for a variety of reasons, such as when a participant terminates employment or does not comply with the terms of repayment. Plan loan offsets are treated as actual distributions and are reported in box 1 of Form 1099-R, Distributions From Pensions, Annuities, Retirement or Profit-Sharing Plans, IRAs, Insurance Contracts, etc., but are not eligible for special tax treatment (i.e., 10-year forward income averaging or the 20 percent capital gains election).

Q 3:157   What is an "eligible retirement plan?"

Qualified disaster recovery assistance distributions can be made from and repaid to any eligible retirement plan. For this purpose, the term eligible retirement plan means any of the following:

- A qualified pension, profit-sharing, or stock bonus plan (including a 401(k) plan).
- A qualified annuity plan.
- A tax-sheltered annuity contract.
- An eligible governmental 457(b) deferred compensation plan.
- A traditional, SEP, SIMPLE, or Roth IRA.

Qualified Disaster Distributions for the Purchase or Construction of a Main Home (Midwestern Disaster Areas)

Q 3:158   If a qualified disaster distribution is used to purchase or construct a main home in the Midwestern disaster area can it be repaid?

If a qualified disaster distribution to purchase or construct a main home in the Midwestern disaster area is received, all or part of that distribution can be repaid to an eligible retirement plan on or after the applicable disaster date (see Q 3:154) and before March 4, 2009. For this purpose, an eligible retirement plan is any plan, annuity, or IRA to which a qualified rollover can be made (see Q 3:132).

To be a qualified disaster distribution, the distribution must meet all of the following requirements.

1. The distribution is a hardship distribution from a 401(k) plan, a hardship distribution from a tax-sheltered annuity contract, or a qualified first-time homebuyer distribution from an IRA.

2. The distribution was received within six months prior to the day after the applicable disaster date.

3. The distribution was to be used to purchase or construct a main home in the Midwestern disaster area that was not purchased or constructed because of the storms, tornadoes, and flooding.

Note. A qualified disaster distribution is subject to the income tax withholding rules applicable to distributions which are not eligible rollover distributions (except for a distribution which would be treated as a qualified distributions, see Qs 4:9, 4:23). Thus, the 20-percent mandatory income tax withholding rules do not apply. [I.R.C. §§ 1400Q(a)(6)(A), 3405]

Q 3:159 How are qualified disaster distributions that are repaid treated?

Amounts that are repaid before March 4, 2009, are treated as a qualified rollover and are not included in income. Also, for purposes of the one-rollover-per-year limit for IRAs, a repayment to an IRA is not considered a qualified rollover.

Q 3:160 How are qualified disaster distributions that are not repaid treated?

If qualified disaster distributions are not repaid before March 4, 2009, they may be taxable and subject to the additional 10 percent tax (or the additional 25 percent tax for certain SIMPLE IRAs) on early distributions). (See Qs 3:149, 3:150, 3:151.) Unless earnings (gain) were distributed from a Roth IRA in a qualified disaster recovery distribution, none of the amount distributed would be taxable. The taxability of a qualified reservist distribution depends upon the plan type making the distribution. In the case of a Roth IRA, special ordering rules apply, and contributions previously made may be withdrawn tax-free and without penalty (see Qs 3:122, 4:1).

Q 3:161 How are qualified disaster distributions that are repaid reported?

Form 8930, Qualified Disaster Recovery Assistance Retirement Plan Distributions and Repayments, is used to report qualified disaster recovery assistance distributions and repayments.

Specific instructions for reporting qualified disaster recovery assistance distributions and repayments on Form 8930 are contained in the instructions to that form.

Note 1. A repayment reduces the amount of qualified disaster recovery assistance distributions. If a repayment is made in 2009, after the 2008 return has been filed, the repayment will reduce amount of the qualified disaster recovery assistance distributions for 2009, unless the taxpayer is eligible to amend his or her 2008 return.

Note 2. If all or part of a qualified disaster distribution is repaid before March 4, 2009, the taxpayer may file an amended return for that part of a distribution that was previously included in income.

Chapter Note. The following two Midwest disaster-area related benefits are also available to qualified individuals.

Qualified individual. To be a qualified individual, the taxpayer's main home has to be located in the Midwestern disaster area on the applicable date (see Q 3:154) and the taxpayer had an economic loss because of the storms, tornadoes, or flooding. Examples of an economic loss include, but are not limited to: loss, damage to, or destruction of real or personal property from fire, flooding, looting, vandalism, theft, wind, or other cause, loss related to displacement from the taxpayer's home, or loss of livelihood due to temporary or permanent layoffs.

1. Increases to the limits for distributions treated as loans from employer plans.

Limits on plan loans. The $50,000 limit for distributions treated as plan loans is increased to $100,000. In addition, the limit based on 50 percent of the vested accrued benefit is increased to 100 percent of that benefit. If the taxpayer's home was located in the Midwestern disaster area, the higher limits apply only to loans received during the period beginning on October 3, 2008, and ending on December 31, 2009.

2. A one-year suspension for payments due on plan loans.

One-year suspension of loan payments. Payments on plan loans outstanding on or after the applicable disaster date (see Q 3:154), may be suspended for one year by the plan administrator. To qualify for the suspension, the due date for any loan payment must occur during the period beginning on the applicable disaster date and ending on December 31, 2009.

Rollover of Airline Payments

Q 3:162   May an "airline payment" be rolled over to a Roth IRA?

Yes. A qualified airline employee (see Q 3:167) may contribute any portion of an airline payment (see Q 3:166) to a Roth IRA. A rollover of an airline payment may only be rolled over to a Roth IRA. The rollover period is very short (see Q 3:163).

Note. Any reduction in the airline payment amount on account of employment taxes is disregarded when figuring the amount that can be contributed to a Roth IRA.

Q 3:163   How long does a taxpayer have to roll over an airline payment to a Roth IRA?

The contribution must be made within 180 days from the date the payment was received, or before June 23, 2009, whichever is later.

Q 3:164   How is the rollover of an airline payment to a Roth IRA treated?

The contribution will be treated as a qualified rollover contribution.

Note. The modified AGI limits that generally apply to Roth IRA rollovers do not apply to airline payments.

Q 3:165   Are rollovers of airline payments to a Roth IRA included in income?

Yes. The rollover contribution is included in income to the extent it would be included in income if it were not part of the rollover contribution. Also, any reduction in the airline payment amount on account of employment taxes shall be disregarded when figuring the amount that can be contribute to a Roth IRA.

Q 3:166   What is an "airline payment?"

An airline payment is any payment of money or other property that is paid to a qualified airline employee from a commercial airline carrier. The payment also must be made both:

- Under the approval of an order of federal bankruptcy court in a case filed after September 11, 2001, and before January 1, 2007 and
- In respect of the qualified airline employee's interest in a bankruptcy claim against the airline carrier, any note of the carrier (or amount paid in lieu of a note being issued), or any other fixed obligation of the carrier to pay a lump-sum amount.

An airline payment amount may not include any amount payable on the basis of the carrier's future earnings or profits.

Q 3:167   Who is a "qualified airline employee?"

A qualified airline employee is an employee or former employee of a commercial airline carrier who was a participant in a qualified defined benefit plan maintained by the carrier which was terminated or became subject to restrictions regarding the special funding rules under Section 402(b) of the Pension Protection Act of 2006.

Q 3:168   How does a taxpayer determine how much of an airline payment can be rolled over?

Form 8935, Airline Payment Report, will be sent to the taxpayer by the commercial airline carrier to a taxpayer that pays one or more airline payment amounts to the taxpayer. The form will indicate the amount of the airline payment that is eligible to be rolled over to a Roth IRA.

The form is also filed with the IRS using Form 8935-T, Transmittal of Airline Payment Reports, or electronically using the Filing Information Returns Electronically (FIRE) system. [WRERA § 125]

Chapter 4

Voluntary Distributions

In general, distributions of amounts contributed to a Roth IRA are not taxable. Distributions of earnings (gain), however, may be taxable and may be subject to penalty if not received in a qualified distribution. Additionally, distributions of conversion amounts may be subject to penalty, if the conversion had not aged for five years in the Roth IRA and/or the distribution is nonqualified.

This chapter considers the ordering rules that apply to distributions from a Roth IRA and defines qualified and nonqualified distributions. The chapter also examines the effect of exclusion periods on Roth IRA distributions and indicates when the 10 percent premature distribution penalty applies.

Transfers between Roth IRAs, including those incident to a divorce, are also discussed in this chapter. Required minimum distributions are discussed in chapter 5. Distributions from designated Roth accounts (DRAs) are discussed in chapter 10.

From time to time, Congress has permitted penalty-free distributions to be made from an eligible retirement plan for special purposes (e.g., hurricane distributions, qualified recovery assistance distributions, qualified disaster recovery distributions, and qualified reservist distributions). These distributions are eligible for repayment (rollover) to an eligible retirement plan, including a Roth IRA, and are discussed in chapter 3. The rollover of airline payments, military death gratuities, Exxon Valdez settlements, and Servicemembers' Group Life Insurance (SGLI) are also discussed in chapter 3.

Overview

Q 4:1   In what order are distributions from a Roth IRA considered to be made, and how are such distributions generally treated for federal income tax (and penalty) purposes?

For purposes of Section 408A of the Internal Revenue Code (Code), relating to Roth IRAs, and Code Section 72, relating to the taxation of distributions from a Roth IRA, the taxation of a distribution depends on the source of Roth IRA funding for the amount distributed. [I.R.C. § 408A(d)(4)]

Distributions that are not qualified distributions may be partially or wholly taxable (see Qs 4:9, 4:12). There is a specified order in which contributions (including conversion contributions and rollover contributions from qualified retirement plans) and earnings are considered as distributed from a Roth IRA. For this purpose, the distribution of excess contributions and earnings thereon are disregarded (see Qs 2:25–2:35, 4:25). Subject to certain aggregation (grouping and adding) rules discussed below, any amount distributed from a Roth IRA is treated as being made in the following order (determined at the end of the taxable year and exhausting each category before moving on to the next category):

- **First:** From regular contributions.

    Exceptions:

    — When a qualified charitable contribution is made from a Roth IRA (which is not generally recommended), the amount distributed from the Roth IRA is deemed coming from the taxable portion (the earnings) first.

    — When a qualified health savings account (HSA) distribution is transferred from a Roth IRA to an HSA, the amount distributed from the Roth IRA is deemed coming from the taxable portion (from earnings) first.

    Note 1. If a repayment is made of a qualified hurricane distribution, qualified recovery assistance distributions, or qualified disaster recovery distributions to a Roth IRA, the repayment is first considered to be a repayment of earnings (see Third category). Any repayments of qualified hurricane distributions in excess of earnings will increase the basis in the Roth IRA by the amount of the repayment in excess of earnings (see Second category item).

- **Second:** From conversion and rollover contributions, on a first-in-first-out basis (generally, total conversions and rollovers from the earliest year first). Aggregation (grouping and adding) rules apply, which are discussed below. Disregard rollover contributions from other Roth IRAs for this purpose. Take these conversion and rollover contributions into account as follows:

  — Taxable portion (the amount required to be included in gross income because of the conversion or rollover) first and then the

  — Nontaxable portion.

  This category includes:

       — Any repayment of qualified reservist distributions.

       — Any repayment of hurricane distributions, qualified recovery assistance distributions, and qualified disaster recovery distributions, to the extent the repayment exceeds earnings (see Qs 3:132–3:161).

       — Rollovers of certain airline payments, military death gratuities, Exxon Valdez settlements, and SGLI (see Qs 3:104, 3:111).

  Note 2. Technically, in any given year, qualified rollover contributions from an eligible retirement plan (other than a Roth IRA) are treated as distributed *after* any other rollover contributions (see, e.g., three items above) are distributed for that year. [I.R.C. § 408A(d)(4)(B)] As a practical matter, the IRS does not seem to address this issue (see Table 4-1).

- **Third:** Earnings on contributions. Earnings received in a qualified distribution are not taxable.

  This category also includes any earnings that are distributed in a nonqualified distribution from DRA under an employer's plan that are rolled over to a Roth IRA.

  Exceptions:

  — When a qualified HSA distribution is transferred from a Roth IRA to an HSA, the amount distributed from the Roth IRA is deemed as coming from the taxable portion (the earnings) first.

  — When a qualified charitable contribution is made from a Roth IRA (which is not generally recommended), the amount transferred is deemed as coming from the taxable portion (the earnings) first. [Treas. Reg. § 1.408A-6, Q&A 8]

Aggregation (grouping and adding rules). For purposes of the ordering rules, determine the taxable amounts distributed (withdrawn), distributions, and contributions by grouping and adding them together as follows:

- *All Roth IRA distributions aggregated.* All distributions from all of an individual's Roth IRAs made during a taxable year are aggregated.

- *Regular contributions.* All regular contributions made for the same taxable year to all the individual's Roth IRAs are aggregated and added to the undistributed total regular contributions for prior taxable years. Regular contributions for a year include contributions made in the following taxable year that are identified by the taxpayer as being made for the prior taxable year.

- *Roth-to-Roth rollovers disregarded.* A distribution from an individual's Roth IRA that is rolled over to another Roth IRA of the individual is disregarded for purposes of determining the amount of both contributions and distributions.

- *Aggregation of contributions.* Add all conversion and rollover contributions made during the year together. For purposes of the ordering rules:

  — In the case of any conversion or rollover in which the conversion or rollover distribution is made in 2008 and the conversion or rollover contribution is made in 2009, treat the conversion or rollover contribution as contributed before any other conversion or rollover contributions made in 2009.

  — However, a conversion contribution made by an individual during 2010, and subject to the two-year spread, is treated for purposes of the ordering rules as distributed before any other conversion contribution that is made by the individual during 2010, 2011, or 2012.

Note 3. A conversion contribution made by an individual during 2010, and subject to the two-year spread, is taxable to the extent of any unrecovered spread income (which is, in effect, an untaxed contribution made to the Roth IRA). In that case, the amount included in income in the year of the distribution is increased by the amount distributed, and the amount included in income in 2012 (or 2011 and 2012 in the case of a distribution in 2010) is the lesser of: (1) half of the amount includible in income as a result of the conversion; and (2) the remaining portion of such amount not already included in income. Special rules apply in the event of death, or when the spouse is the beneficiary of the entire account. Unless a penalty exception applies (or the distribution is a qualified distribution), the taxable amount withdrawn (accelerated into income) may also be subject to the 10 percent premature distribution penalty (see Examples 2 and 3 below). (See Qs 3:15, 4:14, 4:17, 4:18.)

Note 4. If a conversion amount is distributed within five years beginning with the year of the conversion, the amount distributed is treated as if it were taxable for purposes of the 10 percent premature distribution penalty tax under Code Section 72(t) even though the amount distributed is not taxable (a return of basis) under the ordering rules, except for the possible acceleration of income resulting from a 2010 conversion. Thus, unless the distribution is a qualified distribution, or another exception applies, the amount distributed from a conversion made in 2010 within five years is subject to the 10 percent penalty tax under Code Section 72.

Note 5. If the Roth IRA owner died before all amounts are included in income under the two-year spread rule for a 2010 conversion, any amount not included in income is includible on the final income tax return filed on behalf of the decedent for the taxable year that includes the date of death. If the surviving spouse is the sole beneficiary of all of the decedent's Roth

IRAs, however, the spouse may elect to continue to include in income the remaining portion of the taxable amount over the remaining portion of the two-year spread (see Q 3:117). [I.R.C. § 408A(d)(3)(E)(ii)(II); Treas. Reg. § 1.408A-4, Q&A 11]

- *Date of recharacterized Roth contributions.* An individual recharacterizes a contribution made to a traditional IRA (IRA 1) by transferring the contribution to a Roth IRA (Roth IRA 2). The contribution to Roth IRA 2 is treated as contributed on the same date and for the same taxable year that the contribution was made to traditional IRA 1.

  Note 6. Add any recharacterized contributions that end up in a Roth IRA to the appropriate contribution group for the year that the original contribution would have been taken into account if it had been made directly to the Roth IRA.

- *Recharacterized contributions disregarded.* An individual recharacterizes a regular or conversion contribution made to Roth IRA 1 by transferring the contribution to a traditional IRA (IRA 2). The contribution to Roth IRA 1 and the recharacterizing transfer are disregarded in determining the amount of both contributions and distributions from Roth IRA 1 for the taxable year with respect to which the original contribution was made to Roth IRA 1.

- *Multiple beneficiaries.* Each type of contribution is allocated to each beneficiary on a pro-rata basis. For example, a Roth IRA owner dies in 2009, when the Roth IRA contains a regular contribution of $2,000, a conversion contribution of $6,000, and earnings of $1,000. The owner leaves his Roth IRA equally to four children, and each child receives one quarter of each type of contribution. Under the ordering rules, an immediate distribution of $2,000 to one of the children is deemed to consist of $500 of regular contributions and $1,500 of conversion contributions.

[I.R.C. §§ 72(t)(1), 408A(c)(1), 408A(d)(4)(B)(i); Treas. Reg. § 1.408A-6, Q&A 8]

Example 1. On October 15, 2004, Justin converted all $80,000 in his traditional IRA to his Roth IRA. His Forms 8606 from prior years show that $20,000 of the amount converted is his basis. Justin included $60,000 ($80,000 − $20,000) in his gross income.

On February 23, 2009, Justin made a regular contribution of $5,000 to a Roth IRA. On November 7, 2009, at age 60, Justin took a $7,000 distribution from his Roth IRA.

The first $5,000 of the distribution is a return of Justin's regular contribution and is not includible in his income. The next $2,000 of the distribution is not includible in income because it was included previously.

Example 2. Tyrone has a traditional IRA with a value of $1,000, consisting of deductible contributions and earnings. Tyrone does not have a Roth IRA. Tyrone converts the traditional IRA to a Roth IRA in 2010, and, as a result of the conversion, $1,000 is includible in his gross income. Unless Tyrone elects otherwise, $500 of the income resulting from the conversion is includible in income in 2011 and $500 in 2012. Later in 2010, Tyrone takes a $200 distribution, which is not a qualified distribution and all of which, under the ordering rules, is attributable to amounts includible in gross income (accelerated) because of the conversion. Under the accelerated inclusion rule, the $200 distribution is included in income in 2010. In addition, because converted amounts were distributed within the five-year period beginning in 2010, the $200 distributed may be subject to the 10 percent premature distribution penalty tax in 2010. The amount included in income in 2011 is the lesser of (i) $500 (half of the income resulting from the conversion) or (ii) $800 ($1,000 – $200), the remaining income from the conversion). Thus, $500 is included in income in 2011. The amount included in income in 2012 is the lesser of (i) $500 (half of the income resulting from the conversion) or (ii) $300 (the remaining income from the conversion, i.e., $1,000 – $700 ($200 included in income in 2010 and $500 included in income in 2011)). Thus, $300 is included in income in 2012.

If, instead, the $200 amount distributed in 2011 was a qualified distribution (which it technically could not have been, because this was Tyrone's first Roth IRA and he has not met the five-year period for a qualified distribution), the 10 percent penalty tax would not apply. All qualified distributions satisfy the penalty exceptions under Code Section 72.

Note 7. Qualified distributions of converted amounts are not subject to penalty, although any spread income from a conversion made in 2010 may have to be accelerated if distributed (under the ordering rules) before 2012. If the distribution is not a qualified distribution and the five-year aging period applicable to each conversion has not expired, the amount distributed may be subject to the 10 percent premature distribution penalty tax if under age 59½, unless another exception applies.

Example 3. Assume the same facts as in Example 2, except Tyrone takes the $200 distribution in 2011, instead of in 2010. Under the accelerated inclusion rule, the $200 distribution is included in income in 2011. In addition, Tyrone will include the lesser of (i) $500 (half of the income resulting from the conversion) or (ii) $800 ($1,000 – $200) the remaining income from the conversion). Thus, $700 is included in income in 2011. In addition, because converted amounts were distributed within the five-year period beginning in 2011, the $200 distributed may be subject to the 10 percent premature distribution penalty tax in 2011 (see Example 1).

The amount included in income in 2012 is the lesser of (i) $500 (half of the income resulting from the conversion) or (ii) $300 (the remaining income from the conversion, i.e., $1,000 –$700 ($200 + $500) included in income in 2011). Thus, $300 is included in income in 2012.

Example 4. Same facts as in Example 3, except Tyrone removes the $1,000 in the same year the conversion was made (2010). The conversion income will be taxable in 2010 and may be subject to the 10 percent additional tax for premature distributions, unless an exception applies.

Example 5. Amber, age 30, established a Roth IRA in 2010 and made an annual contribution of $100. In 2010, she also converted a traditional deductible IRA worth $40,000 to the Roth IRA (and elected to pay the taxable amount over a two-year period). Twelve years later (2022), Amber converts a traditional deductible IRA worth $10,000 to a Roth IRA, which is credited with a gain of $10. In 2023, Amber removes $50,110 from her Roth IRAs. The following is a summary of what actions Amber must take and how the amounts distributed are taxed:

1. With respect to the 2010 conversion, Amber will have to include $20,000 (one-half of the taxable amount of $40,000) on her Federal Income Tax Return for 2011 and 2012.

2. With respect to the 2022 conversion, Amber will have to include $10,000 (the taxable amount) on her Federal Income Tax Return for 2022.

3. The $100 is treated as distributed first. Although more than five years have elapsed since Amber made that annual contribution, the $100 is not a qualified distribution because that amount was not distributed for one of the four permitted reasons (discussed later). Nonetheless, the $100 amount is not taxable, because of the contribution-first recovery rule and the ordering rules, nor subject to penalty.

4. The $40,000 is treated as distributed next; it is not a qualified distribution either. Under the contribution-first recovery rule and the ordering rules, however, the $40,000 is not subject to federal income tax because the tax was already paid in 2011 and 2012. Additionally, it is not subject to the early distribution penalty because it has been converted for at least five years.

5. The $10,000 is treated as distributed next; it too is not taxable because the tax was paid on Amber's 2022 tax return.

6. Under the special rule, the $10,000 is subject to the 10 percent premature distribution penalty unless one of the Section 72(t) exceptions applies. (Under the special rule, the five-year period started in 2022, the year for which the conversion amount being withdrawn was contributed.) [I.R.C. § 408A(d)(3)(F)(i)(II)]

7. The earnings (gain) of $10 are treated as distributed last. Because Amber is under age 59½, and none of the other three exceptions set forth in Code Section 408A(d)(2)(A) applies, the $10 is not a qualified distribution; therefore, that amount is subject to federal income tax in 2023. In addition, because none of the exceptions in Code Section 72(t) apply, the $10 is also subject to the 10 percent premature distribution penalty.

Practice Pointer. The Roth IRA owner is required to keep track of the ordering provisions to verify the nontaxable portion of a distribution from a Roth IRA (or deemed Roth IRA in an employer's plan, see Q 2:46). A Roth IRA owner should keep a copy of Form 5498, IRA Contribution Information (or similar statements), that show contributions made to the Roth IRA, and Form 1099-R, Distributions from Pensions, Annuities, Retirement or Profit-Sharing Plans, IRAs, Insurance Contracts, etc., that show distributions from Roth accounts. Maintaining Form 8606, Nondeductible IRAs, and the first page of the federal income tax return (Forms 1040, 1040A, 1040NR, or 1040T) may be helpful for other purposes. Form 8606 must be filed if the Roth IRA owner received a distribution from a Roth IRA (other than a rollover or recharacterization and certain contributions that were returned) or converted an amount from a traditional, SEP, or SIMPLE IRA to a Roth IRA (unless the entire amount was recharacterized).

Tax-free distributions from individual retirement plans for charitable purposes. Under current law, if an amount withdrawn from an IRA or Roth IRA is donated to a charitable organization, the rules relating to the tax treatment of withdrawals from IRAs apply to the amount withdrawn and the charitable contribution is subject to the normally applicable limitations on deductibility of such contributions.

The PPA provides an exclusion from gross income for otherwise taxable IRA distributions from a traditional or a Roth IRA in the case of qualified charitable distributions. The provision does not apply to distributions from employer-sponsored retirement plans, including SIMPLE IRAs and simplified employee pensions (SEPs) if a SIMPLE/SEP contribution was made to the plan for the plan year that ends with or within the taxable year that the qualified charitable distribution is made.

The exclusion may not exceed $100,000 per taxpayer per taxable year. Distributions are eligible for the exclusion only if made on or after the date the IRA owner attains age 70$\frac{1}{2}$, and if made by December 31, 2009 (see effective date below). Special rules apply in determining the amount of an IRA/Roth-IRA distribution that is otherwise taxable. The present-law rules regarding taxation of IRA distributions and the deduction of charitable contributions continue to apply to distributions from an IRA or Roth IRA that are not qualified charitable distributions.

An IRA or Roth IRA does not fail to qualify merely because qualified charitable distributions have been made from the account. It is intended that the Treasury Department will prescribe rules under which IRA owners are deemed to elect out of withholding if they designate that a distribution is intended to be a qualified charitable distribution.

A *qualified charitable distribution* is any distribution from an IRA or Roth IRA directly by the IRA/Roth IRA trustee to an organization described in Code Section 170(b)(1)(A) (other than an organization described in Code Section 509(a)(3) or a donor advised fund (as defined in Code Section 4966(d)(2)).

Caution. The exclusion applies only if a charitable contribution deduction for the entire distribution otherwise would be allowable (under present law), determined without regard to the generally applicable percentage limitations. Thus, for example, if the deductible amount is reduced because of a benefit received in exchange, or if a deduction is not allowable because the donor did not obtain sufficient substantiation, the exclusion is not available with respect to any part of the distribution.

If the IRA/Roth-IRA owner has any IRA that includes nondeductible contributions, a special rule applies in determining the portion of a distribution that is includible in gross income (but for the provision) under Code Section 72(t), and thus is eligible for qualified charitable distribution treatment. Under the special rule, the distribution is treated as consisting of income first, up to the aggregate amount that would be includible in gross income (but for the provision) if the aggregate balance of all IRAs (or Roth IRAs) having the same owner were distributed during the same year. In determining the amount of subsequent IRA or Roth-IRA distributions includible in income, proper adjustments are to be made to reflect the amount treated as a qualified charitable distribution under the special rule.

Note. Distributions that are excluded from gross income by reason of the provision are not taken into account in determining the deduction for charitable contributions under Code Section 170.

Effective date. The provision relating to qualified charitable distributions is effective for distributions made in taxable years beginning on or after January 1, 2006, and as extended, taxable years beginning before January 1, 2010. [PPA § 1201(c); I.R.C. §§ 408(d)(8), as amended by PPA § 1201(a), extended for two years by the Emergency Economic Stabilization Act of 2008 (Pub. L. No. 110-343), Division C, § 205]

Qualified HSA funding distribution. An IRA owner may take a one-time (once-in-a-lifetime) IRA (or Roth IRA) distribution to fund a Health Savings Account (HSA). The amount is part of an HSA owner's regular contribution and is subject to his or her HSA regular contribution limit. The Roth IRA distribution is tax-free as long as the HSA owner remains HSA eligible from the month of the HSA contribution through the last day of the 12th month following. No special reporting is required for qualified HSA funding distributions. Generally, it is more beneficial to make such distributions from a non-Roth IRA.

Q 4:2   What are the basis recovery rules for a Roth IRA?

Ordering rules are used to determine whether basis (contributions) is being withdrawn (see Qs 2:25, 3:17). In some cases, taxable amounts are treated as distributed before the aggregate amount of contributions is recovered. The following basis recovery rules apply to a Roth IRA:

1. All of a taxpayer's Roth IRAs are aggregated and treated separately from traditional IRAs.

2. Annual Roth IRA contributions are treated separately from conversion Roth IRA contributions.

3. Conversions are distributed on a first-in, first out basis. [Treas. Reg. § 1.408A-6, Q&A 8(a)(2)]

[I.R.C. § 408A(d)(4)(B); Treas. Reg. § 1.408A-6, Q&A 9(b)]

Table 4-1 can be used to figure the taxable portion of a distribution (other than a qualified distribution) from a Roth IRA (see Q 4:3).

Table 4-1. Figuring the Taxable Part of a Distribution (Other Than a Qualified Distribution from a Roth IRA

1. Enter the total of all distributions made from individual's Roth IRA(s), other than qualified charitable distributions or a one-time distribution to fund an HSA, during the year   *1.* $_____

2. Enter the amount of qualified distributions made during the year   2. − $_____

3. Subtract line 2 from line 1   3. = $_____

4. Enter the amount of distributions made during the year to correct excess contributions made during the year. (Do not include earnings.)   4. − $_____

5. Subtract line 4 from line 3   5. = $_____

6. Enter the amount of distributions made during the year that were contributed to another Roth IRA in a qualified rollover contribution (other than the repayment of a qualified disaster recovery assistance or qualified recovery assistance distribution).   6. − $_____

7. Subtract line 6 from line 5   7. = $_____

8. Enter the amount of *all* prior distributions from Roth IRA(s), other than qualified charitable distributions, or one-time distributions to fund an HSA, whether or not they were qualified distributions)   8. + $_____

9. Add lines 3 and 8   9. = $_____

10. Enter the amount of the distributions included on line 8 that were previously includible in income   10. − $_____

11. Subtract line 10 from line 9   11. = $_____

12. Enter the total of all contributions to all Roth IRAs   12. $_____

13. Enter the total of all distributions made (this year and in prior years) to correct excess contributions, including any earnings.   13. − $_____

14. Subtract line 13 from line 12. (If the result is less than 0, enter 0.)   14. = $_____

15. Subtract line 14 from line 11. (If the result is less than 0, enter 0.)   15. = $_____

16. Enter the smaller of the amount on line 7 or the amount on line 15. This is the taxable part of the Roth IRA distribution   16. = $_____

Q 4:3 Are Roth IRAs aggregated for distribution purposes?

Yes. All of an owner's Roth IRAs are treated as a single Roth IRA for distribution purposes. [I.R.C. § 408A(d)(4); Treas. Reg. § 1.408A-6, Q&A 9(a)]

Practice Pointer. Maintaining separate Roth IRAs has little value, other than perhaps offering some convenience if there are both nonspouse and spouse beneficiaries (see chapter 5).

It is important to note, however, that for distribution purposes, a beneficiary's inherited Roth IRA may not be aggregated with any other Roth IRA maintained by the beneficiary (except for other Roth IRAs that the beneficiary inherited from the same decedent), unless the beneficiary, as the spouse of the decedent and sole beneficiary of the Roth IRA, elects to treat the Roth IRA as his or her own (see Q 5:32). [Treas. Reg. § 1.408A-6, Q&A 11, 1.408A-8, Q&A 1(b)(10)]

Q 4:4 What is the tax basis in annual Roth IRA contributions distributed?

No deduction is allowed for an annual Roth IRA contribution; therefore, the tax basis in annual Roth IRA contributions distributed is equal to the sum of the annual Roth IRA contributions. [Treas. Reg. § 1.408A-6, Q&A 1(b)]

If a qualified hurricane, qualified disaster recovery assistance, or qualified recovery assistance distributions is repaid to a Roth IRA, the repayment is first considered to be a repayment of earnings (i.e., the taxable portion of the distribution or distributions). Any repayments of qualified hurricane, qualified disaster recovery assistance, or qualified recovery assistance distributions in excess of earnings will increase the taxpayer's basis in the Roth IRA by the amount of the repayment in excess of earnings.

The rollover of airline payments, military death gratuities, Exxon Valdez settlements, and SGLI to a Roth IRA increases a taxpayer's basis (in all Roth accounts) (see chapter 3).

Q 4:5 What does the term *conversion amount* refer to?

The term *conversion amount* refers to the total of all amounts contributed (rolled over or transferred) from an eligible retirement plan to a Roth IRA (see chapter 3). To the extent that federal income taxes are paid (or, in some cases, will be paid as in the case of certain disaster distributions; see chapter 3), a tax basis is created in the conversion amount (see Qs 1:10, 1:11, 3:135, 3:150, 4:1, 4:17). [Treas. Reg. § 1.408A-8, Q&A 1(b)(3)]

Q 4:6 What does the term *taxable conversion amount* refer to?

The term *taxable conversion amount* refers to the total of all amounts contributed (rolled over or transferred) from a traditional IRA or an employer's plan (see Q 3:52) to a Roth IRA (conversions) to the extent that the amounts would have been taxable had the amounts been distributed from the traditional

IRA or the employer's plan and not properly converted to a Roth IRA. [Treas. Reg. § 1.408A-8, Q&A 1(b)(8)]

> **Note.** The taxable conversion amount is more technically referred to in the Code as the *qualified rollover contribution includible in gross income.*

Q 4:7   What is the tax basis in converted amounts distributed from a Roth IRA?

Converted amounts distributed from a Roth IRA are treated as basis to the extent federal income taxes were paid as a result of the conversion. In most cases, a tax must be paid when a traditional IRA or an employer's plan account is converted to a Roth IRA (see Qs 3:17, 4:1, item 5, regarding conversions made in 2010). [*See* I.R.C. § 408A(d)(3)(E)(i)(I), 408A(d)(3)(F)(ii)(I)]

Q 4:8   May a corrective distribution be made from a Roth IRA after the due date of the Roth IRA owner's federal income tax return, including extensions?

Yes. Although the rules under Code Section 408(d)(5) regarding corrections after the due date of an IRA owner's federal income tax return for the tax-free distribution of certain excess traditional IRA contributions do not apply to Roth IRAs, excess amounts may be withdrawn after the due date of the federal income tax return (including extensions) (see Qs 2:25, 4:1, 4:9, 4:21, 4:25). The only method of correction available is to recharacterize the excess back to a traditional IRA (if permitted), remove the excess (a nontaxable distribution), or undercontribute in the following year. If not timely removed or recharacterized or used up, the 6 percent penalty tax will apply (see Q 2:24, 4:21).

Qualified Distributions

Q 4:9   What is a *qualified distribution* from a Roth IRA?

A *qualified distribution* from a Roth IRA is a distribution that satisfies two requirements:

1. The amount must not be distributed within the exclusion period (i.e., the five-taxable-year period beginning with the first year for which a contribution is made to *any* Roth IRA).
2. The amount must be distributed
   a. On or after the date on which the owner attains age 59½;
   b. To the beneficiary after the death of the owner;
   c. After the owner becomes disabled under Code Section 72(m)(7); or
   d. For a qualified special purpose (e.g., the distribution meets the requirements for a first-time homebuyer expense).

Note 1. A distribution received before 2003 cannot be a qualified distribution. It should also be noted that conversion amounts that are distributed (under the ordering rules), which are not qualified distributions, may be subject to a 10 percent penalty if withdrawn before the five-year period beginning on the date of such conversion, unless an exception applies.

[I.R.C. § 408A(d)(2)(A); Treas. Reg. § 1.408A-6, Q&A 1(b)]

Note 2. A qualified distribution of earnings (gain) from a Roth IRA is entitled to tax-free treatment. [I.R.C. § 408A(d)(1)] All contributions to a Roth IRA are recovered without any federal income tax liability, although the taxable amount converted may have to be accelerated into income (see Qs 3:17, 4:1). Qualified distributions does not include the return of excess contributions and any net income attributable to the excess contribution that is returned before the due date of the return for the year that the excess contribution was made under Code Section 408(d)(4). (See Qs 2:25–2:35, 4:25.)

Note 3. In contrast to a Roth IRA, in a designated Roth account under an employer's plan, the five-taxable-year period of participation begins on the first day of the employee's taxable year for which the employee first had designated Roth contributions made to the plan and ends when five consecutive taxable years have passed (see Q 10:28).

Q 4:10 Is a qualified distribution from a Roth IRA subject to the 10 percent premature distribution penalty?

No. A qualified distribution from a Roth IRA must be distributed for at least one of four reasons (see Q 4:9); each of those reasons also qualifies as an exception to the 10 percent premature distribution penalty under Code Section 72(t) (see Q 4:22).

Q 4:11 May a qualified distribution from a Roth IRA include a distribution of excess contributions and the earnings attributable to the excess?

No. The definition of a *qualified distribution* does not include an amount distributed in a corrective distribution before the due date of the Roth IRA owner's federal income tax return, including extensions, under Code Section 408. [I.R.C. § 408A(d)(2)(C)]

Nonqualified Distributions

Q 4:12 How is a nonqualified distribution from a Roth IRA treated?

A distribution from a Roth IRA that is not a qualified distribution (see Q 4:9) is a nonqualified distribution. A nonqualified distribution is generally treated as coming first from contributions to the Roth IRA to the extent that the distribution, when added to all previous distributions from the Roth IRA, does not exceed the aggregate amount of contributions to the Roth IRA (see Q 4:1). [I.R.C. § 408A(d)(2)(B); Treas. Reg. § 1.408A-6, Q&A 4] In other words, nonqualified distributions are treated as taken from the nontaxable portion first (the contributions) until the aggregate distributions exceed the aggregate contributions. When that occurs, earnings are treated as part of the distribution for tax purposes. There are two exceptions which apply to the untaxed portion of a conversion contribution; one has expired, and the other will be effective in 2011 and 2012. Thus, neither will apply in 2009 (see Q 4:1).

Practice Pointer. Roth IRA owners must keep track of their aggregate contributions (basis) to all Roth IRAs.

Furthermore, in a nonqualified distribution, generally, if the Roth IRA owner withdraws earnings in addition to contributions, the earnings are taxable; therefore, the earnings are also subject to the 10 percent premature distribution penalty under Code Section 72(t), unless any of the exceptions apply (see Q 4:22). [Treas. Reg. § 1.408A-6, Q&A 5]

Practice Pointer. If the distribution is not a qualified distribution (either the event tests or aging period rules are not met), the individual can generally recover the full amount contributed before any (taxable) earnings are received.

Five-Year Exclusion Periods

Q 4:13 What do the terms *exclusion period* and the *nonexclusion date* refer to?

The term *exclusion period* refers to the five-taxable-year period beginning with the first year for which a contribution is made to a Roth IRA. [I.R.C. § 408A(d)(2)(B)]

The term *nonexclusion date* refers to the end of the exclusion period.

Note. For the purpose of determining whether a distribution of earnings is a qualified distribution, there is only one five-year holding period (see Q 4:17). [I.R.C. § 408A(d)(2)(B)]

Q 4:14 How many exclusion periods are there, and when does each begin?

There are two exclusion (i.e., five-year) periods:

1. For the purpose of determining whether a converted amount is being distributed, the exclusion period begins with the taxable year for which the conversion contribution was made (see Q 4:17). [I.R.C. § 408A(d)(3)(F)(i)(II); Treas. Reg. § 1.408A-6, Q&A 5(c)]

2. For the purpose of determining whether a distribution of earnings is a qualified distribution (see Q 4:9), the exclusion period starts with the year

for which the first contribution (annual or conversion) was made to the Roth IRA. [I.R.C. § 408A(d)(2)(B)]

Example 1. Maureen, a calendar-year taxpayer, makes a conversion contribution on February 25, 2009, and makes a regular contribution for the prior year (2008) on the same date. The five-year period for the conversion begins on January 1, 2009, while the five-year period for the regular contribution begins on January 1, 2008.

Example 2. Brian's taxable year is the calendar year, and he makes a first-time regular Roth IRA contribution any time between January 1, 2009, and April 15, 2010, for 2009. The five-taxable-year period for determining whether the distribution is a qualified distribution begins on January 1, 2009. Brian makes another annual contribution to his Roth IRA in 2011. Because of the requirement of the five-taxable-year period, no qualified distributions can occur before taxable years beginning in 2014 (see Q 4:9).

Example 3. Same facts as in Example 2, except Brian also converts amounts from his traditional IRA and his qualified plan to a Roth IRA in 2010. The five-year exclusion period for determining whether the penalty tax applies to converted amounts distributed before the end of exclusion period does not occur before taxable years beginning in 2015 (see Q 4:17). (See Q 4:1, item 5, regarding the possible acceleration of income if a conversion made in 2010 is withdrawn (under the ordering rules) before 2013.)

Practice Pointer. It is advisable to start contributing to a Roth IRA as soon as possible. Doing so starts the five-year exclusion period running and thus achieves qualified status for the account as soon as possible.

Q 4:15 When does an exclusion period not start?

The five-taxable-year period for determining whether a distribution is a qualified distribution does not start over for subsequent Roth IRA contributions unless the entire account balance in a Roth IRA is distributed to the Roth IRA owner before the owner makes any other Roth IRA contributions. [I.R.C. § 408A(d)(2)(B)]

If an initial contribution is made to a Roth IRA and the Roth IRA is subsequently revoked within seven days, or if an initial Roth IRA contribution is recharacterized, the initial contribution does not start the five-year period (see Qs 9:45–9:46). [*See* preamble to final regulations under Code Section 408A, T.D. 8816, 64 Fed. Reg. 5597–5611 (Feb. 4, 1999)]

An excess contribution that is distributed in accordance with Code Section 408(d)(4) does not start the five-year period. Code Section 408(d)(4) requires that when a correction is made on or before the due date of the IRA owner's federal income tax return (including extensions), the correcting distribution must include any net income attributable to the contribution. Additionally, if an excess or unwanted contribution or conversion contribution is recharacterized as a traditional IRA, the correcting distribution has to be adjusted for any net income; if there are no remaining assets in the Roth IRA, the five-year period does not begin.

Q 4:16   What is the effect on the five-year exclusion period if a Roth IRA owner makes a regular Roth IRA contribution and a conversion contribution to the same Roth IRA?

None. Two separate five-year periods are used. The five-year period used for determining whether the 10 percent premature distribution tax applies to a distribution from a conversion amount is separately determined for each conversion and is not necessarily the same as the five-year period used for determining whether a distribution is a qualified distribution. The five-year period that is used for the purpose of determining whether an amount is a qualified distribution starts with the year for which the first contribution is made to the Roth IRA (see Q 4:14). [I.R.C. § 408A(d)(2)(B); Treas. Reg. § 1.408A-6, Q&A 2]

Q 4:17   What is the result if a converted amount is distributed from a Roth IRA before the end of the applicable exclusion period?

If a converted amount is distributed from a Roth IRA before the five-year period beginning with the taxable year for which the conversion contribution was made has elapsed, the amount is treated as taxable for purposes of the Code Section 72(t) early withdrawal penalties to the extent that it would have been taxable had it been distributed from the traditional IRA and not converted. Thus, the distribution is subject to the 10 percent premature distribution penalty under Code Section 72(t), unless the Roth IRA owner is age 59½ or older or one of the other penalty exceptions applies (see Q 4:22). [I.R.C. § 408A(d)(3)(F); Treas. Reg. § 1.408A-6, Q&As 4 and 5] A qualified distribution would also satisfy the penalty exceptions under Code Section 72(t). The premature distribution penalty is based only on the portion of the distribution that had to be included in gross income because of the conversion. This is true, even though the amount generally may be received under the ordering rules without any federal income tax liability (subject to acceleration for any unrecovered spread income resulting from a 2010 conversion).

> **Example 1.** Abigail makes nondeductible contributions to a traditional IRA. There is no gain. She converts that IRA to a new Roth IRA. Abigail has no other IRAs or Roth IRAs, and she makes no additional contributions. Within five years Abigail removes the amount that she originally converted. The amount distributed is subject neither to federal income tax nor to the 10 percent premature distribution penalty (see Q 4:1).

> **Example 2.** Lola makes deductible contributions to a traditional IRA that has increased in value. She converts that IRA to a new Roth IRA in 2009 and pays all income taxes on the amount converted. Lola has no other IRAs or Roth IRAs, and she makes no additional contributions. Within five years of the conversion (before 2014), Lola distributes the entire account value. The conversion amount distributed is not subject to federal income tax, but the 10

percent premature distribution penalty may apply, if Lola is under age 59½, and none of the other exceptions apply. The taxation of the gain distributed to Lola would depend upon whether the distribution (of gain) was a qualified distribution, which in this case, it does not appear to be (see Q 4:9).

Q 4:18   What special rule applies with regard to the exclusion period if a conversion contribution is distributed when a Roth IRA owner is under age 59½?

If a Roth IRA owner is under the age of 59½ and there is no remaining basis attributable to annual Roth IRA contributions, a converted amount withdrawn before the end of the five-year period starting with the year for which the conversion amount being withdrawn was contributed is treated for purposes of Code Section 72(t) as if it were includible in income (to the extent of the taxable amount). [I.R.C. § 408A(d)(3)(F)] As a result, the amount is subject to the 10 percent premature distribution penalty, unless an exception applies (see Q 4:22), to the extent that the distributed amount would have been taxable had it been distributed from the traditional IRA and not converted. That is so even though the amount may be received under the ordering rules without any federal income tax liability.

> **Practice Pointer.** A Roth IRA owner must keep track of the five-year period for the special rule applicable to distributions of converted amounts (see Q 4:1).

Q 4:19   What is the result if a distribution of earnings is made from a Roth IRA before the exclusion period elapses?

A distribution of earnings (gain) made before the end of the five-year period (see Q 4:17) is a nonqualified distribution (see Q 4:12) and is taxable. Taxable earnings are subject to the 10 percent premature distribution penalty if the Roth IRA owner has not yet attained age 59½, unless one of the other exceptions applies (see Q 4:22). [Treas. Reg. § 1.408A-6, Q&A 5]

Q 4:20   Does the 10 percent premature distribution penalty apply if earnings are withdrawn after the exclusion period has elapsed?

Maybe. Whether or not the 10 percent premature distribution penalty applies to earnings (gain) distributed after the end of the five-year period depends on the reason for the distribution (see Q 4:9). The 10 percent penalty tax does not apply to a qualified distribution.

> **Example 1.** Horace makes a regular Roth contribution in June 2009. In December 2014, at the age of 59½, he makes another annual contribution to his Roth IRA. The applicable five-year period ends in 2014. In 2014, Horace takes a distribution of the total amount in his Roth IRA. Since he is now age 59½, Horace satisfies the five-year rule and the age requirement (one of the

conditions for a qualified distribution); this allows him to take the entire amount of gain tax free and penalty free. Of course, distributions of annual contributions to a Roth IRA are always tax free and penalty free.

Example 2. The facts are the same as those in Example 1, except that Horace is age 25 and removes the account balance to meet his educational expenses. Even though the distribution is made after the five-year period, it is not a qualified distribution because it is made before age 59½ and not made because of disability, on account of death, or for a first-time home purchase (see Q 4:9). Thus, the gain is taxable, but none of the gain is subject to the 10 percent early distribution penalty tax (see Q 4:22).

10 Percent Premature Distribution Penalty

Q 4:21   When does the 10 percent premature distribution penalty apply to distributions from a Roth IRA?

Unless the recipient taxpayer is age 59½ or older or one of the other exceptions under Code Section 72(t) applies (see Q 4:22), an amount distributed from an IRA (including a Roth IRA) that is taxable (e.g., nonqualified distribution of gain) is also subject to a nondeductible penalty of 10 percent. [I.R.C. § 72(t)] Likewise, unless an exception applies, a conversion amount that is distributed before the applicable five-year period ends (see Qs 4:1, 4:17) is subject to the penalty (but not to federal income tax) to the extent of the conversion contribution includible in gross income (see Qs 3:14, 3:15).

Q 4:22   What are the exceptions to the 10 percent premature distribution penalty?

The 10 percent premature distribution penalty under Code Section 72(t) is imposed on most distributions made from a Roth IRA before the Roth IRA owner attains age 59½. The following types of distributions are exceptions from the premature distribution penalty:

1. Distributions made on or after the date on which the Roth IRA owner attains age 59½. [I.R.C. § 72(t)(2)(A)(i)]

2. Distributions made to a beneficiary (or to the estate of the owner) on or after the death of the Roth IRA owner. [I.R.C. § 72(t)(2)(A)(ii)]

3. Distributions attributable to the Roth IRA owner's becoming disabled within the meaning of Code Section 72(m)(7) (as defined in Treasury Regulations Section 1.72-17A(f)). [I.R.C. § 72(t)(2)(A)(iii)]

4. Distributions that are part of a series of substantially equal periodic payments (not less frequently than annually) made for the life (or life expectancy) of the Roth IRA owner or for the joint lives (or joint life expectancies) of the owner and his or her designated beneficiary. [I.R.C. § 72(t)(2)(A)(iv)] Distributions that qualify under this exception generally may not be modified for five years (other than on account of death or

disability) unless another exception applied to the distribution when it initially commenced. Attaining age 59½ during the five-year payment period does not eliminate the penalty if the method of payment is modified. [*See* I.R.C. §§ 72(t)(2)(A), 72(t)(3)(A); *see also* Ltr. Rul. 9739044 (July 1, 1997) (regarding a situation in which a spouse received a partial interest in an IRA under a divorce decree and the total payments from both IRAs were substantially equal to the payments made under the substantially equal periodic payment exception before the division); *see also* Ltr. Ruls. 200202076 (Dec. 15, 2001), 200202074 (Dec. 15, 2001) (regarding situations in which a spouse received a partial interest in an IRA under a divorce decree and the original IRA owner spouse was allowed to reduce payments proportionate to his/her new balance); 200925044 (Mar. 23, 2009), modification resulted when assets from IRA making substantially equal periodic payment under the exception were transferred to another IRA; but see, PLR 200929021 (Apr. 21, 2009), providing relief where an amount was erroneously rolled over into the IRA from which periodic payments were being taken following a rollover from the original IRA.]

Note. In three letter rulings, the IRS permitted distributions under the substantially equal periodic exception to be *recalculated* each year (based on the account balance as of the end of December 31 of the prior year *and* on a current life expectancy or annuity factor) under the "fixed" amortization method. Under the fixed amortization method, annual payments are fixed once calculated. [Rev. Rul. 2002-62, 2002-42 I.R.B. 710, modifying I.R.S. Notice 89-25 (Mar. 12, 1989), which provides three methods of determining substantially equal periodic payments for purposes of the Code Section 72(t) exception from the 10 percent penalty tax] Recalculation may offer advantages when interest rates fluctuate and for investments that either increase or decrease in value. In both cases, the IRS determined that the mortality and interest rate in Private Letter Ruling 200432023 (May 11, 2004) and the life expectancy and interest rate used in Private Letter Rulings 200432028 (May 11, 2004) and 200432021 (May 11, 2004) did not circumvent the requirements of the Code (through the use of an unreasonably high interest rate, a mortality table, or an unreasonable life expectancy). [I.R.C. §§ 72(t)(2)(A)(iv), 72(t)(4)] Because private letter rulings cannot be relied on by others, it would be advisable for an IRA owner to first obtain his or her own ruling before adopting such a payment structure. [*See also* Ltr. Ruls. 200503036 (Oct. 25, 2004); 200437038 (June 17, 2004), method not approved; 200432024 (May 11, 2004), IRA annuity contract; 200432023 (May 11, 2004), IRA annuity contract; 200432021 (May 11, 2004), change approved; 200225040 (Mar. 25, 2002), divorce-driven change allowed]

Practice Pointer. Using recalculation from the beginning may offer more flexibility and may avoid having to utilize the one-time switch exception (to the required minimum distribution method) in Revenue Ruling 2002-62 in the event account balances decline substantially.

5. Distributions for unreimbursed medical expenses to the extent that the distributions do not exceed the amount allowable as a deduction under Code Section 213, relating to amounts paid during the taxable year for medical care (determined without regard to whether the Roth IRA owner itemizes deductions for that taxable year). [I.R.C. § 72(t)(2)(B)]

6. Distributions for medical insurance made to an unemployed individual after separation from employment if the individual has received unemployment compensation for 12 consecutive weeks under any federal or state unemployment compensation law by reason of the separation from employment. [I.R.C. §§ 72(t)(2)(D)(i), 213(d)(1)(D)]

7. Distributions used to pay qualified higher education expenses (including graduate education expenses) for the Roth IRA owner, the owner's spouse, or any child or grandchild of either. [I.R.C. § 72(t)(2)(E)]

8. Distributions made for first-time homebuyer expenses. (There is a lifetime maximum of $10,000. The distribution must be used within 120 days to buy, build, or rebuild the principal residence of the Roth IRA owner, his or her spouse, or any child, grandchild, or ancestor of either. An individual qualifies as a first-time homebuyer if the individual (and his or her spouse) had no present ownership interest in a principal residence during the preceding two years. [I.R.C. § 72(t)(2)(F)]

9. Distributions made on account of an IRS levy under Code Section 6331 on the Roth IRA. (This provision applies to distributions after December 31, 1999.) The provision would not apply to a distribution to a taxpayer that is then used to satisfy an IRS levy, but would apply to a seizure as part of a plea agreement. [I.R.C. §§ 72(t)(2)(A)(vii), 4974(c); Larotonda v. Comm'r, 89 T.C. 287 (1987); Murillo v. Comm'r, T.C. Memo 1998-13, *aff'd,* 166 F.3d 1201 (2d Cir. 1998)]

   Note. It is not known whether distributions made under the Mandatory Victims Restitution Act of 1996 (MVRA), which are treated as "federal tax liens," would be exempt from the 10 percent premature distribution tax penalty. [United States v. Novak, 441 F.3d 819 (9th Cir. 2006).

10. Distributions to individuals called to active duty after September 11, 2001, for at least 180 days (or an indefinite period). Under the PPA, the 10-percent early withdrawal tax does not apply to a qualified reservist distribution from a traditional IRA or Roth IRA (see Qs 3:122–3:123). [I.R.C. § 72(t)(2)(G)(3)(iii)(I)]

Note. The qualified reservist distribution exception does not apply to a SARSEP IRA or a SIMPLE IRA.

An individual who receives a qualified reservist distribution may, at any time during the two-year period beginning on the day after the end of the active duty period, make one or more contributions to an IRA of such individual in an aggregate amount not to exceed the amount of such distribution (see Q 3:124). The dollar limitations otherwise applicable to contributions to IRAs do not apply to any contribution made pursuant to the provision. No deduction is allowed for any contribution made under the provision.

Example. Kendra, a qualified reservist, was called to active duty on August 1, 2007. For personal reasons, Kendra takes a Roth IRA distribution on September 14, 2007. The 10 percent penalty tax for early withdrawal will not apply. Assuming that Kendra is relieved of active duty on May 20, 2009, she will have until May 20, 2011 (the later of two years after the date of enactment or two years after the end of his active duty) to roll over the 2007 distribution amount into a Roth IRA and avoid having to pay federal income tax.

11. Certain disaster distributions received:

   Kansas disaster area

   a. In 2007 and 2008—qualified recovery assistance distributions in the Kansas disaster area (see Qs 3:132–3:142).

   b. After May 3, 2008, and before October 22, 2008—qualified disaster distribution used to purchase or construct a main home in the Kansas disaster area that was not purchased or constructed, if not repaid before October 23, 2008 (see Qs 3:143–3:146).

   Midwestern disaster area

   a. On or after applicable disaster date and before 2010—qualified disaster recovery assistance distributions in the Midwestern disaster area (see Qs 3:147–3:157).

   b. On or after applicable disaster date and before March 4, 2009—qualified disaster distribution used to purchase or construct a main home in the Midwestern disaster area that was not purchased or constructed, if not repaid before March 4, 2009 (see Qs 3:158–3:161).

   Caution. Although certain disaster distributions are exempt from the 10 percent tax, if a disaster distribution for the purchase or construction of a main home is not used to purchase or construct a main home and not timely repaid, any distribution of gain (other than in a qualified distribution described in Q 4:9) will be subject to the additional 10 percent penalty tax.

12. In 2006 through 2009, tax-free distributions from individual retirement plans for charitable purposes (see Q 4:1).

13. In 2005 and 2006, qualified hurricane distribution (see Qs 3:125, 3:129).

14. In 2008, timely removal of an Economic Stimulus Payment directly deposited (see following Note).

Note. Economic Stimulus Payments (but not regular federal tax refunds) directly deposited into IRAs and other tax-favored accounts may be withdrawn tax-free and penalty-free, notwithstanding any restrictions in the Code. This relief is available for amounts withdrawn from these tax-favored accounts that are less than or equal to a taxpayer's directly deposited stimulus payment. To the extent that the withdrawal is made no later than the time for filing the taxpayer's income tax return for 2008, plus extensions (or in the case of a Coverdell Education Savings Account (CESA), the later of May 31, 2009, or the time for filing the taxpayer's income tax return for 2008, plus extensions), the amount withdrawn is treated as neither contributed to nor distributed from the account. Thus, the amount withdrawn will not be subject to regular federal income tax or to any additional tax or penalty under the Code. Thus, for example, a 40-year-old taxpayer whose $1,500 stimulus payment is directly deposited into his or her IRA can withdraw anywhere up to $1,500 from the IRA, tax-free and penalty-free. The IRS recognizes that financial institutions may not be able to distinguish these contributions and distributions from others that may occur. Therefore the financial institution receiving the direct deposit of the economic stimulus payment and making the distribution should report the deposit and distribution in the usual manner. Taxpayers who choose to withdraw their economic stimulus payments will receive instructions in their Form 1040 package that will allow them to report the distribution on their individual income tax return in a manner that shows that the amount withdrawn is not subject to taxes or penalties. [IR-2008-68 (Apr. 30, 2008); I.R.S. Ann. 2008-44, 2008 I.R.B. 20 (Apr. 30, 2008)]

Withholding

Q 4:23　Do the withholding rules apply to distributions from a Roth IRA?

Sometimes. The Consolidated Appropriations Act [Pub. L. No. 106–554], enacted in December 2000, amended the last sentence of Code Section 3405(e)(1)(B) to exclude a Roth IRA from the term *individual retirement plan*. In general, Code Section 3405(e)(1)(B) provides that a payer need not withhold on any payment or distribution that it is reasonable to believe is not includible in gross income. The change was effective as of January 1, 1998, when Roth IRAs first became available. The amendment to the last sentence of Code Section 3405(e)(1)(B) clearly excludes distributions from a Roth IRA from being automatically subject to withholding because, as a general rule, it is reasonable to believe that distributions from a Roth IRA are not includible in gross income. Generally (see Notes below), only the taxable portion of a distribution of gain in a nonqualified distribution (see Q 4:12), a revoked contribution (see Q 9:45) with earnings, or in a corrective distribution with earnings is subject to withholding (see Q 4:25).

> **Practice Pointer.** The withholding requirements only apply to earnings being distributed. In those cases, 10 percent must be withheld on the earnings portion, unless the recipient elects no withholding.

> **Note 1.** Withholding may apply to a distribution from a traditional IRA that is converted to a Roth IRA (see Q 3:18). [Treas. Reg. § 1.408-6, Q&A 13] Estimated tax payments may also be required on a conversion to a Roth IRA (see Q 6:34). [I.R.S. Legal Memo 200105062 (Dec. 12, 2000)]

> **Note 2.** Qualified hurricane, recovery assistance, and recovery disaster distributions are subject to the income tax withholding rules applicable to distributions that are not eligible rollover distributions (except for a distribution that would be treated as a qualified distribution; see Q 4:9).

Thus, the 20 percent mandatory income tax withholding rules do not apply and the taxpayer may elect that there be no withholding. [I.R.C. §§ 1400Q(a)(6)(A), 3405]

Q 4:24   What changes to the withholding rules, as they affect distributions from a Roth IRA, have been enacted?

Buried in the technical corrections section of the final budget bill signed by President William J. Clinton in December 2000 are several changes affecting Roth IRAs. [Consolidated Appropriations Act, Pub. L. No. 106–554] The most significant change exempts most distributions from Roth IRAs from being subject to federal income tax withholding under Code Section 3405 (see Q 4:23). The change is effective retroactively to January 1, 1998 (the original effective date of the Taxpayer Relief Act of 1997) (but see Notes 1 and 2 in Q 4:23).

Q 4:25   How does the Consolidated Appropriations Act affect the correction of excess contributions to a Roth IRA?

The definition of a *qualified Roth IRA distribution* provides that any distribution of an excess contribution plus earnings will never be treated as a qualified distribution. [I.R.C. §§ 408(d)(4), 408A(d)(2)(C)] That means that the earnings being distributed in a corrective distribution will *always* be taxable, even when the distribution would otherwise satisfy the definition of a qualified distribution (see Q 4:9). [Treas. Reg. § 1.408A-6, Q&A 1(d)] Withholding rules may also apply (see Q 4:24).

Transfers Between Roth IRAs

Q 4:26   How should transfers between Roth IRAs be effected?

Transferring assets between Roth IRAs is the most unrestricted method of moving Roth IRA funds from one Roth IRA trustee (or custodian) to another. There are no restrictions on the number of times an individual may request such a transfer. Furthermore, because no distribution occurs, no reporting is required.

Although the IRS allows transfers between Roth IRAs to occur at any time and in any amount, no specific guidance has been issued with respect to proper documentation by the trustees (or custodians) involved. It is strongly recommended, however, that the trustee (or custodial) organization document any and all requests for transfers, whether the transfer is going out from or coming into the trustee (or custodial) organization. It is further recommended that the transferor (losing) organization obtain the signature of the transferee (receiving) organization acknowledging that the receiving institution accepts the funds as a Roth IRA and is the successor fiduciary.

Caution. A trustee (or custodial) organization receiving funds in a direct transfer from another trustee (or custodial) organization should be prepared to act properly if the Roth IRA owner attempts to revoke the newly established IRA at the receiving organization. That is, a timely revocation of an IRA (including a Roth IRA) must be reported (even when the IRA was established with a direct transfer). [Rev. Proc. 91-70, 1991-2 C.B. 899]

Q 4:27   How may a transfer of a deceased Roth IRA owner's account be accomplished?

There are no provisions in the Code or the Treasury regulations that allow a beneficiary of a deceased IRA owner to request a direct transfer between trustees or custodians. [*See* Rev. Rul. 78-406, 1978-2 C.B. 157] There have been letter rulings issued on the subject of transfers by beneficiaries. In Letter Ruling 200027064 a transfer by a widow in the deceased spouse's name was permitted because the widow was the sole beneficiary. In Letter Ruling 8716058 a nonspouse beneficiary was allowed to transfer the mother's IRA to another institution; however, special circumstances applied to the ruling. [*see also* Ltr. Ruls. 9416037 (Jan. 24, 1994), 9802046 (Oct. 18, 1997), 200221048 (Oct. 31, 2001), 200109051 (Dec. 7, 2000), allowing nonspouse transfers]

Generally, if the proceeds of a decedent's IRA are payable to the decedent's estate, and are paid to the personal representative of the estate who then pays them to the decedent's surviving spouse as intestate beneficiary of the estate, said surviving spouse is treated as having received the IRA proceeds from the estate and not from the decedent. Similarly, a surviving spouse may not treat an IRA as his or her own if a trust is beneficiary, even if the surviving spouse is a (or sole) beneficiary of a trust. [Treas. Reg. § 1.408-8, Q&A-5(a); Ltr. Ruls. 200343029 (Jul. 29, 2003), 200324059 (Mar. 18, 2003)] Accordingly, such surviving spouse, generally, is not eligible to roll over (or have transferred) said distributed IRA proceeds into his or her own IRA. Thus, a conversion would generally not be possible under such circumstances.

Although not specifically stated in the RMD regulations, a surviving spouse may not elect to treat the IRA of a decedent as his or her own if an estate is the beneficiary of the IRA even if the spouse is both the sole executor or executrix of the estate and also the sole beneficiary of the estate. [*See, e.g.,* Ltr. Rul. 200343029] However, the Preamble to the final RMD regulations provides, in relevant part, that a surviving spouse who *actually receives* a distribution from an IRA is permitted to roll that distribution over into his or her own IRA even if the spouse is not the sole beneficiary of the deceased's IRA as long as the rollover is accomplished within the requisite 60-day period. A rollover may be accomplished even if IRA assets pass through either a trust or an estate. [Preamble, Treas. Reg. § 1.401(a)(9), 67 Fed. Reg. 74, 18988, 18952 (Apr. 17, 2002)] Thus, the general rule will not apply in a case where the surviving spouse is the sole personal representative of the decedent's estate who must pay the decedent's IRA to himself or herself, as sole intestate beneficiary of the estate, and who, after such payment timely rolls them into an IRA set up and maintained in his or her name. [Ltr. Rul. 200324059 (Mar. 18, 2003); *see also* Ltr.

Rul. 200317032 (Nov. 22, 2002), involving a residuary bequest (under a will) directed in favor of the sole executrix]

In a letter ruling involving the transfer of assets from a qualified plan to an IRA of the child of the deceased, the IRS held that a rollover or transfer necessitates that the actual transfer of plan assets occur during the lifetime of the participant. The IRS reasoned that, although this is not explicitly stated in either Code Section 402(c) (relating to rollovers) or Code Section 401(a)(31) (relating to direct transfers from qualified plans), or in the regulations thereunder, "a valid rollover, even if intended to be accomplished as a direct transfer . . . , necessitates the actual transfer of plan assets occur during the lifetime of the employee for whose benefit the plan account is maintained and for whose benefit the IRA is established." Otherwise, according to the IRS, any transfer occurring after death will be "treated as a distribution that is not a rollover and immediately taxable to the beneficiary." [Ltr. Rul. 200204038 (Oct. 30, 2001] Had the beneficiary been the deceased IRA owner's spouse, the post-death transfer would likely have been permitted.

> **Note.** Letter Ruling 200204038 is a tortured technical reading of statutes to come up with an absurd result. Whether, on death, an incomplete transfer is valid under state law should have been the controlling issue. The IRS now has authority to extend the 60-day rollover period (see Q 3:69).

Transfers Incident to Divorce

Q 4:28   How are transfers between IRAs incident to divorce treated?

When a transfer (see Q 4:30) occurs from an IRA owned by one individual (including a Roth IRA) to an IRA (including a Roth IRA) established for the benefit of the IRA owner's divorced spouse, the transfer is not considered a taxable distribution, and after the transfer the transferee IRA is treated as belonging to the divorced spouse. [I.R.C. § 408(d)(6); Treas. Reg. § 1.408A-1, Q&A 1(b); Ltr. Ruls. 7948054 (Aug. 29, 1979), 8007024 (Nov. 21, 1979), 8025026 (Mar. 2, 1979), 8504079 (Oct. 31, 1984), 8820086 (Feb. 25, 1988), 9011031 (Dec. 19, 1989), 200027060 (Apr. 12, 2000), 200202076 (Dec. 15, 2001), and 200116056 (Dec. 26, 2001); Harris v. Comm'r, T.C. Memo 1991-375, 14 Employee Benefits Cas. (BNA) 1274 (1991) (the withdrawal of funds from an IRA to pay the amount of cash awarded to the IRA owner's ex-spouse in the divorce decree was found to be a taxable transfer); *see also* Bunney v. Comm'r, 114 T.C. 259, 262 (2000) (amounts not "transferred" to spouse in community property state)] Such a transfer may occur only after a divorce decree or a written instrument incident to the divorce has been issued (see Q 4:31). [I.R.C. § 408(d)(6), 408(g)]

Q 4:29   Is a transfer between IRAs incident to legal separation permissible?

Yes. The Omnibus Budget Reconciliation Act of 1989 (OBRA '89) expanded Code Section 408(d)(6) to allow tax-free transfers to occur between spouses'

IRAs as the result of a legal separation. This amendment is effective with respect to legal separations occurring after December 19, 1989.

Q 4:30   What constitutes a transfer between IRAs incident to divorce?

It appears that the IRS interprets the word *transfer* as used in the Code to mean the IRA assets being awarded (or transferred) to the former spouse at the point of the divorce decree itself—that is, before they are physically transferred. In other words, when the divorce decree is finalized, there is one IRA plan that has two IRA participants and contains the assets belonging to the original IRA owner and the assets now belonging to the spouse or former spouse under the terms of the divorce decree. The so-called transfer has already occurred, except for the fact that all of the assets are still in just one IRA plan. [I.R.S. Pub. 590 (2008), at 29]

Q 4:31   How should an IRA trustee or custodian address a transfer between IRAs incident to divorce?

The IRS has not formally addressed the procedures to be followed by an IRA trustee or custodian with regard to a transfer between IRAs (including Roth IRAs) pursuant to a divorce decree or written separation instrument. The authors recommend that when a divorce decree is issued and part or all of an individual's IRA is to be given to the former spouse, the IRA trustee or custodian should internally transfer the amount involved to an IRA set up in the name of the former spouse. The former spouse could then take a taxable and reportable distribution, transfer the IRA to another organization, or leave the IRA at the existing organization.

Q 4:32   How may a Roth IRA owner go about transferring the amounts in his or her IRA affected by a divorce?

IRS Publication 590, Individual Retirement Arrangements, provides two methods that an IRA owner can use to transfer an amount under a divorce decree to a former spouse:

1. *Changing the name on the Roth IRA.* If all the assets in a Roth IRA are to be transferred, the IRA owner can make the transfer by changing the name on the Roth IRA from his or her name to the name of the owner's spouse or former spouse.

2. *Direct transfer.* The Roth IRA owner can direct the trustee (or custodian) of the Roth IRA to transfer the affected assets directly to the trustee (or custodian) of a new or existing Roth IRA set up in the name of the owner's spouse or former spouse. If the spouse or former spouse is allowed to keep his or her portion of the IRA assets in the original owner's Roth IRA, the original owner may direct the trustee to transfer the assets the original owner is permitted to keep directly to a new or existing traditional IRA set up in the original owner's name. The name on the Roth IRA containing the spouse's or former spouse's portion of the assets would then be changed to show his or her ownership.

Practice Pointer. The authors recommend the direct transfer method, except that an internal transfer should occur before any external transfer to another organization.

Note 1. It is assumed that the foregoing IRS interpretation is based on the fact that the divorce decree has already technically transferred all or a portion of the original owner's interest in the Roth IRA to the spouse or former spouse, thereby creating two Roth IRAs within a single Roth IRA plan.

Note 2. The method used may be determined by the internal operational policies of the trustee or custodian.

Caution. The Roth IRA owner should not withdraw the funds from the Roth IRA to pay his or her ex-spouse the amount of the IRA awarded. [Harris v. Comm'r, T.C. Memo 1991-375; Bunney v. Comm'r, 114 T.C. 259 (2000)]

Q 4:33   Do the QDRO rules apply to transfers between IRAs incident to divorce?

No. The qualified domestic relations order (QDRO) rules do not apply to IRAs. [I.R.C. § 414(p)(9)]

Caution. The way a divorce decree is worded should indicate how an IRA trustee (or custodian) should proceed. The divorce decree may call for a "transfer incident to divorce" of a portion or all of the IRA assets. If, however, the divorce decree states that the spouse will "receive a distribution" of the owner's IRA without mentioning a transfer, there may be a question with respect to taxation. That is, in such a case, the original IRA owner may be subject to taxes and the early distribution penalty on the amount distributed, while the former spouse receives the assets tax and penalty free. If there is doubt with respect to the wording in the divorce decree, the matter should be discussed with the legal counsel before proceeding.

Note. For a Roth IRA, only a nonqualified distribution of earnings would be subject to income tax.

Deductions for Losses

Q 4:34   Can a deduction be claimed for a loss in a Roth IRA?

Yes, to the extent that the taxpayer distributes all amounts from all Roth IRAs owned by the taxpayer and the total distributions are less than the taxpayer's unrecovered basis (see Qs 1:11, 4:1). All Roth IRAs maintained for an individual must be aggregated and treated as one Roth IRA for purposes of determining the loss. If the aggregate account balance of all Roth IRAs is less than the basis in all Roth IRAs, distributions are treated as consisting entirely of basis. A Roth IRA loss may be claimed as a miscellaneous itemized deduction (see Q 4:35). [I.R.S. Notice 87-16, A-5, 1987-1 C.B. 446; I.R.S. Notice 89-25, 1989-1 C.B. 662; I.R.S. Pub. No. 590 (2002), at 36, 62]

Example. Several years ago, Quark made contributions to a Roth IRA totaling $1,000. Because all contributions to a Roth IRA are fully taxed, Quark's basis is $1,000. By the end of 2008, Quark's Roth IRA earns $200 in interest income. In that year, Quark receives a distribution of $300, reducing the value of his IRA to $900 ($1,000 + $200 − $300). In 2009, Quark's Roth IRA has a loss of $250. At the end of that year, his Roth IRA balance is $650 ($900 − $250). Quark's remaining basis in his Roth IRA is $700 ($1,000 − $300). Quark receives the $650 balance remaining in the Roth IRA. Subject to the 2 percent-of-adjusted-gross-income limit (see Q 4:35), he can claim a loss for 2009 of $50 (the $700 basis minus the $650 distribution of the Roth IRA balance).

Q 4:35   Is there a limit to the amount of loss that can be deducted in a Roth IRA?

The deduction that can be taken for a Roth IRA is subject to the 2 percent-of-adjusted-gross-income limit that applies to certain miscellaneous itemized deductions on Schedule A, Form 1040. [I.R.S. Pub. No. 590 (2003), at 38]

Caution. The "wash-sale" rules prohibit the claiming of any loss when the same or substantially identical securities are purchased within 30 days before or after the sale. [Rev. Rul. 2008-5, 2008-3 I.R.B. 271]

Q 4:36   Can you take an itemized deduction for a loss in one Roth IRA while maintaining a second Roth IRA?

No. *All* amounts must be withdrawn from *all* Roth IRAs held by an individual to be eligible to take an itemized deduction on any loss. Traditional IRAs and Roth IRAs are treated separately; thus, amounts need be distributed only from all Roth IRAs. Conversely, if an individual is taking a loss on a traditional IRA, that individual must distribute all amounts from all traditional IRAs, but may maintain Roth IRAs. [I.R.S. Notice 87-16, A-5, 1987-1 C.B. 446; I.R.S. Notice 89-25, 1989-1 C.B. 662; I.R.S. Pub. No. 590 (2006), at 66]

Caution. A 10 percent premature withdrawal penalty tax may apply if a taxpayer makes a conversion to a Roth IRA and then withdraws such amounts within the five-year period beginning with the tax year in which the conversion took place (see Q 4:17). [*See* I.R.C. § 408A(d)(3)(F)]

Caution. There is no time period that prevents a taxpayer from subsequently establishing another Roth IRA. In the authors' opinion, the subsequent establishment of a Roth IRA for the same (or subsequent) taxable year would not have any effect on claiming the loss (see Q 4:35).

Demutualization

Q 4:37   Is a life insurer's contribution of policy credits to a Roth IRA as part of the life insurer's demutualization treated as a distribution?

No. The issuance of policy credits to a Roth IRA as part of a life insurer's demutualization does not constitute a distribution of such credits to the Roth IRA owner. The conversion of membership interests to policy credits is a mere change in form of one element within the arrangement to another. Since the conversion increases the accumulation value of the annuity contracts, the policy credits are treated, for purposes of Code Section 408(a)(6) and Code Section 408(b)(3), as any other return of, or return on, an investment within the arrangement and not regarded as having been received by the policyholder. Amounts representing the policy credits will be considered part of the balance to the credit of the Roth IRA owner. [I.R.C. §§ 72, 4972, 4973, 4979; *see* Rev. Rul. 71–233, 1971-1 C.B. 113; *cf.* Treas. Reg. § 1.72-2(a)(3)(i); Ltr. Rul. 200121072 (June 12, 2001)]

Q 4:38   Does a life insurer's contribution of policy credits to a Roth IRA as part of the life insurer's demutualization result in penalties?

No. The contribution of the policy credits to a Roth IRA is not a taxable distribution (see Q 4:36); therefore, there are no penalties. [I.R.C. §§ 72, 4972, 4973, 4979; Ltr. Rul. 200121072 (June 12, 2001)]

Deemed Roth IRAs

Q 4:39   Do the qualified plan distribution rules apply to the deemed Roth IRA portion of a qualified plan?

No. The Roth IRA distribution rules apply to deemed Roth IRAs (see Q 3:100) in a qualified plan (see Q 3:81). Special rollover rules apply (see Q 3:101).

Qualified Roth IRA Contribution Programs (Designated Roth Contributions)

Q 4:40   Do the qualified plan rules apply for purposes of distributions of designated Roth contributions under a qualified Roth IRA contribution program?

Yes. Distributions of designated Roth contributions (see Q 10:28) are subject to the distribution requirements under the employer's plan of which it is a part. Thus, the minimum required distribution rules apply to designated Roth contributions (see Qs 10:26–10:47). [Treas. Reg. § 1.401(k)-1(f)(3)] Excess contributions not timely distributed from a designated Roth account (DRA) are subject to (double) taxation (see Q 10:68).

Chapter 5

Required Minimum Distributions

Although a Roth IRA owner is not required to take any distributions from the Roth IRA during his or her lifetime, the beneficiary (or beneficiaries) of the Roth IRA is subject to the required minimum distribution (RMD) rules upon the death of the Roth IRA owner. This chapter examines those rules as they apply to various beneficiaries under various circumstances. Also considered are how RMDs are to be calculated and what penalties apply when RMDs are not taken timely. What options a beneficiary has when naming his or her beneficiary of the remaining Roth IRA assets are reviewed as well.

This chapter also looks at the effect the final Treasury regulations issued by the Internal Revenue Service in April 2002 have on the Roth IRA (and the RMD rules).

Overview

Q 5:1   When do the required minimum distribution rules apply to a Roth IRA?

No minimum distributions are required to be made from a Roth IRA while the Roth IRA owner is alive. [Treas. Reg. § 1.408A-6, Q&A 14(a)] Once the owner dies, however, the post-death required minimum distribution (RMD) rules under Section 401(a)(9)(B) of the Internal Revenue Code (Code) that apply to the traditional IRA also apply to the Roth IRA (with the exception of the at-least-as-rapidly rule; see Q 5:2). Further, the RMD rules apply to the Roth IRA as though the owner had died before his or her required beginning date, regardless of actual age at death. [Treas. Reg. § 1.408A-6, Q&A 14(b)]

Generally, the entire interest in a Roth IRA must be distributed to the beneficiary (or beneficiaries) by the end of the fifth calendar year after the year of the owner's death (the five-year rule) unless the interest is payable to a designated beneficiary over the life or life expectancy of the designated beneficiary (see Q 5:15). If the entire interest is paid as an annuity, the RMD may never exceed the entire account balance. The RMD must be payable over a period not greater than the designated beneficiary's life expectancy and distributions must begin before the end of the calendar year following the year of death. [Treas. Reg. § 1.401(a)(9)-5, Q&A 1]

If the sole beneficiary of the Roth IRA is the owner's spouse, he or she can either delay distributions until the decedent would have reached age 70½, or treat the Roth IRA as his or her own (see Q 5:32). [Treas. Reg. §§ 1.401(a)(9)-3, Q&A 1, 1.408A-6, Q&A 14(b)]

Note. The Worker, Retiree, and Employer Recovery Act of 2008 (WRERA) suspended the requirement for a beneficiary to take RMDs in 2009. [I.R.C. § 401(a)(9)(H)] IRS Notice 2009-9 summarizes the suspension of 2009 RMDs. In addition, if a beneficiary must take RMDs under the five-year rule (see Q 5:12), he or she can now waive the distribution for 2009, effectively taking distributions over a six-year rather than a five-year period. [I.R.S. Notice 2009-9, 2009-5 I.R.B. 419]

Q 5:2   Does the "at-least-as-rapidly" death distribution rule apply to a Roth IRA?

No. A Roth IRA owner is always treated as dying before his or her required beginning date (see Q 5:1). If distributions were never required to begin with, logic demands that the "at least as rapidly" rule under Code Section 401(a)(9)(B)(i) regarding required lifetime distributions can never apply.

Q 5:3   May a beneficiary of a Roth IRA satisfy a required minimum distribution for the Roth IRA from his or her traditional IRA?

No. An individual required to take a distribution from a Roth IRA may not choose to receive the RMD with respect to the Roth IRA from a traditional IRA (or SIMPLE IRA) that is owned by the individual either as a participant or as a beneficiary. [Treas. Reg. §§ 1.408.8, Q&A 9, 1.408A-6, Q&A 15]

Likewise, an individual required to take a distribution from a traditional IRA (or SIMPLE IRA) may not choose to receive the RMD with respect to the traditional IRA (or SIMPLE IRA) from a Roth IRA that is owned by the individual either as a participant or as a beneficiary. [Treas. Reg. § 1.408A-6, Q&A 15]

> **Example.** Esmeralda inherited a Roth IRA and a traditional IRA. In 2008, the RMD for the Roth IRA is $3,000 and the RMD for the traditional IRA is $4,000. Esmeralda withdrew $7,000 from the traditional IRA in January 2008. Because the distribution from the traditional IRA cannot satisfy the RMD from the Roth IRA, Esmeralda must still withdraw $3,000 from the Roth IRA by the end of 2008.
>
> The beneficiary may, however, satisfy the RMD for one Roth IRA by distributing from another Roth IRA if the Roth IRAs were inherited from the same decedent (see Q 5:7).

Q 5:4   May the beneficiary of a Roth IRA withdraw more than the required minimum distribution?

Yes. Code Section 401(a)(9) merely places a floor on how much must be withdrawn by a beneficiary from a Roth IRA on an annual basis. That is, the beneficiary must withdraw the RMD but may withdraw a greater amount at his or her discretion. It is generally advisable, however, for a beneficiary to take a distribution of only the minimum amount required so as to maximize the advantages of keeping funds in the tax free environment of a Roth IRA.

Q 5:5   May a distribution in excess of the required minimum distribution for a particular year be credited against future required minimum distributions?

No. A distribution in excess of the RMD for a particular year does not create a credit that is available for subsequent RMDs. [Treas. Reg. § 1.401(a)(9)-5, Q&A 2]

> **Example.** Nick's 2010 RMD is $3,000, but he decides to take out $3,500 in 2010. Nick cannot use the excess $500 toward his 2011 RMD.

Q 5:6   May a first-year required minimum distribution from a Roth IRA be deferred until the following April 1?

No. The ability to defer the first RMD from an IRA is reserved for the RMD for the year in which a traditional IRA owner reaches age 70½. The beneficiary of a Roth IRA must receive all RMDs by December 31 of the particular calendar year for which they are to be distributed.

> **Example.** Giovanni inherited a Roth IRA. In 2008, the RMD for the Roth IRA is $3,000. Giovanni must withdraw the $3,000 no later than December 31, 2008. (See Q 5:1 regarding the suspension of the RMD rules for 2009.)

Q 5:7 How do the aggregation rules apply for purposes of satisfying a required minimum distribution?

The aggregation rules for satisfying required distributions under Notice 88-38 [1988-1 C.B. 524] only apply to RMDs from Roth IRAs if the Roth IRAs at issue were inherited from the same decedent (see Qs 5:27, 5:54). [Treas. Reg. § 1.408A-6, Q&A 15]

Under the aggregation rules, the RMD for each Roth IRA is still calculated separately, but the aggregate RMD can be taken from any one or more of the individual's Roth IRAs. (See Q 5:1 regarding the suspension of the RMD rules for 2009.)

> **Example 1.** Molly inherited two Roth IRAs (Roth IRA1 and Roth IRA2) from her mother. In 2008, the RMD for Roth IRA1 is $1,000 and the RMD for Roth IRA2 is $500. Molly can take the entire $1,500 ($1,000 + $500) RMD from Roth IRA1 if she so chooses. Alternatively, Molly can take $750 from Roth IRA1 and $750 from Roth IRA2. As long as the total distribution that Molly takes from Roth IRA1 and Roth IRA2 in 2008 equals at least $1,500, she will have satisfied the RMD for the year.

> **Example 2.** Adrian inherited a Roth IRA from his mother (Roth IRA1) and a Roth IRA from his father (Roth IRA2). In 2008, the RMD for Roth IRA1 is $1,000 and the RMD for Roth IRA2 is $500. Because the two Roth IRAs were inherited from different decedents, Adrian must take the $1,000 RMD from Roth IRA1 and the $500 RMD from Roth IRA2.

Q 5:8 Are qualified charitable contributions taken into account when computing the RMD after the death of the Roth IRA owner?

Yes. Qualified charitable contributions (see Qs 4:1 and 4:22) are taken into account for purposes of the minimum distribution rules applicable to traditional IRAs, and after the death of the owner, Roth IRAs (see Q 5:1), to the same extent the distribution would have been taken into account under such rules had the distribution not been directly distributed under the provision for qualified charitable contributions. This charitable contribution rule is set to expire at the end of 2009 (see Q 4:1). (See Q 5:1 regarding the suspension of the RMD rules for 2009.)

> **Example.** Delbert, age 73, inherited a Roth IRA from his daughter. In 2008, the RMD for the Roth IRA is $10,000. Delbert makes a qualified charitable contribution from the Roth IRA of $20,000 in 2008. The $20,000 charitable contribution satisfies the $10,000 RMD.

Final Treasury Regulations

Q 5:9   How do the Code Section 401(a)(9) Treasury regulations affect Roth IRAs?

The Code Section 401(a)(9) Treasury regulations (issued by the Internal Revenue Service in April 2002) are incorporated by reference into the extant Roth IRA regulations. [I.R.C. § 408A(c)(5); Treas. Reg. §§ 1.408A-1–1.408A-9]

Because the Roth IRA does not have a lifetime distribution requirement, the 401(a)(9) regulations are generally only applicable to Roth IRAs after the death of the Roth IRA owner. One significant planning tool in the 401(a)(9) regulations that affect Roth IRA distributions is the opportunity to finalize the identity of the Roth IRA beneficiary through a valid disclaimer any time up to September 30 of the year following the year in which the Roth IRA owner died (see Q 5:27). [Treas. Reg. § 1.401(a)(9)-4, Q&A 4]

Other significant portions of the 401(a)(9) Treasury regulations affecting Roth IRAs include the following:

1. The life expectancy table, reflecting current mortality (see Q 5:19), provides a benefit to many beneficiaries because distributions may be extended over a longer period than under prior law.

2. The deemed assumption rule for a surviving spouse beneficiary of a Roth IRA owner (see Q 5:1) will only apply if the spouse is the sole beneficiary and has an unlimited right to withdraw from the account.

3. In the case of multiple beneficiaries, if a Roth IRA owner's account is divided into separate accounts for each beneficiary no later than the end of the year following the year of the owner's death, each beneficiary may use his or her own life expectancy in determining the RMD (see Q 5:45).

4. Trusts can be named as a beneficiary, including testamentary trusts. However, the requirements with respect to remainder beneficiaries of a QTIP (qualified terminable interest property) trust (see chapters 6 and 7) are somewhat confused. Also, documentation with respect to the trust's beneficiaries is not required until October 31 of the year following the year of the Roth IRA owner's death (see Q 5:43).

Q 5:10   When do the final Treasury regulations apply for purposes of determining required minimum distributions?

The final Treasury regulations applied at the beginning in 2003 for purposes of determining RMDs. [Treas. Reg. § 1.401(a)(9)-1, Q&A 2] It should be noted, however, that the regulations could be used to calculate RMDs for the 2002 calendar year. The final regulations could not be used to calculate calendar year 2001 RMDs even if they were not required to be distributed until 2002. Alternatively, the 1987 or 2001 proposed regulations could still be relied on when determining RMDs for the 2002 calendar year. [Preamble to the 2002 Final Regulations]

Q 5:11   How do the final Treasury regulations apply to Roth IRA owners who died before 2003?

If the Roth IRA owner died before 2003, the designated beneficiary must be redetermined in accordance with the provisions of Treasury Regulations Section 1.401(a)(9)-4 (see Qs 5:9–5:22) and the applicable distribution period must be reconstructed for purposes of calculating RMDs for calendar years after 2002. [Treas. Reg. § 1.401(a)(9)-1, Q&A 2]

Five-Year Rule

Q 5:12   What does the five-year rule for determining a required minimum distribution require?

The five-year rule set forth in Code Section 401(a)(9)(B)(ii) generally requires that the entire interest of the beneficiary of a Roth IRA be distributed within five years of the Roth IRA owner's death; there is, as may be expected, an exception to the five-year rule (see Q 5:15). [Treas. Reg. § 1.401(a)(9)-3, Q&A 1]

Note. However, because of the suspension of 2009 RMDs (see Q 5:1), if a beneficiary must take RMDs under the five-year rule (see Q 5:1), he or she can now waive the distribution for 2009, effectively taking distributions over a six-year rather than a five-year period. [Notice 2009-9, 2009-5 I.R.B. 419] A 2009 RMD would have normally been required in cases where the Roth IRA owner died in the years 2004 through 2008 with no designated beneficiary.

Example. Tamar dies on January 15, 2008, after naming her estate as beneficiary of her Roth IRA. The beneficiary of her Roth IRA must take distributions out over the five-year rule. Because 2009 is one of the years in the five-year rule, under Notice 2009-9, Tamar does not have to take any distributions until December 31, 2014, at which time the entire Roth IRA must be liquidated.

Q 5:13   If a Roth IRA beneficiary takes distributions under the five-year rule, when exactly must the entire interest be distributed?

A distribution to a beneficiary of a Roth IRA under the five-year rule must be completed no later than December 31 of the calendar year that contains the fifth anniversary of the date of the Roth IRA owner's death. [Treas. Reg. § 1.401(a)(9)-3, Q&A 2]

Example. Linda dies on January 15, 2009. The beneficiary of Linda's Roth IRA will have until December 31, 2014, to withdraw the entire Roth IRA unless an exception to the five-year rule applies.

If a Roth IRA beneficiary elects to take a distribution from a Roth IRA under the five-year rule, the beneficiary need not receive any distribution until the end of the fifth calendar year following the year of the Roth IRA owner's death.

Example. Linda dies on January 15, 2009. The beneficiary of Linda's Roth IRA is taking distributions out over the five-year rule. Accordingly, the beneficiary does not have to take any distributions until December 31, 2014, at which time the entire Roth IRA must be liquidated.

(See, however, Q 5:12 for how the suspension of 2009 required minimum distributions affects those taking distributions under the five-year rule.)

Q 5:14   If a Roth IRA beneficiary elects to receive the entire balance on or before December 31 of the year containing the fifth anniversary, will the 50 percent penalty apply for the years in which no distribution is made?

No. Under Treasury Regulations Section 54.4974-2, Q&A 7, the 50 percent penalty is automatically waived if the individual's entire benefit is distributed by the end of the fifth calendar year following the calendar year of the owner's death.

Q 5:15   What is the exception to the five-year rule?

The exception to the five-year rule (see Q 5:12) is as follows:

When a Roth IRA is payable to a designated beneficiary (see Q 5:23) and distributions begin before the end of the calendar year immediately following the calendar year of the Roth IRA owner's death, RMDs are to be calculated based on the life expectancy of the designated beneficiary. [I.R.C. § 401(a)(9)(B)(iii); Treas. Reg. § 1.401(a)(9)-3, Q&A 1]

Practice Pointer. The exception to the five-year rule should be exercised (when available) when the objective is to maximize the benefit to the Roth IRA beneficiary by minimizing RMDs and thereby maximizing growth in a tax-free environment.

Note. Whether a designated beneficiary may elect to receive benefits under the five-year rule or the life expectancy rule depends on the particular Roth IRA trust or custodial agreement or annuity contract. While most custodians do allow the life expectancy rule, a trustee or custodian need not allow such an option. [Treas. Reg. § 1.401(a)(9)-3, Q&A 4(c)] It is recommended that the Roth IRA contract be reviewed to ascertain the payout options.

Q 5:16   When must required minimum distributions to a Roth IRA beneficiary begin under the exception to the five-year rule?

When RMDs to a Roth IRA beneficiary must begin under the life expectancy rule (i.e., the exception to the five-year rule) depends on the status of the beneficiary.

In the case of a nonspouse beneficiary, RMDs must begin no later than December 31 of the year following the year of the Roth IRA owner's death (see, however, Q 5:17). [Treas. Reg. §§ 1.401(a)(9)-3, Q&A 3(a), 1.408A-6, Q&A 14(b)]

When a spouse is the sole beneficiary (see also Q 5:32), RMDs must begin on or before the later of:

1. December 31 of the year following the calendar year in which the Roth IRA owner died, or

2. The end of the calendar year in which the Roth IRA owner would have attained age 70½.

[Treas. Reg. §§ 1.401(a)(9)-3, Q&A 3(b), 1.408A-6, Q&A 14(b)]

> **Example 1.** Morgan dies on October 20, 2009, after naming her sister, Olivia, as beneficiary of her Roth IRA. Olivia must begin taking RMDs by December 31, 2010.

> **Example 2.** Devon dies on April 20, 2009, after naming his wife, Lydia, as beneficiary of his Roth IRA. Lydia does not perform a spousal rollover. Devon was age 52 at the time of his death. Lydia may wait until Devon would have turned age 70½ (i.e., 2027) to begin taking RMDs.

> **Example 3.** Devon dies on April 20, 2009, after naming his wife, Lydia, as beneficiary of his Roth IRA. Lydia does not perform a spousal rollover. Devon was age 72 at the time of his death. Because Devon was already age 70½, Lydia must begin taking RMDs by December 31, 2010.

Q 5:17   Does the failure to withdraw the required minimum distribution for the year following the year of death preclude use of the life expectancy rule?

No. It appears that a beneficiary can pay the 50 percent penalty for the failure to withdraw the proper RMD and thereafter take life expectancy distributions (see Qs 5:56–5:58). [Treas. Reg. § 54.4974-2]

Letter Ruling 200811028 (Mar. 14, 2008) allowed a beneficiary to utilize the life expectancy method even when the beneficiary failed to begin taking RMDs by the end of the year following the year of the IRA owner's death.

Q 5:18   How is it determined whether the five-year rule or the life expectancy rule applies to a distribution to the beneficiary of a Roth IRA?

If a Roth IRA plan does not include a provision specifying the method of distribution after the death of the Roth IRA owner, the following rules apply:

1. If the owner has a designated beneficiary, distributions are to be made in accordance with the life expectancy rule. [*See* I.R.C. § 401(a)(9)(B)(iii), 401(a)(9)(B)(iv)]

2. If the owner has no designated beneficiary, distributions are to be made in accordance with the five-year rule. [*See* I.R.C. § 401(a)(9)(B)(ii)]

It should be noted that a Roth IRA plan may adopt a provision specifying either that the five-year rule will apply to certain distributions after the death of a Roth IRA owner even if the owner has a designated beneficiary or that in every case distributions will be made in accordance with the five-year rule. [Treas. Reg. § 1.401(a)(9)-3, Q&A 4(a)–(c)]

Alternatively, a plan may adopt a provision that permits a Roth IRA owner (or his or her beneficiaries) to elect on an individual basis whether the five-year rule or the life expectancy rule will apply to distributions after the death of an owner who has a designated beneficiary. Such an election must be made no later than the earlier of the end of the calendar year in which distributions would be required to commence in order to satisfy the requirements for the life expectancy rule (see Q 5:15) or the end of the calendar year that contains the fifth anniversary of the date of death of the owner. As of the date determined under the life expectancy rule, the election must be irrevocable with respect to the beneficiary (and all subsequent beneficiaries) and must apply to all subsequent calendar years.

If a Roth IRA plan provides for an election between the five-year rule and the life expectancy rule, the plan may also specify the method of distribution that applies if neither the owner nor the beneficiary makes such an election. If no election is made and the plan does not specify which method applies, distribution must be made as if there were no plan provision.

Q 5:19   What life expectancy table is used to calculate required minimum distributions for Roth IRA beneficiaries under the exception to the five-year rule?

The Single Life Table found under Treasury Regulations Section 1.401(a)(9)-9, Q&A 1 (shown below) is used to calculate distributions to beneficiaries after the death of a Roth IRA owner under the exception to the five-year rule (i.e., the life expectancy rule). The applicable life expectancy factor is the beneficiary's attained age in the applicable year.

Example. Jack will turn age 37 in 2010. His applicable life expectancy factor for 2010 is 46.5.

Single Life Table

Age	Life Expectancy	Age	Life Expectancy	Age	Life Expectancy
0	82.4	6	76.7	12	70.8
1	81.6	7	75.8	13	69.9
2	80.6	8	74.8	14	68.9
3	79.7	9	73.8	15	67.9
4	78.7	10	72.8	16	66.9
5	77.7	11	71.8	17	66.0

Single Life Table *(con'd)*

Age	Life Expectancy	Age	Life Expectancy	Age	Life Expectancy
18	65.0	52	32.3	86	7.1
19	64.0	53	31.4	87	6.7
20	63.0	54	30.5	88	6.3
21	62.1	55	29.6	89	5.9
22	61.1	56	28.7	90	5.5
23	60.1	57	27.9	91	5.2
24	59.1	58	27.0	92	4.9
25	58.2	59	26.1	93	4.6
26	57.2	60	25.2	94	4.3
27	56.2	61	24.4	95	4.1
28	55.3	62	23.5	96	3.8
29	54.3	63	22.7	97	3.6
30	53.3	64	21.8	98	3.4
31	52.4	65	21.0	99	3.1
32	51.4	66	20.2	100	2.9
33	50.4	67	19.4	101	2.7
34	49.4	68	18.6	102	2.5
35	48.5	69	17.8	103	2.3
36	47.5	70	17.0	104	2.1
37	46.5	71	16.3	105	1.9
38	45.6	72	15.5	106	1.7
39	44.6	73	14.8	107	1.5
40	43.6	74	14.1	108	1.4
41	42.7	75	13.4	109	1.2
42	41.7	76	12.7	110	1.1
43	40.7	77	12.1	111 +	1.0
44	39.8	78	11.4		
45	38.8	79	10.8		
46	37.9	80	10.2		
47	37.0	81	9.7		
48	36.0	82	9.1		
49	35.1	83	8.6		
50	34.2	84	8.1		
51	33.3	85	7.6		

Q 5:20   What account balance is used to calculate required minimum distributions for Roth IRA beneficiaries under the exception to the five-year rule?

The account balance that should be used in determining the RMD in any given year is the account balance of the Roth IRA as of December 31 of the calendar year immediately preceding the calendar year for which the RMD is required to be made. [Treas. Reg. § 1.401(a)(9)-5, Q&A 3(a)]

> **Example.** Julian needs to take a 2008 RMD. The applicable account balance that he will use to calculate his RMD is December 31, 2007.

Q 5:21   Are any adjustments allowed to the account balance used to calculate RMDs for Roth IRA beneficiaries under the exception to the five-year rule?

Yes. The account balance is increased by the amount of any contributions or forfeitures allocated to the Roth IRA balance as of dates in the valuation calendar year after the valuation date. For this purpose, contributions that are allocated to the account balance as of dates in the valuation calendar year after the valuation date, but that are not actually made during the valuation calendar year, are permitted to be excluded. In addition, the account balance is decreased by distributions made in the valuation calendar year after the valuation date. [Treas. Reg. § 1.401(a)(9)-5, Q&A 3]

Contributions made after the calendar year that are allocated as of a date in the prior calendar year are not required to be added back. The only exceptions are rollover amounts and recharacterized conversion contributions that are not in any account on December 31 of a particular year. [Preamble, Treas. Reg. § 1.401(a)(9), T.D. 8987; 67 Fed. Reg. 18988–19028, 18993 (Apr. 17, 2002)]

Q 5:22   How does a Roth IRA beneficiary calculate required minimum distributions?

An RMD is calculated by dividing the applicable account balance (see Q 5:20) by the applicable life expectancy factor (see Q 5:19).

> **Example.** Garrett inherited a Roth IRA. The Roth IRA account balance on December 31, 2009, was $1 million. If his applicable life expectancy factor in 2010 is 58.2, Garrett's RMD equals $17,182.13 ($1,000,000 ÷ 58.2).

Beneficiaries

Designated Beneficiary

Q 5:23   What is a *designated beneficiary*?

A *designated beneficiary* is an "individual" designated under the plan or affirmative election by the Roth IRA owner who is entitled to receive all or a portion of a Roth IRA upon the death of the Roth IRA owner. [I.R.C. § 401(a)(9)(E); Treas. Reg. § 1.401(a)(9)-4, Q&A 1; Treas. Reg. § 1.408-8, Q&A 1] Most often a beneficiary will be named by the owner. In some cases, however, the default provisions of the Roth IRA trust or custodial agreement (or annuity contract) will determine the beneficiary when the Roth IRA owner (or beneficiary) has failed to name a primary or contingent beneficiary. [Treas. Reg. §§ 1.401(a)(9)-4, Q&A 2, 1.408-8, Q&A 1]

Q 5:24 May a person other than an individual be a designated beneficiary?

No. Only an individual may be designated as a beneficiary for purposes of calculating RMDs from a Roth IRA. That is so because only an individual has an ascertainable life expectancy. It follows, then, that a person that is not an individual (e.g., the Roth IRA owner's estate or a charity) may not be a designated beneficiary. It further follows that if a person other than an individual is designated as a beneficiary, the Roth IRA will be deemed to have no designated beneficiary. In some instances where certain requirements are met, a trust that is named as beneficiary receives the status of a designated beneficiary of a Roth IRA. In that instance, the regulations will allow one to look through the trust to determine whether the beneficiaries are individual beneficiaries (see Qs 5:43, 7:2). [Treas. Reg. § 1.401(a)(9)-4, Q&As 3, 5]

Q 5:25 What advantage flows from creating a designated beneficiary?

When a designated beneficiary has been created, that beneficiary is entitled to receive distributions from the Roth IRA over the designated beneficiary's life expectancy (provided the plan or custodial agreement allows for this) rather than under the five-year rule (see Q 5:15).

Example. Ann, who died in 2009, named her son Brian as the sole beneficiary of her Roth IRA. Brian will turn age 50 in 2010 (the year following the year of Ann's death). Brian is entitled to receive distributions based on his life expectancy of 34.2 years as the designated beneficiary. Clearly, the ability to receive distributions over 34.2 years will allow for tremendous tax-free accumulation that would not be available under the five-year rule.

Q 5:26 May a class of beneficiaries be a designated beneficiary?

Yes. The members of a class of beneficiaries capable of expansion or contraction (e.g., children) will be treated as being identifiable (and thus as a designated beneficiary) if it is possible, as of the date the beneficiary is determined (see Q 5:27), to identify the class member with the shortest life expectancy. The class member with the shortest life expectancy will be used to determine RMDs and therefore will be the designated beneficiary. [Treas. Reg. § 1.401(a)(9)-4, Q&A 1]

Example 1. Keith fills out the beneficiary designation form for his Roth IRA by writing "my children" in the primary beneficiary box. Keith dies in 2009, when he has three children: Melissa, age 20; Alex, age 30; and James, age 32. On September 30, 2010, Melissa, Alex, and James are clearly identifiable as his children, and James, as the oldest child, would therefore be the class member with the shortest life expectancy.

Note. Multiple beneficiaries may segregate a Roth IRA into separate accounts and thereafter each beneficiary is independently tested to determine whether such individual beneficiary constitutes a "designated beneficiary." Taxpayers have until December 31 of the year following the year of death to create separate accounts. For purposes of calculating required minimum distributions, Treasury Regulations Section 1.401(a)(9)-8, Q&A 2(a), as amended in June 2004, makes it clear that if separate accounts are actually established by the end of the calendar year following the year after the Roth IRA owner's death, the separate accounts can be used to determine RMDs for the year following the year of the Roth IRA owner's death.

Example 2. Same facts as Example 1, except that by December 31, 2010, the Roth IRA is divided into three separate Roth IRAs—one for the benefit of each child. Melissa, Alex, and James can each use their individual life expectancies to calculate RMDs of their respective Roth IRAs.

Q 5:27   Upon what date is it determined whether a designated beneficiary exists?

A Roth IRA owner's designated beneficiary is determined based on the beneficiaries designated as of September 30 of the calendar year following the calendar year of the owner's death. Consequently, any person or entity that was a beneficiary as of the date of the Roth IRA owner's death but is not a beneficiary as of the later date is not taken into account in determining the owner's designated beneficiary. [Treas. Reg. § 1.401(a)(9)-4, Q&A 4(a)-(c)]

The rule just described provides a significant opportunity for ensuring designated beneficiary status. That is, it allows for subtraction of beneficiaries through qualified disclaimers or the "cashing out" of beneficiaries. A qualified disclaimer (under Code Section 2518) will eliminate the disclaiming beneficiary from consideration when determining the oldest beneficiary for purposes of RMDs. When multiple beneficiaries are named, including non-individual beneficiaries (e.g., a charity), a cash-out of the non-individual beneficiaries would allow the remainder beneficiaries to receive life expectancy distributions.

Example 1. Jim, at his death in 2009, had named his three children as a 50 percent beneficiary and the Salvation Army as a 50 percent beneficiary of his Roth IRA. By distributing 50 percent of the Roth IRA to the Salvation Army by September 30 of the year following the year of Jim's death (2010), and by segregating the Roth IRA into separate shares, each child will be entitled to calculate RMDs from their inherited account based on his or her own life expectancy.

Example 2. Juanita dies in 2009, after naming her mother, age 70, as 50 percent beneficiary of her Roth IRA and her granddaughter, age 10, as the other 50 percent beneficiary. If Juanita's mother makes a qualified disclaimer of her 50 percent interest, she is no longer considered in determining the oldest beneficiary of the Roth IRA (*but* the beneficiary who is entitled to Juanita's mother's share of the Roth IRA because of her disclaimer (i.e., the contingent beneficiary) is considered; see the following note).

Note. Taking advantage of the rule that allows for beneficiaries of a Roth IRA to be determined (and, thus, eliminated) after the Roth IRA's owner's death by, for example, a qualified disclaimer or cash-out will not generally cause the RMD amount to increase. It is important to note, however, that if the disclaimant is younger than the resulting beneficiary or the resulting beneficiary is not an individual, larger RMDs will be required. It is, therefore, important to ascertain the named contingent beneficiary of the account before a disclaimer is executed.

Q 5:28   How is the beneficiary of a Roth IRA determined when the primary beneficiary is living on the date of the Roth IRA owner's death but dies before September 30 of the year following the year of the owner's death?

If a beneficiary dies after the Roth IRA owner, yet prior to September 30 of the year following the year of the owner's death, such deceased beneficiary (provided there is no qualified disclaimer by such beneficiary before his or her death) will continue as a beneficiary (rather than his or her estate or the successor beneficiary) for determining if there is a designated beneficiary as of September 30 of the year following the year of the owner's death and the applicable life expectancy. [Treas. Reg. § 1.401(a)(9)-4, Q&A 4(c)]

Example 1. Edy dies in 2009, after naming one brother, Ben, as 50 percent beneficiary and her other brother, Jerry, as 50 percent beneficiary of her Roth IRA. Ben dies in February 2010. Ben is still used in determining Edy's "designated beneficiary" as of September 30, 2010.

Example 2. Same as the Example 1, except that, before his death, Ben executed a qualified disclaimer of his 50 percent share in the IRA. Because of the disclaimer, he is no longer considered in determining the designated beneficiary as of September 30, 2010.

Q 5:29   When an estate is a beneficiary of a Roth IRA, can the executor of the estate assign the Roth IRA to the beneficiaries of the estate and thereby allow the beneficiaries to become designated beneficiaries?

No. The final regulations make it clear that an estate cannot qualify as a designated beneficiary. Thus, an interest in a Roth IRA payable to an estate cannot be assigned to the beneficiaries of the estate to achieve designated beneficiary status. [Treas. Reg. § 1.401(a)(9)-4, Q&A 1, 3]

Note, however, that a surviving spouse may be able to perform a spousal rollover when the Roth IRA is payable to an estate (see Q 5:40).

Additionally, in Letter Ruling 200343030, an IRA was payable to an estate. The IRS allowed an estate beneficiary to transfer her portion (as estate beneficiary) of the IRA, via trustee-to-trustee transfer, to an inherited IRA in her name. While doing so does not achieve designated beneficiary status, it alleviates the need to keep the estate open until the Roth IRA is completely distributed.

Practice Pointer. Although the Roth IRA cannot be assigned out of the estate for purposes of utilizing the beneficiary's life expectancy, one can assign the Roth IRA to the estate beneficiaries for purposes of closing the estate. In doing so, it is critical that the Roth IRA remain titled in the name of the deceased Roth IRA owner, so that no unintended taxable distribution occurs. Distributing the Roth IRA to the estate beneficiaries *in-kind* should not cause a taxable distribution to occur. This treatment has been supported in several letter rulings. [*See* Ltr. Ruls. 200538030 (Sept. 23, 2005), 200433019 (Aug. 13, 2004)]

Q 5:30   Is a contingent beneficiary that is entitled to a Roth IRA only upon the death of the primary beneficiary taken into consideration when determining which designated beneficiary has the shortest life expectancy?

No. If a successor beneficiary's entitlement to a benefit (here, a Roth IRA) is merely that of a potential successor to the interest of the primary beneficiary, such contingent beneficiary is not considered for purposes of determining which designated beneficiary has the shortest life expectancy. [Treas. Reg. § 1.401(a)(9)-5, Q&A 7(c)]

Example. Ben names his wife, Diane, as primary beneficiary of his Roth IRA and the American Heart Association as contingent beneficiary. Upon Ben's death, Diane may receive distributions based on her life expectancy; that is, she need not take the contingent beneficiary into consideration.

Q 5:31   Must a beneficiary that is entitled to receive a portion of a Roth IRA based on a contingency other than merely a potential successor interest to another beneficiary be taken into account for purposes of calculating required minimum distributions?

Yes, but a contingent beneficiary is not to be taken into consideration for purposes of determining the designated beneficiary with the shortest life expectancy when the contingency is that of a potential successor. [Treas. Reg. § 1.401(a)(9)-5, Q&A 7(b)] This issue arises frequently when a trust is named beneficiary. When this is the case, special consideration must be given to all potential trust beneficiaries whose entitlement to the Roth IRA is not contingent. For example, where a trust includes a power of appointment, all potential appointees must be taken into consideration (see chapter 7).

Spouse

Q 5:32   What options are available to a surviving spouse who is a designated beneficiary of a Roth IRA?

If a Roth IRA owner designates his or her spouse as the sole beneficiary (see Q 5:34), the surviving spouse may elect to treat the Roth IRA as his or her own account. Alternatively, the surviving spouse may receive the Roth IRA as an inherited Roth IRA. In that case, the surviving spouse may delay the commencement of life expectancy distributions from a Roth IRA until December 31 of the year the Roth IRA owner would have attained age 70½ (see Q 5:16). While this option is available, a rollover will forestall RMDs until the death of the surviving spouse, and will therefore be the better option. [Treas. Reg. § 1.408A-6, Q&A 14(b)]

Q 5:33   How does a surviving spouse elect to treat the Roth IRA as his or her own account?

The surviving spouse may elect to treat the Roth IRA as his or her own account by not withdrawing an RMD, by making a contribution to the account, retitling the account in the surviving spouse's name as owner, or by performing a rollover to or from the account. [Treas. Reg. § 1.408-8, Q&A 5(b)]

Q 5:34   When is a surviving spouse considered to be the sole beneficiary of a Roth IRA for purposes of the special deferral rule?

Clearly, when there is only one designated beneficiary of a Roth IRA and that beneficiary is the Roth IRA owner's spouse, the surviving spouse is the sole beneficiary and is entitled to apply the special deferral rule (see Q 5:32).

If the spouse of a Roth IRA owner is named as one of many beneficiaries of the Roth IRA, he or she is no longer the sole beneficiary and therefore would have to begin distributions no later than December 31 of the year following the year of the owner's death, unless the separate share rule applies (see Q 5:45). If the separate share rule applies, the spouse is considered the sole beneficiary of his or her portion of the Roth IRA.

If the requirements regarding the naming of a trust as beneficiary [Treas. Reg. § 1.401(a)(9)-4, Q&A 5] (see Q 5:43) are met and the surviving spouse alone is entitled to receive any and all distributions made from the Roth IRA to the trust during his or her lifetime, the spouse will be considered the sole beneficiary. [Treas. Reg. § 1.401(a)(9)-5, Q&A 7, Ex. 2; *see also* Ltr. Rul. 200831025 (Aug. 1, 2008)] (See Qs 5:39, 7:12.)

> **Caution.** Roth IRA agreements sometimes treat a surviving spouse as assuming the Roth IRA as his or her own Roth IRA as of the date of the original owner's death.

Many Roth IRA agreements provide that a spouse beneficiary may choose from any of the rules applicable to a nonspouse beneficiary (e.g., the five-year rule; the life expectancy rule) and receive the distributions as a *nonspouse* beneficiary (see Q 5:18).

Q 5:35   How are required minimum distributions from a Roth IRA determined for a designated beneficiary who is the surviving spouse?

If the designated beneficiary of a Roth IRA is the surviving spouse and he or she elects not to perform a spousal rollover, the RMD may not be less than the quotient obtained by dividing the balance in the account as of the end of the preceding calendar year by the spouse's applicable life expectancy. Life expectancy is computed by use of the expected return multiples in the Single Life Table (see Q 5:19). For each subsequent year, this process is repeated.

Example 1. Linda inherited a Roth IRA as the sole beneficiary from her deceased husband who was born on June 30, 1940, and died before 2010. On December 31, 2009, the balance of the Roth IRA is $1 million. Linda is 65 in 2010. Linda's RMD for 2010 is $47,619.05 ($1,000,000 ÷ 21.0). On December 31, 2010, the balance of the Roth IRA is $950,000. Linda is 66 in 2011. Linda's RMD for 2011 is $47,029.70 ($950,000 ÷ 20.2). Had Linda's husband been one day younger, she would not have an RMD for 2010 (see Example 2).

Example 2. Linda inherited a Roth IRA as the sole beneficiary from her deceased husband who was born on July 1, 1940, and died before 2010. On December 31, 2009, the balance of the Roth IRA is $1 million. Linda is 65 in 2010. Linda has no RMD for 2010 (see Q 5:36). On December 31, 2010, the balance of the Roth IRA is $950,000. Linda is 66 in 2011, the year in which her husband would have attained age 70½. Linda's RMD for 2011 is $47,029.70 ($950,000 ÷ 20.2).

Q 5:36   If a surviving spouse is designated as the sole beneficiary of a Roth IRA and the Roth IRA owner dies before attaining age 70½, is the surviving spouse's first required minimum distribution delayed until the end of the calendar year in which the owner would have attained age 70½?

Yes. A surviving spouse who is the sole beneficiary of a Roth IRA does not start RMDs until the later of the year following the year in which owner died or the year in which the owner would have attained age 70½. [Treas. Reg. § 1.401(a)(9)-3, Q&A 3(b)]

Example. Richard was born on April 26, 1944, and died in 2009, at age 65, leaving his Roth IRA to his wife, Elizabeth. Elizabeth can wait until 2014 (the year when Richard would have turned 70½ had he lived) to begin taking RMDs.

Practice Pointer. Despite the apparent benefit of the rule just stated, in most circumstances a surviving spouse will be better off treating the Roth IRA as his or her own (because a Roth IRA owner need not take distributions during his or her lifetime). An exception is when the surviving spouse is younger than age 59½ and wishes to make a penalty-free withdrawal (see Q 5:38).

Q 5:37 What is the result if a surviving spouse who is the designated beneficiary of a Roth IRA elects to treat the Roth IRA as his or her own or rolls over the Roth IRA?

Among the ways in which a surviving spouse who is the designated beneficiary of a Roth IRA may treat the Roth IRA as his or her own is to transfer or roll over his or her interest in the Roth IRA to his or her own Roth IRA. If a surviving spouse who is the designated beneficiary of a Roth IRA elects to treat the Roth IRA as his or her own, the surviving spouse's interest in the Roth IRA would then be subject to the distribution requirements applicable to the spouse as the Roth IRA owner rather than as a beneficiary. That means no RMDs must be made during the lifetime of the surviving spouse. Further, a new beneficiary may be named by the surviving spouse. [Treas. Reg. § 1.408-8, Q&A 5]

> **Note.** If a Roth IRA owner dies after reaching age 70½ and the surviving spouse elects to treat the Roth IRA as his or her own in the year of the owner's death, no RMD must be made. If, however, the surviving spouse elects to treat the Roth IRA as his or her own in the year following the owner's death, an RMD must be distributed for that year (the year following the year of the owner's death). Thereafter no RMDs are necessary until the surviving spouse's death.

> **Practice Pointer.** In almost all circumstances, a spousal rollover of a Roth IRA produces a greater benefit than would be the case if the surviving spouse merely treats the Roth IRA as inherited.

Q 5:38 Is there a time frame during which a spousal rollover of a Roth IRA must occur?

No. A surviving spouse who is the beneficiary of a Roth IRA may elect to perform a rollover at any time after the death of the Roth IRA owner. [Treas. Reg. § 1.408-8, Q&A 5(a); Ltr. Rul. 200110033 (Dec. 13, 2000)] If the surviving spouse is younger than age 59½, it may be wise to wait until attaining such age to perform a rollover. If the spouse performs a rollover before age 59½ and takes a distribution, he or she may be subject to the 10 percent early distribution penalty (see Q 4:21). In the alternative, the surviving spouse can treat the Roth IRA as inherited, take penalty-free distributions, and then perform a rollover upon reaching age 59½.

Q 5:39 May a spouse perform a rollover of a Roth IRA if he or she is the beneficiary of a trust?

Maybe. To be permitted to make an election to treat a Roth IRA as his or her own, a spouse must be the sole beneficiary of the Roth IRA and have an unlimited right to withdraw amounts from the Roth IRA. [Treas. Reg. § 1.408-8, Q&A 5] This requirement is not satisfied if a trust is named beneficiary of the Roth IRA even if the spouse is the sole beneficiary of the trust. However, several letter rulings [Ltr. Ruls. 200707159 (Feb. 16, 2007), 200603036 (Jan. 20, 2006), 200603032 (Jan. 20, 2006), 200646026 (Nov. 17, 2006), 200703047 (Jan. 19, 2007)] suggest that the IRS will allow a rollover when a trust is named as beneficiary under certain circumstances. That is, when the spouse is the trustee and has the immediate and unilateral power to appoint the assets of the trust to him or herself, it appears that a rollover of a Roth IRA will likely be respected. If, however, someone other than the surviving spouse has the ability to control the disposition of the Roth IRA, the surviving spouse cannot be said to have exclusive control of the Roth IRA and therefore a rollover will not likely be allowed. [*See* Ltr. Ruls. 200245055 (Nov. 8, 2002), 200221051 (May 24, 2002), 200106047 (Nov. 17, 2000), 200052045 (Oct. 3, 2000)]

> **Note.** Many financial institutions require that a distribution be made to the trust and, if allowable, rolled over by the surviving spouse rather than by the trust because only a surviving spouse may perform a rollover. [I.R.C. § 408(d)(3)(C)]

> **Practice Pointer.** The protection afforded by a letter ruling request should be sought when a spousal rollover is intended and the spouse is a beneficiary of a trust. Further, when a spousal rollover is sought through a trust, trust reformation or qualified disclaimers can often be implemented to give the surviving spouse the requisite foundation to perform a rollover.

Q 5:40   May a spouse perform a rollover of a Roth IRA when an estate is named as beneficiary and the Roth IRA owner died intestate?

In many cases, yes. Based on letter rulings issued under the Final Regulations, it appears that the IRS will continue to respect spousal rollovers (including those involving a Roth IRA) where it is possible for the spouse to receive outright ownership of the IRA (see Q 5:34). [Ltr. Ruls. 200831025 (Aug. 1, 2008), 200720024 (May 18, 2007), 200703035 (Jan. 19, 2007), 200644031 (Nov. 3, 2006), 200611037 (Mar. 17, 2006), 200433026 (Aug. 13, 2004)] The key factor in cases where a spousal rollover is sought is the unilateral ability of the surviving spouse to control the disposition of the IRA (e.g., as executor) or, where there is no discretion as to disposition, the outright entitlement of the IRA to the surviving spouse. [*See* Ltr. Ruls. 200544032 (Nov. 4, 2005), 200510039 (May 11, 2005), 200453016 (Dec. 31, 2004)]

> **Example.** Gordon dies intestate; he also failed to name a beneficiary of his Roth IRA. The default provisions of the custodial agreement direct the Roth IRA to be payable to his estate. Under state law, Gordon's assets are payable to his spouse, Jennifer. Jennifer is the executrix of Gordon's estate. Jennifer assigns the Roth IRA to herself and thereafter performs a spousal rollover. Upon rollover, Jennifer is treated as the owner of the Roth IRA.

Practice Pointer. The protection afforded by a letter ruling should be sought when a spousal rollover is intended and the Roth IRA owner has died intestate.

Nonspouse

Q 5:41 What options apply to required minimum distributions for a nonspouse beneficiary of a Roth IRA?

If a Roth IRA owner designates some person other than his or her spouse as the beneficiary, the entire remaining interest in the Roth IRA will, in accordance with the custodial agreement and at the election of the owner or, if the owner has not so elected, at the election of the beneficiary or beneficiaries, either

1. Be distributed by December 31 of the year containing the fifth anniversary of the owner's death (the five-year rule) or
2. Be distributed over the life expectancy of the designated beneficiary starting no later than December 31 of the year following the year of the owner's death. [Treas. Reg. § 1.401(a)(9)-3]

If distributions do not begin by the date described in the second distribution method, it appears that the beneficiaries would have the option of paying the 50 percent penalty under Code Section 4974 for the failure to withdraw the RMD (see Qs 5:56–5:59) and still have the life expectancy distribution option.

Q 5:42 How are required minimum distributions determined for a designated beneficiary who is a nonspouse individual?

The designated beneficiary of a Roth IRA who is an individual who is not the spouse of the Roth IRA owner is entitled to receive distributions based on his or her life expectancy. The annual RMD is determined by dividing the account balance as of December 31 of the previous year by the applicable distribution period. The applicable distribution period for the first distribution year (the year following the year of the Roth IRA owner's death) is determined under the Single Life Table (see Q 5:19) by referencing the corresponding multiple to the beneficiary's age as of the beneficiary's birthday in the calendar year immediately following the calendar year of the owner's death. In subsequent calendar years, the multiple is reduced by one for each calendar year that has elapsed since the calendar year immediately following the calendar year of the owner's death. Redetermining the life expectancy on an annual basis is not permitted for a nonspouse beneficiary. [Treas. Reg. § 1.401(a)(9)-5]

Example. Joe names his son Jeff as beneficiary of his Roth IRA. Joe dies in August of 2009. As of December 31, 2009, the Roth IRA balance is $400,000. Jeff's attained age in 2010 is 56. Referencing the Single Life Table, Jeff determines that his distribution multiple is 28.7. Therefore, Jeff must withdraw $13,937.28 ($400,000 ÷ 28.7) in 2010. For each subsequent year, the 2010 factor is reduced by one (i.e., 2011 = 27.7, 2012 = 26.7, etc.).

Q 5:43   If a trust is named as the beneficiary of a Roth IRA, may designated beneficiary status be obtained to allow for life expectancy distributions?

Yes, if certain requirements are met. Although only an individual may be a designated beneficiary, when certain requirements are met, the IRS will look through the trust to the beneficiaries of the trust. The beneficiaries will then be treated as having been designated by the Roth IRA owner. [Treas. Reg. § 1.401(a)(9)-4, Q&A 5] (See chapter 7 for additional discussion regarding the naming of a trust as beneficiary of a Roth IRA.)

The following four requirements must be met for a trust to obtain designated beneficiary status for the purpose of determining the distribution period:

1. The trust must be a valid trust under state law, or would be but for the fact that there is no corpus;

2. The trust must be irrevocable or will, by its terms, become irrevocable upon the death of the owner;

3. The beneficiaries of the trust who are beneficiaries with respect to the trust's interest in the Roth IRA must be identifiable from the trust instrument; and

4. Certain documentation must be provided to the plan administrator (see below).

[Treas. Reg. § 1.401(a)(9)-4, Q&A 5]

No later than October 31 of the year following the year of the Roth IRA owner's death, the trustee of the trust must provide to the plan administrator either

1. A final list of all beneficiaries of the trust (including contingent and remainder beneficiaries with a description of the conditions on their entitlement) and certify that, to the best of the trustee's knowledge, the list is correct and complete and that the other three requirements of naming a trust as beneficiary are satisfied, and agree to provide a copy of the trust instrument to the plan administrator upon demand or

2. A copy of the actual trust document for the trust that is named as a beneficiary under the Roth IRA as of the owner's date of death.

[Treas. Reg. § 1.401(a)(9)-4, Q&A 6(b)]

Note. For purposes of the requirement just discussed, the Roth IRA trustee or custodian is treated as the plan administrator. [Treas. Reg. § 1.408-8, Q&A 1]

Q 5:44   If a qualified trust is named as the beneficiary of a Roth IRA, on whose life are required minimum distributions calculated?

If a qualified trust is named as the beneficiary of a Roth IRA, the beneficiary of the trust with the shortest life expectancy will be used to determine RMDs. It should be noted, however, that the separate share rule of Treasury Regulations

Section 1.401(a)(9)-8, Q&A 2, is not available with respect to separate interests created under a trust. [Treas. Reg. § 1.401(a)(9)-4, Q&A 5(c)]

> **Example.** Charles dies after naming a qualified trust as beneficiary of his Roth IRA. His two sons, Harry, age 20, and William, age 24, are the only beneficiaries of the trust. William's life expectancy will be used to determine RMDs.

> **Practice Pointer.** Separate share treatment may not be available even where separate shares are created by beneficiary designation. [Ltr. Ruls. 200317041, 200317043, 200317044 (Apr. 25, 2003)] However, if the beneficiary designation actually names each separate subtrust as beneficiary of the Roth IRA, separate share treatment may be allowed. [*See* Ltr. Rul. 200537044 (Sept. 16, 2005)] (See Qs 5:46 and 7:18.)

Multiple Beneficiaries

Q 5:45   When a Roth IRA names multiple beneficiaries, how are required minimum distributions determined?

If as of September 30 of the year following the year of death, more than one individual is designated as a beneficiary of a Roth IRA, the designated beneficiary with the shortest life expectancy will be the designated beneficiary for purposes of determining the distribution period. [Treas. Reg. § 1.401(a)(9)-5, Q&A 7]

The final regulations clarify that where multiple beneficiaries are named, separate accounts can be established under certain circumstances. This issue is significant where multiple beneficiaries exist and one such beneficiary is a charity or where significant age differences exist among beneficiaries. In such instances, the creation of separate shares allows for independent testing to determine whether a designated beneficiary exists and also independent calculation of RMDs for each separate account.

With respect to the determination of whether a designated beneficiary exists, the final regulations require the determination of beneficiaries as of September 30 of the year following the year of the Roth IRA owner's death. Note that the regulations indicate that separate accounts must be established no later than December 31 of the year following the year of death; however, this appears inconsistent with the September 30 deadline for determining whether a designated beneficiary exists (see Q 5:27). [Treas. Reg. § 1.401(a)(9)-8, Q&A 2] This issue was clarified in June 2004 with the amendment to Treasury Regulations Section 1.401(a)(9)-8, Q&A 2(a). The amended section states that if separate accounts are actually established by the end of the calendar year following the year after the Roth IRA owner's death, the separate accounts can be used to determine RMDs for the year following the year of the Roth IRA owner's death.

> **Example.** Ben dies in 2009. Ben named his two children, Pete, age 21, and Jane, age 25, as equal beneficiaries of his Roth IRA. As of September 30, 2010, the beneficiary with the shortest life expectancy is identifiable as Jane.

Waiting to create separate shares until December 31, 2010, does not change the fact that Ben has a designated beneficiary. Separate shares are created on December 31, 2010. For 2010 and subsequent years, Pete and Jane can use their individual life expectancies to calculate RMDs for their separate accounts.

Caution. If one of the beneficiaries is a non-individual (e.g., a charity), a separate share (or the charity could be "cashed out") should be created by September 30 of the year following the year of death to avoid the entire Roth IRA as being treated as not having a designated beneficiary (see Q 5:27).

Q 5:46 May separate accounts be established when a trust is named as the beneficiary of a Roth IRA?

The regulations state that separate shares created by a trust instrument will not be respected as separate shares for RMD purposes. [Treas. Reg. § 1.401(a)(9)-4, Q&A 5(c)] In Letter Rulings 200317041, 200317043, and 200317044 (Apr. 25, 2003), even though the beneficiary designation directed the trust and the Roth IRA to be segregated into separate accounts, separate shares were not respected (see Q 7:18) and the oldest trust beneficiary's life expectancy had to be used. However, on March 29, 2005, the IRS released Letter Ruling 200537044, which clarifies that if a beneficiary designation form names separate shares for each individual beneficiary of a trust, each trust beneficiary's life will be used for purposes of determining the measuring life under the required minimum distribution rules. In Letter Ruling 200537044, the IRS allowed each individual beneficiary of each trust share to use his or her individual life expectancy to calculate required minimum distributions for his or her share of the IRA. Upon the death of the trustor, the trust created separate subtrusts for each beneficiary. Each separate trust that was created under the master trust instrument was named a beneficiary of the IRA (e.g., 50 percent to Subtrust A and 50 percent to Subtrust B).

Q 5:47 If a non-individual beneficiary is named as the beneficiary of a portion of a Roth IRA and that beneficiary cannot be cashed out, must the entire Roth IRA be liquidated under the five-year rule?

It depends. If a non-individual is included among the multiple beneficiaries of a Roth IRA and it is impossible to cure that beneficiary by September 30 of the year following the year of the Roth IRA owner's death, the distribution period is determined by reference to the beneficiary with the shortest life expectancy. Inasmuch as a non-individual has no life expectancy, the entire designation is infected and therefore the entire Roth IRA will have to be distributed under the five-year rule (see Q 5:12). [Treas. Reg. § 1.401(a)(9)-5, Q&A 7] If, however, it is possible to cash out or segregate that portion of the Roth IRA payable to the non-individual beneficiary and create a separate account (see Q 5:45) by September 30 of the year following the year of the owner's death, the remaining individual beneficiaries should be entitled to life expectancy distributions.

Subsequent Beneficiaries

Q 5:48   May a spouse beneficiary of a Roth IRA designate a subsequent beneficiary?

Yes. When a spouse beneficiary of a Roth IRA elects not to treat the Roth IRA as his or her own (see Q 5:32), the spouse is permitted to name a subsequent beneficiary in the event that the spouse dies before taking the entire balance of the deceased Roth IRA owner's account. [I.R.C. § 401(a)(9)(B)(iv)(II); Treas. Reg. § 1.401(a)(9)-3, Q&A 5] It is important to note, however, that how rapidly the RMDs must be made to a subsequent beneficiary depends on whether the surviving spouse beneficiary dies before or after the date distributions are *required* to commence to the surviving spouse (the calendar year in which the original participant would have attained the age of 70½) (see Qs 5:51, 5:52).

Practice Pointer. Given the nature of a Roth IRA and the ability to stretch RMDs over life expectancy, it is quite likely that a spouse will die during the payout phase. Where that is the case, the ability of the initial beneficiary to designate a successor beneficiary is an important property right. [Treas. Reg. § 1.401(a)(9)-5, Q&A 7]

Further, given the ability of a spousal beneficiary to receive payments and thereafter perform a spousal rollover, in virtually all cases the surviving spouse should perform a spousal rollover prior to the date upon which distributions are to commence, and in so doing, name a new beneficiary (see Q 5:36).

Q 5:49   Must required minimum distributions from a Roth IRA be made under the five-year rule if the surviving spouse beneficiary does not have a designated beneficiary?

Yes. The beneficiary (or beneficiaries) of a surviving spouse who is the beneficiary of a Roth IRA is determined by the September 30 of the calendar year following the calendar year in which the surviving spouse dies. If the surviving spouse beneficiary elects not to treat the Roth IRA as his or her own and dies prior to the date of the commencement of RMDs and there is no designated beneficiary as of that date, RMDs must be made in accordance with the five-year rule. [Treas. Reg. § 1.401(a)(9)-4, Q&A 4(b)]

Example. Peter dies in 2009 at age 50, after naming his wife, Suzanne, as beneficiary of his Roth IRA. Suzanne does not roll the Roth IRA into a Roth IRA in her own name. Suzanne dies in 2010, having never named a beneficiary of her inherited Roth IRA. The entire Roth IRA will now have to be distributed by the end of 2015.

Practice Pointer. In the preceding example, Peter's contingent beneficiary does not receive the account because of Suzanne's death. Once Suzanne inherits the Roth IRA, Peter's beneficiary designation no longer controls. Instead, a beneficiary of a Roth IRA must execute a new beneficiary designation form to dispose of the account at that beneficiary's death.

Q 5:50   **If a surviving spouse is the beneficiary of a Roth IRA and dies before the year in which the Roth IRA owner would have attained age 70½, may the surviving spouse be deemed to be the owner of the Roth IRA, thereby allowing for the naming of a designated beneficiary?**

Yes. If a spouse beneficiary of a Roth IRA dies after the Roth IRA owner, but before RMDs were required to begin to the surviving spouse (even if distributions were made before that date), the five-year rule and the life expectancy rule start all over again with respect to the surviving spouse beneficiary's subsequent beneficiary (or beneficiaries). [Treas. Reg. § 1.401(a)(9)-3, Q&A 5, 1.401(a)(9)-4, Q&A 4(b)] In such case, *only* the surviving spouse "steps into the shoes" of the original owner in determining the distribution period after the spouse's death; consequently, the five-year rule or the life expectancy rule, whichever is applicable, is applied to the subsequent beneficiary.

Q 5:51   **How is the period for distributing required minimum distributions determined when a surviving spouse beneficiary of a Roth IRA designated a subsequent beneficiary, and the Roth IRA owner had died prior to reaching age 70½, and the surviving spouse dies *before* distributions are required to commence?**

When the original owner of a Roth IRA dies before the calendar year in which he or she would have been age 70½ and the surviving spouse beneficiary dies before RMDs are required to commence, the five-year rule and exception start over again with respect to the spouse's subsequent beneficiary (or beneficiaries), and the relevant beneficiary for determining the distribution period is the designated beneficiary of the surviving spouse (see Q 5:50). As noted earlier (see Q 5:49), the designated beneficiary of a surviving spouse is determined on September 30 of the calendar year following the calendar year in which the spouse dies.

For a designated beneficiary, the distribution period for RMDs after a surviving spouse's death is determined by reference to the Single Life Table, using the life expectancy factor of the subsequent designated beneficiary based on the subsequent beneficiary's birthday in the calendar year following the calendar year in which the original surviving spouse beneficiary dies. For subsequent calendar years, the subsequent beneficiary's single life expectancy is reduced by one year for each year that lapses.

> **Example.** Joanne dies in 2008, at age 50, after naming her husband, Jack, as beneficiary of her Roth IRA. Jack does not roll the Roth IRA into a Roth IRA in his own name. Jack dies in 2010, having named his son, John, as beneficiary of the Roth IRA. John must begin taking RMDs from the Roth IRA by the end of 2011. John is 30 in 2011, and therefore the applicable life expectancy factor is 53.3. For subsequent years, subtract one from 53.3 (i.e., for 2012, the life expectancy factor is 52.3).

Q 5:52 How are required minimum distributions determined when the Roth IRA owner died *before* attaining the age of 70½ and the surviving spouse dies on or *after* the date distributions are required to commence to the surviving spouse?

If a surviving spouse who is the beneficiary of a Roth IRA dies on or after the date RMDs are required to commence to the surviving spouse, special rules apply. When a spouse beneficiary begins single life RMDs, the spouse's single life expectancy is redetermined each year based on the spouse's attained age in each distribution calendar year (the surviving spouse's "first distribution calendar year" for such purpose is the calendar year in which the Roth IRA owner would have attained the age of 70½ had he or she lived). When the spouse beneficiary dies, however, distributions will be made to the spouse's subsequent designated beneficiary using the surviving spouse's single life expectancy based on the spouse's birthday in the calendar year of the spouse's death. In subsequent calendar years, the spouse's single life expectancy is reduced by one year for each year that lapses in calculating RMDs to the spouse's subsequent beneficiary. [Treas. Reg. § 1.401(a)(9)-5, Q&A 5(c)(2)]

> **Example.** Brian dies in 2008 at age 69 after naming his wife, Pamela, as beneficiary of his Roth IRA. Pamela does not perform a spousal rollover. Pamela dies in 2012 at age 72 having named her daughter, Susan, as beneficiary of Brian's Roth IRA. If Pamela did not take the RMD in 2012 before she died, the RMD must be taken based on Pamela's age in that year under the Single Life Table (i.e., using the 2012 factor of 15.5). For 2013, the 2012 factor is reduced by one. Thus, Susan must take a 2013 RMD using a life expectancy factor of 14.5 (15.5 – 1). For each subsequent year, Susan would continue to subtract one.

Q 5:53 How is a new spouse of a surviving spouse who is a beneficiary of a Roth IRA treated for purposes of commencing required minimum distributions under the life expectancy rule?

A new spouse of a surviving spouse who is a beneficiary of a Roth IRA is treated as a nonspouse beneficiary for purposes of commencing RMDs under the life expectancy rule. Thus, if the beneficiary of the original surviving spouse is the new spouse of the surviving spouse, the new spouse may not wait until the original surviving spouse would have attained the age of 70½ to begin RMDs. In other words, the rules in Code Section 401(a)(9)(B)(iv) are not available to the new surviving spouse of the original surviving spouse. [Treas. Reg. § 1.401(a)(9)-3, Q&A 5]

Q 5:54 May a new spouse of a surviving spouse who is a beneficiary of a Roth IRA roll over that Roth IRA to another IRA?

No. A new spouse of a surviving spouse who is a beneficiary of a Roth IRA may not roll over that Roth IRA to his or her own IRA or Roth IRA because the new spouse was not the spouse of the original owner. Be that as it may, the surviving spouse of the Roth IRA owner could roll over the Roth IRA to a Roth IRA in his or her own name and designate the new spouse as beneficiary. The new spouse would then be treated as a surviving spouse for all purposes.

Q 5:55   How are required minimum distributions determined when a nonspouse beneficiary designates a subsequent beneficiary?

When a Roth IRA owner dies and the designated beneficiary is not the spouse, the RMD is calculated using the single life expectancy of the non-spouse beneficiary, which is determined based on the beneficiary's birthday in the calendar year following the calendar year in which the owner dies by reference to the Single Life Table. In subsequent calendar years, the single life expectancy of the nonspouse beneficiary is reduced by one year for each year that lapses.

When the nonspouse beneficiary of the Roth IRA dies, any remaining amount is distributed to the nonspouse beneficiary's subsequent beneficiary by continuing to use the nonspouse beneficiary's single life expectancy already determined in the calendar year following the calendar year in which the Roth IRA owner dies and then reduced by one year for each year that lapses. [Treas. Reg. § 1.401(a)(9)-5, Q&A 7(c)(2)]

The life expectancy of the nonspouse beneficiary's subsequent beneficiary is *not* considered for determining the remaining distribution period. [Treas. Reg. § 1.401(a)(9)-5, Q&A 7(c)(1)]

Penalties

Q 5:56   Is a penalty imposed upon a beneficiary of a Roth IRA for failing to take the entire required minimum distribution for a particular year?

Yes. If the amount distributed to a beneficiary of a Roth IRA in a particular year is less than the RMD for that year, an excise tax is imposed on the beneficiary under Code Section 4974 for the taxable year beginning with or within the calendar year during which the amount is required to be distributed. The tax is equal to 50 percent of the amount by which such RMD exceeds the actual amount distributed during the calendar year. [Treas. Reg. § 54.4974-2, Q&A 1]

Example. John's RMD for 2008 was $20,000, but he only took a distribution of $15,000. John's penalty equals $2,500 [($20,000 − $15,000) × 50%].

Q 5:57   Is a penalty imposed each year when a beneficiary of a Roth IRA is receiving distributions under the five-year rule and no required minimum distributions are taken during the first four years?

No. If the five-year rule applies to the distribution to a Roth IRA beneficiary (see Q 5:12), no amount is required to be distributed for any calendar year to satisfy an RMD until the calendar year containing the fifth anniversary date of the Roth IRA owner's death. It follows then that no penalty is imposed for the earlier years. For the calendar year that contains the date five years after the owner's death, however, the RMD amount is the beneficiary's entire remaining interest. Therefore, if the entire interest is not distributed at that time, the 50 percent penalty applies to the undistributed portion. [Treas. Reg. § 54.4974-2, Q&A 7]

Q 5:58   Are there circumstances under which the penalty for failure to take required minimum distribution may be waived?

Yes. When the Commissioner of Internal Revenue Service determines reasonable cause exists, the 50 percent penalty for failure to take RMDs may be waived. A beneficiary must establish to the satisfaction of the Commissioner that the shortfall in the amount to be distributed in any taxable year was due to reasonable error and that reasonable steps are being taken to remedy the shortfall. [Treas. Reg. § 54.4974-2, Q&A 7]

Q 5:59   What is the procedure for obtaining a waiver of the 50 percent penalty for failure to take an adequate RMD?

To obtain a waiver of the penalty, the taxpayer should file IRS Form 5329 and attach a letter explaining why the full RMD was not taken. If the IRS grants the waiver, the penalty will be waived. Prior to the issuance of the 2005 Form 5329, taxpayers had to include the tax with Form 5329 and if the waiver was granted, the penalty tax would be refunded. Beginning with the 2005 Form 5329, however, the instruction to include the tax along with the waiver request was removed.

Tax Matters

Q 5:60   Are all distributions made from a Roth IRA upon the death of the Roth IRA owner free of federal income tax?

No. Distributions to a beneficiary from a Roth IRA that are not qualified distributions (see Q 5:62) are includible in the beneficiary's gross income to the extent that any such distribution is treated as made from earnings. Qualified distributions, however, will not be subject to federal income tax. [I.R.C. § 408A(d)(3)(E)(ii); Treas. Reg. § 1.408A-6, Q&A 14(c)]

Q 5:61   Does the 10 percent premature distribution penalty apply to death distributions to a beneficiary of a Roth IRA?

No. In no event does the 10 percent premature distribution penalty apply to any RMDs from a decedent's Roth IRA, unless a spouse rolls over the inherited Roth IRA into his or her own Roth IRA. [I.R.C. §§ 72(t)(2)(A)(ii), 408A(d)(3)(F)]

Example 1. Tori inherits an IRA from her father. At the age of 21, Tori takes a distribution from her inherited IRA to go on a vacation. Because Tori inherited the IRA, the 10 percent premature distribution penalty does not apply.

Example 2. Josie inherits an IRA from her husband. Josie decides to roll the IRA into an IRA in her own name (a spousal rollover). At age 52, Josie takes a distribution from her IRA to pay for a down payment on a new car. Because Josie rolled the IRA into her own name and it therefore is no longer an inherited IRA, the 10 percent premature distribution penalty applies.

Qualified Distributions

Q 5:62   Are distributions to a beneficiary of a Roth IRA qualified distributions?

Maybe. Regardless of when the Roth IRA owner dies, the five-year rule or the life expectancy rule will apply in the same manner for the designated beneficiary of the Roth IRA. When distributions are made to the beneficiary, however, such distributions may or may not be qualified distributions; thus, any taxable distribution will be subject to federal income tax paid by the beneficiary (see Qs 4:12, 4:19). [Treas. Reg. § 1.408A-6, Q&A 14]

The ordering rules of Code Section 408A(d)(4)(B) apply to a beneficiary who takes distributions from a Roth IRA. Consequently, until the beneficiary is "deemed" to take earnings, no distribution to the beneficiary will be considered taxable. For purposes of the definition of *qualified distribution* and the five-year aging requirement (see Qs 4:13, 4:14), the number of years the Roth IRA was held by the original deceased owner count toward the five-year aging period.

Example. Ben names his daughter, Beth, as the beneficiary of his Roth IRA. Ben dies during calendar year 2009; his five-year aging period began on January 1, 2006. Beth is required to receive distributions under the five-year rule or the life expectancy rule. If Beth waits until January 2011 and then closes out her father's Roth IRA, the distribution will be a qualified distribution and none of it will be taxable.

On the other hand, if Beth wants to spread the distributions over her single life expectancy, she must begin taking distributions by December 31, 2010. Although such distributions will not be considered qualified distributions until 2011, Beth would not be treated as withdrawing earnings. As a result, none of the life expectancy distributions would be considered as taxable distributions.

It should be noted that beginning at any time in 2008 or thereafter, Beth may accelerate distributions at any time; if she does so, she would be considered as receiving qualified distributions.

Depending on the governing Roth IRA agreement, a surviving spouse is sometimes treated as "assuming" the Roth IRA as his or her own Roth IRA as of the date of the original owner's death. In such a case, any distributions to the spouse will be treated as if the spouse were the Roth IRA owner and not the beneficiary. Many Roth IRA agreements have been modified to provide that a spouse beneficiary may choose from any of the rules applicable to a nonspouse beneficiary, such as the five-year rule or the life expectancy rule, and take distributions as a beneficiary rather than as the Roth IRA owner. Also, many Roth IRA agreements provide that when the surviving spouse is the sole beneficiary, the spouse may wait until the original Roth IRA owner would have attained age 70½ to begin distributions if that date is later than December 31 of the calendar year following the calendar year in which the Roth IRA participant died. Alternatively, a spouse beneficiary could roll over the Roth IRA into his or her own Roth IRA (but not into a traditional IRA) and would then be treated as the Roth IRA owner and not the beneficiary.

Practice Pointer. It is important to check the Roth IRA agreement carefully to determine how a spouse beneficiary is treated upon the Roth IRA owner's death.

Q 5:63 How is the five-year period used in determining whether a distribution of gain is a qualified distribution determined for distributions made to the beneficiary of a Roth IRA?

The five-year period used in determining whether a distribution of gain is a qualified distribution (see Q 4:14) does not start over when a Roth IRA owner dies. Thus, the period during which the Roth IRA is held in the name of the beneficiary includes the period during which it was held by the deceased owner. This rule also applies to a surviving spouse who treats the Roth IRA as his or her own Roth IRA.

Example 1. Victor named his son, Timmy, as the beneficiary of his Roth IRA. The five-year period for Victor's Roth IRA began on January 1, 2006. Victor dies in 2009. The five-year period for determining whether Timmy has received a qualified distribution from Victor's Roth IRA expires on December 31, 2010.

Note. The five-year period for a Roth IRA held by the beneficiary of a deceased Roth IRA owner is determined separately from the five-year period for the beneficiary's own Roth IRA.

Example 2. Assume that Timmy, from Example 1, owns his own Roth IRA. The five-year period for his Roth IRA began on January 1, 2004. The expiration of the five-year period for Timmy's Roth IRA is December 31, 2008, whereas the expiration of the five-year period for the Roth IRA of which Timmy is the beneficiary in Example 1 expires on December 31, 2010.

Q 5:64   If a spouse beneficiary treats the Roth IRA as his or her own, how is the five-year period used in determining whether a distribution is a qualified distribution determined?

If a Roth IRA owner's surviving spouse treats the Roth IRA as his or her own, the five-year period used in determining whether a distribution is a qualified distribution for the Roth IRA ends on the earlier of the end of

1. The five-year period for the deceased Roth IRA owner's Roth IRA or
2. The five-year period for the spouse's own Roth IRA.

Example. Mikhail named his wife, Amy, as the beneficiary of his Roth IRA. The five-year period for Mikhail's Roth IRA began on January 1, 2005, and ends on December 31, 2009. Amy also has her own Roth IRA. The five-year period for her Roth IRA began on January 1, 2006, and ends on December 31, 2010. If she treats Mikhail's Roth IRA as her own Roth IRA, her five-year period for all her Roth IRAs ends on December 31, 2009, because that date occurs earlier than the expiration of the Roth IRA she owned before treating Mikhail's Roth IRA as her own Roth IRA.

Q 5:65   If the distribution to beneficiaries of a Roth IRA consists of different types of contributions, how is taxation to the beneficiaries determined?

If a Roth IRA owner dies before the end of the five-year period for determining qualified distributions (or before the end of the five-year period for determining the 10 percent recapture tax on conversion contributions), different types of contributions must be allocated to multiple beneficiaries on a pro rata basis.

Example. Timothy has a Roth IRA that contains a regular contribution of $4,000, a conversion contribution of $6,000, and earnings of $1,000. He has named his two children, Holly and Heather, as equal beneficiaries. Timothy's Roth IRA will be allocated to Holly and Heather as follows:

Holly	*Heather*
$2,000 Regular	$2,000 Regular
$3,000 Conversion	$3,000 Conversion
$500 Earnings	$500 Earnings

Withholding

Q 5:66   Do the federal income tax withholding rules apply to distributions from a Roth IRA?

Generally, no. Code Section 3405 was amended to exempt *most* distributions from Roth IRAs from federal income tax withholding because it is reasonable to believe that such distributions are not generally includible in gross income (see Q 5:62). That is, Section 314 of the Community Renewal Tax Relief Act of 2000 amended the last sentence of Code Section 3405(e)(1)(B) by inserting "(other than a Roth IRA)" after "individual retirement plan."

The change exempting most Roth IRA distributions from federal income tax withholding is effective retroactively to January 1, 1998 (the original effective date of the Taxpayer Relief Act of 1997).

Previously, Code Section 3405 did not differentiate Roth IRAs from other IRAs. As a result, distributions from Roth IRAs, whether or not in fact taxable, were subject to withholding at the rate of 10 percent, unless the recipient was eligible for and elected no withholding as permitted by law. [*See* I.R.C. § 3405(a)(2), 3405(b)(2)]

> **Note.** Withholding may apply to a distribution from a traditional IRA that is converted to a Roth IRA (see Q 3:34). [Treas. Reg. § 1.408A-6, Q&A 13] Estimated tax payments may also be required on a conversion to a Roth IRA (see Q 6:34).

Deemed Roth IRAs

Q 5:67 How are required minimum distributions calculated for deemed Roth IRAs?

Under Code Section 408(q), a qualified employer plan may elect to allow employees to make voluntary employee contributions to a separate account or annuity established under the plan. If the separate account meets the requirements of Code Section 408A, the account is treated for purposes of this title in the same manner as a Roth IRA. Accordingly, the distribution rules applicable to a Roth IRA, as explained in this chapter, are applicable to a deemed Roth IRA. Rules applicable to distributions from qualified employer plans do not apply to distributions from deemed Roth IRAs. Instead, the rules applicable to distributions from Roth IRAs apply to distributions from deemed Roth IRAs. [Treas. Reg. § 1.408(q)-1(e)(1)]

Q 5:68 Can required minimum distributions taken from a deemed Roth IRA be used to satisfy required minimum distributions from the qualified plan?

No. The required minimum distribution rules of Code Section 401(a)(9) must be met separately with respect to the qualified employer plan and the deemed Roth IRA. The determination of whether a qualified employer plan satisfies the required minimum distribution rules of Code Section 401(a)(9) is made without regard to whether a participant satisfies the required minimum distribution requirements with respect to the deemed Roth IRA that is established under such plan. [Treas. Reg. § 1.408(q)-1(e)(2)]

Q 5:69   Are minimum distributions required from a designated Roth account?

Yes. In Treasury Decision 9237 (Dec. 30, 2005), the IRS reasoned that even though Roth IRAs are not subject to the lifetime required minimum distribution rules under Code Section 401(a)(9), Code Section 402A does not provide comparable rules regarding the application of Section 401(a)(9) to designated Roth accounts under a cash or deferred arrangement. Accordingly, the IRS has determined that designated Roth accounts are subject to the rules of Code Section 401(a)(9)(A) and (B) in the same manner as pre-tax elective contributions. [Treas. Reg. § 1.401(k)-1(f)(3)]

Therefore, an owner of a designated Roth account must begin taking distributions by his or her required beginning date (i.e., April 1 of the year following the year in which the owner reaches age 70½). [I.R.C. § 401(a)(9)(A) and (C)] Lifetime required distributions are determined by reference to the Uniform Lifetime Table found under Treasury Regulations Section 1.401(a)(9)-9. [Treas. Reg. § 1.401(a)(9)-5, Q&A-4(a)] The only exception to this general rule is where the owner names a spouse as "sole beneficiary" and such spouse is more than 10 years younger than the owner. In this case, the joint life expectancy is calculated on an annual basis under the Joint and Last Survivor Table found under Treasury Regulations Section 1.401(a)(9)-9. [Treas. Reg. § 1.401(a)(9)-5, Q&A-4(b)]

Q 5:70   What are the required minimum distributions rules for a designated Roth account after the owner dies?

After the death of the owner, post-death required minimum distributions are calculated based upon the life expectancy of the "designated beneficiary." (See Qs 5:19–5:28.) Once the designated beneficiary is ascertained, required minimum distributions are determined based upon the December 31 prior year balance, and the designated beneficiary's life expectancy factor is determined by the designated beneficiary's attained age for the first year of distribution by reference to the Single Life Table (see Q 5:19) under Treasury Regulations Section 1.401(a)(9)-9.

Q 5:71   Is a corrective distribution of excess deferrals (and income) treated as a distribution for purposes of determining whether the plan meets the required minimum distribution rules of Code Section 401(a)(9)?

No, a distribution of excess deferrals (and income) under Treasury Regulations Section 1.402(g)-1(e)(2) and (e)(3) is not treated as a distribution for purposes of determining whether the plan meets the minimum distribution requirements of Code Section 401(a)(9). [Treas. Reg. § 1.402(g)-1(e)(9)]

Chapter 6

Financial Planning

The decision whether to convert an existing traditional IRA to a Roth IRA is thoroughly examined in this chapter. Many factors are used to make this decision—including the decision's income, gift, and estate tax implications.

Tax rates, inflation, the availability of a source of funds outside the IRA to pay the conversion tax, whether a taxpayer needs the IRA funds for retirement, and the rate of return may also influence the decision.

The Basic Considerations

Q 6:1 What statutory features may make a Roth IRA more advantageous than a traditional IRA?

If a taxpayer takes advantage of the statutory features of the Roth IRA, establishing a Roth IRA may be a better alternative than establishing a traditional IRA (deductible or nondeductible). Those features include the following:

- Suspension of the required minimum distribution (RMD) rules (see Qs 5:1, 5:2, 6:10, 6:24, 6:46)

- Qualified distributions of gain that are not subject to federal income tax (see Q 4:9)
- Contributions that are permitted to be made after age 70 (see Q 2:10)
- After-death tax-free growth (see Q 5:1)
- Possibility of beneficial state income tax treatment

These features, coupled with other factors (e.g., tax rates, interest, and growth), will determine whether a traditional IRA or a Roth IRA is a better choice for a particular taxpayer (see Qs 6:22–6:29, 6:37).

In general, the longer a taxpayer waits to withdraw funds, the more attractive the Roth IRA becomes. If a taxpayer can take advantage of that longer deferral, he or she is probably better off with a Roth IRA. Of course, if a lump-sum distribution is taken (e.g., at age 70), the taxpayer's tax bracket at that time plays a more critical role in determining which alternative is better.

Example. Sally has the option of creating a Roth IRA, a deductible traditional IRA, or a bank savings account. During the accumulation period, her tax bracket remains at 30 percent. At the time of distribution, it is assumed that her traditional IRA will be taxed at 30 percent or 15 percent (as indicated below). All growth is projected at 10 percent, distributions are made in a lump sum, and there are no penalties. In the case of the traditional IRA, Sally would also invest her tax savings of $600 ($2,000 × 0.30) in a bank savings account. Roth IRA distributions of gain are assumed to be withdrawn in a qualified (nontaxable) distribution. A comparison of after-tax growth in a Roth IRA, a traditional IRA, and a bank savings account over various time periods follows.

Traditional IRA Taxed at

Years	Roth IRA[1]	30%[2]	15%[3]	Bank[4]
1	4,400	4,784	5,024	4,280
5	6,442	6,642	7,159	5,610
10	10,375	10,221	11,179	7,869
15	16,709	15,985	17,513	11,036
20	26,910	25,268	27,517	15,479
25	43,339	40,218	43,351	21,710
30	69,798	64,296	68,463	30,449
35	112,410	103,073	108,360	42,706
40	181,037	165,524	171,851	59,898
45	291,562	266,101	273,031	84,010
50	469,563	428,083	434,477	117,828

---

[1] $4,000 × 1.10n
[2] $1,200 (savings) + .70 (($4,000 × $1,200) × 1.10n − $1,200)
[3] ($4,000 × 1.10n × .85) + ($1,200 × 1.07n)
[4] $4,000 × 1.07n

Example. Sally will have more spendable income with a Roth IRA if her tax bracket during distribution remains at 30 percent. If she is in the 15 percent bracket at the time of distribution, she will be better off with a traditional deductible IRA. The bank savings account will always be the least attractive alternative. A nondeductible IRA (not shown) would be somewhat better than a bank savings account because of the tax-deferred growth in a traditional IRA. By taking better advantage of some of the deferral features of a Roth IRA (see Q 6:28), Sally may find that the Roth IRA is the most attractive alternative even if she is in a lower marginal tax bracket when the assets are withdrawn.

Inasmuch as annual Roth IRA contributions are never subject to tax and never subject to penalty if removed before the owner attains age 59½ (see chapter 4), a Roth IRA is a better choice for an individual who has an immediate or short-term need to access assets, especially when it is considered that in a Roth IRA, contributions are removed before any gain is deemed distributed (see Q 4:1). The increase in the estate tax applicable exclusion amount under the Economic Growth and Tax Relief Reconciliation Act of 2001 (EGTRRA) also supports this choice.

Q 6:2 What nonstatutory features may make a Roth IRA more advantageous than a traditional IRA?

In addition to its statutory features (see Q 6:1), several nonstatutory features may make a Roth IRA more attractive than a traditional IRA. For example, it may be more efficient to fund (designate as beneficiary) an applicable exclusion bypass trust, also known as a credit shelter trust, a B trust, or a family trust with a Roth IRA (see Q 6:30). The advantages of using a Roth IRA trust include discipline, management (control), and (in some states) creditor protection (see chapter 7 generally, Q 7:7). Using a Roth IRA trust in connection with the generation-skipping tax exemption may also prove advantageous (see Q 7:24).

Q 6:3 Are there any statutory features that may make a *deductible* traditional IRA more advantageous than a Roth IRA?

Yes. If a taxpayer's contribution to a traditional IRA is deductible, there may be an advantage to establishing a traditional IRA (rather than a Roth IRA) provided the taxpayer's marginal tax bracket falls significantly during the distribution phase; for example, from 35 percent to 27 percent. Even if the tax bracket falls, however, that advantage can be easily overcome by other factors and benefits provided by a Roth IRA (see Qs 6:1, 6:2).

Q 6:4 Is a *nondeductible* traditional IRA ever likely to be more advantageous than a Roth IRA?

Rarely. In nearly all cases, a Roth IRA is more advantageous than a nondeductible traditional IRA because federal income taxes do not have to be paid on earnings distributed in a qualified distribution (see Q 4:10) from a Roth

IRA. Furthermore, earnings are distributed pro rata in a traditional IRA but are deemed distributed last in a Roth IRA (see Q 4:1).

Practice Pointer. The only time to contribute to a nondeductible traditional IRA is when a taxpayer is not eligible to contribute to a Roth IRA.

Q 6:5 Who can convert an existing traditional IRA to a Roth IRA?

Any married taxpayer who files a joint federal income tax return, any head of a household, or any single individual whose modified adjusted gross income (MAGI) is not more than $100,000 in the year of conversion may convert an existing traditional IRA to a Roth IRA (see Qs 3:7–3:9, Q 3:10). [I.R.C. § 408A(c)(3)(B)(i)] Married taxpayers filing separate returns are not eligible to convert. [I.R.C. § 408A(c)(3)(B)(ii)] Beginning in 2010, both this income requirement and the filing requirement are eliminated. [I.R.C. § 408A(c)(3)(B) as amended by § 512(a)(1), Pub. L. No. 109-222 (May 17, 2006)]

The Internal Revenue Code (Code) specifically provides that Roth IRA conversion income is *not* included in a taxpayer's MAGI for purposes of the $100,000 limit on MAGI (see Q 6:9). [I.R.C. § 408A(c)(3)(C)(i)(I); Treas. Reg. § 1.408A-4, Q&A 2]

Example. Ron and Nancy, a married couple, have MAGI of $80,000 in 2009. Ron converts his deductible traditional IRA with a value of $500,000 to a Roth IRA. No part of the $500,000 is considered in determining whether the $100,000 MAGI limit is exceeded. Therefore, either Ron or Nancy may convert.

Practice Pointer. Previously, the direct conversion from a qualified plan to a Roth IRA was not permitted and individuals who wanted to convert their qualified plan to a Roth IRA had to first roll over their plan to a traditional IRA and then perform a Roth conversion (see chapter 3). Similar rules applied to distributions from a 403(b) tax-sheltered annuity plan or governmental 457 plan. Under the Pension Protection Act of 2006 (PPA), however, for distributions taken after December 31, 2007, individuals can convert their qualified plan, 403(b) tax-sheltered annuity, and governmental Section 457 plan directly to a Roth IRA (see chapter 3). [PPA § 824 (Pub. L. No. 109-48); I.R.C. § 408A(e), as amended] This avoids the added step of first rolling the plan to an IRA followed by a conversion to a Roth IRA.

Q 6:6 May a participant in a qualified plan convert an existing traditional IRA to a Roth IRA?

Yes. If the taxpayer's MAGI limit does not exceed the $100,000 limit and the taxpayer is not married and filing a separate return (see Q 6:5), a taxpayer who participates in an employer-sponsored qualified plan (e.g., a 401(k) plan or savings incentive match plan for employees (SIMPLE)) is eligible to convert an existing traditional IRA to a Roth IRA.

Q 6:7   May a spouse beneficiary of a qualified plan convert the plan to a Roth IRA?

Yes. Because of their ability to perform spousal rollovers into an account in their own name, a spouse has the option of converting an inherited qualified plan to a Roth IRA. Non-spousal beneficiaries, however, did not have always have this right (see Q 6:8).

A surviving spouse who makes a rollover to a Roth IRA may elect either to treat the Roth IRA as his or her own or to establish the Roth IRA in the name of the decedent with the surviving spouse as the beneficiary (see Q 5:1).

Q 6:8   May a nonspouse beneficiary of a qualified plan convert the plan to a Roth IRA?

Yes, according to Notice 2008-30. [2008-12 I.R.B. 638] The notice provides guidance regarding certain distribution-related provisions of the PPA. This Notice allows nonspouse beneficiaries of inherited retirement plans to convert to a Roth IRA. Previously, only spousal beneficiaries, because of their ability to perform spousal rollovers into an account in their own name, had the option of converting an inherited qualified plan to Roth IRA. Non-spousal beneficiaries, however, did not have this option. Q&A 7 of Section II in Notice 2008-30 expands the conversion power to nonspousal beneficiaries. The Notice states that in the case of a distribution from an eligible retirement plan other than a Roth IRA, the MAGI and filing status of the beneficiary are used to determine eligibility to make a qualified rollover contribution to a Roth IRA (before 2010). Pursuant to Code Section 402(c)(11), a plan may but is not required to permit rollovers by nonspouse beneficiaries. However, beginning in 2010, all qualified plans must be amended to allow for non-spousal rollovers. A rollover by a nonspouse beneficiary must be made by a direct trustee-to-trustee transfer.

> **Practice Pointer.** A nonspouse beneficiary who is ineligible to make a qualified rollover contribution to a Roth IRA may recharacterize the contribution pursuant to Section 408A(d)(6). [I.R.S. Notice 2008-30, 2008-12 I.R.B. 638]

> **Caution.** A nonspouse beneficiary cannot elect to treat the Roth IRA as his or her own. [*See* I.R.S. Notice 2007-7, Part V, 2007-5 I.R.B. 395]

AGI/MAGI

Q 6:9   What is *modified adjusted gross income*?

For Roth IRA purposes, MAGI is a taxpayer's adjusted gross income (AGI) as shown on the taxpayer's Federal Income Tax Return, modified as follows:

1. Subtract any income resulting from the conversion of an IRA to a Roth IRA (conversion income) (see below).

2. Add the following deductions and exclusions—

a. Traditional IRA deduction

b. Student loan interest deduction

c. Qualified tuition and related expense deduction

d. Foreign earned income exclusion

e. Foreign earned income and housing exclusion or deduction

f. Exclusion of qualified bond interest used to pay higher education expenses shown on Form 8815

g. Exclusion of employer-paid adoption expenses shown on Form 8839

(see Qs 6:10–6:15, 6:29, 2:8). [I.R.C. §§ 219(g)(3), 408A(c)(3)(C)(i); Treas. Reg. § 1.408A-3, Q&A 5]

Q 6:10   Does a taxpayer's required minimum distribution count toward his or her MAGI?

Only until 2005. Beginning in 2005, RMDs from an IRA (regular or inherited) do not count toward MAGI for purposes of the Roth IRA conversion limit. (It appears that RMDs from a qualified plan or a 403(b) plan will not be excluded; see Qs 2:8, 3:7–3:9) [I.R.C. § 408A(c)(3)(C)(i)(II) Treas. Reg. § 1.408A-3, A-6]

Example 1. Bill, age 73, expects to earn approximately $40,000 of interest and dividend income with no significant tax deductions in 2003 and is considering conversion to a Roth IRA. Bill's RMD from his traditional IRA for 2004 is $75,000. That will make Bill's MAGI $115,000 for 2004, which is greater than the $100,000 limit, and he will be ineligible for conversion to a Roth IRA. [I.R.C. §§ 219(f), 408A(c)(3)(A)]

Example 2. The facts are the same as those in Example 1, except that the year is 2008 and the $40,000 is from wages reported on Form W-2. Bill is eligible for conversion because, beginning in 2005, RMDs are not considered part of his MAGI for purposes of Roth IRA conversion. Therefore, Bill's MAGI for purposes of eligibility for a Roth IRA conversion will be $40,000, which is less than the $100,000 limit (which applies before 2010).

Example 3. The facts are the same as those in Example 1, except that the year is 2009 and the $40,000 is from wages reported on Form W-2. Although RMDs are not required for 2009 (see Q 5:1), the $75,000 is nonetheless distributed. Thus, the distribution is not treated as a RMD and is taken into account in determining Bill's MAGI for 2009. Therefore, Bill's MAGI for purposes of eligibility for a Roth IRA conversion will be $115,000 ($40,000 + $75,000), which is more than the $100,000 limit (which applies before 2010).

Reduction Below $100,000

Q 6:11   What are some planning strategies that may help reduce a taxpayer's MAGI below $100,000?

The following planning strategies may help reduce a taxpayer's income in the year of a Roth IRA conversion in order to meet the $100,000 MAGI limit:

1. Traditional IRA distributions should be avoided by a taxpayer who has not reached the year in which he or she attains age 70½. [Note that the initial RMD for a taxpayer who attains age 70½ may be postponed until April 1 of the following year. Beginning in 2005, however, an RMD from an IRA is not taken into account when determining if the individual meets the $100,000 MAGI limit.]

2. Discretionary income may be invested in tax-exempt securities or low-dividend-paying equities.

3. Deferred compensation agreements may be modified or created.

4. Certificates of deposit (CDs) and one-year Treasury bills designed to defer income to the following year can be purchased.

5. Recognition of capital gains should be avoided; unrecognized capital losses (to the extent they may be used currently) should be recognized.

6. Exercising nonqualified stock options should be avoided.

7. A taxpayer who is a qualified plan participant could increase or maximize contributions.

8. The taxpayer can increase contributions to flexible spending plans.

9. A self-employed taxpayer may fund a qualified retirement plan or a defined benefit plan.

10. For shareholder-employees of closely held C corporations who have control of their own compensation, current-year salaries can be reduced or deferred.

11. Taxpayers who report income from pass-through entities (i.e., partnerships, S corporations, and limited liability companies) that operate on a cash basis may have some control over income and expense recognition. If the taxpayer can defer the year-end billings of the entity or accelerate the payment of deductible expenses, pass-through income may be reduced.

12. Oil and gas investments should be reviewed (see the following paragraph).

13. The taxpayer who has debt on which he or she is paying interest (especially deductible interest) may want to pay off some or all of the debt by selling income-producing property.

A sophisticated planning strategy available for reducing a taxpayer's income appears to be investing in an oil and gas partnership. Although Code Section 469 was introduced in 1986 to prevent taxpayers from reducing income by generating passive losses, there is a critical exception to the passive loss rules. Code Section 469 includes the following statement:

The term "passive activity" shall not include any working interest in any oil or gas property which the taxpayer holds directly or through an entity which does not limit the liability of the taxpayer with respect to such interest. [I.R.C. § 469(c)(3)(A)]

That provision allows a general partner of an oil and gas venture to enjoy passive losses that may reduce MAGI below the $100,000 conversion limit.

Example. Cecelia's AGI is predicted to be approximately $120,000. She has a $1 million IRA and outside investment assets to pay the income taxes on a Roth IRA conversion. If Cecelia invests $25,000 in an oil and gas partnership of which her portion of the current year's intangible drilling costs is $22,000, her AGI will be reduced to $98,000 and her MAGI will also be $98,000. To make the strategy work, Cecelia needs to make certain that a valid partnership is in existence and that the partnership has in fact incurred the drilling costs. If Cecelia pursues such a strategy, it would also be prudent for her to defer the Roth IRA conversion election until after the partnership has incurred the intangible drilling costs.

Savings Bond Interest Income Used to Pay Education Expenses

Q 6:12   How does income from U.S. savings bonds affect a taxpayer's AGI?

A taxpayer's AGI generally includes the interest income from U.S. savings bonds. The Code provides, however, that a taxpayer who pays "qualified higher education expenses" during the taxable year with "qualified U.S. savings bonds" does not have to include interest income on the redemption in gross income to the extent that the proceeds from the redemption (both principal and interest) do not exceed the expenses. [I.R.C. § 135]

Q 6:13   What is a *qualified U.S. savings bond*?

The term *qualified U.S. savings bond* refers to any U.S. savings bond issued at discount under Section 3105 of Title 31 of the United States Code after December 31, 1989, to an individual who has attained age 24 before the date of issuance. [I.R.C. § 135(c)(1)]

Q 6:14   What are qualified higher education expenses for purposes of the U.S. savings bond interest income exclusion?

In general, the term *qualified higher education expenses* refers to tuition and fees required for the enrollment or attendance at an eligible educational institution of

1. The taxpayer;
2. The taxpayer's spouse; or
3. Any dependent of the taxpayer with respect to whom the taxpayer is allowed a personal deduction under Code Section 151.

[I.R.C. § 135(c)(2)(A)]

There is an exception for education involving sports. The term *qualified higher education expenses* does not include expenses with respect to any course or other education involving sports, games, or hobbies other than as part of a degree program. [I.R.C. § 135(c)(2)(B)]

Q 6:15   How does the exclusion of interest income from U.S. savings bonds from a taxpayer's AGI affect the taxpayer's MAGI for purposes of a Roth IRA conversion?

In determining a taxpayer's MAGI for a Roth IRA conversion, interest income from U.S. savings bonds used to pay qualified higher education expenses during the taxable year must be added back to the taxpayer's AGI (to the extent excluded). [I.R.C. § § 219(g)(2)(A), 408A(c)(3)(C)(i)]

Other Exclusions from AGI

Q 6:16   Besides U.S. savings bond interest income, what amounts may be excluded from AGI (but must be included in MAGI) for Roth IRA conversion purposes?

Exclusions besides that for U.S. savings bond interest income used to pay higher qualified education expenses (see Q 6:14) may affect AGI or MAGI for Roth IRA conversion purposes (see Q 2:8). For one, Code Section 137 states that the gross income of an employee does not include amounts paid or expenses incurred by the employer for qualified adoption expenses. If, however, an employee excludes from income employer-paid adoption expenses, that amount has to be added back to the taxpayer's MAGI for purposes of determining eligibility for converting to a Roth IRA. [I.R.C. §§ 137(a), 219(g)(3)(A)(ii), 408A(c)(3)(C)]

Likewise, Code Section 911 provides an exclusion from gross income for any foreign earned income and for any housing costs paid by an individual's employer. Here, too, for purposes of determining eligibility for converting to a Roth IRA, MAGI must be increased by those amounts. [I.R.C. §§ 219(g)(3)(A)(ii), 408A(c)(3)(C), 911(a)]

> **Example**   Rashid's AGI for 2009 as reported on Form 1040 is $96,000. Rashid excluded $2,000 of employer-paid adoption expenses and $10,000 of foreign earned income from his AGI. After adjustment for those amounts, Rashid's MAGI is $108,000. Therefore, Rashid is not eligible to make a Roth IRA conversion in 2009.

(See Qs 2:8, 6:10–6:17.)

Social Security Taxation

Q 6:17   Is the Roth IRA taxable conversion amount part of the Social Security inclusion formula?

Yes. Under Code Section 86(b)(2) the base for calculating whether a taxpayer's Social Security benefit is subject to income tax is the taxpayer's AGI, which *includes* the Roth IRA taxable conversion amount. If a taxpayer's AGI (including the Roth IRA taxable conversion amount) exceeds the Social Security threshold ($25,000 for single taxpayers and $32,000 for married taxpayers), a portion of any Social Security benefit paid to the taxpayer is subject to income tax, potentially up to 85 percent.

Practice Pointer. A practitioner providing advice to taxpayers whose Social Security income is not currently subject to tax should ensure that income associated with a Roth IRA conversion does not inadvertently subject Social Security benefits to income tax.

Example. Sue's AGI is $20,000 before she performs a conversion to a Roth IRA. The conversion amount is $40,000, which pushes Sue's AGI to $60,000. A portion of Sue's Social Security benefits will now be subject to income tax.

Q 6:18   How does the two-year spread affect the taxation of Social Security benefits?

The two-year spread (see Q 3:17), can negatively affect the taxability of a taxpayer's Social Security by subjecting it to income tax for two years instead of just one year. On the other hand, if the taxpayer can stay under the Social Security threshold of $25,000 for single taxpayers or $32,000 for married taxpayers by using the two-year spread, the taxpayer may be able to avoid taxation of his or her Social Security benefits.

Q 6:19   Are qualified distributions from a Roth IRA included in a taxpayer's AGI for purposes of determining the taxability of Social Security benefits?

No. Qualified distributions from a Roth IRA are treated as income specifically excluded from income tax under Code Section 408A(d)(1). Therefore, any qualified distribution from a Roth IRA does not subject a taxpayer's Social Security to income tax because it is not included as part of the taxpayer's Social Security base, which is used to calculate the taxability of his or her Social Security benefits.

Other Effects of Roth IRA Conversion Income

Q 6:20   Does Roth IRA conversion income affect AGI limits other than that for the taxing of Social Security benefits?

Yes. Because Roth IRA conversion income is included in AGI for all purposes other than the $100,000 MAGI limit on Roth IRA conversion eligibility and the Roth IRA contribution phaseout rules, any limit that references a taxpayer's AGI is affected by a Roth IRA conversion. For example, all of the limits on Form 1040, Schedule A (relating to itemized deductions), are affected by Roth IRA conversion income—negatively so for such items as medical deductions and miscellaneous itemized deductions but in a positive manner for the charitable deduction.

Q 6:21   Does Roth IRA conversion income affect a taxpayer's ability to claim credits?

Yes, Roth IRA conversion income affects a taxpayer's ability to claim credits. The child tax credit and lifetime learning credit, to name two, have AGI limits; converting to a Roth IRA may make the taxpayer's AGI exceed those limits. As a result, such credits may not be available or may be substantially phased out for a taxpayer who converts to a Roth IRA.

Example. George has AGI of $80,000 before inclusion of any Roth IRA conversion income. He has five children and is contemplating a $125,000 Roth IRA conversion. If George converts his $125,000 IRA to a Roth IRA, his AGI for purposes of determining whether he is eligible for the child tax credit will be $205,000. Because his AGI will be well above the $110,000 AGI limit for married taxpayers claiming the child tax credit, George will not be eligible for the child tax credit. He will, in effect, lose $2,500 ($500 child tax credit times five children).

Q 6:22   Does the Roth IRA have a mathematical advantage over the traditional IRA?

No. When considering the conversion of a traditional IRA to a Roth IRA, it is important that a taxpayer understand the basic mathematics of Roth IRA conversions; when the pure math of paying income tax first is compared to the pure math of paying income tax last, there is no difference. That is, absent the advantages discussed in this chapter (see Qs 6:1, 6:24–6:40, and chapter 7 on Roth IRA Trusts), the Roth IRA and the traditional IRA are mathematically indifferent. In other words, if a client's current and future tax rates remain the same, the client will receive no benefit (and no detriment) if the client converts a traditional IRA to a Roth IRA. [Starr, Lawrence C., "Roth 401(k): Still Dumber," 13 JBP 2 (Spring 2006); Watson, Derrin, "Roth 401(k): Not SO Dumb After All," 13 JPB 3 (Spring 2006); Hu, Wei-Yin, "Who Should Save in a Roth 401(K)? (It's Not Just About Tax Rates) (May 27, 2009), available at SSRN: http://ssrn.com/abstract=1410821]

Example. Peter is considering converting $100,000 to a Roth IRA. At the present time, Peter is in the 28 percent tax bracket and expects to be in that tax bracket for all future tax years. Given these assumptions, the amount of IRA assets available for Peter in 20 years, assuming an 8 percent growth rate is as follows:

Table 6-1. "Pure Math" Comparison of Traditional IRA to Roth IRA

	Traditional IRA	Roth IRA
2009 value	$100,000	$100,000
Less tax at 28% rate	($ 0)	($28,000)
Subtotal	$100,000	$ 72,000
Balance after 20 years at 8% interest	$466,096	$335,589

Table 6-1. "Pure Math" Comparison of Traditional IRA to Roth IRA (*cont'd*)

	Traditional IRA	*Roth IRA*
Less tax at 28% rate	($103,507)	($ 0)
Net IRA balance	$ 335,589	$335,589

Practice Pointer. Everything else being equal—and it rarely is, the value of a Roth contribution and the value of a non-Roth contribution to a retirement account is exactly equal on a present value basis. Thus, it is also true—all things being equal, that a Roth deferral is mathematically equivalent to a larger pre-tax deferral.

Only when other factors are introduced (changes in the status quo) can one argue that a Roth contribution is better or worse than a non-Roth contribution. In some cases, it may be possible to undo a contribution or conversion to a Roth IRA in a process called a recharacterization. This may be especially helpful if a Roth IRA has substantially declined in value shortly after the contribution or conversion is made (see Qs 3:29–3:48) or the taxpayer becomes involved in a lawsuit (see Qs 3:30, 3:54).

Q 6:23 When a taxpayer converts his or her traditional IRA to a Roth IRA, is all of the income included in the year of conversion?

If a taxpayer converts a traditional IRA to a Roth IRA in 1999 or later (or made a special election to include the full taxable conversion amount in income for a 1998 conversion—see Q 3:15), the entire taxable conversion amount is taxable in the year of conversion. For a conversion occurring in 2010, however, unless the taxpayer elects otherwise, the taxable conversion amount is spread ratably over two taxable years, beginning with 2011 (i.e., spread over 2011 and 2012) —see Q 3:17. [I.R.C. § 408A(d)(3)(A)(iii)]

Conversion Considerations

Q 6:24 Must a Roth IRA owner take required minimum distributions from the Roth IRA during his or her lifetime?

No. Unlike a traditional IRA owner, a Roth IRA owner does not have to take distributions from the Roth IRA beginning at age 70½ (see Q 5:1). [I.R.C. § 408A(c)(5)] As a result, rather than taking funds from the Roth IRA and reinvesting them elsewhere, the owner can simply continue the deferral within the Roth IRA.

Example. Friedrich, age 60, has a traditional IRA with a balance of $500,000 and a personal fund balance (stocks, bonds, and cash) of $250,000. He consults with Consuela, his financial planning adviser, about the wisdom of converting his IRA to a Roth IRA in 2009. Consuela informs Friedrich that with the traditional IRA, he must begin taking RMDs at age 70. Consuela then prepares the following table using the assumptions that the RMDs are invested, after tax (28 percent tax rate), in an outside account that grows at a 10 percent rate, that the outside account growth is taxed at 20 percent, and that there is no estate tax. The Roth IRA, of course, is not subject to the RMD rules during Friedrich's lifetime. (In her table, Consuela uses the assumption that the entire tax liability is withdrawn from the Roth IRA.) Therefore, the $500,000 beginning balance will continue to grow tax-free until his death. The advantage of being able to defer distributions from the Roth IRA because there are no RMDs from the Roth IRA amounts to $1,179,083.

	Traditional IRA			Roth IRA		
Year	Ending IRA and Outside Fund Balance	Taxes on IRA	Net to Family	Ending IRA and Outside Fund Balance	Taxes on IRA	Net to Family
Jan 1, 2009	$ 750,000	($140,000)	$ 610,000	$ 750,000	($140,000)	$ 610,000
Dec 31, 2009	$ 820,000	($154,000)	$ 666,000	$ 680,000	$ 0	$ 680,000
Dec 31, 2014	$1,282,499	($248,019)	$1,034,480	$1,057,027	$ 0	$1,057,027
Dec 31, 2019	$1,993,511	($384,191)	$1,609,320	$1,646,343	$ 0	$1,646,343
Dec 31, 2024	$2,985,175	($497,711)	$2,487,464	$2,569,156	$ 0	$2,569,156
Dec 31, 2029	$4,422,816	($613,172)	$3,809,644	$4,016,731	$ 0	$4,016,731
Dec 31, 2034	$6,483,563	($702,758)	$5,780,805	$6,291,313	$ 0	$6,291,313
Dec 31, 2039	$9,416,256	($724,171)	$8,692,085	$9,871,168	$ 0	$9,871,168

Q 6:25   How does the deferral period affect the advisability of a Roth IRA conversion?

In general, the longer a taxpayer waits to withdraw funds, the more attractive the Roth IRA becomes. If a taxpayer can take advantage of that longer deferral, he or she is probably better off with a Roth IRA. The longer the funds can grow in a tax-deferred environment, the better the economic result.

Example. Ginger, age 45, has a $400,000 Roth IRA and $112,000 of nonqualified liquid assets. Ginger is currently in the 28 percent tax bracket and expects to be in the 25 percent tax bracket during her retirement years. Assuming a pretax growth rate in the Roth IRA of 7 percent and an after-tax growth rate of 6 percent in the taxable brokerage account, the amount of wealth Ginger will have in the future is as follows:

	Do Nothing			Roth IRA Conversion			Difference ($)	Difference (%)
	Traditional IRA	Brokerage Account	Total	Roth IRA	Brokerage Account	Total		
Pre-Tax Account Balance (Current)	$ 400,000	$112,000	$ 512,000	$ 400,000	$ 112,000	$ 512,000		
Less: Income Tax on Roth IRA Conversion @ 28%	-	-	-	-	(112,000)	(112,000)		
Less: "Built-In" Income Tax @ 25%	(100,000)	-	(100,000)	-	-	-		
After-Tax Account Balance (Current)	$ 300,000	$112,000	$ 412,000	$ 400,000	$ -	$ 400,000	$(12,000)	-3.00%
Pre-Tax Account Balance (Year 10)	$ 786,861	$200,575	$ 987,435	$ 786,861	$ -	$ 786,861		
Less: "Built-In" Income Tax @ 25%	(196,715)	-	(196,715)	-	-	-		
After-Tax Account Balance (Year 10)	$ 590,145	$200,575	$ 790,720	$ 786,861	$ -	$ 786,861	$ (3,860)	-0.49%
Pre-Tax Account Balance (Year 20)	$1,547,874	$359,199	$1,907,073	$1,547,874	$ -	$1,547,874		
Less: "Built-In" Income Tax @ 25%	(386,968)	-	(386,968)	-	-	-		
After-Tax Account Balance (Year 20)	$1,160,905	$359,199	$1,520,105	$1,547,874	$ -	$1,547,874	$ 27,769	1.83%
Pre-Tax Account Balance (Year 30)	$3,044,902	$643,271	$3,688,173	$3,044,902	$ -	$3,044,902		
Less: "Built-In" Income Tax @ 25%	(761,226)	-	(761,226)	-	-	-		
After-Tax Account Balance (Year 30)	$2,283,677	$643,271	$2,926,948	$3,044,902	$ -	$3,044,902	$ 117,954	4.03%

[Robert S. Keebler and Stephen J. Bigge, To Convert or Not to Convert, That Is the Question, *Journal of Retirement Planning*, May–June 2007]

Q 6:26   Is it more advantageous to pay income tax before paying estate tax?

Although the mathematical rule of commutation would indicate that it doesn't matter which tax is paid first, if a taxpayer resides in a state that has either a state estate tax or a state income tax, there may be an advantage to using a Roth conversion before death so that income tax is paid before estate tax.

When the income tax is computed on withdrawals from a traditional IRA, a deduction is given for federal estate tax paid when computing federal taxable income. [I.R.C. § 691(c)] No such deduction is given for state estate tax paid, however. In addition, many states do not incorporate the Code Section 691(c) deduction into their income tax rules. As a result, state income tax may be computed on the entire IRA balance, with no reduction for any estate tax, state or federal.

Therefore, by doing a Roth conversion before death, the amount used to pay state income tax is taken out of the taxable estate and is not subject to either state or federal estate tax.

Because the Code Section 691(c) deduction is an itemized deduction, there is also an advantage to doing a Roth conversion before death if the beneficiaries' income situation will not allow them to use itemized deductions.

Table 6-2 shows the benefit that is achieved by paying income tax before estate tax despite the Code Section 691(c) deduction in a situation where there is state estate tax.

Table 6-2. Section 691(c) Deduction Compared to Paying Income Tax First

	Estate Tax First (Traditional IRA)	*Income Tax First (Roth IRA)*
IRA balance:	**$100,000**	**$100,000**
Less Federal Tax on Roth conversion at 35%*	-	($ 35,000)
Net	$100,000	$ 65,000
Less Federal Estate Tax at 45%*	($ 45,000)	($ 29,250)
Less State Estate Tax at 7%*	($ 7,000)	($ 4,550)
Remaining Balance of IRA	**$ 48,000**	**$ 31,200**
IRA Balance Subject to Income Tax	$100,000	—
Less Section 691(c) deduction	($ 45,000)	—
Balance Subject to Income Tax	$ 55,000	—

Table 6-2. Section 691(c) Deduction Compared to Paying Income Tax First (cont'd)

	Estate Tax First (Traditional IRA)	Income Tax First (Roth IRA)
Less Federal Tax on distributions at 35%[*]	($19,250)	—
Net to Family:	**$ 28,750**	**$31,200**

_____

[*] Rates assumed.

Q 6:27 Should the taxes on a conversion be paid from assets outside the Roth IRA or traditional IRA?

Yes. Being able to pay the income taxes on a conversion to a Roth IRA from outside assets is one of the main factors that drive a conversion. Doing so allows a taxpayer to move assets from a taxable environment to a tax-free environment.

Example. Sarah, age 60, has a traditional IRA with a balance of $500,000 and a $250,000 personal fund balance (stocks, bonds, and cash). She converts her IRA to a Roth IRA in 2009. The entire tax liability of $14,000 ($50,000 × 0.28) is paid from the personal fund. Isaac, Sarah's financial planning adviser, notes that had Sarah kept the traditional IRA, distribution would have had to begin in 2019. Assuming 10 percent growth, a capital gain rate of 20 percent, and no estate tax, Isaac prepares the following table, which shows a $2,213,245 ($10,905,330 − $8,692,085) advantage to the Roth IRA over a 20-year period.

	Traditional IRA			Roth IRA		
Year	Ending IRA and Outside Fund Balance	Taxes on IRA	Net to Family	Ending IRA and Outside Fund Balance	Taxes on IRA	Net to Family
Jan 1, 2010	$ 750,000	($140,000)	$ 610,000	$ 750,000	($140,000)	$ 610,000
Dec 31, 2010	$ 820,000	($154,000)	$ 666,000	$ 680,000	$ 0	$ 680,000
Dec 31, 2015	$1,282,499	($248,019)	$1,034,480	$ 1,076,793	$ 0	$ 1,076,793
Dec 31, 2020	$1,993,511	($384,191)	$1,609,320	$ 1,707,220	$ 0	$ 1,707,220
Dec 31, 2025	$2,985,175	($497,711)	$2,478,464	$ 2,709,872	$ 0	$ 2,709,872
Dec 31, 2030	$4,422,816	($613,172)	$3,809,644	$ 4,306,054	$ 0	$ 4,306,054
Dec 31, 2035	$6,483,563	($702,758)	$5,780,805	$ 6,849,397	$ 0	$ 6,849,397
Dec 31, 2040	$9,416,256	($724,171)	$8,692,085	$10,905,330	$ 0	$10,905,330

Q 6:28 **What variables affect decisions regarding Roth IRA conversions and financial planning other than technical requirements and elections?**

In addition to the technical requirements and the elections a taxpayer may make, Roth IRA conversion analysis is driven by the following factors:

- Tax rates at time of contribution and deduction
- Tax rates at time of distribution and taxation
- Rate of return (growth)
- Deferral period
- Inflation rate
- Current and future cash flow needs

The degree to which any factor affects the decision to convert a traditional IRA to a Roth IRA cannot be determined easily. A small percentage change in one variable may cause the advantage of such a conversion to disappear.

Each variable has a different sensitivity influence on the result, depending on the circumstances. That sensitivity has been effectively demonstrated in a comprehensive series of case studies prepared by Gobind Daryanani, Ph.D., after reviewing software from many sources and developing his own algorithm and proprietary software. [G. Daryanani, *Roth IRA Book: An Investor's Guide* (Bernardsville, N.J.: Digiqual Inc., 1998)] The case studies look at how a small (2 percent to 4 percent) increase in an assumption—future tax rates, for example—can affect decision making. Daryanani defines *sensitivity* as the percentage change in the advantage or disadvantage of a Roth conversion (or contribution) resulting from a 1 percent change in the variable.

> **Example.** Felicity, age 40, calculates that by converting her traditional IRA to a Roth IRA she will have about $100 more per year to spend (taking inflation into account) when she begins withdrawals at age 75. If, however, Felicity starts distributions earlier, say at age 74, the conversion would provide only about $90 extra per year. There is a 10 percent sensitivity to a one-year reduction in the deferral period; here, the sensitivity to that variable is not particularly high.

The following conclusions regarding the relative advantage of a Roth IRA over a traditional IRA are based on a number of observations from various case studies:

A Roth IRA will do significantly better than a traditional IRA even if a tax deduction from a traditional IRA contribution is available *and* that amount is invested. In most cases, individuals do not invest their tax savings; thus, the loss of the current year's deduction will not be significant. The Roth IRA will be an even better choice if the tax savings are *not* invested.

> **Example.** Angela can contribute $4,000 to a deductible traditional IRA. She has a marginal tax rate of 35 percent. If Angela invests her tax savings of $1,400 ($4,000 × 0.35), she will have $5,400 invested (of which $1,400 is in a taxable account and $4,000 is in the traditional IRA and taxable upon

withdrawal). If Angela contributes $4,000 to a Roth IRA, she will have only $4,000 invested. Even so, Angela is better off with a Roth IRA. Assuming an annual growth of 10 percent for 20 years, Angela would be $2,245 ($26,910 − $22,425) ahead with a Roth IRA and no outside savings.

Roth IRA: $4,000 × 1.10^{20} = $26,910 available from Roth IRA (no taxes)

Traditional IRA with tax savings invested:

$4,000 × 1.10^{20} = $26,910; $26,910 − taxes (35%) of $9,418

= $17,492 from traditional IRA

$1,400 × $(1.10 − 0.035)^{20}$ = $4,933 from invested tax savings

1. $17,492 + $4,933 = $22,425 available from traditional IRA with tax savings invested

Even if Angela contributed to a traditional IRA and invested her tax savings in a tax-exempt investment portfolio, it would still be better to convert her traditional IRA to a Roth IRA. If she earned 7 percent tax-free on her outside savings, Angela would generate only $5,418 ($1,400 × 1.07^{20}) from her invested tax savings of $1,400, or $22,910 ($17,492 + $5,418) in total. In this case, the Roth IRA would be better by $4,000 ($26,910 − $22,910).

As the example illustrates, even if traditional IRA tax savings are invested, the Roth IRA may still be the better choice. The tax-free growth in the Roth IRA can offset lower taxes paid during the retirement years when withdrawals are made from a traditional IRA. Of course, the lower those taxes, the longer the Roth IRA has to be held for its owner to break even.

2. Significantly lower tax rates at retirement may make the traditional IRA more advantageous.

3. It takes five years of tax-free growth in the Roth IRA to nullify the advantage of a 5 percent lower average tax at retirement.

4. The Roth IRA advantage increases as the duration of the deferral period increases. Conversely, the traditional IRA advantage increases as the deferral period decreases.

5. An estate will be worth significantly more if Roth IRA assets are left intact until age 80.

6. Inflation affects all IRAs almost equally.

7. Higher rates of return favor the Roth IRA.

8. A plan that makes matching contributions of 50 percent to 100 percent (e.g., a 401(k) plan or a 403(b) plan) will be a better choice than the Roth IRA. At lower percentages, 0 percent to 25 percent, a Roth IRA is generally a better choice.

9. Roth IRA assets are generally the last assets that should be used for retirement income.

Specific observations regarding Roth IRA conversions are as follows:

1. A Roth IRA conversion will generally provide an advantage if the conversion taxes are paid from outside assets.

2. A partial conversion may be appropriate. For example, if funds are needed within five years, a taxpayer may be better off not converting all of his or her traditional IRA. Penalties may also have to be considered (see Qs 4:17–4:22). In addition, if tax rates are lower in retirement and funds from a traditional IRA are needed within 15 years, a partial conversion may be better.

Income and Estate Tax Advantages

Q 6:29   Can a Roth IRA conversion affect a taxpayer's enjoyment of the charitable deduction and investment tax credit carryforwards?

Yes. If a taxpayer has favorable tax attributes such as charitable deduction carryforwards or investment tax credit carryforwards, conversion to a Roth IRA may be desirable.

A charitable deduction, for instance, may not exceed a percentage of the taxpayer's AGI. The deduction percentage further depends on whether the gift was a gift of cash or a gift of appreciated property; for example, if a taxpayer made a contribution of appreciated property to a charity, the deduction is limited to 30 percent of the taxpayer's AGI. By converting to a Roth IRA, a taxpayer increases his or her AGI for purposes of calculating the charitable deduction.

> **Example.** Ian makes a contribution of $130,000 of appreciated securities to a charity. Before a Roth IRA conversion, Ian and his wife, Simone, have AGI of $100,000. If Ian and Simone do not make a Roth conversion election, the charitable deduction will be limited to $30,000, which is 30 percent of their AGI of $100,000. If they convert $200,000 to a Roth IRA, they will be able to deduct $90,000 ($300,000 of AGI × 30% charitable deduction limitation). That allows Ian and Simone to use their charitable deduction earlier than they would otherwise.

> **Note.** A Roth IRA conversion may make it possible to use deductions that would otherwise be lost under the carryforward rules. A charitable deduction carryforward, for example, must be used within five years. Without a Roth IRA conversion, a portion of the charitable deduction could be lost.

Q 6:30   What is meant by the terms *exclusion trust, credit shelter trust, bypass trust,* and *family trust,* and may a Roth IRA be used to fund any such trust?

The terms *exclusion trust, credit shelter trust, bypass trust* (B trust), and *family trust* refer to a trust designed to use a taxpayer's estate tax exemption. Creating such a trust in 2009 allows $3.5 million of property to be sheltered from federal estate taxes in each spouse's estate by using the applicable exclusion. This is a dollar amount that each taxpayer may exclude from the federal estate tax. [I.R.C. §§ 2001, 2010–2016] Such a trust may be created for the benefit of the surviving spouse as the sole or primary beneficiary. On the surviving spouse's death, the remaining assets will not be taxed in his or her estate if the surviving spouse did not have sufficient "control" over the disposition of such property.

A taxpayer may consider making a Roth IRA conversion if he or she needs to fund a bypass trust with retirement assets. It is better to fund a bypass trust with a Roth IRA than with a traditional IRA because the Roth IRA is not generally subject to federal income tax (see chapter 4), as the following calculations indicate:

	Traditional IRA	*Roth IRA*
Exemption amount	$ 3,500,000	$3,500,000
Less income taxes at 35%	($1,225,000)	0
Net to family	$ 2,275,000	$3,500,000
Additional wealth transfer		$1,225,000

Accordingly, for a taxpayer who needs to fund a bypass trust with IRA assets, it may be advantageous to convert a portion of an IRA to a Roth IRA. (See Q 7:2 for requirements that a trust must meet to be a designated beneficiary of a Roth IRA.)

Q 6:31 Will converting a traditional IRA to a Roth IRA reduce a taxpayer's estate?

Yes. If a taxpayer converts a traditional IRA to a Roth IRA, the taxpayer's total taxable estate is reduced by the income taxes paid on the conversion. For example, if a taxpayer converts a $1 million IRA to a Roth IRA and has a 35 percent tax rate, the estate is reduced by $350,000. If the taxpayer is in the 45 percent estate tax bracket, the conversion immediately saves $147,500 ($350,000 × .45) of estate tax.

Q 6:32 Can a taxpayer with a Roth IRA name a new beneficiary after attaining age 70½?

Yes. For a Roth IRA (as well as a traditional IRA), the designated beneficiaries at death will be the persons named at that time who remain beneficiaries on September 30 of the year following the year of death. Because there are no required distributions during lifetime for a Roth IRA, the persons named as beneficiaries will have no impact on the calculation of distributions until after the owner's death.

Q 6:33   What special concerns arise for a taxpayer who converts to a Roth IRA before age 59½?

A taxpayer who converts to a Roth IRA before age 59½ must take care to avoid the 10 percent premature distribution penalty under Code Section 72(t). Although the conversion to a Roth IRA does not trigger that penalty, it is very likely that if a taxpayer takes distributions in excess of the contributions made to the Roth IRA or takes distributions of converted funds from the Roth IRA within five years of the conversion and before attaining age 59½, the Section 72(t) penalty will be imposed (see Q 4:17). [I.R.C. § 408A(d)(3)(F)(i)]

Example 1. Elise converts her $50,000 IRA to a Roth IRA when she is 35 years old. At age 55, when the Roth IRA is worth $340,000, Elise takes a distribution of $75,000 for a down payment on a beach house. Because the distribution is in excess of her $50,000 basis (assume no other contributions were made to the account), Elise's distribution would be subject to income tax on the $25,000 in excess of basis, and the same $25,000 would be subject to the 10 percent premature distribution penalty.

Example 2. Jane, age 50, converts $200,000 to a Roth IRA in 2006. In 2009, she needs more cash to pay the conversion tax and withdraws $10,000. The $10,000 is subject to the 10 percent premature distribution penalty because it is a distribution of converted funds made within five years of the conversion. It is not subject to income tax because it is considered a withdrawal of basis.

Estimated Tax Payments

Q 6:34   Must a taxpayer make estimated tax payments when he or she converts to a Roth IRA?

Probably. If required, estimated tax payments are due April 15, June 15, September 15, and January 15.

The Internal Revenue Service (IRS) imposes interest on underpayments that equals the current statutory interest rate (computed monthly) times the amount of the underpayment. [I.R.C. § 6654(a)] The underpayment is the amount of the required installment that is greater than any amount paid on or before the due date of the installment. [I.R.C. § 6654(b)] Therefore, if an installment payment is not made, the IRS imposes an assessment of interest that is calculated based upon the applicable interest rate times the amount that was not paid by the specified due date times the number of days the installment was overdue.

Because Code Section 408(d) expressly provides that any amount converted to a Roth IRA is includible in gross income, the IRS will not abate estimated tax underpayment penalties, absent a waiver for casualty disaster or other unusual circumstances, as provided by Code Section 6654(e)(3). [I.R.S. Service Center Advice 200105062]

Example. Jeff is required to make an estimated tax payment of $2,000 on June 15. He fails to make the payment by June 15 and instead makes it on July 15. The assessed interest is based on the amount of the estimated payment ($2,000), the length of time from the due date of the payment to the time it was actually paid (30 days), and the current interest rate. If we assume an applicable interest rate of 8 percent, Jeff's underpayment would be $13.15 ($2,000 × 30/365 × 0.08).

Q 6:35   How should a taxpayer make estimated tax payments when he or she converts to a Roth IRA?

A taxpayer who converts to a Roth IRA must make quarterly installments of estimated tax due so that the amount paid through withholding and estimated tax payments causes the taxpayer to qualify for one of the following safe harbors. The amount paid must be greater than or equal to the lesser of (1) 90 percent of the tax shown on the current year's tax return or (2) 100 percent of the amount shown on the prior year's return. However, under I.R.C. § 6654(d)(1)(D)(i), in the case of any taxable year beginning in 2009, the "100 percent" in the second requirement is changed to "90 percent" for any qualified individual.

The term *qualified individual* means any individual if (1) the adjusted gross income shown on the return of such individual for the preceding taxable year is less than $500,000 and (2) such individual certifies that more than 50 percent of the gross income shown on the return of such individual for the preceding taxable year was income from a small business. [I.R.C. § 6654(d)(1)(D)(ii)]

Example. The amount of tax calculated on Asad's 2009 tax return is $10,000. Assuming his 2008 AGI was less than $150,000, Asad was required to pay a minimum of $9,000 through withholding and estimated tax payments unless his 2008 tax liability was less than $9,000. In the latter case, Asad was required to pay, through withholding and estimated tax payments, 100 percent of the tax paid for 2008 for purposes of 2009 income tax.

Note. For an individual with AGI for the preceding year in excess of $150,000, the prior-year safe harbor for required estimated tax installment due for tax years beginning in or after 2003 remains at 110 percent. [I.R.C. § 6654(d)(1)(C)]

Q 6:36   How might a Roth IRA conversion that occurs in the later months of the year cause a problem vis-à-vis estimated tax payments?

In the case of a Roth IRA conversion that occurs in the later months of the year, quarterly estimated payments made earlier in the year may not be adequate because of the extra income that will be recognized later in the year of conversion. A taxpayer can, however, increase withholding toward the end of the year and the payments will be considered made pro rata throughout the year, so no penalty will be imposed. Also, if a taxpayer can show the IRS that the income occurred in the later months of the year, using Form 2210, Underpayment of Estimated Tax by Individuals, Estates, and Trusts, no penalty will be imposed.

Financing Conversions

Q 6:37   How should a taxpayer finance his or her Roth IRA conversion?

The most advantageous way to finance a Roth IRA conversion is with outside liquid assets (see Q 6:38). By using outside assets to fund the Roth IRA conversion tax, the taxpayer, in effect, moves assets from a taxable environment to a tax-free environment.

> **Example.** Elizabeth has a $100,000 traditional IRA and $50,000 in outside liquid assets. She converts the traditional IRA to a Roth IRA. Elizabeth's tax rate is 40 percent. If Elizabeth pays the $40,000 income tax on the conversion out of the IRA, she will have $60,000 in the IRA and $50,000 in outside assets. If she pays the tax from the outside assets, she will have $10,000 in outside assets and $100,000 in the IRA. Her net assets after taxes are $110,000 in both cases, but if she pays the tax out of outside liquid assets instead of out of the IRA, $100,000 instead of $60,000 (a difference of $40,000) will be in the Roth IRA and $10,000 instead of $50,000 (a difference of $40,000) will be in the outside account. In effect, by paying the tax from outside liquid assets, Elizabeth will move $40,000 from a taxable environment to a tax-free environment.

Q 6:38   Should assets that have a low basis be used to pay the taxes on a Roth IRA conversion?

No. Generally, the best source of funds to pay taxes on a Roth IRA conversion is outside cash or high-basis investment accounts. If assets that have a low basis are used, more taxes will have to be paid and more assets will have to be sold to generate the cash needed to pay the tax (see Q 6:37).

Q 6:39   Is interest incurred on indebtedness used to finance a Roth IRA conversion deductible on Form 1040 as an itemized deduction?

It depends. For interest expense to be deductible by an individual taxpayer, it must be interest on home equity indebtedness or interest on home acquisition indebtedness or the money borrowed must be used for a deductible purpose such as business or investment. Simply borrowing on a personal unsecured note or against investments or nonhome real estate does not generate deductible investment interest. [I.R.C. § 163(h)]

The term *home acquisition indebtedness* refers to indebtedness that is used in acquiring, constructing, or substantially improving a taxpayer's qualified residence and that is secured by the residence. Interest incurred to purchase a qualified residence is deductible at the time the interest is paid. The aggregate amount of debt that may be treated as acquisition indebtedness for any period may not exceed $1 million. [I.R.C. § 163(h)(3)(B)(i)(II)]

The term *home equity indebtedness* refers to indebtedness on the taxpayer's principal residence and one other residence that the taxpayer (1) used during the year for personal purposes for more than 14 days or, if greater, more than 10 percent of the number of days it was rented at a fair market value, or (2) used as a residence but not as a rental. [I.R.C. § 163(h)(4)] The aggregate amount of debt that may be treated as home equity indebtedness for any period may not exceed $100,000 (unless the taxpayer is married and files a separate return, in which case the limit is $50,000). [I.R.C. § 163(h)(3)(c)(ii)]

State Law Considerations

Q 6:40   How do the states treat Roth IRAs?

Income tax treatment of Roth IRAs may vary from state to state. Taxpayers should consult their applicable state law to determine if the taxation of Roth IRAs is tied to the federal method of taxation, whether it is independent of federal treatment or whether there is no income tax at all.

Inherited IRA

Q 6:41   What is an *inherited IRA*?

An *inherited IRA* is an IRA that is inherited intact (i.e., the assets remain in a tax-deferred environment) after the death of its owner where the spouse is not the beneficiary (or if the spouse is the beneficiary, he or she does not perform a spousal rollover). An inherited IRA is titled in the deceased owner's name (see Q 6:42), and distributions are made to the beneficiary. [*See* I.R.C. § 408(d)(3)(C)(ii)]

Q 6:42   How should an inherited IRA be titled?

An inherited IRA should remain in the name of the deceased owner for the benefit of the beneficiary. Failure to keep an inherited IRA in the name of the deceased will result in a deemed distribution of the entire amount.

Example. John Smith, deceased, Roth IRA for the benefit of Thomas Smith

Q 6:43   What is the advantage of an inherited IRA?

The Code allows a designated beneficiary of an inherited IRA to stretch out distributions over the beneficiary's life expectancy if distributions begin on or before the end of the calendar year immediately following the calendar year in which the IRA owner died. [Treas. Reg. § 1.401(a)(9)-3] (See Q 5:13.) That allows the funds to remain in the IRA—and thus remain in a tax-deferred (or tax-free, in the case of a Roth) environment—for a longer time (see Qs 5:1, 5:12, 5:15).

> **Example.** Alex dies in 2009, owning a Roth IRA. Alex named his son, Nicholas, as beneficiary of the Roth IRA. Nicholas must begin taking required minimum distributions by December 31, 2010.

Q 6:44   How should an inherited IRA be structured to achieve the maximum wealth transfer?

To achieve the maximum wealth transfer, the beneficiary of an inherited IRA must be a designated beneficiary; that is, only a designated beneficiary can stretch out distributions over his or her lifetime (see Q 5:23). A *designated beneficiary* is generally an individual or a group of individuals [I.R.C. § 401(a)(9)(E); Treas. Reg. § 1.401(a)(9)-4, Q&As 1, 3], although certain trusts may also qualify for designated beneficiary status (see Q 7:2). [Treas. Reg. § 1.401(a)(9)-4, Q&A 5]

> **Note.** If a beneficiary of a Roth IRA is not a designated beneficiary (as determined by September 30 of the year following the year of the Roth IRA owner's death), the entire balance must be distributed no later than the December 31 of the fifth year following the year of death (see Q 5:18).

Q 6:45   What is the mathematical advantage of stretching out distributions from an inherited IRA?

Stretching out distributions from an inherited IRA creates greater wealth to pass to future generations, because the funds will be in a tax-free environment until they are distributed. Alternatively, if the funds are withdrawn immediately after the death of the taxpayer, they will be in a taxable environment and subject to income tax (unless it is a qualified distribution from a Roth IRA).

Table 6-3 illustrates the advantage of stretching out distributions from an inherited IRA over a person's life expectancy versus taking an immediate distribution. It assumes a $500,000 beginning inherited Roth IRA balance and a 40-year-old beneficiary (initial life expectancy of 43.6 years). The personal fund grows at 10 percent and is taxed at 30 percent. The Roth IRA growth is 10 percent. It also shows a $1,304,734 advantage (greater assets) over a 22-year period if distributions are paid over a life expectancy rather than as a single sum on the death of the Roth IRA owner.

Table 6-3. Immediate Withdrawal Versus Distributions over Life Expectancy

	Roth IRA—Immediate Withdrawal			Roth IRA—Distributions over Life Expectancy		
Year	Beginning Roth IRA Balance	Distribution from Roth IRA	Ending Roth IRA and Outside Balance	Beginning Roth IRA Balance	Required Minimum Distribution	Ending Roth IRA and Outside Balance
1	$500,000	$500,000	$535,000	$500,000	$11,765	$549,647
2			$572,450	$537,059	$12,941	$603,846
3			$612,522	$576,529	$14,235	$662,984
4			$655,398	$618,524	$15,659	$727,479
5			$701,276	$663,151	$17,225	$797,780

Table 6-3. Immediate Withdrawal Versus Distributions over Life Expectancy
(cont'd)

	Roth IRA—Immediate Withdrawal			Roth IRA—Distributions over Life Expectancy		
Year	Beginning Roth IRA Balance	Distribution from Roth IRA	Ending Roth IRA and Outside Balance	Beginning Roth IRA Balance	Required Minimum Distribution	Ending Roth IRA and Outside Balance
6			$ 750,365	$ 710,519	$18,947	$ 874,372
7			$ 802,891	$ 760,729	$20,842	$ 957,774
8			$ 859,093	$ 813,876	$22,926	$1,048,547
9			$ 919,230	$ 870,045	$25,219	$1,147,290
10			$ 983,576	$ 929,309	$27,741	$1,254,648
11			$1,052,426	$ 991,725	$30,515	$1,371,309
12			$1,126,096	$1,057,331	$33,566	$1,498,014
13			$1,204,923	$1,126,142	$36,923	$1,635,551
14			$1,289,267	$1,198,141	$40,615	$1,784,766
15			$1,379,516	$1,273,279	$44,676	$1,946,557
16			$1,476,082	$1,351,463	$49,144	$2,121,886
17			$1,579,408	$1,432,550	$54,059	$2,311,773
18			$1,689,966	$1,516,341	$59,464	$2,517,303
19			$1,808,264	$1,602,564	$65,411	$2,739,629
20			$1,934,842	$1,690,869	$71,952	$2,979,971
21			$2,070,281	$1,780,809	$79,147	$3,239,618
22			$2,215,201	$1,871,828	$87,062	$3,519,935

Q 6:46   May a taxpayer achieve a stretch-out IRA with a traditional IRA?

As with a Roth IRA, a taxpayer may achieve a stretch-out IRA using a traditional IRA under certain circumstances. In the right circumstances, distributions may be made over an individual beneficiary's life expectancy.

The Code allows a designated beneficiary to receive distributions over his or her single life expectancy if the distributions begin by December 31 of the year following the year of the IRA owner's death. This is usually far more advantageous than the five-year rule for death before the required beginning date when there is no designated beneficiary or over the life expectancy of the deceased IRA owner for death after the required beginning date when there is no designated beneficiary (see Q 5:1). Therefore, having a designated beneficiary is critical to preserving the deferral that can be achieved with proper planning. [I.R.C. § 401(a)(9)(B)(iii)]

Example. Preston, age 62, died in 2009 and had previously named his daughter Claire as the designated beneficiary of his traditional IRA. If Claire begins taking distributions from the IRA by December 31, 2010, she may stretch distributions out over her single life expectancy.

Q 6:47 At the death of a Roth IRA owner, what distribution options are available to the individual Roth IRA beneficiary?

The traditional IRA distribution rules govern postmortem distributions from a Roth IRA. Thus, an individual Roth IRA beneficiary is allowed to take distributions over his or her life expectancy. [I.R.C. § § 401(a)(9), 408A(c)(5)] If the Roth IRA beneficiary is the account owner's spouse, the rollover rules also apply (see Q 6:49).

Example. Marie leaves a $100,000 Roth IRA to her daughter Sophie, age 40. Sophie has a life expectancy of 43.6 years and the Roth IRA grows at 10 percent. The distributions will be as shown below.

Year	Roth IRA Beginning value	Life Expectancy	Annual Distribution
1	$100,000	43.6	$ 2,294
2	$107,477	42.6	$ 2,523
3	$115,450	41.6	$ 2,775
4	$123,942	40.6	$ 3,053
5	$132,978	39.6	$ 3,358
6	$142,582	38.6	$ 3,694
7	$152,777	37.6	$ 4,063
8	$163,585	36.6	$ 4,470
9	$175,027	35.6	$ 4,916
10	$187,122	34.6	$ 5,408
11	$199,885	33.6	$ 5,949
12	$213,329	32.6	$ 6,544
13	$227,464	31.6	$ 7,198
14	$242,292	30.6	$ 7,918
15	$257,812	29.6	$ 8,710
16	$274,012	28.6	$ 9,581
17	$290,874	27.6	$10,539
18	$308,369	26.6	$11,593
19	$326,454	25.6	$12,752
20	$345,072	24.6	$14,027

The table shows that after 20 years, the Roth IRA is worth more than $345,000 and is still growing, and that Sophie has received more than $130,000 of distributions from the $100,000 Roth IRA.

Q 6:48   At the death of a Roth IRA owner, what distribution options are available when a Roth IRA trust is the beneficiary of the Roth IRA?

When a trust is the beneficiary of a Roth IRA, the minimum distribution rules in the regulations under Code Section 401(a)(9) that govern distributions from a traditional IRA when they are payable to a trust apply. The trust must meet the requirements of the regulations for the trust beneficiaries to be deemed designated beneficiaries. [*See generally* I.R.C. § 401(a)(9); Treas. Reg. § 1.401(a)(9)-4, Q&A 5] If the trust qualifies, distributions are calculated based on the life expectancy of the oldest trust beneficiary (see Q 7:2).

Q 6:49   If a Roth IRA owner's spouse is the beneficiary, may the spouse roll over the Roth IRA to his or her own Roth IRA?

Yes. Code Section 402(c)(9), along with many letter rulings, supports the general concept that a surviving spouse who is "sole beneficiary" may roll over his or her deceased spouse's IRA (including a Roth IRA) to an IRA in the surviving spouse's own name. That is generally done in a trustee-to-trustee transfer in which the surviving spouse requests that the decedent spouse's trustee (or custodian) transfer the funds to an IRA in the surviving spouse's name. [Ltr. Ruls. 200438045 (Sept. 17, 2004), 200106047 (Nov. 17, 2000), 200027064 (Apr. 12, 2000), 200052040 (Oct. 2, 2000), 9608042 (Feb. 23, 1996), 9433031 (May 26, 1994)] Once the funds are transferred to an IRA in the surviving spouse's name, the surviving spouse should name a new beneficiary. [*See* Treas. Reg. § 1.408-8, Q&A 5]

Life Insurance to Pay Estate Tax

Q 6:50   How does life insurance complement the Roth IRA?

In many instances, a taxpayer's estate may not have sufficient liquidity to pay the estate tax on the taxpayer's death. Life insurance can be used to provide liquidity for estate taxes, thereby protecting the Roth IRA (see Qs 1:20, 6:52).

Example. Drew has an IRA valued at $3.8, 2.3 million and $200,000 of additional probate assets. A federal estate tax of $155,800 (for 2009) would be imposed on $500,000, which is the amount above the $3.5 million exemption equivalent (see Qs 6:30, 7:43). In the absence of life insurance, Drew's beneficiaries would need to liquidate a portion of the Roth IRA to pay the estate tax. Such a withdrawal of funds from the Roth IRA would negate the substantial deferral that is available into the future.

Q 6:51   How can a taxpayer use life insurance to protect an IRA?

When planning to use life insurance to protect an IRA (including a Roth IRA), a taxpayer usually sets up an irrevocable life insurance trust so that estate tax does not have to be paid on the death benefit of the life insurance. Most typically, an irrevocable life insurance trust with the taxpayer's children as beneficiaries is established. The taxpayer then makes gifts of cash to the trust. The trustee uses the cash to purchase a survivorship life insurance policy covering both the taxpayer and his or her spouse. At the second death, the life insurance proceeds are paid to the trust. To the extent needed to pay the estate tax, cash can be either loaned to the estate or used to purchase estate assets. That obviates the need to withdraw funds from the IRA in order to pay the tax. After the second death, the taxpayer's children may receive distributions from the IRA over their life expectancies.

Q 6:52   May an IRA invest in a life insurance policy?

No. Neither a Roth IRA nor a traditional IRA may invest in a life insurance contract (see Q 1:20). [I.R.C. § 408(a)(3)]

Q 6:53   Does federal law exempt Roth IRAs from a bankruptcy estate?

Under the Bankruptcy Abuse and Consumer Protection Act of 2005 (BACPA), signed into law on April 20, 2005, Roth IRAs are exempt from the bankruptcy estate up to a $1 million limit (as adjusted for inflation). Previously only stock bonus, pension, profit sharing, annuity, or "similar plans or contracts" were protected from creditors. The $1 million limit for Roth IRAs does not apply to amounts attributable to rollover contributions and related earnings. [11 U.S.C. § 522(b)(2), 522(b)(3), 522(d)(12), 522(n)] In addition, a state that treats a Roth IRA as a "spendthrift trust" under state law (e.g., common law) might be granted additional protection under BACPA. [*See* 11 U.S.C. § 541(c)(2), providing an exclusion from the bankruptcy estate for trust property upon which there is a "restriction on the transfer of a beneficial interest of the debtor . . . that is enforceable under applicable nonbankruptcy law. . . ." (i.e., a "spendthrift trust" pursuant to state law)]

Q 6:54   Can the federal $1 million limit protecting Roth IRAs from creditors be adjusted?

Yes. Under BACPA, the $1 million limit can be increased if the "interests of justice so require" (see Q 6:53). [11 U.S.C. § 522(n)]

Chapter 7

Roth IRA Trusts

A Roth IRA trust is a trust specifically designed to be the beneficiary of a Roth IRA, which is itself by definition a trust or custodial account. This chapter examines the benefits of naming a Roth IRA trust as the beneficiary of a Roth IRA—including discipline, management (control), and, in some states, creditor protection. Drafting considerations that must be addressed when naming a Roth IRA trust as the beneficiary of a Roth IRA are discussed herein, as are the generation-skipping aspects of a Roth IRA trust.

Overview

Q 7:1   What is a *Roth IRA trust*?

A *Roth IRA trust* is a trust specifically designed to be the beneficiary of a Roth IRA. Typically, a Roth IRA trust contains language consistent with the distribution rules for a Roth IRA, including the required minimum distribution rules under Code Section 401(a)(9).

Q 7:2   What requirements must a trust meet to be a designated beneficiary of a Roth IRA?

To be considered a *designated beneficiary* of a Roth IRA a trust must be a qualified trust. A *qualified trust* is a trust that meets each of the following requirements:

1. The trust is a valid trust under state law or would be but for the fact that there is no corpus;
2. The trust is irrevocable or will, by its terms, become irrevocable on the death of the grantor;
3. The beneficiaries of the trust who are beneficiaries with respect to the trust's interest in the grantor's benefit are identifiable from the trust instrument; and
4. The proper documentation has been provided to the plan administrator (see Q 7:5).

[Treas. Reg. § 1.401(a)(9)-4, Q&As 5, 6]

If a trust meets the requirements for being qualified, distributions may be made over the oldest trust beneficiary's life expectancy. [Treas. Reg. § 1.401(a)(9)-5, Q&A 7] If an entity other than an individual (e.g., an estate or a trust other than one meeting the above requirements) is designated as beneficiary under the plan, the deceased will be treated as having no designated beneficiary, even if there are individuals as ultimate beneficiaries (e.g., estate beneficiaries).

Further, in the case of a beneficiary who is not a designated beneficiary and is not a trust meeting the above requirements, special rules apply; for example, the exception to the five-year rule for certain amounts payable over the life of the beneficiary or beneficiaries does not apply (see Q 5:15). [I.R.C. § 401(a)(9)(B)(iii)]

Q 7:3   What are the distribution requirements when a Roth IRA is payable to a trust that does not qualify as a designated beneficiary?

When a Roth IRA is payable to a trust that does not meet the requirements discussed in Q 7:2, the five-year rule applies, and the Roth IRA must be completely distributed no later than December 31 of the calendar year that contains the fifth anniversary of the date of the Roth IRA owner's death (see Qs 5:11, 5:12). [Treas. Reg. § 1.401(a)(9)-3, Q&A 4(a)(2)]

Q 7:4   Who may serve as trustee of a Roth IRA trust?

There are no unique characteristics of a Roth IRA that require that the trustee selection process be altered beyond that of the standard estate planning and tax considerations. Therefore, a qualified individual or corporate trust may serve as the trustee of a Roth IRA trust.

Q 7:5   **Do the provisions requiring that the IRA trustee (or custodian) be provided with a copy of the trust document for a beneficiary trust apply to the Roth IRA?**

Yes. Unless specifically stated otherwise in Section 408A of the Internal Revenue Code (Code), all rules applicable to traditional IRAs apply to Roth IRAs. [I.R.C. § 408A(a)] Therefore, the documentation rules that govern traditional IRAs are applicable to Roth IRAs. Inasmuch as the 2002 regulations require only that documentation be furnished "during any period during which required minimum distributions are determined by treating the beneficiaries of the trust as designated beneficiaries of the employee" [Treas. Reg. § 1.401(a)(9)-4, Q&A 5(b)], documentation is required only after the death of the Roth IRA owner.

By October 31 of the year following the year of the Roth IRA owner's death, the trustee of the Roth IRA trust must provide to the IRA custodian (sometimes called the IRA trustee or issuer) either

1. A final list of all beneficiaries of the trust (including contingent and remainder beneficiaries, with a description of the conditions of their entitlement) as of September 30 of the year following the calendar year of the owner's death, and certify that, to the best of the trustee's knowledge, the list is correct and complete and that the requirements for a trust (see Q 7:2) are satisfied, and agree to provide a copy of the trust instrument to the IRA trustee (or custodian) upon demand; or

2. A copy of the actual trust document for the trust that is named as a beneficiary of the IRA as of the owner's date of death. [Treas. Reg. § 1.401(a)(9)-4, Q&A 6(b)]

A plan will not fail to satisfy Code Section 401(a)(9) merely because the actual terms of the trust instrument are inconsistent with the information previously provided to the IRA trustee, provided the trustee "reasonably relied" on the information and follows the actual trust agreement in the year following the year in which the discrepancy is discovered. [Treas. Reg. § 1.401(a)(9)-4, Q&A 6(c)]

Q 7:6   **May a revocable trust be named as the beneficiary of a Roth IRA?**

Yes. A revocable trust may be named as the beneficiary of a Roth IRA trust. Of course, the four requirements for a qualified trust must be met (see Q 7:2), including the requirement that the trust become irrevocable upon the death of the grantor. [Treas. Reg. § 1.401(a)(9)-4, Q&A 5(b)(2)]

Practice Pointer. Some trusts become irrevocable only upon the death of the surviving spouse. Such a trust would need to become irrevocable upon the death of the Roth IRA owner to satisfy the irrevocable requirement of Treasury Regulations Section 1.401(a)(9)-4, Q&A 5.

Q 7:7 **What are the benefits of naming a Roth IRA trust as the beneficiary of a Roth IRA and naming a child as the beneficiary of the trust rather than naming the child as the beneficiary of the Roth IRA outright?**

There are at least five advantages to naming a Roth IRA trust as the beneficiary of a Roth IRA and naming a child as the beneficiary of the Roth IRA trust rather than naming the child directly as the beneficiary of the Roth IRA:

1. *Discipline.* In the absence of a Roth IRA trust, the child may accelerate IRA distributions and thereby negate the benefit of deferral.

2. *Management/advice.* A financially unsophisticated child may not obtain proper investment counsel regarding the management of an inherited IRA.

3. *Creditor/divorce protection.* Under the Bankruptcy Abuse Prevention and Consumer Protection Act of 2005 (BAPCPA), an inherited Roth IRA may be subject to the claims of creditors. In some states, such an account may also be subject to the claims of the Roth IRA holder's spouse.

4. *Generation skipping.* Direct payment to the child will generally result in 100 percent of the remaining value being included in the estate of the child; a Roth IRA trust may preserve more value for future generations (see Q 7:26).

5. *Disabled beneficiaries.* In the event that a beneficiary becomes disabled or incapacitated and cannot manage his or her affairs, the trustee of a trust can continue to manage the assets of the trust.

The first advantage to naming a Roth IRA trust as the beneficiary of a Roth IRA is that a trustee can impose discipline (restraint) regarding the withdrawal of funds from the IRA. Naming a child as the direct beneficiary of a Roth IRA gives the child the unlimited ability to withdraw funds from the IRA immediately. If the child does so, one of the main benefits of a Roth IRA—the ability to continue the tax-free accumulation of growth and income—is lost.

Example. Ebenezer owns a Roth IRA that he plans to leave to Timothy, who is a child. He consults with Robert, an expert on Roth IRAs, to determine whether he should name Timothy directly or establish a Roth IRA trust with Timothy as the beneficiary of the trust. Robert presents Ebenezer with the following table, which shows that an immediate withdrawal of a $500,000 Roth IRA will ultimately cost Timothy $1 million in only 20 years. The funds that are withdrawn immediately will be in a taxable environment, and the income and gains may be subject to income tax. On the other hand, the funds left in the Roth IRA will continue to accumulate tax-free.

This chart assumes a 10 percent growth rate and a 30 percent tax rate on invested distributions.

	Roth IRA—Immediate Withdrawal			Roth IRA—Distributions over Life Expectancy		
Year	Beginning Roth IRA Balance	Distribution	Ending Roth IRA and Outside Balance	Beginning Roth IRA Balance	Required Minimum Distribution	Ending Roth IRA and Outside Balance
1	**$500,000**	($500,000)	$ 535,000	**$ 500,000**	($11,468)	$ 549,656
2	$ 0	$ 0	$ 572,450	**$ 537,385**	($12,615)	$ 603,875
3	$ 0	$ 0	$ 612,522	**$ 577,248**	($13,876)	$ 663,047
4	$ 0	$ 0	$ 655,398	**$ 619,709**	($15,264)	$ 727,594
5	$ 0	$ 0	$ 701,276	**$ 664,889**	($16,790)	$ 797,969
6	$ 0	$ 0	$ 750,365	**$ 712,909**	($18,469)	$ 874,660
7	$ 0	$ 0	$ 802,891	**$ 763,884**	($20,316)	$ 958,193
8	$ 0	$ 0	$ 859,093	**$ 817,925**	($22,348)	$1,049,134
9	$ 0	$ 0	$ 919,230	**$ 875,135**	($24,582)	$1,148,090
10	$ 0	$ 0	$ 983,576	**$ 935,608**	($27,041)	$1,255,713
11	$ 0	$ 0	$1,052,426	**$ 999,424**	($29,745)	$1,372,703
12	$ 0	$ 0	$1,126,096	**$1,066,647**	($32,719)	$1,499,810
13	$ 0	$ 0	$1,204,923	**$1,137,320**	($35,991)	$1,637,837
14	$ 0	$ 0	$1,289,267	**$1,211,462**	($39,590)	$1,787,642
15	$ 0	$ 0	$1,379,516	**$1,289,059**	($43,549)	$1,950,142
16	$ 0	$ 0	$1,476,082	**$1,370,061**	($47,904)	$2,126,316
17	$ 0	$ 0	$1,579,408	**$1,454,372**	($52,695)	$2,317,209
18	$ 0	$ 0	$1,689,966	**$1,541,845**	($57,964)	$2,523,930
19	$ 0	$ 0	$1,808,264	**$1,632,269**	($63,761)	$2,747,660
20	$ 0	$ 0	$1,934,842	**$1,725,360**	($70,137)	$2,989,653

The second advantage to naming a Roth IRA trust as the beneficiary of a Roth IRA is that the child beneficiary may not be financially wise. In naming a Roth IRA trust as the beneficiary, the trustee designated by the Roth IRA owner, not the child, will be responsible for making investment choices. That should result in greater wealth for the beneficiary.

The third advantage to naming a Roth IRA trust as the beneficiary of a Roth IRA is that a properly drafted trust may provide significant protection from creditors. If the child is the direct beneficiary, the Roth IRA may be subject to the claims of the child's creditors. While BAPCPA provides protection to Roth IRAs, it is not yet clear if this protection will be afforded to inherited accounts. The Roth IRA trust device ensures that the child will have the benefit of the funds within the trust despite the claims of his or her creditors.

The full extent of creditor protection will depend on the state statutes that control the trust as well as use of appropriate language in the trust instrument invoking the protection of the statute. Statutes in Alaska, Delaware, Nevada, Rhode Island, South Dakota, Utah, Oklahoma, and Missouri attempt to increase the extent of creditor protection, especially for "self-settled trusts" in these states. More states can be expected to adopt these types of changes to protect trusts in their own jurisdiction and stem the flow of trust funds to states with more favorable legislation.

The fourth advantage to naming a Roth IRA trust as the beneficiary of a Roth IRA is that the trust can be designed as a generation-skipping trust. That is, if a child is named the direct beneficiary of a Roth IRA, the Roth IRA will be included in the child's estate at death; however, by using a Roth IRA trust one can avoid the imposition of the estate tax at the child's death, thereby passing greater wealth to the grandchildren. Combining a Roth IRA trust with the allocation of the IRA owner's generation-skipping transfer tax (GSTT) exemption can be a powerful tool in increasing the wealth available to future generations. (See Qs 7:26, 7:32, 7:33, 7:44.)

The fifth advantage to utilizing a Roth IRA trust is the protection afforded when a beneficiary becomes disabled. A trust can provide maximum care and financial support for a disabled beneficiary without jeopardizing the beneficiary's eligibility for government benefits.

Q 7:8   What is the effect of naming a charity as a vested remainder beneficiary of a Roth IRA trust?

Because the rules in Treasury Regulations Section 1.401(a)(9)-4, Q&A 4, determine the designated beneficiary "as of September 30 of the calendar year following the calendar year of the employee's death," it is no longer a problem for a charity to be one of the named beneficiaries. Paying the charity's share (and the share of any other nonqualifying beneficiary) before the beneficiary determination date will allow the other beneficiaries to take distributions over their life expectancies (see Q 5:25). Although it is now possible to use a Roth IRA to carry out charitable intents, this is the least tax favorable method for funding charitable bequests. Because of the tax-free nature of Roth IRA distributions, virtually any other asset is better suited for this purpose. (See also Q 7:9 regarding naming a charity as a contingent remainder beneficiary of a Roth IRA trust.)

Q 7:9   What is the effect of naming a charity as a contingent remainder beneficiary of a Roth IRA trust?

Since a charity is a beneficiary that is not a human being, the charity may disqualify the trust as a designated beneficiary unless two requirements are met: (1) the charity's right to receive a benefit from the trust must be contingent upon the death of the human beneficiary and (2) during the life of the human beneficiary, that beneficiary must receive the full amount of the required minimum distributions and all amounts withdrawn from the Roth IRA. [*See* Treas. Reg. § 1.401(a)(9)-5, Q&A 7] The second requirement results in what is commonly referred to as a "conduit" trust; that is, any and all amounts distributed from the Roth IRA must be distributed out of the trust. If both requirements are met, naming the charity as a contingent beneficiary will have no effect until payment is made to the charity at the death of the human beneficiary. Note that naming a charity as contingent beneficiary will not produce an estate tax charitable deduction unless the trust meets the requirements of a qualified split interest trust under Code Section 664.

Practice Pointer. If it is the account owner's desire to name a charity as the remainder beneficiary of a trust, and the owner wants the trust to have the right to accumulate Roth IRA distributions within the trust, the owner should consider naming a qualified charitable remainder trust as the beneficiary of the Roth IRA. [I.R.C. § 664] This will not only provide a charitable estate tax deduction but also allow distributions from the trust to be made for the life of the beneficiary or beneficiaries pursuant to the annuity or unitrust rules of Code Section 664. Naming the charity as remainder beneficiary of a trust that is not a "conduit" trust (i.e., one that distributes all Roth IRA distributions out of the trust) will disqualify the trust and result in application of the five-year rule for distributions.

Q 7:10 May an irrevocable life insurance trust be the beneficiary of a Roth IRA?

For some, naming an irrevocable life insurance trust (ILIT) as the designated beneficiary of a Roth IRA will be a good choice. If the beneficiaries of the ILIT are the persons that the IRA owner would like to receive the benefits of the IRA, using an ILIT may allow the owner to avoid the need to create an additional separate trust.

If an ILIT is designated as the beneficiary of an IRA, it must meet the four requirements of Treasury Regulations Section 1.401(a)(9)-4, Q&A 5(b). These are set forth at Q 7:2.

The payment of expenses and taxes from a trust or the share of the taxable estate allocated to a trust could, in some circumstances, disqualify the trust as a designated beneficiary because, in theory, the IRS could argue that the estate, a non-individual, is a beneficiary of the trust. Because of this, there is still some risk in naming a trust as designated beneficiary if the trust or the trust's share of the taxable estate is required to pay these items. Since an ILIT is outside of the taxable estate, the legal obligation to pay such items would not be imposed on it. Although this may allow the trust to qualify as a designated beneficiary, there may still be a question of how the taxes and expenses will be paid if there are not enough liquid assets outside of the ILIT.

Practice Pointer. There are several planning approaches that can effectively prevent such a negative result:

Loan. The frequently used method of allowing an ILIT to loan money to an estate or trust that has primary responsibility for payment of taxes should be feasible, even if some of the assets of the trust are Roth IRAs. A loan will allow the ILIT trustee to decide whether to use insurance proceeds to pay estate taxes or to take distributions from the IRAs or to do both. Of course, generally, early distributions from an IRA should be avoided to maximize the benefit of tax deferral.

Payment by Trust. Under the 2002 Treasury regulations, the beneficiaries of a Roth IRA trust are not determined until September 30 of the year after the year of death. That span of time allows nonqualified beneficiaries to be eliminated, by payout or otherwise, before the deadline arrives. Such leeway would seem to allow debts and taxes to be paid by a Roth IRA trust without disqualifying the trust as a beneficiary, provided that the payments are made before the deadline for determining beneficiaries. Letter Rulings 200432027–200432029 (Aug. 6, 2004) support this theory. Including language in the trust agreement to the effect that no tax payments may be made after September 30 of the year after the year of the decedent's death should prevent disqualification. This strategy has the disadvantage of paying taxes with assets that might otherwise have been invested without income tax on their gains or growth. Requiring payment made from an ILIT (which is outside of the taxable estate) also jeopardizes the tax-exempt status of some of the assets. Also, if state law protects the Roth IRA from creditors, the trust would not be disqualified as a designated beneficiary. [*See* Ltr. Rul. 200440031 (Oct. 1, 2004)]

Merger. A Roth IRA owner could create a separate trust from the ILIT to receive the Roth IRA proceeds. That trust and the ILIT would have the same beneficiaries and contain identical distribution provisions. Both trusts would also contain clauses facilitating their merger in the future. At the owner's death, the trustee of the ILIT would lend funds to the Roth IRA trust for the payment of taxes. Later, after an estate tax closing letter is obtained, the trustees would merge the trusts in a nontaxable transaction. If the trusts are properly designed, this strategy would allow the Roth IRA to be retained intact, with distributions over the life expectancy of the oldest beneficiary that would not jeopardize the tax-exempt status of the ILIT.

In Letter Ruling 200147039, the taxpayers had established an irrevocable trust that was the beneficiary of a second-to-die life insurance policy. After the death of the second of the taxpayers, the trust paid the proceeds to the taxpayer's children. The trust language also allowed the trustee to pay any death taxes arising from the death of the taxpayers, stating that the trustee "shall be under no compulsion to do so." The IRS ruled that, since the proceeds of the life insurance policy were subject "only to discretionary use by the trustee to pay estate taxes, or other expenses of the estate," the proceeds would not be included in the taxable estate under the provisions of Code Section 2042.

Although this technique worked well for the taxpayers who received the letter ruling, it must be remembered that every letter ruling ends with this warning: "This ruling is directed only to the taxpayer who requested it. Section 6110(k)(3) of the Code provides that it may not be used or cited as precedent." Language allowing a trust to pay taxes must be very carefully structured to avoid the possibility that it will cause inclusion of the assets in the taxable estate.

Drafting Considerations

Q 7:11   What special provisions should be considered when drafting a Roth IRA trust?

In addition to the usual powers given to a trustee, the drafter of a Roth IRA trust should consider including provisions that grant the following powers:

- Power to pay out nonqualified beneficiaries before September 30 of the year following the year of the grantor's death if such payment allows the trust to better accomplish the goals and objectives of the grantor
- Power to change investment advisers or custodians
- Power to amend the trust to bring it into conformity with the provisions of the Code and applicable Treasury regulations as amended so that the intent of the grantor may be carried out
- Power to make elections regarding distributions
- Power to establish subaccounts (see Qs 5:41, 5:42). (A subaccount may facilitate distribution of the account in kind or the ability to treat individual beneficiaries uniquely.)
- Power to distribute accounts or subaccounts in kind as inherited accounts to the extent permitted by law
- Power to withdraw account assets in amounts greater than the required minimum distributions
- Power to pay penalty tax on early withdrawals if, in the trustee's discretion, withdrawal is necessary or in the best interest of the trust or its beneficiaries
- Power to convert qualified plans, 403(b) plans, and governmental 457(b) plans to Roth IRAs to the extent permitted by law.
- Power to convert traditional IRAs to Roth IRAs to the extent permitted by law
- Instruction to trustee to satisfy charitable bequests, to the extent possible, from property that constitutes income in respect of the decedent. [See CCM 200644020 (Dec. 15, 2005).]
- Power to employ accountants or attorneys who have expertise in IRA planning to advise the trustee

(See appendix C for model language for a Roth IRA trust.)

Roth IRA Trust Distribution Rules

Q 7:12   Over what period of time must distributions from a Roth IRA to a qualified trust be paid?

Distributions from a Roth IRA to a qualified trust must be paid over the life expectancy of the oldest beneficiary of that trust [Treas. Reg. § 1.401(a)(9)-5, Q&A 5(c)(1)], determined as follows:

1. *Nonspouse beneficiary trust.* The applicable distribution period is measured by the oldest trust beneficiary's remaining life expectancy determined using the beneficiary's age as of the beneficiary's birthday in the calendar year immediately following the calendar year of the Roth IRA owner's death using the Single Life Table of Treasury Regulations Section 1.401(a)(9)-9. In subsequent years, the distribution factor is reduced by one for each calendar year that has elapsed since the year immediately following the calendar year of the owner's death.

Example 1. Hubert dies. His trust is the beneficiary of his Roth IRA. Lola is the oldest beneficiary of the trust. The following year, Lola, has a 48.5-year life expectancy. Distributions will be made as shown in the following table.

Year	Fund Value	Life Expectancy	Annual Distribution
1	$1,000,000	48.5	$ 20,619
2	$1,077,320	47.5	$ 22,680
3	$1,160,103	46.5	$ 24,948
4	$1,248,670	45.5	$ 27,443
5	$1,343,349	44.5	$ 30,188
6	$1,444,478	43.5	$ 33,206
7	$1,552,399	42.5	$ 36,527
8	$1,667,459	41.5	$ 40,180
9	$1,790,007	40.5	$ 44,198
10	$1,920,390	39.5	$ 48,617
11	$2,058,950	38.5	$ 53,479
12	$2,206,018	37.5	$ 58,827
13	$2,361,910	36.5	$ 64,710
14	$2,526,920	35.5	$ 71,181
15	$2,701,313	34.5	$ 78,299
16	$2,885,316	33.5	$ 86,129
17	$3,079,106	32.5	$ 94,742
18	$3,282,800	31.5	$104,216

Year	Fund Value	Life Expectancy	Annual Distribution
19	$3,496,443	30.5	$114,637
20	$3,719,986	29.5	$126,101

This table assumes a 10 percent growth rate and that all distributions are made on the first day of each year.

2. *Spouse beneficiary-accumulation trust.* If the spouse of the deceased Roth IRA owner is the oldest trust beneficiary and no rollover occurs, the distribution period is measured by the spouse's remaining life expectancy determined using the spouse's age as of the spouse's birthday in the calendar year immediately following the calendar year of the Roth IRA owner's death using the Single Life Table of Treasury Regulations Section 1.401(a)(9)-9. In subsequent years, the distribution factor is reduced by one for each calendar year that has elapsed since the year immediately following the calendar year of the owner's death.

Example 2. Danny dies in 2009. He named an accumulation trust for the benefit of his wife, Sandy, as beneficiary of his Roth IRA. Sandy turns age 62 in 2010. The trustee must begin taking distributions by December 31, 2010. The life expectancy factor for 2010 is 23.5. For 2011, the factor is 22.5, for 2012 it is 21.5, and so on.

3. *Spouse beneficiary-conduit trust.* If the spouse of the deceased Roth IRA owner is the sole trust beneficiary, no rollover occurs, *and* the trust mandates that any and all distributions from the Roth IRA will be distributed outright to the spouse, the distribution period is measured as if the spouse inherited the IRA outright. [*See* Treas. Reg. § 1.401(a)(9)-5, Q&A 7(c)(3), Ex. 2] In other words, required minimum distributions (RMDs) can be delayed until the deceased owner would have reached age 70½. In such year, the RMD is calculated based upon the spouse's life expectancy by referencing his or her attained age for the year of distribution based on the Single Life Table. For each succeeding year, the trustee references the surviving spouse's age under the Single Life Table for his or her attained age for that year.

Example 3. Danny dies in 2008. Danny would have turned age 70½ in 2013. He named a conduit trust for the benefit of his wife, Sandy, as beneficiary of his Roth IRA. The trustee does not have to begin taking distributions until 2013—the year Danny would have turned age 70½. Sandy turns age 62 in 2013. The life expectancy factor for 2013 is 23.5. Under the Single Life Table, for 2014, the factor is 22.7, for 2015 it is 21.8, and so on.

Practice Pointer. One unintended result can occur when utilizing a conduit trust for the benefit of the spouse. Because the spouse will be treated as the sole beneficiary for purposes of determining RMDs, if the spouse dies before the Roth IRA owner would have turned 70½, the five-year rule will apply upon the death of the surviving spouse. [Ltr. Rul. 200644022 (Nov. 3, 2006)]

This results from the rule that if the surviving spouse dies before the Roth IRA owner would have turned 70½, the five-year rule and the life expectancy rule are to be applied as if the surviving spouse performed a rollover. [Treas. Reg. § 1.401(a)(9)-3, Q&A 5] Accordingly, because the trust, not the surviving spouse, mandates the beneficiary upon the death of the surviving spouse, the surviving spouse is deemed to have not named a beneficiary.

Note. The Worker, Retiree, and Employer Recovery Act of 2008 (WRERA) suspended the requirement to take RMDs in 2009. [I.R.C. § 401(a)(9)(H)] (See Q 5:1.)

Q 7:13   How are distributions calculated if the trust beneficiary whose life expectancy is being used to calculate the distributions dies after the beneficiary determination date but before the entire account has been distributed?

If the trust beneficiary whose life is being used to calculate distributions dies before the Roth IRA has been distributed, that beneficiary's remaining life expectancy is used to calculate the distributions. [Treas. Reg. § 1.401(a)(9)-5, Q&A 7(c)(2)] However, see the Practice Pointer in Q 7:12 for an exception to this rule when a conduit trust for the benefit of a spouse is used.

Example. Terry dies in 2006, after naming a trust as beneficiary of his Roth IRA. Jesse, age 18 (in 2007), is the oldest beneficiary of the trust and therefore, his life expectancy of 65.0 is used to determine the RMD from the inherited Roth IRA in 2007. For subsequent years, this factor is reduced by one. Jesse dies in 2010, well before the Roth IRA is fully distributed. Jesse's life expectancy will continue to be the measuring life for determining RMDs. Therefore, for 2010, a factor of 61.0 (65.0 – 4 (one for each year since 2007)) is used, and so on for each year thereafter.

Q 7:14   When must distributions from a Roth IRA begin?

Distributions from a Roth IRA must generally begin by December 31 of the year following the year of the Roth IRA owner's death.

Example 1. Michael died in 2009. Generally, RMDs must begin to be taken from the Roth IRA by December 31, 2010.

There are, however, two exceptions.

1. If a Roth IRA owner dies before reaching age 70½ and the sole beneficiary, for purposes of determining distributions, is the spouse, distributions will not need to start until the end of the calendar year in which the deceased owner would have attained age 70½. (If the surviving spouse performs a spousal rollover, the Roth IRA will be treated as being owned by the surviving spouse; therefore, distributions need not start until after the surviving spouse's death.) [Treas. Reg. § 1.408A-6, Q&A 14]

Example 2. Maria was born on October 5, 1947, and died in 2009, at age 62, leaving her Roth IRA to her husband, Gary. Gary can wait until 2018 (the year Maria would have turned 70½ had she lived) to begin taking RMDs.

2. If a Roth IRA owner dies and no qualified beneficiary has been determined by beneficiary designation, the plan or account document, or otherwise by September 30 of the year after the year of the owner's death, the five-year rule of Code Section 401(a)(9)(B)(ii) applies. Under that rule, distributions are not required to start at a specific time; however, the entire account must be distributed by December 31 of the year in which the fifth anniversary of the owner's death occurs.

Example 3. Becky dies in 2010 without naming a beneficiary. Under the default provision of the Roth plan, the account is payable to Becky's estate. The entire Roth IRA must be distributed by December 31, 2015.

Note. However, because of the suspension of 2009 RMDs (see Q: 5:1), if a beneficiary must take RMDs under the five-year rule (see Q: 5:1) he or she can now waive the distribution for 2009, effectively taking distributions over a six-year rather than a five-year period. [I.R.S. Notice 2009-9, 2009-5 I.R.B. 419]

Example 4. Gary dies on January 15, 2008, after naming his estate as beneficiary of his Roth IRA. The beneficiary of his Roth IRA must take distributions out over the five-year rule. Because 2009 is one of the years in the five-year rule, under Notice 2009-9, the beneficiary does not have to take any distributions until December 31, 2014, at which time the entire Roth IRA must be liquidated.

Q 7:15 When must distributions from a Roth IRA begin when the Roth IRA is payable to a qualified trust?

When a qualified trust is the named beneficiary of a Roth IRA, distributions from a Roth IRA must generally begin by December 31 of the year following the year of the Roth IRA owner's death. However, if the surviving spouse is the sole beneficiary of the trust and the trust is a conduit trust, distributions to do not have to begin until the Roth IRA owner would have been age 70½ (see Q 7:12).

Example. Maria was born on October 5, 1947, and died in 2009, at age 62, leaving her Roth IRA to a conduit trust in which her husband, Gary, is the sole beneficiary. The trustee of the trust can wait until 2018 (the year Maria would have turned 70½ had she lived) to begin taking RMDs.

Q 7:16 If the beneficiary of a Roth IRA dies after the account owner but before September 30 (the beneficiary determination date) of the year following the account owner's death, whose life is the measuring life?

The final regulations make it clear that if a beneficiary dies after the account owner but before the beneficiary determination date (September 30 of the year following the year of death) without disclaiming, that beneficiary's actuarial life expectancy will continue to be used for the purpose of calculating required distributions (see the Example in Q 5:26). [Treas. Reg. § 1.401(a)(9)-4, Q&A 4(c)]

> **Example.** Sue dies in 2009 after naming her son, Fred, as beneficiary of her Roth IRA. Fred dies before September 30, 2010. Fred did not disclaim the Roth IRA. The Roth IRA is now payable to Fred's estate. Fred's life expectancy will still be used to determine RMD from the Roth IRA.

Q 7:17   If more than one person or trust is named as the beneficiary of a Roth IRA, how soon must separate shares or accounts be established to use each individual beneficiary's life as the measuring life for purposes of computing required distributions?

The Regulations allow until September 30 of the year following the year of the Roth IRA owner's death to determine beneficiaries, but allow until December 31 of that year to create separate shares [Treas. Reg. § 1.401(a)(9)-8, Q&A 2(a)(2)] and start distributions. Therefore, for the beneficiaries to utilize their individual life expectancies, separate shares or accounts must be created by December 31 of the year following the year of the account owner's death. Even if separate shares or accounts are not created until December 31 of the year following the year of the Roth IRA owner's death, the beneficiaries can utilize their individual life expectancies for that year. [*See* Treas. Reg. § 1.401(a)(9)-8, Q&A 2(a)] (See Q 5:42.) (See Q 7:18 regarding separate share treatment in relation to a single trust.)

> **Example.** Krista dies in 2009, after naming her children as beneficiaries of her Roth IRA. Krista's children have until December 31, 2010, to create separate shares if they wish to utilize each of their individual life expectancies.

Q 7:18   When a person wishes to create separate shares for each beneficiary of a single trust, what are the requirements that must be met so that each trust share may calculate required distributions over the life expectancy of that share's beneficiary?

Proposed Treasury Regulations Section 1.401(a)(9) that was issued in 2001 stated that "if the beneficiary of the trust named as beneficiary is another trust, the beneficiaries of the other trust will be treated as having been designated as beneficiaries . . . for purposes of determining the distribution period under Section 401(a)(9)(A)(ii) provided that all of the requirements of Proposed Treasury Regulations Section 1.401(a)(9)-4 Q&A 5(b) are satisfied (see Q 7:2).

This permitted a trust that was named as the beneficiary of an IRA to divide into subtrusts for the benefit of other individuals or groups of individuals, and, in some cases, still have the separate share rules apply to each subtrust. A number of letter rulings affirmed this position in situations where the account owner died before the required beginning date (RBD), including Letter Rulings

200234073 and 200234074 (rulings where the 1987 regulations applied). Other letter rulings held that the separate share rules did not apply if death occurred after the RBD. [*See, e.g.*, Ltr. Ruls. 200209058 and 200209059 (Dec. 4, 2001)]

When the final regulations were published, however, there was a significant change to Proposed Treasury Regulations Section 1.401(a)(9)-4, Q&A-5(c). The language that is quoted above was omitted. In its place is language that says that separate account rules are not available to beneficiaries of a trust with respect to the trust's interest in the employee's benefit.

On April 25, 2004, the IRS released three substantially identical rulings that disallowed separate share treatment in the context of a trust. Letter Rulings 200317041, 200317043, and 200317044 dealt with three different taxpayers who are beneficiaries of the same trust. The letter rulings tell us that the account owner died before his RBD. In addition, his beneficiary designation form provided that, at his death, the IRA was to be distributed to the trustee of a trust. The beneficiary designation form as well as the terms of the trust provided that the trust was to be divided into equal accounts for the three beneficiaries. The beneficiary designation form also stated that the trustee may establish separate IRAs in the name of the decedent for the benefit of the three beneficiaries.

The rulings concluded that the account could be divided into three accounts, one for each subtrust, but that distributions from each account must be paid over the life expectancy of the oldest of the three beneficiaries.

However, on March 29, 2005, the IRS released Letter Ruling 200537044, which added greater clarity to this situation. This ruling clarifies that if a beneficiary designation form names separate shares for each individual beneficiary of a trust, each trust beneficiary's life will be used for purposes of determining the measuring life under the required minimum distribution rules.

In Letter Ruling 200537044, the IRS allowed each individual beneficiary of each trust share to use his or her individual life expectancy to calculate required minimum distributions for his or her share of the IRA. Upon the death of the trustor, the trust created separate subtrusts for each beneficiary. Each separate trust that was created under the master trust instrument was named beneficiary of the IRA. The beneficiary designation form named the specific subtrusts as beneficiaries of the IRA. After the IRA owner's death, the IRA was divided into separate IRAs for each of the named beneficiaries.

This fact pattern in Letter Ruling 200537044 can be differentiated from Letter Rulings 200317041, 200317043, and 200317044 in that the IRA owner in Letter Ruling 200537044 expressly named each separate trust as a beneficiary of his IRA, with differing percentile interests. In Letter Rulings 200317041, 200317043, and 200317044, it appears that the taxpayer named the master trust as beneficiary of the IRA with direction that it then be divided into equal shares and payable to the separate subtrusts. The beneficiary designation form in Letter Ruling 200537044 named the separate subtrusts *directly*. The IRA does not pass through the master trust and then get divided. Instead, the IRA is divided at the beneficiary designation level and payable to the separate trusts that were created upon the trustor's death.

Letter Ruling 200537044 provides much needed guidance on how beneficiary designation forms need to be structured to obtain separate share treatment. Instead of simply naming the master trust as beneficiary of the IRA with directions to separate the trust and the IRA into separate shares, each separate subtrust should be specifically named as partial beneficiary in the beneficiary designation form. This should allow each trust beneficiary to utilize his or her individual life expectancy as opposed to using the life expectancy of the oldest primary beneficiary to calculate required minimum distributions.

Example. John Smith creates a trust for the benefit of his four children. Upon John's death, the trust is divided into separate shares for each of his children. John's IRA beneficiary designation form was worded as follows:

- 25% to the Child 1 Trust, as a separate share under the John Smith Trust dtd. 1-1-06
- 25% to the Child 2 Trust, as a separate share under the John Smith Trust dtd. 1-1-06
- 25% to the Child 3 Trust, as a separate share under the John Smith Trust dtd. 1-1-06
- 25% to the Child 4 Trust, as a separate share under the John Smith Trust dtd. 1-1-06

Because the separate subtrusts were named directly as beneficiaries of a separate IRA share, each child should be able to use his or her individual life expectancy to calculate required minimum distributions. Had John's beneficiary designation form instead stated "100% of the IRA to the John Smith Trust dtd. 1-1-06," separate share treatment would not be available.

Q 7:19   Does the age of the Roth IRA owner at the time of his or her death affect distributions to a trust?

No. A Roth IRA owner is always deemed to have died before his RBD (see Q 5:2). If the trust is a qualified trust (see Qs 7:2, 7:5), the trustee may look through the trust and make distributions over the oldest beneficiary's life expectancy. If the trust is not a qualified trust, distributions will be paid under the five-year rule. [Treas. Reg. § 1.401(a)(9)-3 Q&A 3] (See Q 5:11.)

Q 7:20   Does the 10 percent premature distribution penalty apply to distributions from an inherited Roth IRA to a trust?

No. The 10 percent premature distribution penalty never applies to distributions from an inherited Roth IRA—unless a spouse rolls over the inherited Roth IRA into his or her own Roth IRA. [I.R.C. §§ 72(t)(2)(A)(ii), 408A(d)(3)(F)]

Example 1. Tori inherits an IRA from her father. At the age of 21, Tori takes a distribution from her inherited IRA to go on a vacation. Because Tori inherited the IRA, the 10 percent premature distribution penalty does not apply.

Example 2. Josie inherits an IRA from her husband. Josie decides to roll the IRA into an IRA in her own name (a spousal rollover). At age 52, Josie takes a distribution from her IRA to pay for a down payment on a new car. Because Josie rolled the IRA into her own name and it therefore is no longer an inherited IRA, the 10 percent premature distribution penalty applies.

Practice Pointer. If the surviving spouse is younger than age $59\frac{1}{2}$, it may be wise to wait until attaining such age to perform a rollover (see Q 5:35). If the spouse performs a rollover before age $59\frac{1}{2}$ and takes a distribution, he or she may be subject to the 10 percent early distribution penalty (see Q 4:21). In the alternative, the surviving spouse can treat the Roth IRA as inherited, take penalty-free distributions, and then perform a rollover upon reaching age $59\frac{1}{2}$.

Q 7:21 Does the required beginning date affect Roth IRA distributions to a Roth IRA trust?

No. Because distributions are not required until the Roth IRA owner's death, the required beginning date has no effect on distributions from a Roth IRA to a Roth IRA trust. [*See* I.R.C. § 408A] As long as the trust is a qualified trust, distributions after the owner's death can be made over the oldest trust beneficiary's life expectancy (see Qs 5:41, 7:12). The required beginning date matters for the Roth IRA only when a spouse is the named beneficiary and the owner dies before attaining the age of $70\frac{1}{2}$ (see Qs 7:12, 7:14).

Q 7:22 Are penalties imposed if a trust fails to take the proper distributions from a Roth IRA?

Yes. If a Roth IRA trust fails to take the proper distributions from a Roth IRA, the Code imposes a 50 percent penalty on the required minimum distribution less the amount actually distributed for the tax year. [I.R.C. § 4974(a)] (See Q 5:53 for how this penalty may be waived.)

Example. Annika, as trustee of the John Smith Trust, is the beneficiary of a Roth IRA that the trust inherited several years ago. Because the trust beneficiaries do not currently need any income from the trust, she decided not to take the RMD from the inherited Roth IRA, which is $10,000. The Trust, as owner of the Roth IRA, will be assessed a penalty of $5,000 (($10,000 required distribution – $0 actual distribution for current year) × 50%).

Q 7:23 May a Roth IRA trust be used to "freeze" the distribution period of a Roth IRA?

Yes. If the Roth IRA contract and the beneficiary forms are coordinated with the trust document, it should be possible to take distributions over the life expectancy of the oldest trust beneficiary using a "frozen" method. That is, once distributions have started based on the life expectancy of the oldest beneficiary,

distributions to the trust may continue on that schedule even if that beneficiary dies.

> **Example.** Matt died, leaving his Roth IRA payable to a trust for the benefit
> of his three children, Peter, Steven, and Michelle. The trust is designed to
> continue for the benefit of the three children and their issue until the
> youngest of the children attains the age of 50. Because Peter is the oldest of
> the three, his life expectancy will be used to calculate minimum distributions.
> If Peter dies before the trust is terminated, the trustee may continue to take
> minimum distributions from the Roth IRA under the same schedule that
> would be in effect if Peter were still alive. Therefore, the advantage of tax-free
> growth within the Roth IRA will continue despite the early death of the
> beneficiary whose life was the measuring life.

In-Kind Distributions upon Termination of Trust

Q 7:24   When a Roth IRA trust terminates, may a Roth IRA be distributed from the trust in an in-kind distribution?

Whether a Roth IRA may be distributed in kind upon the termination of a
Roth IRA trust generally depends on the trust document. If the document gives
the trustee of the trust the power to distribute assets in kind, such a distribution
should be possible. [Ltr. Rul. 200449041 (Dec. 3, 2004)]

To make it more likely that the IRS will allow a Roth IRA to be distributed in
kind, the following language could be included in the trust document:

> *The Trustee shall have the power to deal with and make elections with respect
> to IRAs, Roth IRAs, 403(b) plans, and qualified plans, including the power to
> create subaccounts within such accounts and to distribute accounts or subac-
> counts as inherited accounts when appropriate. The Trustee may make distribu-
> tions or divisions of the Trust property in cash or in kind or both. In the event that
> the law is not well settled in this area at the time that the Trustee may choose to
> make any such elections or distributions, the Trustee is encouraged to seek
> competent tax advice and to obtain a private letter ruling if that step is
> recommended by the Trustee's advisers.*

> **Practice Pointer.** If the Roth IRA is distributed in kind from the Roth IRA
> trust, the Roth IRA should remain titled in the name of the deceased IRA
> owner. (See Q 6:42 for an example of an acceptable title.) It is also prudent to
> ensure that the Roth IRA custodian will not treat such in-kind distribution as
> a taxable distribution.

Q 7:25   What is the advantage of distributing a Roth IRA in kind at the termination of a trust rather than distributing the assets of the Roth IRA?

If the Roth IRA can be distributed in kind as a Roth IRA, the growth and
income within the Roth IRA will continue to be free of tax. If the Roth IRA is first

liquidated, any income produced by the assets thereafter will be subject to tax. It will almost always be best for the beneficiaries to receive the assets inside of the Roth IRA and continue to take only the required minimum distributions.

> **Example.** Trent, age 81, dies, leaving his $250,000 Roth IRA to a Roth IRA trust of which his three grandchildren are the beneficiaries. The trust dictates that when the youngest of the three grandchildren reaches age 35 the trust will terminate and pass outright to the grandchildren. Absent a provision that allows the trustee to distribute the IRA in kind, the IRA may have to be liquidated. Thereafter, interest dividends and realized capital gains would be subject to tax.

Generation-Skipping Trust

Q 7:26   What is a *generation-skipping trust*?

A *generation-skipping trust* is a trust that is designed to skip a generation of estate tax. That is, by creating a generation-skipping trust a taxpayer is able to avoid one or more generations of estate tax, ultimately passing greater wealth to his or her grandchildren.

In general, the GSTT is imposed on a transfer that either skips a generation within a family or is made to a nonfamily member who is more than $37\frac{1}{2}$ years younger than the person making the gift. [*See* I.R.C. § 2613] Each individual has (in 2009) $3.5 million of GSTT exemption available.

Q 7:27   May a Roth IRA trust be a generation-skipping trust?

Yes. A Roth IRA trust may be a generation-skipping trust. In fact, there are key advantages to using a generation-skipping trust. (See Qs 7:28, 7:29, 7:31.) The younger the beneficiary of the Roth IRA is, the longer the life expectancy period and thus, the longer that the assets can stay within the Roth resulting in more tax-free growth.

> **Example.** Grandfather names his 10-year-old granddaughter, Kathleen, as the beneficiary of his $500,000 Roth IRA. Required minimum distributions over Kathleen's life expectancy at an assumed 10 percent growth rate on the Roth IRA are shown in the table below. The table shows that Kathleen will have received more than $1.1 million in distributions from the $500,000 Roth IRA and the Roth IRA will have grown to over $4.7 million in a 30-year period. In addition, by the time the IRA is liquidated (not shown), Kathleen will have received over $64.7 million of tax-free distributions. (All numbers are rounded.)

Year	Beginning Roth IRA Balance	Life Expectancy	Annual Distribution
1	$ 500,000	72.8	$ 6,868
2	$ 542,445	71.8	$ 7,555
3	$ 588,379	70.8	$ 8,310
4	$ 638,076	69.8	$ 9,141
5	$ 691,827	68.8	$ 10,056
6	$ 749,949	67.8	$ 11,061
7	$ 812,777	66.8	$ 12,167
8	$ 880,670	65.8	$ 13,384
9	$ 954,015	64.8	$ 14,722
10	$1,033,222	63.8	$ 16,195
11	$1,118,730	62.8	$ 17,814
12	$1,211,007	61.8	$ 19,596
13	$1,310,553	60.8	$ 21,555
14	$1,417,897	59.8	$ 23,711
15	$1,533,605	58.8	$ 26,082
16	$1,658,276	57.8	$ 28,690
17	$1,792,544	56.8	$ 31,559
18	$1,937,084	55.8	$ 34,715
19	$2,092,606	54.8	$ 38,156
20	$2,259,862	53.8	$ 42,005
21	$2,439,643	52.8	$ 46,205
22	$2,632,781	51.8	$ 50,826
23	$2,840,151	50.8	$ 55,908
24	$3,062,667	49.8	$ 61,499
25	$3,301,284	48.8	$ 67,649
26	$3,556,998	47.8	$ 74,414
27	$3,830,842	46.8	$ 81,856
28	$4,123,886	45.8	$ 90,041
29	$4,437,229	44.8	$ 99,045
30	$4,772,002	43.8	$108,950

Q 7:28   What is the estate tax advantage of using a Roth IRA to fund a generation-skipping trust?

Naming a generation-skipping trust as the beneficiary of a Roth IRA prevents the imposition of estate tax at the child's death. In designing the generation-skipping trust, it is important to remember the generation-skipping tax exemption. That is, each individual is allowed a GSTT exemption equal to the federal estate tax exemption. For the year 2009, this amount is $3.5 million. This amount may be allocated by the individual or his or her executor. [I.R.C. § 2631] Table 7-1 shows the advantage of a generation-skipping trust and illustrates how the estate tax, in a single-generation trust, has a detrimental effect on future generations. As can be shown in Table 7-1, 45 percent of the child's estate is lost to estate tax upon the child's death. If, instead, the assets were placed in a generation-skipping trust and GSTT exemption was allocated to it by the parent, the assets would transfer tax-free to the grandchild at the child's death.

    Practice Pointer. In large estates it may be advisable to use a taxpayer's GSTT exemption to avoid one or more levels of estate tax.

Table 7-1. Single-Generation Trust Compared to Generation-Skipping Trust

	Single-Generation Trust	Generation-Skipping Trust
Children's taxable estate above unified credit	$1,000,000	$1,000,000
Less estate tax	−450,000	−0
Net to grandchildren	$ 550,000	$1,000,000

Q 7:29   What is the key income tax advantage of naming a generation-skipping trust as the beneficiary of a Roth IRA?

The key income tax advantage of naming a generation-skipping trust as the beneficiary of a Roth IRA is the ability to defer distributions from the Roth IRA for many years: the Roth IRA can be paid out over the oldest trust beneficiary's life expectancy (see Q 7:12), which would be 72.8 years in the case of a 10-year-old grandchild. That may be 20 to 30 years longer than would be the case if a child were named the beneficiary of the Roth IRA or if a child were the oldest beneficiary of the trust. Because qualified Roth IRA distributions are tax-free, part of the GSTT exemption is not lost to income tax, as would be the case with a traditional IRA.

Q 7:30   How can a taxpayer avoid overfunding a generation-skipping trust?

The preferred way to avoid overfunding a generation-skipping trust is to use a formula clause in the beneficiary designation. The formula clause should provide that the generation-skipping trust is to be funded with an amount equal to the deceased account owner's remaining GSTT exemption. Any remaining balance could be payable to other nonskip individuals or trusts. As with any formula funding clause, expressing the amount as a fraction of the available fund will allow the bequest to share in appreciation (or depreciation) after the date of death and before the date of funding (see Q 7:36).

Q 7:31   How can a husband and wife transfer $7 million to a generation-skipping trust and enjoy an exemption for the entire amount?

As noted above (see Q 7:28), each individual may transfer up to $3.5 million free of GSTT in 2009. It must be remembered, however, that for lifetime gifts, only $1 million may be transferred before a gift tax is imposed. Nonetheless, with proper planning a husband and wife should be able to transfer up to $7 million free of tax to generation-skipping trusts if that is the objective of their estate plan.

Example. John and Mary Jo want to maximize their transfer of funds to a generation-skipping trust. John has a $7 million Roth IRA. The beneficiary designation requires that upon John's death, an amount equal to his remaining GSTT exemption will be paid to a generation-skipping trust. The balance of the Roth IRA will be paid to Mary Jo. Upon John's death (if death occurs in 2009) up to $3.5 million will pass to the trust. After John dies, Mary Jo will roll over her share of the Roth IRA into a Roth IRA in her own name. Mary Jo will name the generation-skipping trust as the beneficiary of her Roth IRA to the extent of her remaining GSTT exemption. Upon Mary Jo's death, an additional amount will transfer to the trust, allowing total funding of $7 million, or more if the Roth IRA appreciates and Mary Jo's death occurs in a year when the exemption is greater than $3.5 million.

Note 1. Because the federal estate tax exemption as well as the federal GSTT exemption increases in years after 2005, some persons may wish to limit transfers to these types of trusts by a dollar amount or as a percentage of their total estate to provide for other gifts and to ensure that the surviving spouse is not effectively disinherited.

Note 2. Although transfers may be free of federal estate tax and GSTT, planners will need to consider the impact of state death taxes, if any.

Other Estate Tax Exemption Trusts

Q 7:32   May a Roth IRA be paid directly to a family trust created under the revocable trust?

Yes. In fact, this may be the preferred method for funding the family trust from the Roth IRA. Bypassing the revocable trust may eliminate issues that might call into question the ability of that trust to be a qualified beneficiary. If the family trust is funded directly by the beneficiary designation, it will be important that the beneficiary designation contain appropriate formula language that considers other funding sources and funds the trust only to the extent of available exemption or according to other limitations chosen by the owner.

Q 7:33   Will any portion of the Roth IRA be considered income in respect of a decedent?

Possibly. Typically, there will be no income in respect of a decedent on a Roth IRA; however, if a taxpayer dies within the first five years of the Roth IRA's existence, distributions may be taxable (see Qs 4:14, 4:17). To that extent, the distribution will be treated as income in respect of a decedent. [I.R.C. §§ 408A(d)(1)(A), 408A(d)(2)(B), 691]

Q 7:34   Is it more advantageous to use a traditional IRA or a Roth IRA to fund a bypass trust?

If IRA assets are needed to fund a bypass trust, a Roth IRA is a better vehicle with which to fund the trust than a traditional IRA. That is because a traditional IRA will be subject to income tax and therefore result in substantially less wealth transfer. If a Roth IRA is used to fund the bypass trust, the beneficiaries will receive more wealth since favorable income tax treatment can be stretched out over the oldest trust beneficiary's life expectancy. Table 7-2 shows an additional $1,400,000 of wealth transfer when a Roth IRA rather than a traditional IRA is used to fund a bypass trust.

Table 7-2. Value of Assets Passing to the Bypass Trust

	Traditional IRA	*Roth IRA*
Exemption amount	$ 3,500,000	$3,500,000
Less income taxes at 40%	−1,400,000	−0
Net to family	$ 2,100,000	$3,500,000
Additional wealth transfer		$1,400,000

Funding Clauses

Q 7:35   What is a *funding clause*?

Typically, a *funding clause* is a clause used to accomplish a taxpayer's funding objective—often that is, to achieve no estate tax or to use the generation-skipping trust exemption (see Qs 7:27, 7:28). There are two basic types of funding clauses, a pecuniary funding clause and a fractional funding clause.

A sample pecuniary funding clause may read as follows:

> I give the smallest pecuniary amount that, if allowed as a federal estate tax marital deduction, would result in the least possible federal estate tax being payable by reason of my death.

A fractional funding clause may read as follows:

> I give a fractional share of my residuary estate of which (a) the numerator is the smallest amount that, if allowed as a federal estate tax marital deduction, would result in the least possible federal estate tax being payable by reason of my death, and (b) the denominator is the value of my residuary estate as finally determined for federal estate tax purposes.

Q 7:36 What type of funding clause should be used for purposes of a Roth IRA trust?

Generally, distributing either traditional IRAs or Roth IRAs through an administrative trust should be avoided; however, if this must be done, it is preferable to use a fractional funding clause rather than a pecuniary funding clause. Although the law is not well developed in this area, there is a risk that if an IRA is used to fund a pecuniary bequest it will trigger recognition of income accrued both before and after death. The IRS has ruled that all accrued interest on a Series E bond would be recognized if the bonds were distributed in satisfaction of a pecuniary bequest. [See Ltr. Ruls. 9507008 (Nov. 10, 1994), 9315016 (Jan. 15, 1993)] More recently, CCM 200644020 indicates that a charitable pecuniary bequest in a trust which is satisfied by an in-kind distribution of an IRA will trigger immediate income taxation. In addition, no charitable deduction was allowed because the trust did not direct the trustee to pay charitable bequests from income. The IRS treats such a distribution as a sale of the asset in the estate or trust followed by a distribution of the cash. Therefore, if a pecuniary funding clause is used with an IRA, it is likely the IRS will rule not only that accrued income will be realized but also that the character of the assets as an IRA could be lost. Generally, income would only be taxable in a Roth IRA if the account was still subject to the five-year rule (see Q 4:9), engaged in a prohibited transaction, or was subject to tax on its unrelated business income. [I.R.C. §§ 408(e)(1), 408(e)(2), 408A(a), 408A(d)(2)(B), 4975] Nonetheless, if there is risk that the distribution will cause the account to be treated as sold, the benefits of the characterization of the asset as a Roth IRA could be lost. Therefore, fractional funding clauses should be used to avoid this possibility.

Q 7:37 May a funding clause be used to divide a Roth IRA between individuals and trusts?

Yes. A funding clause may be used to divide a Roth IRA between individuals and trusts. Typically, a fractional funding clause will be used to do so to avoid the acceleration of income in respect of a decedent (see Q 7:36).

Q 7:38 May a funding clause be used in a beneficiary designation?

Yes. Funding clauses may be used in beneficiary designations as well as in wills or trusts. Dividing Roth IRAs by means of a funding clause in the beneficiary designation will allow the appropriate amount of the account to be transferred to trusts or other beneficiaries with less risk that the funds will be subject to creditor claims or administration expenses. If the account owner has a taxable estate, it will be important to understand the allocation of taxes and expenses under local law and to tailor those allocations appropriately in the will or trust document that controls the distribution of the other assets. Under optimum circumstances, Roth IRA funds should be the last assets to be used to pay taxes or expenses of the estate.

As a practical matter, many beneficiary designation forms used by IRA custodians are not well suited to customized or formula funding clauses. Some custodians that do not allow the use of beneficiary designation forms other than their own will allow funding clauses to be used as an attachment to the standard forms.

Q 7:39 Will the funding of a trust's pecuniary bequest to charity using a Roth IRA cause acceleration of income?

Yes, according to the IRS. Under CCM 200644020, a charitable pecuniary bequest in a trust that is satisfied by an in-kind distribution of a Roth IRA will trigger immediate income taxation. This, of course, would only trigger income if the Roth IRA distribution would otherwise be subject to income tax. Typically, no income will be generated on a Roth IRA distribution; however, if a taxpayer dies within the first five years of the Roth IRA's existence, such deemed distribution may be taxable (see Qs 4:14, 4:17). Therefore, fractional funding clauses should be used to avoid this possibility.

Q 7:40 Can a trust take a charitable deduction for the income produced by the funding of a trust's pecuniary bequest to charity using a Roth IRA?

One of the requirements for a trust to take a charitable deduction is that the amount must be paid to the charity "pursuant to the terms of the governing instrument." [I.R.C. § 642(c)(1)]

The amount paid to charity must be paid from gross income. [I.R.C. § 642(c)(1)] Because the Code specifically requires that a charitable deduction is available only if the source of the contribution is gross income, tracing of the contribution is required in determining its source. [Rev. Rul. 2003-123, 2003-50 I.R.B. 1200]

According to CCM 200644020, no charitable deduction will be allowed unless the trust directs the trustee to pay charitable bequests from income. For this reason, it is recommended that the following language be included in trusts:

> I instruct my Trustee to satisfy any charitable bequest or gift, to the extent possible, from property that constitutes income in respect of a decedent.

Disclaimers

Q 7:41 What is a *qualified disclaimer*?

A *qualified disclaimer* is an irrevocable and unqualified refusal by a person to accept an interest in property but only if

1. The refusal is in writing and is received by the transferor of the interest, his or her legal representative, or the holder of the legal title to the

property to which the interest relates not later than the date that is nine months after the later of

    a. The day on which the transfer creating the interest in such person is made or

    b. The day on which such person attains age 21;

2. The person has not accepted the interest or any of its benefits; and

3. As a result of the refusal, the interest passes without any direction on the part of the person making the disclaimer and passes either to the spouse of the decedent or to a person other than the person making the disclaimer.

[I.R.C. § 2518(b)]

Q 7:42   How does a spousal disclaimer work in the overall estate plan?

Under the property law in most states, a spouse is allowed to disclaim assets passing under a beneficiary designation form. When a spouse executes a disclaimer, the funds within the Roth IRA trust will pass to the next beneficiary. In many instances the next beneficiary may be a trust for the benefit of the surviving spouse or the children of the couple (or both). [G.C.M. 39858 (Sept. 9, 1991)]

Example. Enrique dies having named a trust for the benefit of his wife, Marta, as the beneficiary of his Roth IRA. Enrique's children are named as alternate beneficiaries within the trust. Distributions will be made over Marta's remaining life expectancy because she is the oldest beneficiary of the trust. However, if Marta disclaims her interest in the trust, the trust will continue for the benefit of Enrique's children and RMDs can be made over the life expectancy of the oldest child.

Q 7:43   May a qualified disclaimer be used to fund an exemption equivalent bypass trust?

In the event that the beneficiary designation appropriately names the exemption equivalent bypass trust as the alternate beneficiary in the event that the primary beneficiary disclaims, a disclaimer by the primary beneficiary will have the effect of funding that trust.

Example. Troy dies having named his wife, Lisa, as the beneficiary of his entire $10 million estate. Troy's bypass trust is the alternate beneficiary of his estate. Lisa can disclaim an amount necessary to fund Troy's bypass trust up to the exemption equivalent, thereby taking full advantage of Troy's exemption amount.

Note A bypass trust is a trust that shields assets from federal (or federal and state) taxation in the estate of the second spouse to die. Usually the bypass trust is funded at the death of the first spouse with the amount that is allowed to pass free of federal (or federal and state) tax. For the years 2006 through 2008, the federal estate tax exemption amount is $2 million and increased to

$3.5 million in 2009. The amount that may be transferred free of state death or transfer tax varies by state and is less than the federal exemption amount in many cases.

Q 7:44 May a qualified disclaimer be used to fund a generation-skipping trust?

In the event that the beneficiary designation appropriately names the generation-skipping trust as the alternate beneficiary and the primary beneficiary disclaims, a disclaimer by the primary beneficiary will have the effect of funding that trust (see Qs 7:28, 7:41).

Q 7:45 Will a qualified disclaimer by the oldest beneficiary of a trust change the measuring life for calculating required distributions?

If a person disclaims (the disclaimer must be qualified under Code Section 2518—see Q 7:41) all interests in the Roth IRA or all interests in a trust that is a beneficiary of a Roth IRA, that person's life will no longer be the measuring life for calculation of distributions. [*See* Treas. Reg. § 1.401(a)(9)-4, Q&A 4]

> **Example.** Bob dies, leaving his Roth IRA payable to a family trust. The trust is required to distribute income to Bob's wife, Bonnie, and may make discretionary distributions of principal to Bonnie and the children. The trust will pay out to the children after Bonnie's death when the youngest child has attained the age of 40. The required distributions will be calculated based on Bonnie's life expectancy, since she is the oldest beneficiary of the trust. If, however, Bonnie disclaims her interests in the trust, the required distributions will be calculated based on the age of the oldest child who is also a beneficiary of the trust. This will allow substantially longer avoidance of tax on the gains within the Roth IRA.

Q 7:46 Is a beneficiary's disclaimer of an interest in an IRA or a Roth IRA a qualified disclaimer even though prior to making the disclaimer, the beneficiary receives an RMD from the IRA or a Roth IRA for the year of the decedent's death?

Yes. Under Revenue Ruling 2005-36 [2005-26 I.R.B. 1368], a beneficiary's acceptance of the RMD for the year of death does not preclude the beneficiary from making a qualified disclaimer (if all of the requirements of Code Section 2518 are met; see Q 7:41) with respect to all or a portion of the balance of the IRA. The beneficiary may make a qualified disclaimer under Code Section 2518 with respect to all or a portion of the balance of the account, other than the income attributable to the RMD that the beneficiary received, provided that at the time the disclaimer is made, the disclaimed amount and the income attributable to the disclaimed amount are paid to the beneficiary entitled to receive the disclaimed amount, or are segregated in a separate account.

While a beneficiary of a Roth IRA does not need to take an RMD in the year of death (see Q 5:15) (unless the Roth IRA inherited was also an inherited Roth IRA; see Example 2), there is no reason to believe the treatment of a Roth IRA RMD for the year after the year of death would be any different than a traditional IRA under the reasoning of Revenue Ruling 2005-36 [2005-26 I.R.B. 1368] (see Example 3).

Example 1. Christopher's spouse, Krista, is designated as the primary beneficiary of Christopher's IRA. Gabrielle, Christopher and Krista's child, is designated as the contingent beneficiary of the IRA. Three months after Christopher's death, the IRA custodian pays Krista $100,000, the RMD for the year of Christopher's death. No other amounts have been paid from the IRA since Christopher's date of death. Seven months after Christopher's death, Krista disclaims the pecuniary amount of $600,000 of the IRA account balance plus the income attributable to the $600,000 amount earned after the date of death. The income earned by the IRA between the date of Christopher's death and the date of Krista's disclaimer is $40,000. As soon as the disclaimer is made, Gabrielle is paid the $600,000 amount disclaimed, plus that portion of IRA income earned between the date of death and the date of the disclaimer attributable to the $600,000. Krista's disclaimer is a valid disclaimer.

Example 2. Peter inherited a Roth IRA from his mother, Bernice. Peter dies owning the inherited Roth IRA. Peter's beneficiary, Joseph, would like to disclaim the Roth IRA. Four months after Peter's death, the Roth IRA custodian pays Joseph $15,000, the RMD for the year of Peter's death. No other amounts have been paid from the Roth IRA since Peter's date of death. Seven months after Peter's death, Joseph disclaims the Roth IRA. Under Revenue Ruling 2005-36 [2005-26 I.R.B. 1368], Joseph's disclaimer is valid as long as he also disclaims that portion of Roth IRA income earned between the date of death and the date of the disclaimer attributable to the non-RMD portion.

Example 3. Jillian's spouse, Jackson, is designated as the primary beneficiary of Jillian's Roth IRA. Phillip, Jillian and Jackson's child, is designated as the contingent beneficiary of the Roth IRA. Jillian dies in December 2008. In early 2009, the Roth IRA custodian pays Jackson $50,000, the RMD for 2009. No other amounts have been paid from the IRA since Jillian's date of death. Within nine months of Jillian's death, Jackson disclaims the pecuniary amount of $500,000 of the Roth IRA account balance plus the income attributable to the $500,000 amount earned after the date of death. The income earned by the Roth IRA between the date of Jillian's death and the date of Jackson's disclaimer is $20,000. As soon as the disclaimer is made, Phillip is paid the $500,000 amount disclaimed, plus that portion of IRA income earned between the date of death and the date of the disclaimer attributable to the $500,000. Although Revenue Ruling 2005-36 [2005-26 I.R.B. 1368] only refers to the year of death RMD, Jackson's disclaimer should be a valid disclaimer under the same logic.

Taxation

Q 7:47 How are Roth IRA distributions to a Roth IRA trust taxed?

Generally, distributions from a Roth IRA (to a Roth IRA trust or otherwise) are tax free as long as they are qualified distributions (see Qs 4:1, 4:7).

Q 7:48 Does federal tax law address apportionment of estate taxes when a Roth IRA is payable to a trust?

No. Federal tax law addresses apportionment issues in only a few narrowly defined areas, which do not include the apportionment of estate taxes when a Roth IRA is payable to a trust.

Note. Some states have laws that address apportionment issues if a decedent has failed to do so.

Practice Pointer. The best course is to address the issues of apportionment of estate taxes in the estate planning documents.

Permissible Transfer

Q 7:49 May the trustee of a Roth IRA trust transfer the Roth IRA from the decedent's IRA trustee (or custodian) to a new IRA trustee or custodian?

Yes. The trustee of a Roth IRA trust should be able to transfer a Roth IRA to a new IRA trustee or custodian. Several letter rulings have allowed a beneficiary of an inherited IRA to initiate a trustee-to-trustee transfer of the IRA from one investment adviser to another, affording the beneficiary tremendous flexibility with regard to investment options. [Ltr. Ruls. 9416037 (Jan. 25, 1994), 9433032 (May 28, 1994), 9504045 (Jan. 27, 1995), 9623037 (June 7, 1996), 200228025 (July 12, 2002)]

Practice Pointer. If such a trustee-to-trustee transfer occurs, it is important that the Roth IRA at the new custodian remains titled in the name of the deceased IRA owner. (See Q 6:42 for an example of an acceptable title.) [*See* Ltr. Rul. 200228023 (July 12, 2002)]

QTIPing a Roth IRA

Q 7:50 What is a *QTIP trust*?

Generally, an individual may leave an unlimited amount of property to a surviving spouse at death under the estate tax marital deduction. [*See* I.R.C. § 2056(b)] However, the exception to this general rule holds that interests subject to termination would not automatically qualify for the marital deduction. Examples of interests that terminate are typically the ones left by donors who wish to control to whom the assets will ultimately pass. These interests are known as "terminable interests." The terminating event may be the passage of time, a contingency, or conditioned upon an event or failure of an event to occur. For example, property passing to a trust for the benefit of a spouse, which is conditioned upon his or her non-remarriage, is a terminable interest.

A *QTIP trust* or a *qualified terminable interest property trust* is a trust that qualifies for the marital deduction under Code Section 2056(b)(7), despite being a terminable interest. It provides for life income to a surviving spouse, with the remainder usually going to the children. QTIP trust assets remaining at the surviving spouse's death will be taxable in the surviving spouse's estate, even though the first-deceased effectively controlled the subsequent distribution. [*See* I.R.C. § 2056(b)(7)]

Q 7:51   May a Roth IRA be paid to a QTIP trust?

Yes. The rules regarding Roth IRAs payable to a QTIP trust are very similar to those relating to the payment of a traditional IRA to a QTIP trust. Treasury Regulations Section 1.401(a)(9)-5, Q&A 7, Example 2, makes it clear that to receive the special life expectancy calculation allowed under Code Section 401(a)(9)(B)(iv) in which the spouse's life expectancy is used as the measuring life and is recalculated each year, the trust must pay all distributions from the IRA to the spouse. Trusts that meet this requirement are sometimes referred to as "conduit" trusts, since they act as a conduit in paying all IRA distributions to the spouse. A trust may meet the QTIP (marital deduction) requirements by paying the total of income earned by the trust, including income earned within an IRA (see Q 7:53). In some years, however, income may be less than the total of the distributions from the IRA. The IRS takes the position that if some of the distribution may be accumulated in the trust, there is a possibility that it will be held for the remainder beneficiaries. (See Q 7:53 for further discussion on the QTIP requirements when a Roth IRA is payable to a trust.) Therefore, the spouse is not the sole beneficiary despite the fact that during his or her lifetime he or she is the only person entitled to receive distributions. Consequently, the spouse's life is used as the measuring life, since he or she is ordinarily the oldest beneficiary of the trust; however, since he or she is not the "sole" beneficiary, the special recalculated life expectancy rule cannot be used.

QTIP trusts are usually set up with the primary objective of preserving principal assets for the family of the first decedent. Often, QTIP trusts are used in second-marriage situations. When IRAs are used to fund QTIP trusts, there is a conflict between the objective of structuring the trust to maximize the benefit of tax-free growth within the Roth IRA and the objective of keeping principal inside of the trust for distribution at the end of the life of the second spouse.

Practice Pointer. As discussed in Q 7:52, if preservation of principal for later distribution is not the primary objective, paying the Roth IRA outright to the surviving spouse may be preferable so that the surviving spouse may obtain the additional deferral provided by a rollover.

Q 7:52 Is a spousal Roth IRA rollover advantageous when compared to a Roth QTIP trust?

Yes. A rollover is mathematically more advantageous than a QTIP trust. In the context of Roth IRA planning, the overall objective is to maximize deferral of taxation by minimizing the distributions from the Roth IRA. In the context of a rollover, no distributions are required until the surviving spouse's death. In the context of a Roth QTIP trust, it will be necessary to begin distributions by December 31 of the year following the year of the Roth IRA owner's death (see Q 7:13 for an exception to this rule). [I.R.C. §§ 401(a)(9)(B)(iii), 408A(c)(5)] Generally, a trust will be used when non-tax objectives, such as preserving assets for distribution to children or grandchildren, outweigh the potential tax benefits of a spousal rollover.

In addition, where a QTIP trust is funded with a Roth IRA, it will be necessary for an executor of the estate to file an estate tax return (regardless of the size of the estate) and make a QTIP election for both the IRA and the QTIP trust.

Q 7:53 When is a surviving spouse considered to have a qualifying income interest for life in a Roth IRA for purposes of election to treat both the Roth IRA and the trust as QTIP?

Revenue Ruling 2006-26 [2006-22 I.R.B. 939] outlines three different factual situations involving application of the Uniform Principal and Income Act (UPIA) when a marital trust is named beneficiary of decedent's IRA.

The revenue ruling began by laying out the following facts: *A* dies in 2004, at age 68, survived by spouse, *B*. Prior to death, *A* established an IRA. *A*'s will creates a testamentary marital trust (Trust) that is funded with assets in *A*'s probate estate. Prior to death, *A* named Trust as the beneficiary of all amounts payable from the IRA after *A*'s death. The IRA is properly included in *A*'s gross estate for federal estate tax purposes. The IRA is currently invested in productive assets and *B* has the right (directly or through the trustee of Trust) to compel the investment of the IRA in assets productive of a reasonable income. The IRA document does not prohibit the withdrawal from the IRA of amounts in excess of the annual RMD. The executor of *A*'s estate elects to treat both the IRA and Trust as QTIP. Under Trust's terms, all income is payable annually to *B* for *B*'s life, and no person has the power to appoint any part of the Trust principal to any person other than *B* during *B*'s lifetime. *B* has the right to compel the trustee to invest the Trust principal in assets productive of a reasonable income. On *B*'s death, the Trust principal is to be distributed to *A*'s children, who are younger than *B*. Under the trust instrument, no person other than *B* and *A*'s children has a beneficial interest in Trust (including any contingent beneficial interest). Further, under Trust's terms, *B* has the power, exercisable annually, to compel the trustee to withdraw from the IRA an amount equal to all the income of the IRA for the year and to distribute that income to *B*. If *B* exercises this power, the trustee is obligated under Trust's terms to withdraw the greater of all of the income of the IRA or the annual RMD, and distribute currently to B at least the income of the IRA. The Trust provides that any excess of the RMD over the income of the IRA for that year is to be added to Trust's principal. If B does not exercise the power to compel a withdrawal from the IRA for a particular year, the trustee must withdraw from the IRA only the RMD.

The revenue ruling then laid out the following three scenarios:

Situation 1—Authorized Adjustments Between Income and Principal. The facts and the terms of Trust are as described above. Trust is governed by the laws of State X. State X has adopted a version of the UPIA including a provision similar to section 104(a) of the UPIA providing that, in certain circumstances, the trustee is authorized to make adjustments between income and principal to fulfill the trustee's duty of impartiality between the income and remainder beneficiaries. More specifically, State X has adopted a provision providing that adjustments between income and principal may be made, as under section 104(a) of the UPIA, when Trust assets are invested under State X's prudent investor standard, the amount to be distributed to a beneficiary is described by reference to the Trust's income, and the Trust cannot be administered impartially after applying State X's statutory rules regarding the allocation of receipts and disbursements to income and principal. In addition, State X's statute incorporates a provision similar to section 409(c) of the UPIA providing that, when a payment is made from an IRA to a trust: (1) if no part of the payment is characterized as interest, a dividend, or an equivalent payment, and all or part of the payment is required to be distributed currently to the beneficiary, the trustee must allocate 10 percent of the required payment to income and the balance to principal; and (2) if no part of the payment made is required to be distributed from the trust or if the payment received by the trust is the entire amount to which the trustee is contractually entitled, the trustee must allocate the entire payment to principal. State X's statute further provides that, similar to section 409(d) of the UPIA, if in order to obtain an estate tax marital deduction for a trust a trustee must allocate more of a payment to income, the trustee is required to allocate to income the additional amount necessary to obtain the marital deduction.

For each calendar year, the trustee determines the total return of the assets held directly in Trust, exclusive of the IRA, and then determines the respective portion of the total return that is to be allocated to principal and to income under State X's version of section 104(a) of the UPIA in a manner that fulfills the trustee's duty of impartiality between the income and remainder beneficiaries. The amount allocated to income is distributed to B as income beneficiary of Trust, in accordance with the terms of the Trust instrument. Similarly, for each calendar year the trustee of Trust determines the total return of the assets held in the IRA and then determines the respective portion of the total return that would be allocated to principal and to income under State X's version of section 104(a) of the UPIA in a manner that fulfills a fiduciary's duty of impartiality. This allocation is made without regard to, and independent of, the trustee's determination with respect to Trust income and principal. If B exercises the withdrawal power, Trustee withdraws from the IRA the amount allocated to income (or the RMD amount, if greater), and distributes to *B* the amount allocated to income of the IRA.

Situation 2—Unitrust Income Determination. The facts, and the terms of Trust, are as described above. Trust is governed by the laws of State *Y.* Under State *Y* law, if the trust instrument specifically provides or the interested parties consent, the income of the trust means a unitrust amount of 4 percent of the fair market value (FMV) of the trust assets valued annually. In accordance with procedures prescribed by the State *Y* statute, all interested parties authorize the trustee to administer Trust and to determine withdrawals from the IRA in accordance with this provision. The trustee determines an amount equal to 4 percent of the FMV of the IRA assets and an amount equal to 4 percent of the FMV of Trust's assets, exclusive of the IRA, as of the appropriate valuation date. In accordance with the terms of Trust, trustee distributes the amount equal to 4 percent of the Trust assets, exclusive of the IRA, to *B,* annually. In addition, if *B* exercises the withdrawal power, Trustee withdraws from the IRA the greater of the RMD or the amount equal to 4 percent of the value of the IRA assets, and distributes to *B* at least the amount equal to 4 percent of the value of the IRA assets.

Situation 3—"Traditional" Definition of Income. The facts, and the terms of Trust, are as described above. Trust is governed by the laws of State *Z.* State *Z* has not enacted the UPIA, and therefore does not have provisions comparable to sections 104(a) and 409(c) and (d) of the UPIA. Thus, in determining the amount of IRA income *B* can compel the trustee to withdraw from the IRA, the trustee applies the law of State *Z* regarding the allocation of receipts and disbursements to income and principal, with no power to allocate between income and principal. As in Situations 1 and 2, the income of Trust is determined without regard to the IRA, and the income of the IRA is separately determined based on the assets of the IRA.

The IRS ruled that if a marital trust is the named beneficiary of a decedent's IRA, the surviving spouse, under the circumstances described in Situations 1, 2, and 3 in this revenue ruling, will be considered to have a qualifying income interest for life in the IRA and in the trust for purposes of an election to treat both the IRA and the trust as QTIP under Code Section 2056(b)(7). The IRS pointed out that if the marital deduction is sought, the QTIP election must be made for both the IRA and the trust.

The principles illustrated in Situations 1 and 2 of Revenue Ruling 2006-26 will not be applied adversely to taxpayers for taxable years beginning prior to May 30, 2006, in which the trust was administered pursuant to a state statute described in Treasury Regulations Sections 1.643(b)-1, 20.2056(b)-5(f)(1), and 20.2056(b)-7(d)(1) granting the trustee a power to adjust between income and principal or authorizing a unitrust payment in satisfaction of the income interest of the surviving spouse.

Q 7:54   What is the benefit of utilizing a QTIP trust rather than paying outright to a spouse?

The most important benefit of utilizing a QTIP trust is the ability of the creator of the QTIP to determine the ultimate disposition of the trust assets. In many second marriage situations where children exist from a prior marriage, an individual wants to provide for the surviving spouse, yet ensure assets will pass to his or her children. Rather than making the Roth IRA payable to children directly, which may give rise to estate taxation, the IRA owner may make use of the unlimited marital deduction via the QTIP trust. Similarly, where one is concerned about the redirection of the Roth IRA from his or her children and is also concerned about leaving the surviving spouse with insufficient assets to live upon, consideration should be given to the a QTIP trust.

Q 7:55   For a Roth IRA payable to a qualified trust, if a trust beneficiary is living on the date of the Roth IRA owner's death but dies before September 30 of the year following the year of the owner's death, is the beneficiary still considered in determining who is the oldest trust beneficiary?

Yes. If a trust beneficiary dies after the Roth IRA owner, yet prior to September 30 of the year following the year of the owner's death, such deceased trust beneficiary (provided no qualified disclaimer is declared by such beneficiary before his or her death) will continue as a trust beneficiary for determining if a designated beneficiary has been declared as of September 30 of the year following the year of the owner's death and the applicable life expectancy. [Treas. Reg. § 1.401(a)(9)-4, Q&A 4(c)]

> **Example.** Austin dies in 2009, after naming a trust for the benefit of his children, Vincent, age 30, and Gabrielle, age 23. Vincent dies in February 2010. Vincent is still considered in determining the oldest beneficiary of the trust as of September 30, 2010.

Q 7:56   Is a contingent trust beneficiary who is entitled to a Roth IRA only upon the death of the primary trust beneficiary taken into consideration when determining whether the trust is a qualified designated beneficiary and which trust beneficiary has the shortest life expectancy?

No. If a successor beneficiary's entitlement to a Roth IRA is merely that of a potential successor to the interest of the primary trust beneficiary, such contingent beneficiary is not considered for purposes of determining which designated beneficiary has the shortest life expectancy and whether the trust qualifies as a designated beneficiary. [Treas. Reg. § 1.401(a)(9)-5, Q&A 7(c)]

> **Example.** Alexander creates a trust for the benefit of his son, Nicholas. At Nicholas's death, the trust is distributed to Alexander's niece, Ginny, free of trust. If Ginny does not survive Nicholas, the trust is paid to a charity. At Alexander's death, Ginny is alive. Because the trust will pay outright to

Ginny at Nicholas's death, the charity is disregarded for purposes of determining whether the trust is a qualified designated beneficiary and which trust beneficiary has the shortest life expectancy.

Q 7:57 Must a trust beneficiary that is entitled to receive a portion of a Roth IRA based on a contingency, other than merely a potential successor interest to another trust beneficiary, be considered in determining whether the trust is a qualified designated beneficiary and which trust beneficiary has the shortest life expectancy?

Yes, but a contingent beneficiary is not to be taken into consideration for purposes of determining the designated beneficiary with the shortest life expectancy when the contingency is that of a potential successor. [Treas. Reg. § 1.401(a)(9)-5, Q&A 7(b)] This issue arises frequently when a trust is named as the beneficiary. When this is the case, special consideration must be given to all potential trust beneficiaries whose entitlement to the Roth IRA is not contingent. For example, where a trust includes a power of appointment, all potential appointees must be taken into consideration.

> **Example.** Alexander creates a trust for the benefit of his son, Nicholas. At Nicholas' death, the trust is distributed to Alexander's niece, Ginny. Ginny's share is distributed free of trust if she is over age 40. If Ginny does not survive Nicholas and dies before age 40, the trust is paid to a charity. At Alexander's death, Ginny is alive but is only age 35. Because the trust will not (as the facts exist at Alexander's death) pay outright to Ginny at Nicholas' death, the charity is not disregarded for purposes of determining whether the trust is a qualified designated beneficiary. As a result, the trust does not qualify as a designated beneficiary because the charity (a non-individual) is a beneficiary of the trust.

Q 7:58 Is a remainder beneficiary of a conduit trust a mere potential beneficiary?

Yes. The examples under Treasury Regulations Section 1.401(a)(9)-5, A-7 illustrate that a beneficiary of what is commonly referred to as a "conduit trust" is also a mere potential successor. In this context, a conduit trust is a trust that requires the trustee to distribute to the trust beneficiary any and all amounts withdrawn from the IRA. Thus, in a conduit trust, IRA assets are not allowed to accumulate in trust (outside of the IRA wrapper) for future beneficiaries.

To illustrate this point, assume that under the terms of Trust A, any and all amounts that the trustee withdraws from retirement accounts payable to the trust must be immediately distributed to the primary beneficiary, Child A. In other words, Trust A is a conduit trust. Child A is given a testamentary general power of appointment. If the trust were *not* a conduit trust, the fact that the child is given a general power of appointment would disqualify the trust as a designated beneficiary because not only is a non-individual a potential beneficiary of the trust (i.e., an estate or a creditor), but by September 30 of the year following the year of the IRA owner's death, it would not be possible to determine who is the oldest potential beneficiary of the trust. However, because the trust *is* a conduit trust, any beneficiaries beyond Child A can be disregarded in determining whose life expectancy is used and if the trust qualifies as a designated beneficiary.

Utilizing a conduit trust can be a useful tool when the grantor wishes to name a charity or an older relative as a contingent beneficiary of the trust. It also tends to eliminate many of the traps that exist in trying to draft an accumulation trust to qualify as a designated beneficiary. While a conduit trust does not provide maximum spendthrift protection, it does provide a safeguard against the beneficiary taking accelerated payments from the IRA—a protection that would not exist if the trust beneficiary were named as the outright beneficiary of the IRA.

Chapter 8

Beneficiary Designations and Estate Planning

Peter Gulia, Esq.
Fiduciary Guidance Counsel

This chapter focuses on a retirement plan participant's use of his or her valuable right under a Roth account to name a beneficiary. The chapter explains some of a participant's opportunities and restrictions in making a beneficiary designation, including marriage and family rights that restrain a beneficiary designation. And because a participant might have a *Roth account* under a retirement plan that includes a qualified Roth contribution program (see chapter 10), this chapter explains survivor-annuity and spouse's-consent provisions that could apply under those plans.

Making a beneficiary designation is an important part of estate planning. Because a Roth account benefit will not pass under or be transferred by a will, a Roth account beneficiary designation affects the individual's overall estate plan.

The subject of tax-oriented estate planning warrants a book of its own. This chapter introduces the concept because many participants mistakenly assume that they lack sufficient wealth for estate tax issues to be of concern. Because a taxable estate can include nonprobate assets, including retirement benefits, this chapter describes some tax-treatment rules and planning opportunities. Estate planning ideas are explained in chapter 7.

Last but not least, this chapter ends with a "top-ten" list of common mistakes that people make when designating beneficiaries, and how a practitioner might help his or her client avoid those mistakes.

Roth account. This chapter refers to the following kinds of plans:

- a Roth IRA described by Internal Revenue Code Section 408A(b);

- a 401(k) or 403(b) plan's designated Roth account described by Code Section 402A(b)(2)(A).

The following words are used in this chapter in a specially defined manner:

IRA. An individual retirement account under Code Section 408(a), an individual retirement annuity under Code Section 408(b), or a trust that is treated as an individual retirement account under Code Section 408(c).

Non-ERISA. A governmental plan, a church plan that has not elected to be governed by ERISA, or an IRA that is not held under a plan.

Non-probate. Property that is transferred or contract rights that are provided without a court-supervised administration or succession.

Participant. A participant (instead of a beneficiary or alternate payee) under a retirement plan or the original participant of an IRA. Participant also refers to the person who is the original holder or "owner" of an IRA.

Payer. Any custodian, insurer, plan administrator, or other person responsible for deciding or paying a claim under a plan or IRA.

Probate. Property that is transferred through a court-supervised administration or succession.

Retirement plan. Either of the plans mentioned above — a Roth IRA or a designated Roth account.

State. The District of Columbia or any state, commonwealth, territory, possession, or similar jurisdiction of the United States. Because this chapter includes many references to state law, it makes parallel references to a state (instead of the lawyers' word, jurisdiction) for reading ease. For example, although the District of Columbia is not a state, law that applies to a person because he or she resides in the District of Columbia is state law, as distinguished from U.S. law or federal law, which applies throughout the United States.

Citations. This chapter includes many general explanations of state laws. To support each such statement with citations to more than 50 state laws would be unwieldy in this chapter's summary. Moreover, an employee-benefits practitioner usually is interested first, in a general sense, in the state laws. To these ends, the chapter frequently cites the Uniform Probate Code, Uniform Trust Code, and other uniform acts recommended by the Uniform Law Commission (*http://www.nccusl.org*) (visited on June 25, 2009). A reader who wants to find whether a particular state enacted a statute based on a uniform law might begin with this chapter's citations to Uniform Laws Annotated (U.L.A.), which includes citations for states' adoptions of, and variations from, the recommended uniform laws.

Because most employee-benefits practitioners do not use printed volumes to read federal or state statutes or regulations, this chapter's citations to statutes and regulations omit publisher and year references. A reader may find statutes efficiently and inexpensively using Wolters Kluwer's Loislaw service; for more information, visit *http://www.loislaw.com* (visited on June 25, 2009), or call 1-800-354-2512.

Specialty citations are in the forms and with the abbreviations customary to employee-benefits or tax practitioners, including the abbreviations listed in the book's front matter. Other citations generally follow the Association of Legal Writing Directors' *ALWD Citation Manual*, Third edition (Aspen Publishers, 2005), except as modified by the abbreviation and punctuation style of this book. To order any Aspen Publishers title, go to www.aspenpublishers. com, or call 1-800-638-8437.

Making a Beneficiary Designation

Q 8:1   Is a Roth benefit disposed by the participant's will?

No. A retirement plan or a Roth IRA contract usually will include a provision by which the participant may name his or her beneficiary or beneficiaries. The beneficiary designation applies even if the participant's will attempts to state a contrary disposition or to revoke a beneficiary designation. [Restatement (Third) of Property: Wills and Other Donative Transfers § 7.1 comment d (2003)] Indeed, if a beneficiary change could be effected by the participant's will, a responsible insurer or custodian would be unwilling to make any payment until a court had determined the correct distribution of a participant's estate or at least had appointed an executor. [*See, e.g.,* Stone v. Stephens, 155 Ohio 595, 600–601, 99 N.E.2d 766 (1951)] Understanding that a will does not change a contract's beneficiary results simply from applying the terms of the contract. Yet, some states, for convenience, provide a statute to recognize these non-testamentary transfers. [*See generally* Unif. Probate Code §§ 1-201(4), 8 pt. I U.L.A. 33–46 (1998) & Supp. 7–20 (2008), 6-101(a)(3), 8 pt. II U.L.A. 430–432 (1998) & Supp. 183–184 (2008), 6-104, 8 pt. II U.L.A. 467–474 (1998), 6-201, 8 pt. II U.L.A. 480–482 (1998)] Even without a statute, courts have held that a will cannot "override" a beneficiary designation. [*See generally* Restatement (Third) of Property: Wills and Other Donative Transfers § 7.1 comment d (2003)]

> **Note.** A beneficiary's right under a non-ERISA retirement plan arguably might be subject to the State of Washington's Testamentary Disposition of Nonprobate Assets Act. [*See* Wash. Rev. Code §§ 11.11.003 to 11.11.903] But even concerning a participant who is a resident or domiciliary of Washington, that statute might not always apply because many IRA "products" include a governing-law clause and few of these choose Washington law. Concerning a non-ERISA plan, state law may supplement an IRA's provisions concerning the manner of making a beneficiary designation. For instance, New York law requires that a beneficiary designation be signed. [New York Estates, Powers and Trusts Law § 13-3.2]

> For an ERISA plan, only the plan's provisions govern a beneficiary designation. [ERISA § 514; Kennedy v. Plan Adm'r for DuPont Sav. & Inv. Plan, 129 S. Ct. 865 (2009); Egelhoff v. Egelhoff, 532 U.S. 141 (2001)]

> **Caution.** In some circumstances, a will might be a beneficiary designation that supersedes an earlier designation if the plan's documents do not require that a beneficiary designation be made only on the form prescribed by the plan's administrator and the will is submitted to the administrator according to the plan's conditions. [*See, e.g.,* Liberty Life Assurance Co. of Boston v. Kennedy, 358 F.3d 1295 (11th Cir. 2004)]

Q 8:2   What law governs a beneficiary designation?

If a retirement plan or a Roth IRA is not governed by the Employee Retirement Income Security Act of 1974 (ERISA), state law may supplement the plan's or IRA's provisions concerning the manner of making a beneficiary designation.

For an ERISA plan, a participant must make a beneficiary designation according to the plan's provisions, a plan administrator must administer a plan according to its provisions, and ERISA preempts state laws. [ERISA § § 401, 403, 514; Kennedy v. Plan Adm'r for DuPont Sav. & Inv. Plan, 129 S. Ct. 865 (2009); Egelhoff v. Egelhoff, 532 U.S. 141 (2001)]

Caution. Some practitioners mistakenly assume that ERISA does not govern a payroll-deduction-only plan that helps participants buy an IRA (including a Roth IRA). Such an IRA-only plan is exempt from Parts 2 and 3 of Subtitle B of Title I of ERISA. [ERISA §§ 201(6), 301(a)(7); *see also* Cline v. Indus. Maint. Eng'g & Contracting Co., 200 F.3d 1223 (9th Cir. 2000)] A plan might be excused from some of ERISA's reporting and disclosure requirements. [DOL Reg. §§ 2520.104-48, 2520.104-49] But Parts 4 and 5 apply to a plan if an employer "endorsed" the plan or became involved in the plan's administration. [DOL Reg. § 2510.3-2(d)(1); *see also* DOL Interpretive Bulletin 99-1, reprinted in 29 C.F.R. § 2509.99-1] This means that ERISA's fiduciary responsibility, claims-procedure, and civil enforcement provisions govern such an employer-maintained plan.

Q 8:3 Are there other reasons (beyond providing a death benefit) why a participant would want to name a beneficiary?

Yes. There are at least two kinds of benefits—other than the death benefit itself—that might be obtained by naming a beneficiary. They are described below.

1. *A beneficiary, even if he or she is not a surviving spouse, may direct a rollover.* If an eligible retirement plan so provides, a designated beneficiary, even if he or she is not the participant's surviving spouse, may instruct a direct rollover into his or her IRA (including a Roth IRA). [I.R.C. § 402(c)(11) added by Pension Protection Act of 2006 (PPA), Pub. L. No. 109-280, § 829 (Aug. 17, 2006), amended by Worker, Retiree, and Employer Recovery Act of 2008 § 108(f)]

Caution. A state might have an income tax law that does not follow the Internal Revenue Code. Before a beneficiary directs a rollover (or even decides to take a distribution), he or she should get expert advice about whether each state of which he or she is a resident or a domiciliary [*see* 4 U.S.C. § 114] would recognize the rollover, or would tax the distribution, even if rolled over for federal income tax purposes.

A hardship distribution can be based on the need of a beneficiary who is not a spouse or dependent. Without waiting for a participant to meet a plan's severance or other condition that may permit a distribution, a retirement plan may permit a payment to meet a participant's hardship. A hardship must be based on the participant's need, which can include some needs concerning a participant's spouse or dependent. Further, a plan may provide that an event (including a medical expense) that would meet the plan's hardship conditions if it happened concerning a participant's spouse or dependent is a hardship if it happens concerning "a person who is a beneficiary under the plan with respect to the participant." [Pub. L. No. 109-280, § 826 (Aug. 17, 2006)] In the IRS's view, such a rule applies only concerning a primary beneficiary—that is, one who "has an unconditional right to all or a portion of the participant's account balance under the plan upon the death of the participant." [I.R.S. Notice 2007-7, 2007-5 I.R.B. 395 (Jan. 29, 2007) at Q&A-5(a)]

Practice Pointer. For a plan year that begins on or after January 1, 2010, a plan must permit a nonspouse beneficiary's direct rollover of an eligible rollover distribution.

Note. Even before 2010, to the extent that the state law of California, Connecticut, Iowa, Massachusetts, New Hampshire, New Jersey, Oregon, or Vermont applies, state law might require a non-ERISA plan that allows a direct rollover by an opposite-sex spouse to include this beneficiary rollover provision to the extent that the provision is needed so that the plan does not discriminate against a same-sex marriage, civil union, or domestic partnership that has legal rights and burdens equal to another marriage. (See Q 8:47.)

Q 8:4   Who may make a beneficiary designation?

Before a participant's death, only the participant may make a beneficiary designation.

A typical retirement plan usually does not state a provision that permits a beneficiary to name his or her further beneficiary. But some plans, especially IRAs, provide that after a beneficiary's right has become fixed, he or she may name a further beneficiary for the portion of his or her separate share that remains after the designating beneficiary's death. In addition, some IRAs permit a beneficiary to name a further contingent beneficiary if the IRA participant had not (before his or her death) designated all of the IRA benefit and the IRA contract lacked a "default" provision. [Ltr. Rul. 199936052 (June 16, 1999)]

Caution. Depending on the plan's and account's provisions, as well as other facts and circumstances, a power to name further beneficiaries might cause a retirement benefit that remains undistributed at each beneficiary's death to be subject to federal estate tax and state estate and inheritance taxes, notwithstanding that the same benefit was previously so taxed on the participant's death (and on a preceding beneficiary's death). [I.R.C. § 2041(a)(2); Treas. Reg. § 20.2041-1(b)] A federal estate tax may be postponed if the beneficiary names his or her spouse as the succeeding beneficiary, and that spouse has power to take the entire remaining benefit. [I.R.C. § 2056; Ltr. Rul. 199936052 (June 16, 1999)]

Note. If any plan does not provide for a beneficiary to name his or her succeeding beneficiary and a benefit remains after all participant-named beneficiaries are dead, a plan administrator or payer may determine under the plan's terms which person a retirement plan might provide that the personal representative of the participant's estate is the "default" beneficiary. Although a participant's estate might have been closed before this time, an estate may be "reopened" for subsequent administration on the discovery of property that was not disposed by the previous administration. [*See generally* Unif. Probate Code § 3-1008, 8 pt. I U.L.A. 300–302 (1998) & Supp. 83 (2006)]

Practice Pointer. A careful participant would make a complete beneficiary designation that contemplates all possibilities. If a participant does not want to specify alternate takers, the participant could create a trust, which could include a power of appointment for a beneficiary to name a further beneficiary.

Practice Pointer. Whether a retirement plan or an IRA "product" permits a beneficiary to name his or her further beneficiary, or precludes such a designation, is not "hard-wired" by federal tax law, but rather is a provision of the particular plan and account documents together with applicable law. [Phil Royce, Beneficiaries Naming Beneficiaries: Examples and a new form—IRA Successor Beneficiary Form (Wolters Kluwer, Apr. 18, 2008), available at *http://www.complianceheadquarters.com/ComplianceArticles/ IRA_041808.aspx* (subscription required (visited on June 25, 2009)] A person who cares about whether a particular plan or "product" allows a beneficiary to name his or her further beneficiary should read carefully all relevant documents.

Q 8:5 Why should a participant read a beneficiary designation form?

Plan administrators, trustees, custodians, and insurers design beneficiary-designation forms anticipating the possibility that a participant might give incomplete or ambiguous instructions. For example, many forms provide that if a participant has not specified how to divide his or her retirement plan or IRA, it will be divided among all beneficiaries in equal shares.

A beneficiary-designation form might include other "gap-fillers" or "default" provisions, some of which might be surprising to a participant. For example, a beneficiary-designation form might provide that a beneficiary change for one IRA will change the beneficiary for every IRA with the provider. Some retirement plans provide that the beneficiary designated under a pension or life insurance plan is the default beneficiary.

Practice Pointer. Because default provisions might frustrate a participant's intent, a participant should read, complete, sign, and deliver his or her beneficiary-designation form.

Q 8:6 Must a beneficiary designation be witnessed?

Usually, no. For a non-ERISA plan or IRA, most states' laws do not require that a beneficiary designation be signed in the presence of a notary or otherwise witnessed. Even if a plan's administrator adopts a form that calls for witnesses, a plan administrator might have discretion to excuse an absence of witnesses. [*See, e.g.*, Lowing v. Pub. Sch. Employees' Ret. Bd., 766 A.2d 306 (Pa. Cmmw. 2001)]

For an ERISA plan, a beneficiary designation must be made according to the plan and the plan's procedures. [*See* ERISA § 514]

Q 8:7   Will a beneficiary designation made under a power of attorney be accepted?

Maybe. A trustee, custodian, insurer, or plan administrator may (but need not) accept a beneficiary designation made by an agent under a power of attorney. Typically, a trustee, custodian, insurer, or plan administrator will decline to act unless the power-of-attorney document expressly states a power to change beneficiary designations. [*See, e.g.*, Pension Comm. Heileman-Baltimore Local 1010 IBT Pension Plan v. Bullinger, 16 Employee Benefits Cas. (BNA) 1024 (D. Md. 1992); Clouse v. Philadelphia, Bethlehem & New England R.R. Co., 787 F. Supp. 93, 15 Employee Benefits Cas. (BNA) 1347 (E.D. Pa. 1992); *see also* Restatement (Second) of Agency § 37 (1957)]

> **Practice Pointer.** If ERISA does not preempt state law, a practitioner should consider which state's law might apply, and should draft a power-of-attorney document to meet the state laws of all states that might be involved.

> **Example.** Bill resides in Kentucky, but works in Ohio, and while there bought a Roth IRA. This Roth IRA provides that it is governed by Massachusetts law, and neglects to state any provision concerning conflict of laws. Rather than assume that a power of attorney that meets the requirements of Kentucky's statute would be sufficient, Bill's lawyer drafts a document that conforms not only to Kentucky law but also to Ohio law and Massachusetts law. Doing so is less expensive than researching which law would apply. And following all states' laws gives Bill a better likelihood that his document will be used.

Q 8:8   Will a participant's attempt to make a beneficiary designation be honored?

Maybe. For "standard-form" contracts, some states recognize the contract interpretation fiction of substantial compliance (see Q 8:9).

Substantial Compliance

Q 8:9   What is the doctrine of substantial compliance?

When recognized, the *doctrine of substantial compliance* might excuse a contract holder's failure to effect a change of beneficiary according to the contract's terms if he or she intended to change his or her beneficiary and did everything reasonably in his or her power to effect the change. Some courts find that this equitable doctrine of substantial compliance circumvents "a formalistic, overly technical adherence to the exact words of the change of beneficiary provision in a given [contract]." [Phoenix Mut. Life Ins. Co. v. Adams, 30 F.3d 554, 563 (4th Cir. 1994)]

The doctrine of substantial compliance, which is one manifestation of the doctrine of substantial performance of a contract, has been criticized as defeating freedom of contract. [*See, e.g.,* G. Gilmore, *The Death of Contract* (Ohio Univ. Press 1974)

Note. The doctrine of substantial compliance in making a beneficiary designation is one manifestation of the doctrine of substantial performance of a contract. Some law professors have criticized the doctrine as defeating the freedom of contract. [*See, e.g.,* Grant Gilmore, *The Death of Contract,* at 74 (1974)]

A payer's interpleader or other circumstances that make a payer a mere stakeholder do not lessen the need for a claimant to show the participant's substantial compliance with a plan's or contract's procedure for making a beneficiary designation. [*See, e.g.,* McCarthy v. Aetna Life Ins. Co., 681 N.Y.S.2d 790 (1998)]

Q 8:10 Does the doctrine of substantial compliance apply to a Roth IRA not held under a plan?

Yes, under most states' laws. If ERISA does not preempt state law, a state court would likely apply a relevant state's doctrine of substantial compliance.

Q 8:11 Does the doctrine of substantial compliance apply to a Roth account under a non-ERISA plan?

Yes, in most states. If ERISA does not preempt state law, a state court would likely apply a relevant state's doctrine of substantial compliance.

Caution. Even if the decedent resided and all claimants reside in the same state, that state's law is not necessarily the governing law. A plan or a contract might include provisions concerning which state's law governs.

Q 8:12 Does the doctrine of substantial compliance apply to an ERISA plan?

If a plan is governed by ERISA, the doctrine of substantial compliance should apply only if the plan administrator in its discretion decides to use the concept to aid its own interpretation or administration of the plan.

To determine the beneficiary under an ERISA plan, a court should hold that any state's doctrine of substantial compliance is preempted. [ERISA § 514; *see* Egelhoff v. Egelhoff, 532 U.S. 141 (2001); *see, e.g.,* Schmidt v. Sheet Metal Workers' Nat'l Pension Fund, 128 F.3d 541 (7th Cir. 1997); *see, e.g.,* Phoenix Mut. Life Ins. Co. v. Adams, 30 F.3d 554 (4th Cir. 1994); Continental Assurance

Co. v. Davis, 24 Employee Benefits Cas. (BNA) 2273, 2000 U.S. Dist. LEXIS 810 (N.D. Ill. Aug. 11, 2000); Metro. Life Ins. Co. v. Hall, 9 F. Supp. 2d 560 (D. Md. 1998); Fortis Benefits Ins. Co. v. Johnson, 966 F. Supp. 987 (D. Nev. 1997); First Capital Life Ins. Co. v. AAA Commc'ns, Inc., 906 F. Supp. 1546 (N.D. Ga. 1995)] At least two federal courts of appeals, however, have held that a state's common-law doctrine of substantial compliance supplements an ERISA plan's provisions. [BankAmerica Pension Plan v. McMath, 206 F.3d 821 (9th Cir.), *cert. denied sub nom.* McMath v. Montgomery, 531 U.S. 952 (2000); Peckham v. Gem State Mut. of Utah, 964 F.2d 1043 (10th Cir. 1992)] In the absence of findings by the plan administrator, the Fourth Circuit found that a state's doctrine of substantial compliance may be replaced by a federal common-law doctrine of substantial compliance. [Metropolitan Life Ins. Co. v. Johnson, 297 F.3d 558, 567–569 (7th Cir. 2002); Phoenix Mut. Life Ins. Co. v. Adams, 30 F.3d 554 (4th Cir. 1994)] Although some federal courts considering the question have held that ERISA does not necessarily preempt a state's doctrine of substantial compliance, the contributing author's view is that ERISA preempts any such law relating to an ERISA plan. [ERISA § 514]

> **Practice Pointer.** Unless a plan provision is contrary to ERISA, an ERISA plan administrator must administer a plan according to the plan's documents. [ERISA § 404(a)] Therefore, if a plan states that any doctrine of substantial compliance will not apply, the plan administrator must interpret and administer the plan without using such a doctrine.
>
> Further, if a plan grants the plan's administrator discretion in interpreting or administering the plan, a court will not interfere with the plan administrator's decision unless it was an abuse of discretion. [*See* Firestone Tire & Rubber Co. v. Bruch, 489 U.S. 101 (1989)]
>
> **Practice Pointer.** If a plan's administrator is worried that a court might decide that ERISA does not preempt the doctrine of substantial compliance or that ERISA permits a court to consider the doctrine as supplementary federal common law of ERISA, the administrator might, in appropriate circumstances, make an alternative discretionary finding on whether the participant's efforts to change his or her beneficiary designation were sufficient to meet such a doctrine. It is difficult for a plaintiff to prove that a decision was so obviously wrong that it must have been an abuse of discretion.

Lost Beneficiary Designation

Q 8:13   What should a payer do if it cannot locate a beneficiary designation because records were destroyed?

Even with prudent efforts to safeguard records, circumstances beyond an insurer's or custodian's control might result in the destruction of Roth IRA records. If so, a payer should try to "reconstruct" a beneficiary designation using the best evidence available to it.

That records are lost or destroyed does not discharge a payer from its obligation to administer a Roth account. When deciding whether to pay any benefit to a potential beneficiary, a payer must act in good faith and must use reasonable procedures, especially when deciding who is a participant's beneficiary. When a record is lost or destroyed, a payer may use the most reliable evidence available to it. For example, a claimant might furnish a copy of a beneficiary designation. A payer might use its discretion to rely on a document that appears to be a copy of a participant's beneficiary designation. A payer should do so, however, only if it has adopted and uses reasonable procedures designed to detect a forgery. Further, when a claimant submits evidence that he or she is the participant's beneficiary, a payer must take reasonable steps to consider whether the evidence is credible.

[*See generally* DOL PWBA (now EBSA), FAQs for Plan Sponsors, Fiduciaries and Service Providers Related to the Events of September 11th, *http://www.dol. gov/ebsa/faqs/faq_911_3.html* (visited June 26, 2009]

Default Beneficiary Designation

Q 8:14   What happens when a participant did not make a beneficiary designation?

A retirement plan or a Roth IRA contract may state a "default" beneficiary designation that applies when a participant did not make a valid beneficiary designation. A typical default provision pays the nondesignated benefit to the personal representative of the participant's estate. Or a plan governed by ERISA's Part 2 (see Qs 8:28, 8:64) might provide the plan's death benefit to a participant's surviving spouse and, subsequently, to a participant's personal representative only if there is no surviving spouse.

If, under community-property law (see Qs 8:89–8:94), a portion of a participant's Roth benefit belongs or belonged to the participant's spouse, the spouse (or the spouse's beneficiaries or heirs) may have a claim against the participant's personal representative for payment of the spouse's community property. In Alaska, Arkansas, Colorado, Connecticut, Florida, Hawaii, Kentucky, Michigan, Montana, New York, North Carolina, Oregon, Virginia, and Wyoming, a statute based on the Uniform Disposition of Community Property Rights at Death Act might apply. [*See generally* Unif. Disp. Comm. Prop. Rights at Death Act, 8A U.L.A. 213–227 (2003) & Supp. 128 (2008)]

Laws and External Documents That Might Affect a Beneficiary Designation

Q 8:15   Does a divorce revoke a beneficiary designation?

Whether a divorce revokes a beneficiary designation turns on (1) whether ERISA or state law governs the retirement plan or Roth account, (2) which state law (if any) applies, and (3) what the chosen state law (if applicable) provides.

If a Roth account is not part of an ERISA plan, state law may apply. In many states, a divorce will not revoke a beneficiary designation that names the ex-spouse. [*See, e.g., In re* Declaration of Death of Santos, Jr., 282 N.J. Super.

509, 660 A.2d 1206 (1995); Hughes v. Scholl, 900 S.W.2d 606 (Ky. 1995); Stiles v. Stiles, 21 Mass. App. Ct. 514, 487 N.E.2d 874 (1986); O'Toole v. Central Laborers' Pension & Welfare Funds, 12 Ill. App. 3d 995, 299 N.E.2d 392 (1973); Gerhard v. Travelers Ins. Co., 107 N.J. Super. 414, 258 A.2d 724 (Ch. Div. 1969)] Some states have a statutory provision that attempts to provide that a divorce or annulment makes the former spouse not a beneficiary except as otherwise specified by a court order. [*See generally* Unif. Probate Code § 2-804(b), 8 pt. I U.L.A. 217–222 (1998) & Supp. 61–64 (2008)] Even when the relevant state has such a statute, however, it might not apply if the contract has contrary provisions. In any case, state law will protect a payer that pays the beneficiary of record unless the payer has received a court order restraining payment or at least a written notice that states a dispute about who is the lawful beneficiary. [*See generally* Unif. Probate Code § 2-804(g), (h), 8 pt. I U.L.A. 218–219 (1998) & Supp. 61–64 (2008)]

If a Roth account is part of an ERISA plan, ERISA preempts all state laws. [ERISA § 514] Therefore, only the plan's terms will govern whether a divorce or other circumstance has any effect on the plan beneficiary designation. [ERISA §§ 404(a), 514; Kennedy v. Plan Adm'r for DuPont Sav. & Inv. Plan, 129 S. Ct. 865 (2009); Egelhoff v. Egelhoff, 532 U.S. 141(2001); *see also* Boggs v. Boggs, 520 U.S. 833 (1997), *reh'g denied*, 521 U.S. 1138 (1997)]

> **Practice Pointer.** A plan sponsor should consider whether it might be helpful for a plan to state expressly that any annulment, divorce, marital separation, or other event or circumstance has no effect under the plan.

> **Practice Pointer.** After a divorce, a participant should remember to change or confirm his or her beneficiary designation.

Q 8:16 What happens when a beneficiary designation is contrary to an external agreement?

A payer pays according to the plan's or contract's provisions and applicable law, and need not consider external documents. However, once a payer has paid a beneficiary, a person who has rights under an external agreement may pursue remedies against the payee under state law (if ERISA does not preempt state law). [*See, e.g.*, Kinkel v. Kinkel, 699 N.E.2d 41 (Ohio 1998) (A custodian correctly paid an IRA participant's named beneficiary, but the participant's children later recovered from the participant's surviving spouse.)]

Q 8:17 May an executor participate in a court proceeding concerning a disputed benefit?

Often, no. A personal representative of a participant's estate may participate in a court proceeding concerning a disputed benefit only if the personal representative is a bona fide claimant. If a personal representative does not make any claim of right to the benefit, however, such a personal representative has no justiciable claim or standing to participate in a court proceeding. [*See, e.g.*, Deaton v. Cross, 184 F. Supp. 2d 441 (D. Md. 2002)]

Q 8:18   Why would a divorced participant not want to name his or her young child as a beneficiary?

A divorced participant might not want to name his or her young child as a beneficiary if doing so might have the effect of putting money in the hands of the child's other parent—the participant's former spouse.

A retirement plan or a Roth IRA is a contract. A payer wants to be sure that a payment is a complete satisfaction of that contract. Ordinarily, a beneficiary's deposit or negotiation of a check that pays a Roth account distribution is the beneficiary's acceptance of the payer's satisfaction of the beneficiary's claim under the Roth account.

A *minor* is a person still young enough that he or she cannot make a binding contract. At common law, the age of majority was 21. Now, all but three state's laws generally end a person's minor status at 18.

Before a child reaches 18 (or the other age of competence to make binding contracts), his or her guardian or conservator may disaffirm an agreement or promise the child made. After a child reaches 18 (or the other "full age"), he or she may disaffirm an agreement or promise he or she made before he or she reached the age of competence to make contracts.

A payer will not take the risk that paying a distribution is not a complete satisfaction of Roth account obligations. Thus, payers usually are unwilling to pay a retirement benefit to a minor.

To facilitate payment in these circumstances, most retirement plans and IRAs permit payment to a minor's conservator, guardian, or Uniform Transfers to Minors Act custodian. [*See generally* Susan N. Gary and Nancy E. Shurtz, Nontax considerations in testamentary transfers to minors, in Carmine Y. D'Aversa, ed., *Tax, Estate, and Lifetime Planning for Minors*, chapter 10, at 295–336 (ABA, 2006)] If a participant named his or her child as a beneficiary (rather than naming as beneficiary a custodian), a payer is likely to honor a claim made by the child's guardian. If a child's other parent is living, most courts would maintain or appoint the parent as the child's conservator. In some states, the law presumes that a court should consider a child's parent or natural guardian to serve also as the child's conservator. [*Compare* Manley v. Detroit Auto Inter-Insurance Exch., 127 Mich. App. 444, 339 N.W.2d 205 (1983), *motion denied*, 357 N.W.2d 644 (Mich. App. 1983), *remanded on other grounds*, 425 Mich. 140, 388 N.W.2d 216 (1986) *with In re* Estate of Fisher, 503 So .2d 962 (Fla. App. 1987) (child's "natural guardian" of his person was not the guardian of his property); *see generally* Unif. Probate Code § 5-413(6)-(7), 8 pt. II U.L.A. 390–395 (1998) & Supp. 178 (2008)]

Q 8:19   Can a participant name his or her dog or cat as a beneficiary?

No. A beneficiary must be a person, whether a natural person or a nonnatural person (such as a corporation), that can endorse a negotiable instrument—such as the check that pays the plan distribution.

For many people, living with a pet is an important and comforting part of life, and providing for the care of the pet is a real concern. Although it is usually more effective for a pet owner to plan for the care of the pet in the pet owner's will, some people might have insufficient probate property to provide for the pet's care and instead may use a beneficiary designation.

Under the laws of every state, an individual cannot give any part of his or her estate to a non-human animal. However, a pet owner may leave a sum of money to a trustee (see Q 8:20) or to a person designated to care for the pet, along with a request (but not a direction) that the money be used for the pet's care.

Practice Pointer. The pet owner should select a caretaker he or she trusts, because the caretaker often has no legal obligation to use the money for the purpose specified. If there is no suitable relative or friend who would take the pet, the pet owner or guardian might consider a charitable organization whose function is to care for, or place, companion animals.

Q 8:20   May a trust provide for a pet animal's care?

State laws differ widely concerning whether and how a trust may provide for the care of animals; these differences may be grouped in the following broad categories.

1. In some states, a trust for the support of an animal is invalid because there is no beneficiary. However, a trust for a human beneficiary may include a provision that the trustee may use trust property to pay for the care of an animal because the animal's care may benefit the human beneficiary.

2. In some states, a person may create a valid trust for an animal (if the trust satisfies other trust law concerning the duration of a trust), but such a trust is an honorary trust. [*See generally* Restatement (Third) of Trusts § 47 (2003)] A court will not order any remedy if the trustee fails to perform the honorary trust.

3. In some states, a trust for an animal's care may be enforced in the courts. [*See generally* Unif. Probate Code § 2-907, 8 pt. I U.L.A. 239–242 (1998) & Supp. 63 (2006)]

In some states, a trust recognized under categories in item 2 or item 3 above cannot exceed 21 years, even if the life span of a particular animal is longer. [*See generally* Unif. Probate Code § 2-907, 8 pt. I U.L.A. 239–242 (1998) & Supp. 63 (2006)] But Colorado permits a valid pet trust for the life of the animal and "the animal's offspring in gestation." [Colo. Rev. Stat. Ann. § 15-11-901]

A trust does not necessarily mean that the trustee must be the animal's caretaker. If the trustee cannot or prefers not to take physical possession of the animal, a separate person may be named as the caretaker. But it is usually more efficient for one person to serve as both caretaker and trustee.

Q 8:21   How might a participant make a beneficiary designation to provide for his or her pet animal's care?

For an illustration of how to provide for the care of a pet without using a trust, consider the following example.

Example. Gary desires that his cat be properly cared for after Gary's death. Gary is a man of modest income and little wealth. Gary anticipates that almost none of his property will pass by his will. Gary has a small balance (to which he no longer contributes) under a Roth IRA. To provide for his cat, Gary makes the following provisions:

Beneficiary designation

Mary Johnson 100%

Will

I give my cat, Lady Lucy of Canterbury Tails, and any other pet animals that I may own at the time of my death, to Mary Johnson (who currently resides at 234 Sunset Road, Indianapolis, Indiana) with the request that she treat them as companion animals. To provide for the care of these animals, I have made a separate financial provision for Mary Johnson and I request (but do not direct) that she use that money for the care of these animals.

Practice Pointer. If a participant has relatives who might challenge the beneficiary designation, the participant should consider providing only a reasonable amount of money for the care of any pet. A large sum of money for a pet may prompt relatives to challenge the beneficiary designation.

A bequest, gift, trust, or beneficiary designation in favor of a pet animal that is unreasonably large may be capricious and therefore legally ineffective. [*See generally* Restatement (Third) of Trusts § 29 (2003)] Sometimes, a court will reduce the amount set aside for the care of the pet animal. [*See, e.g., In re* Templeton Estate, 4 Fiduc. Rep. 2d (Bisel) 172 (Pa. Common Pleas Orphans' Ct. 1984); *In re* Lyon's Estate, 1974 Pa. D. & C. Dec. LEXIS 444 (C.P. 1974); *see generally* Unif. Probate Code § 2-907(c)(6) (1998)]

Q 8:22   Who is taxed on a Roth account distribution set aside for the care of a pet animal?

If a Roth account distribution is paid to a pet's caretaker who does not serve as a trustee, the distribution is that individual's income.

If a Roth account distribution is paid to a trustee who serves under a valid trust, the distribution is the trust's income. A valid pet trust that is legally unenforceable will nevertheless be treated as a trust for federal income tax purposes.

Although a trust normally has a deduction in the amount of trust distributions, "since the amounts of income required to be distributed . . . and amounts properly paid, credited, or required to be distributed under [the relevant Internal Revenue Code sections] are limited to distributions intended for beneficiaries, a deduction under those sections is not available for distributions for the benefit of a pet animal. Similarly, such distributions are not taxed to anyone . . . [.]" [Rev. Rul. 76-476, 1976-2 C.B. 192] These rules are consistent with the idea that trust income generally should not be taxed more than once.

Using Trusts

Q 8:23   What is a living trust?

A trust refers to a person's right to the beneficial enjoyment of property to which another person holds the legal title. A *living trust* is a trust that is created and takes effect during the settlor's lifetime. [*See generally* Bryan A. Garner, Black's Law Dictionary 999 (8th ed. 2004)] A typical living trust is revocable. If a living trust is irrevocable, it necessarily involves at least one beneficiary other than the trust's creator. [*See generally* Restatement (Third) of Trusts § 2 (2003)]

Q 8:24   Can a participant hold his or her Roth account in a living trust?

No. Whether a Roth account is a Roth 401(k), a Roth 403(b), or a Roth IRA, the retirement plan must provide that a participant cannot transfer any right he or she has under the plan or contract. [I.R.C. § § 401(a)(13), 401(f)-(g), 403(b)(1)(C), 408(a)(4), 408(b)(1), 408A(b)] If a living trust can be revoked or amended, as is customarily permitted with the kind of trust that many people call a "living trust" (see Q 8:23), the trust declaration or agreement could not ensure that during the participant's lifetime the Roth account benefit would be used only for the participant's benefit.

> **Practice Pointer.** There is no particularly good reason to try to put a Roth account benefit into a living trust. A Roth account benefit already is nonprobate property that will pass according to the plan's or contract's beneficiary designation (see Q 8:1).

Q 8:25   Can a trust be a beneficiary of a Roth account?

Yes. Usually, a participant may name a trust as beneficiary under a retirement plan or IRA. To make a correct beneficiary designation, a participant should name the trustee, as trustee of the trust, as beneficiary. Most payers, however, will treat a designation of the trust as if it were a designation of the duly appointed and then-currently serving trustee of the trust. The trust must be legally in existence (or completed such that it would be legally in existence on the trustee's receipt of money or property) *before* the participant makes the beneficiary designation.

> **Note.** A beneficiary of a trust is not a designated beneficiary for minimum-distribution purposes (see chapter 5) unless the trust meets specified requirements, which include that the beneficiaries are identifiable under the trust instrument. [Treas. Reg. § 1.401(a)(9)-4, Q & A D-5]

Family Rights That Restrain a Beneficiary Designation

Q 8:26 Is a beneficiary designation that does not provide for the participant's spouse valid?

Whether a beneficiary designation that does not provide for a participant's spouse is valid turns on whether the retirement plan is governed by ERISA, or the plan otherwise has a spouse's-consent provision.

Q 8:27 May an ERISA plan participant make a beneficiary designation that does not provide for his or her spouse?

No, unless his or her spouse consents. If a Roth account is part of an ERISA plan, a participant's beneficiary designation that fails to provide for his or her spouse will be invalid, either for 100 percent of the death benefit or the value of the plan's qualified preretirement survivor annuity (QPSA), whichever is provided by the plan, unless the participant made a qualified election that was supported by the spouse's notarized consent. [ERISA § 205] Likewise, many church plans and governmental plans have their own survivor-annuity or spouse's-consent provisions.

Just as a person who is not yet a spouse cannot give a spouse's consent (see Q 8:97), a participant who is not yet divorced or separated cannot change his or her beneficiary without his or her spouse's consent. [ERISA § 205; *see also* Merchant v. Corder, 1999 WL 486590 (4th Cir. July 12, 1999)]

If an ERISA plan was not amended to state a QPSA or other spouse's death benefit as required by the Retirement Equity Act of 1984, a surviving spouse (who has not consented otherwise) is nonetheless entitled to a QPSA or, if the plan does not provide any benefit as an annuity, the entire account balance. [Lefkowitz v. Arcadia Trading Co., 996 F.2d 600 (2d Cir. 1993)]

The rule that a spouse's consent must be witnessed by a notary or plan representative is strict. Even when a spouse admitted that she signed the spouse's consent, it was not valid without a notary's certificate. [Lasche v. George W. Lasche Basic Profit Sharing Plan, 111 F.3d 863 (11th Cir. 1997)]

Q 8:28 Can a Roth IRA participant make a beneficiary designation that does not provide for his or her spouse?

Yes, unless the IRA contract provides otherwise. Even if a Roth IRA is part of an ERISA-governed plan, an IRA is exempt from Part 2 of Subtitle B of Title I of ERISA. Thus, the survivor–annuity or spouse's-consent rules of ERISA Section 205 do not apply to an IRA. [ERISA § 201(6)]

A trustee, custodian, insurer, or plan administrator will, in the absence of any court order or written notice of a dispute, give effect to the participant's valid beneficiary designation.

If a participant's spouse did not receive his or her share provided by state law, a distributee might be liable to the participant's personal representative to the extent that state law provides for a spouse's elective share to be payable from nonprobate property. [*See generally* Unif. Probate Code § 2-204, 8 pt. I U.L.A. 104–105 (1998)]

In Louisiana, a payer may follow the participant's beneficiary designation. [La. Rev. Stat. Ann. §§ 23:638, 23:652] To the extent necessary to satisfy the spouse's community-property rights and usufruct, a distributee who receives benefits under a nongovernmental (and non-ERISA) retirement plan (e.g., a church plan that has not elected to be governed by ERISA) must account for and pay over benefits to the participant's surviving spouse. [T.L. James & Co. Inc. v. Montgomery, 332 So. 2d 834 (La. 1976)] A distributee who receives benefits under a retirement plan of "any public or governmental employer" is *not* subject to the claims of forced heirs. [La. Civ. Code Ann. art. 1505]

Caution. That ERISA's Part 2 of Subtitle B of Title I (which includes ERISA's surviving-spouse protection) does not apply to a plan for IRAs does not mean that state law applies. If ERISA governs a plan (even without applying some Parts), ERISA preempts state laws. [ERISA § 514]

Different laws may apply to members of a Native American Indian tribe. [Jones v. Meehan, 175 U.S. 1 (1899); *see also* Davis v. Shanks, 15 Minn. 369 (1870); Hasting v. Farmer, 4 N.Y. 293 (1850); Dole v. Irish, 2 Barb. 639 (N.Y. Sup. Gen. Term. 1848)] A Native American Indian tribe's law usually applies, however, between or among members of the tribe, and often cannot be enforced against persons outside the tribe.

Even when a participant's beneficiary change has an obvious potential to frustrate a divorcing spouse's equitable-distribution rights, a participant remains free to make his or her beneficiary designation unless a court's restraining order binds him or her. [*E.g.*, Titler v. State Employees' Ret. Bd., 768 A.2d 899 (Pa. Cmmw. Ct. 2001)] Further, an order that binds a participant might not bind a plan administrator or payer.

Note 1. If a distributee received a plan distribution in one year but paid over an amount to the participant's surviving spouse in a later year, the distributee recognizes income for the year he or she received the distribution and claims a deduction for the year he or she paid restoration to the surviving spouse. [I.R.C. § 1341; United States v. Lewis, 340 U.S. 590 (1951)]

Note 2. A surviving spouse who is not the participant's named beneficiary and instead receives a benefit because of an elective share law or community property law is not a designated beneficiary when applying the plan's minimum distribution provisions. [Treas. Reg. § 1.401(a)(9)-4, A-1] Thus, it might become necessary to compute a minimum distribution by reference to a different person's life.

Q 8:29   Must a payer tell an ex-spouse when a participant changes his or her beneficiary designation contrary to a court order?

No, in the absence of a court order that commands the payer to furnish specified information, a payer has no duty to furnish information about a particular beneficiary-designation change:

> Absent a promise or misrepresentation, the courts have almost uniformly rejected claims by plan participants or beneficiaries that an ERISA administrator has to volunteer individualized information taking account of their peculiar circumstances. This view reflects ERISA's focus on limited and general reporting and disclosure requirements [citations omitted], and also reflects the enormous burdens an obligation to proffer individualized advice would inflict on plan administrators[.]

[Barrs v. Lockheed Martin Corp., 287 F.2d 202, 27 Employee Benefits Cas. (BNA) 2409, Pens. Plan Guide (CCH) ¶ 23,979F (1st Cir. 2002)]

Even when a plan administrator is governed by ERISA Section 404's greatest fiduciary duties, courts have not required a plan administrator to furnish an alternate payee or beneficiary information beyond that required by an express statutory or plan provision. If a Roth IRA is not governed by ERISA, it seems unlikely that a court would impose a duty greater than federal courts have applied concerning ERISA plans.

Failing to Provide for a Child

Q 8:30   Can a participant make a beneficiary designation that does not provide for his or her child?

In the United States, only Louisiana and Puerto Rico have a forced-share provision for a decedent's children. [See La. Civ. Code Ann. arts. 1493–1495; P.R. Laws tit. 31, § § 2362, 2411–2463] Therefore, a participant can usually "disinherit" his or her children. In some states, a modest family allowance is sometimes required for a decedent's children if there is no surviving spouse. [See generally Unif. Probate Code § § 2-403–2-404, 8 pt. I U.L.A. 141, 142 (1998) & Supp 37–38 (2008)]

In Louisiana, a payer may follow the participant's beneficiary designation. [La. Rev. Stat. Ann. §§ 23:638, 23:652] A distributee who receives benefits under a nongovernmental (and non-ERISA) retirement plan, however, must account for and pay over benefits to the participant's surviving spouse to the extent that payment is necessary to satisfy his or her community-property rights and usufruct and to the participant's children or forced heirs to the extent that payment is necessary to satisfy their légitime. [T.L. James & Co. v. Montgomery, 332 So. 2d 834 (La. 1976)] A distributee who receives benefits under a retirement plan of "any public or governmental employer" is *not* subject to the claims of forced heirs. [La. Civ. Code Ann. art. 1505]

Different laws may apply to members of a Native American tribe. [Jones v. Meehan, 175 U.S. 1 (1899); see also 25 U.S.C. § 1301(1); Davis v. Shanks, 15

Minn. 369 (1870); Hasting v. Farmer, 4 N.Y. 293 (1850); Dole v. Irish, 2 Barb. 639 (N.Y. Sup. Gen. Term. 1848); *see generally* United States v. Wheeler, 435 U.S. 313 (1978)]

Whether it is called légitime, legitimate portions, or compulsory portions in civil-law nations, family provision or family maintenance in nations following English law, or ahl alfara-id under the Koran, in most nations a person is limited in his or her right or privilege to disinherit his or her children.

Practice Pointer. A participant who resides in a nation other than the United States should consult an expert lawyer before he or she makes a beneficiary designation that does not provide for his or her spouse and children.

Charitable Gifts

Q 8:31   May a participant name a charity as beneficiary?

Yes, a participant may name a charitable organization as a beneficiary.

Although some states previously had statutes that would void some charitable gifts made soon before a donor's death or of more than a specified portion of his or her estate, those statutes were unconstitutional. [*See, e.g.*, Estate of Cavill, 329 A.2d 503 (Pa. 1974)] States repealed all of these statutes.

For a participant who already has fairly provided for his or her spouse and children, a charitable gift may be worthwhile. Many people who have worked for charity or in education are inclined to continue that work by making a gift to a charitable organization.

Caution. A charitable-organization employer should avoid inappropriately inducing its employees to name the charity as a beneficiary. In addition to consequences under other laws, doing so could interfere with rights under an ERISA plan. [*See* ERISA § 510]

Practice Pointer. For someone who already has decided to make charitable gifts on death and expects his or her estate to be subject to a significant federal estate tax, some financial planners suggest that using a retirement plan benefit might be an efficient way to provide the gift. They suggest this because deferred compensation is subject to both federal income tax and federal estate tax, while a capital asset enjoys a "stepped-up" basis (except for deaths in 2010) and is not subject to income tax until the beneficiary sells the asset. Other planners point out that the federal income tax deduction for federal estate tax attributable to property that is income in respect of a decedent partially mitigates the "double tax." [*See* I.R.C. § 691(c)] Along with this, they argue that a retirement plan might permit longer income tax deferral while post-death income on capital assets will subject the beneficiary to income tax. Considering which course might be "right" turns on the donor's (and the planner's) assumptions. Further, non-tax factors might favor a particular approach.

Of course, a charity should avoid inappropriately influencing any person to name the organization as a beneficiary.

Q 8:32   If a charity is a beneficiary, what is the tax treatment of that Roth IRA benefit?

Although a Roth IRA benefit will be included in the participant's taxable estate for federal estate tax purposes, the estate will have a deduction for the amount that properly passes to charity. [I.R.C. § 2055] Further, although some portion of a distribution from a Roth IRA otherwise might be included in income for federal income tax purposes, a charitable organization does not recognize income or pay federal income tax on its receipts from charitable gifts. [I.R.C. § 501(a)]

Simultaneous Death; Absentees

Q 8:33   What should a payer do if there is doubt about the order of deaths?

For many retirement plans, the order of deaths between a participant and a beneficiary is irrelevant.

> **Practice Pointer.** A carefully drafted plan should state that a person cannot be a beneficiary if he or she is not living, or it is not in existence, when the plan administrator receives the person's claim or, if later, a benefit is to be paid or becomes payable.

If an ERISA plan administrator must decide the order of deaths between a participant and a beneficiary (or among potential beneficiaries) and the plan does not provide a presumption concerning the order of deaths, the plan administrator need not follow any state's simultaneous-death statute. [ERISA § 514(b); *cf.* Apostal v. Laborer's Welfare & Pension Fund, 195 F. Supp. 2d 1052, 27 Employee Benefits Cas. (BNA) 2670 (N.D. Ill. 2002)] If the plan does not provide a specific rule, a plan administrator might choose to follow the general pattern of state laws (see Q 8:34), treating such an invented rule as the plan administrator's interpretation.

Q 8:34   What is the typical simultaneous-death rule?

The "old" Uniform Simultaneous Death Act, adopted by many states, provides that if "there is no sufficient evidence that the persons have died otherwise than simultaneously, the property of each person shall be disposed of as if he [or she] had survived [the other person]." [Unif. Simultaneous Death Act § 1 (1940)] The 1991 version of the Uniform Simultaneous Death Act and the Uniform Probate Code each generally provides that a person cannot qualify as an heir unless he or she survives the first decedent for 120 hours. Further, the person who would claim through the heir has the burden of proving the duration that the heir survived the first decedent. [Unif. Probate Code §§ 2-104, 2-702, 8 pt. I U.L.A. 84, 182–186 (1998) & Supp. 29, 54 (2008)]

Practice Pointer. For tax-planning purposes, a wealthy participant may prefer to vary these "default" rules by express language in his or her beneficiary designation. [*See, e.g.*, Treas. Reg. § 20.2056(e)-2(e)] Even if state law applies to the plan, state law will permit a different provision if it is stated by the plan or the participant's beneficiary designation. [*See, e.g.*, 20 Pa. Consol. Stat. § 8505]

Alternatively, a common-disaster clause or a delay clause of up to six months does not disqualify property for the federal estate tax marital deduction. [I.R.C. § 2056(b)(3); Treas. Reg. § 20.2056(b)-3(b)]

If it becomes necessary for an ERISA plan's administrator to determine the order of deaths between or among potential beneficiaries and the retirement plan does not provide a presumption concerning the order of deaths, it might be prudent for the plan administrator to indulge a presumption that all persons who died within a few days of one another died at the same time and survived to the relevant time.

If a plan's administrator decides claims under a non-ERISA plan, the plan administrator might be required to follow state law.

Q 8:35 Is there a federal common law of ERISA concerning simultaneous deaths?

No. At common law, when two or more persons died in a common disaster, there was no presumption for or against any person surviving another. [*See, e.g.*, People v. Eulo, 482 N.Y.S.2d 436, 472 N.E.2d 286 (1984)] Moreover, there is no clear consensus in states' statutes. [*See generally* Restatement (Third) of Property: Wills and Other Donative Transfers § 1.2, statutory note (2003)]

Q 8:36 What should a payer do when someone says a participant or beneficiary is absent and presumed dead?

In ordinary circumstances, a plan administrator or payer should not presume a participant's or beneficiary's death. Instead, a plan administrator or payer should require the claimant (usually, the next beneficiary) to prove the absentee's death by an appropriate court order.

Under the common law, a person was presumed dead if he or she had been absent for a continuous period of seven years. Likewise, an absentee's exposure to a specific peril was a sufficient ground for presuming death. Further, death may be inferred if survival of the absentee would be beyond human expectation or experience. [*See, e.g., In re* Katz's Estate, 135 Misc. 861, 239 N.Y.S. 722 (Sup. Ct. 1930)] Courts sometimes required considerable evidence of an unexplained absence. For example, a person's absence from the places where his relatives resided together with his failure to communicate with his relatives was not enough to show that he was absent from his residence without explanation. [Estate of Morrison v. Roswell, 92 Ill. 2d 207, 441 N.E.2d 68, 65 Ill. Dec. 276 (1982)]

In 1939, the Uniform Absence as Evidence of Death and Absentees Property Act reversed the common-law rules: the fact that a person had been absent for seven years (or any duration) or had been exposed to a specific peril did not set up a presumption of death; instead, these facts were merely evidence for a court or jury to consider in making its own finding of whether the absentee's death had occurred. [*See* Armstrong v. Pilot Life Ins. Co., 656 S.W.2d 18 (Tenn. Ct. App. 1983)]

The Uniform Probate Code, portions of which have been adopted in many states, returns to a presumption. A person is presumed dead after he or she has been absent for a continuous period, such as three, four, five, or seven years. [*Cf.* Minn. Stat. § 576.141; N.J. Stat. Ann. § 3B:27-1; N.Y. Est. Powers & Trusts Law § 2-1.7; 20 Pa. Cons. Stat. Ann. § 5701(c)] However, a person who seeks a declaration of the absentee's death must demonstrate to a court's satisfaction that the absentee has not been heard from after diligent search or inquiry and that his or her absence is not satisfactorily explained. [*E.g.*, 20 Pa. Cons. Stat. Ann. §§ 5702–5705] Unless sufficient evidence proves that death occurred sooner, the end of the waiting period is deemed the date of death. [*See, e.g.*, Hubbard v. Equitable Life Assurance Society of the United States, 248 Wis. 340, 21 N.W.2d 665 (1946); Hogaboam v. Metropolitan Life Ins. Co., 248 Wis. 146, 21 N.W.2d 268 (1946)]

The presumption of an absentee's death does not necessarily apply to all property in the same way. For example, some states do not use the presumption to provide a life insurance death benefit. [*E.g.*, Armstrong v. Pilot Life Ins. Co., 656 S.W.2d 18 (Tenn. Ct. App. 1983)]

Usually, the person who would benefit from the absentee's death bears the burden of proof.

Note. The terrorist attacks of September 11, 2001, and Hurricane Katrina in 2005 focused renewed attention on laws that permit a finding of death based on exposure to a specific peril. [*See* La. Civil Code art. 54; N.J. Stat. Ann. §§ 3B:27-1, 3B:27-6; N.Y. Est. Powers & Trusts Law § 2.17(b); 20 Pa. Cons. Stat. Ann. § 5701(c); *see also* Chiaramonte v. Chiaramonte, 435 N.Y.S.2d 523 (Sup. Ct. 1981); Zucker's Will, 219 N.Y.S.2d 72 (Sup. Ct. 1961); *In re* Estate of Bobrow, 179 N.Y.S.2d 742 (Sup. Ct. 1958); *In re* Brevoort's Will, 73 N.Y.S.2d 216 (Sup. Ct. 1947)]

An ERISA plan's administrator need not follow state law and instead may make its own rules and use discretion in deciding whether or when a person's death occurred. [*See* Estate of Slack ex rel. Apostal v. Laborer's Welfare & Pension Fund, 195 F. Supp. 2d 1052, 27 Employee Benefits Cas. (BNA) 2670 (N.D. Ill. 2002)]

Marriage

These questions explain some basics of marriage, as well as the differences between ceremonial marriage and informal or common-law marriage. Also, questions under this heading refer to same-sex marriages, including civil unions and domestic partnerships.

Q 8:37   Why is understanding the law of marriage important to beneficiary designations?

An important restraint on a beneficiary designation is a spouse's rights. Of course, these rights turn on a person's showing that he or she was a participant's spouse. Although many people are accustomed to thinking of a marriage certificate as evidence that a valid marriage occurred, sometimes it is unclear whether a marriage existed.

Q 8:38   What is marriage?

Marriage is a civil contract and a relation or status by which each of two persons agrees to live with the other as spouses, to the exclusion of others. States regulate marriage as part of their police power. Most states recognize a marriage contracted in another state, unless the marriage is contrary to a strong public policy of the forum state.

Q 8:39   What is a void marriage?

A void marriage is one that is invalid from its inception, and cannot be made valid. A marriage is void if:

- The parties are too closely related or
- Either party is married to someone else.

In some states, a later "marriage" becomes valid on the end of an earlier marriage, if both parties to the later "marriage" were unaware that the earlier marriage was undissolved when they entered into the later "marriage."

In some states, a marriage is void if the parties are of the same sex and a restriction against such a marriage is not contrary to the state's constitution or the United States Constitution (see Q 8:62).

Either party may "walk away" from a void marriage without waiting for a divorce or annulment.

Note. A fraudulently obtained marriage license, or a failure to obtain a license, might not by itself invalidate a marriage. [*See, e.g.*, Carabetta v. Carabetta, 182 Conn. 344, 438 A.2d 109 (1980)]

Q 8:40   What is a voidable marriage?

A voidable marriage is one that is initially invalid but remains in effect unless ended by a court order. For example, a marriage is voidable if either party was underage, drunk, or otherwise legally incompetent. Likewise, a marriage is voidable if someone used fraud, duress, or force to induce a party to "agree" to the marriage. The parties may ratify an otherwise voidable marriage by words or conduct after the removal of the impediment that made the marriage voidable.

Ceremonial Marriage

Q 8:41   What is a ceremonial marriage?

A ceremonial marriage is a marriage performed according to a state statute (other than a statute that recognizes common-law marriage). Many people prefer a ceremonial marriage to an informal or common-law marriage because a ceremonial marriage is easier to prove.

A license to marry is required, and is furnished by a state court or official upon approval of an application designed to check the parties' eligibility to marry. In most states, an application must state identifying information, information about each prior marriage of either applicant, and other facts necessary to find whether there is a legal impediment to the proposed marriage. A refusal to issue a marriage license is reviewable by a court. An application for a marriage license is a public record.

If either party is a minor or mentally incapacitated, most states require at least a guardian's approval, and sometimes a court's approval.

Most states provide that a judge, government official, or minister of a church may perform a ceremony. Some people use the term "civil marriage" to describe a ceremony led by a judge or government official, as distinguished from one solemnized by a church's minister. Some states permit the parties to perform their marriage ceremony. Some states permit (and others prohibit) a proxy marriage, a ceremony in which someone stands in for an absent party.

A failure to comply with statutory rules does not necessarily result in a void marriage. Sometimes a defect makes a marriage voidable rather than void. If a state recognizes common-law marriage, a defective ceremonial marriage often results in a valid common-law marriage.

Q 8:42   What is the effect of a marriage certificate?

A person who wants to prove that a marriage exists (or existed until the other person's death) may refer to the marriage certificate as evidence of the marriage's validity. Unless someone else shows persuasive evidence of a defect, a marriage certificate usually is strong evidence that the marriage occurred.

Common-Law Marriage

Q 8:43   What is a common-law marriage?

A common-law marriage (perhaps more appropriately called an informal marriage) is a marriage that was not solemnized by a ceremony but was created by the simple agreement of the parties. Each person must be legally capable of making a marriage contract and must state, orally or in writing, his or her present agreement to the relation of spouses, agreeing to live with his or her spouse to the exclusion of all others. In general, the exchange of words that makes the marriage must be in the present tense, and must state the marriage itself rather than an intent to marry.

Some people mistakenly assume that a period of cohabitation results in a common-law marriage, but that is not true under any state's law. Conversely, cohabitation is not necessary; the present agreement to the marriage is all that is needed. [*See generally* James Kent, Commentaries on American Law, vol. II, part IV, lect. XXVI, at 86–93 (1794)] However, Alabama law seems to require cohabitation as further evidence of the agreement to a marriage. [Herd v. Herd, 194 Ala. 613, 69 So. 885 (1915)] Likewise, Texas law suggests that an informal marriage "may be proved by evidence that . . . a man and woman . . . lived together in [Texas] as husband and wife[.]" [*See* Texas Family Code Ann. § 2.401(a)] Further, a "holding out" as spouses, while sometimes presented as evidence of a common-law marriage, is not always required. Even those who expressly denied to a third person that they were married may be married if they agreed (between themselves) to be married. [Polly v. Coffey, 2003 Ohio 509 (Ohio Ct. App. Feb. 3, 2003)] Nonetheless, because a court's consideration of whether a common-law marriage existed usually involves disputed or ambiguous facts, courts often consider cohabitation and "reputation"(whether third persons believed the couple were spouses) as evidence that might suggest how likely it is that the couple agreed to a marriage.

Note. Although England and Wales did not recognize common-law marriages (other than of Jews or Quakers) made after 1753, early America (even before the 1776 Declaration of Independence) was permitted to recognize common-law marriage because Britain's statute did not apply to Scotland, the Channel Islands, or Britain's colonies. [Lord Hardwicke's Act (Marriage Act), 1753, 26 Geo. II. c. 33 (Eng.)]

If the law of a state that recognizes common-law marriage (see Q 8:44) applies, a couple might be married, notwithstanding the absence of any ceremony or writing. Even an implication of consent to a marriage might be sufficient. [*In re* Garges' Estate, 474 Pa. 237, 378 A.2d 307 (Pa. 1977)] Also, a marriage ceremony that had a defect is likely to result in a common-law marriage. [*See, e.g., In re* Larry's Estate, 29 Fiduc. Rep. (Bisel) 298 (Pa. Common Pleas Orphans' Ct. Div. 1979)]

Practice Pointer. Usually, the absence of a ceremony (and of witnesses, other than the parties) makes it difficult to prove that a common-law marriage exists or existed. Often, there is an evidence law rule or presumption against the claimant testifying to the creation of the relationship. [*See, e.g.,* 20 Pa. Consol. Stat. § 2209; 42 Pa. Consol. Stat. § 5930; *see also* Estate of Stauffer v. Stauffer, 476 A.2d 354 (Pa. 1984); Wagner's Estate, 398 Pa. 531 (1960); Estate of Corace v. Graeser, 527 A.2d 1058 (Pa. Super. Ct. 1987)] Courts consider evidence of how each person described the relationship to third persons and how third persons understood the relationship. The use of names might be significant. [*E.g., In re* Erlanger's Estate, 145 Misc. 1, 259 N.Y.S. 610 (N.Y. Sur. 1932)] However, either spouse's denial of the marriage in records such as a driver's license, Social Security claims, tax returns, insurance applications, bank accounts, and wage records does not necessarily deny a common-law marriage. [*E.g.*, Dalworth Trucking Co. v. Bulen, 924 S.W.2d 728 (Tex. App. 1996); Estate of Giessel, 734 S.W.2d 27 (Tex. App. 1987)] The burden of proving a common-law marriage is on the person who asserts that it existed. [*E.g.*, Driscoll v. Driscoll, 220 Kan. 225, 227, 552 P.2d 629 (1976); *In re* Estate of Gavula, 490 Pa. 535, 417 A.2d 168 (Pa. 1980); *In re* Estate of Stauffer, 315 Pa. Super. 591, 462 A.2d 750 (1983), *rev. on other grounds,* 504 Pa. 626, 476 A.2d 354 (1983); *but see* Fiedler v. Nat'l Tube Co., 161 Pa. Super. 155, 53 A.2d 821 (1947)]

Usually, the burden of proof is on the person who claims that a common-law marriage was made. [*See, e.g.*, White v. State Farm Mutual Auto Ins. Co., 907 F. Supp. 1012 (E.D. Texas 1995)]

If a couple ever lived or even traveled in a state that recognizes or previously recognized common-law marriage (see Q 8:44), the couple could be married, notwithstanding the absence of any ceremony or writing.

Q 8:44   Which states recognize common-law marriage?

As of early 2009, Alabama, Colorado, Iowa, Kansas, Montana, New Hampshire, Oklahoma, Rhode Island, South Carolina, Texas, Utah, and the District of Columbia recognize a common-law marriage. [*Ex parte* Deborah Maudlin Creel, 719 So. 2d 783 (Ala. Sup. Ct. 1998); Colo. Rev. Stat. §§ 14-2-104 to 14-2-109.5 (on and after September 1, 2006 only those who are at least age 18 may contract a common-law marriage; earlier common-law marriages made when a party was under age 18 continue to be recognized); Nugent v. Nugent, 955 P.2d 584 (Colo. Ct. App. 1998); Iowa Dep't of Human Servs. *ex rel.* Greenhaw v. Stewart, 579 N.W.2d 32 (Iowa Sup. Ct. 1998); Shaddox v. Schoenberger, 19 Kan. App. 2d 361, 869 P.2d 249 (1994); Mont. Code Ann. § 40-1-403; N.H. Rev. Stat. Ann. § 457:39; Boyd v. Monsey Constr. Co., 959 P.2d 612 (Okla. Civ. App. 1998); Lovegrove v. McCutcheon, 712 A.2d 874 (R.I. Sup. Ct. 1998); Barker v. Barker, 330 S.C. 361, 499 S.E.2d 503 (App. 1998); Tex. Fam. Code § 1.91-101; Utah Code Ann. § 30-1-4.5; Berryman v. Thorne, 700 A.2d 181 (D.C. Ct. App. 1997)] New Hampshire recognizes common-law marriage for survivorship, but not for divorce. [N.H. Rev. Stat. Ann. § 457:39] States that abolished common-law marriage in the 1990s and later include Georgia, Idaho, Ohio, and Pennsylvania. [Ga. Code Ann. § 19-3-1.1; Idaho Code § 32-201; Ohio Rev. Code Ann. § 3105. 12; 23 Pa. Cons. Stat. Ann. § 1103]

Note. Pennsylvania abolished common-law marriage for marriages made *after* January 1, 2005, and expressly preserved those "contracted *on* or before January 1, 2005[.]" [23 Pa. Cons. Stat. § 1103] Thus, words spoken on that New Year's eve might have resulted in a marriage.

All states recognize a marriage that, even if it does not meet all requirements of local law, was valid under the laws of the state in which the spouses lived at the time they entered into the marriage. [*See, e.g.*, *In re* Estate of Lamb, 99 N.M. 157, 655 P.2d 1001 (1982); People v. Badgett, 10 Cal. 4th 330, 41 Cal. Rptr. 635,

895 P.2d 877 (1995); *see generally* Restatement (Second) of Conflict of Laws § 283(2) (1971)] Likewise, states recognize a marriage made according to a Native American Indian law or custom. [*See, e.g.*, Buck v. Branson, 34 Okla. 807, 127 P. 436 (1912); People *ex rel.* La Forte v. Rubin, 98 N.Y.S. 787 (1905); Kobogum v. Jackson Iron Co., 76 Mich. 498, 43 N.W. 602 (1899); Earl v. Godley, 42 Minn. 361, 44 N.W.254 (1890); Wall v. Williamson, 8 Ala. 48 (1844); Morgan v. McGhee, 24 Tenn. 13 (1844)] Further, some states that recognize common-law marriage internally recognize a marriage that the spouses entered into while they lived in another state, notwithstanding that the marriage was invalid in the other state. [*See, e.g.*, Dibble v. Dibble, 88 Ohio App. 490, 100 N.E.2d 451 (1950)] In many states that do not recognize a common-law marriage made in the state, children born during the invalid marriage may nevertheless be presumed to be the children of both the child's mother and the man who would be her common-law husband.

Because of the recognition that states give to other states' and nations' laws, it is possible for a common-law marriage to exist anywhere in the United States. Although the states that recognize informal marriage are the minority, the mobility of the American people enables many informal marriages. Indeed, even a weekend or one-day trip across state lines can result in a marriage. [*See, e.g.*, Tornese v. Tornese, 233 A.D.2d 316, 649 N.Y.S.2d 177 (App. Div. 1996); Carpenter v. Carpenter, 208 A.D.2d 882, 617 N.Y.S.2d 903 (App. Div. 1994); Kellard v. Kellard, 13 Fam. L. Rep. (BNA) 1490 (N.Y. Sup. Ct. 1987); In re Seymour, 113 Misc. 421, 185 N.Y.S. 373 (N.Y. Sur. 1920)] Further, among states that currently do not recognize common-law marriage, almost half allowed it when persons still alive might have married.

Q 8:45 How does common-law marriage affect a non-ERISA benefit?

State law (or a Native American tribe's law) may provide that if a participant has a spouse, some or all of a retirement plan benefit belongs to the spouse (see Q 8:26). If the law of a state that recognizes common-law marriage (see Q 8:44) applies, the couple may be married notwithstanding the absence of any ceremony or writing.

A payer is protected in making a payment according to the beneficiary designation. For a benefit paid under a non-ERISA plan, the distributee receives any payment subject to the spouse's rights.

Example. George and Carmen lived in Pennsylvania throughout their working lives. In early 1999, before George met Carmen, George named his brother, Bill, as the beneficiary on George's Roth IRA. Even after his marriage to Carmen in late 1999, and the birth of their children, Diana in 2000 and Samuel in 2001, it never occurred to George that he should change any beneficiary designation. After George's retirement, George and Carmen moved to a retirement community in Cazenovia, New York. George died without having made any will. After George died, Bill sent in a claim to the custodian, which paid Bill all of George's Roth IRA balance. On his death,

George's Roth IRA balance was $200,000, and his probate assets were $60,000. There was nothing else.

(For ease of illustration, both parts of this example omit family exemption, homestead allowance, funeral and administration expenses, debts, taxes of all kinds, and lawyers' fees.)

If Carmen does not elect to take an elective share of George's augmented estate (which includes non-probate retirement plan benefits), George's estate would be divided as follows:

	Roth IRA	Probate Estate	Augmented Estate	Share
Carmen	$ 0	$ 55,000	$ 55,000	21%
Diana	$ 0	$ 2,500	$ 2,500	1%
Samuel	$ 0	$ 2,500	$ 2,500	1%
Bill	$200,000	$ 0	$200,000	77%
Total	$200,000	$ 60,000	$260,000	

[N.Y. Est. Powers & Trusts § 4-1.1(a)(1)]

If Carmen elects to take an elective share of George's augmented estate, George's estate would be divided as follows:

	Augmented Estate	Share
Carmen	$ 86,666.67	33.33%
Diana	$ 0	0 %
Samuel	$ 0	0 %
Bill	$173,333.33	66.66%
Total	$260,000.00	100.00%

[N.Y. Est. Powers & Trusts § 5-1.1-A(a)(2), (c)]

Because George's probate estate is insufficient to pay Carmen the amount to which she is entitled, Bill must pay Carmen $26,666.67. [N.Y. Est. Powers & Trusts § 5-1.1-A(c)]

In some states, dower and curtesy might provide additional or related rights to a spouse. In some states, a spouse's election of (or right to elect) a forced share is "in lieu of" dower and curtesy rights. [E.g., N.Y. Est. Powers & Trusts Law §§ 5-1.1(d)(9), 5-1.1-A(c)(8)] Many states simply abolished dower and curtesy. [See generally Unif. Probate Code § 2-112, 8 pt. I U.L.A. 90–91 (1998); Restatement (Third) of Property: Wills and Other Donative Transfers § 9.1 comment c (2003)]

Q 8:46   How does common-law marriage affect a beneficiary designation?

A plan might provide that some or all of a death benefit belongs to a spouse (see Q 8:27). State law may provide that if a participant has a spouse, some or all of a retirement plan benefit belongs to the spouse (see Q 8:28). If a couple ever lived (or even traveled) in a state that recognizes or then recognized common-law marriage (see Q 8:44), the couple may be married notwithstanding the absence of any ceremony or writing. A recognized common-law marriage is no less a marriage than a ceremonial marriage. [*Cf.* 5 C.F.R. § 630.1202] Many states recognize common-law marriage (see Q 8:44).

> **Example.** Harold and Wendy lived together in Alabama. Harold never made any beneficiary designation under his employer's ERISA-governed 401(k) plan (which included Roth accounts). The plan provides that, in the absence of a beneficiary designation, a surviving spouse is entitled to the participant's account. When Wendy calls to ask about this plan benefit, the employer tells Wendy that it has no record that Wendy is Harold's spouse. Wendy files the plan's claim form, and attaches to it an affidavit that states facts that, if correct, would prove that her relationship with Harold was a common-law marriage under Alabama law. Because the employer, acting as plan administrator, does not receive any contrary information, it decides that Wendy is Harold's surviving spouse. The plan administrator decides to pay the full benefit as Wendy requested.

> **Practice Pointer.** A plan administrator must act as an expert when deciding plan claims. [ERISA § 404(a)(1)] Therefore, a plan administrator should obtain expert legal advice to evaluate a person's claim that he or she is the common-law spouse of a participant. Although a plan administrator should consult a lawyer who has sufficient expert knowledge and skill, the lawyer need not be admitted to law practice in the state in which the claimant asserts that he or she married the participant; it is enough that the lawyer is admitted to law practice in *any* state. [D.O.L. ERISA Adv. Op. 2005-16A (June 10, 2005)]

Some people assume that common-law marriage does not apply to a couple in which both persons are of the same sex. At least one court decision found that common-law marriage does not apply to a couple in which both persons are of the same sex. However, that decision has limited value as precedent because the intermediate appeals court did not consider arguments that had not been presented to the trial court. [DeSanto v. Barnsley, 328 Pa. Super. 181, 476 A.2d 952 (1984)] Discrimination against a same-sex couple or their marriage might be contrary to the U.S. Constitution or a state constitution (see Qs 8:47–8:62).

Same-Sex Marriage

Q 8:47   In what ways might a same-sex couple be recognized as spouses?

There are at least five ways a same-sex couple might be recognized as spouses:

1. The couple married in another nation.
2. The couple married in a state that provides same-sex marriage.
3. The couple married in a state that previously provided same-sex marriage.
4. The couple are parties to a civil union or domestic partnership governed by the laws of a state that provides that the rights and burdens of such a relationship are identical to the rights and burdens of another marriage.
5. The couple are domestic partners under a state's law and, for the particular plan purpose involved, a relevant state's law provides a right or burden that makes a domestic partner a spouse for the purpose involved.

Note. New Jersey law has four sets of statutes for marriage: two different statutes for opposite-sex couples and two different statutes for same-sex couples. Concerning same-sex couples, New Jersey law recognizes a civil union that has the same legal rights and burdens as an opposite-sex marriage. New Jersey also recognizes, if it was made before February 19, 2007 or was or is made by persons who are 62 or older, a domestic partnership, which under New Jersey law provides fewer rights and burdens.

Caution. New Jersey recognizes a same-sex relationship established under the law of another state or of a foreign nation. But the other state's or nation's name for a relationship does not control its treatment under New Jersey law. "Rather, it is the nature of the rights conferred by another jurisdiction that will determine how a relationship will be treated under New Jersey law." [N.J. Atty. Gen. Formal Opinion No. 3-2007 (Feb. 16, 2007) (available at *http://www.state.nj.us/health/vital/documents/legal_advice_ssm.pdf*) (visited on June 25, 2009)] Therefore, a domestic partnership made under California law is a civil union under New Jersey law.

States recognize a marriage that, even if it does not meet all requirements of local law, was valid under the laws of the state in which the spouses lived at the time they entered into the marriage. [*See generally* Restatement (Second) of Conflict of Laws § 283(2) (1971)] This rule is so strong that states have recognized an incestuous marriage. [*See, e.g., In re* Estate of May, 305 N.Y. 486, 114 N.E.2d 4 (1953); *see also* Campione v. Campione, 201 Misc. 590 (N.Y. Sup. Ct. 1951)]

Q 8:48   Does a state of the United States recognize a foreign nation's marriage?

Yes, a state of the United States will recognize a marriage made according to the law of a foreign nation in which the marriage was made. [*See, e.g.,* Hallett v. Collins, 51 U.S. 174 (1850); Montano v. Montano, 520 So. 2d 52 (Fla. Dist. Ct. App. 1988); People v. Imes, 68 N.W. 157 (Mich. 1896); Miller v. Miller, 128 N.Y.S. 787 (Sup. 1911); Ferrie v. Pub. Adm'r, 3 Bradf. Sur. 151 (N.Y. Sur. 1855)] Even common-law or defective marriages in a foreign nation have been recognized as legitimate marriages in the United States. [*See, e.g.,* Overseers of Poor of Town of Newbury v. Overseers of Poor of Town of Brunswick, 2 Vt. 151 (1829). *Cf.* Metropolitan Life Ins. Co. v. Holding, 293 F. Supp. 854 (E.D. Va.

1968); Matter of Lamb's Estate, 655 P.2d 1001 (N.M. 1982) *But see* Randall v. Randall, 345 N.W.2d 319 (Neb. 1984)] A court will even recognize a marriage that might be contrary to the norms of the forum state. [*See, e.g.*, United States v. Lee Sa Kee, 3 U.S. Dist. Ct. Haw. 265 (1908); Estate of Dalip Singh Bir, 83 Cal. App. 2d 256, 188 P.2d 499 (1948) (More than 50 years before the decedent's death in California, two women had married him in the Punjab Province of British India "according to the law and manner of the Jat community"); *see also* Sousa v. Freitas, 10 Cal. App. 3d 660, 89 Cal. Rptr. 485 (1970)] However, a court will not recognize as a marriage a relationship that under foreign law does not provide the usual rights of marriage. [*See, e.g.*, American Airlines v. Mejia, 766 So. 2d 305 (Fla. Dist. Ct. App. 2000)]

A state's refusal to recognize a foreign nation's marriage could lead to an international conflict. [*See generally* Universal Declaration of Human Rights; Covenant on Civil and Political Rights; Covenant on Economic, Social and Cultural Rights; Restatement (Third) Foreign Relations Law of the United States § 701 (1987)]

Q 8:49   Do other nations recognize same-sex marriages?

Belgium, Canada, the Netherlands, South Africa, and Spain recognize same-sex marriage.

At least Andorra, Argentina, Australia, Brazil, Colombia, Croatia, the Czech Republic, Denmark, Finland, France, Germany, Greenland, Hungary, Iceland, Israel, Italy, Luxembourg, Mexico, Namibia, New Zealand, Norway, Portugal, Slovenia, South Africa, Sweden, Switzerland, and the United Kingdom (including England, Wales, Scotland, and Northern Ireland) recognize various forms of same-sex marriages. However, not all of these relationships have the same rights and burdens as those of a U.S. state's opposite-sex marriage, and so some might not be recognized for some purposes under a state's law.

Q 8:50   Does Massachusetts provide marriage for same-sex couples?

Yes. The Massachusetts constitution requires that the Commonwealth provide marriage to a same-sex couple (who are Massachusetts residents) if it provides marriage to an opposite-sex couple. [Goodridge v. Dep't of Pub. Health, 440 Mass. 309, 798 N.E.2d 941 (Mass. 2003); *see also In re* Opinions of the Justices to the Senate, 440 Mass. 1201, 802 N.E.2d 565 (Mass. 2004); Cote-Whitacre v. Dep't of Pub. Health, 446 Mass. 350 (2006)]

Q 8:51   Does California provide marriage for same-sex couples?

Maybe. For a marriage (other than a domestic partnership) made in California, California law recognizes a marriage of a same-sex couple if the marriage was made on or after 5 p.m. June 16, 2008 and no later than November 4, 2008. [Strauss v. Horton, 46 Cal. 4th 364, 207 P.3d 48, 93 Cal. Rptr. 3d 591, 2009 Cal. LEXIS 4626 (May 26, 2009) (An amendment to California's constitution to restrict the use of the word *marriage* to opposite-sex couples is not a precluded revision if California law provides for a same-sex couple equal rights of marriage under a different word or phrase.), *later proceedings*, 2009 Cal. LEXIS 5433, 5434, 5474, *modified by* 2009 Cal. LEXIS 5416 (June 17, 2009), *reh'g denied*, 2009 Cal. LEXIS 5652 (Cal. June 17, 2009)] A California domestic partnership has rights and burdens identical to those of an opposite-sex couple's marriage. [Cal. Fam. Code § 297.5; *see also In re* Domestic Partnership of Ellis, 76 Cal. Rptr. 3d 401 (Ct. App. 2008)]

Q 8:52   How does a Vermont civil union of a same-sex couple affect a beneficiary designation?

As discussed elsewhere in this chapter, applicable law might provide that after the death of a participant who was a party to a Vermont civil union, some or all of a retirement plan benefit must be provided to the other party to the civil union to the extent necessary to provide such a spouse his or her property rights.

Vermont law provides that same-sex couples must have the opportunity to obtain the same benefits and protections afforded by Vermont law to married opposite-sex couples. [Vt. Const. ch. I, art. 7; Baker v. Vermont, 744 A.2d 864 (Vt. 1999)] Under Vermont statutes, the same-sex parties to a civil union have the same benefits, protections, and responsibilities as those provided for spouses in any other marriage. [15 Vt. Stat. Ann. §§ 1201(2), 1204(a)] This rule applies whether the source of law is statute, administrative regulation, court rule, policy, common law, or any other source of civil law. [15 Vt. Stat. Ann. § 1204(a)] Further, a party to a civil union is included in any definition or use of the term spouse as that term is used in any Vermont law. [15 Vt. Stat. Ann. § 1204(b)]

Vermont law provides that a surviving spouse has a right to at least one-third of his or her spouse's personal estate. [14 Vt. Stat. Ann. §§ 401-402] A court has power to enter an order relating to nonprobate property, such as a retirement plan benefit, when necessary to give effect to a surviving spouse's property rights. [14 Vt. Stat. Ann. § 1721]

Q 8:53   What is a domestic partnership?

A domestic partnership is a quasi-marriage recognized for some (but not all) purposes under some states' laws.

Q 8:54   Which states provide for a domestic-partnership relationship?

Currently, the District of Columbia, Hawaii, Maine, New Jersey, and Washington register these relationships. [*See, e.g.,* Hawaii Rev. Stat. § 572C-4; Maine RSA § 1-201, subsections 10-A and 10-B; N.J. Domestic Partnership Act § 4.b; Wash 60th Legislature 2007 Regular Session, An act relating to protecting individuals by granting certain rights and benefits (enacted Apr. 20, 2007) (effective 90 days after the adjournment of that session)] Other states, including California, use the "domestic partner" label to refer to a relationship that has rights and burdens identical to those of an opposite-sex couple's marriage. [*See, e.g.,* Cal. Fam. Code § 297.5; *see also In re* Domestic Partnership of Ellis, 76 Cal. Rptr. 3d 401 (Ct. App. 2008)]

Note. New Jersey recognizes domestic partnerships made before February 19, 2007, and allows a couple (whether opposite-sex or same-sex) to register a domestic partnership on or after that date only if *both* parties are 62 or older. [N.J. Stat. Ann. § 26:8A-4.b.(5)]

Q 8:55   Who may form a domestic partnership?

In the states that register domestic partnerships (see Q 8:54), a same-sex couple may form a domestic partnership.

In New Jersey, an opposite-sex or same-sex couple may form a domestic partnership if both persons are 62 or older. [N.J. Stat. Ann. § 26:8A-4.b.(5)] In California, an opposite-sex couple may form a domestic partnership if one person is older than 62 and is eligible for Social Security old-age benefits. [Cal. Family Code § 297(b)(6)(B)]

For either a same-sex or an opposite-sex domestic partnership, both partners must:

- Be 18 or older
- Be unrelated
- Live together
- Be financially responsible for one another's living expenses
- Have some joint financial arrangements
- Be in a committed relationship of mutual caring

In addition, neither partner can be a spouse or domestic partner with anyone else. [*See, e.g.,* Haw. Rev. Stat. Ann. § 572C-4 (referring to a "reciprocal beneficiary" rather than a "domestic partner")]

Q 8:56   What are some of the rights of a domestic partner?

In the states that provide a domestic-partner relationship, a domestic partner's rights typically include civil rights concerning personal dignity, autonomy, and nondiscrimination; rights concerning health insurance (other than an employer-funded or noninsured health plan). Some states make a domestic partner similar to a spouse for state income tax purposes. [*See, e.g.,* N.J. Stat. Ann. §§ 54A:1-2.e, 54A:3-1(b)2, 54A:3-1(b)1] Likewise, some states treat a domestic partner as a spouse for inheritance tax purposes. [N.J. Rev. Stat. §§ 54:34-1.f, 54:34-2.a.(1), 54:34-4.j]

Q 8:57   Does a surviving domestic partner have a right to "inherit" from the other's estate?

A domestic partner in California has the same community-property rights as a spouse. [Cal. Family Code §§ 297-299] A reciprocal beneficiary in Hawaii has the same elective-share rights as a spouse. [Haw. Rev. Stat. § 560:2-202] A domestic partner in Maine has the same elective-share rights as a spouse. [Me. Rev. Stat. Ann. § 102]

Q 8:58   Is an opposite-sex domestic partner a spouse under federal laws?

It is unclear whether an opposite-sex domestic partner is a spouse. A domestic partner might be a spouse under some federal laws but not be a spouse under other federal laws.

The state legislatures that enacted domestic-partner laws appear to have intended that an opposite-sex domestic partner enjoy some or all incidents of marriage while avoiding some burdens of marriage under federal laws. [*See, e.g.*, N.J. Senate, Judiciary Committee Statement on a substitute for S. 2820 (Dec. 15, 2003) ("In authorizing domestic partnerships only for opposite sex couples who are age 62 and older, the committee recognizes that older persons often refrain from entering into marriage because remarriage could jeopardize their status as surviving spouse with regard to retirement income and benefits."); *see also* Cal. Stats. 2003, c. 421 (AB 205) § 15 ("This act shall be construed liberally in order to secure to eligible couples who register as domestic partners the full range of legal rights, protections and benefits, as well as all of the responsibilities, obligations, and duties to each other, to their children, to third parties [,] and to the state, as the laws of California extend to and impose upon spouses.") (emphasis added)]

But it is not clear that an opposite-sex couple can have it both ways; an opposite-sex domestic partner might be a spouse under some federal laws. [*See* 1 U.S.C. § 7] A domestic partnership includes the usual attributes of marriage: cohabitation, exclusivity, mutual dependence, financial responsibility, and (in many states) a presumed transfer of property to a surviving spouse. Therefore, a government agency or court might find that opposite-sex domestic partners live together as husband and wife and that the rights not provided by state law (if any) are irrelevant or insignificant in deciding whether the partners are spouses under a particular federal law.

Q 8:59   Is a same-sex domestic partner a spouse under federal laws?

If Section 7 of Title 1 of the United States Code is not unconstitutional, a same-sex domestic partner is not a spouse under any federal statute. [1 U.S.C. § 7] If Section 7 of Title 1 of the United States Code is unconstitutional, a same-sex domestic partner might be a spouse under some or all federal laws if the rights not provided by state law (if any) are irrelevant or insignificant in deciding whether the partners are spouses under a particular federal law. [*See* 1 U.S.C. § 7]

Q 8:60   Does the United States Constitution require recognition of a same-sex marriage?

Maybe. A discrimination against a same-sex couple or their marriage might be contrary to the United States Constitution, and therefore of no legal effect. [*See* U.S. Const. art. IV sec. 1 & Fifth Amendment]

Q 8:61   Could a state constitution require recognition of a same-sex marriage?

Maybe. A discrimination against a same-sex couple or their marriage might be contrary to a state constitution, and therefore of no effect. [*Compare* Goodridge v. Dep't Pub. Health, 440 Mass. 309, 798 N.E.2d 941 (2003) (Massachusetts' constitution requires that the Commonwealth provide full marriage to a same-sex couple to the same extent that it provides marriage to an opposite-sex couple); Lewis v. Harris, 188 N.J. 415 (2006) (New Jersey constitution requires same-sex marriage); Baker v. Vermont, 744 A.2d 864 (Vt. 1999) (Vermont's constitution requires that a same-sex couple must have the opportunity to obtain the same benefits and protections afforded by Vermont law to a married opposite-sex couple) *with* Hernandez v. Robles, 2006 N.Y. slip op. 5239, 2006 LEXIS 1836 (Ct. App. July 6, 2006) (New York constitution does not require same-sex marriage); Andersen v. King County, 138 P.3d 963 (Wash. 2006) (Washington constitution does not require same-sex marriage)]

Q 8:62   Must a state recognize a same-sex marriage made in another state?

Maybe. A federal statute states that a state need not recognize a same-sex marriage established in another state:

> No State . . . shall be required to give effect to any public act, record, or judicial proceeding of any other State . . . respecting a relationship between persons of the same sex that is treated as a marriage under the laws of such other State . . . or a right or claim arising from such relationship.

[28 U.S.C. § 1738C] It is unclear whether this statute is law, because it might be unconstitutional. [*See* U.S. Const. art. IV sec. 1 & Fifth Amendment]

Spouse's Rights

Q 8:63   What are the ways a participant's surviving spouse might have rights to a participant's retirement plan benefit?

A participant's surviving spouse might have rights to a participant's retirement plan or IRA benefit as:

- Spouse's-consent rights provided by the plan (see Qs 8:64–8:94)
- Elective-share rights under state law (see Qs 8:86–8:88)
- Community-property rights under state law (see Qs 8:89–8:84)

ERISA Survivor Benefits or Spouse's-Consent Rights

Q 8:64   What rights does ERISA provide for a participant's surviving spouse?

A plan that is governed by Part 2 of Subtitle B of Title I of ERISA (or a Section 401 qualified plan that is not a governmental plan or a church plan) must provide some kind of benefit to a participant's spouse. The form of the required benefit turns on whether a distribution begins before or after the participant's death.

For a distribution that begins before a participant's death, a plan must, unless an exception applies, provide a qualified joint and survivor annuity (QJSA). [ERISA §§ 205(a)(1), 205(b)] Ordinarily, a defined contribution plan that is not governed by ERISA funding standards need not provide a QJSA as long as a participant does not elect that his or her retirement plan benefit be paid as a life annuity. [ERISA § 205(b)(1)(C)(ii)]

> **Practice Pointer.** Previously, the IRS had an informal view that merely providing an annuity as a plan's default distribution option was, in effect, a participant's election of that annuity for the purposes of the survivor-annuity rule. The IRS no longer takes that position. Nonetheless, if a plan provides a life annuity as a normal form of benefit, a plan sponsor may amend the plan to provide that every annuity is an optional form of benefit, or to eliminate every annuity option. Such an amendment is not a cutback of accrued benefits. [ERISA § 204(g)(2)(B); Treas. Reg. § 1.411(d)-4/Q & A-2(e)] Once the amendment is effective, the plan need not provide a QJSA unless (if the plan permits) a participant affirmatively chooses it or chooses a different life annuity and fails to deliver a qualified election.

> **Practice Pointer.** A practitioner should thoroughly consider all significant tax treatments before he or she suggests that a participant choose a single-sum or other short-term payout. In some states, only a life annuity or periodic payments similar to a life annuity will qualify for favorable treatment as a "pension" under state income tax laws. [*See, e.g.,* N.Y. Tax Law §§ 612, 617-a; 72 Pa. Consol. Stat. § 7301(d)(3), 7303; 61 Pa. Code § 101.6(c); Bickford v. Commonwealth, 533 A.2d 822 (Pa. 1987)]

For a distribution that begins after a participant's death, a plan must provide a qualified pre-retirement survivor annuity or an alternate survivor benefit. [ERISA § 205(a)(2), 205(b)]

Q 8:65   What is a qualified joint and survivor annuity?

A *qualified joint and survivor annuity* is an annuity for the participant's life with a survivor annuity for his or her surviving spouse's life. The periodic payment of the survivor annuity must be no less than 50 percent (and no more than 100 percent) of the payment during the joint lives of the participant and his or her spouse. A QJSA is the actuarial equivalent of an annuity only on the participant's life. [ERISA § 205(d)]

Note. If a plan governed by Part 2 of Subtitle B of Title I of ERISA provides a qualified joint and survivor annuity, the plan must permit a participant to elect that his or her benefit be paid as a *qualified optional survivor annuity*. A qualified optional survivor annuity (QOSA) means a joint-and-survivor annuity that includes a recurring payment in its survivor phase that is equal to the *applicable percentage* of the payment during the participant's life. If a plan's normal QJSA provides a survivor-phase payment that is less than 75 percent of the payment during the participant's life, the applicable percentage is 75. If a plan's normal QJSA provides a survivor-phase payment that is at least 75 percent of the payment during the participant's life, the applicable percentage is 50. As with other survivor-annuity forms, a qualified optional survivor annuity must be at least the actuarial equivalent of a single-life annuity for the participant's life. A plan that is required to provide a survivor annuity must provide at least two different QJSAs, in addition to a QPSA. A plan administrator's written explanations of a plan's survivor-annuity options must explain *all* of the options, including the new qualified optional survivor annuity. The minimum election period for survivor-annuity choices is 180 days. A plan amendment made solely to meet the QOSA requirement generally does not violate the anti-cutback rule. However, this anti-cutback relief does not protect taking away a subsidized QJSA unless an equivalent or greater subsidy remains in at least one of the amended plan's other payout forms of that kind. The new law requiring these QOSA provisions applies to plan years that began or begin on or after January 1, 2008. A later date could apply to a plan maintained under a collective-bargaining agreement. [ERISA § 205(c)-(d), as amended by Pension Protection Act of 2006 (PPA) § 1004]

A surviving-spouse benefit under a QJSA vests irrevocably as of the annuity starting date. Only the person who was the participant's spouse on the annuity starting date—not any subsequent spouse—is entitled to the survivor benefit (if that spouse survives the participant). [Hopkins v. AT&T Global Info. Solutions Co., 105 F.3d 153 (4th Cir. 1997); Carmona v. Carmona, 544 F.3d 988 (9th Cir. 2008); Robinson v. New Orleans Employers ILA AFL-CIO Pension, Welfare, Vacation & Funds Holiday Funds, 40 Employee Benefits Cas. (BNA) 2937 (E.D. La. Apr. 2, 2007); *see also* McGowan v. NJR Serv. Corp., 423 F.3d 241 (3d Cir. 2005), *cert. denied*, 127 S. Ct. 1118 (2007)]

Practice Pointer. An exception to the rule that a participant's surviving spouse is the person that was his or her spouse on the relevant date—the participant's death for a QPSA or alternate survivor benefit, or the annuity starting date for a QJSA—is that a qualified domestic-relations order may specify that a person, even if he or she no longer is the participant's spouse, is deemed to be the participant's surviving spouse.

Q 8:66   What is a qualified optional survivor annuity?

Sometimes, a joint-and-survivor annuity provides the same recurring payment to the survivor as was payable to the first annuitant—this is a 100 percent survivor annuity. But sometimes the recurring payment of the survivor phase is less than that of the first phase. Under current law, the payment in the survivor phase of a QJSA may be at any percentage from 50 to 100.

If a plan must provide a survivor annuity, the plan must (for plan years that begin on or after January 1, 2008) permit a participant to elect that his or her retirement benefit be paid as a qualified optional survivor annuity.

A qualified optional survivor annuity means a joint-and-survivor annuity that includes a recurring payment in its survivor phase that is equal to the applicable percentage of the payment during the participant's life. If a plan's normal QJSA provides a survivor-phase payment that is less than 75 percent of the payment during the participant's life, the applicable percentage is 75. If a plan's normal QJSA provides a survivor-phase payment that is at least 75 percent of the payment during the participant's life, the applicable percentage is 50.

> **Example.** A plan that provides a participant a choice between a QJSA with a 100 percent survivor annuity and a QJSA with a 50 percent survivor annuity would meet the QOSA rule.

As with other survivor-annuity forms, a QOSA must be at least the actuarial equivalent of a single-life annuity for the participant's life.

Thus, a plan that is required to provide a survivor annuity (and does not subsidize the QJSA, which would be unlikely for a defined-contribution plan) must provide at least two different QJSAs, in addition to a QPSA.

A plan administrator's written explanation of a plan's survivor-annuity options must explain all of the options, including the qualified optional survivor annuity. The minimum election period for survivor-annuity choices is 180 days.

> **Note.** A plan amendment made solely to meet the QOSA requirement generally does not violate the anti-cutback rule.

> **Practice Pointer.** Although the QOSA rule applies to plan years that begin on or after January 1, 2008, an in-operation provision may be confirmed by a plan amendment made by the last day of the first plan year that began or begins on or after January 1, 2009—that is, by December 31, 2009 for a calendar-year plan. [PPA of 2006 § 1107]

Q 8:67   What is a qualified pre-retirement survivor annuity?

For a defined-contribution plan, a *qualified pre-retirement survivor annuity* (QPSA) is the annuity that results from using no less than half the participant's vested account balance to buy an annuity for the surviving spouse's life. [ERISA § 205(e)(2)]

Q 8:68   What is an alternative survivor benefit?

For a defined contribution plan that is not governed by ERISA's or the Internal Revenue Code's funding standards, a plan may omit both a qualified joint and survivor annuity and a qualified preretirement survivor annuity if the plan (in addition to meeting other conditions) provides that, absent a qualified election, the benefit that remains after a participant's death belongs to the participant's surviving spouse. [ERISA § 205(b)(1)(C)]

Q 8:69   What is a qualified election?

An ERISA plan must include a provision that assures a participant's surviving spouse some retirement income after the participant's death, and must include a provision that assures a survivor benefit if the participant dies before he or she receives or begins a distribution. [ERISA § 205] A plan must permit a participant to "waive" one or more of these benefits. [ERISA § 205(c)(1)(A)] To do so, a participant must deliver to the plan administrator a qualified election. [ERISA § 205(c)(2)] Ordinarily, such an election has no effect unless the participant's spouse consents to the election. [ERISA § 205(c)(2)(A)] Also, a participant's qualified election must meet several form, content, and procedure requirements.

Q 8:70   Who is a spouse?

In some circumstances, it can be unclear, for the purposes of ERISA Section 205, whether a person is or is not a spouse, and which of two or more persons is a participant's spouse or surviving spouse.

ERISA states no definition for its use of the word *spouse*. Further, ERISA states no provision concerning whether a putative spouse is or is not a spouse for any purpose of ERISA Section 205.

> **Practice Pointer.** If a plan administrator makes a discretionary decision on whether a person does or does not have a spouse, the administrator should follow ERISA's claims-procedure rules, obtain information necessary to evaluate the claims and other questions presented, compile a sound administrative record, explain its decisions, and further act with care so that a court may defer to the administrator's decisions. [*See, e.g.*, Blessing v. Deere & Co., 985 F. Supp. 886–899, 899–907 (S.D. Iowa 1997)]

Q 8:71   Is a separated spouse a spouse for survivor-annuity or spouse's-consent purposes?

Yes. No matter how long a separation continues, a marriage does not end until a court orders the divorce.

> **Example.** In 1984, Barbara and Alfred separated. In 1986, Alfred sued for divorce. In 1991, Alfred died. A divorce had not been ordered. Despite seven years' separation, Barbara was Alfred's wife until his death. Although the plan had previously paid distributions, she was entitled to the survivor portion of the qualified joint and survivor annuity that would have been paid in the absence of her consent. [Davis v. College Suppliers Co., 813 F. Supp. 1234 (S.D. Miss. 1993)]

Even a finding of fact that the spouse abandoned the participant would be irrelevant. [*In re* Lefkowitz, 767 F. Supp. 501, 508 (S.D.N.Y. 1991), *aff'd sub nom.* Lefkowitz v. Arcadia Trading Co. Ltd. Defined Benefit Pension Plan, 969 F.2d 600, 16 Employee Benefits Cas. (BNA) 2516, Pens. Plan Guide (CCH) ¶ 23880Z (2d Cir. 1993)]

Q 8:72   When a participant is survived by a spouse and a putative spouse, which one is treated as the participant's surviving spouse?

No rule exists; whether a putative spouse, a real spouse, both, or neither is treated as a participant's spouse depends on a plan administrator's, arbitrator's, or judge's thoughts about what might be desirable in the particular circumstances.

The following two cases had opposite results. In the contributing author's view, neither court explained the real reason for its decision.

Example 1. In 1965, John and Susie married in Louisiana. In 1970, a Louisiana court ordered a judgment of separation, but not any divorce or dissolution of John and Susie's marriage. In 1973, Susie, while still married to John, "married" Milton. In 2000, John, while still married to Susie, "married" Gwendolyn in Texas. In 2001, John died (while still married to Susie and "married" to Gwendolyn). He was domiciled in Texas when he died. After John's death, Susie and Gwendolyn each submitted claims to his pension plan for a survivor annuity; each claimed that she was John's surviving spouse. The pension plan included the following provision: "All questions pertaining to the validity of construction of this Pension Plan shall be determined in accordance with the laws of the State of Illinois and, to the extent of preemption[,] with the laws and regulations of the United States." (As cited below, these are the relevant facts of a real case.)

In resolving the plan administrator's interpleader, the court considered whether to apply Louisiana law, Texas law, Illinois law, or some combination of them in deciding which claimant (if either) was John's surviving spouse. Notwithstanding that neither of the claimants had argued for it, the court chose Texas law. Further, the court used Texas *property* law to resolve the *status* question needed to apply an ERISA plan's provision that preempts state law. Following this, the court found that Susie's acceptance of the benefits of her fraudulent "marriage" to Milton precluded her from asserting that she was John's surviving spouse, and recognized Gwendolyn as an innocent putative spouse to be treated as if she had been a spouse. [Cent. States, Se. & Sw. Areas Pension Fund v. Gray, 2003 WL 22339272 (N.D. Ill. Oct 10, 2003)]

Example 2. In 1966, Douglas married Ann in Ohio. They lived together in Ohio from 1966 to 1982. In 1972, Douglas began a relationship with Rita. In 1982, Ann left Douglas and moved to Tennessee. In 1985, Douglas and Rita "married" in Nevada. Ann and Rita each submitted claims for several benefits to be provided to Douglas' surviving spouse. The pension plan provided that it "shall be construed, governed[,] and administered in accordance with the laws of the State of Michigan[,] except where [sic] otherwise required by Federal law."

In resolving the plan administrator's interpleader, the court considered whether to apply Federal law, Michigan law, or Ohio law, or some combination of them in deciding which claimant (if either) was John's surviving spouse. [Croskey v. Ford Motor Co.-UAW, 2002 U.S. Dist. LEXIS 8824 (S.D.N.Y. May 6, 2002)]

Note 1. In both of these cases, the court did not apply the contractual choice of law and, even further, ignored the plan's provision that the plan be construed using the plan-specified State law.

Note 2. Courts' procedures for interpleaders, which focus on the arguments of the competing claimants and often do not require a stakeholder to assert a position, increase the likelihood that a court will render a decision that is unhelpful for future plan administration.

Practice Pointer. Before deciding to interplead competing claims, a fiduciary should consider which person or persons will pay the attorneys' fees and other expenses of the interpleader. If the plan might bear the expenses, a fiduciary should consider whether paying the expenses is a prudent or necessary use of plan assets. Instead, a plan administrator might use claims procedures and the deference afforded to a discretionary decision maker to protect the plan against "double" liability, while setting up some opportunity for lower expenses (or, at least, delaying an expense) or even no incremental expense.

Q 8:73   What is a spouse's consent?

Usually, an election is a qualified election only if the participant's spouse consents to it. In addition to meeting other form, content, and procedure requirements, a spouse's consent to a participant's election must

1. Be in writing;
2. Name a beneficiary that cannot be changed without the spouse's consent, or expressly consent to the participant's beneficiary designations (without further consent);
3. Acknowledge the effect of the participant's election; and
4. Be "witnessed by a plan representative or a notary public[.]"

[ERISA § 205(c)(2)(A)(i)-(iii)]

The courts have held that a plan administrator must comply strictly with these requirements, even if there is no doubt that a spouse's consent was informed, voluntary and genuine. [*See, e.g.,* McMillan v. Parrott, 913 F.2d 310 (6th Cir. 1990); Lasche v. George W. Lasche Basic Ret. Plan, 870 F. Supp. 336 (S.D. Fla. 1994); *see also* Alfieri v. Guild Times Pension Plan, 446 F. Supp. 2d 99, 112–113 (E.D.N.Y. 2006)] A spouse's sworn statement in his or her spouse's consent that the spouse consents to the participant's beneficiary designation is ineffective if in fact the beneficiary-designation part of the documents had not been completed when the spouse signed. [ERISA§ 205(c)(2)(A); Davis v. Adelphia Commc'ns Corp., 475 F. Supp. 2d 600 (W.D. Va. 2007); *but see* Vilas v. Lyons, 702 F. Supp. 555 (D. Md. 1988) (a plan administrator may rely on a spouse's sworn statement that he or she received and read the required explanation of the spouse's rights)]

A premarital agreement cannot be a spouse's consent (see Q 8:97).

Q 8:74   May a spouse's guardian sign the spouse's consent?

A spouse's guardian may sign the spouse's consent, even if the electing participant is the spouse's guardian. [Treas. Reg. § 1.401(a)-20/Q & A-27] However, a guardian must act in the best interests of his or her ward. A guardian serves under a court's supervision and must account for his or her actions in court. Further, some guardianship decisions require a court's approval before the guardian implements the decision. [*See generally* Unif. Probate Code § 206, 8 pt. I U.L.A. 115–118 (1998)] It might be difficult to persuade a court that turning away money was in a surviving spouse's best interest. Although a participant might suggest making an irrevocable designation naming a trust for his or her spouse's benefit as the plan beneficiary, most retirement plans do not permit an irrevocable beneficiary designation.

Q 8:75   May proof of a spouse's consent be given in an electronic notarization?

Yes, but not really.

A Treasury regulation allows a notary's or plan representative's certificate to be furnished by electronic means, but requires that the spouse's consent have been signed in the physical presence of the notary or plan representative. [Treas. Reg. § 1.401(a)-21(d)(6)(i)&(ii)]

> **Note.** An electronic notarization is useful if each relying person has arranged in advance to receive and inspect an electronic apostille concerning a particular notary's electronic credentials. A capacity to accept electronic notarizations can be useful to those businesses and government agencies that process a large volume of transactions that depend on authenticated signatures. A typical retirement plan, however, even if it has many claims and distributions, does not have enough claims that require a spouse's consent to motivate the plan's administrator to put effort and resources into arrangements for receiving electronic notarizations.

Q 8:76   Who is a plan representative?

ERISA does not define its use of the words "plan representative." [ERISA § § 3, 205] The Retirement Equity Act of 1984's legislative history does not explain what Congress meant. [S. Rep. No. 98-575 to accompany H.R. 4280, 98th Cong., 2d Sess. (1984), reprinted in 1984 U.S.C.C.A.N. 2547, 2560]

A person might be a plan representative for the limited purpose of administering a plan's provisions required or permitted by ERISA's spouse's-consent rule or a plan's spouse's consent provision if the plan administrator has authorized the person to witness such a spouse's consent.

In a case that involved facts and forms typical of a retirement plan's service arrangements, a federal court found that the litigants who asserted that a spouse's consent had been witnessed did not offer enough evidence even to allege that a securities broker-dealer's employee was a plan representative. [Lasche v. George W. Lasche Basic Ret. Plan, 870 F. Supp. 336, 339, Pens. Plan Guide (CCH) ¶ 23905L (S.D. Fla. 1994)]

Q 8:77   Must a plan representative be independent of the participant?

Yes. Although nothing in ERISA Section 205 requires that a witness to a spouse's consent be independent of the electing participant, at least one federal court has interpreted the statute to include such a requirement. A plan administrator who was the same person as the electing participant could not, even though he was a plan representative (or even if he was the only plan representative), witness his spouse's consent. [Lasche v. George W. Lasche Basic Ret. Plan, 870 F. Supp. 336, 339, Pens. Plan Guide (CCH) ¶ 23905L (S.D. Fla. 1994)]

> **Practice Pointer.** If a lawyer or financial planner who advises a participant about making a beneficiary designation that would provide for anyone other than the participant's spouse knows that the participant also is a plan administrator, trustee, or other fiduciary, the lawyer or planner should advise the participant to ask his or her spouse to sign the consent in the presence of an independent notary. Failing to give that advice might be malpractice.

Because ERISA permits a plan administrator to rely on a spouse's consent witnessed by a notary, it seems unlikely that a federal court would find that it could be prudent for a plan administrator to rely on a spouse's consent witnessed only by the interested participant or someone who is subordinate to the interested participant. [ERISA §§ 205(c)(6), 404(a)(1)]

Q 8:78   Who is a notary?

ERISA does not define its use of the term *notary public*. [ERISA §§ 3, 205] Nor does the legislative history of the Retirement Equity Act of 1984 explain what Congress meant by a notary public. [S. Rep. No. 98-575 to accompany H.R. 4280, 98th Cong., 2d Sess. (1984), reprinted in 1984 U.S.C.C.A.N. 2547, 2560]

Many practitioners assume that Congress intended to describe a person state law recognizes as one whose certificate that he or she witnessed an acknowledgment will be recognized as conclusive evidence that the acknowledgment was made. Usually, a recognized official's certificate that he or she witnessed an acknowledgment is nearly conclusive evidence that the acknowledgment was made. In most states, an acknowledgment may be made before a judge, court clerk, recorder of deeds, or notary. [*See generally* Uniform Law on Notarial Acts § 3(a)] In New Jersey, a lawyer, if he or she is a licensed attorney, may certify an acknowledgment or affidavit. [N.J. Stat. Ann. § 41:2-1]

Q 8:79 How may a person in a foreign nation make an acknowledgment?

When a person is not present in the United States, his or her acknowledgment may be made before a United States ambassador, consul, consular officer, or consular agent. [22 U.S.C. §§ 4215, 4221] A consular officer must officiate and perform a notarial act that an applicant properly requests. [22 U.S.C. § 4215]

Further, some state's laws recognize an acknowledgment made before a judge, court clerk, or notary of the nation where the acknowledgment is made. [*See generally* Unif. Acknowledgment Act § 4(2)–(3), 12 U.L.A. 10–11 (1996)] It is unclear, however, whether a plan administrator would adopt such a rule. [ERISA §§ 404(a)(1)(D), 514(a)]

Q 8:80 How may a person in military service make an acknowledgment?

A person who is (1) a member of the armed forces; (2) a former member of the armed forces entitled to retired or retainer pay and legal assistance, or the dependent of an active or former member if the dependent is entitled to legal assistance; (3) a person "serving with, employed by, or accompanying the armed forces outside the United States"; or (4) a person subject to the Uniform Code of Military Justice outside the United States may make his or her acknowledgment, affidavit, deposition, or other statement that calls for a notarial act before a military officer described below. [10 U.S.C. §§ 1044, 1044a(a)(1)–(4)]

The following persons may officiate and certify a notarial act:

1. A judge advocate or reserve judge advocate;
2. A civilian attorney who serves as a legal assistance attorney;
3. An adjutant, assistant adjutant, or personnel adjutant, whether on active or reserve duty; or
4. A person designated by another statute or by a regulation of any of the armed forces.

[10 U.S.C. § 1044a(b)(1)–(4)]

Further, some state's laws recognize an acknowledgment that a person serving in any of the armed forces or his or her dependent, even if not entitled to military legal assistance, makes before a commissioned officer. [*See generally* Unif. Acknowledgment Act § 10, 12 U.L.A. 18–19 (1996) & Supp. 2 (2003)] It is unclear, however, whether a plan administrator would adopt such a rule. [ERISA §§ 404(a)(1)(D), 514(a)]

Q 8:81   Must a notary be independent of the participant?

Yes. Although nothing in ERISA Section 205 specifies that a witness to a spouse's consent be independent of the electing participant, at least two courts have interpreted the statute to include such a requirement:

In *Howard v. Branham & Baker Coal Co.*, the district court focused on the fact that the notary public before whom Mr. Jensen had purportedly signed the document was Mrs. Jensen herself—a circumstance that the court concluded would render the document ineffective as a spouse's consent. The court explained its thinking thus:

> Generally, it is considered contrary to public policy for a notary to take an acknowledgement of an instrument to which he or she is a party[.] [citation omitted] [C]ongress, through the [Retirement Equity Act], wanted a spouse to carefully consider a decision to waive retirement benefits without pressure from the other spouse and so imposed the requirement that the waiver be witnessed by a plan representative or a notary. To permit a spouse to act as notary to an instrument concerning their own benefits would appear to undermine this congressional intent.

[Howard v. Branham & Baker Coal Co., 968 F.2d 1214 (Table), 1992 WL 154571, *slip op.* at 3 (6th Cir. July 6, 1992) (unpublished disposition), quoting and affirming No. 90-00115 (E.D. Ky.) (unpublished order); *accord* Lasche v. George W. Lasche Basic Ret. Plan, 870 F. Supp. 336, 339, Pension Plan Guide (CCH) ¶ 23905L (S.D. Fla. 1994)]

The federal courts' view is consistent with state laws concerning when a notary properly may officiate and the legal effect of a notary's certificate that he or she witnessed an acknowledgment. [1 Am. Jur. 2nd Acknowledgments § 16]

Q 8:82   Must a plan representative be independent of the participant?

Yes. Although nothing in ERISA Section 205 requires that a witness to a spouse's consent be independent of the electing participant, at least two federal courts have interpreted the statute to include such a requirement. A plan administrator who was the same person as the electing participant could not, even though he was a plan representative (or even if he was the only plan representative), witness his spouse's consent. [Lasche v. George W. Lasche Basic Ret. Plan, 870 F. Supp. 336 (S.D. Fla. 1994)]

Practice Pointer. If a lawyer or financial planner who advises a participant about making a beneficiary designation that would provide for anyone other than the participant's spouse knows that the participant also is a plan administrator, trustee, or other fiduciary, the lawyer or planner should advise the participant to ask his or her spouse to sign the consent in the presence of an independent notary. Failing to give that advice might be malpractice.

Because ERISA permits a plan administrator to rely on a spouse's consent witnessed by a notary, it seems unlikely that a federal court would find that it could be prudent for a plan administrator to rely on a spouse's consent witnessed only by the interested participant or someone who is subordinate to the interested participant. [ERISA § § 205(c)(6), 404(a)(1)]

Q 8:83   May a plan administrator rely on a notary's certificate?

Yes, usually. If a plan administrator acted according to ERISA's fiduciary duties when it decided whether to accept a spouse's consent, the consent, even if not properly witnessed, nonetheless discharges the plan from liability to the extent of the payments made before the plan administrator knew that the consent did not meet the plan's requirements. [ERISA § 205(c)(6)] If a plan administrator acted according to ERISA's fiduciary duties, it is not liable to the non-consenting spouse. [ERISA § 404(a)(1)] Of course, the plan administrator must promptly correct or restrain payments once it knows that a spouse's consent was not properly witnessed.

Q 8:84   What should a plan administrator do if it relied on a notary's false or incorrect certificate?

If a plan administrator acted according to ERISA's fiduciary duties when it decided to accept a spouse's consent, the consent (or purported consent), even if not properly witnessed, nonetheless discharges the plan from liability to the extent of the payments made before the plan administrator knew that the consent did not meet the requirements of ERISA Section 205 and of the plan. [ERISA § 205(c)(6)] If the plan administrator acted according to ERISA's fiduciary duties, it is not liable to the spouse. [ERISA § 404(a)(1)] Of course, the plan administrator must promptly correct or stop payments once it knows that a spouse's consent was not properly witnessed.

Practice Pointer. A plan administrator may rely on a notary's certificate only if it acted according to ERISA's fiduciary duties, which include relying on a document only if a prudent expert familiar with administering retirement plans would, after exercising sufficient diligence, do so. A plan administrator must not ignore an internal inconsistency or other warning signs of fraud.

Example 1. Harold's election form states that he has no spouse. But the form's part for a spouse's consent is signed and notarized. A prudent administrator would not ignore this inconsistency, and instead must inquire into the facts. [Rice v. Rochester Laborers' Annuity Fund, 888 F. Supp. 494 (W.D.N.Y. 1995)]

Example 2. Wilma submits an election that states that she has no spouse. There is no inconsistency or irregularity in this form. The retirement plan's administrator also administers a health plan under which the same group of employees and their spouses are eligible. Would a prudent-expert fiduciary check the health plan's record to confirm that Wilma had not told the other plan that she has a spouse?

If a plan incurs or might incur an expense because the plan administrator relied on a notary's certificate, the plan's fiduciary might have a duty to evaluate whether it is in the plan's best interest to pursue a claim or lawsuit against the notary (and the notary's surety). [ERISA § 404(a)(1)] A notary is responsible for damages caused by his or her negligent performance of his or her duties. [John D. Perovich, Annotation, Liability of Notary Public or His Bond for Negligence in Performance of Duties, 44 A.L.R. 3d 555 (1972); Kenneth W. Biedzynski, 58 Am. Jur. 2d Notaries Public (Liability for Notarial Acts—Negligent Acknowledgment) § 60 (2002)] Also, a spouse who did not receive what he or she would have been entitled to had the notary performed correctly may sue the notary.

An employer might be vicariously liable for a notary's fraudulent or negligent performance of his or her office, depending on the relevant facts, surrounding circumstances, and which state's law governs the employer's duty of care. [*Compare* Vancura v. Katris, 2008 App. LEXIS 1317 Ill. App. LEXIS 1317 (Dec. 26, 2008) *with* Commercial Union Ins. Co. of New York v. Burt Thomas-Aitken Constr. Co., 49 N.J. 389, 230 A.2d 498 (1967); *see generally* Model Notary Act of 2002, 12-1, Liability of Notary, Surety, and Employer, Comment, at 68–69]

Q 8:85   Is a plan administrator protected from liability if it relied on a participant's statement about why his or her spouse's consent was not needed?

Maybe. ERISA includes the following protection from liability: "If a plan fiduciary acts in accordance with part 4 of this subtitle [ERISA's fiduciary-responsibility provisions] in . . . making a determination under paragraph (2) [concerning whether the participant's spouse consented to the participant's election, or whether such a consent was excused], then such . . . determination shall be treated as valid for purposes of discharging *the plan* from liability *to the extent of* payments made pursuant to such Act [sic]." [ERISA § 205(c)(6) (emphasis added)]

Some statements in the Retirement Equity Act's legislative history suggest total relief: "If the plan administrator acts in accordance with the fiduciary standards of ERISA . . . in accepting the representations of the participant that the spouse's consent cannot be obtained, then the plan will not be liable for payments to the surviving spouse." [Senate Rep. No. 575, 98th Cong., 2d Sess. 14 (1984), *reprinted in* 1984 U.S.C.C.A.N. 2547, 2560] But one court construed the "to the extent" phrase to mean that a plan must pay the surviving spouse an amount or amounts based on what remains of the benefit that would have been provided in the absence of the participant's false election, after subtracting the amounts the plan paid. [Hearn v. W. Conference of Teamsters Pension Trust Fund, 68 F.3d 301, 19 Employee Benefits Cas. (BNA) 1954 (9th Cir. 1995)]

Caution. Under the Ninth Circuit's precedent, a *plan* might be liable to pay some benefit to a participant's surviving spouse despite the fact that, because the plan administrator did not breach any fiduciary duty, the plan has no claim by which the plan can obtain extra money to pay the surviving spouse. Thus, the expense of paying a benefit to the surviving spouse might be an expense that the plan administrator must allocate to other plan accounts and, unless the plan provides otherwise, may allocate to other participants' and beneficiaries' accounts.

Elective-Share Rights

Q 8:86   What is an elective-share right?

In almost all states that do not provide community property (see Qs 8:89–8:94) a decedent's surviving spouse may elect to take a share of the decedent's property, even if the decedent's will and other transfers had not provided for his or her spouse. [*See generally* Restatement (Third) of Property: Wills and Other Donative Transfers § 9.1(a) (2003)]

Q 8:87   How much is a surviving spouse's elective share?

In many states, a surviving spouse's elective share is one-third of the decedent's estate. In a few, it is one-half. [*See generally* Restatement (Third) of Property: Wills and Other Donative Transfers § 9.1(a) (2003)]

In some states, the elective-share percentage increases under a schedule based on the duration of the marriage. For those states, a typical schedule has an elective-share percentage that ranges from 3 percent for a marriage that lasted one year to 50 percent for a marriage of 15 years or more. [*See generally* Restatement (Third) of Property: Wills and Other Donative Transfers § 9.2(a) (2003)]

Q 8:88   Is an elective share computed on all property?

Some states compute an elective share only on probate property. However, many states now provide that an elective share is computed on an "augmented estate" that includes several items of nonprobate property. [*See generally* Restatement (Third) of Property: Wills and Other Donative Transfers § 9.1(b)-(c) (2003)] Some states have detailed rules for counting this augmented estate. [*See generally* Unif. Probate Code § 2-203–2-210, 8 pt. I U.L.A. 103–125 (1998) & Supp. 33–35 (2008)]

Community Property

Q 8:89   What is community property?

In a separate-property regime, which applies in 41 states and all U.S. territories and possessions except Puerto Rico, an item of property normally belongs to the person who has title to it, paid for it, earned it, or otherwise acquired it. Although any property owned by a married person may become subject to equitable distribution on a divorce or other marital dissolution, the property belongs to the person who owns it until a court makes an order.

Community property is a term that lawyers use to refer to a regime that treats each item of property or an aggregate of property acquired by either spouse of a married couple during the marriage and while the couple are domiciled in a community-property state (see Q 8:91) as owned equally by each spouse. Each spouse's ownership exists presently, notwithstanding that the other spouse currently may hold title to or have control over the property.

> **Caution.** Income derived from separate property might be separate property or community property based on the kind of property that produced income and which state's laws apply. [*See, e.g.,* Alsenz v. Alsenz, 101 S.W.3d 648 (Tex. Ct. App. 2003) (income received during a marriage from a patent was community property notwithstanding that all work was performed and the patent was issued before the marriage); *see generally* Internal Revenue Manual Part 25.18.1.2.13 (available at *http://www.irs.gov/irm/part25/irm_25-018-001.html* (visited June 26, 2009)]

Ordinarily, community property is property acquired during marriage except property acquired by gift. [*See generally* Black's Law Dictionary 297 (8th ed. 2004)

> **Note.** A typical community-property statute refers to a community of *spouses*, and often provides no useful definition concerning what the word "spouse" means. Even if a state does not recognize same-sex marriages made in the state, it is less clear whether a state would recognize a same-sex couple's marriage or quasi-marriage made in another state. Further, a court might apply community-property law to protect the expectations of a nonspouse in a relationship that, in a judge's view, resembled marriage. (See Q 8:112.)

Q 8:90   How does community-property law apply to a retirement plan benefit?

If community-property law applies, a retirement plan benefit is community property to the extent that it accrued during the marriage and while the participant was domiciled in a community-property state. Beyond the usual tracing and accounting challenges of a community-property regime, a retirement plan might involve extra difficulty because a retirement plan might receive rollover contributions from IRAs and other eligible retirement plans, and it might be difficult to trace when the contributions to those plans were made.

> **Practice Pointer.** Even a practitioner who works primarily or exclusively in a small geographic area that has no community-property state should maintain some general awareness about community-property law. People in America relocate, and property that was community property when a couple was domiciled in a community-property state ordinarily remains community property when the couple relocates to a separate-property state.

In Wisconsin, the non-participant's community-property right in a retirement plan or deferred compensation plan ends on the non-participant's death if the non-participant's death occurs before the participant's death. [Wis. Stat. Ann. § § 766.31(3), 766.62(5)]

Q 8:91   Which states are community-property states?

Currently, Arizona, California, Idaho, Louisiana, Nevada, New Mexico, Puerto Rico, Texas, Washington, and Wisconsin are community-property states.

Alaska gives a married couple a choice of whether to use a separate-property regime or a community-property regime. [Alaska Stat. § 34.77.090] The separate-property regime applies unless the married couple agree to use a community-property regime. If the couple choose Alaska's community-property regime, they may use a written community-property agreement or a community-property trust to vary some of the state-law provisions that otherwise would govern their community property. [Alaska Stat. § 34.77.020]

California law permits a married couple to accept a conveyance as "community property with right of survivorship." [Cal. Civ. Code § 682.1]

In Texas, community-property law is a right protected by the state constitution. [Tex. Const. [1845], art. VII, § 19]

Although American community-property regimes are based primarily on the Spanish system, community-property law varies considerably from state to state. For example, if all contributions to a retirement plan were made before the participant was married, but investment earnings accrued during the marriage, some states would classify the entire retirement plan (including investment earnings) as separate property, while others might classify the investment earnings that accrued during the marriage as community property.

Wisconsin is the only state to have adopted as its community-property law any form of the Uniform Marital Property Act recommended by the National Conference of Commissioners on Uniform State Laws. [Wis. Stat. Ann. §§ 766. 001-766.97; see generally Unif. Marital Prop. Act, 9A pt. I U.L.A. 103–158 (1998) & Supp. 58–62 (2008)]

Q 8:92   Can community-property law be applied to nonspouses?

Maybe. In a state that applies community-property law to determine the property rights of married persons but does not recognize common-law marriage, a court might apply community-property law to protect the expectations of a nonspouse in a relationship that, in a judge's view, resembled marriage. Arizona, California, and Louisiana provide community-property rights to a putative spouse, but not to a meretricious nonspouse. [Stevens v. Anderson, 75 Ariz. 331, 256 P.2d 712 (1953); Cal. Civ. Code § 4452; La. Civ. Code Ann. arts. 117-118] Even for a couple in which neither person believed that he or she was married or had a spouse, Washington applies community-property law to a couple who have or had a "committed intimate relationship" (whether opposite-sex or same-sex), and may have even after a relationship's end that results from either person's death. [Olver v. Fowler, 168 P.3d 348, 33 Fam. L. Rptr. (BNA) 1520 (2007); Vasquez v. Hawthorne, 145 Wash. 2d 103, 33 P.3d 735 (Wash. 2001); Connell v. Francisco, 127 Wash. 2d 339, 898 P.2d 831 (Wash. 1995); Warden v. Warden, 36 Wash. App. 693, 676 P.2d 1037 (1984); *In re* Marriage of Lindsey, 101 Wash. 2d 299, 678 P.2d 328 (1984); *In re* Brenchley's Estate, 96 Wash. 223, 164 P. 913 (1917)]

Other legal theories for adjusting the property rights of putative spouses or meretricious spouses include express or implied contract, partnership, and unjust enrichment.

Q 8:93   How does community-property law affect payment of benefits under an ERISA plan?

ERISA preempts state laws that relate to an ERISA plan. [ERISA § 514] Nonetheless, a domestic relations court may order a participant to transfer an amount or property to his or her spouse or former spouse.

Q 8:94   How does community-property law affect death benefits under a non-ERISA plan?

If a participant names a beneficiary other than his or her spouse for more than half of (or, more precisely, for more than the participant's separate property plus community-property rights in) his or her benefit under a retirement plan, the participant's spouse might have a right under state law to get a court order invalidating the beneficiary designation, or at least as much of it as would leave the spouse with less than half of (or more precisely, with less than the spouse's community-property rights in) the retirement plan benefit. Nevertheless, a payer may pay based on the beneficiary designation it has on record until a payer receives a court order restraining payment or a written notice that the spouse asserts his or her rights.

Premarital Agreements

Q 8:95   What is a premarital agreement?

A *premarital agreement* is an agreement made between two persons who are about to marry concerning property rights that arise from marriage. Typically, a premarital agreement provides that each of the soon-to-be spouses waives one or more of the property rights that a spouse otherwise would have. A premarital agreement can waive a spouse's right to a share of the other's estate. Within limits required by public policy and basic fairness, a premarital agreement may specify what property division will apply if the marriage ends in divorce.

In a state with a law based on the Uniform Premarital Agreement Act, the parties to a premarital agreement may contract concerning property rights, the support of a spouse or former spouse, making a will or trust, and "the participantship rights in and disposition of the death benefit from a life insurance policy." [Unif. Premarital Agreement Act § 3(a)(6), 9C U.L.A. 43–46 (2001) & Supp. 10–12 (2008)]

A court will not enforce an agreement to the extent that it would cause a spouse or former spouse to become eligible for public assistance. [*See generally* Unif. Premarital Agreement Act § 6(b) (1983), 9C U.L.A. 48–55 (2001) & Supp. 12–15 (2008)] A party to a premarital agreement may not waive child support, and a premarital agreement cannot adversely affect child support. [Unif. Premarital Agreement Act § 3(a)(7), 3(b), 9C U.L.A. 43–46 (2001) & Supp. 10–12 (2008)]

Generally, a premarital agreement must be written. In New York, a premarital agreement must be in writing, signed by both parties, and acknowledged by each party in the presence of a notary public or similar officer. [*See, e.g.,* N.Y. Dom. Rel. Law § 236B(3)]

Many state statutes or court decisions add further requirements. Typically, each party should fully disclose his or her financial circumstances to the other. [*See, e.g.,* 23 Pa. Consol. Stat. Ann. § 3106(a)(2)] In particular, a waiver of a spouse's right to take a portion of the other spouse's estate might be enforced only if preceded by adequate disclosure of the other's net worth. [*See, e.g.,* Thies v. Lowe, 903 P.2d 186 (Mont. 1995); Rosenberg v. Lipnick, 389 N.E.2d 385 (Mass. 1979)] In some states, however, a person need not disclose an asset, which never will become a part of his or her estate, that could be the subject of the other spouse's election or waiver. [*See, e.g., In re* Perelman's Estate, 438 Pa. 112, 263 A.2d 375 (1970)] Although not expressly required under most states' laws, the better practice is for each party to get the advice of a lawyer of his or her choosing. [*E.g., In re* Slaughter Estate, 14 Fiduc. Rep. 2d (Bisel) 349 (Pa. C.P. Orphans' Ct. Div. 1994); *see also In re* Matson, 730 P.2d 668 (Wash. 1986)]

Even when the proponent's lawyer warns the other party to seek independent legal advice, an agreement might be invalid if the proponent's lawyer fails to explain to the unrepresented party that person's disadvantages under the agreement and why he or she needs legal advice. [Bonds v. Bonds, 99 Cal. Rptr. 2d 252, 5 P.3d 815 (2000); *In re* Estate of Lutz, 563 N.W.2d 90, 97–98 (N.D. 1997); *In re* Marriage of Foran, 834 P.2d 1081 (Wash. Ct. App. 1992)]

Practice Pointer. When a litigant attacking a premarital agreement asserts that the agreement is invalid because he or she did not receive sufficient legal advice or did not understand his or her lawyer's advice, such an assertion likely waives the evidence-law privilege for confidential communications between a client and his or her lawyer. [*See, e.g., In re* Marriage of Niklas, 211 App. 3d 28 Cal. App. 3d 28, 258 Cal. Rptr. 921 (1989); Weingarten v. Weingarten, 234 N.J. Super. 318, 560 A.2d 1243 (1989); Jarvis v. Jarvis, 141 Misc. 2d 207, 533 N.Y.S.2d 207 (1988)]

Note. Courts are especially reluctant to enforce an agreement that was presented just before the wedding ceremony. Although some suspect that judges are sympathetic to the "pressure" to sign that might come from an understandable desire to avoid the embarrassment of canceling a wedding, the formal reason for not enforcing a "last-minute" agreement is that a lack of time interfered with the offeree's opportunity to obtain legal advice. [*See, e.g.*, Hoag v. Dick, 799 A.2d 391 (Me. 2002)]

Practice Pointer. A guidebook—Gary N. Skoloff, Richard H. Singer Jr., and Ronald L. Brown, *Drafting Prenuptial Agreements* (Aspen Publishers 2007)—organizes its authors' explanations of relevant law and drafting suggestions based on whether the couple are both young, both old, or of different ages, and whether the spouses or soon-to-be spouses are similar or different in wealth.

In states that do not regulate premarital agreements by statute, courts apply ordinary contract law principles but with extra scrutiny, recognizing the confidential relationship of those engaged to marry. [*See generally* Restatement of Property: Wills and Other Donative Transfers § 9.4 (2003)]

In some states, a premarital agreement that makes reasonable provision for the surviving spouse will be enforced even in the absence of full and fair disclosure. An unreasonable agreement will be enforced only if there was full and fair disclosure. [*See generally* Unif. Premarital Agreement Act § 6(a)(2), 9C U.L.A. 48–55 (2001) & Supp. 12–15 (2008)] Under the laws of some states, an agreement that was reasonable when made may become unreasonable through changed circumstances. [*See, e.g.*, Rider v. Rider, 22 Fam. L. Rep. (BNA) 1454 (Ind. 1996)]

Q 8:96　Can a premarital agreement waive a right to a non-ERISA Roth IRA benefit?

Yes. Even if a surviving spouse is entitled to an elective share, community property, or other protective rights under state law, an expertly prepared premarital agreement—or marital agreement (see Qs 8:98–8:100)—should be sufficient to eliminate or waive those rights. [*See generally* Unif. Probate Code § 2-207; Unif. Premarital Agreement § 3, 9C U.L.A. 43–46 (2001) & Supp. 10–12 (2008)]

In some circumstances, it might be difficult to enforce the terms of a premarital agreement. At least one court has held that an offset against agreement rights in recognition of a surviving spouse's receipt of retirement benefits (that were not provided by the premarital agreement) could be an ERISA violation notwithstanding that the person applying the offset had no connection to any ERISA plan. This was so because the offset had the effect of "discriminating" against the spouse because she exercised her right to a benefit under an ERISA plan. [*See, e.g.*, Mattei v. Mattei, 126 F.3d 794 (6th Cir. 1997) (construing ERISA § 510)] Although this case interpreted ERISA's non-interference provision, state law might impose a similar principle concerning a person's rights under a non-ERISA plan.

Q 8:97 Can a premarital agreement waive a spouse's right to a Roth IRA benefit under an ERISA plan?

No. First, a premarital agreement rarely includes all of the form requirements necessary to constitute a valid spouse's consent to waive rights under ERISA. [ERISA § 205] Second, the Department of the Treasury has stated its interpretation that a premarital agreement cannot constitute a waiver of survivor annuity rights. [Treas. Reg. § 1.401(a)-20, Q & A 28] Most important, the spouse's consent to a participant's qualified election must be signed by the spouse, and a person making a premarital agreement is not yet a spouse.

All federal court decisions on this question have held that a premarital agreement cannot be used to waive a spouse's ERISA Section 205 rights. [*See* Hurwitz v. Sher, 789 F. Supp. 134 (S.D.N.Y. 1992), *aff'd*, 982 F.2d 778 (2d Cir. 1992), *cert. denied*, 508 U.S. 912 (1993); Callahan v. Hutsell, Callahan & Buchino, 813 F. Supp. 541 (W.D. Ky. 1992); Howard v. Branham & Baker Coal Co., 968 F.2d 1214 (6th Cir. 1992); Nellis v. Boeing, 15 Employee Benefits Cas. (BNA) 1651, 18 Fam. L. Rep. (BNA) Rep. 1374 (D. Kan. 1992); Zinn v. Donaldson Co., 799 F. Supp. 69 (D. Minn. 1992)]

At least one court has held that a premarital agreement (or, presumably, a marital agreement) cannot waive a qualified joint and survivor annuity if the spouse could not know what he or she would waive because the plan had not yet been created. [Pedro Enters. v. Perdue, 998 F.2d 491 (7th Cir. 1993)]

Marital Agreements

Q 8:98 What is a *marital agreement*?

A *marital agreement* is an agreement made between two persons who already are spouses concerning property rights that arise from their marriage. Typically, a marital agreement provides that each spouse waives one or more of the property rights that a spouse would otherwise have. A marital agreement can waive a spouse's right to a share of the other's estate. [*See generally* Restatement (Third) of Property: Wills and Other Donative Transfers § 9.4(a) (2003)] Within limits required by public policy and basic fairness, a marital agreement can specify what property division will apply if the marriage ends in divorce or when it ends by a party's death.

Generally, a marital agreement must be written. In New York, a marital agreement must be in writing, signed by both parties, and acknowledged by each party in the presence of a notary public or similar officer. [N.Y. Dom. Rel. Law § 236B(3)]

Many state statutes or court decisions add additional requirements meant to ensure basic fairness. Even if no statute applies specified conditions, courts use heightened scrutiny, recognizing the confidential relationship of spouses. [*See generally* Restatement (Third) of Property: Wills and Other Donative Transfers § 9.4(b)-(c) (2003)] Typically, each party should fully disclose his or her financial circumstances to the other. The better practice is for each party to get the advice of a lawyer of his or her choosing. [*In re* Slaughter Estate, 14 Fiduc.

Rep. 2d (Bisel) 349 (Pa. C.P. Orphans' Ct. Div. 1994); *see also In re* Matson, 730 P.2d 668 (Wash. 1986)] Even when the proponent's lawyer warns the other party to seek independent legal advice, an agreement might be invalid if the proponent's lawyer fails to explain to the unrepresented party that person's disadvantages under the agreement and why he or she needs legal advice. [Bonds v. Bonds, 99 Rptr. 2d 252 Cal. Rptr. 2d 252, 5 P.3d 815 (2000); *In re* Estate of Lutz, 563 N.W. 2d 90, 97, 98 (N.D. 1997); *In re* Marriage of Foran, 834 P.2d 1081 (Wash. Ct. App. 1992)] But Pennsylvania will enforce a premarital or marital agreement even if a party received no disclosure concerning his or her statutory right. [Stoner v. Stoner, 572 665 Pa. 665, 819 A.2d 529 (2003)]

> **Caution.** An agreement between a couple who already are married might fail to provide what lawyers call consideration—that is, a promise to do something one is not already under a legal duty or obligation to do, or to refrain from doing something that one has a legal right to do. An agreement merely to stay married might be insufficient to support a legally binding marital agreement. [Bratton v. Bratton, 136 S.W.3d 595 (Tenn. 2004)]

> A marital agreement is void if it was signed under the threat of a divorce. [*See, e.g.*, *In re* Sharp's Estate, 1979 Pa. D. & C. Dec. LEXIS 267 (C.P. 1979)]

Q 8:99   Can a marital agreement waive a spouse's right to a non-ERISA Roth IRA benefit?

Yes. Even if a surviving spouse is entitled to an elective share, community property, or other protective rights under state law, an expertly prepared marital agreement should be sufficient to eliminate or waive those rights. [*See generally* Unif. Probate Code § 2-207, 8 pt. I U.L.A. 118–121 (1998)]

Q 8:100   Can a marital agreement waive a spouse's right to an ERISA plan benefit?

Yes. A marital agreement can waive a spouse's right to an ERISA plan benefit if the marital agreement states all of the form requirements necessary to constitute a valid spouse's consent under the plan. To accomplish this, a family lawyer should consult an expert employee benefits lawyer and each plan administrator.

Tenancy by the Entirety

Q 8:101   What is *tenancy by the entirety*?

A *tenancy by the entirety* is a form of concurrent property ownership that recognizes the special unity of a married couple. A tenancy by the entirety can be created only if required unities of title, interest, possession, time, and person (a valid marriage) all exist. [*See generally* Restatement (First) of Property § 67 (1936)] Along with other requirements, two people can become co-tenants in a tenancy by the entirety only if they are legally married.

Under a tenancy by the entirety, each of the two spouses owns all the property, and neither spouse acting alone can dispose of the property. A tenancy by the entirety ends on the death of either spouse, or on the divorce or other dissolution of the marriage. [*See, e.g.*, 23 Pa. Cons. Stat. § 3507, *In re Sharp's Estate*, 11 D. & C. 3d 371Pa. D. & C. 3d 371 (Common Pleas Orphans Ct. Div. 1979)]

Q 8:102   What kind of property may be owned as a tenancy by the entirety?

Of the states that recognize tenancy by the entirety as an available form of property ownership, some allow it only for *real property* (such as a couple's home), and some allow it for both real property and *personal property*. [*See generally* Restatement (Third) of Property: Wills and Other Donative Transfers § 6.2, reporter's note 13 to comment f (2003)]

Q 8:103   Why might a person want property to be owned in a tenancy by the entirety?

Because neither spouse acting alone can dispose of the property (see Q 8:101), a tenancy by the entirety may provide useful protection against the claims of creditors. For example, if only one of the two spouses is bankrupt, a bankruptcy trustee generally cannot reach property held in a tenancy by the entirety. [*See* 11 U.S.C. § 110]

Practice Pointer. For a detailed explanation of protections from creditors that might result from a tenancy by the entirety, *see* Lewis D. Solomon and Lewis J. Saret, *Asset Protection Strategies* (2007) (available at *http://onlinestore.cch.com* (visited June 25, 2009)]

A participant might not need the protection that a tenancy-by-the-entirety ownership, when available, could provide. Usually, a retirement plan benefit is excluded from a participant's bankruptcy estate. [11 U.S.C. § 522, as amended by the Bankruptcy Abuse Prevention and Consumer Protection Act of 2005, Pub. L. No. 109-8, 119 Stat. 23 (2005); *see also* 11 U.S.C. § 541(c)(2); Rousey v. Jacoway, 544 U.S. 320 (2005); Patterson v. Shumate, 504 U.S. 753 (1992)]

Note. For either ERISA or non-ERISA Roth account benefits, a federal tax lien supersedes any ERISA, plan, or contract restraints. [I.R.C. §§ 6321, 6331; Treas. Reg. § 1.401(a)-13(b)(2)] A federal tax lien may attach to a taxpayer's property rights in a tenancy by the entirety, even if the taxpayer's spouse is not a debtor. [United States v. Craft, 535 U.S. 274 (2002)]

Finally, a married person might prefer a tenancy by the entirety simply because it reflects his or her beliefs about the nature of marriage.

Q 8:104   Can a participant transfer a Roth account benefit into a tenancy by the entirety?

No, a participant will be unable to transfer his or her rights under a Roth IRA contract or a plan-based Roth account into a tenancy by the entirety for one or more of the following reasons:

1. State law does not recognize tenancy by the entirety.

2. The Roth IRA contract rights are personal property that cannot be the subject of a tenancy by the entirety.

3. State law precludes a conveyance of property into a tenancy by the entirety.

4. The Roth IRA contract, in a provision required by the Internal Revenue Code (Code), precludes any transfer.

5. ERISA preempts state law.

At common law, a married couple cannot hold *personal property* (property other than land and the buildings fixed onto the land) in a tenancy by the entirety. This is still the rule in some states.

At common law, one spouse who solely owns property cannot convey that property into a tenancy by the entirety. Some states now allow such a transfer, but those provisions are of no use to a participant because a participant lacks the power to transfer his or her rights under a retirement plan or Roth IRA contract. A plan or contract will provide that benefits cannot be assigned, alienated, or transferred. [I.R.C. §§ 401(a)(13), 401(f)-(g), 403(b)(1)(C), 408(a)(4), 408(b)(1), 408A(b)] Thus, even in states that recognize tenancy by the entirety as an available form of property ownership, tenancy by the entirety cannot apply to a Roth account benefit because a participant cannot transfer ownership of it.

Disclaimers

Q 8:105   What is a *disclaimer*?

A *disclaimer* (also called a *renunciation* in some states) is a writing in which a beneficiary states that he or she does not want to receive a benefit. To be valid and to achieve tax planning purposes, the disclaimer must meet certain requirements (see Q 8:111).

Q 8:106   Is a disclaimer permitted under a Roth IRA?

A retirement plan or a Roth IRA will not permit a participant to disclaim his or her benefit because a plan or contract provides that a participant cannot forfeit or transfer any right he or she has under the contract. A Roth IRA might, however, permit a disclaimer made by a beneficiary. [*See* G.C.M. 39858 (Sept. 9, 1991); Ltr. Ruls. 9226058, 9037048, 8922036 (Mar. 31, 1992)]

A trustee, custodian, insurer, or plan administrator may (but need not) accept a beneficiary's disclaimer.

Q 8:107   What is the effect of a disclaimer?

If a beneficiary makes a legally valid disclaimer that the plan administrator or payer accepts, the retirement plan or Roth IRA benefit will be distributed (or distributable) as if the disclaimant had died before the participant's death or before the creation of the benefit disclaimed. [*See generally* Unif. Disclaimer of Property Interests Act (1999), 8A U.L.A. 159–189 (2003), Unif. Disclaimer of Property Interests Act (1978), 8A U.L.A. 191–208 (2003)]

Q 8:108   What is the tax effect of a disclaimer?

If a beneficiary makes a valid disclaimer that also meets all requirements of Code Section 2518, the disclaimed benefit will not be in the disclaimant's estate for federal estate tax purposes, and will not be the disclaimant's income for federal income tax purposes. [I.R.C. § 2518; Treas. Reg. § 25.2518-1] Many states have a similar rule for state death tax purposes. [*See, e.g.*, 72 Pa. Consol. Stat. Ann. § 9116(c)]

Q 8:109   Why would someone want to make a disclaimer?

Although most people do not lightly turn away money, sometimes there might be a good reason to make a disclaimer.

A typical reason is to complete tax-oriented estate planning. For example, a beneficiary might prefer to make a disclaimer to help accomplish one or more of the following estate-planning objectives:

1. Changing a restricted transfer in favor of the beneficiary into an unrestricted transfer to the same beneficiary;
2. Changing an unrestricted transfer to the beneficiary into a restricted transfer in favor of the same beneficiary;
3. Limiting a transfer to a child or other nonspouse to permit the participant's spouse to delay the required beginning date;
4. Limiting a transfer to a child or other nonspouse to permit the participant's spouse to make a rollover;
5. Limiting a transfer to a child or other nonspouse to increase the marital deduction;
6. Limiting a transfer to a spouse as needed to "equalize" the effective transfer tax rate of each spouse;
7. Limiting a transfer to a spouse as needed to fully use the generation-skipping tax exemption of the first spouse to die;
8. Limiting a transfer to a spouse as needed to avoid an estate transfer surtax [I.R.C. § 2001(c)(2)]; or

9. Providing a designated beneficiary so as to lengthen tax deferral for the plan benefit and thereby increase a gift to charity.

If a beneficiary makes a legally valid disclaimer that also meets all requirements of Code Section 2518, the disclaimed benefit will not be in the disclaimant's estate for federal estate tax purposes, and will not be the disclaimant's income for federal income tax purposes (see Q 8:111). Most states have a similar rule for state death tax purposes.

Another frequent use is to correct a "wrong" beneficiary designation.

Example. Matthew saved for retirement using a Roth IRA. When he applied for this Roth IRA contract, he was single and named his parents as beneficiaries. Recently, Matthew married Laura. Shortly after returning from their honeymoon, Matthew was killed in an accident. Matthew's parents believe that if Matthew had thought about it, he would have wanted his wife to be his beneficiary. Therefore, each of them files a disclaimer with the Roth IRA custodian. Although the parents cannot directly control who gets the benefit, their lawyer advises them that the contract's "default" provision (see Q 8:14), together with their state's intestacy law, will result in Laura getting the benefit. All family members feel that this is a morally sound result and what Matthew would have wanted. Disclaimers allow the family to achieve this good result.

Another reason to make a disclaimer is to not receive a benefit that would be taken by the disclaimant's creditors. Some courts find that such a disclaimer is a fraudulent transfer, and thus is void. [*See, e.g.,* Pennington v. Bigham, 512 So. 2d 1344 (Ala. 1987); Stein v. Brown, 480 N.E.2d 1121 (Ohio 1985)] And some states by statute bar a disclaimer by an insolvent beneficiary. [*See, e.g.,* Fla. Stat. Ann. § 732.801(6); Mass. Gen. Laws Ann. ch. 191A § 8; Minn. Stat. Ann. § 525.532(c)(6)] Federal law or state law is most likely to bar a disclaimer that could interfere with a government's opportunity to collect on a debt to the government. [*See, e.g.,* State v. Murtha, 427 A.2d 807 (Conn. 1980); *accord* Dep't of Income Maint. v. Watts, 558 A.2d 998 (Conn. 1989); *but see In re* Estate of Kirk, 591 N.W.2d 630 (Iowa 1999)] If these rules do not apply, a disclaimer is not a fraudulent transfer. [*See, e.g.,* Cal. Probate Code § 283; Essen v. Gilmore, 607 N.W.2d 829 (Neb. 2000)] Even a valid disclaimer does not avoid a federal tax lien. [Drye v. United States, 528 U.S. 49 (1999)]

Caution. A beneficiary should not make a disclaimer unless he or she first gets his or her lawyer's advice that doing so will not be a federal health care crime. [*See* 42 U.S.C. § 1320a-7b(a)(6)]

Q 8:110   Can a beneficiary's executor or agent disclaim?

If a retirement plan or a Roth IRA permits a beneficiary to disclaim a benefit, whether that power can be exercised only by the beneficiary personally or by the beneficiary's executor, personal representative, guardian, or attorney-in-fact as a fiduciary depends on the plan's or contract's language. Some courts have held that only a beneficiary personally may exercise the power to disclaim, unless specific plan or contract language provides for recognizing a personal representative's or agent's disclaimer. [*See, e.g.,* R. Scott Nickel, as Plan Benefit Administrator of the Thrift Plan of Phillips Petroleum Co. v. Estate of Lurline Estes, 122 F.3d 294, 21 Employee Benefits Cas. (BNA) 1762, Pens. Plan Guide (CCH) ¶ 23937U (5th Cir. 1997)]

For a non-ERISA plan, it is unclear whether a similar result would apply under state law. In some states, a personal representative may disclaim an interest and the disclaimer relates back to the disclaimant's death or even to the death of the person making the disclaimant a beneficiary. [*See, e.g.,* Texas Probate Code § 37A; Rolin v. I.R.S., 588 F.2d 368 (2d Cir. 1978) (applying New York law)]

Even if a fiduciary has power under applicable law to make a disclaimer [*see generally* Unif. Disclaimer of Property Interests Act (1999) § 11, 8A U.L.A. 180 (2003)], such a disclaimer might not be a qualified disclaimer for federal tax purposes. [*Compare* Ltr. Ruls. 200013041 (Jan. 4, 2000), 9615043 (Jan. 17, 1996), 9609052 (Dec. 7, 1995) (disclaimer recognized) *with* Ltr. Rul. 9437042 (June 22, 1994) (disclaimer not recognized); *see also* Rev. Rul. 90-110, 1990-2 C.B. 209 (disclaimer by trustee not a qualified disclaimer)]

Q 8:111   What are the requirements for a legally valid disclaimer?

To be effective for federal tax and retirement plan purposes, a disclaimer usually must meet all of the following requirements:

1. The disclaimer must be made before the beneficiary accepts or uses the disclaimed benefit.
2. The disclaimant must not have received any consideration for the disclaimer.
3. The benefit must pass without any direction by the disclaimant.
4. The disclaimer must be in writing and must be signed by the disclaimant.
5. The writing must state an irrevocable and unqualified refusal to accept the benefit.
6. The writing must be delivered to the trustee, custodian, insurer, or plan administrator.
7. The writing must be so delivered no later than nine months after
   a. The date of the participant's death, or
   b. The date the beneficiary attains age 21, whichever is later.
8. The disclaimer must meet all requirements of applicable or relevant state law (if any).

[I.R.C. § 2518; Treas. Reg. § 25.2518-2; G.C.M. 39858, 1991 WL 776304 (Sept. 9, 1991); *see generally* Unif. Disclaimer of Property Interests Act, 8A U.L.A. 151 (1993)] A disclaimer may renounce a specified portion of what the beneficiary/disclaimant otherwise would be entitled to.

Note. The Fifth Circuit has interpreted the tax regulations' no-consideration condition as limited to bargained-for consideration. In the view of that court, leading a disclaimant to understand that he or she would otherwise be provided for or that his or her needs would be considered does not necessarily vitiate the tax-qualified treatment of a disclaimer if the disclaimer is valid under non-tax law. [Estate of Monroe v. Comm'r, 124 F.3d 699 (5th Cir. 1997); *see also* Estate of Lute v. United States, 19 F. Supp. 2d 1047 (D. Neb. 1998)]

State law may provide additional requirements. For example, in some states a disclaimer must state the disclaimant's belief that he or she has no creditor that could be disadvantaged by the disclaimer. In some situations, especially when the beneficiary is a minor or an incapacitated person, a disclaimer may require court approval. [*E.g.*, N.Y. Est. Powers & Trusts Law § 2-1.11(c); 20 Pa. Consol. Stat. § 6202] Even when court approval is not required, state law may require that a disclaimer is not valid unless it is filed in the appropriate probate court. [*See generally* Unif. Probate Code § 2-801, 8 pt. I U.L.A. 206–210 (1998) & Supp. 100–101 (2008)]

In addition to state law and tax law requirements, a retirement plan or Roth account may impose further requirements.

Caution. Even a valid disclaimer does not defeat a federal tax lien against a disclaimant's property, including property that he or she would receive in the absence of his or her disclaimer and a tax lien. [I.R.C. § 6321; Drye v. United States, 528 U.S. 49 (1999); *see also* United States v. Irvine, 511 U.S. 224 (1994); United States v. Mitchell, 403 U.S. 190 (1971)]

Practice Pointer. If a surviving spouse wants to make a tax-qualified disclaimer of a portion of what otherwise would be his or her rights under a QTIP trust (see Q 8:126), the estate's executor and the QTIP trust's trustee might first divide the QTIP trust into separate trusts. An assignment of any portion of a spouse's interest in a QTIP trust is a taxable gift of that trust's principal. [Treas. Reg. § 25.2519-1(a)] But a disclaimer is not an assignment. [*Cf.* Ltr. Ruls. 200122036 (Mar. 1, 2001), 200044034 (Aug. 8, 2000); *see generally* Unif. Disclaimer of Property Interests Act (amended 2002) § 5(f), 8A U.L.A. 166–170 (2003)]

Q 8:112 Can a beneficiary's disclaimer be a qualified disclaimer even though the beneficiary received a required minimum distribution for the year of the decedent's death?

Yes. The Treasury Department ruled that a disclaimer of a remaining beneficial interest in a decedent's IRA was a qualified disclaimer even though, before making the disclaimer, the disclaimant received the required minimum distribution for the year of the decedent's death. The Treasury Department reasoned that a disclaimer may renounce a specified portion of what the beneficiary/disclaimant otherwise would be entitled to. For information about minimum-distribution rules, see chapter 5.

Q 8:113   Is a person who disclaimed his or her remaining interest in a retirement plan benefit after receiving a required distribution considered a designated beneficiary for minimum distribution purposes?

A person who disclaims a retirement plan benefit under a qualified disclaimer (see Q 8:111) by September 30 of the year following the year of the participant's death is not taken into account in determining the participant's designated beneficiary. For information about minimum-distribution rules, see chapter 5.

Government Claims

Q 8:114   Is a Roth IRA counted as an asset for Medicaid eligibility?

A Roth IRA probably is counted as an "available resource" for Medicaid eligibility purposes to the extent that the patient or his or her spouse currently has a legal right to get payment under the Roth IRA. [42 U.S.C. §§ 1396a–1396p] Because a typical Roth IRA contract does not provide any distribution restrictions, it appears likely that a Roth IRA will be counted as an available resource for Medicaid purposes.

> **Note.** An explanation of Medicaid and its complex eligibility rules is beyond the scope of this book. Medicaid is covered in Aspen Publishers' *Elder Law Answer Book* (Aspen Publishers, 2007) and CCH's *Estate and Retirement Planning Answer Book* (CCH, 2007).

> **Practice Pointer.** A participant might consider not selecting as his or her beneficiary a person likely to need Medicaid benefits if the participant can make a more appropriate beneficiary designation. A beneficiary should not make a disclaimer without first getting his or her lawyer's advice that doing so will not be a federal health care crime. [*See* 42 U.S.C. § 1320a-7 b(a)(6)]

Q 8:115   Is a Roth IRA counted as an asset for the Medicaid eligibility of the participant's spouse?

After the community spouse resource allowance is used, a Roth IRA benefit probably is counted as an available or includible resource to determine the Medicaid eligibility of a participant's spouse. [*See generally* 42 U.S.C. §§ 1396–1396v]

Q 8:116   Can an Internal Revenue Service levy take a participant's Roth IRA?

Maybe. Although a Roth IRA's anti-alienation clause reflects a policy view that a participant's retirement benefits should not be available to ordinary creditors, an IRS lien or levy applies to Roth IRA amounts, even if the Roth IRA is held under an ERISA plan. [*See, e.g.,* Shanbaum v. United States, 32 F.3d 180,

183 (5th Cir. 1994); Ameritrust Co. v. Derakhshan, 830 F. Supp. 406, 410–411 (N.D. Ohio 1993); Travelers Ins. Co. v. Ratterman, 77 A.F.T.R. 2d (RIA) 96-956, 96-1 U.S. Tax Cas. (CCH) ¶ 50,143 (S.D. Ohio 1996); Palmore v. United States *ex rel.* I.R.S. (*In re* Palmore), 71 A.F.T.R. 2d (PH) 93-1588 (N.D. Okla. 1993); Schreiber v. United States (*In re* Schreiber), 163 B.R. 327, 334 (Bankr. N.D. Ill. 1994); Raihl v. United States (*In re* Raihl), 152 B.R. 615, 618 (BAP 9th Cir. 1993); Jacobs v. I.R.S. (*In re* Jacobs), 147 B.R. 106, 108–109 (Bankr. W.D. Pa. 1992); *In re* Perkins, 134 B.R. 408, 411 (Bankr. E.D. Cal. 1991); *In re* Reed, 127 B.R. 244, 248 (Bankr. D. Haw. 1991); *see also* ERISA § 514(d); I.R.C. § 6334(c); Treas. Reg. § 1.401(a)-13(b)(2)]

However, a levy extends only to property rights that exist at the time of the levy. [Treas. Reg. § 301.6331-1(a); *see also* I.R.S. Internal Legal Memo 200102021]

Q 8:117 When will the IRS file a levy on a participant's Roth IRA benefit?

If a participant has not yet severed from employment or otherwise completed the conditions that entitle him or her to a retirement plan benefit, the IRS usually will not levy on the participant's retirement plan benefit. [I.R.S. Internal Legal Memo 200032004 (May 18, 1998)] If a participant has completed the conditions that entitle him or her to a retirement plan benefit, the IRS usually will levy on a retirement plan benefit only if the participant has been abusive. A levy on retirement savings might require the approval of an IRS supervisor. [Internal Revenue Manual ¶ 5.11.6.2]

Q 8:118 When will the IRS levy a beneficiary's retirement plan benefit?

Because a levy concerning a beneficiary, especially a nonspouse beneficiary, does not involve disturbing retirement income in the same way that a levy regarding a participant would, the IRS might be less reluctant to levy on a retirement plan benefit to which a beneficiary has become entitled after the participant's death.

Practice Pointer. If a participant knows that a person whom the participant might prefer to name as a beneficiary has shown irresponsibility in handling money by failing to meet tax obligations, the participant might consider naming as his or her beneficiary a responsible trustee under a spendthrift trust.

Unclaimed Property

Q 8:119 Is an ERISA plan governed by a state's unclaimed property law?

No. An unclaimed property law would require delivery of plan assets and liabilities and hence such a law relates to the plan and its administration. Therefore, it is preempted by ERISA. [ERISA §§ 403(c)(1), 514(a);

Commonwealth Edison Co. v. Vega, 174 F.3d 870 (7th Cir. 1999), *cert. denied sub nom.* Topink v. Commonwealth Edison Co., 120 S. Ct. 176 (1999)] The Department of Labor (DOL) has consistently advised that ERISA preempts state unclaimed property laws. [D.O.L. ERISA Adv. Ops. 78-32A (Dec. 22, 1978), 79-30A (May 14, 1979), 83-39A (July 29, 1983), 94-14A (Dec. 7, 1994)] Likewise, the DOL has taken that position as a friend of the court. [*See, e.g.,* Commonwealth Edison Co. v. Casillas, No. 97 C 0006, 1998 U.S. Dist. LEXIS 7236 (N.D. Ill. May 12, 1998), *aff'd sub nom.* Commonwealth Edison Co. v. Vega, 174 F.3d 870 (7th Cir. 1999), *cert. denied sub nom.* Topink v. Commonwealth Edison Co., 120 S. Ct. 176 (1999)]

At least one federal court found that an unclaimed property law was not preempted by ERISA in specific circumstances. [Aetna Life Ins. Co. v. Borges, 869 F.2d 142, 10 Employee Benefits Cas. (BNA) 2001 (2d Cir. 1989), *cert. denied*, 493 U.S. 811 (1989)] That court stated, "[W]e think that the impact of Connecticut's escheat law on ERISA benefit plans is too tenuous, remote, and peripheral to require preemption . . . ." [*Id.* at 147] However, the court appears to have found that the effect of the unclaimed property law was remote because the ERISA plan administrator had already approved the claims that resulted in uncollected bank drafts on the insurer's account and the government sought to apply its unclaimed property law only to the insurer. Further, the insurer's health insurance contract accounting and insurance premiums were affected by the application or nonapplication of the unclaimed property law. Thus, the unclaimed-property law had the effect of regulating insurance. ERISA preemption does not apply to "*any* law of any State which [sic] regulates insurance." [ERISA § 514(b)(2)(A) (emphasis added)]

In the contributing author's view, the *Borges* decision cannot be fairly understood as applying to a plan administrator (as distinguished from an insurer), because the point of ERISA preemption is to "overrule" all state laws. [ERISA § 514(a)] Also, careful readers will observe that the court's finding applies only to Connecticut's abandoned-property law, and only under the specific facts of the case.

Q 8:120   Is a non-ERISA Roth IRA governed by a state's unclaimed-property law?

Yes. Each of the 50 states (and the District of Columbia and U.S. possessions) has a law regulating abandoned or unclaimed property. A typical unclaimed-property law requires any person in possession of intangible property that is unclaimed by its owner for a specified number of years to transfer that property to the custody of the state. [*See generally* Unif. Unclaimed Property Act (1995) § 1(12), 8C U.L.A. 97–102 (2001) & Supp. 7–10 (2003); Unif. Disposition of Unclaimed Property Act (1981) § 1(13), 8C U.L.A. 177–185 (2001) & Supp. 11–26 (2003)]

Q 8:121 When is a retirement plan benefit considered abandoned?

The "waiting period" that sets up a legal presumption that property is abandoned or unclaimed varies by state law. Under typical state laws, the waiting period starts when the benefit became payable or distributable. Under many retirement plans, a benefit usually is paid within a month from the date that the benefit became distributable. Therefore, as a practical matter many payers start the waiting period on the check date.

Tax-Oriented Estate Planning

Q 8:122 What is the *federal estate tax*?

The *federal estate tax* is a tax on the right to transfer property on death. The tax is imposed on a decedent's taxable estate, which includes nonprobate property and rights. An unlimited marital deduction allows an individual to transfer any amount to his or her surviving spouse (if the spouse is a U.S. citizen) without federal estate tax at that time, but tax may apply when the survivor dies. [I.R.C. § 2056] A tax credit allows an individual to transfer about $3.5 million for deaths in 2009 without federal estate tax. [I.R.C. § 2010(b)]

Normally, an estate will not incur federal estate tax unless the estate is worth more than the applicable amount shown in the following table:

For estates of decedents dying during	Applicable exclusion amount
2001	$ 675,000
2002	$1,000,000
2003	$1,000,000
2004	$1,500,000
2005	$1,500,000
2006	$2,000,000
2007	$2,000,000
2008	$2,000,000
2009	$3,500,000
2010	no federal estate tax
2011	$1,000,000

[I.R.C. § 2001 as in effect before EGTRRA, during EGTRRA's effect, and after EGTRRA's expiration; for estates of decedents dying before 2002 or after 2010, the federal estate tax's highest rate is 55 percent; however, a 5 percent surtax is imposed on cumulative taxable transfers between $10 million and $17,184,000, which practically results in a marginal tax rate up to 60 percent.]

Q 8:123   Should a person who is not "wealthy" care about estate tax planning?

Many people have more wealth (at least for tax purposes) than they think. For estate tax purposes, a taxable estate includes nonprobate property, such as the following:

- A home
- Personally owned life insurance benefits
- Employment-based life insurance benefits
- Retirement benefits

Q 8:124   What is a *state death transfer tax*?

A *state death transfer tax* is a state tax imposed on the transfer or receipt of wealth at death. Almost every state imposes some form of death transfer tax.

An *estate tax* is a tax on the privilege of transferring property from a decedent.

An *inheritance tax* is a tax on the privilege of receiving property from a decedent, including even property that a person did not own at the time of his or her death.

Unlike the federal estate tax law's marital deduction, an inheritance tax or a state estate tax may apply even when the beneficiary is the decedent's spouse.

In some states, the amount of the state death tax is the maximum amount for which the state death tax credit is available under federal estate tax law. [*See* I.R.C. § 2011] In other states, the state death tax may be greater. Some states also have a state or local gift tax.

Q 8:125   Is a Roth account benefit subject to federal estate tax?

Yes. The value of a participant's Roth account as of the date of his or her death, or if annuity payments have begun, the value of the remaining payments (if any), is included in the participant's estate for federal estate tax purposes. [*See generally* I.R.C. §§ 2033–2046]

Q 8:126   Is a Roth IRA subject to state death tax?

An explanation of each state's death taxes is beyond the scope of this book. Some states tax retirement benefits for death tax purposes according to rules similar to the rules of the federal estate tax, but often without an exemption amount. Other states have their own rules. In several states, the tax may vary based on the relationship of the beneficiary to the participant. [*See, e.g.,* 72 Pa. Consol. Stat. § 9116(a)]

Q 8:127   Does a beneficiary designation of the spouse qualify for the marital deduction?

Yes, as long as the spouse is the only person who can benefit, at least until his or her death. [I.R.C. § 2056; Ltr. Rul. 199936052]

Q 8:128   Does a beneficiary designation of a QTIP trust qualify for the marital deduction?

Yes. If the trust agreement includes necessary provisions (explained below) and the executor and the trustee properly make the election, a qualified terminable interest property (QTIP) trust qualifies for the marital deduction.

Q 8:129   What provisions must a QTIP trust include?

In addition to the usual requirements for a QTIP trust, participant and his or her estate planning lawyer should make sure that the trust (or at least the subtrust that will hold the Roth IRA benefit) provides all of the following:

1. During the spouse's life, no one (including the spouse) can have any power to appoint any part of the Roth IRA benefit or QTIP property resulting from it to anyone other than the surviving spouse.
2. The trustee has power to make the Roth IRA and any trust property resulting from it productive or income-earning.
3. The spouse has a right to require the trustee to make the Roth IRA and any trust property resulting from it productive or income-earning.
4. The trust document does not change the definition of principal and income in a way that might result in less income distributable to the spouse.
5. The trustee must have the power under the trust and the right under the Roth IRA to get a distribution of the retirement benefit, at least for the amount described in (10) below.
6. The surviving spouse must have the right to require the trustee to get a Roth IRA distribution, at least for the amount described in (10) below.
7. The QTIP trust's fiduciary accounting income must include the Roth IRA's income.
8. To ensure the spouse's right to all of the income, the trust must provide that all administration expenses normally charged to corpus (including any income tax payable with respect to the distribution of principal) be charged to corpus and not to income.
9. If it is necessary to administer the trust, the trustee must compute the Roth IRA's fiduciary accounting income and the QTIP trust's fiduciary accounting income.
10. If (for a year) the surviving spouse exercises his or her right to get all of the trust's fiduciary accounting income, the QTIP trustee must claim a distribution from the retirement plan in an amount not less than the

greater of the Section 401(a)(9) minimum distribution (including any incidental benefit required distribution) or the QTIP trust's fiduciary accounting income attributable to the Roth IRA.

11. The participant-decedent's executor and the trustee of the QTIP trust must make the QTIP election for the QTIP trust and for the Roth IRA.

[I.R.C. § 2056(b)(7); Treas. Reg. §§ 20.2056(b)-5(f)(8), 20.2056(b)-7; Rev. Rul. 2006-26, 2006-1 C.B. 939; Rev. Rul. 2000-2, 2000-3 I.R.B. 305]

Caution. A trust creator (and his or her estate-planning lawyer) also should consider what provisions qualify a trust for an exemption or deduction under a state's inheritance, estate, or other transfer tax. Qualifying for a state's marital treatment might require more restrictive, or less restrictive, conditions. For example, a Pennsylvania inheritance tax exemption for "a transfer of property for the sole use of the transferor's surviving spouse" does not require that income be paid if the surviving spouse does not request it. [72 Pa. Stat. § 9113; *cf.* Estate of Goldman, 781 A.2d 259, 2001 Pa. Commw. LEXIS 533 (2001)]

Practice Pointer. In drafting QTIP trust provisions, an estate-planning lawyer should recognize that a retirement plan or Roth IRA does not state provisions for determining fiduciary accounting income. Therefore, the trust must provide for the trustee to make its own computation of fiduciary accounting income based on the information available to it. (See Q 8:130.)

Caution. A surviving spouse who does not exercise his or her right to obtain the retirement plan benefit and thereby the QTIP trust's income should consider whether his or her waiver or non-exercise of that right constitutes a taxable gift of a future interest.

Practice Pointer. A careful drafter of a QTIP trust might consider provisions that would preclude (or at least not authorize) an excessive trustee fee. When a trustee is a family member who is a natural object of the QTIP trust beneficiary's bounty, an excessive trustee fee is a taxable gift from the surviving spouse to the trustee. [T.A.M. 200014004; *see generally* Merill v. Fahs, 324 U.S. 308 (1945); Comm'r v. Wemyss, 324 U.S. 303, 306 (1945); Harwood v. Comm'r, 82 T.C. 239, 259 (1984); Estate of Reynolds v. Comm'r, 55 T.C. 172 (1970); Estate of Anderson v. Comm'r, 8 T.C. 706, 720 (1947); Estate of Hendrickson v. Comm'r, T.C. Memo 1999-357] In addition to gift tax on the portion of the trustee's fee that is in excess of reasonable compensation, a surviving spouse's acquiescence in an excessive fee calls into question whether the surviving spouse truly had a right to all of the trust's income, and thereby whether the trust is or was a QTIP trust. [I.R.C. § 2056(b)(7)]

Q 8:130   What is a trust's fiduciary accounting income?

In trust or fiduciary accounting, *income* refers to money or property the trust receives as a year's (or shorter period's) return from a principal asset.

Example. Imagine a fruit-bearing tree. A year's harvest of fruit is income. If the tree grows taller and wider (and becomes more valuable if it can bear more fruit than the year before), those are changes in the principal. If the tree's owner chops it down and sells it for more than she paid to get the tree, she has a capital gain.

The amount of a retirement plan distribution treated as income is likely to be determined under:

1. A traditional income rule (see Q 8:131)
2. An adjustment rule (see Q 8:132)
3. A unitrust rule (see Q 8:133)

In the absence of an adjustment (see below) or a unitrust measure of income (see below), a trust counts as fiduciary accounting income the trust's interest, dividends, rents, and similar income, but not capital gains (or other changes to the principal value of a trust asset). How much of a retirement plan distribution is treated as income is likely to be determined under: (1) a traditional income rule; (2) an adjustment rule; or (3) a unitrust rule.

Q 8:131   What is the traditional income rule for measuring income?

In many states, a trustee ordinarily allocates to principal all of a payment that a retirement plan was not required to make, and 10 percent of a payment that the retirement plan was required to pay. For this rule, a payment is not "required to be made" merely because the trustee exercises its right to a distribution or withdrawal. The rule applies whether the payments begin soon after the beneficiary's right first becomes subject to the trust or are deferred until a future date. As long as the distributee had a right to take a payment, the rule applies whether a distribution is paid in money or delivered in property. The rule is based on the payment right rather than on the assets held under a plan or as a contract under which the payments are made. [See generally Unif. Principal and Income Act § 409 (before 2008 amendment), 7B U.L.A. 170–172 (2000) & Supp. 66–69 (2005)] This rule includes a "fail-safe" to preserve QTIP or other marital-deduction tax treatment: "If, to obtain an estate tax marital deduction for a trust, a trustee must allocate more of a payment to income than provided for by this [rule], the trustee shall allocate to income the additional amount necessary to obtain the marital deduction." [Unif. Principal and Income Act § 409 (before 2008 amendment), 7B U.L.A. 170–172 (2000) & Supp. 66–69 (2005)]

In the IRS's view, a trust or subtrust does not qualify as QTIP property unless the surviving spouse has unqualified rights to all of the trust's fiduciary accounting income, including all income attributable to a retirement plan. [Rev. Rul. 2006-26, 2006-1 C.B. 939] A 2008 revision to the recommended uniform law would, to the extent that a state adopts it, provide rules designed to conform to those IRS views. Among other provisions, the uniform law could permit applying a unitrust rule (see Q 8:133) to determine a retirement plan's income that otherwise would be unknown. [Unif. Principal and Income Act § 409 (available at *http://www.law.upenn.edu/bll/archives/ulc/upaia/2008_final. htm*) (visited on June 25, 2009)]

Q 8:132   What is the adjustment rule for apportioning income?

If a trustee invests a trust's assets according to a prudent-investor or total-return investment policy, even a trust with very good investment results might have little income. Using a traditional principal-and-income accounting method for a trust that achieves investment returns through capital gains could result in only a small distribution (or none) to a trust's income beneficiary. Under the Uniform Principal and Income Act, a trustee may use fiduciary discretion to make an adjustment between principal and income. [*See generally* Unif. Principal and Income Act §§ 104, 506, 7B U.L.A. 141–149, 188–190 (2000) & Supp. 37–46, 77–78 (2005)] For example, a trustee might decide to treat a portion of the trust principal's change in value as though it were income. For a QTIP or other marital-deduction trust that requires regular income distributions to a surviving spouse, a trustee may use this adjustment power to increase the income to which a surviving spouse is entitled, but not to decrease income. [*See generally* Unif. Principal and Income Act §§ 104(c)(1), 7B U.L.A. 141–149 (2000) & Supp. 37–46 (2005)] Further, a trustee must use an adjustment power according to applicable law, the terms of the trust, and the trustee's fiduciary duties, including especially the duty to be impartial. A court may prevent or remedy an abuse of the trustee's discretion. [*See generally* Unif. Principal and Income Act § 105, 7B U.L.A. Supp. 46–54 (2005); Restatement (Second) of Trusts §§ 183, 187, 232, 233 (1959); *see also* Restatement of Restitution § 22 (1937)]

Q 8:133   What is the unitrust rule for measuring income?

If a trust is governed by, or its trustee voluntarily adopted, a total-return investment policy, many states provide varying opportunities to treat a percent- age of a trust's assets (counted as an average of recent years' closing balances) as income. [*See generally* Unif. Principal Income and Act general notes 7B U.L.A. 131–135 (2000) & Supp. 4–32 (2006)] For Internal Revenue Code provisions that call for income to be distributable, regulations allow a trust to treat this measure of income as meeting those requirements if, along with the necessary total- return investment policy and other conditions, the income percentage is no less than 3 percent and no more than 5 percent. [Treas. Reg. § 1.643(b)-1] In addition to these tax-law constraints on an income percentage, some states specify a presumed percentage—for example, 4 percent. [*E.g.*, 20 Pa. Consol. Stat. § 8105(d)(3)]

> **Note.** During a time when a trustee of a QTIP subtrust must take a minimum distribution, if the subtrust holds only one retirement benefit and counts income as 4 percent of recent years' trust assets, that subtrust's income usually will be less than the plan's minimum distribution. Income might be more than the minimum distribution if the minimum distribution is mea- sured based on an age of 72 or younger. [*See* Treas. Reg. § 1.401(a)(9)-5] Or

income might be more than the minimum distribution if there were investment losses that reduced the balances on which income is determined.

Q 8:134 When would a participant want to name a QTIP trust as beneficiary?

A QTIP trust may be desirable whenever a participant wants the federal estate tax marital deduction but does not want his or her spouse to receive the Roth IRA benefit directly.

> **Example 1.** Bob and Cathy, a married couple, have no children together, but Bob has children from a previous marriage. A QTIP trust can allow Bob to provide for Cathy during Cathy's life, while preserving some of his Roth IRA benefit for his children.

> **Example 2.** Annabelle cares very much for her husband, Jim, and wants her Roth IRA benefit to provide for Jim if she dies first; but Annabelle believes that Jim is irresponsible in handling money and prefers that a professional trustee manage his financial needs. A QTIP trust can allow Annabelle to provide for Jim without putting all the money in his hands.

Qualified Domestic Trust for an Alien

Q 8:135 How is the marital deduction different when a decedent's spouse is an alien?

Normally, an unlimited deduction is available for property passing to a decedent's surviving spouse. [I.R.C. § 2056] This deduction can apply to all or a portion of the value of a Roth IRA to the extent that it becomes payable to the participant's surviving spouse or becomes held under a QTIP trust for the spouse's benefit (see Qs 8:125–8:128). If a participant's spouse is an alien, the availability of the marital deduction is severely restricted. These restrictions apply even if the alien spouse resides in the United States. [I.R.C. §§ 2056, 2056A]

Q 8:136 How can a participant preserve the marital deduction when his or her spouse is an alien?

The federal estate tax marital deduction is not available for an alien spouse unless the property passing to the spouse is provided through a qualified domestic trust (QDOT). [I.R.C. § 2056(d)(2)]

Q 8:137 What is a *qualified domestic trust*?

A *qualified domestic trust*, or QDOT, is a trust that holds assets for the benefit of (but not subject to the control of) the spouse during the spouse's life. The trust must restrict distributions during the spouse's life to trust income and hardship distributions, or else pay a special tax on any other distribution. [I.R.C. § 2056A(b)] A QDOT must have at least one trustee who is a U.S. citizen, or a U.S. corporation must be responsible for paying any federal estate tax due from the trust. [I.R.C. § 2056A] Further technical conditions are specified by Treasury regulations. [Treas. Reg. § 20.2056A-1 *et seq.*]

Q 8:138   How can a participant obtain QDOT treatment?

It is unlikely that a Roth IRA contract will by its own terms satisfy the conditions for a surviving spouse's benefit to be treated as a QDOT.

A participant who wants QDOT treatment for his or her spouse's benefit should, with his or her estate planning lawyer's advice, select an appropriate trustee and create a QDOT. To cause any Roth IRA benefit remaining on the participant's death to pass into the QDOT, the participant should change his or her Roth IRA beneficiary designation—but only on the advice of his or her expert estate planning lawyer. The following is a sample beneficiary designation:

> Thomas Tertius, or the duly appointed and then currently serving U.S. trustee of my Qualified Domestic Trust dated February 2, 1991

The parties and the trustee should be careful to follow any additional requirements particular to QDOT treatment for a Roth IRA. [*See, e.g.,* Ltr. Rul. 9713018 (Dec. 17, 1996) (involving a 403(b) arrangement)]

Q 8:139   How can a surviving spouse obtain QDOT treatment?

To preserve the marital deduction for a benefit passing to an alien spouse, the spouse must "transfer" his or her Roth IRA distribution to a QDOT before the decedent's estate's federal estate tax return is filed. [I.R.C. § 2056(d)(2)(B)(i)] Of course, a beneficiary cannot assign or transfer a Roth IRA distribution; however, if the alien spouse receives a lump-sum distribution and pays the proceeds into a QDOT before the estate tax return is filed the distribution may qualify for the marital deduction.

The regulations also provide a special rule for annuity payments [Treas. Reg. § 20.2056A-4], but it is unlikely to be desirable for the parties.

Giving Advice

Q 8:140   May a financial-services representative give advice about beneficiary designations?

A financial-services representative may give practical information about how to fill-in a retirement plan's or account's form that seeks beneficiary information. He or she must not, however, give advice about the legal effect of a beneficiary designation. Further, a nonlawyer must warn a person about the risks of acting without advice. [*See, e.g., In re* Opinion No. 26 of the Committee on Unauthorized Practice, 654 A.2d 1344 (N.J. 1995); *see generally* Restatement (Second) of Torts § 552 (1977)]

Except when done by a properly admitted lawyer, giving legal advice, even for free, is a crime or offense in most states. Even if the nonlawyer explicitly states that he or she is not a lawyer, it is still a crime to give legal advice.

Note. The contributing author asks readers to understand that this chapter's description of the law does not reflect his view about what the law ought to be. Rather, he believes that any person should be free to give legal advice (and to bear responsibility for his, her, or its advice).

Unfortunately, many people believe (often incorrectly) that they cannot afford legal advice. Although a financial-services representative should urge a participant to get expert legal advice, it might be impractical to avoid participants' questions asked in the course of filling out an IRA application. Perhaps it is not unauthorized practice of law to furnish widely known general information that does not involve applying the law to a specific factual situation.

Q 8:141 Is a nonlawyer who gives legal advice liable for damages that result from reliance on his or her incorrect or incomplete advice?

Yes, a nonlawyer is liable if his or her "client" suffered harm because he or she relied on the nonlawyer's inappropriate advice. Courts have not hesitated to impose liability on a nonlawyer for giving incorrect or even incomplete advice. Moreover, a nonlawyer is held to at least the same standard of care and expertise as a competent lawyer. [*See, e.g.*, Williams v. Jackson Co., 359 So. 2d 798 (Ala. Civ. App. 1978), *writ denied*, 359 So. 2d 801 (1978); Wright v. Langdon, 274 Ark. 258, 623 S.W.2d 823, 826 (1981); Biakanja v. Irving, 49 Cal. 2d 647, 320 P.2d 16 (1958); Banks v. District of Columbia Dep't of Consumer & Regulatory Affairs, 634 A.2d 433 (D.C. 1993); Buscemi v. Intachai, 730 So. 2d 329, 330 (Fla. Dist. Ct. App. 1999), *review denied*, 744 So. 2d 452 (Fla. 1999); Miller v. Whelan, 42 N.E. 59, 63 (Ill. 1895); Torres v. Fiol, 110 Ill. App. 3d 9 (1982); Ford v. Guarantee Abstract & Title Co., 553 P.2d 254, 264 (Kan. 1976); Webb v. Pomeroy, 655 P.2d 465 (Kan. Ct. App. 1982); Busch v. Flangas, 837 P.2d 438, 440 (Nev. 1992); Mezzaluna v. Jersey Mortgage & Title Guar. Co., 162 A. 743, 745 (N.J. 1932); Sandler v. New Jersey Realty Title Ins. Co., 169 A.2d 735, 740–741 (N.J. Super Ct. Law Div. 1961), *rev'd on other grounds*, 178 A.2d 1 (N.J. 1961); Leather v. United States Trust Co. of New York, 279 A.D.2d 311; 720 N.Y.S.2d 448, 2001 N.Y. App. Div. LEXIS 154 (2001); Latson v. Eaton, 341 P.2d 247 (Okla. 1959); Jones v. Allstate Ins. Co., 45 P.3d 1068, 1081 (Wash. 2002); Cultum v. Heritage House Realtors, Inc., 694 P.2d 630, 633 (Wash. 1985); Bowers v. Transamerica Title Ins. Co., 675 P.2d 193, 200–201 (Wash. 1983); Tegman v. Accident & Med. Investigations, Inc., 30 P.3d 8, 13 (Wash. Ct. App. 2001); Bishop v. Jefferson Title Co., 28 P.3d 802, 808 (Wash Ct. App. 2001); Hangman Ridge Training Stables, Inc. v. Safeco Title Ins. Co., 652 P.2d 962, 965 (Wash. Ct. App. 1982); Hecomovich v. Nielsen, 518 P.2d 1081, 1085

(Wash. Ct. App. 1974); Burien Motors, Inc. v. Balch, 513 P.2d 582, 586 (Wash. Ct. App. 1974); Andersen v. Nw. Bonded Escrows, Inc., 484 P.2d 488, 491 (Wash. Ct. App. 1971); *see also* McKeown v. First Interstate Bank of California, 194 Cal. App. 3d 1225, 240 Cal. Rptr. 127, 1987 Cal. App. LEXIS 2125 (1987); Correll v. Goodfellow, 125 N.W.2d 745 (Iowa 1964); Brown v. Shyne, 242 N.Y. 176 (1926); Mattieligh v. Poe, 57 Wash. 2d 203, 356 P.2d 328, 329 (1960)] Further, a court might treat a nonlawyer's unlicensed practice of law as negligence per se to result in strict liability. [*See generally* Restatement (Second) of Torts § 288A (1965), *accord* Restatement (Third) of Torts § 14 (Proposed Final Draft Apr. 6, 2005)]

Practice Pointer. This duty, even for a nonlawyer, includes the duty to have and use specialist expertise, or to refer one's "client" to an appropriate specialist.

A nonlawyer plan administrator also will be liable for incorrect or incomplete advice. Although a lawsuit against an ERISA plan's administrator or other fiduciary for negligent misrepresentation or negligent communication is preempted [Griggs v. EI DuPont de Nemours & Co. 237 F.3d 371 (4th Cir. 2001); Farr v. U.S. West, 151 F.3d 908 (9th Cir. 1998)], a plan administrator's incorrect statement might be a breach of its fiduciary duty to furnish accurate and non-misleading information. [*See, e.g.*, Griggs v. EI DuPont de Nemours & Co., 237 F.3d 371 (4th Cir. 2001)]

Practice Pointer. If a participant expresses a desire to make a beneficiary designation that would provide anything less than all of his or her death benefit to his or her spouse, a practitioner should urge the participant to get the advice of an expert lawyer.

Q 8:142   Can written materials give guidance about beneficiary designations?

Maybe. In Texas, any restriction against the unauthorized practice of law does not preclude "written materials, books, forms, computer software, or similar products if the products clearly and conspicuously state that the products are not a substitute for the advice of an attorney." [Texas Government Code § 81.101(c)]

In other states, it is unclear whether such publications would be so protected. Despite the United States' constitutional protections for free speech, at least one court found that mere written publications, without oral communication, was the unauthorized practice of law. [*See, e.g.*, Unauthorized Practice of Law Comm. v. Parsons Tech., Inc. d/b/a Quicken Family Lawyer, No. 3:97-CV-2859H, 1999 WL 47235 (N.D. Tex. Jan. 22, 1999) (before enactment of Texas Government Code § 81.101(c)), *vacated*, 179 F.3d 956 (5th Cir. 1999)] In the contributing author's view, the court's decision, had it not been vacated, would have been reversed on rehearing, appeal, or review.

Although some ERISA plan administrators might guess that ERISA preempts state laws, ERISA does not preempt criminal laws, which might include some laws that restrain the unauthorized practice of law. [ERISA § 514(b)(7)]

Q 8:143   Can liability result from a reader's reliance on incorrect information?

Yes, a person that presents information may be liable for damages that result from a reader's reliance on incorrect information. [*See, e.g.*, *In re* Thompson, 574 S.W.2d 365, 369 (Mo. 1978) (holding sellers of divorce kits liable to consumers harmed by use of the kits)] In addition to other sources of liability, a person that is or should be aware that a recipient of its written or oral communication may rely on it is liable for harm that results because the communication lacks the accuracy, completeness, or other care that would be used by a person who is in the business of presenting that kind of information. [*See generally* Restatement (Second) of Torts § 552 (1977)]

Q 8:144   Does the lawyer who writes a person's will need to know about his or her beneficiary designation?

Professor John Langbein, an authority on the law of wills, trusts, and estates, observed that many Americans die with several "wills"—maybe one that was written in a lawyer's office, and a dozen others that were filled out on standard forms. For most people, those forms—beneficiary designations—dispose of far more money and property than the will does. [Langbein, "The Nonprobate Revolution and the Future of the Law of Succession," 97 *Harv. L. Rev.* 1108 (Mar. 1984)]

Making a beneficiary designation under a retirement plan or a Roth IRA is an important part of estate planning. Although a retirement benefit will not pass by a will (see Q 8:1), a beneficiary designation affects a person's overall estate plan. A participant should make sure his or her lawyer knows the beneficiary designation he or she made under every retirement plan, including a Roth IRA, and should ask for the lawyer's advice about whether to consider changing any beneficiary designation.

Q 8:145   May a lawyer give advice about a beneficiary designation?

Yes. A lawyer may render advice about law as long as he or she writes or speaks his or her advice while present in a state in which he or she is admitted to practice law (even if the advised person is domiciled in a state in which the lawyer is not admitted to practice law). [*See e.g.*, Estate of Condon, 64 Cal. Rptr. 2d 789 (Ct. App. 1997)] Also, a lawyer may render advice while in a state in which he or she is not admitted if the advice is reasonably related to the lawyer's proper practice in a state in which he or she is admitted. [*See generally* Restatement (Third) Law Governing Lawyers § 3(3) (2001); Model Rules of Professional Conduct, Rule 5.5(c)(4) (ABA 2008)] In addition, a lawyer may render advice while in a state in which he or she is not admitted if the lawyer's practice is permitted under federal law. [*See, e.g.*, The Florida Bar re Advisory Opinion—Nonlawyer Preparation of Pension Plans, 571 So. 2d 430 (1990); *see generally* Model Rules of Professional Conduct, Rule 5.5(d)(2) (ABA 2008)]

Common Mistakes

Q 8:146   What are some of the common mistakes people make with beneficiary designations?

Because people enroll in a Roth IRA quickly, they sometimes make beneficiary designations that are less than carefully considered. Consider the following explanation of some common mistakes.

1. *Failing to coordinate a beneficiary designation's provisions with those made in other nonprobate designations, trusts, and a will.* Although a beneficiary designation's provisions need not be the same as those of a participant's will or other dispositions, if they are different the maker should understand why he or she has made different provisions and whether they are likely to add up to a combined result that he or she wants.

2. *Failing to consider whether a beneficiary designation is consistent with tax-oriented planning.* A participant might have had a lawyer's or CPA's advice about how to leave his or her estate, including both probate and nonprobate property, to achieve a desired tax outcome. Making a beneficiary designation without considering its effect on the maker's tax-oriented plan could result in an unanticipated tax.

3. *Making a beneficiary designation that a payer will refuse to implement.* For example, a person might try to make a beneficiary designation that refers to terms that one may use in a will or trust but are precluded by his or her Roth IRA contract. A payer's interpretation of the beneficiary designation without the offending terms might result in a disposition quite different from what the participant would have wanted.

4. *Trying to name beneficiaries by writing "all my children, equally" or describing a class.* Whenever a beneficiary designation refers to information not in a custodian's or insurer's records, a payer may decide that the participant did not make a beneficiary designation, or might allow a claimant an opportunity to name every person in the class and prove that there are no others. Because it is difficult to prove the nonexistence of an unidentified person, even the opportunity to correct such a beneficiary designation would result in significant frustration and delay.

5. *Neglecting to use a beneficiary's Social Security number or Individual Taxpayer Identification Number.*

   Example. Gary Smith named his three children—Reid Smith, Catherine Smith, and Alice Smith—as his beneficiaries, and used only their names. By the time of Gary's death many years later, Reid and Alice had married. Reid had no special difficulty claiming his benefit. But Alice Carpenter (who had taken her husband's surname) was required to submit proof that she is the same person as Alice Smith. Because an identifying number assigned by the Social Security Administration or Internal Revenue Service is unique, this burden could have been avoided had Gary put Alice's number on the beneficiary-designation form.

Caution. Some participants will want to balance this use of a clear identifier against concerns about a potential for identity theft.

6. *Naming a minor as a beneficiary without considering who the minor's guardian would be.* For example, a divorced person might not want to name his or her young child as a beneficiary if doing so might have the effect of putting money in the hands of the child's other parent—the participant's former spouse. Instead, a participant might name a suitable trustee or custodian.

7. *Naming a son or daughter as a beneficiary without considering his or her prudence.*

   Example. Ralph names his daughter, Britney, as beneficiary of Ralph's custodial account. When Ralph dies, Britney is 19 years old, and no longer is a minor under applicable law. Although Britney should pay her sophomore year's $25,000 tuition at the Newark College of Fashion Arts, Britney buys a new car, and then neglects to pay the second insurance premium. When the uninsured car is stolen, Britney has nothing left from her father's gift.

8. *Forgetting to give a copy of the beneficiary designation to the beneficiary.* A payer has no duty or obligation to contact a participant's beneficiaries to invite them to submit a claim. Indeed, many financial services providers particularly avoid doing so because such a communication might invite fraudulent claims. A beneficiary might not claim a benefit if he or she is unaware that he or she is a beneficiary. Likewise, a beneficiary might face difficulty in claiming a benefit if he or she does not know the name of the Roth IRA custodian or insurer.

9. *Naming one's estate as his or her beneficiary.* Some people think that naming one's estate as beneficiary is a way to avoid inconsistency in his or her estate plan. While such a beneficiary designation might fulfill a goal of avoiding inconsistency, it bears other consequences, which might be disadvantageous. Amounts paid or payable to an executor or personal representative for the estate are available to a decedent's creditors. And a benefit's "run" through an estate might, because of accounting and timing differences, result in income taxes greater than the income tax that would result if the recipient received the benefit directly. (*See* I.R.C. §§ 1, 72, 641–691)

10. *Failing to make a beneficiary designation.* Although this observation might seem somewhat inconsistent with some just described, another common mistake is failing to make a beneficiary designation. A person who has difficulty making up his or her mind about a beneficiary designation is unlikely to have read a Roth IRA contract carefully enough to understand the effect of its "default" provision. Although a young person might assume that death is far away, the point of a beneficiary designation is to provide for the possibility of death.

    Practice Pointer. A planner might suggest that the risks of failing to make a beneficiary designation outweigh the risks of a less than perfectly considered beneficiary designation. In those circumstances, a planner might remind a participant that a typical Roth IRA contract allows a participant to change his or her beneficiary designation at any time.

11. *Forgetting to review one's beneficiary designation.* A participant should review his or her beneficiary designations periodically, and whenever there is a significant change in his or her family or wealth.

    Example. Nancy named her husband, Larry, as her beneficiary under a Roth IRA. Although Nancy wanted to make sure that her children would be provided for, she trusted her husband to take care of the whole family. Nancy and Larry divorced, and Nancy neglected to change her beneficiary designation. After Nancy's death, Larry submits his claim to the Roth IRA custodian. The custodian follows the Roth IRA contract's terms, which do not revoke a beneficiary designation because of a participant's divorce. The custodian pays Larry, and he spends the money without considering any needs of Nancy's children.

The examples and common mistakes explained above are only a few of the many ways a participant might make an unwise beneficiary designation. A participant should use his or her valuable right to name a beneficiary, and use that right with care.

Chapter 9

Required Reporting for Roth IRAs

This chapter discusses in detail the information required to be reported regarding contributions to and distributions from Roth IRAs, the various deadlines for such reporting, and the penalties for failing to supply all the required information in a timely fashion.

Reporting requirements for Roth IRA trustees and custodians with respect to contributions are twofold: Certain information must be reported to the IRA owner (or to beneficiaries in certain cases) and to the Internal Revenue Service (IRS).

Reporting requirements for IRA trustees and custodians with respect to distributions are also twofold: Certain information must be reported to the recipient of the distribution and to the IRS. All distributions must be reported, even those that result when the initial establishment of an IRA is revoked.

Reporting Roth IRA Contributions on Form 5498

Q 9:1   What information regarding Roth contributions is required to be reported to the Internal Revenue Service?

Each year, trustees and custodians of Roth IRAs must submit contribution information to the Internal Revenue Service (IRS). [I.R.C. §§ 408A(d)(3)(D), 408(i); Treas. Reg. § 1.408–5] Form 5498, IRA Contribution Information, is designed for this purpose.

Following is a summary of Roth information required for the 2009 tax year (see Q 9:8).

1. Rollover contributions to a Roth IRA received during 2009. (Even if the rollover is within the same institution, a rollover from a traditional IRA to a Roth IRA should not be included.)

2. The amount converted from a traditional IRA, SEP IRA, or SIMPLE IRA to a Roth IRA during 2009. (A rollover from one Roth IRA to another Roth IRA should not be included.)

3. Recharacterized contribution from a traditional IRA to a Roth IRA.

4. The fair market value (FMV) of the account as of December 31, 2009.

5. A checkbox to indicate a Roth IRA or Roth conversion IRA contribution.

6. Any regular contributions made to a Roth IRA in 2009 and through April 15, 2010, designated for 2009.

Note. A Form 5498 must be issued for any IRA with a year-end balance, regardless of current activity, just to report the IRA's FMV. Of course, if any reportable activity occurred, Form 5498 must be submitted even if the account was closed before year-end.

Q 9:2   What recent changes/clarifications were made to Form 5498?

The following changes were made to Form 5498 for 2009:

Enlarged and reformatted. There are two forms to a page instead of three to provide additional boxes for reporting information formerly reported in the blank box next to box 10. New boxes 12a through 15b have been added for reporting (see Q 9:8):

- Box 12a The required minimum distribution (RMD) date applicable to a beneficiary Roth IRA account (see chapter 5)
- Box 12b RMD amount
- Box 13a Postponed (made for a prior year) contribution (see chapter 3)
- Box 13b Year for which postponed contribution made
- Box 13c Postponed contribution reason code

Note. In addition to codes for service in the combat zone service or hazardous duty area, a code for affected taxpayers, as described in IRS news releases relating to federally designated disaster areas, is provided. (See chapter 3.)

- Box 14a Repayments of a qualified reservist distribution or disaster distribution (see Qs 3:16, 9:8)
- Box 14b Repayment codes for a box 14a qualified reservist distribution or disaster distribution
- Box 15a Other contributions such as catch-up contributions made in the case of certain employers in bankruptcy (see Qs 2:1, 9:8)
- Box 15b Reason code for box 15a contribution

The following changes were made to Form 5498 for 2008:

Qualified rollover contributions. Instructions have been added for reporting qualified rollover contributions (conversions) from an employer's plan to a Roth IRA (see Q 3:52).

The following changes were made to Form 5498 for 2007:

Additional contributions. Information for reporting additional contributions for some participants in a 401(k) plan of certain employers in bankruptcy is provided (see Qs 2:1, 9:8).

Qualified charitable distributions. Guidance on the treatment of qualified charitable distributions is provided by referring to Notice 2007-7 [2007-5 I.R.B. 395] (see Q 4:1).

Nonspouse designated beneficiaries. Guidance on reporting for Roth IRAs of nonspouse designated beneficiaries has been added (see Q 9:14).

Qualified reservist distributions. Reporting instructions have been added regarding the repayment of qualified reservist distributions (see Qs 3:16, 9:8).

Q 9:3   What recent changes/clarifications were made to Form 1099-R?

The following changes were made to Form 1099-R for 2009:

Corrective distributions. Provides that excess contributions (except for designated Roth contributions) are taxable in the year of distribution (see chapter 10).

Charitable contributions. Provides that distributions from IRAs, including Roth IRAs, for charitable purposes may be made through December 31, 2009 (see Q 4:1). Roth IRAs are generally not used for charitable giving purposes.

The following changes were made to Form 1099-R for 2008:

Permissible withdrawals from eligible automatic contribution arrangements. Permissible withdrawals from eligible automatic contribution arrangements have been added to the list of distributions that are not eligible rollovers. [I.R.C. § 414(w)]

Qualified rollover contributions. Reporting instructions for qualified rollover contributions from an employer's plan have been added (see Q 3:52).

Box 4. Federal Income Tax Withheld. Instructions for withholding on non-qualified distributions from designated Roth accounts have been added.

Guide to Distribution Codes. The following changes were made to the Guide to Distribution Codes (see Q 9:30).

- An exception was added to Distribution Code 2 on page 11 for distributions that are permissible withdrawals under an eligible automatic contribution arrangement under Section 414(w).

- New Distribution Code H (direct rollover of a designated Roth account distribution (only) to a Roth IRA) was added. Code BG is still used for designated Roth contributions that are directly transferred to another designated Roth account under an employer's 401(k) or 403(b) plan.

- Distribution Codes B (nonqualified designated Roth account (DRA) distribution) and D (returns of excess deferral plus earnings taxable in 2006). Code D does not apply to a Roth IRA.

The following changes were made to Form 1099-R for 2007:

Certain qualified distributions. Guidance has been added to indicate that there is no special reporting for qualified charitable distributions. Recipients of these distributions claim the associated tax benefits on their own income tax returns (see Q 4:1).

Nonspouse designated beneficiaries. Notice 2007-7 provides guidance on provisions in the Pension Protection Act of 2006 (PPA) regarding the tax treatment of certain distributions to nonspouse designated beneficiaries (see Q 3:1, 3:52).

Q 9:4   What is the deadline for filing Form 5498 with the IRS?

The deadline for submitting Form 5498 to the IRS is May 31 of each year. Thus, 2009 Forms 5498 are due on Monday, June 1, 2010.

Note. If a regular due date falls on a Saturday, a Sunday, or a legal holiday, the due date is the next business day (see Q 2:13).

Q 9:5   How can an extension of time to file Form 5498 with the IRS be requested?

For paper or magnetic media filing, a request for an extension of time to file Form 5498 with the IRS can be made by completing Form 8809, Request for Extension of Time to File Information Returns, and sending it to the following address:

Enterprise Computing Center—Martinsburg
Information Reporting Program
Attn: Extension of Time Coordinator

240 Murall Drive
Kearneysville, WV 25430

To avoid delays, be sure the attention line is included on all envelopes and packages containing Form 8809.

Form 8809 must be filed no later than the due date for Form 5498—that is, May 31 (June 1, 2010 for 2009 reporting)—in order for the IRS to consider granting the extension. If the IRS approves the extension request, an additional 30 days to file is granted. If more time is needed to file, up to an additional 30 days can be requested by submitting another Form 8809 before the end of the initial extension period.

> **Practice Pointer.** The IRS suggests that Form 8809 be filed as soon as it is known that an extension is necessary.

> **Note.** If a request to extend the time to file Form 5498 with the IRS is approved, the extension applies only to the due date for filing the form with the IRS. Such approval does not extend the due date for providing extension statements to IRA owners or beneficiaries.

Q 9:6   Does the IRS grant automatic extensions?

Yes. Under Treasury Regulations Section 1.6081-8, filers and transmitters of certain information returns may obtain an automatic 30-day extension of time to file. Forms covered by this regulation include Form 1042-S, Form 8027, and forms in the 1099, 1098, 5498, and W-2 series.

Filers may request an automatic 30-day extension by filing Form 8809. No signature or explanation is required. The form may be submitted on paper, or through the Filing Information Returns Electronically (FIRE) system either as a fill-in form or electronic file. Requests for additional time generally are granted only in cases of extreme hardship or catastrophic event. The IRS will send a letter of explanation approving or denying the request for an additional extension.

However, an extension beyond the initial 30-day period will not be granted unless the filer (1) has first obtained an automatic extension and (2) provides a signed Form 8809 and a detailed explanation.

> **Note.** An extension of time to file an information return with the IRS does not extend the due date for providing a statement to the individual whose information is required to be reported.

Q 9:7   May an extension be requested to provide returns to the form recipient?

Yes. As stated earlier, an extension of time to file an information return with the IRS does not extend the due date for providing a statement to the person with respect to whom the information is to be reported. The payer may request an extension of time to provide the returns to the form recipient by sending a letter to Enterprise Computing Center—Martinsburg (see Q 9:5). The letter must include (a) the payer's name, (b) the payer's TIN, (c) the payer's address, (d) type of return, (e) a statement that the payer's extension request is for providing statements to recipients, (f) reason for delay, and (g) the signature of the payer or authorized agent. The request must be postmarked by the date on which the statements are due to the recipients. If the request for an extension is approved, the payer will generally be granted a maximum of 30 days to furnish the recipient statements. See General Instructions for Forms 1099, 1098, 3921, 3922, 5498, and W-2G, Statements to Participants, page 11 (2009).

Q 9:8 How should the 2009 Form 5498 be completed?

The following is a box-by-box explanation of the 2009 Form 5498.

Note. If an individual has only one IRA agreement, only one Form 5498 should be issued. If, on the other hand, an individual has established more than one Roth IRA multiple Forms 5498 must be issued.

Box 1: IRA Contributions (Other Than Amounts in Boxes 2–4, 8–10, 13a, 14a, and 15a). This box is used to report contributions made to a traditional IRA in 2009 and from January 1 through April 15, 2010, which are designated *for* 2009.

Box 1 is left blank in the case of a Roth IRA (see box 10 below).

Box 2: Rollover Contributions. Enter any 60-day rollover contributions made to a Roth IRA during 2009. Also include a direct rollover to a traditional IRA from an employer-sponsored qualified plan (Section 401(a) or Section 403(a) plan), a tax-sheltered annuity (Section 403(b) plan), a governmental 457(b) plan, or the Federal Employee's Thrift Savings Plan. Designated Roth contributions that are rolled over from a 401(k) or 403(b) are also reported in box 2.

If the rollover consists of property other than cash, enter its FMV on the date of distribution.

Note 1. The value the property on the day it is received may differ from the value of the property on the day of distribution from the original plan.

Do not report as rollovers direct transfers between like plans that involve no payment or distribution to the individual. If a distribution is directly transferred from a Roth IRA to another Roth IRA, do not report the amount rolled over in this box.

Note 2. Also report in box 2 a military death gratuity, a Servicemembers' Group Life Insurance (SGLI) payment, qualified Exxon Valdez settlement income, and certain airline payment amounts (see chapter 3).

Note 3. The repayment of a qualified reservist distribution is not treated as a rollover and is not reported in box 2. Such amounts are entered in box 14a (see below). The repayment of qualified hurricane distributions (see Qs 3:125–3:131) is reported in box 14a. A code is entered in box 14b (see below).

Box 3: Roth IRA Conversion Amount. Enter the amount of a conversion (or a reconversion) from a traditional IRA, SEP IRA, or SIMPLE IRA (that has met the two-year period) to a Roth IRA during 2009 regardless of how the conversion was accomplished.

Box 4: Recharacterized Contributions. A recharacterization transfer from a traditional IRA to a Roth IRA or from a Roth IRA to a traditional IRA, plus earnings, is reported in box 4. All recharacterization transfers received by the same IRA during the same year are aggregated and reported on a single Form 5498. Mark the appropriate checkbox in box 7 to indicate the type of IRA that received the recharacterization.

Box 5: FMV of Account. Enter the FMV of the Roth IRA being reported on this Form 5498 as of December 31, 2009, in this box. This value includes all assets of the plan. An IRA *plan* means all of the assets under the trust or custodial agreement (or in the case of an IRA annuity, the value of the annuity contract). The December 31, 2009, FMV does not include regular contributions made in 2010 for 2009.

For example, an individual may have signed only one Roth IRA agreement and has various investments. In this case, only one Form 5498 should be issued. On the other hand, an individual may have established more than one Roth IRA agreement. For example, one agreement was established for regular contributions, a second agreement for conversion contributions, and a third agreement for a direct rollover from another Roth IRA. In this case, three Forms 5498 should be issued, because the individual has three Roth IRA plans.

Caution. If more than one Form 5498 is being provided, only show the FMV in box 5 on only one of those forms.

Traditional IRAs must be reported separately from Roth IRAs. Likewise, SIMPLE IRAs must be reported on a separate Form 5498.

Box 6: Life Insurance Cost Included in Box 1. This box is used for endowment contracts only. Enter the amount included in box 1 allocable to the cost of life insurance. Life insurance is not a permissible Roth IRA investment. Therefore, no amount should be entered in this box for a Roth IRA.

Box 7: Checkboxes. This series of checkboxes is used to identify the character of the IRA contribution or assets in the account. The boxes are IRA, SEP, SIMPLE, and Roth IRA.

Roth IRA Checkbox. Check this box if Form 5498 is being filed to report information about any Roth IRA account.

Box 8: SEP Contribution. This box is used to report any amount that the employer (including a self-employed) has contributed to a SEP IRA (including salary deferrals under a SARSEP IRA) *during* 2009, including contributions made in 2009 for 2008 but not including contributions made in 2010 for 2009. No amount should be entered in this box for a Roth IRA.

Box 9: SIMPLE Contribution. This box is used to report employer contributions to a SIMPLE IRA (including salary deferrals and employer matching or nonelective) *during* 2009. No amount should be entered in this box for a Roth IRA.

Box 10: Roth IRA Contributions. Enter any regular contributions made to a Roth IRA in 2009 and through April 15, 2010, which are designated *for* 2009. Do not report a Roth IRA conversion (see box 3) or 60-day rollovers (see box 2) in this box.

Box 11: Check if RMD for 2010. Check the box if the participant must take a RMD in 2010 or reached age 70½ during the year. Roth IRAs are not subject to RMD reporting (but see chapter 4 regarding beneficiaries).

Note. The blank boxes to the left of box 10 have been replaced with boxes 12 through 15 beginning in 2009.

Box 12a: RMD Date. If Form 5329 is used to report RMD dates and amounts, the RMD date is entered in this box. No entry should be entered in this box for a Roth IRA.

Box 12b: RMD Amount. If Form 5329 is used to report RMD dates and amounts, the RMD amount is entered in this box.

Box 13a: Postponed Contribution. Report the amount of any postponed contributions made in 2009 for a prior year. If contributions were made for more than one prior year, each year's postponed contribution must be reported on a separate Form 5329.

Box 13b: Year. Enter the year for which the postponed contribution reported in box 13a was made.

Box 13c. Code. Enter a reason code for the postponed contribution. For participant's service in the combat zone or hazardous duty area, enter AF for Allied Force, JE for Joint Endeavor, EF for Enduring Freedom, and IF for Iraqi Freedom. For affected participants in a federally designated disaster area, enter FD.

Box 14a: Repayments. Enter amount of any repayment of a qualified reservist distribution (see Q 3:119) or a designated disaster distribution repayment (e.g., a qualified hurricane distribution, see Q 3:125).

Box 14b: Code. Enter QR for the repayment of a qualified reservist distribution, or DD for repayment of a federally designated disaster distribution.

Box 15a: Other Contributions. Enter the amount of special catch-up contributions made in the case of certain employer bankruptcies (up to $3,000). The regular catch-up contribution ($1,000 for 2009) does not apply if the special catch-up contribution is made (see Q 2:1). [I.R.C. § 219(c)(5)(C)]

Box 15b: Code. Enter BK for special catch-up contributions (see above).

Note. If box 13 or 14 is used to report more than one type of contribution to the same account, a separate Form 5498 is required for each type of contribution. Only enter the FMV on one of the forms.

Q 9:9 What information or important reminders are contained in the instructions for Form 5498?

Important reminders in the general instructions for the 2009 version of Form 5498 include the following.

E-filers are reminded that using the Filing Information Returns Electronically (FIRE) system requires following the specifications contained in Publication 1220, Specifications for Filing Forms 1098, 1099, 3921, 3922, 5498, and W-2G Electronically. In addition, the IRS does not provide a fill-in form option. See part F on page 5 for information on e-file.

Information to Be Provided to IRA Owner (or Beneficiary)

Q 9:10 Must Form 5498 be provided to a Roth IRA owner?

In general, a copy of the Form 5498 that is submitted to the IRS must be provided to the Roth IRA owner (or beneficiary as the case may be). The deadline for providing that copy is May 31, the same deadline as the deadline for IRS submission.

Additionally, an FMV statement, also referred to as an "annual participant statement," must be issued to all Roth IRA owners before the May 31 deadline. That is, by Monday, February 1, 2010, for 2009 reporting, the trustee of a Roth IRA must provide the owner with a statement of the FMV of the account on December 31, 2009, in any written format. If using Form 5498 to report this information, that FMV is to be reflected in box 5 on Form 5498.

Q 9:11 May a substitute statement for Form 5498 be furnished to an IRA owner?

Yes. An exact copy of the official Form 5498 need not be furnished to the IRA owner. A trustee (or custodial) organization may use a substitute for Form 5498 that meets the requirements of IRS Publication 1179, *General Rules and Specifications for Substitute Forms 1096, 1098, 1099, 5498, and W-2G , and 1042-S.*

IRS Publication 1179, updated each year, contains the current year's revenue procedure dealing with sending substitute statements to form recipients. It may be ordered from the IRS by calling (800) 829-3676. [Also available as Rev. Proc. 2008-36, 2008-33 I.R.B. 340 (Aug. 18, 2008)]

Substitute statements (including those issued in lieu of Form 5498) to form recipients must meet the following requirements:

1. They must contain the same tax year, form number, and form name as those on the official IRS form, prominently displayed together in one area of the statement; for example, in the upper right part of the statement.

2. The filer and form recipient identification information that is required on the official IRS form must be included.

3. All applicable dollar amounts and information, including box numbers, required to be reported to the form recipient must be titled on the form recipient statement in substantially the same manner as they are on the official IRS form.

4. Appropriate instructions to the form recipient, similar to those on the official IRS form, must be provided to aid in the proper reporting of the items on the form recipient's income tax return.

5. The following language must be included—"The information in boxes 1, 2, 3, 4, 5, 6, 7, 8, 9, 10, and 11 is being furnished to the Internal Revenue Service."

6. The Office of Management and Budget (OMB) number must be shown as it appears on the official IRS form.

7. The quality of carbon used to produce substitute statements to recipients must meet the following standards—

   a. All copies must be clearly legible;

   b. All copies must have the capability to be photocopied; and

   c. Fading must not be of such a degree as to preclude legibility and the ability to photocopy.

8. Although not required, payers reporting 5498 (or 1099-R) information on substitute forms are encouraged to furnish a direct access telephone number of an individual who can answer questions about the statement.

9. The box caption "Federal income tax withheld" must be in boldface type on the form recipient statement.

[Rev. Proc. 2008-36, §§ 4.1.3, 4.4.3, 2008-33 I.R.B. 340 (Aug. 18, 2008)]

In general, black chemical transfer inks are preferred; other colors are permitted only if the above standards are met. Hot wax and cold carbon spots are generally not permitted.

Q 9:12   Must Form 5498 (or a substitute statement) be sent to an IRA owner for a year with no contributions?

No. If a statement regarding an IRA's FMV was furnished to the IRA owner by January 31, 2009 (Monday, February 1, 2010, for 2009 reporting), and no reportable contributions were made, it is not necessary to furnish another statement (i.e., Form 5498) to the owner to report no contributions for 2009 reporting purposes.

Be that as it may, IRS Publication 1179 contains the following note:

Note 1. If the trustee does not issue Form 5498 to a participant because no contributions were made to an IRA for the year, a year-end statement issued to the participant reporting the FMV of the account must contain a similar legend designating which information is being furnished to the IRS.

Furthermore, the instructions to Form 5498 contain the following note:

Note 2. If no statement is provided to the participant because no contributions were made for the year, the statement of the FMV of the account must contain a legend designating which information is being furnished to the Internal Revenue Service.

[Rev. Proc. 2008-36, § 4.3.3, 2008-33 I.R.B. 340 (Aug. 18, 2008)]

Practice Pointer. It may be appropriate for a Roth IRA trustee or custodian to plan ahead and include the necessary language on the FMV statement sent to the Roth IRA owner in January to cover the contingency that no Form 5498 (or substitute) is sent in May.

Q 9:13   May the FMV statement and the Form 5498 requirements be coordinated?

Yes. Many organizations coordinate the FMV statement and the Form 5498 requirements in the following manner:

1. In January, the official Form 5498 (or an acceptable substitute) for the prior year is issued for each Roth IRA owner who has already made the prior year's Roth contribution, completed a conversion from a traditional IRA to a Roth IRA, or made a rollover or direct rollover contribution during the prior year (see Q 3:4). The prior year-end value is also included on Form 5498 (or the acceptable substitute).

2. After April 15, the official Form 5498 (or an acceptable substitute) may be issued for each IRA owner who made a regular contribution for a prior year to a traditional IRA or Roth IRA between January 1 and April 15 of the following year. Only those individuals need to receive a new Form 5498 before the May 31 deadline.

3. All information (both the January information and the later information) is transmitted to the IRS at the same time, after April 15 but before the May 31 deadline.

Many financial reporting institutions have found the foregoing procedure to be a most efficient and economical way to handle both the FMV and Form 5498 requirements.

Practice Pointer. Because reporting requirements change every year, it is best to discuss them with the data processing department at least annually.

Deceased IRA Owner

Q 9:14   Are there special reporting requirements for a deceased Roth IRA owner?

Yes. In the year of a Roth IRA owner's death, Form 5498 (and the year-end FMV information due by January 31) must be issued in both the decedent's name and in the name of each primary beneficiary (the latter because a Roth IRA owner must be able to identify the source of each Roth IRA he or she holds for purposes of figuring the taxation of a distribution from an IRA). [Rev. Proc. 89-52, 1989-2 C.B. 632]

The beneficiary's Form 5498 must be styled, for example, as "Robert Patrick as beneficiary of Greg Yarnell"; the only information to be reported is the FMV of the beneficiary's portion of the decedent's Roth IRA as of year-end. The trustee or custodian continues issuing Form 5498 on behalf of the beneficiary until the IRA is reduced to zero.

Unless a spouse beneficiary makes the decedent's Roth IRA his or her own Roth IRA (see Qs 5:32, 5:34), the spouse is treated as any other beneficiary for the special reporting purposes. If the spouse is sole beneficiary and makes the decedent's Roth IRA his or her own in the year of death, however, Form 5498 and the annual FMV statement are prepared without the beneficiary designation—because the spouse becomes the Roth IRA owner.

On the decedent's Form 5498 and annual FMV statement, either the FMV of the Roth IRA as of the date of death or the FMV as of the end of the year in which the decedent died may be used.

Q 9:15   What is the alternative method of reporting a deceased IRA owner's balance under Revenue Procedure 89-52?

Under the alternative method of reporting a deceased Roth IRA owner's balance contained in Revenue Procedure 89-52 [1989-2 C.B. 632], any FMV reported on the beneficiary's Form 5498 should not also be reported on the decedent's Form 5498 for that year. Consequently, the value of the decedent's account as of the end of the year will frequently be zero even though the money is still in the account.

In other words, under the alternative method, for the year in which the IRA owner dies, the trustee or custodian prepares a Form 5498 in the name of the original IRA owner (and with the owner's Social Security number) reflecting rollover contributions (box 2), any Roth conversions for the year (box 3), the FMV as zero (box 5), the proper box checked (box 7), or Roth IRA contributions (box 10). That Form 5498 will be the last such form to be issued in the name of the deceased IRA owner. If the trustee (or custodian) uses this alternative method, it must inform the executor of the decedent's estate of his or her right to secure the Roth IRA's FMV as of the date of death of the Roth IRA owner, provided that the Roth IRA has not yet been withdrawn by the beneficiary.

Usually no entry is required in a box if the value is zero. Under the alternative method, the money is in fact still in the account at year-end; therefore, the preparer is specifically instructed to enter a zero in box 5.

Q 9:16   If the beneficiary of a Roth IRA receives a total distribution by year-end, how is it reported?

If a beneficiary of a Roth IRA takes a total distribution of his or her share of a Roth IRA in the year of the IRA owner's death, it is not necessary to file a Form 5498 or to furnish an annual statement for that beneficiary. Instead, Form 1099-R in the name of the beneficiary reports the amount of the death distribution. Form 5498 must still be issued for the decedent, however, even if the only information being reported is zero in box 5.

Q 9:17   How do the reporting requirements for a deceased Roth IRA owner apply if the IRA trustee (or custodian) had no knowledge of the owner's death until after the reporting date?

If a trustee (or custodian) had no knowledge of the death of the Roth IRA owner until after the reporting deadline (generally May 31), no corrective filing of Form 5498 is required for that year nor furnish a corrected annual statement. The trustee (or custodian) should probably prepare Forms 5498 for the year it becomes aware of the owner's death, provided the Roth IRA has not yet been withdrawn by the beneficiary.

Whether or not the trustee (or custodian) was notified timely of the death of the Roth IRA owner, the trustee (or custodian) must inform the executor of the decedent' estate of the executor's right to receive the IRA's FMV statement as of the IRA owner's death. Normally, using the language for box 5 on the back of copy B of the official Form 5498, or using the official copy B, automatically satisfies that requirement. [Rev. Proc. 89-52, 1989-2 C.B. 632]

> **Example.** Sarah Mock had a Roth IRA, the beneficiaries of which were her three nephews: Brian Snake, Brad Snake, and Bob Snake. In the year of Sarah's death, but before she died, a rollover conversion in the amount of $75,000 was added to Sarah's Roth IRA from her traditional IRA. Brad and Bob both took a total distribution of their beneficial interest in the Roth IRA. Brian decided to have his portion paid out over a five-year period, leaving the year-end FMV of Sarah's IRA as $25,000.
>
> In the year of Sarah's death, two Forms 5498 will be issued. First, a Form 5498 will be issued in Sarah Mock's name and Social Security number with $75,000 in box 3, representing her conversion amount from her traditional Roth IRA, and $0 in box 5, reflecting the use of the *alternative method* for reporting FMV. Brian will receive a Form 5498 styled "Brian Snake as beneficiary of Sarah Mock," using Brian's Social Security number and reporting $25,000 FMV in box 5. That dollar amount represents Brian's one-third beneficial interest in his aunt's Roth IRA. (No Form 5498 will be

issued for Brad and Bob because each took a total distribution of his beneficial interest in the IRA before year-end.)

Brad will receive a Form 1099-R styled "Brad Snake as beneficiary of Sarah Mock," using Brad's Social Security number and reflecting the $25,000 death distribution he received from his aunt's Roth IRA during the year. Bob will receive Form 1099-R styled "Bob Snake as beneficiary of Sarah Mock," using Bob's Social Security number and reflecting the $25,000 death distribution he received from his aunt's Roth IRA during the year.

Recharacterization Contributions

Q 9:18   What are the *first IRA* and *second IRA* with respect to recharacterization contribution reporting for purposes of Form 5498?

For purposes of Form 5498, the *first IRA* is the IRA from which the recharacterization is being made, and the *second IRA* is the IRA to which the recharacterization is being made.

Q 9:19   For purposes of Form 5498, what reporting requirements apply to the first IRA involved in a recharacterization?

The first IRA involved in a recharacterization reports the original contribution on Form 5498 showing the character of the contribution (rollover, conversion, or regular). The trustee of the first IRA must also report the distribution on Form 1099-R.

Q 9:20   For purposes of Form 5498, what reporting requirements apply to the second IRA involved in a recharacterization?

The second IRA involved in a recharacterization reports the contribution as a recharacterized contribution on Form 5498 in box 4.

Furthermore, the trustee (or custodian) of the second IRA checks the box that identifies the type of IRA involved. The FMV will *not* be entered in box 5 of the separate Form 5498 that is reporting the recharacterization. (It will be shown on the Form 5498 issued with respect to the other contributions made to the same plan.) If, however, there are no other contributions or rollovers to the recharacterized IRA, the FMV of the account and the recharacterization of the IRA contribution may be reported on the same Form 5498.

Note. All recharacterization transfers received by the same IRA for the "prior year" are aggregated and reported on a single Form 5498.

Revoked Roth IRAs

Q 9:21   Must a revoked Roth IRA be reported on Form 5498?

Yes. Revenue Procedure 91-70 [1991-2 C.B. 899] outlines the reporting requirements that apply whenever an IRA is timely revoked (see Qs 1:36–1:38, 4:26). Before issuance of Revenue Procedure 91-70, an IRA that was timely revoked was treated as though it had never existed and no reporting was required.

Q 9:22   How are the different types of contributions made to a Roth IRA that is timely revoked reported on Form 5498?

If a traditional or Roth IRA is revoked during its first seven days or is closed at any time by the IRA trustee or custodian due to a failure of the taxpayer to satisfy the Customer Identification Program (CIP) requirements, the distribution from the Roth IRA must be reported. [See Treas. Reg. § 1.408-6(d)(4)(ii); USA Patriot Act (Pub. L. No. 107-37) § 326]

In addition, Form 5498, IRA Contribution Information, must be filed to report a regular, rollover, Roth IRA conversion, SEP IRA, or SIMPLE IRA contribution to an IRA that is subsequently revoked or closed by the trustee or custodian.

If a regular contribution is made to a traditional or Roth IRA that later is revoked or closed, and distribution is made to the taxpayer, enter the gross distribution in box 1 of Form 1099-R. If no earnings are distributed, enter 0 (zero) in box 2a and code 8 in box 7 for a traditional IRA and code J for a Roth IRA. If earnings are distributed, enter the amount of earnings in box 2a. For a traditional IRA, enter codes 1 and 8, if applicable, in box 7; for a Roth IRA, enter codes J and 8, if applicable. These earnings could be subject to the 10 percent early distribution tax under Code Section 72(t). If a rollover contribution is made to a traditional or Roth IRA that later is revoked or closed, and distribution is made to the taxpayer, enter in boxes 1 and 2a of Form 1099-R the gross distribution and the appropriate code in box 7 (code J for a Roth IRA). See chart in Q 9:46. Follow this same procedure for a transfer from a traditional or Roth IRA to another IRA of the same type that later is revoked or closed. The distribution could be subject to the 10 percent early distribution tax under Code Section 72(t).

If an IRA conversion contribution is made to a Roth IRA that later is revoked or closed, and a distribution is made to the taxpayer, enter the gross distribution in box 1 of Form 1099-R. If no earnings are distributed, enter 0 (zero) in box 2a and code J in box 7. If earnings are distributed, enter the amount of the earnings in box 2a and code J in box 7. These earnings could be subject to the 10 percent early distribution tax under Code Section 72(t). [See also Rev. Proc. 91-70, 1991-2 C.B. 899]

Q 9:23   What happens if the revocation of an IRA "crosses" a calendar year-end?

In most situations, a revocation of an IRA (including a Roth IRA) occurs in the same calendar year as the contribution. Therefore, a year-end FMV statement and completing box 5 of Form 5498 will not be required. If, however, the contribution is made in one calendar year and revoked in the next calendar year (but within seven days), an FMV statement and box 5 of Form 5498 must be prepared accordingly.

Penalties

Q 9:24   What are the penalties for noncompliance with the filing requirements for Form 5498?

The following penalties apply to a trustee or custodial organization required to file Form 5498 with the IRS:

1. A $50-per-failure penalty applies to each failure to timely file an original Form 5498.

2. A $50-per-failure penalty applies to each failure to file a corrected Form 5498 when required.

3. A $50-per-failure penalty applies to each failure to timely furnish a statement to a participant as required.

4. If the trustee or custodian files on paper returns, a $50-per-failure penalty applies to each failure to furnish paper forms that are machine scannable.

Failure to transmit Form 5498 via magnetic media or electronically when required and failure to follow the paper submission format are treated as failure to file the form unless the trustee or custodial organization has an approved waiver on file or can establish reasonable cause, or in some cases, due diligence.

Penalties also apply to reporting an incorrect tax identification number (TIN) and failing to report a TIN. The penalties are different depending on the type of information return being filed.

All of the foregoing penalties apply unless the failures were due to reasonable cause and not willful neglect. In the case of intentional disregard of the filing and correct information requirements, higher penalties of $100 per failure may be imposed. [I.R.C. § 6693; Treas. Reg. § 1.408-5]

Records Retention

Q 9:25   How long should copies of Form 5498 be kept?

Copies of information returns filed with the IRS (including Form 5498), or the ability to reconstruct the data, should be retained for at least three years from the due date of the returns. However, for a Roth IRA owner to verify the nontaxable part of distributions from his or her Roth IRA (and other IRAs), keep a copy of the following forms and records until all distributions are made:

- Page 1 of Forms 1040 (or Forms 1040A, 1040, NR, or 1040-T) filed for each year a nondeductible contribution was contributed to an IRA.
- Forms 8606 and any supporting statements, attachments, and worksheets for all applicable years.
- Forms 5498 or similar statements received each year showing contributions (and FMV) made to a traditional IRA or Roth IRA.
- Form 1099-R or Form W-2P each year a distribution was received.

Note. Forms 1040-T and W-2P are forms that were used in prior years.

Reporting Roth IRA Distributions on Form 1099-R

Q 9:26 What information regarding distributions from Roth IRAs is required to be reported to the IRS and to the recipient?

Each year, trustees and custodians of IRAs (including Roth IRAs) are required to report distribution information to the IRS and to the recipient of the distribution. [I.R.C. § 408(i); Treas. Reg. § 1.408-7] Form 1099-R, Distributions from Pensions, Annuities, Retirement or Profit-Sharing Plans, IRAs, Insurance, Contracts, etc., is designed for that purpose. The distributions at issue are those that have been made during the calendar year to which the report relates.

Note. Beginning in 2006, Roth 401(k) and Roth 403(b) distributions will be reported on separate 1099-R forms. In addition, if a participant terminates service, they will receive two separate 1099-Rs, one for the Roth account, and another for the distribution of any non-Roth balances under the plan.

Q 9:27 What is the deadline for filing Form 1099-R?

Form 1099-R must be provided to recipients of distributions no later than January 31 following the calendar year in which the distribution was made. Form 1099-R must be transmitted to the IRS no later than February 28 following the calendar year in which the distribution was made. (Leap years are ignored for this deadline.) [I.R.S. Ann. 91-179, 1991-49 I.R.B. 78] If a regular due date falls on a Saturday, Sunday, or legal holiday, the due date becomes the next business day.

Q 9:28 How can an extension of time to file Form 1099-R with the IRS be requested?

For paper or magnetic media filing, a request for an extension of time to file Form 1099-R with the IRS can be made by completing Form 8809, and sending it to the following address:

Enterprise Computing Center—Martinsburg
Information Reporting Program
Attn: Extension of Time Coordinator
240 Murall Drive
Kearneysville, WV 25430

Form 8809 must be filed no later than the due date for Form 1099-R in order for the IRS to consider granting the extension. If the IRS approves the extension request, an additional 30 days to file is granted. If more time is needed to file, an additional 30 days can be requested by submitting another Form 8809 before the end of the initial extension period. (See Q 9:8 for additional information.)

Practice Pointer. The IRS suggests that Form 8809 be filed as soon as it is known that an extension is necessary.

Note. If a request to extend the time to file Form 1099-R with the IRS is approved, the extension applies only to the due date for filing the returns with the IRS. Such approval does not extend the due date for providing statements to IRA owners or beneficiaries.

Q 9:29 How can an extension of time for providing Form 1099-R to Roth IRA owners or beneficiaries be requested?

An extension of time for providing Form 1099-R to IRA owners or beneficiaries can be requested by sending a letter to the following address:

Enterprise Computing Center—Martinsburg
Information Reporting Program
Attn: Extension of Time Coordinator
240 Murall Drive
Kearneysville, WV 25430

The letter must include the following information:

- Payer's name
- Payer's TIN
- Payer's address
- Type of return (in this instance, Form 1099-R)
- Statement that the request is for an extension for providing forms to recipients
- Reason for the delay
- Signature of the payer or authorized agent

The request must be postmarked by the due date of the return—in this case, January 31.

If the request for extension is approved, an additional 30 days is granted to furnish the recipient statements.

Q 9:30   How should the 2009 Form 1099-R be completed for a Roth IRA?

Following is a box-by-box explanation of the 2009 Form 1099-R, including the reporting codes applicable to Roth IRA distributions.

Box 1: Gross Distribution. Report the total amount of the distribution, *including* income taxes that were withheld (if any), but do *not* include any fees that were charged (e.g., CD penalties for early withdrawal). For a distribution of property other than cash, report the FMV of the property on the date of distribution. Include direct rollovers.

Recharacterizations. Recharacterizations of eligible Roth IRA contributions are reportable on Form 1099-R. Enter the amount of the recharacterized contribution plus earnings in this box. In the case of a loss on the recharacterized contribution, enter the actual amount recharacterized in this box. Recharacterizations *must* be accomplished via a trustee-to-trustee transfer, rather than a distribution and rollover.

The IRA *from which* the recharacterized amount is being transferred is referred to as the *first IRA*. Therefore, that trustee must issue Form 1099-R. (The trustee of the first IRA must also report the original contribution and its character on Form 5498 issued with respect to the first IRA.)

If the first IRA is a traditional IRA, the only type of contribution that is eligible to be recharacterized to a Roth IRA is a regular contribution. If the first IRA is a Roth IRA, the eligible recharacterized contribution to a traditional IRA can be either a regular contribution or a conversion. Earnings (or losses) attributable to the recharacterized contribution must be included in the transfer. "Prior year" recharacterizations must be reported on a separate Form 1099-R from "same year" recharacterizations because different reporting codes apply for Box 7. Code R is used for a prior year recharacterization, and code N is used for a same year recharacterization.

A prior year recharacterization is a recharacterization of a contribution made *for* 2008 and recharacterized in 2009, even if the 2008 contribution was made in 2009. In the case of a recharacterization of a conversion that came from a traditional IRA in 2008 but was not converted until 2009 (but within the requisite 60-day period), treat this recharacterization as a prior year recharacterization for these reporting purposes. A same year recharacterization is a recharacterization of a contribution made *for* 2009 and recharacterized in 2009 (see Q 9:44).

Conversions/reconversions. The trustee must report in this box an IRA that is converted or reconverted to a Roth IRA, even if the conversion or reconversion is accomplished as a trustee-to-trustee transfer or is internally converted with the same trustee.

Revocations and CIP failures. If a regular contribution is made to a Roth IRA (or a traditional IRA) that is revoked within the plan's first seven days, and distribution is made to the taxpayer, enter the gross distribution in this box. If an IRA conversion contribution is made to a Roth IRA that is revoked within the plan's first seven days, and distribution is made to the taxpayer, enter the gross distribution in this box. (See contribution revocations in Q 1:35.) If a Roth IRA is involuntarily closed by the trustee or custodian because it did not receive the information necessary to satisfy the CIP under the USA Patriot Act (Pub. L. No. 107-37) (see Q 1:19) it is treated, for reporting purposes, the same as a revocation.

> **Note.** *Designated Roth Account.* For distribution from a designated Roth account, enter the gross distribution in box 1, the taxable portion of the distribution in box 2a, the basis included in the distributed amount in box 5, and the first year of the five-taxable-year period in the box to the left of box 10. Also, enter the applicable code(s) in box 7 (see Q 9:31).

Box 2a: Taxable Amount. For a distribution from a Roth IRA, report the total distribution in box 1 and leave box 2a blank except in the case of an Roth IRA revocation (see Q 1:35) or CIP account closure (see Q 1:19) and a recharacterization (see Q 3:29). Use code J, Q, or T as appropriate in box 7. Use code 8 or P, if applicable, in box 7 with code J. Do not combine code Q or T with any other codes. However, for the distribution of excess Roth IRA contributions, report the gross distribution in box 1 and only the earnings in box 2a. Enter code J, and code 8 or P in box 7. See box 7 contribution codes in Q 9:31.

Roth IRA conversion. Report the total amount converted or reconverted from a traditional IRA, SEP IRA, or SIMPLE IRA to a Roth IRA in boxes 1 and 2a. For a Roth IRA conversion, use code 2 in box 7 if the participant is under age 59½ or code 7 if the participant is at least age 59½. Also check the "IRA/SEP/SIMPLE" box in box 7.

A conversion or reconversion is considered a distribution and must be reported even if it is with the same trustee and even if the conversion is done by a trustee-to-trustee transfer. When an IRA annuity described in Code Section 408(b) is converted to a Roth IRA, the amount that is treated as distributed is the FMV of the annuity contract on the date the annuity contract is converted. This rule also applies when a traditional IRA account holds an annuity contract as an account asset and the traditional IRA is converted to a Roth IRA.

> **Note.** Determining the FMV of an individual retirement annuity issued by a company regularly engaged in the selling of contracts depends on the timing of the conversion (see Qs 3:20–3:28).

Losses (Roth IRA and designated Roth accounts). If a distribution is a loss, do not enter a negative amount in this box (see Qs 4:34–4:35). For example, if stock is distributed from a designated Roth account, enter the value of the stock in box 1, leave box 2a blank, and enter the employee's contributions or designated Roth account contributions in box 5.

Revocation and Other Failures

- *Excess or unwanted contributions.* If an excess (or unwanted) contribution made to a Roth IRA is distributed (including the earnings attributable) by the deadline for filing the individual's federal income tax return (including extensions) for the year *during which* the contribution was made, enter only the earnings in this box. If there are no earnings, enter 0 (zero) in this box. This type of distribution is handled and reported in exactly the same manner as described under Code Section 408(d)(4). These earnings may be subject to the 10 percent penalty on early distributions.

- *Revocation or CIP failure.* If a regular contribution made to a Roth IRA is timely revoked (usually within the first seven days from the date the plan is established), and no earnings are distributed, enter 0 (zero) in this box and code J (early distributions from Roth IRA) in box 7. If earnings are distributed in such revoked distribution, enter only the earnings in this box, and, if applicable, code J (early distribution) and 8 (excess contributions plus earnings) in box 7 regardless of age. These earnings may be subject to the 10 percent penalty on early distributions.

- *Rollover later revoked or closed.* If a rollover is made to a Roth IRA that is later revoked or closed, and a distribution is made to the taxpayer, enter the gross distribution in boxes 1 and 2a and code J in box 7. The distribution may be subject to the 10 percent penalty on early distributions.

- *Conversion or reconversion revocation.* If a conversion made to a Roth IRA is timely revoked, and no earnings are distributed, enter 0 (zero) in this box, and code J in box 7. If earnings are distributed, enter only the earnings in this box, and code J in box 7. These earnings may be subject to the 10 percent penalty on early distributions.

Note. The contribution first recovery rules do not apply to a designated Roth account (DRA) under an employer's plan (see Q 10:28, and the Example below).

Example. Participant A received a nonqualified distribution of $5,000 from the participant's designated Roth account. Prior to the distribution, the participant's account balance was $10,000, consisting of $9,400 of designated Roth contributions and $600 of earnings. The taxable amount of the $5,000 distribution is $300 (600 ÷ 10,000 × 5,000). The nontaxable portion of the distribution is $4,700 (9,400 ÷ 10,000 × 5,000). The issuer would report on Form 1099-R:

- Box 1, $5,000 as the gross distribution;
- Box 2a, $300 as the taxable amount;
- Box 5, $4,700 as the designated Roth contribution basis (nontaxable amount); and
- The first year of the five-taxable-year period in the box to the left of box 10.

Box 2b: Taxable Amount Not Determined. Enter an "X" in this box only if the trustee or custodian is unable to reasonably obtain the data needed to compute the taxable amount.

If the distribution is from a *Roth IRA*, generally mark this box and leave box 2a blank (unless the distribution is a return of excess plus earnings, a recharacterization, or a revocation as explained in box 2a).

Do *not* mark this box if the distribution is a return of an excess contribution plus earnings from a Roth IRA. In this case, the earnings *are* taxable (and reported in box 2a), and thus the taxable amount *is* determined. Do *not* mark this box if the Form 1099-R is reporting a recharacterization transfer from a Roth IRA to a traditional IRA. In this case, 0 (zero) is entered in box 2a, and thus the taxable amount *is* determined to be zero. Do *not* mark this box if the distribution is a revocation of a Roth IRA. In this case, either the earnings or 0 (zero) will be entered in box 2a, and thus the taxable amount *is* determined.

(Second) Box 2b: Total Distribution. Enter an "X" in this box only if the payment shown in box 1 is a total distribution. A total distribution is one or more distributions within one tax year in which the entire balance of the account is distributed. If periodic or installment payments are made, mark this box in the year the final payment is made.

Box 3: Capital Gain (Included in Box 2a). Leave this box blank for any Roth IRA distribution.

Box 4: Federal Income Tax Withheld. Most Roth IRA distributions are exempt from any federal income tax withholding as a result of the Consolidated Appropriations Act of 2000. [Pub. L. No. 106-554] Therefore, do not withhold on any Roth IRA distribution, except in the case of a returned contribution plus earnings before the return due date or a revoked contributions plus earnings. These earnings are always treated as a taxable distribution, even where the Roth IRA owner otherwise meets the definition of a "qualified distribution." [*See* I.R.C. § 408A(d)(2)(C); Treas. Reg. § 1.408A-6, Q&A 1(d)] Thus, withholding applies only on the earnings being distributed. Of course, the recipient can elect no withholding on the earnings.

Recharacterizations. Do not withhold on any IRA recharacterization. Recharacterizations are not treated as distributions.

Note. If a payee fails to furnish his or her taxpayer identification number (TIN), or if the IRS notifies the trustee before any distribution that the TIN furnished is incorrect, the payee cannot claim exemption from these withholding requirements. Backup withholding under Code Section 3406 does not apply to any retirement plan distribution.

Box 5: Employee Contributions or Designated Roth Contributions. This box does not apply to any Roth IRA.

Designated Roth contribution accounts. Distributions from a designated Roth contribution account (DRA) are reported on a separate Form 1099-R. The employee's basis in the DRA are reported in box 5, and earnings in box 2a.

Box 6: Net Unrealized Appreciation in Employer's Securities. This box does not apply to any Roth IRA.

Box 7: Distribution Code. Enter the appropriate code(s) that shows the type of distribution. In certain cases, double codes must be entered. Only three numeric combinations are permitted on one Form 1099: codes 8 and 1, 8 and 2, or 8 and 4. If two or more other numeric codes are applicable, more than one

Form 1099-R must be filed. If an alpha and numeric code is used, there is no required ordering of the codes. Revocations codes are discussed in Q 9:46. For example, if part of a distribution is premature (code 1) and part is not (code 7), file one Form 1099-R for the part to which code 1 applies and another Form 1099-R for the part to which code 7 applies.

Q 9:31   What codes are used to complete box 7 of the 2009 Form 1099-R?

The following codes are used to complete box 7 of the 2009 Form 1099-R for a Roth IRA:

Code 1 (early distribution, no known exception). Indicates that the employee/taxpayer is under age 59½ and the trustee *does not know* if any of the exceptions under distribution codes 2, 3, or 4 apply.

Use code 1 even if the Roth IRA distribution is made for any of the following reasons (since the trustee will not *know* that the exception to the 10 percent premature tax applies):

- Medical expenses [I.R.C. § 72(t)(2)(B)]
- Qualified higher education expenses [I.R.C. § 72(t)(2)(E)]
- First-time homebuyer expenses [I.R.C. § 72(t)(2)(F)]
- Health insurance premiums paid by certain unemployed individuals [I.R.C. § 72(t)(2)(D)]

In these cases, the taxpayer can file Form 5329 with his or her federal income tax return to indicate that the 10 percent premature tax does not apply to the taxable amount.

Use code 1 for a Code Section 408(d)(5) distribution if the taxpayer is under age 59½. See the description of a Code Section 408(d)(5) distribution under box 2a discussion.

Substantially Equal Periodic Payments (SEPPs) Under Code Section 72(t)(2)(A)(iv). In the 2009 instructions, the IRS repeats two times the following statement: "Code 1 must also be used even if a taxpayer is 59 or older and he or she modifies a series of substantially equal periodic payments under Section 72(q), (t) or (v) prior to the end of the 5-year period." If the trustee uses code 2 for SEPPs, the payer is responsible for monitoring and tracking the payments.

Using code 1 for substantially equal payments means:

1. The payer is *not* assuming any responsibility in determining if the amount of the payments meets the exception to the 10 percent premature tax under Code Section 72(t).
2. The payer is *not* monitoring the account for any potential event that would render the account modified (such as additional contributions or partial transfers out of the account).

3. The payer is *not* tracking the modification period (which is the *longer of* attaining age 59½ or the close of the five-year period beginning with the first payment).

Practice Pointer. Substantially equal payments from a Roth IRA are an exception to the 10 percent premature tax to the extent the taxpayer receives any distribution from a Roth IRA that is taxable. However, in these cases, the taxpayer *must* use Forms 8606 and 5329 to indicate that the taxable amount is not subject to the 10 percent tax. This is true even if the payer knows and is tracking the substantially equal payments.

Using code 2 for substantially equal payments means:

1. The payer *is* assuming responsibility in determining if the amount of the payments meets the exception to the 10 percent premature tax under Code Section 72(t).

2. The payer *is* monitoring the account for any potential event that would render the account modified (such as additional contributions or partial transfers out of the account).

3. The payer *is* tracking the modification period (which is the *longer of* attaining age 59½ or the close of the five-year period beginning with the first payment) and thus must switch to code 1 if a modification occurs, even if the taxpayer has attained age 59½.

4. When the taxpayer reaches age 59½, the payer *does not* automatically switch to code 7 (normal) for subsequent distributions. Code 2 would be used until the entire modification period has expired. When the payer uses code 2 for substantially equal payments, switching to code 7 merely because the taxpayer reaches age 59½ is *not* appropriate because the payer would then assume responsibility for the exception to the 10 percent tax until the expiration of the modification period.

5. The taxpayer would not file Form 5329.

Transfers incident to divorce. For Roth IRAs, the rules of Code Section 408(d)(6) apply in making a nonreportable transfer of the affected assets to the IRA of the gaining spouse in the event of a divorce or legal separation.

If applicable, use one of the following codes in addition to code 1: code 8, B, D, L, or P.

Code 2 (early distribution, exception applies (as defined in Code Section 72(q), (t), or(v)). Code 2 is used only if the recipient has not reached age 59½ and for the following specific reasons:

1. A pre-age 59½ distribution is made from an employer's plan or IRA because of an IRS levy under Code Section 6331.

2. A distribution (except from a Roth IRA) is made based on the substantially equal payment rules and the trustee monitors the distribution amounts and the five-year period or attainment of 59½, if later (see explanation under code 1 earlier).

3. Any other distribution that is subject to an exception under Code Section 72(t) that is not required to be reported using code 1 (normal), 3 (disability), or 4 (death). See Q 4:22.

If applicable, use one of the following codes in addition to code 2: code 8, B, D, or P.

Code 3 (disability). Use code 3 if the employee/taxpayer is disabled under Code Section 72(m)(7). [*See* Treas. Reg. § 1.72-17(f)]

Do not use any other code with code 3.

Code 4 (death). Use code 4 regardless of the age of the deceased participant or the age of the beneficiary to indicate that the distribution was made to the decedent's beneficiary, including an estate or a trust.

If applicable, use one of the following codes in addition to code 4: code 8, A, B, D, G, H, L, or P.

Code 5 (prohibited transaction). If it is known that the participant or beneficiary of any IRA has engaged in a prohibited transaction (as defined in Code Section 4975(c)) or if there was an improper use of the account (as defined in Code Section 408(e)(2)), the payer must report the deemed distribution on Form 1099-R.

If the prohibited transaction involves a Roth IRA, use code 5 (instead of code J) regardless of the taxpayer's age.

Do not use any other code with code 5.

Code 6 (Code Section 1035 exchange). Code 6 does not apply to a Roth IRA.

Code 7 (normal distribution). Code 7 does not apply to a Roth IRA.

Code 8 (excess contributions plus earnings/excess deferrals (and/or earnings) taxable in 2009).

1. *IRAs.* Use code 8 for a corrective distribution plus earnings from a Roth IRA where the earnings are taxable in the year of distribution. For a Roth IRA, use the double code J8 regardless of the taxpayer's age.

   Example. A contribution of $5,000 was made in 2009 to a Roth IRA, but the participant was ineligible to make such contribution. Before the end of 2009, the individual withdraws the $5,000 plus $100 of earnings. $5,100 is entered in box 1, $100 is entered in box 2a, and code J8 is reported in box 7 because the earnings are taxable in the year of distribution (2009).

   Example. A contribution of $5,000 was made in January 2009, to a Roth IRA, and designated as a 2008 contribution. However, the participant was ineligible to make such contribution (for the prior year). Before the end of 2009, the individual withdraws the $5,000 plus $100 of earnings. $5,100 is entered in box 1, $100 is entered in box 2a, and code J8 is reported in box 7 because the earnings are taxable in the year *in which* (not *for which*) the contribution was made.

2. If applicable, use one of the following codes in addition to code 8: code 1, 2, 4, B, or J.

Code 9 (cost of current life insurance protection). Code 9 does not apply to a Roth IRA.

Code A (may be eligible for 10-year tax option). Code A does not apply to a Roth IRA.

Code D (excess contributions plus earnings/excess deferrals taxable in 2007). Code D does not apply to a Roth IRA.

Code E (excess annual additions under Code Section 415). Code E does not apply to a Roth IRA.

Code F (charitable gift annuity). Code F does not apply to a Roth IRA.

Code G (direct rollover from one plan to another plan). Code G does not apply to a Roth IRA. For a direct rollover of an eligible rollover distribution to a Roth IRA (from a traditional IRA or eligible retirement plan, other than from a designated Roth account), report the total amount rolled over in box 1, the taxable amount in box 2a, and any basis recovery amount in box 5. Use Code G in box 7.

Code H (direct rollover of a designated Roth account distribution to a Roth IRA). For a direct rollover of a distribution from a designated Roth account to a Roth IRA, enter the amount rolled over in box 1 and 0 (zero) in box 2a. Use Code H in box 7. If a spouse or nonspouse beneficiary makes a direct rollover from a designated Roth account to a Roth IRA, use double Code H4.

If applicable, use with code 4 (death).

Code J (early distribution from a Roth IRA). Use code J to report a distribution from a Roth IRA when code Q or T *do not* apply. In some cases, the taxpayer will need to file Form 5329 to indicate that the 10 percent premature distribution tax does not apply. If the Roth IRA engages in a prohibited transaction, use code 5 as a stand-alone code. Use code 2 (early distribution, exception applies) for an IRS levy instead of Code J.

If applicable, use one of the following codes in addition to code J: code 8 or P.

Code L (loans treated as deemed distributions under Code Section 72(p)). Code L does not apply to a Roth IRA.

Code N (recharacterized IRA contribution made for 2009). Use code N to indicate a recharacterization of a contribution made for 2009 and recharacterized in 2009 to another type of IRA by a trustee-to-trustee transfer or with the same trustee. See the previous discussion under box 1 description.

Do not use any other code with code N.

Code P (excess contributions plus earnings/excess deferrals taxable in 2008). Use code P to indicate that the distribution is taxable in the prior year. See the previous discussions for box 2a and code 8. For corrective distributions of excess contributions plus earnings under any IRA, including a Roth IRA, the IRS suggests that trustees and custodians advise the payee, at the time of the distribution, that the earnings are taxable in the year *during which* the contributions were made.

Example. A regular contribution of $5,000 was made on October 1, 2008, to a Roth IRA. The Roth IRA owner's AGI exceeded the limits in 2008, and therefore, the individual has an excess Roth IRA contribution. On April 5, 2009, a corrective distribution was paid to the individual that included earnings of $250. On the 2009 Form 1099-R, $3,250 is entered in box 1, and $250 in box 2a. If the Roth IRA owner is under age 59½, use the double code JP regardless of the Roth IRA owner's age. Code P indicates that the earnings are taxable in the prior year, 2008.

If applicable, use one of the following codes in addition to code P: code 1, 2, 4, B, or J.

Code Q (qualified distribution from a Roth IRA). Use code Q for a Roth IRA distribution only if the trustee or custodian *knows* that the participant meets the five-year aging period *and* either (1) the participant is age 59½; (2) the participant has died and the distribution is being made to a beneficiary; or (3) the participant is disabled under Code Section 72(m)(7).

Do not use any other code with code Q. If any other code, such as 8 or P applies, use code J.

Code R (recharacterized IRA contribution made for 2008). Use code R to indicate a recharacterization of a contribution made *for* 2008 and recharacterized in 2009 to another type of IRA by a trustee-to-trustee transfer or with the same trustee. See the previous discussion under box 1 description. Do not use any other code with code R. Compare to code N above.

Code S (early distribution from a SIMPLE IRA in first two years, no known exception). Code S does not apply to a Roth IRA.

Code T (Roth IRA distribution, exception applies). Use code T for a distribution from a Roth IRA if the trustee or custodian does not know whether the five-year aging period has been met but does know that the taxpayer is at least 59½, has died, or has become disabled. For example, if the Roth IRA owner is under age 59½ and the distribution is due to disability or death but the trustee or custodian knows if the five-year aging period has been met, use code T. Do not use code T for any reason other than those listed. If the Roth IRA owner is over age 59½, use code T instead of code Q *unless* the trustee or custodian knows that the five-year aging period has been met and the reason for distribution is either death or disability.

Do not use any other code with code T. If any other code, such as 8 or P, applies, use code J.

IRA/SEP/SIMPLE Checkbox. It is not necessary to mark the box for a distribution from a Roth IRA or any recharacterization transfer.

Box 8: Other. Box 8 does not apply to a Roth IRA.

Box 9a: Your Percentage of Total Distribution. Box 9a does not apply to a Roth IRA.

Box 9b: Total Employee Contributions/Designated Roth Contributions. Entering designated Roth contributions in box 9b is not required, but the total employee after-tax DRA contributions that the recipient can recover tax free may be entered in this box. (See Qs 10:56–10:59.) This box does not apply to a Roth IRA.

Boxes 10–15: State and Local Tax Withheld. These boxes and Copies 1 and 2 of Form 1099-R are provided for convenience only and need not be completed for the IRS. If these boxes are used, the state and local information boxes can report distributions and taxes for two states or localities separated by the dotted line.

Q 9:32   What information is entered in the unnumbered boxes on Form 1099-R?

The following information is entered in the unnumbered boxes on Form 1099-R:

1. Payer's name, address, and ZIP code.

2. Payer's federal identification number: The same name, address, and EIN number used to remit federal income tax withholding amounts and to file Form 945 *must* be used here.

3. Recipient's identification number: This box must reflect the Taxpayer Identification Number (TIN) of the *recipient* (the person or entity receiving the distribution). In the case of a distribution to an estate or a trust, the estate's tax identification number or the trust's tax identification number is used, not the Social Security number of the decedent. For multiple beneficiary recipients, prepare a separate Form 1099-R for each beneficiary. In the case of an IRS levy or when the account becomes subject to the unclaimed property laws of the state, issue Form 1099-R in the name and TIN of the participant.

4. Recipient's name, address, and ZIP code: If the recipient is an individual, this box reflects the name of the recipient as it is shown on his or her Social Security card. In the case of a distribution made to a beneficiary, the recipient is the beneficiary, not the deceased participant. In some cases, the beneficiary recipient is not an individual (e.g., estate, trust, charity, university). The appropriate name and tax identification number of the entity should be provided, not the name and Social Security number of the deceased participant.

5. The account number must be unique to identify the specific "plan" being reported. The recipient's TIN cannot be used for this purpose. Also, in cases where multiple reportable distributions are made from the same plan for different reasons that require separate Forms 1099-R, the account number must be able to identify the specific Form 1099-R. The purpose of this box is to identify the proper form if a correction is filed.

For example, the following distributions were made during 2009 from the same Roth IRA, Account Number 123456789:

March distribution that is premature (code 1 applies)

June distribution that is converted to a Roth IRA (code 2 applies)

IRA owner attains age 59½ on July 14

September distribution that is a return of excess (code 8 or P applies)

November distribution that is a normal distribution (code 7 applies)

Although four (4) distributions were made from the same "plan" (in our example Account Number 123456789), separate Forms 1099-R are required because different codes apply. In this example, it would be acceptable to enter Account Number 123456789, along with –1, –2, –3, and –4 (or –A, –B, –C and –D), or some other sequence. If it becomes necessary to correct the Form 1099-R that reported the September distribution, the corrected Form 1099-R would indicate "Account Number 123456789-3" so the IRS will know which form is being corrected.

Q 9:33   What is the minimum amount for which distributions must be reported on Form 1099-R?

Distributions are not required to be reported on Form 1099-R for payments aggregating less than $10 in any calendar year from the same plan.

Q 9:34   May a substitute statement for Form 1099-R be furnished to a recipient of a distribution from an IRA?

Yes. A substitute statement for Form 1099-R may be furnished to a recipient of a distribution from an IRA if the substitute statement meets the following requirements:

1. It must contain the same tax year, form number, and form name as those on the official IRS form, prominently displayed together in one area of the statement; for example, in the upper right part of the statement.

2. The filer and form recipient identification information required on the official IRS form must be included.

3. All applicable dollar amounts and information, including box numbers, required to be reported to the form recipient must be titled on the form recipient statement in substantially the same manner as they are on the official IRS form.

4. Appropriate instructions to the form recipient, similar to those on the official IRS form, must be provided to aid in the proper reporting of the items on the form recipient's income tax return.

5. The following language must be included: "This information is being furnished to the Internal Revenue Service."

6. The OMB number must be shown as it appears on the official IRS form.

7. The quality of carbon used to produce substitute statements to recipients must meet the following standards—

a. All copies must be clearly legible;

b. All copies must have the capability to be photocopied; and

c. Fading must not be of such a degree as to preclude legibility and the ability to photocopy.

In general, black chemical transfer inks are preferred; other colors are permitted only if the above standards are met. Hot wax and cold carbon spots are not permitted.

> **Note.** IRS Publication 1220 is published each year and contains the current year's magnetic media and electronic reporting requirements. It can be ordered from the IRS by calling (800) 829-3676. IRA trustees and custodians should make certain the current Publication 1220 is being used.

Q 9:35   Are distributions to a beneficiary reported on Form 1099-R?

Yes. If distributions from an IRA are made to a beneficiary or the deceased IRA owner's estate, Form 1099-R must be prepared using the name and TIN of the beneficiary or the estate, not those of the decedent. When there is more than one beneficiary recipient, separate Forms 1099-R must be prepared for each beneficiary.

When Form 1099-R Is Not Used

Q 9:36   Are there special rules for reporting distributions to nonresident aliens?

Yes. If income tax is withheld under Code Section 1441 (the nonresident alien section), the distribution and withholding are reported on Form 1042-S, Foreign Person's U.S. Source Income Subject to Withholding, and on Form 1042, Annual Withholding Tax Return for U.S. Source Income of Foreign Persons. Form 1099-R is not used.

Q 9:37   Are trustee-to-trustee transfers reported on Form 1099-R?

No. Form 1099-R is not used to report direct transfers between trustees involving the same type of plan (e.g., Roth IRA to Roth IRA).

Q 9:38   Is a transfer incident to a divorce reported on Form 1099-R?

No. A transfer of an IRA pursuant to a divorce or legal separation is not considered a distribution and is not reportable on Form 1099-R.

Q 9:39   Is an investment that is renewed or reinvested treated as a distribution?

No. Whenever an existing investment (e.g., a CD) within an IRA is renewed or reinvested in some other form of investment, no distribution occurs. Therefore, no Form 1099-R is issued.

Q 9:40   Is an early withdrawal penalty on a CD included in the distribution reported on Form 1099-R?

No. In no event will the assessment of an early withdrawal penalty on a CD or any other permissible transaction fee be included as part of the gross distribution amount reported on Form 1099-R. That is, the reportable distribution amount is determined after the penalty or fee has been subtracted. [Instructions for Forms 1099, 1098, 5498, and W-2G]

Q 9:41   Are fees deducted from an IRA reported on Form 1099-R?

No. When such fees as annual maintenance fees or transaction fees are deducted from an IRA, the amounts are not treated as distributions and are not reportable on Form 1099-R.

Conversion

Q 9:42   How is a conversion of a traditional IRA to a Roth IRA reported?

If a traditional IRA is converted to a Roth IRA, it must be reported as a distribution, even if the assets are transferred in a trustee-to-trustee transfer or transferred within the same financial institution. Form 1099-R is prepared for the traditional IRA. Code 2 is used if the participant is under age $59\frac{1}{2}$; code 7 is used if the participant is over age $59\frac{1}{2}$.

Recharacterization

Q 9:43   What are the *first IRA* and the *second IRA* involved in a recharacterization for purposes of Form 1099-R?

For purposes of Form 1099-R, the *first IRA* is the IRA from which the recharacterization is being made, and the *second IRA* is the IRA to which the recharacterization is being made.

Q 9:44   For purposes of Form 1099-R, what reporting requirements apply to trustees in the case of a recharacterization of a contribution from a first IRA to a second IRA?

Reporting by the Trustee of the First IRA. The trustee of the first IRA reports the recharacterized contribution plus earnings in box 1 of Form 1099-R. In the case of a loss on the recharacterized contribution, the actual amount recharacterized is reported in box 1.

Beginning in 2002, "prior year" recharacterizations and "same year" recharacterizations must be reported on separate Forms 1099-R because different reporting codes now apply for box 7.

A *prior year recharacterization* is a recharacterization of a contribution made for 2008 and recharacterized in 2009, even if the 2009 contribution was made in 2009. In the case of a recharacterization of a conversion that came from a traditional IRA in 2008 but was not converted until 2009 (but within the requisite 60-day period), the trustee should treat this recharacterization as a "prior year" recharacterization for reporting purposes. "Prior year" recharacterizations are reported using code R in box 7.

A *same year recharacterization* is a recharacterization of a contribution made for 2009 and recharacterized in 2009. "Same year" recharacterizations are reported using code N in box 7.

> **Note.** A *contribution recharacterization* is (1) the "undoing" of a current year regular contribution plus earnings to a Roth IRA or (2) the "unwinding" of a conversion or failed conversion (see Q 3:32) to a Roth IRA by transferring the amount plus earnings back to a traditional IRA. [I.R.C. § 408A(d)(6); Treas. Reg. § 1.408A-5, Q&A 1] For tax purposes, upon a conversion gains and losses of the entire Roth IRA must be applied on a pro rata basis, the so called "anti-cherry picking rule," and is applied to all investments within *that* Roth IRA. By using a Roth segregation conversion strategy, it may be possible to recharacterize loss assets while leaving gain assets in a Roth IRA (see Q 3:31).

Revoked Roth IRAs

Q 9:45   Must a revoked Roth IRA be reported on Form 1099-R?

Yes. Revenue Procedure 91-70 [1991-2 C.B. 899] outlines the reporting requirements that apply whenever an IRA is timely revoked. Before issuance of Revenue Procedure 91-70, an IRA that was timely revoked was treated as though it had never existed and no reporting was required. The Roth IRA was first available in 1998; therefore, the revocation of a Roth IRA has had to be reported since the Roth IRA was introduced.

Q 9:46   How are distributions from revoked Roth IRAs reported on Form 1099-R?

The following chart shows the appropriate code or codes to enter in box 7 when reporting the revocation of a contribution to an IRA and the amount to be entered in box 2a of Form 1099-R. The gross amount of the revoked contribution is reported in box 1 of the form (see Q 9:30).

Form 1099-R

Source of Contribution	Box 2a	Box 7
Regular contribution to a Roth IRA without earnings	0	Code J regardless of age
Regular contribution to a Roth IRA with earnings	Earnings	Code J8 regardless of age
Rollover or transfer to a Roth IRA	Same as box 1	Code J regardless of age
Conversion to a Roth IRA without earnings	0	Code J regardless of age
Conversion to a Roth IRA with earnings	Earnings	Code J regardless of age

Correcting 1099-R Forms

Q 9:47   How soon should corrected Forms 1099-R be filed?

It is sometimes necessary to correct a Form 1099-R after the original has been submitted to the IRS. All corrections for a year must be submitted to the IRS in accordance with the following information. [I.R.S. Pub. 1220 as revised annually]

Example. A direct rollover was paid from an employer's plan to an eligible recipient plan, and Form 1099-R was filed with the IRS reporting that none of the direct rollover was taxable by entering a zero in box 2a. It is discovered that part of the direct rollover was not eligible to be rolled over because part of the distribution consisted of the employee's RMD. The original Form 1099-R must be corrected by issuing a new Form 1099-R.

The "Corrected Form 1099-R" section was added to the Form 1099-R instructions to emphasize the requirement to file a corrected Form 1099-R with the IRS if the form has already been filed and it is later discovered that an error was made. Furthermore, a corrected copy, clearly identified as "corrected," must be issued to the recipient as soon as possible.

Q 9:48   How is a corrected Form 1099-R to be completed?

All boxes on the form must be completed with the correct information, not just the boxes needing correction. Some types of corrections (e.g., no payee TIN, incorrect payee TIN, or incorrect name or address) require two separate steps (two separate Forms 1099-R). [Form 1099-R instructions; I.R.S. Pub. 1220, Part A, § 8.14 (June 2009))]

If the corrected Forms 1099-R are submitted on paper documents, an "X" is placed in the "corrected box" at the top of the corrected forms; the accompanying paper transmittal form, Form 1096, must also be marked "corrected" at the top of the form. For magnetic media or electronic submissions, the procedures contained in IRS Publication 1220 for the current year must be followed. [I.R.S. Pub. 1220, Part A, § 8.14 (June 2009)]

Penalties

Q 9:49   How does the IRS treat failure to transmit Forms 1099-R via magnetic media or electronically when required?

The IRS treats failure to transmit Forms 1099-R via magnetic media or electronically when required as failure to file the forms unless the trustee or custodial organization has an approved waiver on file or can establish reasonable cause, or in some cases, due diligence. In the case of intentional disregard of the filing requirements, a penalty of $100 per failure may be imposed.

Q 9:50   What penalties apply if a trustee or custodial organization fails to follow the paper document format for Form 1099-R?

In general, the amount of the penalty for failure to comply with the paper document requirements for Form 1099-R is based on when the correct information return is filed. Penalties include the following:

- $15 per return if a correct filing is made within 30 days (i.e., by March 30 if the due date is February 28), with a maximum penalty of $75,000 per year ($25,000 for small businesses)

- $30 per return if a correct filing is made more than 30 days after the due date but by August 1, with a maximum penalty of $150,000 per year ($50,000 for small businesses)

- $50 per return if a correct filing is made after August 1 or if no filing is made, with a maximum penalty of $250,000 per year ($100,000 for small businesses)

A $100-per-failure penalty (with no ceiling) applies for intentional disregard of the filing requirements. [I.R.C. § 6721; I.R.S. Pub. 1220, Part H (June 2007), reprinted from Rev. Proc. 2007-51, 2007-30 I.R.B. 146 (July 23, 2007)] The following are *exceptions* to the failure to file penalty:

1. The penalty does not apply to any failure that was due to reasonable cause and not to willful neglect.

2. An inconsequential error or omission is not considered a failure to include correct information. An inconsequential error or omission must be such that it does not prevent or hinder the IRS from processing the return, from correlating the information required to be shown on the return with the information shown on the payee's tax return, or from otherwise putting the return to its intended use. Errors and omissions that are never inconsequential are those related to a TIN, a payee's surname, or any dollar amounts.

De minimis Rule for Corrections. Even if reasonable cause cannot be shown, the penalty for failure to file correct information returns does not apply to a certain number of returns if

1. The information returns were filed;

2. There was a failure to include all the information required to be shown on a return or incorrect information was included; and

3. Corrected returns are filed by August 1.

If all three conditions are satisfied, the penalty for filing incorrect returns (but not for filing late) does not apply to the greater of 10 information returns or 0.5 percent of the total number of information returns the entity is required to file for the calendar year. [I.R.S. Pub. 1220, Part O (June 2007)]

Merger of Trustees and Custodians

Q 9:51   What reporting is required in the case of two trustees (or custodians) that merge?

Generally, when two trustees (or custodial organizations) merge and the surviving organization becomes the owner of all of the assets, the reporting requirements for the entire year are the responsibility of the survivor organization. If the successor trustee (or custodian), however, is acquiring a portion of the predecessor's business (i.e., only a portion of the IRA portfolio), the rules under IRS Revenue Procedure 99-50 apply.

This revenue procedure outlines the procedures that permit a successor business to combine all information reporting following a merger or an acquisition. The procedure covers information reporting with respect to Form 1042-S, all forms in the series 1098, 1099, and 5498, and Form W-2G, hereinafter referred to as "appropriate forms."

The provisions of this revenue procedure apply only when all the following conditions are met:

1. One business entity (the "successor") acquires from another business entity (the "predecessor") substantially all the property (a) used in the

trade or business of the predecessor or (b) used in a separate unit of a trade or business of the predecessor;

2. During the preacquisition portion of the calendar year in which the acquisition occurs, the predecessor is required to file any of the information returns covered in this procedure;

3. During the post-acquisition portion of the acquisition year, the predecessor or the separate unit of the predecessor does not make or receive any reportable payments and does not withhold or collect any tax;

4. The requirements described in Section 5 of the revenue procedure (relating to the "alternative procedure") are met; and

5. The IRS instructions to the appropriate forms do not prohibit use of the alternative procedure.

Q 9:52   What is the standard method of reporting after the merger or acquisition?

Under Section 4 of Revenue Procedure 99-50, the standard method (referred to as the "standard procedure") is where each person who makes or receives payments, or withholds or collects taxes, that are reportable on any of the appropriate forms is responsible for separate information reporting of those transactions. Therefore, under the standard procedure, both the predecessor and the successor must file the appropriate forms for reportable transactions occurring in the acquisition year.

Q 9:53   Is there an alternative method?

Yes. The alternative method is when the successor files all returns. For the successor to file combined information reporting, the following requirements must be satisfied:

1. Both the predecessor and the successor must agree that the successor assumes the predecessor's entire information reporting obligations for the appropriate forms to which their agreement applies. In such case, the predecessor is relieved of its information reporting obligations for reportable transactions occurring in the acquisition year, only if and to the extent that their agreement meets, and the successor satisfies, the requirements of this revenue procedure.

2. The predecessor and the successor must agree upon the specific forms to which this alternative procedure applies. They may agree, for example, to use the alternative procedure for all appropriate forms or limit the use of the alternative procedure to (a) certain specific forms or (b) specific reporting entities. In other words, the standard procedure can be used for certain forms or by certain reporting entities, whereas the alternative procedure can be used for other certain forms or by certain other reporting entities.

3. On each appropriate form, the successor must combine (a) any payments made or received on account of a person by the predecessor in the preacquisition portion of the acquisition year with (b) any payments

made or received on account of that person by the successor in that year, if any, and must report the aggregate amount(s) on account of that person for that year.

4. On each appropriate form, the successor must also combine the amount of any withheld income tax for a person by the predecessor in the preacquisition portion of the acquisition year with the amount(s) withheld for that person by the successor in that year and, on the appropriate form(s), must report the aggregate withheld amount for the year.

5. The successor must file a statement with the IRS indicating that the appropriate forms are being filed on a combined basis in accordance with this revenue procedure. Also, if the predecessor has withheld any income tax during the acquisition year and reported it on Form 945, the total of the withholding amounts shown on the successor's Forms 1099 for that year will exceed the total of the withholding amounts shown on the successor's Form 945. Therefore, the statement that must be filed with the IRS must reflect the amount of any income tax that has been withheld by the predecessor and by the successor for each type of form. Identical procedures apply to the filing of Forms 1042 and 1042-S.

6. The statement required to be filed with the IRS must include the name, address, telephone number, and employer identification number of both the successor and predecessor, and the name and telephone number of the person responsible for preparing this statement.

7. The statement for Forms 1042-S must be attached to the Form 1042 and mailed to the address appearing in its instructions on or before the due date of the Form 1042.

8. The statement for the forms in the series 1098, 1099, and 5498, and Form W-2G must be filed separately from such forms and Form 945. Unless otherwise directed by the form's instructions, the statement for forms in the series 1098, 1099, and 5498, and Forms W-2G must be mailed on or before the due date for such forms to

Enterprise Computing Center—Martinsburg
230 Murall Drive
Attn: Chief, Information Returns Branch
Mail Stop 360, Kearneysville, WV 25430

This procedure is generally effective for appropriate forms filed after December 31, 1999. If a successor filed forms before this date, however, and the requirements of this revenue procedure were satisfied, the predecessor's filing obligations are deemed to have been satisfied, as long as the predecessor and successor have substantially complied with all of these requirements, except for the statement requirements described above.

Records Retention

Q 9:54   How long should copies of Form 1099-R be kept?

Copies of information returns filed with the IRS (including Form 1099-R), or the ability to reconstruct the data, should be kept for at least three years from the due date of the returns.

Federal Income Tax Return (Form 8606)

Q 9:55   What is the purpose of Form 8606?

Form 8606, Nondeductible IRAs, has three parts. The three parts are used to report the following:

- Part I
  - Part, but *not* all, of traditional, SEP, or SIMPLE IRAs was converted to Roth IRAs in 2009 (excluding any portion that was recharacterized) *and* nondeductible contributions were made to a traditional IRA in 2009 or an earlier year. In this case, a portion may be taxable and possibly subject to the additional 10 percent tax if under age $59\frac{1}{2}$.

    Part I is also used when nondeductible contributions are made to a traditional IRA in 2009 *and* the taxpayer made a distributed from a traditional IRA (including a SEP or SIMPLE IRA) in 2009.
  - Nondeductible contributions were made to a traditional IRA in 2009.
  - Distributions from traditional, SEP, or SIMPLE IRAs were made in 2009 if the taxpayer ever made nondeductible contributions to a traditional IRA in 2009 or an earlier year. For this purpose, distributions do not include a rollover (other than the repayment of a qualified disaster recovery assistance distribution), qualified charitable distribution, one-time distributions to fund a health savings account (HSA), conversion, recharacterization (correction of unwanted or excess contribution), or return of IRA/Roth IRA contributions.
- Part II
  - A conversions of all or a portion of a traditional, SEP, or SIMPLE IRA to a Roth IRA in 2009 (excluding any portion recharacterized).

  Note. If a 2009 Roth IRA contribution was recharacterized as a traditional IRA contribution, or vice versa, treat the contribution as having been made to the second IRA, not the first IRA.
- Part III
  - For this purpose, distributions do not include a rollover (other than the repayment of a qualified disaster recovery assistance distribution), qualified charitable distribution, one-time distributions to fund an HSA, recharacterization (correction of unwanted or excess contribution), or return of IRA/Roth IRA contributions.

— Complete Part III of Form 8606 only if, after considering the above, there is an amount to report. If not, report the (nontaxable) distribution on Form 1040 (line 15a; Form 1040A, line 11a; or Form 1040NR, line 16a).

Note. Form 8606 is not filed solely to report regular contributions to Roth IRAs.

Q 9:56   How does a taxpayer report distributions from a Roth IRA on his or her federal 2009 income tax return?

The trustee or custodian is not required to compute the taxable portion of a Roth IRA distribution. The taxable portion (if any) is computed in Part III of Form 8606—Nondeductible IRAs. The taxable amount shown on line 25c of Form 8606 is reported on Form 1040 (line 15b; Form 1040A, line 11b; or Form 1040NR, line 16b). Not all amounts withdrawn are treated as distributions for reporting purposes (see Q 9:57).

Q 9:57   How is a recharacterization reported on Form 8606?

Generally, an individual can recharacterize (correct) an IRA or Roth IRA contribution, a Roth IRA conversion, or a Roth rollover from a eligible employer's plan by making a trustee-to-trustee transfer from one IRA to another type of IRA. Trustee-to-trustee transfers are made directly between financial institutions or within the same financial institution. The transfer must be made by the federal income tax return due date (including extensions) and reflected on the return. However, if the return was timely filed without making the transfer, the transfer can be made within six months of the due date of the return, excluding extensions (see Q 3:38).

For reporting purposes, a recharacterized conversion is treated as though the conversion had never occurred. Any recharacterized contribution will be treated as having been originally contributed to the second IRA (or Roth IRA), rather than the first IRA (or Roth IRA). The amount transferred must include related earnings or be reduced by any loss. In most cases, the related earnings that must be transferred are determined by the trustee or custodian of the IRA (see Q 3:41). Any earnings or loss that occurred in the first IRA will be treated as having occurred in the second IRA. Any loss that occurred while the funds were in the first IRA can not be deducted. In addition, no deduction is permitted for a contribution to a traditional IRA if the amount is later recharacterized.

Four different types of recharacterizations may be used. In some cases, a statement must be attached to the return. The four types of recharacterizations are as follows:

1. An amount is converted from a traditional, SEP, or SIMPLE IRA to a Roth IRA in 2009 and all or part of the amount is later recharacterized back to a traditional, SEP, or SIMPLE IRA.

If only part of the amount converted was recharacterized, report the amount not recharacterized on Form 8606. If the entire amount was recharacterized, do not report the recharacterization on Form 8606. In either case, attach a statement to the return explaining the recharacterization and include the amount converted from the traditional, SEP, or SIMPLE IRA in the total on Form 1040, line 15a; Form 1040A, line 11a; or Form 1040NR, line 16a. If the recharacterization occurred in 2009, also include the amount transferred back from the Roth IRA on that line. If the recharacterization occurred in 2010, report the amount transferred only in the attached statement, and not on the 2009 or 2010 tax return (a 2010 Form 1099-R should be sent to the taxpayer by February 1, 2011, stating that a recharacterization was made of an amount converted in the prior year).

> **Example.** Mindy is married and files a joint return. Mindy converted $20,000 from her traditional IRA to a new Roth IRA on May 20, 2009. On April 7, 2010, she determines that her 2009 modified AGI for Roth IRA purposes will exceed $100,000, and she is not allowed to make a Roth IRA conversion. The value of the Roth IRA on that date is $19,000. Mindy recharacterizes the conversion by transferring that entire amount ($19,000) to a traditional IRA in a trustee-to-trustee transfer. Mindy reports $20,000 on Form 1040, line 15a (IRA distribution received). She does not include the $19,000 on line 15a because it did not occur in 2009, nor does she report that amount on her 2010 return because it does not apply to the 2010 tax year. Mindy attaches a statement to Form 1040 explaining that (a) she made a conversion of $20,000 from a traditional IRA on May 20, 2009, (b) she recharacterized the entire amount, which was then valued at $19,000, back to a traditional IRA on April 7, 2010, and (c) she recharacterized because her 2009 modified AGI for Roth IRA purposes exceeded $100,000.

2. Part or all of a contribution made to a traditional IRA is later recharacterized to a Roth IRA.

If only part of the contribution is recharacterized, report the nondeductible traditional IRA portion of the remaining contribution, if any, on Form 8606, Part I. If the entire contribution is recharacterized, do not report the contribution on Form 8606. In either case, attach a statement to the return explaining the recharacterization. If the recharacterization occurred in 2009, include the amount transferred from the traditional IRA on Form 1040, line 15a; Form 1040A, line 11 a; or Form 1040NR, line 16a. If the recharacterization occurred in 2010, report the amount transferred only in the attached statement.

> **Example.** Catrina is single, covered by a retirement plan, and contributed $5,000 to a new traditional IRA on May 27, 2009. On February 24, 2010, Catrina determines that her 2009 modified AGI will limit her traditional IRA deduction to $1,000. The value of her traditional IRA on that date is $4,500. Catrina decides to recharacterize $4,000 of the traditional IRA contribution as a Roth IRA contribution, and have $4,400 ($4,000 contribution plus $400 related earnings) transferred from her traditional IRA to a Roth IRA in a trustee-to-trustee transfer. Catrina deducts the $1,000 traditional IRA contribution on Form 1040. She is not required to file Form 8606, but she must attach a statement to her return explaining the recharacterization. The statement indicates that she contributed $5,000 to a traditional IRA on May

27, 2009; recharacterized $4,000 of that contribution on February 24, 2010, by transferring $4,000 plus $400 of related earnings from her traditional IRA to a Roth IRA in a trustee-to-trustee transfer; and that all $1,000 of the remaining traditional IRA contribution is deducted on Form 1040. Catrina does not report the $4,400 distribution from her traditional IRA on her 2009 Form 1040 because the distribution occurred in 2010. She does not report the distribution on her 2010 Form 1040 because the recharacterization related to 2009 and was explained in an attachment to Catrina's 2009 return.

3. Part or all of a contribution to a Roth IRA is later recharacterized to a traditional IRA.

Report the nondeductible traditional IRA portion, if any, on Form 8606, Part I. If the entire contribution was not recharacterized, do not report the remaining Roth IRA portion of the contribution on Form 8606. Attach a statement to the return explaining the recharacterization. If the recharacterization occurred in 2009, include the amount transferred from the Roth IRA on Form 1040, line 15a; Form 1040A, line 11a; or Form 1040NR, line 16a. If the recharacterization occurred in 2010, report the amount transferred only in the attached statement, and not on the 2009 or 2010 tax return.

Example. Linus is single and contributed $5,000 to a new Roth IRA on June 14, 2009. On December 27, 2009, he determines that his 2009 modified AGI will allow a full traditional IRA deduction. He decides to recharacterize the Roth IRA contribution as a traditional IRA contribution and has $5,250, the balance in the Roth IRA account ($5,000 contribution + $250 related earnings), transferred from his Roth IRA to a traditional IRA in a trustee-to-trustee transfer. Linus deducts the $5,000 traditional IRA contribution on Form 1040. He is not required to file Form 8606, but he must attach a statement to his return explaining the recharacterization. The statement indicates that Linus contributed $5,000 to a new Roth IRA on June 14, 2009; recharacterized that contribution on December 27, 2009, by transferring $5,250, the balance in the Roth IRA, to a traditional IRA in a trustee-to-trustee transfer; and that $5,000 of the traditional IRA contribution is deducted on Form 1040. Linus includes the $5,250 distribution on his 2009 Form 1040, line 15a.

4. An amount from a qualified retirement plan is rolled over to a Roth IRA in 2009 and later recharacterized all or part of the amount to a traditional IRA.

Attach a statement explaining the recharacterization on the tax return and include the amount of the original rollover on Form 1040, line 16a; Form 1040A, line 12a; or Form 1040NR, line 17a. Also, include any taxable amount of the rollover not recharacterized on Form 1040, line 16b; Form 1040A, line 12b; or Form 1040NR, line 17b. If the recharacterization occurred in 2009, also include the amount transferred from the Roth IRA on Form 1040, line 15a; Form 1040A, line 11a; or Form 1040NR, line 16a. If the recharacterization occurred in 2010, report the amount transferred only in the attached statement, and not on the 2009 or 2010 tax return (a 2010 Form 1099-R should be sent to the taxpayer by February 1, 2011, stating that the taxpayer made a recharacterization of an amount in the prior year). Do not report these rollovers or recharacterizations on Form 8606.

> **Example.** Loretta is single and she rolled over $50,000 from her 401(k) plan to a new Roth IRA on July 20, 2009. On March 25, 2010, she determined that her 2009 modified AGI for Roth IRA purposes will exceed $100,000, and she was not allowed to make a Roth IRA conversion rollover. The value of the Roth IRA on that date is $49,000. Loretta recharacterizes the rollover by transferring that entire amount to a traditional IRA in a trustee-to-trustee transfer. She reports $50,000 on Form 1040, line 16a. Loretta does not include the $49,000 on line 15a because it did not occur in 2009 (she also does not report that amount on her 2010 return because it does not apply to the 2010 tax year). Loretta attaches a statement to Form 1040 explaining that (a) she made a rollover of $50,000 from a 401(k) plan to a Roth IRA on July 20, 2009 and (b) she recharacterized the entire amount, which was then valued at $49,000, to a traditional IRA on March 25, 2010.

Q 9:58   How is a return of an IRA or Roth IRA contribution reported on Form 8606?

If traditional IRA contributions or Roth IRA contributions were made in 2009 for 2009 and those contributions were returned to with any related earnings (or less any loss) by the due date (including extensions) of the 2009 federal income tax return, the returned contributions are treated as if they were never contributed. Do not report the contribution or distribution on Form 8606 or take a deduction for the contribution. However, the distribution must be reported along with any related earnings on the 2009 Form 1040, lines 15a and 15b; Form 1040A, lines 11 a and 11 b; or Form 1040NR, lines 16a and 16b. Attach a statement explaining the distribution. No deduction is allowed for any loss that occurred (see Qs 4:34–4:36 for an exception if the entire amount in all traditional or Roth IRAs are distributed). In addition, if under age 59½ at the time of a distribution with related earnings, the 10 percent premature distribution tax may apply.

If the 2009 tax return was filed without withdrawing a contribution made in 2009, the contribution can be returned within six months of the due date of the 2009 tax return, excluding extensions (see Q 2:33). In most cases, the related earnings that must be withdrawn are figured by the trustee or custodian (see Q 2:32). If a contribution was made for 2008 and it was returned in 2009 as described above, do not report the distribution on the 2009 tax return. Instead, report it on the 2008 original or amended return in the manner described above.

> **Example.** On May 31, 2009, Helen contributed $5,000 to her Roth IRA. The value of the Roth IRA was $18,000 prior to the contribution. On December 29, 2009, when Helen is age 57 and the value of the IRA is $24,150, Helen realizes she cannot make the entire contribution because her taxable compensation for the year will be only $4,000. Helen decides to have $1,000 of the contribution ($5,000) returned to her and withdraws $1,050 from her Roth IRA ($1,000 contribution + $50 earnings; see Q 2:32). Helen did not make

any other withdrawals or contributions. Helen reports the distribution in Part III of Form 8606. Helen includes $1,050 on Form 1040, line 15a, and $50 on line 15b. Helen attaches a statement to her tax return explaining the distribution. Because Helen properly removed the excess contribution with the related earnings by the due date of her tax return, Helen is not subject to the additional 6 percent tax on excess contributions. However, because Helen was under age 59½ at the time of the distribution, the $50 of earnings is subject to the 10 percent premature distribution tax. Helen completes Part I of Form 5329, Additional Taxes on Qualified Plans (Including IRAs) and Other Tax-Favored Accounts. Helen includes $5.00 ($50 × .10) on Form 1040, line 59, which is the amount shown on line 4 of Form 5329.

Q 9:59   How is Form 8606 completed in connection with a Roth IRA?

Form 8606, Nondeductible IRAs, contains three parts. The line numbers for Roth IRA reporting in each of those parts are completed as follows.

Part I—Nondeductible Contributions to Traditional IRAs and Distributions from Traditional IRAs, SEP IRAs, and SIMPLE IRAs

Complete Part I of Form 8606 if part, but not all, of a traditional IRA, SEP IRA, or SIMPLE IRA was converted to a Roth IRA in 2009 (excluding any portion that was recharacterized) and nondeductible contributions were made to a traditional IRA in 2009 or an earlier year (see Q 9:57).

Line 8

If, in 2009, an amount was converted from traditional IRA, SEP IRA, or SIMPLE IRA to a Roth IRA, enter on line 8 the net amount converted. To figure that amount, subtract from the total amount converted in 2009 any portion that was recharacterized to traditional IRA, SEP IRA, or SIMPLE IRA in 2009 or 2010. Do not take into account related earnings that were transferred with the recharacterized amount or any loss that occurred while the amount was in the Roth IRA.

Part II—2009 Conversions from Traditional IRAs, SEP IRAs, and SIMPLE IRAs to a Roth IRA

Complete Part II of Form 8606 if part or all of a traditional IRA, SEP IRA, or SIMPLE IRA was converted to a Roth IRA in 2009, excluding any portion that was recharacterized (see Q 9:57).

Caution. There is a limit on number of conversions. If an amount was converted from a traditional IRA, a SEP IRA, or a SIMPLE IRA to a Roth IRA in 2009 and then recharacterized back to a traditional, SEP, or SIMPLE IRA, that amount cannot be reconverted until the later of January 1, 2010, or 30 days after the recharacterization (see Q 3:44).

Note. Until 2010, a taxpayer may not convert any amount to Roth IRAs if his or her modified AGI for Roth IRA purposes is more than $100,000, and, if married, does not file a joint return. If a conversion was erroneously made, the converted amount must be recharacterized (see Q 3:16).

Line 16

If line 8 was not completed, see the instructions for that line above. Then, enter on line 16 the amount that would have been entered on line 8 had line 8 been completed.

Line 17

If line 11 was not completed, enter on line 17 the amount from line 2 (or the amount that would have been entered on line 2 if that line had been completed) plus any contributions included on line 1 that are made before the conversion.

Part III—Distributions from Roth IRAs

Complete Part III to figure the taxable part, if any, of a 2009 Roth IRA distribution (see Q 9:57).

Line 19

In addition to distributions (not excepted below), include all qualified disaster recovery distributions and all recovery assistance distributions received from the Roth IRA even if they were later repaid.

Exceptions. Do not include on line 19 any of the following.

- Distributions that were rolled over, including distributions made in 2009 and rolled over after December 31, 2009 (outstanding rollovers).
- Recharacterizations.
- Distributions that are a return of contributions (see Q 9:58).
- Distributions made on or after age 59½ if a contribution (including a conversion) was made for 2004 or an earlier year.
- A one-time distribution to fund an HSA (see Q 4:1). No special reporting is required for qualified HSA funding distributions.
- Qualified charitable distributions.
- Distributions made upon death or due to disability if a contribution (including a conversion) was made for 2004 or an earlier year.
- Transfer incident to a divorce. The direct transfer of part or all of a Roth IRA to a spouse under a divorce or separation agreement is not taxable to the individual or to his or her spouse (see Qs 5:37, 5:39). The direct transfer is not taxable to the Roth IRA owner or his or her former spouse.

If, after considering the items above, there is no amount to enter on line 19, do not complete Part III; the Roth IRA distribution(s) is(are) not taxable. Instead, include the total Roth IRA distribution(s) on Form 1040, line 15a; Form 1040A, line 11 a; or Form 1040NR, line 16a.

Line 20

If a qualified first-time homebuyer distribution was made from a Roth IRA and a contribution (including a conversion) was made to a Roth IRA for 2004 or an earlier year, enter the amount of the qualified expenses on line 20, but do not enter more than $10,000.

Line 22

Figure the amount to enter on line 22 as follows.

- If a Roth IRA distribution was not made before 2009 (other than an amount rolled over or recharacterized or a returned contribution), enter on line 22 the total of all regular contributions to Roth IRAs for 1998 through 2009 (excluding rollovers from other Roth IRAs and any contributions that are returned), adjusted for any recharacterizations.
- If no distribution was made before 2009, use Table 9-1 to figure the amount to enter on line 22.
- Increase the amount on line 22 by any amount rolled in from a designated Roth account that is treated as investment in the contract.
- Increase or decrease the amount on line 22 by any basis transferred or received incident to divorce (see Qs 5:37, 5:39). Also attach a statement explaining the transfer.
- Increase or decrease the amount on line 22 by the amounts received by the taxpayer as a military death gratuity or SGLI payment that was rolled over to the taxpayer's Roth IRA (see Qs 3:104–3:111).
- Increase or decrease the amount on line 22 by any amount received as qualified Exxon Valdez settlement income (see Qs 3:112–3:118). Also attach a statement explaining the transfer.

Table 9-1. Amount to be entered on line 22 when distributions were made before 2008.

IF the most recent year prior to 2009 in which a Roth IRA distribution[*] was made was in . . .	THEN enter on Form 8606, line 22, this amount . . .	PLUS the total of all regular contributions[**] to Roth IRAs for . . .
2008 (an amount was entered on 2008 Form 8606, line 19)	The excess of 2008 Form 8606, line 22, over line 19 of that Form 8606	2009
2007 (an amount was entered on 2007 Form 8606, line 19)	The excess of 2007 Form 8606, line 22, over line 19 of that Form 8606	2008 and 2009
2006 (an amount was entered on 2006 Form 8606, line 19)	The excess of 2006 Form 8606, line 22, over line 19 of that Form 8606	2007 and 2009
2005 (an amount was entered on 2005 Form 8606, line 19)	The excess of 2005 Form 8606, line 22, over line 19 of that Form 8606.	2006 through 2009
2004 (an amount was entered on 2004 Form 8606, line 19)	The excess of 2004 Form 8606, line 22, over line 19 of that Form 8606.	2005 through 2009

Table 9-1. Amount to be entered on line 22 when distributions were made before 2009. (*cont'd*)

IF the most recent year prior to 2009 in which a Roth IRA distribution* was made was in . . .	THEN enter on Form 8606, line 22, this amount . . .	PLUS the total of all regular contributions** to Roth IRAs for . . .
2003 (an amount was entered on 2003 Form 8606, line 19)	The excess of 2003 Form 8606, line 20, over line 19 of that Form 8606.	2004 through 2009
2002 (an amount was entered on 2002 Form 8606, line 19)	The excess of 2002 Form 8606, line 20, over line 19 of that Form 8606.	2003 through 2009
2001 (an amount was entered on 2001 Form 8606, line 19)	The excess of 2001 Form 8606, line 20, over line 19 of that Form 8606.	2002 through 2009
2000 (an amount was entered on 2000 Form 8606, line 17)	The excess of 2000 Form 8606, line 18d, over line 17 of that Form 8606.	2001 through 2009
1999 (an amount was entered on 1999 Form 8606, line 17)	The excess of 1999 Form 8606, line 18d, over line 17 of that Form 8606.	2000 through 2009
1998 (an amount was entered on 1998 Form 8606, line 18)	The excess of 1998 Form 8606, line 19c, over line 18 of that Form 8606.	1999 through 2009
Did not take a Roth IRA distribution* prior to 2009	$0	1998 through 2009

---

* Excluding rollovers, recharacterizations, and contributions that were returned.
** Excluding rollovers, conversions, Roth IRA contributions that were recharacterized, and any contributions that were returned.

Line 23

Generally, there is an additional 10 percent tax on 2009 distributions from a Roth IRA that are shown on line 23. The additional tax is reported on Form 5329, Part I. The 10 percent tax does not apply to any qualified disaster recovery assistance distribution or qualified recovery assistance distribution (see Qs 3:132–3:161).

Line 24

Figure the amount to enter on line 24 as follows:

- If no Roth IRA conversions were ever made to a Roth IRA and no amount was rolled over from an eligible employer's qualified plan, 403(b) plan, or governmental 457(b) plan, enter -0- on line 24.

- If a Roth IRA distribution (other than an amount rolled over or recharacterized or a returned contribution) was made before 2009 in excess of the basis in regular Roth IRA contributions, use Table 9-2 to figure the amount to enter on line 24. If no such distribution (see above) was taken before 2009, enter on line 24 the total of all conversions made to Roth IRAs (other than amounts recharacterized). These amounts are shown on line 14c of the taxpayer's 1998, 1999, and 2000 Forms 8606 and line 16 of the taxpayer's 2001 through 2009 Forms 8606.

- Increase or decrease the amount on line 24 by any basis transferred or received incident to divorce (see Qs 5:37, 5:39). Also attach a statement explaining the transfer.

Table 9-2. Amount to be entered on line 24 if a Roth IRA distribution (other than an amount rolled over or recharacterized or a returned contribution) was made before 2009 in excess of the basis in regular Roth IRA contributions.

IF the most recent year prior to 2009 in which a distribution was made in excess of the basis in contributions was . . .	THEN enter on Form 8606, line 24, this amount . . .	PLUS the sum of the amounts on the following lines . . .
2008 (2008 Form 8606, line 22, was less than line 19 that Form 8606)	The excess, if any, of 2008 Form 8606, line 24, over line 23[**] of that Form 8606.	Line 16 of 2009 Form 8606
2007 (2007 Form 8606, line 22, was less than line 19 that Form 8606)	The excess, if any, of 2007 Form 8606, line 24, over line 23[**] of that Form 8606.	Line 16 of 2007 and 2008 Form 8606
2006 (2006 Form 8606, line 22, was less than line 19 that Form 8606)	The excess, if any, of 2006 Form 8606, line 24, over line 23[**] of that Form 8606.	Line 16 of 2007 through 2009 Forms 8606
2005 (2005 Form 8606, line 22, was less than line 19 of that Form 8606)	The excess, if any, of 2005 Form 8606, line 24, over line 23[**] of that Form 8606.	Line 16 of 2006 through 2009 Forms 8606
2004 (2004 Form 8606, line 22, was less than line 19 of that Form 8606)	The excess, if any, of 2004 Form 8606, line 24, over line 23[**] of that Form 8606.	Line 16 of 2005 through 2009 Forms 8606
2003 (an amount was entered on 2003 Form 8606, line 21)	The excess, if any, of 2003 Form 8606, line 22, over line 21 of that Form 8606.	Line 16 of 2004 through 2009 Forms 8606

Table 9-2. Amount to be entered on line 24 if a Roth IRA distribution (other than an amount rolled over or recharacterized or a returned contribution) was made before 2009 in excess of the basis in regular Roth IRA contributions. (*cont'd*)

IF the most recent year prior to 2009 in which a distribution was made in excess of the basis in contributions was . . .	THEN enter on Form 8606, line 24, this amount . . .	PLUS the sum of the amounts on the following lines . . .
2002 (an amount was entered on 2002 Form 8606, line 21)	The excess, if any, of 2002 Form 8606, line 22, over line 21 of that Form 8606.	Line 16 of 2003 through 2009 Forms 8606
2001 (an amount was entered on 2001 Form 8606, line 21)	The excess, if any, of 2001 Form 8606, line 22, over line 21 of that Form 8606.	Line 16 of 2002 through 2009 Forms 8606
2000 (an amount was entered on 2000 Form 8606, line 19)	The excess, if any, of 2000 Form 8606, line 25, over line 19 of that Form 8606.	Line 16 of 2001 through 2009 Forms 8606
1999 (an amount was entered on 1999 Form 8606, line 19)	The excess, if any, of 1999 Form 8606, line 25, over line 19 of that Form 8606.	Line 14c of 2000 Form 8606 and line 16 of 2001 through 2009 Forms 8606
1998 (an amount was entered on 1998 Form 8606, line 20)	The excess, if any, of 1998 Form 8606, line 14c, over line 20 of that Form 8606.	Line 14c of 1999 and 2000 Forms 8606 and line 16 of 2001 through 2009 Forms 8606
Did not have such a distribution in excess of basis in contributions	The amount from 2008 Form 8606, line 16.	Line 14c of 1998, 1999, and 2000 Forms 8606 and line 16 of 2001 through 2007 Forms 8606

---

[*] Excluding rollovers, recharacterizations, and contributions that were returned.
^{**} Refigure line 23 without taking into account any amount entered on Form 8606, line 20.

Line 25b

If all distributions are either qualified disaster recovery assistance distributions or qualified recovery assistance distributions, enter the amount from line 25a on line 25b. If there are distributions unrelated to either the Midwestern severe storms, tornadoes, or flooding; or the Kansas storms and tornadoes, as well as qualified disaster recovery assistance distributions or qualified recovery assistance distributions, multiply the amount on line 25a by a fraction. The numerator of the fraction is the total of all disaster recovery assistance distributions or recovery assistance distributions. The denominator of the fraction is the amount from Form 8606, line 21 (see Example below).

Example. Aaron received a distribution from his Roth IRA (that he did not roll over) in the amount of $30,000 on April 1, 2009, unrelated to the severe storms, tornadoes, or flooding in the Midwestern disaster areas. On August 18, 2009, he received a qualified disaster recovery assistance distribution (as a result of the severe storms, tornadoes, or flooding in a Midwestern disaster area) from his Roth IRA in the amount of $10,000. Aaron would report total distributions of $40,000 on Form 8606, line 19. Because he has no first-time homebuyer expenses reported on line 20, he would also enter $40,000 on line 21. Aaron would then complete lines 22 through 24. Form 8606, line 25a shows an amount of $20,000. Aaron would enter $5,000 ($20,000 × $10,000 ÷ $40,000) on line 25b. Aaron would also enter $9,000 on line 14 of Form 8930, Qualified Disaster Recovery Assistance Retirement Plan Distributions and Repayments.

Q 9:60   How are distributions from an IRA reported if the recipient is not an individual?

If the recipient of an IRA distribution is not an individual (e.g., an estate or a trust), the distribution is taxable to the recipient entity. Items of income taxable to the entity for purposes of federal income taxes are reported on Form 1041, U.S. Income Tax Return for Estates and Trusts. Form 1099-R is issued in the name of the recipient entity using the entity's TIN.

Q 9:61   When must a recipient attach Form 1099-R to Form 1040?

A recipient is required to attach Form 1099-R to his or her (or its) federal income tax return only if federal income tax withholding is shown in box 4.

Q 9:62   Do the reporting requirements applicable to IRAs for RMDs apply to Roth IRAs?

No. The Final Required Minimum Distribution (RMD) Regulations issued on April 17, 2002, along with Notice 2002-27, outline the new reporting requirements for trustees of traditional IRAs that became effective in 2003. The new reporting rule affects the trustee of a traditional IRA with respect to the IRA owners only. Decedent (beneficiary) reporting is not required.

Since Roth IRA owners are not subject to the minimum distribution requirement, the new reporting regulations do not apply. In addition, the preamble to the new final regulations specifically excepts from the new reporting requirements: Roth IRAs and beneficiary reporting for all IRAs.

Q 9:63   How are distributions from an IRA reported if the recipient is not an individual?

If the recipient of an IRA distribution is not an individual (e.g., an estate or a trust), the distribution is taxable to the recipient entity. Items of income taxable to the entity for purposes of federal income taxes are reported on Form 1041, U.S. Income Tax Return for Estates and Trusts. Form 1099-R is issued in the name of the recipient entity using the entity's TIN.

Q 9:64   Do the reporting requirements applicable to IRAs for required minimum distributions apply to Roth IRAs?

No. The Final Required Minimum Distribution (RMD) Regulations issued on April 17, 2002, along with Notice 2002-27, outline the new reporting requirements for trustees of traditional IRAs that became effective in 2003. The new reporting rule affects the trustee of a traditional IRA with respect to the IRA owners only. Roth IRA and Roth IRA decedent (beneficiary) reporting is not required.

Because Roth IRA owners are not subject to the minimum distribution requirement, the new reporting regulations do not apply. In addition, the preamble to the new final regulations specifically excludes the following from the new reporting requirements: Roth IRAs, beneficiary reporting for all IRAs, and 403(b) contracts.

Chapter 10

Designated Roth Contribution Programs

This chapter discusses elective contributions that can be treated as *designated Roth contributions* under an employer's 401(k) or 403(b) plan as well as how such contributions are accounted for and maintained. The chapter also addresses qualified and non-qualified distributions from designated Roth accounts under the final and amended regulations issued in 2007 and the treatment of such amounts for income and penalty tax purposes. The rules relating to rollovers, when permitted, and direct transfers, as well as the reporting and recordkeeping requirements for designated Roth accounts are also issues discussed in this chapter (see also chapter 9). The April 2007 final 402A regulations providing guidance on the taxation of distributions from designated Roth accounts (DRAs) under 401(k) and 403(b) plans are also discussed in this chapter, as well as the 60-day and direct rollover rules applicable to distribution of designated Roth contributions. Finally, this chapter discusses the final 403(b) regulations issued in July 2007 relating to elective deferrals under a 403(b) plan that are designated Roth contributions. A chart of rollover contributions from designated Roth accounts follows Q 10:47.

In General

Q 10:1 Is a Roth 401(k) or Roth 403(b) a new type of plan? What is it?

No, a Roth 401(k) or Roth 403(b) is not a new type of plan. *Designated Roth contributions* are a new type of contribution that can be accepted by new or existing 401(k) or 403(b) plans (see Q 10:6). If a plan adopts this feature, employees can designate some or all of their elective contributions as designated Roth contributions (which are included in gross income) rather than as traditional, pretax elective contributions (see Q 10:5). Technically, such a program is called a *designated Roth contribution program* (DRCP). [I.R.C. § 402A(b)] However, the program is more commonly called a *designated* Roth contribution program or "DRCP." The account that holds such contributions is referred to as designated Roth account or "DRA." Therefore, starting in 2006, elective contributions come in two types: traditional, pretax elective contributions (elective contributions are also referred to as elective deferrals) and designated Roth contributions. [I.R.C. § 402A(e)(1)]

> **Note.** Designated Roth contributions are allowed in 401(k) plans and 403(b) plans but not in a SARSEP or SIMPLE IRA plan.

Q 10:2 Have regulations been issued regarding designated Roth contribution accounts under a 401(k) or 403(b) plan?

Yes. On March 1, 2005, the IRS released much-awaited proposed Roth 401(k) regulations. [Treas. Reg. § 1.401(k)-1(f)] The regulations, as amended, were finalized on January 3, 2006. [Treas. Reg. §§ 1.401(k), 1.401(m)(2), 1.401(m)(5) (T.D. 9237, 71 Fed. Reg. 6 (Jan. 3, 2006)] Economic Growth and Tax Relief Reconciliation Act (EGTRRA) authorized the establishment of Roth 401(k) and Roth 403(b) accounts beginning January 1, 2006. The final 401(k) regulations provide guidance only on Roth 401(k) accounts. They do not cover Roth 403(b) arrangements. Guidance on Roth 403(b) was issued in 2007. [T.D. 9340, 72 Fed. Reg. 21128–41160 (July 26, 2007)]

The final regulations under Code Section 401(k) apply to plan years beginning on or after January 1, 2006. The 2006 final regulations closely followed the 2005 proposed regulations and provided clarifications that did the following:

1. Clarified that, in order to provide for designated Roth contributions, a qualified cash or deferred arrangement must also offer pretax elective contributions. Thus, a plan is not permitted to offer only designated Roth contributions. [Treas. Reg. §§ 1.401(k)-1(f)(1), 1.403(b)-3(c)(1)]

2. Provided that elective contributions may only be treated as designated Roth contributions to the extent permitted under the plan. [Treas. Reg. §§ 1.401(k)-1(f)(1), 1.403(b)-3(c)(1)]

3. Retained the rule that, under the separate accounting requirement, contributions and withdrawals of designated Roth contributions must take place in a DRA maintained for the employee and that the plan must retain a record of the investment in that account. Gains, losses, and so on, must

be allocated on a "reasonable and consistent" basis to the DRA and other accounts under the plan. [Treas. Reg. § 1.401(k)-1(f)(3)]

4. Confirmed that forfeitures may not be allocated to the DRA, and no contributions other than designated Roth contributions and rollover contributions described in Code Section 402A(c)(3)(B) can be allocated to a DRA. [Treas. Reg. § 1.401(k)-1(f)(3)]

5. Retained the requirement that the designated Roth contributions are taken into account under the actual deferral percentage test (ADP test). [I.R.C. § 401(k)(3); Treas. Reg. § 1.401(k)-(4)(i)]

6. Clarified that a direct rollover from a DRA under a qualified cash or deferred arrangement can only be made to another DRA under an applicable retirement plan, or to a personal Roth IRA, and only to the extent a direct rollover is permitted under the rules of Code Section 402(c) regarding rollovers from an employer's plan. [Treas. Reg. § 1.401(k)-1(f)(4)(ii)]

   Note. If a participant's Roth balance is less than $200, the plan may provide an involuntary cashout of the benefits and does not have to offer a rollover option. [Treas. Reg. §§ 1.401(k)-1(f)(4)(ii); 1.403(b)-7(b)(2)]

7. Clarified that Roth contributions can be treated as catch-up contributions and serve as the basis for a participant loan. [Treas. Reg. § 1.401(k)-1(f)(4); Preamble, Treas. Reg. § 1.401(k), Other Rules, 71 Fed. Reg. 6 (Jan. 3, 2006)]

8. Retained the rule that a highly compensated employee, with elective contributions that include both pretax and Roth contributions, can elect whether excess contributions are to be attributed to pretax elective contributions or to designated Roth contributions, though there is no requirement that a plan provide this option. [Treas. Reg. § 1.401(k)-2(b)(1)(ii)]

9. Retained the rule that a distribution of excess contributions by April 15 following the year the excess is made, to the extent it represents a distribution of Roth contributions, is not includible in gross income. Income allocable to a corrective distribution is, however, includible in the same manner as income allocable to a corrective distribution of excess pretax elective contributions, that is, in the same manner as income allocable to a corrective distribution of excess aggregate contributions that are not designated as Roth contributions. [Treas. Reg. § 1.401(m)-2(b)(2)(vi)(C)]

10. Clarified that an adopting plan may use Roth contributions as the default in an automatic enrollment/negative election (i.e., an employee who has not made an affirmative election is deemed to have irrevocably designated the contributions as "designated Roth contributions"). [Treas. Reg. § 1.401(k)-1(f)(5)(ii)(A) and (B)]

11. Confirmed that Roth contributions are subject to the RMD rules of Code Section 401(a)(9)(A) and (B) in the same manner as pretax elective contributions made under the plan. It should be noted that Roth IRA contributions are not subject to the rules of Code Section 401(a)(9)

during the lifetime of the owner. [Treas. Reg. §§ 1.401(k)-1(f)(4)(i); 1.403(b)-3(c)(2)]

Note. The 2006 final regulations provided limited guidance with respect to the taxation of distributions of designated Roth contributions (see below). That guidance was issued in January 2006, with the release of proposed regulations (since finalized, see below) issued under Code Sections 402(g), 402A, 403(b), and 408A.

On April 30, 2007, the IRS released final regulations providing guidance on the taxation of distributions from DRAs under 401(k) and 403(b) plans. [T.D. 9324, 72 Fed. Reg. 82, 21103–21116 (Apr. 30, 2007), amended 72 Fed. Reg. 107, 30974 (June 5, 2007)] The final regulations affect administrators of, employers maintaining, participants in, and beneficiaries of 401(k) and 403(b) plans, as well as owners and beneficiaries of Roth IRAs and trustees of Roth IRAs. The following is a summary of the final regulations under Code Section 402A, and amended final regulations under Code Section 401(k). The final Code Section 402A regulations:

- Retain the rule that any transaction or accounting methodology involving an employee's DRA and any other accounts under the plan or plans of an employer that has the effect of directly or indirectly transferring value from another account into the DRA violates the separate accounting requirement (see Q 10:80).

- Clarify that, in the case of distribution to an alternate payee or beneficiary, the age, death, or disability of the participant are used to determine whether the distribution is qualified (e.g., satisfies the five-taxable year period and 59½, death, or disability rules). The only exception is in the case of a rollover by an alternate payee or surviving spouse to a DRA under a plan of his or her own employer (see Q 5:30).

Determination of five-taxable-year period for qualified distributions—

- Confirm that the five-taxable-year period during which a distribution is *not* a qualified distribution begins on the first day of the employee's taxable year for which the employee first had designated Roth contributions made to the plan and ends when five consecutive taxable years have been completed. However, if a direct rollover is made from a DRA under another plan, the five-taxable-year period for the recipient plan begins on the first day of the employee's taxable year for which the employee first had designated Roth contributions made to the other plan, if earlier (see Q 10:29).

- Provide that designated Roth contributions made by a reemployed veteran are treated as made in the taxable year with respect to which the contributions relate (see Q 10:44).

- The determination of whether a payment is a qualified distribution is determined based upon the actual year of the payment from the account and does not take into account whether the payment is part of a series of distributions or whether the payment is attributable to a prior calendar year (see Q 10:37).

- Provide that certain contributions do not start the five-taxable-year period of participation. For example, a year in which the only contributions consist of excess deferrals will not start the five-taxable-year period of participation. Further, excess contributions that are distributed to prevent an ADP failure also do not begin the five-taxable-year period of participation. Finally, contributions returned to the employee pursuant to Code Section 414(w) regarding permissive withdrawals from eligible automatic contribution arrangements also do not start the five-taxable-year period of participation (see Qs 10:40, 10:68).

Taxation of nonqualified distributions

- Retain the rules from the proposed regulations for taxation of nonqualified distributions and provide that a distribution from a DRA that is not a qualified distribution is taxable to the distributee, treating the DRA as a separate contract under Code Section 72 (see Qs 10:41, 10:44, 10:46, 10:63, 10:65–10:68, 10:79).
- Retain the rule that the basis recovery rules in Code Section 408A, which provide that the first distributions from a Roth IRA are a return of contributions (and thus not includible in gross income) until all contributions have been returned as basis, do not apply to DRAs (see Q 10:27).
- Provide that the limit on elective contributions available for hardship distribution is an aggregate limit that takes into account both pretax elective contributions and designated Roth contributions. For example, an employee could take all hardship distributions from the pretax account, even though part of the amount available for hardship is attributable to designated Roth contributions (see Q 10:62).

Rollover of designated Roth contributions

- Retain the rule in the proposed regulation that, in order to roll over any portion of the basis in a DRA into a DRA under another plan, the rollover of the distribution must be accomplished through a direct rollover (i.e., a rollover to another DRA is not available for the portion of the distribution not includible in gross income if the distribution is made directly to the employee) (see Q 10:48). However, the requirement that the receiving plan separately account for designated Roth contributions that are rolled over has been eliminated because such contributions are already independently subject to the separate account requirement. [Treas. Reg. § 1.401(k)-1(f)(3)] Retain the provision in the proposed regulations requiring the distributing plan making the direct rollover is required to report the amount of the investment in the contract and the first year of the five-year period to the recipient plan so that the recipient plan will not need to rely on information from the distributee (see Q 10:73).
- The definition of a DRA has been revised to only include accounts under a plan to which designated Roth contributions are made in lieu of elective contributions or deferrals (see Q 10:23).

- Clarify that a distribution from a DRA may only be rolled over to a 401(k) plan or 403(b) plan if that plan has a designated Roth program (see Q 10:48).

- If the entire account balance of a DRA is rolled over to another DRA, and, at the time of the distribution, the investment in the contract exceeds the balance in the DRA, the final regulations clarify that the investment in the contract in the distributing plan is included in the investment in the contract of the recipient plan (see Q 10:60).

- If a distribution from a DRA is made to an employee, the employee is still able to roll over the entire amount (or any portion thereof) into a Roth IRA within a 60-day period. If only a portion of the distribution is rolled over, the portion that is rolled over is treated as consisting first of the amount of the distribution that is includible in gross income (see Q 10:48). [I.R.C. § 402(c)(2)] The income limits for contributions for Roth IRAs do not apply to rollovers or direct transfers.

- Confirm that the employee's period of participation under the distributing plan is not carried over to the recipient plan for purposes of determining whether the employee satisfies the five-taxable-year requirement under the recipient plan. However, the final regulations provide that such an indirect rollover contribution starts the five-taxable-year period of participation under the receiving plan for a participant who has made no prior designated Roth contributions to that plan (see Q 10:49).

Determination of five-taxable-year period after a rollover to a Roth IRA

- Retain the rule under the proposed regulations that the five-taxable-year periods applicable to Roth IRAs and DRAs are determined independently (see Q 10:27).

- Provide that if a qualified distribution from a DRA is rolled over into a Roth IRA, the entire amount of the distribution will be treated as basis in the Roth IRA (see Q 10:54).

- If the entire account balance of a DRA is distributed and some or all of the distribution is rolled over to a Roth IRA, and, at the time of the distribution, the investment in the contract exceeds the balance in the DRA, the final regulations provide that the investment in the contract in the distributing plan is included in the amount treated as a contribution to the Roth IRA (see Q 10:55).

Certain amounts not qualified distributions

- The final regulations clarify that an amount is not precluded from being a qualified distribution merely because it is described as an amount not eligible for rollover (see Q 10:28). Thus, hardship distributions and required minimum distributions are not precluded from being qualified distributions. Similarly, payments in a stream of periodic payments are not precluded from being qualified distributions. [*See* I.R.C. § 402(c)(4)(A)]

Reporting and recordkeeping

- Clarify that DRA distribution reporting is only required to the extent provided in forms and instructions (see Q 10:73).

Designated Roth contributions as excess deferrals

- Provide that if there are any excess deferrals that are designated Roth contributions that are not corrected prior to April 15th of the year following the excess, the first amounts distributed from the DRA are treated as distributions of excess deferrals and earnings until the full amount of those excess deferrals (and attributable earnings) are distributed (see Qs 10:68–10:73).

Modifications to final Roth 401(k) regulations

- Clarify that the balance of a participant's DRA and a participant's other accounts under the plan are treated as accounts held under two separate plans for purposes of applying not only the special rule for *de minimis* distributions (reasonably expected to total less than $200) but also both the automatic rollover rules for mandatory distributions and the extent to which plans must allow split distributions. Thus, for example, if a participant has less than $1,000 in the participant's DRA and less than $1,000 in the participant's other accounts, the plan will not need to provide the participant with an automatic rollover with respect to the DRA or the other accounts even if the total accrued benefit of the participant under the plan exceeds $1,000. [Treas. Reg. § 1.401(k)-1(f)(4)(ii)]
- Clarify that compensation for foreign missionaries is not precluded from being contributed to a DRA merely because the compensation would not have been includible in gross income if paid directly (see Q 10:8).

On July 26, 2007, final regulations relating to elective deferrals were issued under Code Section 403(b). The final 403(b) regulations generally are effective on January 1, 2009. [T.D. 9340, 72 Fed. Reg. 41128–41160 (July 26, 2007)] For purposes of those final regulations, the term "elective deferral" includes a designated Roth contribution as well as a pretax elective contribution. The final regulations relating to elective deferrals under a 403(b) plan that are designated Roth contributions are substantially unchanged from the proposed regulations regarding designated Roth accounts under a Section 403(b) plan that were issued in January 2006. [REG-146459-05, 71 Fed. Reg. 4320 (Jan. 26, 2006)] Similar to the 2006 proposed regulations, the final 403(b) regulations provide that the rules for designated Roth contributions in a 401(k) plan under Treasury Regulations Sections 1.401(k)-1(f)(1) and 1.401(k)-1(f)(2) also apply to designated Roth contributions under 403(b) plan. A designated Roth contribution under a 403(b) plan is a 403(b) elective deferral that is:

1. Designated irrevocable by the employee at the time of the cash or deferred election a "designated Roth contribution";
2. Made in lieu of all or a portion of the 403(b) elective deferral otherwise permitted to be made under the plan;

3. Treated by the employer as includible in gross income as wages (subject to applicable withholding requirements) at the time the employee would have received the cash had the employee not made the cash or deferred election; and

4. Maintained in a separate account. [Treas. Reg. § 1.403(b)-3(c)(1)]

In addition, designated Roth contributions must meet the timing distribution rules applicable to elective deferrals under the 403(b) plan, as well as, the required minimum distribution rules under Code Sections 401(a)(9)(A) and 401(a)(9)(B). [Treas. Reg. §§ 1.403(b)-3(c)(2), 1.403(b)-6(d)] If any employee has the right to make designated Roth contributions, then all eligible employees must that right (see Q 10:22). [*See* Treas. Reg. § 1.403(b)-11 for effective dates applicable to collectively bargaining agreements, retirement income accounts, and plans that exclude certain types of employees from elective deferrals.]

Contributions to Designated Roth Accounts

Q 10:3   What is a *designated Roth contribution program*?

A *designated Roth contribution program* is a permissive feature that may be added to a qualified 401(k) plan or 403(b) plan and that allows participants to make (designate) Roth-like contributions (Roth elective deferrals) to that plan. [I.R.C. §§ 402A(b)(1), 402A(e)(1); Treas. Reg. § 1.401(m)-5; Treas. Reg. § 1.402A, Q&A 1]

Q 10:4   What are designated Roth contributions under a 401(k) or 403(b) plan?

Designated Roth contributions under a 401(k) or 403(b) plan are defined as elective contributions under a qualified cash or deferred arrangement that are:

1. Designated irrevocably by the employee at the time of the cash or deferred election as designated Roth contributions;

2. Treated by the employer as includible in the employee's income at the time the employee would have received the contribution amounts in cash if the employee had not made the cash or deferred election (e.g., by treating the contributions as wages subject to applicable withholding requirements); and

3. Maintained by the plan in a separate account.

Contributions may be treated as designated Roth contributions only to the extent permitted under the plan. [I.R.C. §§ 402A(c)(2), 402A(e)(2); Treas. Reg. §§ 1.401(k)-1(f)(1); 1.402A-1, Q&A 1; 1.403(b)-2(a)(17)] Thus, the plan must contain provisions regarding designated Roth contributions. Such provisions must be adopted by the end of the plan year for which the provisions are operationally effective. [Notice 2001-42, 2001-2 C.B. 70, regarding "good-faith" EGTRRA amendments]

In Notice 2006-44 (2006-20 I.R.B. 889), the IRS provided a sample plan amendment for plan sponsors that want to provide for designated Roth contributions in their 401(k) plans. Although a 403(b) plan also may allow designated Roth contributions, the sample amendment does not address these plans.

Q 10:5   Must a 401(k) or 403(b) plan accept designated Roth contributions?

No. A 401(k) or 403(b) plan will have to be amended to accept designated Roth contributions. [I.R.C. § 402A(b); Treas. Reg. §§ 1.401(k)-1(f)(1); 1.402A-1, Q&A 1; 1.403(b)-3(b)(3)]

Q 10:6   May a participant in a 401(k) or 403(b) plan designate any or all of the participant's after-tax elective deferral contributions for the year to be designated Roth contributions?

Yes. In taxable years beginning after 2005, a participant in a 401(k) or 403(b) plan will be permitted to designate any or all of the participant's elective deferral contributions for the year to be Roth 401(k) contributions or Roth 403(b) contributions, respectively (see Q 10:3). [I.R.C. § 402A] Contributions made by participants under the DRCP are generally referred to as "designated Roth contributions."

Caution. Because the statute (Code Section 402A) is effective for 2006, the first year that a qualified withdrawal from a DRCP can be made is 2011.

Q 10:7   When may designated Roth accounts be distributed?

Generally, designated Roth accounts may be distributed no sooner than elective deferrals are permitted to be distributed under the plan (see Qs 10:27, 10:41). [I.R.C. § 402A(a)(1)]

Q 10:8   May an employer exclude designated Roth contributions from an employee's gross income?

No. Although designated Roth contributions will generally be treated as elective deferrals, they will not be excluded from gross income. [I.R.C. § 402A(a)(1)] However, in the case of a self-employed individual, an elective contribution is treated as not excludible from gross income only if the individual does not claim a deduction for such amount. If an elective contribution would not have been includible in gross income if the amount had been paid directly to the employee (rather than being subject to a cash or deferral election), the elective contribution is nevertheless permitted to be a designated Roth contribution, provided the employee is entitled to treat the amount as an investment in the contract pursuant to Code Section 72(f)(2) regarding special rules for computing employee's contributions. [Treas. Reg. §§ 1.401(k)-1(f)(2); 1.403(b)-3(a)] Thus, compensation for foreign missionaries is not precluded from being contributed to a DRA merely because the compensation would not have been includible in gross income if paid directly.

A tax credit for contributions may be available to certain lower-income taxpayers (see Q 2:43).

Q 10:9 How are designated Roth contributions tested in a 401(k) plan?

Designated Roth contributions are tested along with pretax deferrals as part of the actual deferral percentage (ADP) test in a 401(k) plan. These contributions will also be treated as Section 402(g) elective deferrals for purposes of nonforfeitability and distribution requirements. [I.R.C. § 402A(c)(1)(A); Treas. Reg. §§ 1.401(k)-2, 1.401(m)-2]

Q 10:10 Are designated Roth contributions subject to wage withholding?

Yes. A designated Roth contribution is treated by the employer as includible in the employee's gross income at the time the employee would have received the amount in cash if the employee had not made the election; hence, designated Roth contributions are subject to all applicable wage withholding requirements. [Treas. Reg. §§ 1.401(k)-1(f)(2); 1.403(b)-3(c)(2)]

Q 10:11 May a participant make both pretax elective and designated Roth contributions in the same year?

Yes, a participant may make contributions to both a DRA and a traditional, pretax account in the same year in any proportion the participant may choose. However, the combined amount contributed in any one year is limited (see Q 10:12).

Q 10:12 Are there any limits as to how much may be contributed to a DRA?

Yes, the combined amount contributed to all DRAs and traditional, pretax accounts in any one year for any participant is limited by Code Section 402(g) to $16,500 (plus an additional $5,500 in catch-up contributions if the individual is age 50 or older) for 2009. [Treas. Reg. § 1.402(g)-1(d)(1) to (2)]

Under the special Code Section 403(b) catch-up limit, the Section 402(g) limit ($16,500/$22,000) is increased by the lowest of the following three amounts: (i) $3,000; (ii) the excess of $15,000 over the amount not included in gross income for prior taxable years by reason of the special Section 403(b) catch-up rules, plus elective deferrals that are designated Roth contributions (see note); or (iii) the excess of (A) $5,000 multiplied by the number of years of service of the employee with the qualified organization, over (B) the total elective deferrals made for the employee by the qualified organization for prior taxable years. For this purpose, a qualified organization is an eligible employer that is a school, hospital, health and welfare service agency (including a home health service agency), or a church-related organization

> **Note.** The Treasury Department has recommended that item "i" above (the $3,000 limit) be further changed to reflect the intent that the reduction for designated Roth contributions be limited to designated Roth contributions that have been made pursuant to the 403(b) plan catch-up rules. [I.R.C. § 402(g)(7)(A)(ii)(II); GOZA § 402(g)(7)(A)(ii), clarifying that the aggregate $16,500 (for 2009) limit on such contributions was reduced not only by pretax elective deferrals made pursuant to the special Section 403(b) catch-up rules, but also by designated Roth contributions.]

Q 10:13   May catch-up contributions be made as a designated Roth contribution?

A participant may elect to treat catch-up contributions (if age 50 or older before the end of the calendar year) as designated Roth contributions. [Treas. Reg. §§ 1.401(k)-1(f)(4)(i); 1.403(b)-2(b)(17)]

Q 10:14   Must the election to make designated Roth contributions be made at the beginning of the year?

No. The rules regarding frequency of elections apply in the same manner to both pretax elective contributions and designated Roth contributions and must be specified under the plan. Thus, an employee must have an effective opportunity to make (or change) an election to make designated Roth contributions at least once during each plan year. A Roth election must be in place before any money can be placed in a DRA. [Treas. Reg. §§ 1.401(k)-1(f)(5)(i); 1.403(b)-5(b)(2)]

Q 10:15   Do the same income restrictions that apply to Roth IRAs apply to designated Roth contributions?

No, there are no limits on income in determining if designated Roth contributions can be made. [I.R.C. § 402A(1)] Of course, the participant must have compensation from which to make designated Roth contributions.

Q 10:16   Can an employer make matching contributions on designated Roth contributions?

Yes. An employer can make matching contributions on designated Roth contributions. [Treas. Reg. §§ 1.401(k)-1(f)(4)(i); 1.403(b)-5(a)(1)(iv)]

Q 10:17   May employer matching contributions be allocated to the participant's DRA?

No. Only an employee's designated Roth contributions can be allocated to DRAs. [Treas. Reg. §§ 1.401(k)-1(f)(3); 1.402A-1 Q&A 1, 1.403(b)-7(e)] The matching contributions made on account of designated Roth contributions must be allocated to a pretax account, similar to matching contributions on traditional, pretax elective contributions.

Q 10:18   May plan forfeitures be placed into a DRA?

No amounts other than designated Roth contributions and rollover contributions (and earnings on such contributions) are permitted to be allocated to a DRA. [Treas. Reg. § 1.401(k)-1(f)(3)] Therefore, forfeitures, matching contributions, or any other employer contributions may not be allocated to the DRA.

Q 10:19   If a participant makes designated Roth contributions and later changes his or her mind, may the designated Roth contributions be treated as pretax elective contributions? Can they be re-characterized and transferred from the DRA to the traditional, pretax account?

No, the election to make designated Roth contributions is irrevocable. Similarly, negative elections that treat contributions as designated Roth contributions are also irrevocable (see Q 10:21). Once contributions are designated as Roth contributions, they cannot later be changed to pretax elective contributions. Thus, they cannot be re-characterized and transferred from the DRA to the traditional, pretax account. [Treas. Reg. §§ 1.401(k)-1(f)(1)(i); 1.403(b)-3(c)(1)]

Q 10:20   Can a plan offer only designated Roth contributions?

No, in order to provide for designated Roth contributions, a 401(k) or 403(b) plan must also offer pretax elective contributions. [Treas. Reg. §§ 1.401(k)-1(f)(1)(i); 1.403(b)-3(c)(1)]

Q 10:21   Can an employer's 401(k) or 403(b) plan automatically enroll participants into making designated Roth contributions if the participant does not affirmatively decline participation?

Yes, a plan that provides for a cash or deferred election can stipulate that contributions will be made in the absence of an affirmative election by the participant declining participation. If such plan has both pretax elective contributions and designated Roth contributions, the plan must set forth the extent to which those default contributions are pretax elective contributions or designated Roth contributions. [Treas. Reg. § 1.401(k)-1(f)(5)(ii)(A)] If the default contributions under the plan are designated Roth contributions, an employee who has not made an affirmative election is deemed to have irrevocably designated the contributions as designated Roth contributions. [Treas. Reg. § 1.401(k)-1(f)(5)(ii)(B)]

Q 10:22   If designated Roth contributions are offered to one participant under a 403(b) tax-sheltered annuity plan, must they be offered to all participants under that TSA plan?

Yes. The universal availability requirement of Code Section 403(b)(12) includes the right to make designated Roth contributions. [I.R.C. § 403(b)(12); Treas. Reg. § 1.403(b)-5(b)] Thus, if any employee is given the opportunity to designate Code Section 403(b) elective deferrals as designated Roth contributions, then all eligible employees must be given that right. [I.R.C. § 403(b)(12)]

Designated Roth Accounts

Q 10:23   What is a designated Roth account?

A designation Roth Account (DRA) is a separate account under a 401(k) plan or 403(b) plan to which designated Roth contributions are made in lieu of elective deferrals, and for which separate accounting of contributions, gains, and losses is maintained (see Q 10:24). This separate accounting requirement applies at the time the designated Roth contribution is contributed to the plan and must continue to apply until the DRA is completely distributed. [Treas. Reg. §§ 1.401(k)-6, 1.403(b)-3(c), 1.401(k)-1(f)(3), 1.402A-1, Q&A 1]

Q 10:24   How will designated Roth contributions be accounted for?

The plan must separately account for designated Roth contributions and any gains or losses on them. Separate records must be maintained with respect to each participant's designated Roth account (see Q 10:23). [I.R.C. § 402A(b)(2); Treas. Reg. § 1.401(k)-1(f)(3)] In general, a participant's DRA and the participant's other accounts under a plan are treated as accounts held under two separate plans. [Treas. Reg. §§ 1.401(k)-1(f)(4)(ii); 1.403(b)-7(e)]

Q 10:25   Does a new account need to be established under the employer's 401(k) or 403(b) plan to receive designated Roth contributions?

Yes, designated Roth contributions must be kept completely separate from previous and current 401(k) or 403(b) pretax elective contributions. A separate account must be established for each participant making designated Roth contributions. [I.R.C. § 402A(b)(2)] A rollover from a Roth IRA to a DRCP may be placed into a separate account (i.e., not combined with designated Roth contributions under the plan) (see Q 10:63).

Q 10:26   How will Roth 401(k) contributions be treated?

Roth 401(k) contributions will be treated like after-tax contributions for income tax purposes; however, they will be treated as pretax contributions for purposes of the maximum deferral limit. For example, for 2006, the first year in which Roth 401(k) contributions may be made, a participant's combined pretax and Roth 401(k) contributions cannot exceed $15,000; $16,500 for 2009. Roth 401(k) contributions will also have to be included in the ADP test and will be subject to the minimum required distribution (MRD) rules. [Treas. Reg. § 1.401(k)-1(f)(4)]

Plans are required to keep records of designated Roth 401(k) contributions and related earnings in a separate account (see Q 10:24). [I.R.C. § 402A(b)(2); Treas. Reg. § 1.401(k)-1(f)(3)] Amounts in Roth 401(k) accounts may generally be rolled over to a Roth IRA or directly transferred to another 401(k) plan or 403(b) program that accepts Roth contributions (see Qs 10:48–10:67). [I.R.C. § 402A(c)(3)]

A plan may permit highly compensated employees who make both designated Roth and traditional pretax 401(k) contributions to elect whether to take ADP test corrective distributions from their pretax or from their Roth contributions (see Q 10:60). [Treas. Reg. § 1.401(k)-2(b)(1)(ii)]

Distributions from Designated Roth Accounts

Q 10:27 How will DRA distributions be taxed?

The taxation of a distribution from a DRA depends on whether or not the distribution is a qualified distribution (see Q 10:28). A qualified distribution from a DRA is not includible in gross income. Distributions from a DRA received before the end of the five-year period starting with the year of the first contribution cannot be a qualified distribution. Because there are no ordering rules, nonqualified distributions from a designated Roth account within five years will be subject to basis recovery rules (see Q 10:42). Thus, such distributions may be partially taxable. [I.R.C. § 402A(d)(2)–(4); Treas. Reg. § 1.402A-1, Q&A 2] However, a direct transfer to another DRCP account may occur within the five-year period (see Q 10:48). [I.R.C. § 402A(d)(4)]

> **Note.** Designated Roth contributions are subject to the RMD rules of Code Section 401(a)(9)(A) and (B) in the same manner as pretax elective contributions made under the plan. It should be noted that Roth IRA contributions are not subject to the rules of Code Section 401(a)(9) during the lifetime of the owner (see Q 10:2). [Treas. Reg. § 1.401(k)-1(f)(4)(i)]

Q 10:28 What is a *qualified distribution* from a DRA?

A *qualified distribution* from a DRA generally is a distribution received after a five-taxable-year period *and* after age 59½, death, or disability (see Q 10:40). [I.R.C. § 402A(d)(2)(A); Treas. Reg. § 1.402A-1, Q&A 2(b)] A qualified distribution is not taxable. [Treas. Reg. § 1.402A-1, Q&A 2(a)] All other distributions are *nonqualified* distributions.

Caution. In the case of distribution to an alternate payee or beneficiary, the age, death, or disability of the participant are used to determine whether the distribution is qualified. The only exception is in the case of a rollover by an alternate payee or surviving spouse to a DRA under a plan of his or her own employer. [Treas. Reg. § 1.402A-1, Q&A 4] Under the plan, designated Roth contributions (elective deferrals) may not be distributed any earlier than the participant's severance from employment (separation from service, for plan years beginning before 2002), death, or disability. A plan may also provide that such amounts may be distributed upon:

1. Termination of the plan without the employer's maintaining another defined contribution plan (other than an employee stock ownership plan as defined in Code Section 4975(e)(7) or 409(a), a simplified employee pension plan as defined in Code Section 408(k), a SIMPLE IRA plan as defined in Code Section 408(p), and beginning in 2006, a plan or contract described in Code Section 403(b) or a plan described in Code Section 457(b) or (f)) at any time during the period beginning on the date of plan termination and ending 12 months after all assets have been distributed from the plan.

2. The attainment of age 59½ in the case of a profit-sharing plan.

3. The hardship of the participant.

Thus, an available distribution must be received after a five-taxable-year period *and* after age 59½, death, or disability, to be treated as a qualified distribution of designated Roth contributions. [I.R.C. §§ 401(k)(2)(B), 402A(d)(2)(A); Treas. Reg. §§ 1.401(k)-1(d)(3), 1.402A-1, Q&A 2(b), 1.403(b)-6(d), 1.403(b)-7(e); Rev. Proc. 2005-16, 2005-10 I.R.B. 674, § 6.03(15)]

The final regulations under Code Section 402A clarify that an amount is not precluded from being a qualified distribution merely because it is described as an amount not eligible for rollover. Thus, hardship distributions and required minimum distributions are not precluded from being qualified distributions (see Q 10:43). Similarly, payments in a stream of periodic payments (see Q 10:37) are not precluded from being qualified distributions. [*See* I.R.C. § 402(c)(4)(A); Treas. Reg. § 1.402A-1, Q&A 11]

Example 1. After making designated Roth contributions under his employer's plan for 10 years, Wally, age 57 and in good physical health, terminates employment and receives an immediate distribution. The distribution is not a qualified distribution because Wally had not attained age 59½ (and he was not disabled).

Example 2. Same facts as in the preceding example, except that Wally is age 64. The distribution is a qualified distribution.

Example 3 Same facts as in the preceding example, except that Wally made his first designated Roth contribution two years ago. The distribution is not a qualified distribution (see Q 10:42).

Practice Pointer. Amounts rolled over from a Roth IRA are not subject to these distribution restrictions unless the rolled-over amounts are placed into the same separate account as designated Roth contributions (see Q 10:65).

Note. All distributions that may be made pursuant to one or more of the foregoing distributable events are subject to the spousal and participant consent requirements (if applicable) contained in Code Sections 401(a)(11) and 417.

[Treas. Reg. § 1.402A-1, Q&A 2(b)] A qualified distribution from a DRA is not includible in the employee's gross income. [Treas. Reg. § 1.402A-1, Q&A 2(a); *see* Listing of Required Modifications (LRM) for Cash or Deferred Arrangements, Item XVI (Jan. 2006); Treas. Reg. § 1.401(k)-2(vi)(c)]

Example. Vincent, age 62, a participant in a profit-sharing plan, receives a $12,000 distribution, which is a qualified distribution that is attributable to his being disabled, from his DRA. Immediately prior to the distribution, the account consisted of $21,850 of investment in the contract (i.e., designated Roth contributions) and $1,150 of income. For purposes of determining recovery of investment in the contract, the distribution is deemed to consist of $11,400 of investment in the contract ($12,000 × $21,850 ÷ ($1,150 + $21,850)), and $600 of income ($12,000 × $1,150 ÷ ($1,150 + $21,850)). Immediately after the distribution, Vincent's DRA consists of $10,450 of investment in the contract and $550 of income. This determination of the remaining investment in the contract will be needed if Vincent subsequently is no longer disabled and takes a nonqualified distribution from the DRA (see Q 10:44). [Treas. Reg. § 1.402A-1, Q&A 7(b)]

Q 10:29   What is a five-taxable-year period of participation, and how is it calculated?

The five-taxable-year period of participation is the period of five consecutive taxable years that begins with the first day of the first taxable year in which the employee makes a designated Roth contribution to any DRA established for the employee under the same plan and ends when five consecutive taxable years have been completed. For this purpose, the first taxable year in which an employee makes a designated Roth contribution is the year in which the amount is includible in the employee's gross income. However, a contribution that is returned as an excess deferral or excess contribution does not begin the five-taxable-year period of participation. Similarly, a contribution returned as a permissible withdrawal under Code Section 414(w) does not begin the five-taxable-year period of participation. [Treas. Reg. § 1.402A-1, Q&A 4(a)]

Q 10:30   How is an employee's five-taxable-year period determined?

Generally, an employee's five-taxable-year period of participation is determined separately for each plan [*see* I.R.C. § 414(l)] in which the employee participates. Thus, if an employee has elective deferrals made to DRAs under two or more plans, the employee may have two or more different five-taxable-year periods of participation, depending on when the employee first had contributions made to a DRA under each plan. [Treas. Reg. § 1.402A-1, Q&A 5]

Q 10:31   Is the five-taxable-year period of participation ever redetermined?

No. The beginning of the five-taxable-year period of participation is not redetermined for any portion of an employee's DRA. This is true even if the entire DRA is distributed during the five-taxable-year period of participation and the employee subsequently makes additional designated Roth contributions under the plan. [Treas. Reg. § 1.402A-1, Q&A 4(c)]

Furthermore, the beginning of the five-taxable-year period of participation is not redetermined even if the employee dies or the account is divided pursuant to a qualified domestic relations order (QDRO), and thus, a portion of the account is not payable to the employee and is payable to the employee's beneficiary or an alternate payee. [Treas. Reg. § 1.402A-1, Q&A 4(d)]

Q 10:32   What factors are used to determine qualified distributions when there is a distribution to an alternate payee or beneficiary or an indirect (60-day) rollover by the alternate payee or beneficiary?

In the case of distribution to an alternate payee or beneficiary, generally, the age, death, or disability of the employee is used to determine whether the distribution to an alternate payee or beneficiary is qualified. However, if an alternate payee or a spousal beneficiary rolls the distribution into a DRA in a plan maintained by his or her own employer, such individual's age, disability, or death is used to determine whether a distribution from the recipient plan is qualified. [Treas. Reg. § 1.402A-1, Q&A 4(d)]

Q 10:33   When does the five-taxable-year period of participation begin when there is a direct rollover contribution to the alternate payee's or spousal beneficiary's own DRA?

If the rollover is a direct rollover contribution to the alternate payee's or spousal beneficiary's own DRA, the five-taxable-year period of participation under the recipient plan begins on the earlier of the date the employee's five-taxable-year period of participation began under the distributing plan or the date the five-taxable-year period of participation applicable to the alternate payee's or spousal beneficiary's DRA began under the recipient plan. [Treas. Reg. § 1.402A-1, Q&A 4(d)]

Q 10:34   When does the five-taxable-year period of participation begin when the designated Roth contribution is made by a reemployed veteran for a year of qualified military service that is before the year in which the contribution is actually made?

If a designated Roth contribution is made by a reemployed veteran for a year of qualified military service that is before the year in which the contribution is actually made (see note), the contribution is treated as having been made in the year of qualified military service to which the contribution relates, as designated by the reemployed veteran. [*See* I.R.C. § 414(u); Treas. Reg. § 1.402A-1, Q&A 4(e)]

> **Note.** Reemployed veterans may identify the year of qualified military service for which a contribution is made for other purposes, such as for entitlement to a match, and the treatment for the five-taxable-year period of participation rule follows that identification. [I.R.C. § 414(u)] In the absence of such designation, for purposes of determining the first year of the five years of participation, the contribution is treated as relating to the first year of qualified military service for which the reemployed veteran could have made designated Roth contributions under the plan, or if later, the first taxable year in which designated Roth contributions could be made under the plan. [Treas. Reg. § 1.402A-1, Q&A 4(e)]

Q 10:35   Is the period after an annuity contract is distributed and before a payment from the annuity contract is made included in determining whether the five-year period of participation is satisfied?

Yes. A distribution of an annuity contract from a DRA is not a distribution event for purposes of Code Section 402 or 402A. [Treas. Reg. § 1.402(c)-2, A-10(a)] Instead, only distributions from the annuity contract are treated as distributions for those purposes. [Treas. Reg. § 1.402A-1, Q&A 14] Thus, the period after the annuity contract is distributed and before a payment from the annuity contract is made is included in determining whether the five-year period of participation is satisfied.

Q 10:36   When is it determined that an annuity contract distributed from a DRA is a qualified distribution?

For purposes of determining if a distribution is a qualified distribution (see Q 10:28), the determination of whether a distribution is made on or after the date the employee attains age 59½, made to a beneficiary or the estate of the employee on or after the employee's death, or attributable to the employee's being disabled, is made based on the facts at the time the distribution is made from the annuity contract. Thus, the determination of whether a payment is a qualified distribution is determined based on the actual year of the payment from the account and does not take into account whether the payment is part of a series of distributions or whether the payment is attributable to a prior calendar year.

Example. Allen first makes a designated Roth contribution to a DRA in 2008 at age 56. An annuity contract purchased only with assets from the DRA is distributed to Allen at age 57. Allen then receives a distribution from the contract in 2013 at age 60, and the distribution is a qualified distribution. [Treas. Reg. § 1.402A-1, Q&A 14]

Q 10:37 How does the five-taxable-year period of participation rule apply to an RMD attributable to an earlier year or a series of periodic payments?

The determination of whether a payment is a qualified distribution is determined based upon the actual year of the payment from the account and does not take into account whether the payment is part of a series of distributions or whether the payment is attributable to a prior calendar year.

Example. John made designated Roth contributions for six years and then retired at age 58 and began to receive payments from that account based on his life expectancy. Payments made after John attains age 59½ are qualified distributions (see Q 10:28), which are not taxable. Payments received before John attained age 59½ are nonqualified distributions (see Q 10:44) and are subject to basis recovery rules.

Q 10:38 How does the five-taxable-year period apply if there is more than one plan?

If there is more than one plan, an employee may have two or more different five-taxable-year periods depending on when the employee first had contributions made to a DRA under each plan. [Treas. Reg. § 1.402A-1, Q&A 4(b)]

Q 10:39 Must the employer ascertain the employee's taxable year?

No. In the absence of actual knowledge to the contrary, the plan administrator or other responsible party is permitted to assume that the employee's taxable year is the calendar year. [Treas. Reg. § 1.402A-2, Q&A 1]

Note. In contrast to a DRA, the five-year period for a Roth IRA [I.R.C. § 408A] begins with the first taxable year for which a contribution is made into any Roth IRA. [I.R.C. § 402A(d)(2)(B)]

Q 10:40 Are there any distributions that cannot be qualified distributions and are includible in income?

Yes, distributions of the following amounts are not treated as qualified distributions, are not eligible rollover distributions, and are includible in income:

1. Corrective distributions of elective deferrals contributed to a DRA in excess of the Code Section 415 limits (lesser of $49,000 or 100 percent of earnings for 2009)

2. Corrective distributions of excess deferrals under Code Section 402(g) (generally $16,500 in 2009, $22,000 if 50 or older, see Q 10:12)

3. Corrective distributions of excess contributions or excess aggregate contributions

4. Deemed distributions under Code Section 72(p), regarding participant loan defaults

[I.R.C. § 408A(d)(2)(C); Treas. Reg. § 1.402A-1, Q&As 2(c) and 11]

Such amounts are taxable under the rules of Treasury Regulations Sections 1.72-16(b), 1.72(p)-1, Q&A-11 through 13, 1.402(g)-1(e)(8), 1.401(k)-2(b)(2)(vi), 1.401(m)-2(b)(2)(vi), or 1.404(k)-1T. [*See* Treas. Reg. § 1.402A-1, Q&A 11] Thus, for example, loans that are treated as deemed distributions pursuant to Code Section 72(p), or dividends paid on employer securities [I.R.C. § 404(k)], are not qualified distributions even if the deemed distributions occur, or the dividends are paid after the employee attains age 59½ and the five-taxable-year period of participation has been satisfied. However, if an applicable dividend is reinvested in qualifying employer securities, the amount of such a dividend is not precluded from being a qualified distribution if later distributed. [*See* I.R.C. § 404(k)(2)(A); Treas. Reg. § 1.402A-1, Q&A 11]

Q 10:41   Will ordering rules apply to DRCP accounts?

No. There are no ordering rules for DRCP accounts. However, the account is treated as a separate contract under Code Section 72. Thus, a nonqualified distribution from a DRA is taxable to the distributee under Code Section 402 or Code Section 403(b)(1), treating the DRA as a separate contract (see Q 10:44). [*See* I.R.C. §§ 72(e)(8), 402A(d)(3); Preamble, Treas. Reg. § 1.401(k), T.D. 9324, 72 Fed. Reg. 82, 21103, 21105 (Apr. 30, 2007)]

Example 1. Veronica has made designated Roth contributions of $18,800. The account has earnings of $1,200 at the time Veronica receives a nonqualified distribution of $10,000 from her DRA. Veronica receives $18,800 of designated Roth contributions that are not includible in her gross income and $600 of earnings that are includible in her gross income. The earnings attributable to the nonqualified distribution ($600) can be computed as follows:

$12,000 × ($10,000 ÷ ($18,800 + $1,200) = $600

Example 2. Assume instead that Veronica has made a Roth IRA contribution of $2,800. The account has earnings of $200 at the time Veronica receives a nonqualified distribution (under the rules of Code Section 408(d)(4)) of $1,000 from her Roth IRA account. Because of the distribution ordering rules applicable to Roth IRAs (see Q 4:12), basis is returned first. Therefore, none of the $1,000 Veronica receives in the nonqualified distribution from her Roth IRA is taxable.

Q 10:42   What happens if a distribution is taken from a DRA before the end of the five-taxable-year period?

Under the regulations, a nonqualified distribution is included in the distributee's gross income to the extent allocable to *income* on the contract and excluded from gross income to the extent allocable to investment in the contract (basis) (see Q 10:44).

Note. For purposes of Code Section 72, designated Roth contributions are described in Code Section 72(f)(1) or 72(f)(2), to the extent applicable.

Example. Bella, a qualified plan participant, receives a $14,000 eligible rollover distribution that is not a qualified distribution from her DRA, consisting of $11,000 of investment in the contract and $3,000 of income. Within 60 days of receipt, Bella rolls over $7,000 of the distribution into a Roth IRA. The $7,000 is deemed to consist of $3,000 of income and $4,000 of investment in the contract. Because the only portion of the distribution that could be includible in Bella's gross income (the income) is rolled over, none of the distribution is includible in her gross income. [Treas. Reg. § 1.402A-1, Q&A 7(b)]

Q 10:43   Since designated Roth contributions are made after-tax, can they be withdrawn from the DRA at any time and without taxes?

No, the plan's restrictions on withdrawals that apply to pretax elective contributions also apply to designated Roth contributions (see Q 10:28). So if an employer's plan permits distributions from the 401(k) or 403(b) accounts on account of hardship, an employee may choose to receive a hardship distribution from the DRA. But such a distribution will consist of a pro rata share of earnings and basis, and the earnings will be included in gross income unless the employee had the DRA for five years and is either disabled or over age 59½ (see Q 10:28).

Q 10:44   How is a distribution from a DRA taxed if it is not a qualified distribution?

Except in the case of a rollover, a distribution from a DRA that is not a qualified distribution is taxable to the distributee under Code Section 402 in the case of a plan qualified under Code Section 401(a) and under Code Section 403(b)(1) in the case of a Section 403(b) plan. For this purpose, a DRA is treated as a separate contract under Code Section 72. Thus, except as otherwise provided for a rollover, if a distribution is before the annuity starting date, the portion of any distribution that is includible in gross income as an amount allocable to income on the contract and the portion not includible in gross income as an amount allocable to investment in the contract is determined under Code Section 72(e)(8), treating the DRA as a separate contract.

Similarly, if a distribution is on or after the annuity starting date, the portion of any annuity payment that is includible in gross income as an amount allocable to income on the contract and the portion not includible in gross income as an amount allocable to investment in the contract is determined under Code Section 72(b), treating the DRA as a separate contract. [Treas. Reg. § 1.402A-1, Q&A 3]

Q 10:45   What is the tax treatment of employer securities distributed from a DRA?

If a distribution of employer securities from a DRA is not a qualified distribution, Code Section 402(e)(4), regarding amounts attributable to employer contributions, applies. Thus, in the case of a lump-sum distribution that includes employer securities, unless the taxpayer elects otherwise, net unrealized appreciation attributable to the employer securities is not includible in gross income; and such net unrealized appreciation is not included in the basis of the distributed securities and is capital gain to the extent such appreciation is realized in a subsequent taxable transaction. [Treas. Reg. § 1.402A-1, Q&A 10(a)]

Q 10:46   What is the basis in employer securities distributed from a DRA in a qualified distribution?

In the case of a qualified distribution of employer securities from a DRA, the distributee's basis in the distributed securities for purposes of subsequent disposition is the FMV of the securities at the time of distribution. [Treas. Reg. § 1.402A-1, Q&A 10(b)] In such a case, the distributee will receive capital gains treatment at the time of any future disposition of the security, to the extent of any post-distribution appreciation. If a distribution with respect to employer securities is not a qualified distribution, the net unrealized appreciation rules [I.R.C. § 402(e)(4)] apply in the same manner as to any other distribution except that the DRA is treated as a separate contract.

> **Note.** The basis of the stock at the time of the disposition will be increased to reflect the NUA amount so that such amount will not be subsequently taxed as appreciation at the time of a subsequent disposition of the stock.

Q 10:47   Must an employee receive special information when an eligible rollover distribution is made from a DRA?

Yes. If an amount is distributed from a DRA, the plan administrator or other responsible party with respect to the plan must provide a statement to the recipient (see Q 10:74).

Rollovers of Designated Roth Contributions

Designated Roth Contribution Rollover Chart

Designated Roth Contribution Program	Direct Rollover to Roth IRA	Participant Rollover (within 60 days) to Roth IRA	Direct Rollover to 401(k) Designated Roth Account	Participant Rollover (within 60 days) to Designated Roth Account
Rollover of designated Roth contributions permitted.	Yes. *See* Treas. Reg. § 1.408A-10, Q&A 1.	Yes. *See* Treas. Reg. § 1.402A-1, Q&A 5a.	Yes. *See* Treas. Reg. § 1.402A-1, Q&A 5(a).	No (only gain can be rolled over, see below). *See* Treas. Reg. § 1.402A-1, Q&A 5(a).
Rollover of *earnings* on designated Roth contributions permitted.	Yes. *See* Treas. Reg. § 1.408A-10, Q&A 1.	Yes. **Note.** If partial rollover, taxable portion of nonqualified distributions treated as rolled over first. *See* Treas. Reg. § 1.402A-1, Q&As 5(a) & 5(d).	Yes. *See* Treas. Reg. § 1.402A-1, Q&A 5(a).	Yes. *See* Treas. Reg. § 1.402A-1, Q&A 5(a).
Determination of Five-Taxable-Year Period	*Nonqualified distributions (applies to earnings)*— based on year first contribution to Roth IRA. *Qualified distributions*— treated as basis in Roth IRA. Ordering rules apply if earnings in Roth IRA not	*Nonqualified distributions (applies to earnings)*— based on year of first contribution to Roth IRA. *Qualified distributions*— treated as basis in Roth IRA. Ordering rules apply if earnings in	Five-taxable-year period begins on the *earlier* of: (a) Year first Roth contribution made to the distributing plan or (b) First year of five-year period in the receiving plan.	No tracking. The five-taxable-year period starts with the first year of the five-taxable-year period in the receiving plan. *See* Treas. Reg. § 1.402A-1, Q&A 5(c).

Designated Roth Contribution Rollover Chart (*cont'd*)

Designated Roth Contribution Program	Direct Rollover to Roth IRA	Participant Rollover (within 60 days) to Roth IRA	Direct Rollover to 401(k) Designated Roth Account	Participant Rollover (within 60 days) to Designated Roth Account
	distributed in a qualified distribution. *See* Treas. Reg. § 1. 408A-10, Q&A 4.	Roth IRA not distributed in a qualified distribution. *See* Treas. Reg. §§ 1. 402A-1, Q&A 5(b), 1.408A-10, Q&A 4.	*See* Treas. Reg. § 1. 402A-1, Q&A 4(b).	
Recipient Plan Tracking of Five-Taxable-Year Period	Five-taxable-year period starts with year rolled over to new Roth IRA, or year first contribution made to existing Roth IRA, if earlier. *See* Treas. Reg. § 1. 408A-10, Q&A 4.	Five-taxable-year period starts with year rolled over to new Roth IRA, or year first contribution made to existing Roth IRA, if earlier. *See* Treas. Reg. § 1. 408A-10, Q&A 4.	Five-taxable-year period begins on the *earlier* of: (a) Year first Roth contribution made to the distributing plan, or (b) First year of five-year period in the receiving plan. *See* Treas. Reg. § 1. 402A-1, Q&A 4(b).	

Designated Roth Contribution Rollover Chart (*cont'd*)

Designated Roth Contribution Program	Direct Rollover to Roth IRA	Participant Rollover (within 60 days) to Roth IRA	Direct Rollover to 401(k) Designated Roth Account	Participant Rollover (within 60 days) to Designated Roth Account
	Note. Annual Roth IRA contribution limits do not apply under this method. *See* Treas. Reg. § 1.408A-10, Q&A 2.	**Note.** Annual Roth IRA contribution limits do not apply under this method. *See* Treas. Reg. § 1.408A-10, Q&A 2.	**Note.** Only this method (direct rollover) permits (after-tax) designated Roth contributions to be rolled over to a DRCP. *See* Treas. Reg. § 1.402A-1, Q&A 5(a).	**Note.** Nonqualified distributions from DRCP requires a pro rata distribution of earnings and after-tax amounts. *See* Treas. Reg. § 1. 402A-2, Q&A 2.
See Questions	See Qs 4:1, 4:9. 10:29, 10:39, 10:49.	See Qs 4:1, 4:9, 10:28, 10:48, 10:49, 10:55.	See Qs 10:48. 10:50.	See Qs 10:44, 10:48, 10:49.

Q 10:48   Can distributions from a DRA be rolled over to a DRA of another employer or into a Roth IRA?

Yes. However, if the portion of a distribution from a DRA under a plan qualified under Code Section 401(a) that is not includible in income is to be rolled over into a DRA under another plan, the rollover of the distribution must be accomplished through a direct rollover (i.e., a 60-day rollover to another DRA is not available for the portion of the distribution not includible in gross income if the distribution is made directly to the employee) and can only be made to a plan qualified under Code Section 401(a) that agrees to separately account for the amount not includible in income (i.e., it cannot be rolled over into a Section 403(b) plan). To the extent of a taxable distribution from a DRA, the participant may roll over the distribution to another plan (401(k) or 403(b)) that accepts rollovers of distributions from a DRA (see Q 10:48). The final regulations clarify that a distribution from a DRA may only be rolled over to a 401(k) plan or 403(b) plan if that plan has a designated Roth contribution program (DRCP). [Treas. Reg. § 1.402A-1, Q&A 5] If a distribution from a DRA is made to the employee, the employee would still be able to roll over the entire amount (or any portion thereof) of an eligible rollover distribution into a Roth IRA within 60 days of receipt. Under Code Section 402(c)(2), if only a portion of the distribution is rolled over, the portion that is rolled over is treated as consisting first of the amount of the distribution that is includible in gross income. Alternatively, the employee is permitted to roll over the taxable portion of the distribution to a DRA under either a Code Section 401(a) or a Code Section 403(b) plan within 60 days of receipt. In addition, in the case of a rollover by the individual, the employee's period of participation under the distributing plan is not carried over to the recipient plan for purposes of determining whether the employee satisfies the five-taxable-year requirement under the recipient plan (see Q 10:49). [I.R.C. § 402A(c)(3); Treas. Reg. §§ 1.402A-1, Q&A 5(c); 1.402A-10, Q&A 3]

Note. The income limits for contributions for Roth IRAs do not apply to rollovers or direct transfers of a DRA.

Example 1. Yolanda, age 62, made $20,000 of contributions to her DRA under her employer's qualified plan before she retired four years later. She does not have a Roth IRA. Yolanda received a $30,000 distribution that included $10,000 of gain. Although the distribution is eligible to be rolled over to a Roth IRA, the distribution is *not* a qualified distribution because it is received within the five-year period.

Yolanda rolls over the taxable amount ($10,000) into a new Roth IRA and removes the amount two years later.

The taxable amount that was rolled over ($10,000) remains "as gain" in the Roth IRA until the five-year period is satisfied, which starts when the rollover is made. Assume, with gain, the Roth IRA is now worth $11,000. If the amount is distributed from the Roth IRA before the end of the five-year period the entire amount received is taxable (all treated as gain).

If the $30,000 was a qualified distribution from the DRA, then only $10,000 would be taxable and the $20,000 would be treated as a return of basis. If the five-year period was satisfied in the Roth IRA, no amount of the $30,000 (and any additional gain), would be taxable when distributed.

In general, a participant may roll over his or her non-Roth 401(k) account to any eligible retirement plan (traditional IRA, qualified plan, 403(b) plan, or governmental 457(b) plan). In many cases, a participant will have two separate rollover distributions (from Roth and non-Roth accounts under the plan).

The portion that is not rolled over is treated as consisting first of the amount that is not includible in gross income, the nontaxable portion of the distribution. Thus, the amount rolled over is treated as consisting first of the taxable portion, that is, the earnings.

Q 10:49   How is the five-taxable-year period calculated in the case of an indirect (60-day) rollover of a distribution from a DRA maintained under a Code Section 401(k) or 403(b) plan to a Roth IRA?

In the case of a rollover of an eligible rollover distribution from a DRA maintained under a Code Section 401(k) or 403(b) plan to a Roth IRA, the period that the rolled-over funds were in the DRA does not count toward the five-taxable-year period for determining qualified distributions from the Roth IRA. However, if an individual had established a Roth IRA in a prior year, the five-year period for determining qualified distributions from a Roth IRA that began as a result of that earlier Roth IRA contribution applies to any distributions from the Roth IRA (including a distribution of an amount attributable to a rollover contribution from a DRA). [Treas. Reg. §§ 1.402A-1, Q&A 5(c), 1.402A-10, Q&A 4(b)] In addition, if a qualified distribution from a DRA is rolled over into a Roth IRA, the entire amount of the distribution will be treated as basis in the Roth IRA. [Treas. Reg. § 1.402A-10, Q&A 3]

> **Example 1.** Karen has been making contributions to a DRA for six years. She then severs employment and receives a distribution of her entire DRA in a qualified distribution. The amount is timely rolled over into a new Roth IRA. The years Karen made designated Roth contributions are not taken into account when determining whether a distribution from her Roth IRA is a qualified distribution (see Q 4:9).

> **Example 2.** Same facts as in the preceding example except Karen established and made contributions to her Roth IRA six years ago. The five-year period for determining qualified distributions from a Roth IRA that began as a result of the earlier Roth IRA contribution (six years ago) applies to any distributions from Karen's Roth IRA (including a distribution of the amount attributable to a rollover contribution from her DRA).

> **Example 3.** Mercury, an employee, began making designated Roth contributions under his employer's 401(k) plan in 2009. Mercury, who is over age 59½, takes a distribution from Mercury's DRA in 2011, prior to the end of the five-taxable-year period of participation used to determine qualified distributions from a DRA. The distribution is an eligible rollover distribution (see Q 10:50) and Mercury rolls it over to his Roth IRA, which was established in 2007. Any subsequent distribution from the Roth IRA of the amount rolled in, plus earnings thereon, would not be includible in gross income (because it would be a qualified distribution).

> **Example 4.** The facts are the same as in the preceding example, except that the Roth IRA is Mercury's first Roth IRA and is established with the rollover in 2011, which is the only contribution made to the Roth IRA. If a distribution is made from the Roth IRA prior to the end of the five-taxable-year period used to determine qualified distributions from a Roth IRA (which begins in 2011, the year of the rollover which established the Roth IRA) the distribution would not be a qualified distribution, and any amount of the distribution that exceeded the portion of the rollover contribution that consisted of investment in the contract is includible in Mercury's gross income.

> **Example 5.** The facts are the same as in the preceding example, except that the distribution from the DRA and the rollover to the Roth IRA occur in 2014 (after the end of the five-taxable-year period of participation used to determine qualified distributions from a DRA). If a distribution is made from the Roth IRA prior to the expiration of the five-taxable-year period used to

determine qualified distributions from a Roth IRA, the distribution would not be a qualified distribution, and any amount of the distribution that exceeded the amount rolled in is includible in Mercury's gross income.

Q 10:50   How is the five-taxable-year period calculated in the case of a direct rollover of a distribution from a DRA maintained under a Code Section 401(k) or 403(b) plan to another DRA?

If a direct rollover contribution of a distribution from a DRA under another plan is made by the employee to the plan, the five-taxable-year period of participation begins on the first day of the employee's taxable year in which the employee first had designated Roth contributions made to such other DRA, if earlier than the first taxable year in which a designated Roth contribution is made to the plan. [Treas. Reg. § 1.402A-1, Q&A 4(b)]

Q 10:51   What is an *eligible rollover distribution*?

In general, the term *eligible rollover distribution* means any distribution to an employee of all or any portion of the balance to the credit of the employee in a qualified trust; except that such term shall not include [I.R.C. § 402(c)(4)]:

- Any distribution which is one of a series of substantially equal periodic payments (not less frequently than annually) made—
  - For the life (or life expectancy) of the employee or the joint lives (or joint life expectancies) of the employee and the employee's designated beneficiary, or
  - For a specified period of 10 years or more.
- Any distribution after death to the extent such distribution is an RMD. [I.R.C. § 401(a)(9)]
- Any distribution which is made upon hardship of the employee.

Q 10:52   Can an eligible rollover distribution from a DRA be rolled over to a Roth IRA?

Yes. An eligible rollover distribution from a DRA may be rolled over to a Roth IRA. [Treas. Reg. § 1.402A-10, Q&A 1]

Q 10:53   Can an eligible rollover distribution from a DRA be rolled over to a Roth IRA even if the distributee is not otherwise eligible to make a conversion contribution to a Roth IRA?

No. The $100,000 MAGI limit and, if married, joint filing requirement, may restrict rollovers to Roth IRAs for some individuals before 2010 (see Qs 1:14, 3:7).

Q 10:54   For purposes of the ordering rules on distributions from Roth IRAs, what portion of a distribution from a rollover contribution from a DRA is treated as contributions (basis)?

Distributions from Roth IRAs are deemed to consist first of regular contributions, then of conversion contributions, and finally, of earnings. [I.R.C. § 408(d)(4)] The amount of a rollover contribution that is treated as a regular contribution is the portion of the distribution that is treated as investment in the contract (basis), and the remainder of the rollover contribution is treated as earnings. Thus, the entire amount of any qualified distribution from a DRA that is rolled over into a Roth IRA is treated as a regular contribution to the Roth IRA. Accordingly, a subsequent distribution from the Roth IRA in the amount of that rollover contribution is not includible in gross income (see Q 4:1).

Q 10:55   For purposes of the ordering rules on distributions from Roth IRAs, what portion of a distribution from a *partial* rollover contribution from a DRA is treated as contributions (basis)?

If the entire account balance of a DRA is distributed to an employee and only a portion of the distribution is rolled over to a Roth IRA, and at the time of the distribution, the investment in the contract exceeds the balance in the DRA, the portion of investment in the contract that exceeds the amount used to determine the taxable amount of the distribution is treated as a regular contribution (i.e., basis, for purposes of the ordering rules, see Q 4:1) to the Roth IRA. [Treas. Reg. § 1.402A-10, Q&A 3] The amount of the investment in the contract (basis) is reported to the employee (see Q 10:74).

> **Note.** If the investment in the contract exceeds the account balance and the entire account balance is distributed (and not rolled over) it is unclear whether the taxpayer would be entitled to a deduction for the difference. [*See* Rev. Proc. 72-305, 1972-1 C.B. 116]

> **Example 1.** Laura made designated Roth contributions of $1,000. She later terminates employment and receives an eligible rollover distribution of $900 representing the balance in her account. Laura rolls over $600 of that distribution to her Roth IRA. Of the $600 amount rolled over, $100 ($1,000 − $900) is treated as a regular contribution. The remaining $500 ($600 − $100) is treated as earnings in the Roth IRA. The portion not rolled over ($300) represents a return of basis and is not taxable.

> **Example 2.** Assume the same facts as in Example 1, except Laura received an eligible rollover distribution, which is not a qualified distribution, of $1,200 and rolled over $800 to a Roth IRA. Of the amount rolled over, $200 would be treated as a regular contribution and $600 as earnings (see Q 10:48). If only a portion is rolled over, the portion that is rolled over is treated as consisting first of the amount that was includible in income (see Q 10:48). The portion not rolled over ($400) represents a return of basis and is nontaxable.

Example 3. Assume the same facts as in Example 2, except Laura does not roll over any portion of the nonqualified distribution. The gain of $200 ($1,200 − $1,000) is taxable and may be subject to penalty (see Q 10:27).

Q 10:56   Can amounts distributed from a Roth IRA be rolled over to a DRA?

No. Amounts distributed from a Roth IRA may be rolled over or transferred only to another Roth IRA and are not permitted to be rolled over to a DRA under a 401(a) or 403(b) plan. The same rule applies even if all the amounts in the Roth IRA are attributable to a rollover distribution from a DRA in a plan. [Treas. Reg. § 1.402A-10, Q&A 5]

Q 10:57   May a Roth IRA be rolled over into a DRCP?

No. A participant may roll over a distribution from a Roth IRA to a deemed IRA, but not to a DRA under an employer's plan. [I.R.C. § 402(c)(8)(B)]

Q 10:58   May DRAs receive conversion contributions?

No. EGTRRA does not authorize direct conversions into a DRA. [*See* I.R.C. § 408A(d)(3)(A), (B)]

Q 10:59   May DRAs be rolled over or transferred to a deemed Roth IRA?

Not directly. DRAs are portable for rollover or direct rollover purposes to either another employer's plan that accepts DRCP accounts or to the individual's own Roth IRA, but not to a deemed Roth IRA. [I.R.C. § 402A(c)(3); Treas. Reg. § 1.401(k)-1(f)(4)(ii)] However, a Roth IRA that contains funds that were rolled over or directly transferred from a DRA may be rolled over to a deemed Roth IRA (see Q 10:57), but not to a DRCP account. [*See* I.R.C. § 402(c)(8)(B)]

Q 10:60   In the case of a rollover contribution to a DRA, how is the amount that is treated as investment in the contract under Code Section 72 determined?

If the entire amount of a distribution from a DRA is rolled over to another DRA, the amount of the rollover contribution allocated to investment in the contract in the recipient DRA is the amount that would not have been includible in gross income—determined without regard to net unrealized appreciation in distributed employer securities if the distribution had not been rolled over. Thus, if an amount that is a qualified distribution is rolled over, the entire amount of the rollover contribution is allocated to investment in the contract. [Treas. Reg. § 1.402A-1, Q&A 6(a)]

However, if the entire account balance of a DRA is rolled over to another DRA in a direct rollover, and, at the time of the distribution, the investment in the contract exceeds the balance in the DRA, the investment in the contract in the distributing plan is included in the investment in the contract of the recipient plan. [Treas. Reg. § 1.402A-1, Q&A 6(b)]

Q 10:61   After a qualified distribution from a DRA has been made, how is the remaining investment in the contract of the DRA determined under Code Section 72?

After a qualified distribution from a DRA has been made, the portion of any qualified distribution that is treated as a recovery of investment in the contract is determined in the same manner as if the distribution were not a qualified distribution. Thus, the remaining investment in the contract in a DRA after a qualified distribution is determined in the same manner after a qualified distribution as it would be determined if the distribution were not a qualified distribution. [Treas. Reg. § 1.402A-1, Q&A 7(a)]

> **Example.** Cathleen receives a $12,000 distribution, which is a qualified distribution that is attributable to her being disabled, from her DRA. Immediately prior to the distribution, the account consisted of $21,850 of investment in the contract (i.e., designated Roth contributions) and $1,150 of income. For purposes of determining recovery of investment in the contract under Code Section 72, the distribution is deemed to consist of $11,400 of investment in the contract ($12,000 × $21,850 ÷ ($1,150 + $21,850)) and $600 of income ($12,000 × $1,150 ÷ ($1,150 + $21,850)). Immediately after the distribution, Cathleen's DRA consists of $10,450 of investment in the contract and $550 of income. This determination of the remaining investment in the contract will be needed if Cathleen subsequently is no longer disabled and takes a nonqualified distribution from the DRA (see Q 10:44).

Q 10:62   What is the relationship between the accounting for designated Roth contributions as investment in the contract for purposes of Code Section 72 and their treatment as elective deferrals available for a hardship distribution under Code Section 401(k)(2)(B)?

No relationship exists between the accounting for designated Roth contributions as investment in the contract for purposes of Code Section 72 and their treatment as elective deferrals available for a hardship distribution under Code Section 401(k)(2)(B). A plan that makes a hardship distribution under Code Section 401(k)(2)(B) from elective deferrals that includes designated Roth contributions must separately determine the amount of elective deferrals available for hardship and the amount of investment in the contract attributable to designated Roth contributions for purposes of Code Section 72. Thus, the entire amount of a hardship distribution is treated as reducing the otherwise maximum distributable amount for purposes of applying the rule in Code Section 401(k)(2)(B) and Treasury Regulations Section 1.401(k)-1(d)(3)(ii) that generally limits hardship distributions to the principal amount of elective deferrals made less the amount of elective deferrals previously distributed from the plan, even if a portion of the distribution is treated as income under Code Section 72(e)(8). [Treas. Reg. § 1.402A-1, Q&A 8(a)]

Example 1. Assume the same facts as in the example in Q 10:61, except that Cathleen is not disabled, the distribution is a hardship distribution, and Cathleen has received no previous distributions of elective deferrals from the plan. The adjustment to the investment in the contract is the same as in Q 10:61, but for purposes of determining the amount of elective deferrals available for future hardship distribution, the entire amount of the distribution is subtracted from the maximum distributable amount. Thus, Cathleen has only $9,850 ($21,850 – 12,000) available for hardship distribution from her DRA. [Treas. Reg. § 1.402A-1, Q&A 8(b)]

Example 2. Jerome, age 45, is a participant in a 401(k) plan that permits hardship distributions and permits the participant to choose whether the hardship distributions come from the DRA or the pretax elective contribution account under the plan. He receives a hardship distribution of $20,000. Jerome never had a prior hardship distribution. He has the following elective deferral accounts under the plan:

	Roth Elective	Pretax Elective	Total
Deferrals	$18,000	$32,000	$50,000
Income	$ 2,000	$ 8,000	$10,000
Total	$20,000	$40,000	$60,000

If the distribution is taken from the Roth account, Jerome would pay tax on the $2,000 of income ($2,000 ÷ $20,000 × $20,000) (see Qs 10:41, 10:60). The $2,000 would also be subject to the 10 percent premature distribution tax penalty (see Q 4:21). If Jerome only received a hardship distribution of $10,000 and it came from the Roth account, he would pay tax and penalty on $1,000. On the other hand, if Jerome took the distribution from his pretax elective contribution account, he would pay income and penalty taxes on the entire amount distributed in the hardship distribution. Before the distribution, $50,000 was available for hardship. After the distribution (assume $20,000), regardless of which account it came from, Jerome is limited to $30,000 of additional hardship distributions ($50,000 – $20,000).

Q 10:63   Can an employee have more than one separate *contract* for designated Roth contributions?

For purposes of the DRA distribution rules, there can be only one contract for purposes of applying Code Section 72 (see Q 10:79). Thus, Roth rollovers (see Qs 10:48–10:67) and designated Roth contributions will be considered a single contract. [Treas. Reg. § 1.402A-1, Q&A 9] However, an employee may have more than one separate *account* (see Qs 10:64–10:67). There may be advantages in having more than one account if rollovers are permitted to be made under the plan (see Q 10:65).

Q 10:64   May a rolled-over Roth IRA account be separately accounted for, or must it be combined with new Roth contributions?

A rolled-over Roth IRA account may be separately accounted for, or it may be combined with new Roth contributions in accordance with plan provisions. There might be an advantage in establishing a separate account to hold an amount that is rolled over into the employer's plan (see Q 10:65). [See I.R.C. § 402A(b)(2), regarding the establishment of separate "accounts for each employee . . . "]

If there is more than one separate account under a plan, the separate accounts are considered to be one contract for purposes of applying Code Section 72 to the distributions from either account.

Q 10:65   What are the possible advantages if a plan provides for the establishment of a different separate account to hold amounts that are rolled over into the employer's plan?

Although there is only one separate *contract* for an employee with respect to the designated Roth contributions under a plan for purposes of Code Section 72, a plan may provide for one separate *account* for designated Roth contributions made under the plan and another separate *account* for rollover contributions. In such case, the separate account consisting of rollover contributions is not subject to the restrictions on distributions otherwise applicable to the account consisting of designated Roth contributions made under the plan (see Q 10:28). However, both separate accounts are considered to be one contract for purposes of applying Code Section 72 to the distributions from either account (see Q 10:63). [Treas. Reg. § 1.402A-1, Q&A 9(a)]

In addition, separate accounting for Roth rollovers may be desirable for top-heavy testing in that the amount of the Roth rollovers would be excluded from consideration. [I.R.C. § 416(g)(4)(a)]

Q 10:66   How is a separate account with respect to an employee's accrued benefit consisting of designated Roth contributions that is established and maintained for an alternate payee pursuant to a qualified domestic relations order treated?

If a separate account with respect to an employee's accrued benefit consisting of designated Roth contributions is established and maintained for an alternate payee pursuant to a qualified domestic relations order and another DRA is maintained for the employee, each account is treated as a separate contract for purposes of Code Section 72. The alternate payee's DRA is also a separate contract for purposes of Code Section 72 with respect to any other account maintained for that alternate payee. [Treas. Reg. § 1.402A-1, Q&A 9(b)]

Q 10:67   How are separate accounts established and maintained for different beneficiaries after the death of an employee treated?

If separate accounts are established and maintained for different beneficiaries after the death of an employee, the separate account for each beneficiary is treated as a separate contract under Code Section 72 and is also a separate contract with respect to any other account maintained for that beneficiary under the plan that is not a DRA. When the separate account is established for an alternate payee or for a beneficiary (after an employee's death), each separate account must receive a proportionate amount attributable to investment in the contract. [Treas. Reg. § 1.402A-1, Q&A 9(b)]

Excess Contributions

Q 10:68   How are excess designated Roth deferrals treated?

Any excess deferral under Code Section 402(g)(2), regarding the limitations on exclusions for elective deferrals, must be distributed by April 1 following the taxable year in which the excess deferral is made. If not timely corrected by April 1 (no extensions), the excess deferral amount is included in gross income for the taxable year in which such excess is distributed from the account. In addition, the excess deferral amount is not treated as an investment in the contract. [I.R.C. § 402A(d)(2)(3)]

The final 2007 regulations under Code Section 402A provided that if any excess deferrals are designated Roth contributions that are not corrected prior to April 15 of the year following the excess, the first amounts distributed from the DRA are treated as distributions of excess deferrals and earnings until the full amount of those excess deferrals (and attributable earnings) are distributed (see Q 10:40). [Treas. Reg. § 1.402(g)-1(a)]

Furthermore, a qualified distribution (which is not includible in gross income) does not include any amount (including any income) on any excess deferrals or excess contributions. Thus, if not timely corrected, the excess amount, including any income thereon, will (eventually) be subject to double taxation: once when the excess is contributed under the plan (and not excluded from income) and again when distributed. [I.R.C. §§ 402A(d)(1), 402A(d)(2)(c); Treas. Reg. § 1.402(g)-1(e)(8)(iii)] Unless an exception applies, the distribution of the excess (and earnings) (treated as a nonqualified distribution, see Q 10:40) may be subject to the 10 percent penalty under Code Section 72, which is applied separately in respect to payments from DRAs and other distributions and payments from the employer's plan. [I.R.C. §§ 72(t), 402A(d)(4)]

> **Caution.** Any distribution of amounts attributable to excess deferrals not timely corrected is includible in gross income without adjustment for any return of investment in the contract under Code Section 72(e)(8).

Note. If not timely corrected excess designated Roth contributions may be distributed no sooner than elective deferrals are permitted to be distributed under the plan (see Q 10:7).

Q 10:69   Is a correcting distribution of an excess contribution includible in income?

A distribution of excess contributions is not includible in gross income to the extent it represents a distribution of designated Roth contributions. However, the income allocable to a corrective distribution of excess contributions that are designated Roth contributions is includible in gross income in the same manner as income allocable to a corrective distribution of excess contributions that are pretax elective contributions.

Q 10:70   How may a plan provide for the correction of excess deferrals after the taxable year?

In general, a plan may provide that if any amount is an excess deferral under Code Section 402(g) and not later than the first April 15 (or such earlier date specified in the plan) following the close of the individual's taxable year (see Q 10:36), the individual may notify each plan under which deferrals were made of the amount of the excess deferrals received by the plan. If any designated Roth contributions were made to a plan, the notification must also identify the extent to which, if any, the excess deferrals are comprised of designated Roth contributions. A plan may provide that an individual is deemed to have notified the plan of excess deferrals (including the portion of excess deferrals that are comprised of designated Roth contributions) to the extent the individual has excess deferrals for the taxable year calculated by taking into account only elective deferrals under the plan and other plans of the same employer, and the plan may provide the extent to which such excess deferrals are comprised of designated Roth contributions. A plan may instead provide that the employer may notify the plan on behalf of the individual under these circumstances. [Treas. Reg. § 1.401(g)-1(e)(2)]

Q 10:71   What must the plan's notification of excess contributions contain?

If any designated Roth contributions were made to a plan, the notification must identify the extent to which, if any, the excess deferrals are comprised of designated Roth contributions. A plan may provide that an individual is deemed to have notified the plan of excess deferrals (including the portion of excess deferrals that are comprised of designated Roth contributions) for the taxable year calculated by taking into account only elective deferrals under the plan and other plans of the same employer, and the plan may provide the extent to which such excess deferrals are comprised of designated Roth contributions. A plan may instead provide that the employer may notify the plan on behalf of the individual under these circumstances. [Treas. Reg. § 1.402(g)-1(e)(3)(i)(A)]

Q 10:72   How is the income on an excess deferral computed?

In general, the income allocable to excess deferrals is equal to the sum of the allocable gain or loss for the taxable year of the individual and, in the case of a distribution in a taxable year beginning on or after January 1, 2007, made to correct an excess deferral, to the extent the excess deferrals are or will be credited with gain or loss for the gap period (i.e., the period after the close of the taxable year and prior to the distribution) if the total account were to be distributed, the allocable gain or loss during that period. [Treas. Reg. § 1.402(g)-1(e)(5)(i)]

Method of Allocating Income. A plan will not fail to use a reasonable method for computing the income allocable to excess deferrals merely because the income allocable to excess deferrals is determined on a date that is no more than seven days before the distribution. [Treas. Reg. § 1.402(g)-1(e)(5)(ii)]

Alternative Method of Allocating Taxable-Year Income. A plan may determine the income allocable to excess deferrals for the taxable year by multiplying the income for the taxable year allocable to elective deferrals by a fraction. The numerator of the fraction is the excess deferrals by the employee for the taxable year. The denominator of the fraction is equal to the sum of:

A. The total account balance of the employee attributable to elective deferrals as of the beginning of the taxable year, plus

B. The employee's elective deferrals for the taxable year.

[Treas. Reg. § 1.402(g)-1(e)(5)(iii)]

Reporting and Recordkeeping Requirements for Designated Roth Accounts

Caution. In order to give plans sufficient time to develop systems to comply with the new reporting requirements, the reporting and record-keeping requirements (Qs 10:73–10:77) are effective for taxable years beginning after 2007. [Treas. Reg. § 1.402A-2, Q&A 4]

Q 10:73   Who is responsible for keeping track of the designated Roth contributions and five-taxable-year period?

Under the 2007 final Code Section 402A regulations, the plan administrator or other responsible party with respect to a plan with a DRA is responsible for keeping track of the five-taxable-year period for each employee and the amount of designated Roth contributions made on behalf of such employee. [Treas. Reg. § 1.402A-2, Q&A 1]

In addition, the plan administrator or other responsible party of a plan directly rolling over a distribution would be required to provide the plan administrator of the recipient plan (i.e., the plan accepting the eligible rollover distribution, see Q 10:51) with a statement indicating either the first year of the five-taxable-year period for the employee and the portion of such distribution attributable to basis or that the distribution is a qualified distribution. [Treas. Reg. § 1.402A-2, Q&A 2(a)(1); *see also* Treas. Reg. § 1.403(b)-10(d)(2)] Additional information must also be provided (see Q 10:75)] The final 2007 regulations clarify that reporting is only required to the extent provided in forms and instructions. [Treas. Reg. § 1.402A-2, Q&A 3]

In the case of a direct rollover from another DRA, the plan administrator or other responsible party of the recipient plan can rely on reasonable representations made by the plan administrator or responsible party with respect to the plan with the other DRA (see Q 10:57, regarding notification statements required in the case of rollovers). [Treas. Reg. § 1.402A-2, Q&A 2(a)(1)]

> **Note.** In the absence of actual knowledge to the contrary, the plan administrator or other responsible party is permitted to assume that the employee's taxable year is the calendar year. [Treas. Reg. § 1.402A-2, Q&A 2(a)(1)]

Q 10:74   In the case of an eligible rollover distribution from a DRA, what additional information must be provided with respect to such distribution?

For taxable years beginning on or after January 1, 2007, if an amount is distributed from a DRA in an eligible rollover distribution (see Q 10:51), the plan administrator or other responsible party with respect to the plan must provide a statement, as described below: [I.R.C. § 6047(f); Treas. Reg. § 1.402A, Q&A 2(a)]

Direct rollover from DRA. In the case of a direct rollover of a distribution from a DRA under a plan to a DRA under another plan, the plan administrator or other responsible party must provide to the plan administrator or responsible party of the recipient plan either a statement indicating the first year of the five-taxable-year period and the portion of the distribution that is attributable to basis (investment in the contract under Code Section 72), or a statement that the distribution is a qualified distribution.

Distributions other than direct rollovers from a DRA. If the distribution is not a direct rollover to a DRA under another plan, the plan administrator or responsible party must provide to the employee the portion of the distribution that is basis, or a statement that the distribution is a qualified distribution.

The statement must be provided within a reasonable period following the direct rollover or distributee request, but in no event later than 30 days following the direct rollover or distributee request. [I.R.C. § 6047(f); Treas. Reg. § 1.402A, Q&A 2(b)] If this information is provided on a statement attached to the check issued to the employee, this requirement would be satisfied.

Q 10:75 Since a qualified distribution from a DRA is not subject to taxation, must the distribution be reported?

Yes. DRA Distributions from a DRA must be reported on Form 1099-R, Distributions from Pensions, Annuities, Retirement or Profit-Sharing Plans, IRA, Insurance Contracts, in accordance with the instructions to the form. [Treas. Reg. § 1.402A-2, Q&A 3]

Q 10:76 Must the amount contributed as designated Roth contributions be identified on Form W-2, in addition to being reported in box 1 of Form W-2?

Yes. Contributions to a DRA must also be separately reported on Form W-2, Wage and Tax Statement, in accordance with the instructions to Form W-2. (See chapter 9.)

Q 10:77 Do employees have any recordkeeping or reporting obligations?

An employee has no reporting obligation with respect to designated Roth contributions under a Code Section 401(k) or 403(b) plan. However, an employee rolling over a distribution from a DRA to a Roth IRA should keep track of the amount rolled over in accordance with the instructions to Form 8606, Nondeductible IRAs. (See chapter 9.)

Miscellaneous

Q 10:78 If a participant is required to take a corrective distribution under a 401(k) plan due to failure of the ADP nondiscrimination tests, can some or all of the corrective distribution be taken from a DRA?

Yes. A plan can provide that the highly compensated employee (HCE), as defined in Code Section 414(q), with elective contributions for a year that include both pretax elective contributions and designated Roth contributions may elect whether excess contributions are to be attributed to pretax elective contributions or designated Roth contributions. There is no requirement that the plan provide this option; and a plan may provide for correction without permitting an HCE to make such an election. [Treas. Reg. § 1.402(g)-1(e)(2)–(3)]

Q 10:79   If any amount from a DRA is included in a loan to an employee, do the plan aggregation rules of Code Section 72(p)(2)(D) apply for purposes of determining the total amount an employee is permitted to borrow from the plan, even though the DRA generally is treated as a separate contract under Code Section 72?

Yes. If any amount from a DRA is included in a loan to an employee, notwithstanding the general rule that the DRA is treated as a separate contract under Code Section 72, the plan aggregation rules of Code Section 72(p)(2)(D) apply for purposes of determining the maximum amount the employee is permitted to borrow from the plan and such amount is based on the total of the designated Roth contribution amounts and the other amounts under the plan, regardless of whether the loan is from the DRA or other accounts under the plan. However, to the extent a loan is from a DRA, the repayment requirement of Code Section 72(p)(2)(C) must be satisfied separately with respect to that portion of the loan and with respect to the portion of the loan from other accounts under the plan. [Treas. Reg. § 1.402A-1, Q&A 12]

Q 10:80   Does a transaction or accounting methodology involving an employee's DRA and any other accounts under the plan or plans of an employer that has the effect of transferring value from the other accounts into the DRA violate the separate accounting requirement of Code Section 402A?

Yes. Any transaction or accounting methodology involving an employee's DRA and any other accounts under the plan or plans of an employer that has the effect of directly or indirectly transferring value from another account into the DRA violates the separate accounting requirement under Code Section 402A. However, any transaction that merely exchanges investments between accounts at FMV will not violate the separate accounting requirement. [Treas. Reg. § 1.402A-1, Q&A 13, which applies to DRAs for taxable years beginning on or after January 1, 2006]

Q 10:81   Will the separate accounting requirement be violated if separate accounts are maintained within a single contract?

Probably. It may be difficult for a single contract to have combined guarantees that apply to both accounts without the potential for a prohibited transfer of value between the accounts, and the IRS has not issued guidance on how to account for these guarantees (including related charges). The IRS may provide additional guidance with respect to the allocation of income, expenses, gains, and losses among accounts within an annuity contract.

Appendix A

Roth IRA Charts and Tables

Traditional IRA and Roth IRA Comparison Chart for 2009

	Traditional IRA	*Roth IRA*
Eligibility	• Individuals (and their spouses) who receive compensation	• Individuals (and their spouses) who receive compensation
	• Individuals age 70½ and over *cannot* contribute	• Individuals age 70½ and over *can* contribute
Deduction for Contributions	• Subject to limitations, contributions are deductible	• No deduction permitted for contributions
Contribution Limits	• Individuals can contribute up to $5,000 ($5,000 if age 50 or older) annually (or 100% of compensation, if less)	• Individuals can generally contribute up to $5,000 ($6,000 if age 50 or older) (or 100% of compensation, if less)

A-1

	Traditional IRA	*Roth IRA*
	• Deductibility depends on income level for individuals who are active participants in an employer-sponsored retirement plan	• Ability to contribute phases out at income levels of $105,000 to $120,000 (single taxpayers) and $166,000 to $176,000 (married taxpayers)
	• Overall limit for contributions to *all* IRAs (traditional and Roth combined) is $5,000 ($6,000 if age 50 or older) annually (or 100% of compensation, if less)	• Overall limit for contributions to *all* IRAs (traditional and Roth combined) is $5,000 ($6,000 if age 50 or older) annually (or 100% of compensation, if less)
Contribution Deadline	• Tax filing deadline, not including extensions (generally April 15)	• Tax filing deadline, not including extensions (generally April 15)
Documents	• IRS model trust	• IRS model trust
	• IRS model custodial account	• IRS model custodial account
	• Prototype IRA	• Prototype Roth IRA
	• Technical Disclosure statement	• Technical Disclosure statement
	• Financial Disclosure statement	• Financial Disclosure statement
Excess Contributions	• 6% excise tax each year until corrected	• 6% excise tax each year until corrected
	• Five methods to correct:	• Presumably, five methods to correct (see Q 2:25):
	1. Before 1040 due date, including extensions, with earnings, no 6% penalty	1. Before 1040 due date, including extensions, with earnings, no 6% penalty
	2. Before 1040 due date including extensions, recharacterize amount treated as a current years contribution	2. Before 1040 due date, including extensions, recharacterize amount treated as a current years contribution
	3. After 1040 due date, including extensions, without earnings, 6% penalty	3. After 1040 due date, including extensions, without earnings, 6% penalty
	4. After return due date plus 6 months, 6% penalty, amended return	4. After return due date plus 6 months, 6% penalty, amended return
	5. Carry over, 6% penalty	5. Carry over, 6% penalty

	Traditional IRA	*Roth IRA*
Earnings	• Earnings and interest are not taxed when received by IRA	• Earnings and interest are not taxed when received by IRA
Rollovers/ Conversions	• Qualified plan to traditional IRA • Traditional IRA to traditional IRA • 403(b), 403(b)(7), or governmental 457(b) to traditional IRA • Qualified 401(k) to traditional IRA • Can recharacterize current year's contribution, plus earnings, tax-free to Roth IRA • Deemed IRA to traditional IRA • Traditional IRA to qualified plan, 403(b), or governmental 457(b) plan • Deemed IRA to deemed IRA • No Roth 401(k) account or Roth 403(b) account to traditional IRA • Traditional IRA conversion to Roth IRA • Rollover of hurricane distributions, airline payments, qualified recovery assistance distributions, and qualified disaster recovery distributions from an eligible retirement plan • Rollover of Exxon Valdez settlements	• Roth IRA to Roth IRA • After 2007, qualified plan to Roth IRA • After 2007, 403(b), 403(b)(7) or governmental 457(b) to Roth IRA • Conversions available from traditional IRA if below MAGI limits • Can recharacterize current year's contribution, plus earnings, tax-free to traditional IRA • Deemed Roth to Roth IRA • Deemed Roth to deemed Roth • Roth 401(k) account or Roth 403(b) account to Roth IRA, Roth 401(k), or Roth 403(b) account • No Roth 401(k) account or Roth 403(b) account to traditional IRA • Rollover of hurricane distributions, airline payments, qualified recovery assistance distributions, and qualified disaster recovery distributions from an eligible retirement plan • Rollover of military death gratuities and Servicemembers' Group Life Insurance (SGLI) • Rollover of Exxon Valdez settlements
Withdrawals	• Generally, total (principal and earnings) taxable as income in year withdrawn (except for any prior nondeductible contributions)	• Generally, qualified distribution not taxable as long as account open for 5 years and participant has attained age 59½

	Traditional IRA	*Roth IRA*
Death Distributions	• If participant dies before the required beginning date (RBD), distributions must commence within 1 year (spouse may roll over) or treat as own; otherwise 5-year rule • Surviving spouse can treat as own or wait until owner would have reached age 70½ • Special rules apply to distributions passing through estates and trusts. • If participant dies after RBD, single life expectancy distribution to designated beneficiary	• If spouse designated sole beneficiary, spouse can become "owner" when owner dies • Special rules apply to distributions passing through estates and trusts. • Spouse can leave account in deceased's name (and be treated as a nonspouse) if document provides • Spouse can roll over interest to another Roth IRA • If a nonspouse is designated as a beneficiary, then 5-year rule or the exception applies to all beneficiaries • Under the exception, distributions must commence by Dec. 31 following year of death over nonrecalculated single life expectancy of each designated beneficiary
Required Distributions	• Minimum withdrawals must begin by April 1 of year after age 70½ is attained (RBD). • 2009 RMDs suspended	• Minimum withdrawals not required during lifetime of owner • 2009 RMDs suspended for nonspouse beneficiaries

Traditional IRA Deduction Restrictions for Active Participants

If an individual or his or her spouse is an active participant in an employer plan during any part of the year, the contribution to the individual's traditional IRA (or his or her spouse's traditional IRA) may be completely, partly, or not at all deductible depending on the individual's filing status and the total modified adjusted gross income (MAGI) shown on the tax return, as follows:

- If you are an active participant and MAGI is any amount up to the lower limit, the contribution is deductible.
- If you are an active participant and MAGI falls between the minimum limit and the maximum limit, the contribution is partly deductible.

- If you are an active participant and MAGI falls above the maximum limit, the contribution is not deductible.

For years other than 2009, substitute the correct minimum limit and maximum limit (shown later) in the chart below to determine deductibility in any particular year.

Minimum and Maximum Limits

	If You Are Single	If You Are Married Filing Jointly	If You Are Married Filing Separately	Then Your Traditional IRA Contribution
	Up to min. limit ($55K for 2009)	Up to min. limit ($89K for 2009)	See below	Is fully deductible
MAGI Level	More than min. limit but less than max. limit ($66K for 2009)	More than min. limit but less than max. limit ($110K for 2009)	More than $0 but less than $10K	Is partly deductible
	Max. limit ($66K for 2009) or more	Max. limit ($110K for 2009) or more	More than $10K	Is not deductible

Note 1. The chart above applies only to an individual who is an active participant.

Note 2. After 1997, in the case of a married individual who files a joint return when only one spouse is an active participant, the minimum limit for the non-active participant spouse is $150,000 and the maximum limit is $160,000. Beginning in 2007, the $150,000 amount will be indexed for inflation (as shown below). For 2009, the indexed limit range is $166,000 to $176,000.

Note 3. If MAGI falls in the partly deductible range, the portion of the contribution that is deductible must be calculated as follows: Multiply your contribution by a fraction. The numerator is the amount by which MAGI exceeds the minimum limit (for 2009, $55,000 if single or $89,000 if married filing jointly). The denominator is $10,000 (note that the denominator for married joint filers is $20,000 starting in 2007). Subtract this from the contribution and then round up to the nearest $10. The deductible amount is the greater of the amount calculated or $200 (provided you contributed at least $200). If the contribution amount was less than $200, the entire contribution is deductible.

The minimum limit and the maximum limit will generally change for each year until 2007, at which time the $50,000 and $80,000 amounts (without indexing for 2007) will be indexed for inflation (as shown below). The minimum limit and maximum limit for these years are shown in the following table. Substitute the correct minimum limit and maximum limit in the chart above to determine deductibility in any particular year. If you are married but filing separate returns, your minimum limit is always zero and your maximum limit is always $10,000.

Minimum and Maximum Limits

Year	Single Minimum Limit	Single Maximum Limit	Married Filing Jointly Minimum Limit[a]	Married Filing Jointly Maximum Limit[a]
1998	$30,000	$40,000	$50,000	$60,000
1999	$31,000	$41,000	$51,000	$61,000

	Single		Married Filing Jointly	
Year	Minimum Limit	Maximum Limit	Minimum Limit[a]	Maximum Limit[a]
2000	$32,000	$42,000	$52,000	$62,000
2001	$33,000	$43,000	$53,000	$63,000
2002	$34,000	$44,000	$54,000	$64,000
2003	$40,000	$50,000	$60,000	$70,000
2004	$45,000	$55,000	$65,000	$75,000
2005	$50,000	$60,000	$70,000	$80,000
2006	$50,000	$60,000	$75,000	$85,000
2007[b]	$52,000	$62,000	$83,000	$103,000
2008	**$53,000**	**$63,000**	**$85,000**	**$105,000**
2009	**$55,000**	**$65,000**	**$89,000**	**$109,000**

[a] If married filing separately, the minimum limit is $0 and the maximum limit is $10,000 for all years.
[b] The base amounts ($50,000 and $80,000) (not shown) are adjusted for inflation starting in 2007 in increments of $1,000. [I.R.C. § 219(g)(8); PPA § 833(b),(c)]

Restrictions on Roth IRA Contributions for High-Income Taxpayers

Contributions to a Roth IRA are not always permitted, or contributions may be limited to an amount less than $5,000 ($6,000 if age 50 or older). This depends on the individual's filing status and the amount of modified adjusted gross income (MAGI). The following chart shows how contributions are restricted for 2009.

	If You Are Single	If You Are Married Filing jointly	Then You Can Make
	Up to $105,000	Up to $166,000	Full contribution
MAGI Level	More than $105,000[*] but less than $120,000	More than $166,000[*] but less than $176,000	Reduced contribution
	$120,000 and up	$176,000 and up	No contribution

Note. The maximum Roth IRA contribution limit phases out over the first $10,000 of MAGI if the individual is a married taxpayer filing separately. In such case, if MAGI is $10,000 or more, no annual contribution can be made to a Roth IRA for the year. See Annual Roth IRA Contribution Limits table on page A-17 for earlier years.

[*]Amounts indexed for inflation starting in 2007 in $1,000 increments. [I.R.C. § 408A(c)(3)(C); PPA § 833(c), (d)]

Roth IRA Distribution Taxation

The chart on the following page applies to distributions of accumulated annual Roth IRA contributions and to amounts converted to a Roth IRA from a traditional IRA. For purposes of federal income taxes, in general, annual Roth IRA contributions and amounts converted are recovered free of federal income tax before any gain is distributed (the contribution-first recovery rule). In addition, annual Roth IRA contributions are treated as distributed before a converted amount (the ordering rules). Although the contribution-first recovery rule is actually part of the ordering rules, the rules are easier to understand if they are treated as separate rules.

There are two exceptions to the contribution-first recovery rule, but not to the ordering rules (see Q 4:1).

1. *Before 2001, spread-income on a 1998 conversion.* The exception applied when the income caused by a 1998 conversion was spread over a four-year period (1998, 1999, 2000, 2001). In such a case, to the extent the converted amount was received (under the ordering rules) (during the first three years) was accelerated into income and was subject to federal income tax to the extent it would have been taxed in a later year under the deferral (and the amount may also have been subject to penalty if the distributee was under age $59\frac{1}{2}$).

Note. The exceptions to the contribution-first recovery rule do not actually cause any gain to be distributed, but rather caused, distribution of the unrecovered spread income (which is, in effect, an untaxed contribution).

2. *In 2010 and 2011, spread-income on a conversion distributed before 2012.* The exception will apply when the income caused by a 2010 conversion that is spread over a two-year period (2011 and 2012) is received (under the ordering rules) before 2012. In such a case, to the extent of the unrecovered spread income, any amount received during the first two years (2010 and 2011) will be accelerated into income and subject to federal income tax to the extent it would have been taxed in a later year under the deferral (and the amount may also be subject to penalty if the distributee is under age $59\frac{1}{2}$).

Even if the taxable income resulting from the conversion (if any) is not spread out over a two-year period (and there is no remaining basis attributable to annual Roth IRA contributions), a converted amount withdrawn before the five-year nonexclusion period is subject to the 10 percent premature distribution penalty tax (unless an exception applies) to the extent that the distributed amount would have been taxable if it had been distributed from the traditional IRA (or, after 2007, certain employer plans) and not rolled over or converted. Thus, the amount may be subject to penalty even though the amount may be received (unless accelerated; see above) without any federal income tax liability. For this purpose, the five-year nonexclusion period starts with the year for which the conversion contribution being withdrawn was made. [I.R.C. § 408A(d)(3)(F)(i)(II)] On the other hand, the five-year nonexclusion period that is used for the purpose of determining whether a distribution of gain is a qualified distribution starts with the year for which the first contribution is made to the Roth IRA. A qualified distribution of gain is not subject to federal income tax or penalty.

Distribution of Roth IRA Earnings

Reason for Distribution	Roth IRA Earnings Paid Out WITHIN 5 Years		Roth IRA Earnings Paid Out AFTER 5 Years	
	Earnings Taxable	Subject to 10% Penalty	Earnings Taxable	Subject to 10% Penalty
On or after age 59½	Yes	No	No	No
Before age 59½, see penalty exceptions 1–8	Yes	Yes	Yes	Yes
1. Death	Yes	No	No	No
2. Disability	Yes	No	No	No
3. First-time home-buyer—$10K limit	Yes	No	No	No
4. Substantially equal periodic payments	Yes	No	Yes	No
5. Medical expenses above 7.5% of AGI	Yes	No	Yes	No
6. Insurance premiums by unemployed	Yes	No	Yes	No
7. Higher education expenses	Yes	No	Yes	No
8. IRS levy	Yes	No	Yes	No
9. Individuals called to active duty	Yes	No	Yes	No
10. Qualified recovery assistance distribution	Yes	No	Yes	No
11. Qualified disaster distribution to purchase or construct main home	Yes	No, if used or repaid	Yes	No, if used or repaid
12. Charitable transfer	Yes, from earnings first	No	Yes, from earnings first	No
13. Qualified hurricane distribution	Yes	No	Yes	No
14. Removal of economic stimulus payment	No	No	No	No
15. Qualified HSA distribution	Yes, from earnings first	No	Yes, from earnings first	No

Note 1. See accompanying information.

Note 2. From time to time, Congress has permitted penalty-free distributions to be made from an eligible retirement plan for special purposes (e.g., hurricane distributions, qualified recovery assistance distributions, qualified disaster recovery distributions, and qualified reservist distributions). These distributions are eligible for repayment (rollover) to an eligible retirement plan, including a Roth IRA, and are discussed in chapter 3. Special rules (not shown above) apply to the distribution and repayment of special purpose distributions.

Traditional/Roth IRA Eligibility for 2009

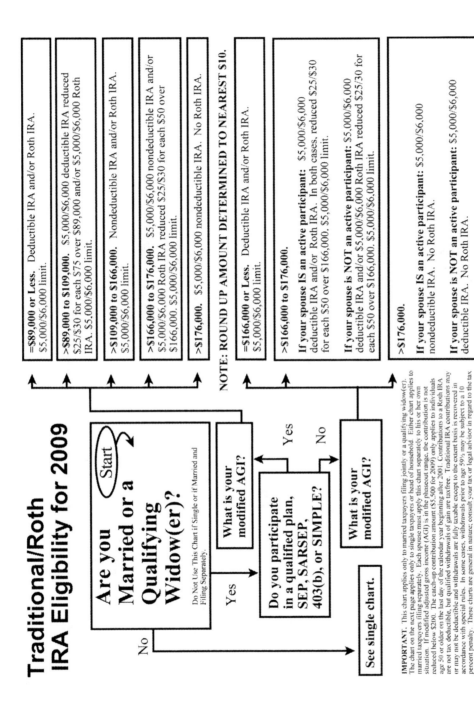

Start

Are you Married or a Qualifying Widow(er)?

Do Not Use This Chart if Single or if Married and Filing Separately.

No → **What is your modified AGI?**

- **=$89,000 or Less.** Deductible IRA and/or Roth IRA. $5,000/$6,000 limit.
- **>$89,000 to $109,000.** $5,000/$6,000 deductible IRA reduced $25/$30 for each $75 over $89,000 and/or $5,000/$6,000 Roth IRA. $5,000/$6,000 limit.
- **>$109,000 to $166,000.** Nondeductible IRA and/or Roth IRA. $5,000/$6,000 limit.
- **>$166,000 to $176,000.** $5,000/$6,000 nondeductible IRA and/or $5,000/$6,000 Roth IRA reduced $25/$30 for each $50 over $166,000. $5,000/$6,000 limit.
- **>$176,000.** $5,000/$6,000 nondeductible IRA. No Roth IRA.

Yes

Do you participate in a qualified plan, SEP, SARSEP, 403(b), or SIMPLE?

Yes → **What is your modified AGI?**

- **=$166,000 or Less.** Deductible IRA and/or Roth IRA. $5,000/$6,000 limit.
- **>$166,000 to $176,000.**
  If your spouse IS an active participant: $5,000/$6,000 deductible IRA and/or Roth IRA. In both cases, reduced $25/$30 for each $50 over $166,000. $5,000/$6,000 limit.
  If your spouse is NOT an active participant: $5,000/$6,000 deductible IRA and/or $5,000/$6,000 Roth IRA reduced $25/$30 for each $50 over $166,000. $5,000/$6,000 limit.
- **>$176,000.**
  If your spouse IS an active participant: $5,000/$6,000 nondeductible IRA. No Roth IRA.
  If your spouse is NOT an active participant: $5,000/$6,000 deductible IRA. No Roth IRA.

No → **See single chart.**

NOTE: ROUND UP AMOUNT DETERMINED TO NEAREST $10.

IMPORTANT. This chart applies only to married taxpayers filing jointly or a qualifying widow(er). The chart on the next page applies only to single taxpayers or head of household. Either chart applies to married taxpayers filing separately. Each spouse must apply this chart separately to his or her own situation. If modified adjusted gross income (AGI) is in the phaseout range, the contribution is not reduced below $200. The catch-up contribution amount ($5,500 for 2009) only applies to individuals age 50 or older on the last day of the calendar year beginning after 2001. Contributions to a Roth IRA are not tax deductible, but qualified withdrawals of gain are taxfree. Traditional IRA contributions may or may not be deductible and withdrawals are fully taxable except to the extent basis is recovered in accordance with special rules. In some cases, withdrawals prior to age 59½ may be subject to a 10 percent penalty. These charts are general in nature; consult your tax or legal advisor in regard to the tax or legal effects of making contributions and/or taking distributions.
© 2009 GSI.

Traditional/Roth
IRA Eligibility for 2009

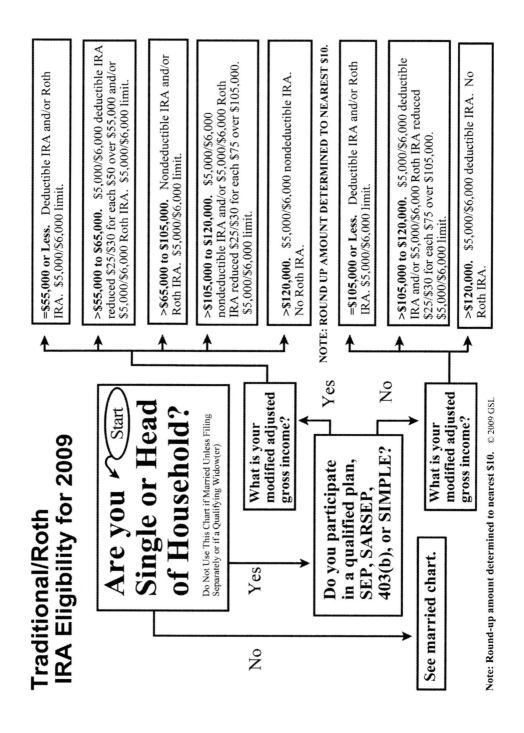

Start

Are you Single or Head of Household?

Do Not Use This Chart if Married Unless Filing Separately or if a Qualifying Widow(er).

Yes → Do you participate in a qualified plan, SEP, SARSEP, 403(b), or SIMPLE?

No → See married chart.

What is your modified adjusted gross income?

(Qualified plan = Yes):

- **=$55,000 or Less.** Deductible IRA and/or Roth IRA. $5,000/$6,000 limit.
- **>$55,000 to $65,000.** $5,000/$6,000 deductible IRA reduced $25/$30 for each $50 over $55,000 and/or $5,000/$6,000 Roth IRA. $5,000/$6,000 limit.
- **>$65,000 to $105,000.** Nondeductible IRA and/or Roth IRA. $5,000/$6,000 limit.
- **>$105,000 to $120,000.** $5,000/$6,000 nondeductible IRA and/or $5,000/$6,000 Roth IRA reduced $25/$30 for each $75 over $105,000. $5,000/$6,000 limit.
- **>$120,000.** $5,000/$6,000 nondeductible IRA. No Roth IRA.

What is your modified adjusted gross income?

(Qualified plan = No):

- **=$105,000 or Less.** Deductible IRA and/or Roth IRA. $5,000/$6,000 limit.
- **>$105,000 to $120,000.** $5,000/$6,000 deductible IRA and/or $5,000/$6,000 Roth IRA reduced $25/$30 for each $75 over $105,000. $5,000/$6,000 limit.
- **>$120,000.** $5,000/$6,000 deductible IRA. No Roth IRA.

NOTE: ROUND UP AMOUNT DETERMINED TO NEAREST $10.

© 2009 GSL

Note: Round-up amount determined to nearest $10.

Distribution to Beneficiary Chart

The following chart can be used as a reference for determining the applicable life expectancy for required minimum distributions after the death of the Roth IRA owner depending on the beneficiary. This chart does not represent tax, accounting, or legal advice. It is meant only to provide guidelines on generic situations. The individual taxpayer is advised to and should rely on the taxpayer's own advisers. This chart was created by Robert S. Keebler, CPA, MST.

Beneficiary	*Distributions to Beneficiary*	*Citation*
Spouse— Inherited IRA (No rollover)	Spouse may defer required distributions until the year the owner would have reached age 70½. In this year, the RMD is calculated based upon spouse's life expectancy by referencing her attained age for the year of distribution based on the Single Life Table of Treas. Reg.§ 1.401(a)(9)-9. For each succeeding year, the surviving spouse references his or her recalculated age under the Single Life Table.	Treas. Reg. § 1.401(a)(9)-3 Q&A 3(b)
	Upon the death of the surviving spouse:	
	1. If the surviving spouse dies prior to the year in which the owner would have been age 70½, the spouse is deemed to be the owner/participant and a beneficiary is determined as of September 30th of the year following death. In this following year, such beneficiary must begin to receive RMDs based upon his or her corresponding life expectancy under the Single Life Table. For each succeeding year, the factor is reduced by one.	Treas. Reg. § 1.401(a)(9)-3 Q&A 5; Treas. Reg. § 1.401(a)(9)-5 Q&A 5(c)(2)
	2. If the surviving spouse dies on or after the date in which the owner would have reached age 70½, an RMD for the current year must be taken. Thereafter, RMDs are calculated based upon the now deceased spouse's life expectancy by reference to his or her attained age in the year of death by reference to the Single Life Table. For each succeeding year, the *factor* is reduced by one.	

Beneficiary	*Distributions to Beneficiary*	*Citation*
Spouse—Rollover	RMDs begin the year the spouse reaches age 70½, (subject to deferral to of year following). If the spouse is already age 70½, RMDs begin by December 31st of the year following the rollover. For such years, RMDs based upon spouse's life expectancy factor determined under the Uniform Lifetime Table. (Recalculated)	Treas. Reg. § 1.408-8 Q&A 5(a)
Child	The first year distribution (year after the year of death) is determined based upon corresponding life expectancy factor for the child's age in the year of the first distribution by reference to the Single Life Table. For succeeding years, this *factor* is reduced by one.	Treas. Reg. § 1.401(a)(9)-3 Q&A l(a); and Treas. Reg. § 1.401(a)(9)-3 Q&A 3(a).
Child by Qualified Disclaimer	The first year distribution is determined based upon corresponding life expectancy factor for the child's age in the year of the first distribution by reference to the Single Life Table. For succeeding years, this *factor* is reduced by one.	Treas. Reg. § 1.401(a)(9)-3 Q&A l(a); and Treas. Reg. § 1.401(a)(9)-3 Q&A 3(a). *See also* Treas. Reg. § 1.401(a)(9)-4 Q&A 4(a).
Grandchild	The first year distribution is determined based upon corresponding life expectancy factor for the grandchild's age in the year of the first distribution by reference to the Single Life Table. For succeeding years, this factor is reduced by one.	Treas. Reg. § 1.401(a)(9)-3 Q&A l(a); and Treas. Reg. § 1.401(a)(9)-3 Q&A 3(a).
Grandchild Qualified Disclaimer	The first year distribution is determined based upon corresponding life expectancy factor for the grandchild's age in the year of the first distribution by reference to the Single Life Table. For succeeding years, this factor is reduced by one.	Treas. Reg. § 1.401(a)(9)-3 Q&A l(a); and Treas. Reg. § 1.401(a)(9)-3 Q&A3(a). *See also* Treas. Reg. § 1.401(a)(9)-4 Q&A 4(a).
Multiple Individual Beneficiaries	As long as the account is segregated prior to December 31st of the year following death, each beneficiary may independently calculate RMDs. Thus, with respect to each beneficiary, the first year distribution is determined based upon corresponding life expectancy factor for the beneficiary's age in the year of the first distribution by reference to the Single Life Table. For succeeding years, this factor is reduced by one.	Treas. Reg. § 1.401(a)(9)-3 Q&A l(a); Treas. Reg. § 1.401(a)(9)-3 Q&A 3(a); Treas. Reg. § 1.401(a)(9)-5 Q&A 7(a); *See also* Treas. Reg. § 1.401(a)(9)-8 Q&A 2 & Q&A 3.

Beneficiary	_Distributions to Beneficiary_	_Citation_
Designated Beneficiary Trust	The first year distribution is determined based upon corresponding life expectancy factor for the oldest beneficiary's age in the year of the first distribution by reference to the Single Life Table. For succeeding years, this factor is reduced by one. If the trust is designed to create "one pot" for the benefit of multiple beneficiaries, RMDs are based upon the oldest beneficiary's life expectancy. However, if the Beneficiary Designation is payable specifically to separate sub-trusts, each separate sub-trust beneficiary should be able to use his or her respective life expectancy to calculate. RMDs (_see_ Ltr. Rul. 200537044). Note, however, multiple shares must be established by December 31st of the year following death	Treas. Reg. § 1.401(a)(9)-3 Q&A 1(a); Treas. Reg. § 1.401(a)(9)-3 Q&A 3(a); Treas. Reg. § 1.401(a)(9)-5 Q&A 7(a); _see also_ Treas. Reg. § 1.401(a)(9)-8 Q&A 2 & Q&A 3.
Non Designated Beneficiary Trust	Entire balance must be distributed no later than December 31st of the fifth anniversary year of the decedent's death. However, consider the potential to cash out non-individual beneficiaries where and if possible.	Treas. Reg. § 1.401(a)(9)-3 Q&A 1(a) & Q&A 2
Charity	Entire balance must be distributed no later than December 31st of the fifth anniversary year of the decedent's death. However, consider the potential to cash out the charity or segregate interests where multiple beneficiaries exist.	Treas. Reg. § 1.401(a)(9)-3 Q&A 1(a) & Q&A 2
Estate	Entire balance must be distributed no later than December 31st of the fifth anniversary year of the decedent's death.	Treas. Reg. § 1.401(a)(9)-3 Q&A 1(a) & Q&A 2. _See also_ Treas. Reg. § 1.401(a)(9)-4 Q&A 3.

IRA and ROTH IRA Distribution Flowchart

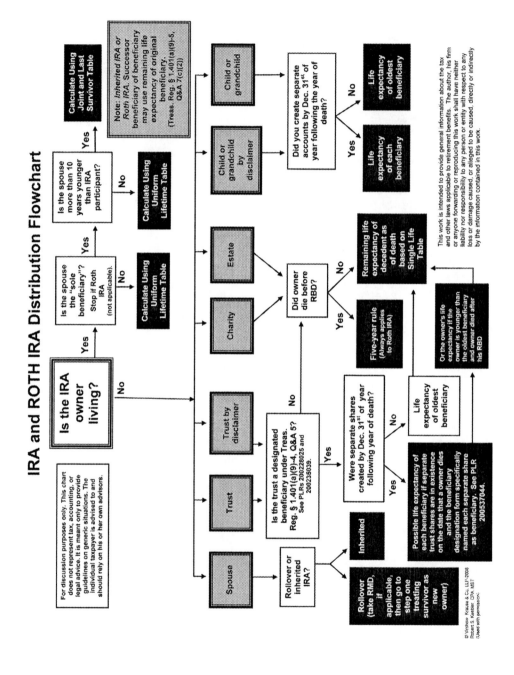

Annual Roth IRA Contribution Limits

Taxable Year	Normal Limit	Catch-up Amount	Total Contribution
1998	$2,000	None	$2,000
1999	$2,000	None	$2,000
2000	$2,000	None	$2,000
2001	$2,000	None	$2,000
2002	$3,000	$ 500	$3,500
2003	$3,000	$ 500	$3,500
2004	$3,000	$ 500	$3,500
2005	$4,000	$ 500	$4,500
2006	$4,000	$1,000	$5,000
2007	$4,000	$1,000	$5,000
2008	**$5,000**	**$1,000**	**$6,000**
2009	**$5,000**	**$1,000**	**$6,000**

[I.R.C. §§ 408A(c)(2), 219(b)(5), 414(v)]

Modified Adjusted Gross Income (MAGI) Phaseout Chart

The annual contribution limit for a Roth IRA is phased out based on the filing status and MAGI of the individual. That is, if an individual's MAGI is more than the minimum phaseout amount but less than the maximum phaseout amount, the contribution is phased out. In general, the phaseout is determined in a ratable manner. If an individual's MAGI is below the minimum phaseout amount, the annual limit applies ($5,000; $6,000 with catch-up contribution for 2009); if the MAGI is above the maximum phaseout amount, no contribution is permitted. (See Qs 2:1, 2:5.) However, if an individual whose MAGI falls within the phaseout range is eligible to make a Roth IRA contribution of more than $0 but less than $200, the individual may make a contribution of up to $200. That rule does not require that such an individual make a $200 contribution. The following chart shows the maximum Roth contribution (before rounding) for 2009 when MAGI is in a phaseout range for single taxpayers, married taxpayers filing jointly, and married taxpayers filing separately.

Single Taxpayers

MAGI	Under Age 50	Age 50 or Older
$120,000	$ 0	$ 0
119,999	200	200
119,900	200	200
119,800	200	200
119,700	200	200
119,600	200	200
119,500	200	200
119,400	200	240
119,300	233	280
119,200	267	320
119,100	300	360
119,000	333	400
118,900	367	440

Married Taxpayers Filing Jointly

MAGI	Under Age 50	Age 50 or Older
$176,000	$ 0	$ 0
175,999	200	200
175,900	200	200
175,800	200	200
175,700	200	200
175,600	200	240
175,500	250	300
175,400	300	360
175,300	350	420
175,200	360	480
175,100	450	540
175,000	500	600
174,900	550	660

Married Taxpayers Filing Separately

MAGI	Under Age 50	Age 50 or Older
$10,000	$ 0	$ 0
9,999	200	200
9,900	200	200
9,800	200	200
9,700	200	200
9,600	200	240
9,500	250	300
9,400	300	360
9,300	350	420
9,200	400	480
9,100	450	540
9,000	500	600
8,900	550	660

Single Taxpayers			Married Taxpayers Filing Jointly			Married Taxpayers Filing Separately		
MAGI	Under Age 50	Age 50 or Older	MAGI	Under Age 50	Age 50 or Older	MAGI	Under Age 50	Age 50 or Older
118,800	400	480	174,800	600	720	8,800	600	720
118,700	433[1]	520[2]	174,700	650	780	8,700	650	780
118,600	467	560	174,600	700	840	8,600	700	840
118,500	500	600	174,500	750	900	8,500	750	900
118,400	533	640	174,400	800	960	8,400	800	960
118,300	567	680	174,300	850	1,020	8,300	850	1,020
118,200	600	720	174,200	900	1,080	8,200	900	1,080
118,100	633	760	174,100	950	1,140	8,100	950	1,140
118,000	667	800	174,000	1,000	1,200	8,000	1,000	1,200
117,900	700	840	173,900	1,050	1,260	7,900	1,050	1,260
117,800	733	880	173,800	1,100	1,320	7,800	1,100	1,320
117,700	767	920	173,700	1,150	1,380	7,700	1,150	1,380
117,600	800	960	173,600	1,200	1,440	7,600	1,200	1,440
117,500	833	1,000	173,500	1,125	1,500	7,500	1,250	1,500
117,400	867	1,040	173,400	1,300	1,560	7,400	1,300	1,560
117,300	900	1,080	173,300	1,350	1,620	7,300	1,350	1,620
117,200	967	1,120	173,200	1,400	1,680	7,200	1,400	1,680
117,100	1000	1,160	173,100	1,450	1,740	7,100	1,450	1,740
117,000	1033	1,200	173,000	1,500	1,800	7,000	1,500	1,800
116,900	1067	1,240	172,900	1,550	1,860	6,900	1,550	1,860
116,800	1067	1,280	172,800	1,600	1,920	6,800	1,600	1,920
116,700	1100	1,320	172,700	1,650	1,980	6,700	1,650	1,980
116,600	1133	1,360	172,600	1,700	2,040	6,600	1,700	2,040
116,500	1167	1,400	172,500	1,750	2,100	6,500	1,750	2,100
116,400	1200	1,440	172,400	1,800	2,160	6,400	1,800	2,160
116,300	1233	1,480	172,300	1,850	2,200	6,300	1,850	2,200

Single Taxpayers			Married Taxpayers Filing Jointly			Married Taxpayers Filing Separately		
MAGI	*Under Age 50*	*Age 50 or Older*	*MAGI*	*Under Age 50*	*Age 50 or Older*	*MAGI*	*Under Age 50*	*Age 50 or Older*
116,200	1267	1,520	172,200	1,900	2,280	6,200	1,900	2,280
116,100	1300	1,560	172,100	1,950	2,340	6,100	1,950	2,340
116,000	1333	1,600	172,000	2,000	2,400	6,000	2,000	2,400
115,900	1367	1,640	171,900	2,050	2,460	5,900	2,050	2,460
115,800	1400	1,680	171,800	2,100	2,520	5,800	2,100	2,520
115,700	1433	1,720	171,700	2,150	2,580	5,700	2,150	2,580
115,600	1467	1,760	171,600	2,200	2,640	5,600	2,200	2,640
115,500	1500	1,800	171,500	2,250	2,700	5,500	2,250	2,700
115,400	1533	1,840	171,400	2,300	2,760	5,400	2,300	2,760
115,300	1567	1,880	171,300	2,350	2,820	5,300	2,350	2,820
115,200	1600	1,920	171,200	2,400	2,880	5,200	2,400	2,880
115,100	1633	1,960	171,100	2,450	2,940	5,100	2,450	2,940
115,000	1,667	2,000	171,000	2,500	3,000	5,000	2,500	3,000
114,900	1,700	2,040	170,900	2,550	3,060	4,900	2,550	3,060
114,800	1,733	2,080	170,800	2,600	3,120	4,800	2,600	3,120
114,700	1,767	2,120	170,700	2,650	3,180	4,700	2,650	3,180
114,600	1,800	2,160	170,600	2,700	3,240	4,600	2,700	3,240
114,500	1,833	2,200	170,500	2,750	3,300	4,500	2,750	3,300
114,400	1,867	2,240	170,400	2,800	3,360	4,400	2,800	3,360
114,300	1,900	2,280	170,300	2,850	3,420	4,300	2,850	3,420
114,200	1,933	2,320	170,200	2,900	3,480	4,200	2,900	3,480
114,100	1,967	2,360	170,100	2,950	3,540	4,100	2,950	3,540
114,000	2,000	2,400	170,000	3,000[3]	3,600[4]	4,000	3,000	3,600
113,900	2,033	2,440	169,900	3,050	3,660	3,900	3,050	3,660
113,800	2,067	2,480	169,800	3,100	3,720	3,800	3,100	3,720
113,700	2,100	2,520	169,700	3,150	3,780	3,700	3,150	3,780

Single Taxpayers			Married Taxpayers Filing Jointly			Married Taxpayers Filing Separately		
MAGI	Under Age 50	Age 50 or Older	MAGI	Under Age 50	Age 50 or Older	MAGI	Under Age 50	Age 50 or Older
113,600	2,133	2,560	169,600	3,200	3,840	3,600	3,200	3,840
113,500	2,167	2,600	169,500	3,250	3,900	3,500	3,250	3,900
113,400	2,200	2,640	169,400	3,300	3,960	3,400	3,300	3,960
113,300	2,223	2,680	169,300	3,350	4,020	3,300	3,350	4,020
113,200	2,267	2,720	169,200	3,400	4,080	3,200	3,400	4,080
113,100	2,300	2,760	169,100	3,450	4,140	3,100	3,450	4,140
113,000	2,333	2,800	169,000	3,500	4,200	3,000	3,500	4,200
112,900	2,367	2,840	168,900	3,550	4,260	2,900	3,550	4,260
112,800	2,400	2,880	168,800	3,600	4,320	2,800	3,600	4,320
112,700	2,433	2,920	168,700	3,650	4,380	2,700	3,650	4,380
112,600	2,467	2,960	168,600	3,700	4,400	2,600	3,700	4,400
112,500	2,500	3,000	168,500	3,750	4,500	2,500	3,750	4,500
112,400	2,533	3,040	168,400	3,800	4,560	2,400	3,800	4,560
112,300	2,567	3,080	168,300	3,850	4,620	2,300	3,850	4,620
112,200	2,600	3,120	168,200	3,900	4,680	2,200	3,900	4,680
112,100	2,633	3,160	168,100	3,950	4,740	2,100	3,950	4,740
112,000	2,667	3,200	168,000	4,000	4,800	2,000	4,000	4,800
111,900	2,700	3,240	167,900	4,050	4,860	1,900	4,050	4,860
111,800	2,733	3,280	167,800	4,100	4,920	1,800	4,100	4,920
111,700	2,767	3,320	167,700	4,150	4,980	1,700	4,150	4,980
111,600	2,800	3,360	167,600	4,200	5,040	1,600	4,200	5,040
111,500	2,833	3,400	167,500	4,250	5,100	1,500	4,250	5,100
111,400	2,867	3,440	167,400	4,300	5,160	1,400	4,300	5,160
111,300	2,900	3,480	167,300	4,350	5,220	1,300	4,350	5,220
111,200	2,933	3,520	167,200	4,400	5,280	1,200	4,400	5,280
111,100	2,967	3,560	167,100	4,450	5,340	1,100	4,450	5,340

Single Taxpayers

MAGI	Under Age 50	Age 50 or Older
111,000	3,000	3,700
110,900	3,033	3,740
110,800	3,067	3,780
110,700	3,100	3,820
110,600	3,133	3,860
110,500	3,167	3,900
110,400	3,200	3,940
110,300	3,233	3,980
110,200	3,267	3,920
110,100	3,300	3,960
110,000	3,333	4,000
109,900	3,367	4,040
109,800	3,400	4,080
109,700	3,433	4,120
109,600	3,467	4,160
109,500	3,500	4,200
109,400	3,533	4,240
109,300	3,567	4,280
109,200	3,600	4,320
109,100	3,633	4,360
109,000	3,667	4,400
108,900	3,700	4,440
108,800	3,733	4,480
108,700	3,767	4,520
108,600	3,800	4,560
108,500	3,833	4,600

Married Taxpayers Filing Jointly

MAGI	Under Age 50	Age 50 or Older
167,000	4,500	5,400
166,900	4,550	5,460
166,800	4,600	5,520
166,700	4,650	5,580
166,600	4,700	5,640
166,500	4,750	5,700
166,400	4,800	5,760
166,300	4,850	5,820
166,200	4,900	5,880
166,100	4,950	5,940
166,000	5,000	6,000

Married Taxpayers Filing Separately

MAGI	Under Age 50	Age 50 or Older
1,000	4,500	5,400
900	4,550	5,460
800	4,600	5,520
700	4,650	5,580
600	4,700	5,640
500	4,750[5]	5,700[6]
400	4,800	5,760
300	4,850	5,820
200	4,900	5,880
100	4,950	5,940
0	5,000	6,000

Single Taxpayers

MAGI	Under Age 50	Age 50 or Older
108,400	3,867	4,640
108,300	3,900	4,680
108,200	3,933	4,720
108,100	3,967	4,760
108,000	4,000	4,800
107,900	4,033	4,840
107,800	4,067	4,880
107,700	4,100	4,920
107,600	4,133	4,960
107,500	4,167	5,000
107,400	4,200	5,040
107,300	4,233	5,080
107,200	4,267	5,120
107,100	4,300	5,160
107,000	4,333	5,200
106,900	4,367	5,240
106,800	4,400	5,280
106,700	4,433	5,320
106,600	4,467	5,360
106,500	4,500	5,400
106,400	4,533	5,440
106,300	4,567	5,480
106,200	4,600	5,520
106,100	4,633	5,560
106,000	4,667	5,600
105,900	4,700	5,640

Married Taxpayers Filing Jointly

MAGI	Under Age 50	Age 50 or Older

Married Taxpayers Filing Separately

MAGI	Under Age 50	Age 50 or Older

Single Taxpayers			Married Taxpayers Filing Jointly			Married Taxpayers Filing Separately		
MAGI	Under Age 50	Age 50 or Older	MAGI	Under Age 50	Age 50 or Older	MAGI	Under Age 50	Age 50 or Older
105,800	4,733	5,680						
105,700	4,767	5,720						
105,600	4,800	5,760						
105,500	4,833	5,800						
105,400	4,867	5,840						
105,300	4,900	5,880						
105,200	4,933	5,920						
105,100	4,967	5,960						
105,000	5,000	6,000						

Note. All numbers are rounded to the next highest multiple of $10 (not shown) to determine the maximum contribution amount (e.g., $213 is rounded to $220).

Note. Minimum $200 amount shown where applicable.

[1] $5,000 — ($118,700 – $105,000)/($120,000 – $105,000) × $5,000 = $433. The maximum contribution is $440 (rounded to the next multiple of $10).

[2] $6,000 — ($118,700 – $105,000)/($120,000 – $105,000) × $6,000 = $520. The maximum contribution is $520.

[3] $5,000 — ($170,000 – $166,000)/($176,000 – $166,000) × $5,000 = $3,000.

[4] $6,000 — ($170,000 – $166,000)/($176,000 – $166,000) × $6,000 = $3,600.

[5] $5,000 — ($500 – $0)/($10,000 – $0) × $6,000 = $4,750.

[6] $6,000 — ($500 – $0)/($10,000 – $0) × $6,000 = $5,700.

Appendix B

Extracts from Relevant Code Sections (As of August 1, 2009)

This appendix includes recent changes made to Code Section 408A by the Heroes Earnings Assistance and Relief Tax Act of 2008 (HEART) (Pub. L. No. 110-245) that was adopted on June 17, 2008.

Code Section 408A: Roth IRAs

[**Note.** Except as provided below, Code Section 408A applies to tax years beginning after December 31, 1997 (TRA '97 (Pub. L. No. 105-34))]

Section 408A—Roth IRAs.

(a) GENERAL RULE.—Except as provided in this section, a Roth IRA shall be treated for purposes of this title in the same manner as an individual retirement plan.

(b) ROTH IRA.—For purposes of this title, the term "Roth IRA" means an individual retirement plan (as defined in section 7701(a)(37)) which is designated (in such manner as the Secretary may prescribe) at the time of establishment of the plan as a Roth IRA. Such designation shall be made in such manner as the Secretary may prescribe.

(c) TREATMENT OF CONTRIBUTIONS.—

(1) NO DEDUCTION ALLOWED.—No deduction shall be allowed under section 219 for a contribution to a Roth IRA.

(2) CONTRIBUTION LIMIT.—The aggregate amount of contributions for any taxable year to all Roth IRAs maintained for the benefit of an individual shall not exceed the excess (if any) of—

(A) the maximum amount allowable as a deduction under section 219 with respect to such individual for such taxable year (computed without regard to subsection (d)(1) or (g) of such section), over

(B) the aggregate amount of contributions for such taxable year to all other individual retirement plans (other than Roth IRAs) maintained for the benefit of the individual.

(3) LIMITS BASED ON MODIFIED ADJUSTED GROSS INCOME.—

(A) DOLLAR LIMIT.—The amount determined under paragraph (2) for any taxable year shall not exceed an amount equal to the amount determined under paragraph (2)(A) for such taxable year, reduced (but not below zero) by the amount which bears the same ratio to such amount as—

(i) the excess of—

(I) the taxpayer's adjusted gross income for such taxable year, over

(II) the applicable dollar amount, bears to

(ii) $15,000 ($10,000 in the case of a joint return or a married individual filing a separate return).

The rules of subparagraphs (B) and (C) of section 219(g)(2) shall apply to any reduction under this subparagraph.

Author's Note. Code Section 408A(c)(3)(B), below, prior to amendment by the Pension Protection Act of 2006 (Pub. L. No. 109-280), applies to distributions on or before December 31, 2007. It was stricken by the Tax Increase Prevention and Reconciliation Act of 2005 (Pub. L. No. 109-222), applicable to taxable years beginning after 2009.

(B) ROLLOVER FROM IRA.—A taxpayer shall not be allowed to make a qualified rollover contribution to a Roth IRA from an individual retirement plan other than a Roth IRA during any taxable year if, for the taxable year of the distribution to which such contribution relates—

(i) the taxpayer's adjusted gross income exceeds $100,000, or

(ii) the taxpayer is a married individual filing a separate return.

Author's Note. Code Section 408A(c)(3)(B), below, as amended by the Pension Protection Act of 2006 (Pub. L. No. 109-280), applies to distributions after December 31, 2007. It was stricken by the Tax Increase Prevention and Reconciliation Act of 2005 (Pub. L. No. 109-222), applicable to tax years beginning after December 31, 2009. Thus, this version is in effect for distributions made in 2008.

> (B) ROLLOVER FROM ELIGIBLE RETIREMENT PLAN.—A taxpayer shall not be allowed to make a qualified rollover contribution to a Roth IRA from an an [sic] eligible retirement plan (as defined by section 402(c)(8)(B)) other than a Roth IRA during any taxable year if, for the taxable year of the distribution to which such contribution relates—
>
>> (i) the taxpayer's adjusted gross income exceeds $100,000, or
>>
>> (ii) the taxpayer is a married individual filing a separate return.

Author's Note. Code Section 408A(c)(3)(C), below, was redesignated as Code Section 408A(c)(3)(B) by the Tax Increase Prevention and Reconciliation Act of 2005 (Pub. L. No. 109-222), applicable to tax years beginning after December 31, 2009.

> (C) DEFINITIONS.—For purposes of this paragraph—

Author's Note. Code Section 408A(c)(3)(C)(i), below, prior to amendment by the Tax Increase Prevention and Reconciliation Act of 2005 (Pub. L. No. 109-222), applies to tax years beginning on or before December 31, 2009.

>> (i) adjusted gross income shall be determined in the same manner as under section 219(g)(3), except that—
>>
>>> (I) any amount included in gross income under subsection (d)(3) shall not be taken into account; and
>>>
>>> (II) any amount included in gross income by reason of a required distribution under a provision described in paragraph (5) shall not be taken into account for purposes of subparagraph (B)(i), and

Author's Note. Code Section 408A (c)(3)(C)(i), below, as amended by the Tax Increase Prevention and Reconciliation Act of 2005 (Pub. L. No. 109-222), applies to tax years beginning after December 31, 2009.

>> (i) adjusted gross income shall be determined in the same manner as under section 219(g)(3), except that any amount included in gross income under subsection (d)(3) shall not be taken into account, and
>>
>> (ii) the applicable dollar amount is—
>>
>>> (I) in the case of a taxpayer filing a joint return, $150,000,
>>>
>>> (II) in the case of any other taxpayer (other than a married individual filing a separate return), $95,000, and
>>>
>>> (III) in the case of a married individual filing a separate return, zero.

Author's Note. Code Section 408A(c)(3)(D), below, was redesignated as Code Section 408A(c)(3)(C) by the Tax Increase Prevention and Reconciliation

Act of 2005 (Pub. L. No. 109-222), applicable to tax years beginning after December 31, 2009.

> (D) MARITAL STATUS.—Section 219(g)(4) shall apply for purposes of this paragraph.

Author's Note. Code Section 408A(c)(3)(C)[(D)], below, as added by the Pension Protection Act of 2006 (Pub. L. No. 109-280), applies to tax years beginning after 2006.

> (C)[(D)] INFLATION ADJUSTMENT.—In the case of any taxable year beginning in a calendar year after 2006, the dollar amounts in subclauses (I) and (II) of subparagraph (C)(ii) shall each be increased by an amount equal to—

>> (i) such dollar amount, multiplied by

>> (ii) the cost-of-living adjustment determined under section 1(f)(3) for the calendar year in which the taxable year begins, determined by substituting "calendar year 2005" for "calendar year 1992" in subparagraph (B) thereof.

> Any increase determined under the preceding sentence shall be rounded to the nearest multiple of $1,000.

(4) CONTRIBUTIONS PERMITTED AFTER AGE 70½.—Contributions to a Roth IRA may be made even after the individual for whom the account is maintained has attained age 70½.

(5) MANDATORY DISTRIBUTION RULES NOT TO APPLY BEFORE DEATH.—Notwithstanding subsections (a)(6) and (b)(3) of section 408 (relating to required distributions), the following provisions shall not apply to any Roth IRA:

> (A) Section 401(a)(9)(A).

> (B) The incidental death benefit requirements of section 401(a).

(6) ROLLOVER CONTRIBUTIONS.—

> (A) IN GENERAL.—No rollover contribution may be made to a Roth IRA unless it is a qualified rollover contribution.

> (B) COORDINATION WITH LIMIT.—A qualified rollover contribution shall not be taken into account for purposes of paragraph (2).

(7) TIME WHEN CONTRIBUTIONS MADE.—For purposes of this section, the rule of section 219(f)(3) shall apply.

(d) DISTRIBUTION RULES.—For purposes of this title—

(1) EXCLUSION.—Any qualified distribution from a Roth IRA shall not be includible in gross income.

(2) QUALIFIED DISTRIBUTION.—For purposes of this subsection—

(A) IN GENERAL.—The term "qualified distribution" means any payment or distribution—

> (i) made on or after the date on which the individual attains age 59½,
>
> (ii) made to a beneficiary (or to the estate of the individual) on or after the death of the individual,
>
> (iii) attributable to the individual's being disabled (within the meaning of section 72(m)(7), or
>
> (iv) which is a qualified special purpose distribution.

(B) DISTRIBUTIONS WITHIN NONEXCLUSION PERIOD.—A payment or distribution from a Roth IRA shall not be treated as a qualified distribution under subparagraph (A) if such payment or distribution is made within the 5-taxable year period beginning with the 1st taxable year for which the individual made a contribution to a Roth IRA (or such individual's spouse made a contribution to a Roth IRA) established for such individual.

(C) DISTRIBUTIONS OF EXCESS CONTRIBUTIONS AND EARNINGS.—The term "qualified distribution" shall not include any distribution of any contribution described in section 408(d)(4) and any net income allocable to the contribution.

Author's Note. The heading for Code Section 408A(d)(3), below, prior to amendment by the Pension Protection Act of 2006 (Pub. L. No. 109-280), applies to distributions on or before December 31, 2007.

> (3) ROLLOVERS FROM AN IRA OTHER THAN A ROTH IRA.—

Author's Note. The heading for Code Section 408A(d)(3), below, as amended by Pension Protection Act of 2006 (Pub. L. No. 109-280), applies to distributions after December 31, 2007.

> (3) ROLLOVERS FROM AN ELIGIBLE RETIREMENT PLAN OTHER THAN A ROTH IRA.—

Author's Note. Code Section 408A(d)(3)(A), below, prior to amendment by the Pension Protection Act of 2006 (Pub. L. No. 109-280) and the Tax Increase Prevention and Reconciliation Act of 2005 (Pub. L. No. 109-222), applies to distributions on or before December 31, 2007.

> (A) IN GENERAL.—Notwithstanding section 408(d)(3), in the case of any distribution to which this paragraph applies—
>
> > (i) there shall be included in gross income any amount which would be includible were it not part of a qualified rollover contribution,
> >
> > (ii) section 72(t) shall not apply, and

(iii) unless the taxpayer elects not to have this clause apply for any taxable year, any amount required to be included in gross income for such taxable year by reason of this paragraph for any distribution before January 1, 1999, shall be so included ratably over the 4-taxable year period beginning with such taxable year.

Any election under clause (iii) for any distributions during a taxable year may not be changed after the due date for such taxable year.

Author's Note. Code Section 408A(d)(3)(A), below, as amended by the Pension Protection Act of 2006 (Pub. L. No. 109-280), but prior to amendment by the Tax Increase Prevention and Reconciliation Act of 2005 (Pub. L. No. 109-222), applies to distributions after December 31, 2007, and to tax years beginning on or before December 31, 2009.

(A) IN GENERAL.—Notwithstanding sections 402(c), 403(b)(8), 408(d)(3), and 457(e)(16), in the case of any distribution to which this paragraph applies—

(i) there shall be included in gross income any amount which would be includible were it not part of a qualified rollover contribution,

(ii) section 72(t) shall not apply, and

(iii) unless the taxpayer elects not to have this clause apply for any taxable year, any amount required to be included in gross income for such taxable year by reason of this paragraph for any distribution before January 1, 1999, shall be so included ratably over the 4-taxable year period beginning with such taxable year.

Any election under clause (iii) for any distributions during a taxable year may not be changed after the due date for such taxable year.

Author's Note. Code Section 408A(d)(3)(A), below, as amended by the Pension Protection Act of 2006 (Pub. L. No. 109-222) and the Tax Increase Prevention and Reconciliation Act of 2005 (Pub. L. No. 109-280), applies to tax years beginning after December 31, 2009.

(A) IN GENERAL.—Notwithstanding sections 402(c), 403(b)(8), 408(d)(3), and 457(e)(16), in the case of any distribution to which this paragraph applies—

(i) there shall be included in gross income any amount which would be includible were it not part of a qualified rollover contribution,

(ii) section 72(t) shall not apply, and

(iii) unless the taxpayer elects not to have this clause apply, any amount required to be included in gross income for any taxable year beginning in 2010 by reason of this paragraph shall be so included ratably over the 2-taxable-year period beginning with the first taxable year beginning in 2011.

Any election under clause (iii) for any distributions during a taxable year may not be changed after the due date for such taxable year.

Author's Note. Code Section 408A(d)(3)(B), below, prior to amendment by the Pension Protection Act of 2006 (Pub. L. No. 109-280), applies to distributions on or before December 31, 2007.

(B) DISTRIBUTIONS TO WHICH PARAGRAPH APPLIES.—This paragraph shall apply to a distribution from an individual retirement plan (other than a Roth IRA) maintained for the benefit of an individual which is contributed to a Roth IRA maintained for the benefit of such individual in a qualified rollover contribution.

Author's Note. Code Section 408A(d)(3)(B), below, as amended by the Pension Protection Act of 2006 (Pub. L. No. 109-280), applies to distributions after December 31, 2007.

(B) DISTRIBUTIONS TO WHICH PARAGRAPH APPLIES.—This paragraph shall apply to a distribution from an eligible retirement plan (as defined by section 402(c)(8)(B)) (other than a Roth IRA) maintained for the benefit of an individual which is contributed to a Roth IRA maintained for the benefit of such individual in a qualified rollover contribution.

(C) CONVERSIONS.—The conversion of an individual retirement plan (other than a Roth IRA) to a Roth IRA shall be treated for purposes of this paragraph as a distribution to which this paragraph applies.

Author's Note. Code Section 408A(d)(3)(D), below, prior to amendment by the Pension Protection Act of 2006 (Pub. L. No. 109-280), applies to distributions on or before December 31, 2007.

(D) ADDITIONAL REPORTING REQUIREMENTS.—Trustees of Roth IRAs, trustees of individual retirement plans, or both, whichever is appropriate, shall include such additional information in reports required under section 408(i) as the Secretary may require to ensure that amounts required to be included in gross income under subparagraph (A) are so included.

Author's Note. Code Section 408A(d)(3)(D), below, as amended by the Pension Protection Act of 2006 (Pub. L. No. 109-280), applies to distributions after December 31, 2007.

(D) ADDITIONAL REPORTING REQUIREMENTS.—Trustees of Roth IRAs, trustees of individual retirement plans, persons subject to section 6047(d)(1), or all of the foregoing persons, whichever is appropriate, shall include such additional information in reports required under section 408(i) or 6047 as the Secretary may require to ensure that amounts required to be included in gross income under subparagraph (A) are so included.

Author's Note. Code Section 408A(d)(3)(E), below, prior to amendment by the Tax Increase Prevention and Reconciliation Act of 2005 (Pub. L. No. 109-222), applies to tax years beginning on or before December 31, 2009.

> (E) SPECIAL RULES FOR CONTRIBUTIONS TO WHICH 4-YEAR AVERAGING APPLIES.—In the case of a qualified rollover contribution to a Roth IRA of a distribution to which subparagraph (A)(iii) applied, the following rules shall apply:
>
> (i) ACCELERATION OF INCLUSION.—
>
>> (I) IN GENERAL.—The amount required to be included in gross income for each of the first 3 taxable years in the 4-year period under subparagraph (A)(iii) shall be increased by the aggregate distributions from Roth IRAs for such taxable year which are allocable under paragraph (4) to the portion of such qualified rollover contribution required to be included in gross income under subparagraph (A)(i).
>>
>> (II) LIMITATION ON AGGREGATE AMOUNT INCLUDED. —The amount required to be included in gross income for any taxable year under subparagraph (A)(iii) shall not exceed the aggregate amount required to be included in gross income under subparagraph (A)(iii) for all taxable years in the 4-year period (without regard to subclause (I)) reduced by amounts included for all preceding taxable years.
>
> (ii) DEATH OF DISTRIBUTEE.—
>
>> (I) IN GENERAL.—If the individual required to include amounts in gross income under such subparagraph dies before all of such amounts are included, all remaining amounts shall be included in gross income for the taxable year which includes the date of death.
>>
>> (II) SPECIAL RULE FOR SURVIVING SPOUSE.—If the spouse of the individual described in subclause (I) acquires the individual's entire interest in any Roth IRA to which such qualified rollover contribution is properly allocable, the spouse may elect to treat the remaining amounts described in subclause (I) as includible in the spouse's gross income in the taxable years of the spouse ending with or within the taxable years of such individual in which such amounts would otherwise have been includible. Any such election may not be made or changed after the due date for the spouse's taxable year which includes the date of death.

Author's Note. Code Section 408A(d)(3)(E), below, as amended by the Tax Increase Prevention and Reconciliation Act of 2005 (Pub. L. No. 109-222), applies to tax years beginning after December 31, 2009.

(E) SPECIAL RULES FOR CONTRIBUTIONS TO WHICH 2-YEAR AVER-AGING APPLIES.—In the case of a qualified rollover contribution to a Roth IRA of a distribution to which subparagraph (A)(iii) applied, the following rules shall apply:

(i) ACCELERATION OF INCLUSION.—

(I) IN GENERAL.—The amount otherwise required to be included in gross income for any taxable year beginning in 2010 or the first taxable year in the 2-year period under subparagraph (A)(iii) shall be increased by the aggregate distributions from Roth IRAs for such taxable year which are allocable under paragraph (4) to the portion of such qualified rollover contribution required to be included in gross income under subparagraph (A)(i).

(II) LIMITATION ON AGGREGATE AMOUNT INCLUDED.—The amount required to be included in gross income for any taxable year under subparagraph (A)(iii) shall not exceed the aggregate amount required to be included in gross income under subparagraph (A)(iii) for all taxable years in the 2-year period (without regard to subclause (I)) reduced by amounts included for all preceding taxable years.

(ii) DEATH OF DISTRIBUTEE.—

(I) IN GENERAL.—If the individual required to include amounts in gross income under such subparagraph dies before all of such amounts are included, all remaining amounts shall be included in gross income for the taxable year which includes the date of death.

(II) SPECIAL RULE FOR SURVIVING SPOUSE.—If the spouse of the individual described in subclause (I) acquires the individual's entire interest in any Roth IRA to which such qualified rollover contribution is properly allocable, the spouse may elect to treat the remaining amounts described in subclause (I) as includible in the spouse's gross income in the taxable years of the spouse ending with or within the taxable years of such individual in which such amounts would otherwise have been includible. Any such election may not be made or changed after the due date for the spouse's taxable year which includes the date of death.

(F) SPECIAL RULE FOR APPLYING SECTION 72.—

(i) IN GENERAL.—If—

(I) any portion of a distribution from a Roth IRA is properly allocable to a qualified rollover contribution described in this paragraph; and

(II) such distribution is made within the 5-taxable year period beginning with the taxable year in which such contribution was made, then section 72(t) shall be applied as if such portion were includible in gross income.

(ii) LIMITATION.—Clause (i) shall apply only to the extent of the amount of the qualified rollover contribution includible in gross income under subparagraph (A)(i).

(4) AGGREGATION AND ORDERING RULES.—

(A) AGGREGATION RULES.—Section 408(d)(2) shall be applied separately with respect to Roth IRAs and other individual retirement plans.

(B) ORDERING RULES.—For purposes of applying this section and section 72 to any distribution from a Roth IRA, such distribution shall be treated as made—

(i) from contributions to the extent that the amount of such distribution, when added to all previous distributions from the Roth IRA, does not exceed the aggregate contributions to the Roth IRA; and

(ii) from such contributions in the following order:

Contributions other than qualified rollover contributions to which paragraph (3) applies.

Qualified rollover contributions to which paragraph (3) applies on a first-in, first-out basis.

Any distribution allocated to a qualified rollover contribution under clause (ii)(II) shall be allocated first to the portion of such contribution required to be included in gross income.

(5) QUALIFIED SPECIAL PURPOSE DISTRIBUTION.—For purposes of this section, the term "qualified special purpose distribution" means any distribution to which subparagraph (F) of section 72(t)(2) applies.

(6) TAXPAYER MAY MAKE ADJUSTMENTS BEFORE DUE DATE.—

(A) IN GENERAL.—Except as provided by the Secretary, if, on or before the due date for any taxable year, a taxpayer transfers in a trustee-to-trustee transfer any contribution to an individual retirement plan made during such taxable year from such plan to any other individual retirement plan, then, for purposes of this chapter, such contribution shall be treated as having been made to the transferee plan (and not the transferor plan).

(B) SPECIAL RULES.—

(i) TRANSFER OF EARNINGS.—Subparagraph (A) shall not apply to the transfer of any contribution unless such transfer is accompanied by any net income allocable to such contribution.

(ii) NO DEDUCTION.—Subparagraph (A) shall apply to the transfer of any contribution only to the extent no deduction was allowed with respect to the contribution to the transferor plan.

(7) DUE DATE.—For purposes of this subsection, the due date for any taxable year is the date prescribed by law (including extensions of time) for filing the taxpayer's return for such taxable year.

Author's Note. Code Section 408A(e), below, prior to amendment by the Pension Protection Act of 2006 (Pub .L. No. 109-280), applies to distributions on or before December 31, 2007. This subsection was further amended by the Heroes Earnings Assistance and Relief Tax Act of 2008 (HEART), Section 109 (Pub. L. No. 110-245). See next Author's Note.

(e) QUALIFIED ROLLOVER CONTRIBUTION.—For purposes of this section, the term "qualified rollover contribution" means a rollover contribution to a Roth IRA from another such account, or from an individual retirement plan, but only if such rollover contribution meets the requirements of section 408(d)(3). Such term includes a rollover contribution described in section 402A(c)(3)(A). For purposes of section 408(d)(3)(B), there shall be disregarded any qualified rollover contribution from an individual retirement plan (other than a Roth IRA) to a Roth IRA.

Author's Note. Code Section 408A(e), as in effect prior to the amendments made by the Pension Protection Act of 2006 (Pub .L. No. 109-280), was amended by the Heroes Earnings Assistance and Relief Tax Act of 2008 (HEART), Section 109 (Pub. L. No. 110-245). The amendment (below) generally applies to distributions on or before December 31, 2007, and to deaths from injuries occurring on or after June 17, 2008, the date the HEART Act was enacted.

(e) QUALIFIED ROLLOVER CONTRIBUTION.—For purposes of this section—

(1) IN GENERAL.—The term "qualified rollover contribution" means a rollover contribution to a Roth IRA from another such account, or from an individual retirement plan, but only if such rollover contribution meets the requirements of section 408(d)(3). Such term includes a rollover contribution described in section 402A(c)(3)(A). For purposes of section 408(d)(3)(B), there shall be disregarded any qualified rollover contribution from an individual retirement plan (other than a Roth IRA) to a Roth IRA.

(2) MILITARY DEATH GRATUITY.—

(A) IN GENERAL.—The term "qualified rollover contribution" includes a contribution to a Roth IRA maintained for the benefit of an individual made before the end of the 1-year period beginning on the date on which such individual receives an amount under section 1477 of title 10, United States Code, or section 1967 of title 38 of such Code, with respect to a person, to the extent that such contribution does not exceed—

(i) the sum of the amounts received during such period by such individual under such sections with respect to such person, reduced by

(ii) the amounts so received which were contributed to a Coverdell education savings account under section 530(d)(9).

(B) ANNUAL LIMIT ON NUMBER OF ROLLOVERS NOT TO APPLY.—Section 408(d)(3)(B) shall not apply with respect to amounts treated as a rollover by subparagraph (A).

(C) APPLICATION OF SECTION 72.—For purposes of applying section 72 in the case of a distribution which is not a qualified distribution, the amount treated as a rollover by reason of subparagraph (A) shall be treated as investment in the contract.

Author's Note. Effective Date—Application Of Amendments To Deaths From Injuries Occurring On Or After October 7, 2001, And Before Enactment. The amendments to Code Section 408A(e) apply to any contribution of a military death gratuity (as defined above and below), for deaths from injuries occurring on or after October 7, 2001, and before June 17, 2008, the date of the enactment of the HEART Act, if such contribution is made not later than 1 year after June 17, 2008.

Author's Note. Code Section 408A(e), below, as amended by the Pension Protection Act of 2006 (Pub. L. No. 109-280), applies to distributions after December 31, 2007. This subsection was further amended by the Heroes Earnings Assistance and Relief Tax Act of 2008 (HEART), Section 109 (Pub. L. No. 110-245). See above Author's Note.

(e) QUALIFIED ROLLOVER CONTRIBUTION.—For purposes of this section, the term "qualified rollover contribution" means a rollover contribution—

(1) to a Roth IRA from another such account,

(2) from an eligible retirement plan, but only if—

(A) in the case of an individual retirement plan, such rollover contribution meets the requirements of section 408(d)(3), and

(B) in the case of any eligible retirement plan (as defined in section 402(c)(8)(B) other than clauses (i) and (ii) thereof), such rollover contribution meets the requirements of section 402(c), 403(b)(8), or 457(e)(16), as applicable.

For purposes of section 408(d)(3)(B), there shall be disregarded any qualified rollover contribution from an individual retirement plan (other than a Roth IRA) to a Roth IRA.

Author's Note. Code Section 408A(e), as in effect after to the amendments made by the Pension Protection Act of 2006 (Pub .L. No. 109-280), was amended by the Heroes Earnings Assistance and Relief Tax Act of 2008 (HEART), Section 109 (Pub. L. No. 110-245). The amendment (below) generally applies to taxable years beginning after December 31, 2007, and to deaths from injuries occurring on or after June 17, 2008, the date the HEART Act was enacted.

(e) Qualified Rollover Contribution.—For purposes of this section—

(1) IN GENERAL.—The term "qualified rollover contribution" means a rollover contribution—

(A) to a Roth IRA from another such account,

(B) from an eligible retirement plan, but only if—

(i) in the case of an individual retirement plan, such rollover contribution meets the requirements of section 408(d)(3), and

(ii) in the case of any eligible retirement plan (as defined in section 402(c)(8)(B) other than clauses (i) and (ii) thereof), such rollover contribution meets the requirements of section 402(c), 403(b)(8), or 457(e)(16), as applicable.

For purposes of section 408(d)(3)(B), there shall be disregarded any qualified rollover contribution from an individual retirement plan (other than a Roth IRA) to a Roth IRA.

(2) MILITARY DEATH GRATUITY. —

(A) IN GENERAL.—The term "qualified rollover contribution" includes a contribution to a Roth IRA maintained for the benefit of an individual made before the end of the 1-year period beginning on the date on which such individual receives an amount under section 1477 of title 10, United States Code, or section 1967 of title 38 of such Code, with respect to a person, to the extent that such contribution does not exceed—

(i) the sum of the amounts received during such period by such individual under such sections with respect to such person, reduced by

(ii) the amounts so received which were contributed to a Coverdell education savings account under section 530(d)(9).

(B) ANNUAL LIMIT ON NUMBER OF ROLLOVERS NOT TO APPLY.—Section 408(d)(3)(B) shall not apply with respect to amounts treated as a rollover by the subparagraph (A).

(C) APPLICATION OF SECTION 72.—For purposes of applying section 72 in the case of a distribution which is not a qualified distribution, the amount treated as a rollover by reason of subparagraph (A) shall be treated as investment in the contract.

(f) INDIVIDUAL RETIREMENT PLAN.—For purposes of this section—

(1) a simplified employee pension or a simple retirement account may not be designated as a Roth IRA; and

(2) contributions to any such pension or account shall not be taken into account for purposes of subsection (c)(2)(B).

Appendix C

IRA Legacy Trust—Sample Provisions

The IRA Legacy Trust^{sm} is a service mark of Robert S. Keebler, CPA, MST.

Peter M. Caplan
IRA Legacy Family Revocable Trust ^{sm}

For use by Legal Counsel only

I, **Peter M. Caplan**, hereinafter referred to as "Trustor," currently residing in Green Bay, Wisconsin, hereby make this agreement between myself and the initial Trustee of the **Peter M. Caplan IRA Legacy Family Trust**. The Trustee agrees to hold, administer, and distribute any assets which are hereby transferred to this Trust and any assets which hereafter may be transferred to this Trust under the terms, provisions, and conditions set forth below.

Article I—Revocation—***

*Article II—Name of Trust—*This Trust shall forever be known as the **Peter M. Caplan IRA Legacy Family Trust**.

*Article III—Inter Vivos Investment Management—*The Trustee shall have no duty to invest the Trust corpus during Trustor's lifetime unless specifically directed by the Trustor. The Trustee shall accumulate any income received and add such income to corpus. Upon receiving written instructions from the Trustor, the Trustee shall collect and return any corpus or accumulated income to the Trustor within reasonable time.

*Article IV—IRA Information—*The Trustor intends, through a properly executed Beneficiary Designation Form, to name the Trustee as the beneficiary of certain Retirement Assets. Although it is Trustor's intent that this Trust be a qualified "designated beneficiary" as that term is used in Internal Revenue Code Section 401(a)(9), this Trust shall not be construed or interpreted as a beneficiary designation of any accounts noted herein or on exhibits attached hereto, nor shall this Trust be construed as an assignment of any interest in any of the aforesaid plans or accounts. The Trustor expressly reserves the right during the Trustor's lifetime to create, modify, and amend beneficiary designations regarding any and all Retirement Assets, accounts, or other assets that may now or hereafter be payable to this Trust.

Information regarding assets the Trustor currently intends to transfer to this Trust is set forth on the attached **Exhibit I**. This information includes:

1. A list of the currently existing plans and accounts that will become payable to this Trust at the death of the Trustor.

2. A list of tax basis information of any nondeductible IRA and Roth IRA that the Trustor currently intends to become payable to this Trust at his death.

3. A list of the dates on which the Trustor established the plans and accounts referred to above.

Article V—Administration Upon Death of Trustor—

1. After the death of the Trustor, the Trustee shall hold, administer, manage, and distribute the Trust Estate subject to the terms of this Trust and the following terms and conditions:

    A. *Annual Distributions*—The Trustee may accumulate the income in Trust or may, at any time, distribute any part or all of the net income and corpus of this Trust to, or for the benefit of, the Trustor's spouse and lineal descendants as the Trustee shall determine to be necessary or advisable for each such beneficiary's health, education, maintenance, and support in such person's accustomed manner of living. Subject to these standards, all distributions of income and corpus shall be at such times and in such amounts as the Trustee determines. The Trustee shall have the power to refrain from making distributions to any one or more individuals among whom distributions could be made or make distributions in unequal amounts to one or more beneficiaries as in the Trustee's sole discretion is deemed appropriate. Attached as **Exhibit II** is a list showing the names, dates of birth, and social security numbers of the Trustor's spouse and lineal descendants living as of the date of this Trust instrument.

    B. *Distribution Priority*—If funds available to the Trustor's spouse from sources other than this Trust are known by the Trustee to be inadequate for the health, education, maintenance, and support in said spouse's accustomed manner of living, it is the Trustor's desire that the Trustee give first consideration to the health, education, maintenance, and support in said spouse's accustomed manner of living in making discretionary distributions.

2. *Minimum Distributions*—After the death of the Trustor, the Trustee shall withdraw the required minimum distributions from any Retirement Asset subject to the minimum distribution rules of IRC Section 401(a)(9) and regulations thereunder. The Trustor believes that the long-term needs of the beneficiaries will be best met by utilizing other trust assets and other resources before liquidating any Retirement Asset payable to this Trust.

3. *Accounting Provisions*—The Trustor directs the Trustee to treat distributions from any Retirement Asset as income of the Trust to the extent that the distribution represents income generated or deemed to be generated by such plan or individual retirement account, notwithstanding the treatment of such portion of the plan or IRA distribution under State law concerning the determination of income and corpus for trust accounting purposes.

4. *Qualified Distributions*—Prior to taking any IRA distribution, the Trustee shall determine when any Roth IRA was established and determine whether a distribution will be a qualified distribution as defined in IRC Section 408A(d)(2), as amended, or would be subject to any State or Federal penalty taxes. The Trustee shall take reasonable measures to ensure treatment as a qualified distribution and to reduce or avoid penalty taxes.

5. *Disclaimer*—The Trustor's spouse may disclaim any interest in this Trust or all or any portion of the assets added to this Trust by reason of the Trustor's death in accordance with the provisions of IRC Section 2518 and applicable local law. Any portion disclaimed shall be held in a separate trust and administered under the same terms and conditions set forth herein for the benefit of the beneficiaries other than the Trustor's spouse.

6. *Designated Beneficiary Provisions*—The Trustee shall comply with the procedural requirements of the Code and Regulations (or applicable proposed Regulations) to allow the beneficiaries of the Trust to be treated as being designated beneficiaries of the Retirement Assets for purposes of determining the distribution period under IRC Section 401(a)(9). These requirements are currently set forth in Treasury Regulations Section 1.401(a)(9)-4, Q&A 5 and 6 and require certain documentation to be furnished to the plan administrator by the October 31 of the year following the year of the death of the Trustor.

Article VI—Limited Testamentary Power of Appointment Vested in Spouse—The Trustor's spouse shall have the power, exercisable solely by specific reference in a Last Will and Testament, to appoint all or any part of the assets of this Trust, to or for the benefit of any one or more of the Trustor's lineal descendants, in Trust or otherwise, as the Trustor's spouse shall choose. This limited testamentary power of appointment shall not apply to any property which has been received by this Trust because of a disclaimer executed by the Trustor's spouse, nor shall such limited power of appointment apply to such property held in this Trust (or any trust created hereunder) with respect to which Trustor's spouse disclaimed an interest.

Article VII—Distribution of Remaining Trust Property—Upon the death of the Trustor's spouse, or upon the Trustor's death in the event that the Trustor's spouse dies first, the Trustee shall distribute all of the property remaining in this Trust, and not disposed of by the effective exercise of the special testamentary power of appointment granted above, as follows:

1. All property shall be distributed, in money and/or in kind, in equal shares to the Trustor's then living children, and to the issue of any deceased child by right of representation.

2. If none of the Trustor's lineal descendants are then living, all the properties remaining distributable from this Trust shall be distributed as provided in Article XV, Paragraph 7.

3. *Payment to Beneficiary Under Age 25*—Notwithstanding the above, if the Trustee would at any time be required to make a distribution in termination of this Trust to a beneficiary who is under the age of 25, the Trustee, in the Trustee's sole discretion may hold such amount in this Trust for said beneficiary until that person has reached age 25. After the creation of this separate trust, the Trustee may pay to or use for the benefit of the trust beneficiary such amount of the income and corpus as the Trustee, in the Trustee's sole discretion and judgment, deems necessary and advisable for the beneficiary's health, support, maintenance, and education, even if

such distribution should exhaust the Trust or Trust share herein established. Any income earned during this period and not distributed to the trust beneficiary shall be accumulated and added to the corpus of the trust. If a trust beneficiary dies after the creation of a Trust under this paragraph and before final trust distribution, the remaining trust corpus shall be distributed to that trust beneficiary's issue by right of representation. If the beneficiary has no issue, the Trust share shall be distributed as provided in Article XV, Paragraph 7.

*Article VIII—Spendthrift Provision—****

*Article IX—Successor Trustees—****

*Article X—Annual Fiduciary Accounting—****

Article XI—Early Termination of Trust—The Trustor's intended purposes in creating this Trust and any following Trusts are to conserve the corpus of the Trust and IRAs payable to this Trust for the benefit of the Trustor's family, to achieve savings in income taxes, generation-skipping taxes, and death taxes, and to provide for the financial needs and benefit of the Trustor's spouse and issue. Notwithstanding whatever may be provided herein to the contrary, if in the opinion of the Trustee there are changes in the law, including tax law, or other circumstances which would frustrate the Trustor's purposes, or if in the Trustee's opinion the amount held in this Trust or any Trust or Trust share herein created is insufficient to justify the administrative expense of continuing such Trust or Trust share, the Trustee may terminate a Trust or Trust share, either all or in part. The Trustee shall have the power to terminate a Trust or Trust share under this Paragraph without obtaining the approval of any court. On termination of the Trust or Trust share hereunder, the Trust assets shall be distributed to the then living beneficiary or beneficiaries by right of representation. In default thereof, the Trust assets shall be distributed under the terms of Article XV, Paragraph 7.

*Article XII—Powers and Duties of the Trustee—****

Powers Related to Retirement Assets

   a. *Account Management*—The Trustee may deal with and make elections with respect to Retirement Assets. The Trustee shall have the power to create subaccounts within such accounts and to distribute accounts or subaccounts as inherited accounts when appropriate.

   b. *Withdrawals of Proceeds*—The Trustee shall have the right in his/her or its sole discretion to withdraw any or all of the remaining qualified plan benefit, IRA balance, Roth IRA balance, or 403(b) account balance, or to direct that the plan benefit or individual retirement account be paid directly to a beneficiary of the Trust who is entitled to income or corpus of the Trust.

   c. *Investment Management*—After the death of the Trustor, the Trustee shall have the right to administer, invest, manage, transfer, and work with the Trustor's IRA, Roth IRA, annuity or plan Custodian with the same rights the Trustor held prior to death. The Trustee, to the extent permitted by law shall have the right to transfer an IRA, Roth IRA, annuity or plan from one custodian to another custodian. The Trustee shall not have the right to change the beneficiary of any IRA, Roth IRA, annuity or plan to any party or entity other then this Trust.

d. *Change Custodians*—The Trustee shall have the power to change custodians and investment advisors of Individual Retirement Accounts and qualified plans and to provide directives for the investment and management of such accounts or plans.

e. *Penalty on Early Withdrawal*—The Trustee may pay any penalty tax imposed because of the early withdrawal of funds from a qualified plan, or IRA, including the withdrawal of funds from a Roth IRA within five years of its creation, in the event that in the Trustee's sole discretion such withdrawal is necessary or is in the best interest of the Trust or its beneficiaries.

f. *Cooperation with Spouse*—The Trustee is instructed to cooperate with the Trustor's surviving spouse in accomplishing transfer or rollover of IRAs or qualified plans in which the Trustor's surviving spouse has a legal interest.

g. *Conversion of IRAs*—The Trustee may convert IRAs held by the Trust to Roth IRAs as those accounts are defined in Internal Revenue Code section 408A, to the extent permitted by law. The Trustee may convert qualified plans to IRAs and generally deal with IRAs and retirement accounts to the extent permitted by the applicable law.

h. *Final Distributions*—The Trustee is encouraged to work with the executor of the Trustor's estate to determine whether sufficient distributions have been taken from Retirement Assets in the year of the Trustor's death to fully fund the required minimum distributions for that year.

i. *Trustee's Limited Power to Amend*—Trustee is authorized to amend the terms of this Trust Agreement in any manner that may be required so that this Trust Agreement will comply with the current or future requirements as a Designated Beneficiary, as the term is defined under IRC § 401(a)(9) and applicable regulations thereunder. Any such amendment may by its terms apply retroactively to the inception of the Trust Agreement.

j. Notwithstanding other provisions of this Trust agreement, the Trustee may fully pay out the interest of any beneficiary who is not an "individual," and is therefore not a qualified beneficiary within the meaning of IRC § 401(a)(9) and the Regulations and Proposed Regulations thereunder, by the September 30 of the year following the year of the Trustor's death, if in the Trustee's judgment failure to do so would result in acceleration of distributions from retirement accounts to the detriment of the other beneficiaries or the objectives of this Trust.

k. In the event that the value of the beneficial interest of any beneficiary who is not a qualified "individual" is not readily ascertainable, the Trustee shall have the authority to negotiate and finalize compromise settlement agreements with such beneficiary. It is intended that such settlements would be reached for the purpose of allowing the trustee to pay out the interest of such non qualified beneficiary thereby qualifying this trust as a trust for which the remaining qualified beneficiary's or beneficiaries' life expectancy will be used to determine required distributions. It is further provided that such settlements must be finalized prior to September 30 the year following the year of the death of the Trustor/Owner of retirement assets payable to this trust.

l. Certain provisions of this Trust Agreement are intended to inform and assist the Trustee to comply with the tax Code and Regulations that were in effect at the time of the execution of the Trust document. It is not the intent of the Trustor to impose additional procedural restrictions or requirements that would not otherwise be imposed by law. To the extent that future changes in the law should diminish procedural requirements that do not protect the interests of the beneficiaries or serve the purposes of this Trust, such restrictions or requirements otherwise imposed by this document shall be of no effect.

Article XIII—Summary of Trust Terms—

1. *Qualified Plan—****
2. *Roth IRA—****
3. *IRA—****
4. *403(b) Plan—****
5. *Qualified Distribution—****
6. *Nonqualified Distribution—****
7. *Basis—Roth IRA—****
8. *Basis—Roth conversion IRA—****
9. *Basis—Nondeductible IRAs—****
10. *Internal Revenue Code—****
11. *Retirement Assets—****
12. *Oldest Primary Beneficiary*—The Oldest Primary Beneficiary is the oldest Trust beneficiary who is entitled to distributions under the terms of this Trust determined as of September 30 of the year following the year of the Trustor's death.

Article XIV—Generation-Skipping Transfer Taxes—***

Article XV—Miscellaneous

1. *Controlling Law*—Irrespective of the situs of the Trust or Trusts created under this Trust Agreement, it is the Trustor's direction that the law of the State of *** shall be controlling for purposes of determining the validity of such Trusts and in the interpretation to be given to the provisions of this Trust Agreement, but that the law of the jurisdiction in which a Trust is being administered shall govern its administration.

2. *Afterborn Issue*—***

3. *Adoption*—For purposes of this Trust Agreement, a legally adopted child shall be considered a natural born child of the adoptive parent. Accordingly, any reference to "issue" and "child" shall include adopted children or series of adopted children in the line of descent. Further, any reference to "issue" and "child" shall refer to the children and issue of the Trustor. Notwithstanding the foregoing, or any other provisions contained in this Trust Agreement, any individual adopted or who may be adopted who is older than the Trustor's spouse shall be deemed to have predeceased the Trustor.

4. *Paragraph Headings*—The underlined headings as to contents of particular paragraphs herein are inserted only for convenience and are in no way to be construed as a part of the provisions of this instrument or as a limitation on the scope of the particular paragraphs to which they refer.

5. *Use of Words*—The use of words of the masculine gender is intended to include, wherever appropriate, the feminine gender, and vice versa. The use of words of the singular is intended to include, wherever appropriate, the plural, and vice versa. This applies to descriptions of Trustee, Retirement Assets, and issue.

6. *Partial Invalidity*—If any provision of this Trust is void, unenforceable, or invalid, the remaining provisions shall nevertheless be valid and carried into effect.

7. *Failure of Beneficiaries*—If at any time prior to final distribution hereunder all the beneficiaries identified by the Trustor are deceased and no other disposition of the property is directed by this Trust, the remaining property of this Trust shall be distributed to the Trustor's lineal descendants by right of representation, provided that any such descendant born before the Oldest Primary Beneficiary shall be deemed deceased. In default thereof, the remaining property of this Trust shall be distributed to the descendants of the Trustor's parents then living by right of representation, provided that any such descendant born before the Oldest Primary Beneficiary shall be deemed deceased. In default thereof, the property shall be distributed to the Trustor's next of kin then living, regardless of how remote their degree of kinship, provided that any such next of kin born before the Oldest Primary Beneficiary shall be deemed deceased.

8. *Beneficiary of Retirement Assets*—It is my intention that all Retirement Assets received by this Trust shall be paid to qualified beneficiaries as that term is used in the Regulations under IRC Section 401(a)(9). Therefore, no benefit from Retirement Assets shall be used by this Trust for the payment of debts, or other nonqualifying distributions at such time as the use would result in the Trust not being a qualified beneficiary. In addition, no benefit shall be paid to a charity or any other person or entity that would not be a qualified beneficiary for purposes of determining required distributions under the provisions of IRC Section 401(a)(9), except that such payment may be made before the beneficiaries of this Trust must be determined, if, as a result of said payment, the nonqualifying beneficiary is

eliminated as a beneficiary of this Trust. This provision shall not apply to any specific bequest to a charity or for a nonqualified person or entity which is funded by Retirement Assets under express language herein.

9. *Charitable Bequests*—I instruct my Trustee to satisfy any charitable bequest or gift, to the extent possible, from property that constitutes income in respect of a decedent

IN WITNESS WHEREOF, this Trust Agreement was executed in duplicate on this _____ day of _____ , 20_____ .

IN THE PRESENCE OF:

_____ (SEAL)

_____

_____ - Trustee

STATE OF _____)

   ss.

COUNTY OF _____)

Personally came before me this _____ day of _____ , 20_____ , the above-named _____ , to me known to be the person who executed the foregoing instrument and acknowledged the same.

   Notary Public, _____ County,

   My Commission Expires:_____

   This instrument was drafted by _____ , Attorney.

EXHIBIT I

   Assets intended to be transferred

EXHIBIT II

   Beneficiaries: names
                     dates of birth
                     addresses
                     Social Security numbers

Harold S. Caplan
IRA Legacy Family Trust sm

(For Benefit of Children and Issue of any Deceased Child—Separate Shares)

For use by Legal Counsel only

I, **Harold S. Caplan**, hereinafter referred to as "Trustor," currently residing in Green Bay, Wisconsin, hereby make this agreement between myself and the initial Trustee of the **Harold S. Caplan IRA Legacy Family Trust**. The Trustee agrees to hold, administer, and distribute any assets which are hereby transferred to this Trust and any assets which hereafter may be transferred to this Trust under the terms, provisions and conditions set forth below.

Article I—Revocation—***

*Article II—Name of Trust—*This Trust shall forever be known as the **Harold S. Caplan IRA Legacy Family Trust**.

*Article III—Inter Vivos Investment Management—*The Trustee shall have no duty to invest the Trust corpus during Trustor's lifetime unless specifically directed by the Trustor. The Trustee shall accumulate any income received and add such income to corpus. Upon receiving written instructions from Trustor, the Trustee shall collect and return any corpus or accumulated income to the Trustor within a reasonable time.

*Article IV—IRA Information—*The Trustor intends, through a properly executed Beneficiary Designation Form, to name the Trustee as the beneficiary of certain Retirement Assets. Although it is Trustor's intent that this Trust be a qualified "designated beneficiary" as that term is used in Internal Revenue Code section 401(a)(9), this Trust shall not be construed or interpreted as a beneficiary designation of any accounts noted herein or on exhibits attached hereto, nor shall this trust be construed as an assignment of any interest in any of the aforesaid plans or accounts. The Trustor expressly reserves the right during the Trustor's lifetime to create, modify and amend beneficiary designations regarding any and all Retirement Assets, accounts or other assets that may now or hereafter be payable to this trust.

Information regarding assets the Trustor currently intends to transfer to this Trust is set forth on the attached **Exhibit I**. This information includes:

1. A list of the currently existing plans and accounts that will become payable to this trust at the death of the Trustor.

2. A list of tax basis information of any nondeductible IRA and Roth IRA that the Trustor currently intends to become payable to this Trust at his death.

3. A list of the dates on which the Trustor established the plans and accounts referred to above.

Article V—Administration Upon Death of Trustor

1. After the death of the Trustor, the Trustee shall divide the Trust Estate into separate shares and distribute such shares subject to the terms of this Trust and the following terms and conditions. If any share lapses, then that share shall be divided and added to the other shares in proportion to their relative percentages to be distributed as if it had been an original part thereof.

   A. Fifty Percent (50%) of the Trust Estate shall be set aside for my child, John Caplan, if surviving, to be held, administered and distributed as set forth below. If John Caplan does not survive me, Fifty Percent (50%) of the Trust Estate shall be set aside for John Caplan's issue by right of representation.

   B. Fifty Percent (50%) of the Trust Estate shall be set aside for my child, Julie Caplan, if surviving, to be held, administered and distributed as set forth below. If Julie Caplan does not survive me, Fifty Percent (50%) of the Trust Estate shall be set aside for Julie Caplan's issue by right of representation.

2. The shares set aside pursuant to the provisions above shall constitute separate and distinct trusts and shall be held, administered and distributed by the Trustee as follows:

   A. *Withdrawal from Retirement Assets* In the year of death and each subsequent year, the Trustee shall withdraw from such Retirement Assets made payable to this trust, the Required Minimum Distribution(s) for such year. Additionally, the Trustee may withdraw so much of the net income and principal of Retirement Assets payable to this trust as is necessary for health, education, support or maintenance of a trust share beneficiary.

   B. *Distributions of Income and Corpus* The Trustee may accumulate the income in Trust or may, at any time, distribute any part or all of the net income and corpus of this Trust to, or for the benefit of, a trust share beneficiary, as the Trustee shall determine to be necessary or advisable for each such beneficiary's health, education, maintenance and support. If funds available to such beneficiary from sources other than this Trust are known by the Trustee to be adequate for such beneficiary's health, education, maintenance and support, it is the Trustor's desire that the Trustee make no distribution of income or corpus for such beneficiary's benefit from this Trust. Subject to these standards, all distributions of income and corpus shall be at such times and in such amounts as the Trustee determines. The Trustee shall have the power to refrain from making distributions to any one or more individuals among whom distributions could be made or make distributions in unequal amounts to one or more beneficiaries as in the Trustee's sole discretion is deemed appropriate.

3. *Minimum Distributions*—After the death of the Trustor, the Trustee shall withdraw the required minimum distributions from any Retirement Asset

subject to the minimum distribution rules of IRC § 401(a)(9) and regulations thereunder. The Trustor believes that the long-term needs of the beneficiaries will be best met by utilizing other trust assets and other resources before liquidating any Retirement Asset payable to this Trust.

4. *Accounting Provisions.* The Trustor directs the Trustee to treat distributions from any Retirement Asset as income of the Trust to the extent that the distribution represents income generated or deemed to be generated by such plan or individual retirement account, notwithstanding the treatment of such portion of the plan or IRA distribution under State law concerning the determination of income and corpus for trust accounting purposes.

5. *Qualified Distributions.* Prior to taking any IRA distribution, the Trustee shall determine when any Roth IRA was established and determine whether a distribution will be a qualified distribution as defined in IRC § 408A(d)(2), as amended, or would be subject to any State or Federal penalty taxes. The Trustee shall take reasonable measures to ensure treatment as a qualified distribution and to reduce or avoid penalty taxes.

6. *Designated Beneficiary Provisions.* The Trustee shall comply with the procedural requirements of the Code and Regulations (or applicable proposed Regulations) to allow the beneficiaries of the Trust to be treated as being designated beneficiaries of the Retirement Assets for purposes of determining the distribution period under IRC § 401(a)(9). These requirements are currently set forth in Treas. Reg. § 1.401(a)(9)-4 Q&A 5 and Q&A 6 and require certain documentation to be furnished to the plan administrator by October 31 of the year following the year of the death of the Trustor.

7. *Creation of Separate Shares.* When, in accordance with Treas. Reg. § 1.401(a)(9)-8, Separate Accounts or Segregated Shares are created under the terms of a beneficiary designation(s), naming this Trust as beneficiary, the Trustee shall create Separate Shares or Segregated Accounts, within the definition of Treas. Reg. § 1.401(a)(9)-8 Q&A 3, as directed. It is the intention of this provision to allow said beneficiaries to enjoy the benefit of distributions from any IRA(s) or qualified plans over their separate life expectancies.

Article VI—Distribution of Remaining Trust Property—Upon the death of the Trustor and at such time as the Beneficiary for whom the Separate Trust Share was established has attained the age of _____ (____) years, the Trustee shall distribute all of the property remaining in such Separate Trust Share as follows:

1. All property shall be distributed, in money and/or in kind to the Beneficiary for whom the Separate Trust Share was established.

2. If the Beneficiary for whom the Separate Trust Share was established dies before final distribution of the Trust, all property shall be distributed, in money and/or in kind the such Beneficiary's issue by right of representation.

3. If the beneficiary has no living issue, the Trust share shall be distributed as provided in Article XIV, Paragraph 7.

4. *Payment to Beneficiary Under Age 25* Notwithstanding the above, if the Trustee would at any time be required to make a distribution in termination of this Trust to a beneficiary who is under the age of 25 years, the Trustee, in the Trustee's sole discretion may hold such amount in this Trust for said beneficiary until that person has reached age 25. After the creation of this separate trust, the Trustee may pay to or use for the benefit of the trust beneficiary such amount of the income and corpus as the Trustee in the Trustee's sole discretion and judgment deems necessary and advisable for the beneficiary's health, education, maintenance and support, even if such distribution should exhaust the Trust or Trust share herein established. Any income earned during this period and not distributed to the trust beneficiary shall be accumulated and added to the corpus of the trust. If a trust beneficiary dies after the creation of a Trust under this paragraph and before final trust distribution, the remaining trust corpus shall be distributed to that trust beneficiary's issue by right of representation. If the beneficiary has no issue, the Trust share shall be distributed as provided in Article XIV, Paragraph 7.

Article VII—Spendthrift Provision— * * *

Article VIII—Successor Trustees— * * *

Article IX—Annual Fiduciary Accounting— * * *

*Article X—Early Termination of Trust—*The Trustor's intended purposes in creating this Trust and any following Trusts are to conserve the corpus of the Trust and IRAs payable to this Trust for the benefit of the Trustor's family, to achieve savings in income taxes, generation-skipping taxes and death taxes, and to provide for the financial needs and benefit of the Trustor's issue. Notwithstanding whatever may be provided herein to the contrary, if in the opinion of the Trustee there are changes in the law, including tax law, or other circumstances which would frustrate the Trustor's purposes, or if in the Trustee's opinion the amount held in this Trust or any Trust or Trust share herein created is insufficient to justify the administrative expense of continuing such Trust or Trust share, the Trustee may terminate a Trust or Trust share, either all or in part. The Trustees shall have the power to terminate a Trust or Trust share under this Paragraph without obtaining the approval of any court. On termination of the trust or trust share hereunder, the trust assets shall be distributed to the then living beneficiary or beneficiaries by right of representation. In default thereof, the Trust assets shall be distributed under the terms of Article XIV, Paragraph 7.

Article XI—Powers and Duties of the Trustee— * * *

Powers Related to Retirement Assets

a. *Account Management—*The Trustee may deal with and make elections with respect to Retirement Assets. The Trustee shall have the power to create subaccounts within such accounts and to distribute accounts or subaccount as inherited accounts when appropriate.

b. *Withdrawals of Proceeds*—***

c. *Investment Management*—***

d. *Change Custodians*—***

e. *Penalty on Early Withdrawal*—***

f. *Cooperation with Spouse*—***

g. *Conversion of IRAs*—***

h. *Final Distributions*—The Trustee is encouraged to work with the executor of the Trustor's estate to determine whether sufficient distributions have been taken from Retirement Assets in the year of the Trustor's death to fully fund the required minimum distributions for that year.

i. *Trustee's Limited Power to Amend*—***

j. Notwithstanding other provisions of this Trust agreement, the Trustee may fully payout the interest of any beneficiary who is not an "individual," and is therefore not a qualified beneficiary within the meaning of IRC § 401(a)(9) and the Regulations and Proposed Regulations thereunder, by the September 30 of the year following the year of the Trustor's death, if in the Trustee's judgment failure to do so would result in acceleration of distributions from retirement accounts to the detriment of the other beneficiaries or the objectives of this Trust.

k. In the event that the value of the beneficial interest of any beneficiary who is not a qualified "individual" is not readily ascertainable, the Trustee shall have the authority to negotiate and finalize compromise settlement agreements with such beneficiary. It is intended that such settlements would be reached for the purpose of allowing the trustee to pay out the interest of such non qualified beneficiary thereby qualifying this trust as a trust for which the remaining qualified beneficiary's or beneficiaries' life expectancy will be used to determine required distributions. It is further provided that such settlements must be finalized prior to September 30 of the year following the year of the death of the Trustor/owner of retirement assets payable to this trust.

3. *Facility of Payment*—***

4. *Creation of Separate Shares and Allocation of Deceased Trustor's Generation Skipping Transfer Tax Exemption*—***

5. *Separate Trust for Property with Different Inclusion Ratio*—***

6. *Trustee Relieved from Bond and Court Accounting*—***

7. *Change of Situs.* The Trustee may change the situs and controlling law of this Trust or any following Trust created by this instrument if the Trustee, in the Trustee's sole discretion, determines that such new situs and controlling law would further protect the assets of this Trust, including Individual Retirement Accounts and Roth IRAs, diminish tax burden of this Trust or its beneficiaries, result in more efficient administration or otherwise serve the needs and best interests of the Trust and its beneficiaries.

In considering any such change the Trustee is encouraged to seek advice of competent CPAs and legal counsel in determining the advantages and disadvantages including tax benefits and creditor protection afforded to Individual Retirement Accounts which may be a part of the Trust corpus.

8. **Trustee Fees.**—***

9. **Perpetuities.** Notwithstanding any other provisions of this Trust, no trust created by this agreement shall extend beyond the period permitted by applicable State law nor shall any interest which under applicable law is required to vest indefeasibly continue beyond the allowed time. In the event that any applicable State law would require termination of this trust or indefeasible vesting of an interest in this Trust, or any trust or trust share created by this trust, within a certain time period, the trust or trust share affected shall terminate or vest, as required, on the later of either (1) the last day on which the trust or trust share could exist (or exist without vesting) pursuant to applicable law or (2) the day before the date on which such law becomes applicable. On termination of the trust or trust share hereunder, the trust assets shall be distributed to the then living beneficiary or beneficiaries by right of representation. In default thereof, the Trust assets shall be distributed under the terms of Article XV, Paragraph 7.

Article XII—Summary of Trust Terms

1. **Qualified Plan**—***
2. **Roth IRA**—***
3. **IRA**—***
4. **403(b) Plan**—***
5. **Qualified Distribution**—***
6. **Nonqualified Distribution**—***
7. **Basis-Roth IRA**—***
8. **Basis-Roth conversion IRA**—***
9. **Basis-Nondeductible IRAs**—***
10. **Internal Revenue Code**—***
11. **Retirement Assets**—***
12. **Oldest Primary Beneficiary**—The Oldest Primary Beneficiary is the oldest Trust beneficiary who is entitled to distributions under the terms of this Trust determined as of September 30th of the year following the year of the Trustor's death.

Article XIII—Generation Skipping Transfer Taxes

If any generation-skipping tax is imposed on any distribution from this Trust, as a taxable distribution or taxable termination, the Trustee may pay, from the Trust Estate,***.

Article XIV—Miscellaneous

1. *Controlling Law*—Irrespective of the situs of the trust or Trusts created under this Trust Agreement, it is the Trustor's direction that the law of the State of*** shall be controlling for purposes of determining the validity of such Trusts and in the interpretation to be given to the provisions of this Trust Agreement, but that the law of the jurisdiction in which a Trust is being administered shall govern it administration.

2. *Afterborn Issue*—***

3. *Adoption*—For purposes of this Trust Agreement, a legally adopted child shall be considered a natural born child of the adoptive parent. Accordingly, any reference to "issue" and "child" shall include adopted children or series of adopted children in the line of descent. Further, any reference to "issue" and "child" shall refer to the children and issue of the Trustor. Notwithstanding the foregoing, or any other provisions contained in this Trust Agreement, any individual adopted or who may be adopted who is older than the Oldest Initial Primary Beneficiary shall be deemed to have predeceased the Trustor.

4. *Paragraph Headings*—***

5. *Use of Words*—***

6. *Partial Invalidity*—***

7. *Failure of Beneficiaries*—If at any time prior to final distribution hereunder, all the beneficiaries identified by the Trustor are deceased and no other disposition of the property is directed by this Trust, the remaining property of this Trust shall be distributed to the Trustor's lineal descendants by right of representation, provided that any such descendant born before the Oldest Primary Beneficiary shall be deemed deceased. In default thereof the property shall be distributed to, the Trustor's next of kin then living, regardless of how remote their degree of kinship is, provided that any such next of kin born before the Oldest Primary Beneficiary shall be deemed deceased. With respect to usage of the term "next of kin," it is my intent to override any State law provision regarding failed transfer, potentially requiring escheat to such State. Rather use of this term is intended to create interests based on consanguinity.

8. *Beneficiary of Retirement Asset*—It is my intention that all Retirement Assets received by this Trust shall be paid to qualified beneficiaries as that term is used in the Regulations under IRC § 401(a)(9). Therefore no benefit from Retirement Assets shall be used by this Trust for the payment of debts or other non-qualifying distributions at such time as the use would result in the Trust not being a qualified beneficiary. In addition, no benefit shall be paid to a charity or any other person or entity that would not be a qualified beneficiary for purposes of determining required distributions under the provisions of IRC § 401(a)(9) except that such payment may be made before the beneficiaries of this Trust must be determined, if, as a result of said payment, the non-qualifying beneficiary is eliminated as a beneficiary of this trust. This provision shall not apply to any specific

bequest to a charity or for a nonqualified person or entity which is funded by Retirement Assets under express language herein.

9. *Charitable Bequests*—***

IN WITNESS WHEREOF, this Trust Agreement was executed in duplicate on this _____ day of _____, 20_____ .

IN THE PRESENCE OF:

_____ (SEAL)

Harold S. Caplan—Trustor

_____ (SEAL)

_____ - Trustee

STATE OF _____)

   ss.

COUNTY OF _____)

Personally came before me this _____ day of _____ , 20_____ , the above-named _____ , to me known to be the person who executed the foregoing instrument and acknowledged the same.

   Notary Public, _____ County,

   My Commission:_____

   This instrument was drafted by _____ , Attorney.

EXHIBIT I

   Assets intended to be transferred

Peter M. Caplan
IRA Legacy Grandchildren's Trust^{sm}

For use by Legal Counsel only

I, **Peter M. Caplan**, hereinafter referred to as "Trustor," currently residing in Green Bay, Wisconsin, hereby make this agreement between myself and the initial Trustee of the **Peter M. Caplan IRA Legacy Grandchildren's Trust**. The Trustee agrees to hold, administer, and distribute any assets which are hereby transferred to this Trust and any assets which hereafter may be transferred to this Trust under the terms, provisions, and conditions set forth below.

Article I—Revocation—***

Article II—Name of Trust

This Trust shall forever be known as the **Peter M. Caplan IRA Legacy Grandchildren's Trust.**

Article III—Inter Vivos Investment Management

The Trustee shall have no duty to invest the Trust corpus during the Trustor's lifetime unless specifically directed by the Trustor.***

Article IV—IRA Information—***

Information regarding assets the Trustor currently intends to transfer to this Trust is set forth on the attached **Exhibit I**. This information includes:***

*Article V—Administration Upon Death of Trustor—*After the death of the Trustor, the Trustee shall hold, administer, manage, and distribute the Trust Estate subject to the terms of this Trust and the following terms and conditions:

1. A. *Withdrawal from Retirement Assets*—In the year of death and each subsequent year, the Trustee shall withdraw from such Retirement Assets made payable to this Trust, the Required Minimum Distribution(s) for such year. Additionally, the Trustee may withdraw so much of the net income and principal of Retirement Assets payable to this Trust as is necessary for health, education, support, or maintenance of the Trustor's grandchildren, and the issue of any deceased grandchildren.

   B. *Distributions of Income and Corpus*—The Trustee may accumulate the income in Trust or may, at any time, distribute any part or all of the net income and corpus of this Trust to, or for the benefit of, the Trustor's grandchildren, and the issue of any deceased grandchildren, as the Trustee shall determine to be necessary or advisable for each such beneficiary's health, education, maintenance, and support. If funds available to such beneficiaries from sources other than this Trust are known by the Trustee to be adequate for their health, education, maintenance, and support, it is the Trustor's desire that the Trustee make no distribution of income or corpus for their benefit from this Trust. Subject to these standards, all distributions of income and corpus shall be at such times and in such amounts as the Trustee determines. The Trustee shall have the power to refrain from making distributions to any one or more individuals among whom distributions could be made or make distributions in unequal amounts to one or more beneficiaries as in the Trustee's sole discretion is deemed appropriate.

Attached as **Exhibit II** is a list showing the names, dates of birth, and Social Security numbers of the Trustor's grandchildren and children of deceased grandchildren living as of the date of this Trust instrument.

2. *Minimum Distributions*—After the death of the Trustor, the Trustee shall withdraw the Required Minimum Distributions from any Retirement Asset subject to the minimum distribution rules of IRC Section 401(a)(9) and regulations thereunder. The Trustor believes that the long-term needs of the beneficiaries will be best met by utilizing other trust assets and other resources before liquidating any Retirement Asset payable to this Trust.

3. *Accounting Provisions*—***

4. *Qualified Distributions*—***

5. *Designated Beneficiary Provisions*—***

6. *Creation of Separate Shares*—***

Article VI—Distribution of Remaining Trust Property—Upon the death of the Trustor and at such time as the youngest living grandchild of the Trustor has attained the age of 25, the Trustee shall distribute all of the property remaining in this Trust as follows:

1. All property shall be distributed, in money and/or in kind, in equal shares, one share to each of the Trustor's then living grandchildren and one share to each issue of any deceased grandchild by right of representation.

2. If none of the above lineal descendants are then living, all the properties remaining distributable from this Trust shall be distributed in accordance with Article XIV, Paragraph 7.

3. *Payment to Beneficiary Under Age 25*—Notwithstanding the above, if the Trustee would at any time be required to make a distribution in termination of this Trust to a beneficiary who is under the age of 25, the Trustee, in the Trustee's sole discretion may hold such amount in this Trust for said beneficiary until that person has reached age 25. After the creation of this separate trust, the Trustee may pay to or use for the benefit of the trust beneficiary such amount of the income and corpus as the Trustee, in the Trustee's sole discretion and judgment, deems necessary and advisable for the beneficiary's health, education, maintenance, and support, even if such distribution should exhaust the Trust or Trust share herein established. Any income earned during this period and not distributed to the trust beneficiary shall be accumulated and added to the corpus of the trust. If a trust beneficiary dies after the creation of a Trust under this paragraph and before final trust distribution, the remaining trust corpus shall

be distributed to that trust beneficiary's issue by right of representation. If the beneficiary has no issue, the Trust share shall be distributed as provided in Article XIV, Paragraph 7.

Article VII—Spendthrift Provision—***

Article VIII—Successor Trustees—***

Article IX—Annual Fiduciary Accounting—***

*Article X—Early Termination of Trust—*The Trustor's intended purposes in creating this Trust and any following Trusts are to conserve the corpus of the Trust and IRAs payable to this Trust for the benefit of the Trustor's family, to achieve savings in income taxes, generation-skipping taxes, and death taxes, and to provide for the financial needs and benefit of the Trustor's issue. Notwithstanding whatever may be provided herein to the contrary, if in the opinion of the Trustee there are changes in the law, including tax law, or other circumstances which would frustrate the Trustor's purposes, or if in the Trustee's opinion the amount held in this Trust or any Trust or Trust share herein created is insufficient to justify the administrative expense of continuing such Trust or Trust share, the Trustee may terminate a Trust or Trust share, either all or in part. The Trustees shall have the power to terminate a Trust or Trust share under this Paragraph without obtaining the approval of any court. On termination of the Trust or Trust share hereunder, the Trust assets shall be distributed to the then living beneficiary or beneficiaries by right of representation. In default thereof, the Trust assets shall be distributed under the terms of Article XIV, Paragraph 7.

Article XI—Powers and Duties of the Trustee—***

   —Powers Related to Retirement Assets—***

Article XII—Summary of Trust Terms—***

*Article XIII—Generation-Skipping Transfer Taxes—*If any generation-skipping tax is imposed on any distribution from this Trust, as a taxable distribution or taxable termination, the Trustee may pay, from the Trust Estate, ***.

Article XIV—Miscellaneous—***

1. *Controlling Law—*Irrespective of the situs of the Trust or Trusts created under this Trust Agreement, it is the Trustor's direction that the law of the State of *** shall be controlling for purposes of determining the validity of such Trusts and in the interpretation to be given to the provisions of this Trust Agreement, but that the law of the jurisdiction in which a Trust is being administered shall govern its administration.

2. *Afterborn Issue—****

3. *Adoption—****

4. *Paragraph Headings—****

5. *Use of Words—****

6. *Partial Invalidity—****

7. *Failure of Beneficiaries*—***
8. *Beneficiary of Retirement Asset*—***
9. *Charitable Bequests*—***

IN WITNESS WHEREOF, this Trust Agreement was executed in duplicate on this _____ day of _____ , 20_____ .

IN THE PRESENCE OF:

_____ (SEAL)

Peter M. Caplan - Trustor

_____ (SEAL)

_____ - Trustee

STATE OF _____)

   ss.

COUNTY OF _____)

Personally came before me this _____ day of _____ , 20_____ , the above-named _____ , to me known to be the person who executed the foregoing instrument and acknowledged the same.

   Notary Public, _____ County,

My Commission Expires:_____

This instrument was drafted by _____ , Attorney.

EXHIBIT I

   Assets intended to be transferred

EXHIBIT II

   Beneficiaries: names
                       dates of birth
                       addresses
                       Social Security numbers

Appendix D

Extracts from Treasury Regulations (As of August 1, 2009)

Preamble, Final Treasury Regulations Section 1.408A (T.D. 8816, 64 FR 5597-5611 (Feb. 4, 1999)), revised by T.D. 9056, 68 FR 23586-23590 (May 5, 2003))

Summary: This document contains final regulations relating to Roth IRAs under section 408A of the Internal Revenue Code (Code). Roth IRAs were created by the Taxpayer Relief Act of 1997 as a new type of IRA that individuals can use beginning in 1998. Section 408A was amended by the Internal Revenue Service Restructuring and Reform Act of 1998. On September 3, 1998, a notice of proposed rulemaking was published in the Federal Register (63 FR 46937) under Code section 408A. Written comments were received regarding the proposed regulations. On December 10, 1998, a public hearing was held on the proposed regulations. The final regulations affect individuals establishing Roth IRAs, beneficiaries under Roth IRAs, and trustees, custodians or issuers of Roth IRAs.

Effective date: The final regulations are effective on February 3, 1999.

Applicability date: The final regulations are applicable to taxable years beginning on or after January 1, 1998, the effective date for section 408A.

* * *

Background

On September 3, 1998, a notice of proposed rulemaking was published in the Federal Register (63 FR 46937) under section 408A of the Internal Revenue Code

(Code). The proposed regulations provide guidance on section 408A of the Code, which was added by section 302 of the Taxpayer Relief Act of 1997, Public Law 105-34 (111 Stat. 788), and established the Roth IRA as a new type of individual retirement plan, effective for taxable years beginning on or after January 1, 1998. The provisions of section 408A were amended by the Internal Revenue Service Restructuring and Reform Act of 1998, Public Law 105-206 (112 Stat. 685). In addition, Notice 98-50 (1998-44 I.R.B. 10) provides guidance on reconverting an amount that had previously been converted and recharacterized. This notice solicited public comments concerning reconversions.

Written comments were received on the proposed regulations and Notice 98-50. A public hearing was held on the proposed regulations and Notice 98-50 on December 10, 1998. After consideration of all the comments, the proposed regulations under section 408A are adopted as revised by this Treasury decision.

Explanation of Provisions

Overview

A Roth IRA generally is treated under the Code like a traditional IRA with several significant exceptions. Similar to traditional IRAs, income on undistributed amounts accumulated under Roth IRAs is exempt from Federal income tax, and contributions to Roth IRAs are subject to specific limitations. Unlike traditional IRAs, contributions to Roth IRAs cannot be deducted from gross income, but qualified distributions from Roth IRAs are excludable from gross income.

In general, comments received on the proposed regulations did not request significant changes. Thus, the final regulations retain the general structure and substance of the proposed regulations.

General Provisions and Establishment of Roth IRAs

Commentators asked for clarification regarding whether a Roth IRA may be established for the benefit of a minor child or anyone else who lacks the legal capacity to act on his or her own behalf. On this point, the IRS and Treasury intend that the rules for traditional IRAs also apply to Roth IRAs. Thus, for example, a parent or guardian of a minor child may establish a Roth IRA on behalf of the minor child. However, in the case of any contribution to a Roth IRA established for a minor child, the compensation of the child for the taxable year for which the contribution is made must satisfy the compensation requirements of section 408A(c) and section 1.408A-3.

Regular Contributions

Several commentators requested clarification of the treatment of excess Roth IRA contributions under sections 4973, 408(d)(5), and 219(f)(6). Commentators asked for clarification regarding the removal of excess Roth IRA contributions after the contributor's Federal tax return due date has passed. The final regulations clarify that, pursuant to section 4973(f), excess contributions may be applied, on a year-by-year basis, against the annual limit for regular contributions to the extent that the Roth IRA owner is eligible to make regular Roth IRA contributions for a taxable year but does not otherwise do so. However, in response to several requests for clarification, the IRS and Treasury note that the rules under section 408(d)(5) for the tax-free distribution of certain excess traditional IRA contributions after the IRA owner's Federal income tax return due date do not apply to Roth IRAs because Roth IRA contributions are always tax-free on distribution (except to the extent that they accelerate income inclusion under the 4-year spread). Similarly, section 219(f)(6), which provides for the deductibility of excess traditional IRA contributions in subsequent taxable years, has no application to Roth IRAs because contributions to Roth IRAs are never deductible.

Another commentator asked for clarification whether contributions to education IRAs are disregarded for purposes of applying the limitation on regular contributions to Roth IRAs. No change has been made to the final regulations on this point because the final regulations retain the definition of an IRA provided in the proposed regulations, which excludes an education IRA under section 530. Thus, contributions to an education IRA are disregarded in applying the Roth IRA contribution limitation (and in applying the contribution limitation for traditional IRAs).

Conversions

In response to certain comments, the final regulations clarify that conversions and recharacterizations made with the same trustee may be accomplished by redesignating the account or annuity contract, rather than by the opening of a new account or the issuance of a new annuity contract for each conversion or recharacterization.

As requested by commentators, the final regulations provide that a change in filing status or a divorce does not affect the application of the 4-year spread for 1998 conversions. Thus, if a married Roth IRA owner who is using the 4-year spread files separately or divorces before the full taxable conversion amount has been included in gross income, the remainder must be included in the Roth IRA owner's gross income over the remaining years in the 4-year period, or, if applicable, in the year for which the remainder is accelerated due to distribution or death.

Two commentators questioned why the proposed regulations require that a surviving spouse be the sole beneficiary of all a Roth IRA owner's Roth IRAs in order to elect to continue application of the 4-year spread after the Roth IRA owner's death. The IRS and Treasury view this result as compelled by the statutory language of section 408A(d)(3)(E)(ii)(II). That section provides that the surviving spouse must acquire the "entire interest" in any Roth IRA to which a conversion contribution to which the 4-year spread applies is "properly allocable." Under the aggregation and ordering rules of section 408A(d)(4), all a

Roth IRA owner's Roth IRAs are treated as a single Roth IRA, and a conversion contribution is therefore allocable to all the owner's Roth IRAs. Thus, a surviving spouse must be the sole beneficiary of all a Roth IRA owner's Roth IRAs in order to acquire the entire interest in any Roth IRA to which a 1998 conversion contribution is properly allocable.

Commentators also asked the IRS and Treasury to clarify whether Roth IRA distributions that are part of a series of substantially equal periodic payments begun under a traditional IRA prior to conversion to a Roth IRA are subject to income acceleration during the 4-year spread period and the 10 percent additional tax on early distributions under section 72(t). The final regulations clarify that those distributions are subject to income acceleration to the extent allocable to a 1998 conversion contribution with respect to which the 4-year spread applies. The final regulations further clarify, however, that the additional 10 percent tax under section 72(t) will not apply, even if the distributions are not qualified distributions (as long as they are part of a series of substantially equal periodic payments).

Under the proposed regulations, if an IRA owner has reached age 70, any amount distributed (or treated as distributed because of a conversion) from the IRA for a year consists of the required minimum distribution to the extent that an amount equal to the required minimum distribution for that year has not yet been distributed (or treated as distributed); as a required minimum distribution, that amount cannot be converted to a Roth IRA. Although one commentator requested that this rule be retained in the final regulations, other commentators objected to it. A number of commentators asked the IRS and Treasury to adopt a rule allowing an IRA owner who wishes to convert a traditional IRA to a Roth IRA in the year he or she turns 70 to leave the amount of his or her required minimum distribution with respect to such IRA in the IRA until April 1 of the following year, provided the conversion is accomplished by means of a trustee-to-trustee transfer. The commentators note that this rule applies in the case of trustee-to-trustee transfers between traditional IRAs. The final regulations retain the rule that the required minimum distribution amount is ineligible for rollover, including such a distribution for the year that the individual reaches age 70, because, pursuant to section 408A(d)(3)(C), a conversion is treated as a distribution regardless of whether the conversion is accomplished by a trustee-to-trustee transfer. Accordingly, the required minimum distribution amount is ineligible for rollover, and as such, is also ineligible to be converted to a Roth IRA.

Additionally, several commentators suggested that the rule in the proposed regulations is inconsistent with section 401(a)(9), which generally requires that IRA distributions begin by April 1 of the calendar year following the calendar year in which the IRA owner reaches age 70. These commentators argued that, under section 401(a)(9), distributions made during the calendar year in which the IRA owner reaches age 70 should not be considered required minimum distributions under sections 401(a)(9) and 408(a)(6) and (b)(3). However, the proposed regulations under sections 401(a)(9) and 408(a)(6) and (b)(3) provide that the first year for which distributions are required under section 401(a)(9) is the year in which the IRA owner reaches age 70, and that distributions made prior to April 1 of the following calendar year are treated as made for that first year. The regulations under section 402(c) and the proposed regulations under sections 401(a)(9) and 408(a)(6) and (b)(3) provide that the first amount distributed during a calendar year is treated as a required minimum distribution to the extent that the amount required to be distributed for that calendar year under section 401(a)(9) has not been distributed. For these reasons, the final regulations retain the rule of the proposed regulations.

Recharacterizations of IRA Contributions

The final regulations clarify that the computation of net income under section 1.408-4(c)(2)(iii) in the case of a commingled IRA may include net losses on the amount to be recharacterized.

Commentators asked the IRS and Treasury to clarify whether an amount converted from a SEP IRA or SIMPLE IRA to a Roth IRA may be recharacterized back to the SEP IRA or SIMPLE IRA from which the amount was converted. The final regulations provide that Roth IRA conversion contributions from a SEP IRA or SIMPLE IRA may be recharacterized to a SEP IRA or SIMPLE IRA (including the original SEP IRA or SIMPLE IRA). Another commentator also asked for clarification whether it is necessary to track the source of assets (i.e., as employer or employee contributions) converted from a SEP IRA or SIMPLE IRA to a Roth IRA for purposes of determining whether such assets may be recharacterized. The prohibition on recharacterizing employer contributions to a SEP IRA or SIMPLE IRA set forth in the final regulations only applies to those contributions at the time they are made to the SEP IRA or SIMPLE IRA. Once such contributions have been made to a SEP IRA or a SIMPLE IRA, the SEP IRA or SIMPLE IRA may be converted to a Roth IRA and subsequently recharacterized (provided, in the case of a SIMPLE IRA, that the two-year rule has been satisfied prior to the conversion).

Commentators asked for clarification regarding whether an election to recharacterize an IRA contribution may be made on behalf of a deceased IRA owner. The final regulations provide that the election to recharacterize an IRA contribution may be made by the executor, administrator, or other person charged with the duty of filing the decedent's final Federal income tax return.

Commentators also asked whether an excess contribution to an IRA made in a prior year, and applied against the contribution limits in the current year under section 4973, may be recharacterized. Only actual contributions may be recharacterized; thus, excess contributions actually made for a prior year and deemed to be current-year contributions for purposes of section 4973 are not contributions that are eligible to be recharacterized (unless the recharacterization would still be timely with respect to the taxable year for which the contributions were actually made). This rule applies to any excess contribution, whether made to a traditional or a Roth IRA.

Commentators asked for clarification regarding a conduit IRA that is converted to a Roth IRA and subsequently recharacterized back to a traditional IRA. The IRS and Treasury note that a conduit IRA that is converted to a Roth IRA and subsequently recharacterized back to a traditional IRA retains its status as a conduit IRA because the effect of the recharacterization is to treat the amount recharacterized as though it had been transferred directly from the original conduit IRA into another conduit IRA.

Commentators also asked whether a recharacterization is subject to withholding. A recharacterization is not a designated distribution under section 3405 and, therefore, is not subject to withholding.

The final regulations also provide rules regarding the "reconversion" of an amount that has been transferred from a Roth IRA to a traditional IRA by means of a recharacterization after having been earlier converted from a traditional IRA to a Roth IRA. After publication of the proposed regulations, the IRS and Treasury issued Notice 98-50, which provides interim rules regarding Roth IRA reconversions made during 1998 and 1999. Notice 98-50 stated that the interim rules were intended to clarify and supplement the proposed regulations and permitted taxpayers to rely on those rules as if incorporated in the proposed regulations. Notice 98-50 noted that the IRS and Treasury were considering whether the final regulations should provide that a taxpayer is not eligible to reconvert an amount before the end of the taxable year in which the amount was first converted (or the due date for that taxable year), or that a taxpayer who transfers a converted amount back to a traditional IRA in a recharacterization must wait until the passage of a fixed number of days before reconverting. Although Notice 98-50 invited interested parties to submit comments on those approaches, little comment was received on that issue. The final regulations provide reconversion rules for 2000 and subsequent years that generally differ from the interim rules of Notice 98-50. However, for 1998 and 1999, the final regulations continue the interim rules of Notice 98-50.

Effective January 1, 2000, an IRA owner who converts an amount from a traditional IRA to a Roth IRA during any taxable year and then transfers that amount back to a traditional IRA by means of a recharacterization may not reconvert that amount from the traditional IRA to a Roth IRA before the beginning of the taxable year following the taxable year in which the amount was converted to a Roth IRA or, if later, the end of the 30-day period beginning on the day on which the IRA owner transfers the amount from the Roth IRA back to a traditional IRA by means of a recharacterization. As under Notice 98-50, any amount previously converted is adjusted for subsequent net income in determining the amount subject to the limitation on subsequent reconversions.

A reconversion made before the later of the beginning of the next taxable year or the end of the 30-day period that begins on the day of the recharacterization is treated as a "failed conversion" (a distribution from the traditional IRA and a regular contribution to the Roth IRA), subject to correction through a recharacterization back to a traditional IRA. For these purposes, only a failed conversion resulting from a failure to satisfy the statutory requirements for a conversion (e.g., the $100,000 modified adjusted gross income limit) is treated as a conversion in determining when an IRA owner may make a reconversion. Thus, an IRA owner whose taxable year is the calendar year and who converts an amount to a Roth IRA in 2000 and then transfers that amount back to a traditional IRA on January 18, 2001 because his or her adjusted gross income for 2000 exceeds $100,000 cannot reconvert that amount until February 17, 2001 (the first day after the end of the 30-day period beginning on the day of the recharacterization transfer) because the failed conversion made in 2000 is treated as a conversion for purposes of the reconversion rules. However, if that IRA owner inadvertently attempts to reconvert that amount before February 17, 2001, the attempted reconversion is not treated as a conversion for purposes of the reconversion rules (although it is otherwise treated as a failed conversion). Therefore, the IRA owner could transfer the amount back to a traditional IRA in a recharacterization and reconvert it at any time on or after February 17, 2001. If the IRA owner does reconvert the amount on or after February 17, 2001, he or she cannot reconvert that amount again until 2002.

As indicated above, the final regulations continue the interim rules of Notice 98-50 applicable for 1998 and 1999. Therefore, an IRA owner who converts an amount from a traditional IRA to a Roth IRA during 1998 and then transfers that amount back to a traditional IRA by means of a recharacterization may reconvert that amount once (but no more than once) on or after November 1, 1998, and on or before December 31, 1998; the IRA owner may also reconvert that amount once (but no more than once) during 1999. Similarly, an IRA owner who converts an amount from a traditional IRA to a Roth IRA during 1999 that has not been converted before and then transfers that amount back to a traditional IRA by means of a recharacterization may reconvert that amount once (but no more than once) on or before December 31, 1999. In contrast to the rule for years after 1999, a failed conversion is not treated as a conversion for these 1998 and 1999 interim rules.

As did Notice 98-50, the final regulations provide that a reconversion made during 1998 or 1999 for which the IRA owner was not eligible is deemed to be an "excess reconversion" and does not change the IRA owner's taxable conversion amount. Instead, the excess reconversion and the last preceding recharacterization are not taken into account for purposes of determining the IRA owner's taxable conversion amount, and the IRA owner's taxable conversion amount is based on the last reconversion that was not an excess reconversion. An excess reconversion is otherwise treated as a valid reconversion. The final regulations grandfather conversions and reconversions made before November 1, 1998.

Distributions

In response to concerns raised in the comments regarding potential double taxation, the final regulations clarify that a nonqualified distribution from a Roth IRA is taxed only to the extent that the amount of the distribution, when added to all previous distributions (whether or not they were qualified distributions) and reduced by the taxable amount of such previous distributions, exceed[s] the owner's contributions to all his or her Roth IRAs.

Commentators also asked for clarification regarding whether a beneficiary may aggregate his or her inherited Roth IRAs with other Roth IRAs maintained by such beneficiary. The final regulations provide that a beneficiary's inherited Roth IRA may not be aggregated with any other Roth IRA maintained by such beneficiary (except for other Roth IRAs that the beneficiary inherited from the same decedent), unless the beneficiary, as the spouse of the decedent and sole beneficiary of the Roth IRA, elects to treat the Roth IRA as his or her own.

In addition, commentators also asked for clarification regarding whether the 5-taxable year period for determining whether a distribution is a qualified distribution starts over for subsequent Roth IRA contributions if the entire account balance in a Roth IRA is distributed to the Roth IRA owner before he or she makes any other Roth IRA contributions. In such a case, the 5-taxable year period does not start over. However, if an initial Roth IRA contribution is made to a Roth IRA that subsequently is revoked within 7 days, or if an initial Roth IRA contribution is recharacterized, the initial contribution does not start the 5-year period. The final regulations provide that an excess contribution that is distributed in accordance with section 408(d)(4) does not start the 5-year period.

One commentator questioned the rule in the proposed regulations providing that a distribution allocable to a conversion contribution is treated as made first from the portion (if any) that was includible in gross income as a result of the conversion. The IRS and Treasury note that this result is plainly compelled by section 408A(d)(4)(B)(ii). Another commentator inquired about the treatment of all conversions as designated distributions under section 3405; the commentator suggested that conversions effected by means of trustee-to-trustee transfers should not be treated as designated distributions subject to withholding. However, section 408A(d)(3) treats all Roth IRA conversions as distributions regardless of how they are effected.

Reporting Requirements

The final regulations retain the reporting rules set forth in the proposed regulations.

Effective Date

The final regulations are applicable to taxable years beginning on or after January 1, 1998, the effective date for section 408A.

* * *

Preamble, Final Treasury Regulations Section 1.408A-4 Converting Amounts to Roth IRAs
(T.D. 9814, 73 Fed. Reg. 43860-43863 (July 29, 2008))

[**Summary:** The final regulations clarify that where an individual retirement annuity or an annuity contract held by an individual retirement account is surrendered with no retained or transferred rights, the amount treated as a distribution is limited to the surrendered cash value (the actual proceeds available to be deposited into the Roth IRA).

The proposed regulations used a methodology from the gift tax regulations (Treas. Reg. § 25.2512-6) to determine fair market value of an annuity contract. Those rules depend on how soon after purchase the contract was converted and whether future premiums were to be paid. The different time periods were "soon after" the contract was sold and after the contract "has been in force for some time." To provide clarity and a more uniform interpretation, the final regulations modify the application of the valuation rules taken from the gift tax regulations (collectively referred to under these regulations as the gift tax method). The gift tax method under the final regulations includes a second alternative for situations where there is no comparable contract and is the same as the third method under the proposed regulations, except that it applies whenever there is no comparable contract.]

Background

Roth IRAs and Conversions

This document contains final regulations that amend the Income Tax Regulations (26 CFR Part 1) under section 408A of the Code relating to Roth IRAs. Section 408A of the Code, which was added by section 302 of the Taxpayer Relief Act of 1997, Public Law 105-34 (111 Stat. 788), establishes the Roth IRA as a type of individual retirement plan, effective for taxable years beginning on or after January 1, 1998.

The identifying characteristic of Roth IRAs is that all contributions to Roth IRAs are after-tax contributions (that is, an IRA owner cannot take a deduction for a contribution made to a Roth IRA) but qualified distributions are tax-free. A qualified distribution from a Roth IRA is a distribution that is made: (1) at least five years after the account owner (or the account owner's spouse) made a Roth IRA contribution, and (2) after age 59, after death, on account of disability, or for a first-time home purchase.

A taxpayer whose modified adjusted gross income for a year does not exceed $100,000 (and who, if married, files jointly)[1] may convert an amount held in a non-Roth IRA (that is, a traditional IRA or SIMPLE IRA) to an amount held in a Roth IRA. If a taxpayer converts an amount held in a non-Roth IRA to a Roth IRA, the taxpayer must include the value of the non-Roth IRA being converted in gross income (to the extent the conversion is not a conversion of basis in the non-Roth IRA).

A conversion may be accomplished by means of a rollover, trustee-to-trustee transfer, or account redesignation. Regardless of the means used to convert, any amount converted from a non-Roth IRA to a Roth IRA is treated as distributed from the non-Roth IRA and rolled over to the Roth IRA. In the case of a conversion involving property, the conversion amount generally is the fair market value of the property on the date of distribution or the date the property is treated as distributed from the traditional IRA.

Final regulations regarding Roth IRAs were published in the Federal Register on February 4, 1999 (64 FR 5597). On August 19, 2005, the IRS issued temporary regulations under section 408A (70 FR 48868) relating to conversions involving annuities. These temporary regulations were also issued in identical form as proposed regulations (70 FR 48924).

Rev. Proc. 2006-13 (2006-1 CB 315), which was issued on January 17, 2006, in response to several comments received on the temporary and proposed regulations, provided interim guidance with respect to the temporary regulations. See § 601.601(d)(2)(ii)(b). After consideration of all comments received on the proposed regulations, these final regulations adopt the provisions of the proposed regulations with certain modifications described in the Explanation of Provisions.

Explanation of Provisions

Like the proposed regulations, these final regulations clarify that when a non-Roth individual retirement annuity is converted to a Roth IRA, the amount that is treated as distributed is the fair market value of the annuity contract on the date the annuity contract is converted. Similarly, when a non-Roth individual retirement account holds an annuity contract as an account asset and the account is converted to a Roth IRA, the amount that is treated as distributed with respect to the annuity contract is the fair market value of the annuity contract on the date the annuity contract is converted (that is distributed or treated as distributed from the non-Roth IRA).

One commentator suggested that the final regulations should clarify that where a conversion is made by surrendering an annuity without retaining or transferring rights, the amount converted, and hence the amount that must be included in income as a result of the conversion, is limited to the surrendered cash value (the actual proceeds to be deposited into the Roth IRA). Rev. Proc. 2006-13 provided that, in such a case, the valuation methods in the temporary regulations do not apply.

The final regulations adopt this suggestion. Thus, to the extent an individual retirement annuity or an annuity contract held by an individual retirement account is surrendered with no retained or transferred rights, the amount treated as a distribution is limited to the surrendered cash value (the actual proceeds available to be deposited into the Roth IRA).The proposed regulations used a methodology from the gift tax regulations (§ 25.2512-6) to determine fair market value of an annuity contract. Those rules depend on how soon after purchase the contract was converted and whether future premiums were to be paid. The different time periods were "soon after" the contract was sold and after the contract "has been in force for some time." A commentator stated that these terms are not defined and do not lend themselves to clear or uniform interpretation.

In response to these comments, the final regulations modify the application of the valuation rules taken from the gift tax regulations (collectively referred to under these regulations as the gift tax method). The applicability of one valuation rule within the gift tax method is based upon whether the company which sold the initial contract sells comparable annuities. If there is such a comparable contract currently being sold, the fair market value of the contract is determined as the price of the comparable contract. For example, assume a taxpayer who is age 60 at the time of the conversion had purchased from an insurance company a contract at an earlier age which will pay him $500 per month for life beginning at age 70. If the insurance company is selling contracts that will provide a taxpayer who is age 60 $500 per month for life at age 70, then the fair market value of the taxpayer's contract, for purposes of determining the amount converted, is the current price of the similar contract. (If the conversion occurs soon after the annuity was sold, the comparable contract is the annuity itself and, thus, the fair market value of the annuity is established by the actual premiums paid for such contract.) This comparable contract valuation rule subsumes the first two methods under the proposed regulations.

The gift tax method under the final regulations includes a second alternative for situations where there is no comparable contract. If no comparable contract is available to make a comparison, the fair market value is established through an approximation that is based on the interpolated terminal reserve at the date of the conversion, plus the proportionate part of the gross premium paid before the date of the conversion which covers the period extending beyond that date. This reserve alternative is the same as the third method under the proposed regulations, except that it applies whenever there is no comparable contract.

Rev. Proc. 2006-13 provided an alternative to the valuation method in the proposed regulations based on the accumulation of premiums and this alternative is included in the final regulations. Under this "accumulation method," the fair market value of an annuity contract is permitted to be determined using the methodology provided in § 1.401(a)(9)-6, A-12, with the following modifications. First, all front-end loads and other non-recurring charges assessed in the twelve months immediately preceding the conversion must be added to the account value. Second, future distributions are not to be assumed in the determination of the actuarial present value of additional benefits. Finally, the exclusions provided under § 1.401(a)(9)-6, A-12(c)(1) and (c)(2), are not to be taken into account.

These final regulations also provide authority for the Commissioner to issue additional guidance regarding the fair market value of an individual retirement annuity, including formulas to be used for determining fair market value.

Effective Date

These regulations are applicable to any Roth IRA conversion where an annuity contract is distributed or treated as distributed from a traditional IRA on or after August 19, 2005. However, taxpayers may instead apply the valuation methods in the temporary regulations and Rev. Proc. 2006-13 for annuity contracts distributed or treated as distributed from a traditional IRA on or before December 31, 2008. See § 601.601(d)(2)(ii)(b). Thus, for example, the adoption of these final regulations does not eliminate the special rule for 2005 conversions set forth in section 4 of Rev. Proc. 2006-13.

Special Analyses***

Section 1.408A-0 Roth IRAs; Table of Contents.
(T.D. 8816, 64 FR 5597-5611 (Feb. 4, 1999))

This table of contents lists the regulations relating to Roth IRAs under section 408A of the Internal Revenue Code as follows:

Section 1.408A-1 Roth IRAs in general.

Section 1.408A-2 Establishing Roth IRAs.

Section 1.408A-3 Contributions to Roth IRAs.

Section 1.408A-4 Converting amounts to Roth IRAs.

Section 1.408A-5 Recharacterized contributions.

Section 1.408A-6 Distributions.

Section 1.408A-7 Reporting.

Section 1.408A-8 Definitions.

Section 1.408A-9 Effective date.

Treasury Regulations Section 1.408A-1
Roth IRAs in General
T.D. 8816, 64 FR 5597-5611 (Feb. 4, 1999)

This section sets forth the following questions and answers that discuss the background and general features of Roth IRAs:

Q-1   What is a Roth IRA?

A-1. (a) A Roth IRA is a new type of individual retirement plan that individuals can use, beginning in 1998. Roth IRAs are described in section 408A, which was added by the Taxpayer Relief Act of 1997 (TRA 97), Public Law 105-34 (111 Stat. 788).

(b) Roth IRAs are treated like traditional IRAs except where the Internal Revenue Code specifies different treatment. For example, aggregate contributions (other than by a conversion or other rollover) to all an individual's Roth IRAs are not permitted to exceed $2,000 for a taxable year. Further, income earned on funds held in a Roth IRA is generally not taxable. Similarly, the rules of section 408(e), such as the loss of exemption of the account where the owner engages in a prohibited transaction, apply to Roth IRAs in the same manner as to traditional IRAs.

Q-2 What are the significant differences between traditional IRAs and Roth IRAs?

A-2. There are several significant differences between traditional IRAs and Roth IRAs under the Internal Revenue Code. For example, eligibility to contribute to a Roth IRA is subject to special modified AGI (adjusted gross income) limits; contributions to a Roth IRA are never deductible; qualified distributions from a Roth IRA are not includible in gross income; the required minimum distribution rules under section 408(a)(6) and (b)(3) (which generally incorporate the provisions of section 401(a)(9)) do not apply to a Roth IRA during the lifetime of the owner; and contributions to a Roth IRA can be made after the owner has attained age 70.

Treasury Regulation Section 1.408A-2
Establishing Roth IRAs
(T.D. 8816, 64 FR 5597-5611 (Feb. 4, 1999))

This section sets forth the following questions and answers that provide rules applicable to establishing Roth IRAs.

Q-1 Who can establish a Roth IRA?

A-1. Except as provided in A-3 of this section, only an individual can establish a Roth IRA. In addition, in order to be eligible to contribute to a Roth IRA for a particular year, an individual must satisfy certain compensation requirements and adjusted gross income limits (see section 1.408A-3 A-3).

Q-2 How is a Roth IRA established?

A-2. A Roth IRA can be established with any bank, insurance company, or other person authorized in accordance with section 1.408-2(e) to serve as a trustee with respect to IRAs. The document establishing the Roth IRA must clearly designate the IRA as a Roth IRA, and this designation cannot be changed at a later date. Thus, an IRA that is designated as a Roth IRA cannot later be treated as a traditional IRA. However, see section 1.408A-4 A-1(b)(3) for certain rules for converting a traditional IRA to a Roth IRA with the same trustee by redesignating the traditional IRA as a Roth IRA, and see section 1.408A-5 for rules for recharacterizing certain IRA contributions.

Q-3 Can an employer or an association of employees establish a Roth IRA to hold contributions of employees or members?

A-3. Yes. Pursuant to section 408(c), an employer or an association of employees can establish a trust to hold contributions of employees or members made under a Roth IRA. Each employee's or member's account in the trust is treated as a separate Roth IRA that is subject to the generally applicable Roth IRA rules. The employer or association of employees may do certain acts otherwise required by an individual, for example, establishing and designating a trust as a Roth IRA.

Q-4 What is the effect of a surviving spouse of a Roth IRA owner treating an IRA as his or her own?

A-4. If the surviving spouse of a Roth IRA owner treats a Roth IRA as his or her own as of a date, the Roth IRA is treated from that date forward as though it were established for the benefit of the surviving spouse and not the original Roth IRA owner. Thus, for example, the surviving spouse is treated as the Roth IRA owner for purposes of applying the minimum distribution requirements under section 408(a)(6) and (b)(3). Similarly, the surviving spouse is treated as the Roth IRA owner rather than a beneficiary for purposes of determining the amount of any distribution from the Roth IRA that is includible in gross income and whether the distribution is subject to the 10-percent additional tax under section 72(t).

Treasury Regulations Section 1.408A-3 Roth IRAs (T.D. 8816, 64 FR 5597-5611 (Feb. 4, 1999))

This section sets forth the following questions and answers that provide rules regarding contributions to Roth IRAs:

Q-1 What types of contributions are permitted to be made to a Roth IRA?

A-1. There are two types of contributions that are permitted to be made to a Roth IRA: regular contributions and qualified rollover contributions (including conversion contributions). The term regular contributions means contributions other than qualified rollover contributions.

Q-2   When are contributions permitted to be made to a Roth IRA?

A-2. (a) The provisions of section 408A are effective for taxable years begin-ning on or after January 1, 1998. Thus, the first taxable year for which contributions are permitted to be made to a Roth IRA by an individual is the individual's taxable year beginning in 1998.

(b) Regular contributions for a particular taxable year must generally be con-tributed by the due date (not including extensions) for filing a Federal income tax return for that taxable year. (See section 1.408A-5 regarding recharacter-ization of certain contributions.)

Q-3   What is the maximum aggregate amount of regular contributions an individual is eligible to contribute to a Roth IRA for a taxable year?

A-3. (a) The maximum aggregate amount that an individual is eligible to con-tribute to all his or her Roth IRAs as a regular contribution for a taxable year is the same as the maximum for traditional IRAs: $2,000 or, if less, that indi-vidual's compensation for the year.

(b) For Roth IRAs, the maximum amount described in paragraph (a) of this A-3 is phased out between certain levels of modified AGI. For an individual who is not married, the dollar amount is phased out ratably between modified AGI of $95,000 and $110,000; for a married individual filing a joint return, between modified AGI of $150,000 and $160,000; and for a married individual filing separately, between modified AGI of $0 and $10,000. For this purpose, a married individual who has lived apart from his or her spouse for the entire taxable year and who files separately is treated as not married. Under section 408A(c)(3)(A), in applying the phase-out, the maximum amount is rounded up to the next higher multiple of $10 and is not reduced below $200 until completely phased out.

(c) If an individual makes regular contributions to both traditional IRAs and Roth IRAs for a taxable year, the maximum limit for the Roth IRA is the lesser of—

(1) The amount described in paragraph (a) of this A-3 reduced by the amount contributed to traditional IRAs for the taxable year; and

(2) The amount described in paragraph (b) of this A-3. Employer contri-butions, including elective deferrals, made under a SEP or SIMPLE IRA Plan on behalf of an individual (including a self-employed individual) do not reduce the amount of the individual's maximum regular contribution.

(d) The rules in this A-3 are illustrated by the following examples:

Example 1. In 1998, unmarried, calendar-year taxpayer B, age 60, has modified AGI of $40,000 and compensation of $5,000. For 1998, B can contribute a maximum of $2,000 to a traditional IRA, a Roth IRA or a com-bination of traditional and Roth IRAs.

Example 2. The facts are the same as in Example 1. However, assume that B violates the maximum regular contribution limit by contributing $2,000 to a traditional IRA and $2,000 to a Roth IRA for 1998. The $2,000 to B's Roth IRA would be an excess contribution to B's Roth IRA for 1998 because an individual's contributions are applied first to a traditional IRA, then to a Roth IRA.

Example 3. The facts are the same as in Example 1, except that B's compensation is $900. The maximum amount B can contribute to either a traditional IRA or a Roth (or a combination of the two) for 1998 is $900.

Example 4. In 1998, unmarried, calendar-year taxpayer C, age 60, has modified AGI of $100,000 and compensation of $5,000. For 1998, C contributes $800 to a traditional IRA and $1,200 to a Roth IRA. Because C's $1,200 Roth IRA contribution does not exceed the phased-out maximum Roth IRA contribution of $1,340 and because C's total IRA contributions do not exceed $2,000, C's Roth IRA contribution does not exceed the maximum permissible contribution.

Q-4 How is compensation defined for purposes of the Roth IRA contribution limit?

A-4. For purposes of the contribution limit described in A-3 of this section, an individual's compensation is the same as that used to determine the maximum contribution an individual can make to a traditional IRA. This amount is defined in section 219(f)(1) to include wages, commissions, professional fees, tips, and other amounts received for personal services, as well as taxable alimony and separate maintenance payments received under a decree of divorce or separate maintenance. Compensation also includes earned income as defined in section 401(c)(2), but does not include any amount received as a pension or annuity or as deferred compensation. In addition, under section 219(c), a married individual filing a joint return is permitted to make an IRA contribution by treating his or her spouse's higher compensation as his or her own, but only to the extent that the spouse's compensation is not being used for purposes of the spouse making a contribution to a Roth IRA or a deductible contribution to a traditional IRA.

Q-5 What is the significance of modified AGI and how is it determined?

A-5. Modified AGI is used for purposes of the phase-out rules described in A-3 of this section and for purposes of the $100,000 modified AGI limitation described in section 1.408A-4 A-2(a) (relating to eligibility for conversion). As defined in section 408A(c)(3)(C)(i), modified AGI is the same as adjusted gross income under section 219(g)(3)(A) (used to determine the amount of deductible contributions that can be made to a traditional IRA by an individual who is an active participant in an employer-sponsored retirement plan), except that any conversion is disregarded in determining modified AGI. For example, the deduction for contributions to an IRA is not taken into account for purposes of determining adjusted gross income under section 219 and thus does not apply in determining modified AGI for Roth IRA purposes.

Q-6 Is a required minimum distribution from an IRA for a year included in income for purposes of determining modified AGI?

A-6. (a) Yes. For taxable years beginning before January 1, 2005, any required minimum distribution from an IRA under section 408(a)(6) and (b)(3) (which generally incorporate the provisions of section 401(a)(9)) is included in income for purposes of determining modified AGI.

(b) For taxable years beginning after December 31, 2004, and solely for purposes of the $100,000 limitation applicable to conversions, modified AGI does not include any required minimum distributions from an IRA under section 408(a)(6) and (b)(3).

Q-7 Does an excise tax apply if an individual exceeds the aggregate regular contribution limits for Roth IRAs?

A-7. Yes. Section 4973 imposes an annual 6 percent excise tax on aggregate amounts contributed to Roth IRAs that exceed the maximum contribution limits described in A-3 of this section. Any contribution that is distributed, together with net income, from a Roth IRA on or before the tax return due date (plus extensions) for the taxable year of the contribution is treated as not contributed. Net income described in the previous sentence is includible in gross income for the taxable year in which the contribution is made. Aggregate excess contributions that are not distributed from a Roth IRA on or before the tax return due date (with extensions) for the taxable year of the contributions are reduced as a deemed Roth IRA contribution for each subsequent taxable year to the extent that the Roth IRA owner does not actually make regular IRA contributions for such years. Section 4973 applies separately to an individual's Roth IRAs and other types of IRAs.

Treasury Regulations Section 1.408A-4 Roth IRAs in General (T.D. 8816, 64 FR 5597-5611 (Feb. 4, 1999), amended by T.D. 9220, 70 FR 48868-48871 (Aug. 22, 2005); T.D. 9418, 73 FR 43860-43863 (July 29, 2008) revising Q-14 and A-14 and removing Temporary Treasury Regulations Section 1.408A-4T)

This section sets forth the following questions and answers that provide rules applicable to Roth IRA conversions:

Q-1 Can an individual convert an amount in his or her traditional IRA to a Roth IRA?

A-1. (a) Yes. An amount in a traditional IRA may be converted to an amount in a Roth IRA if two requirements are satisfied. First, the IRA owner must satisfy the modified AGI limitation described in A-2(a) of this section and, if married, the joint filing requirement described in A-2(b) of this section.

Second, the amount contributed to the Roth IRA must satisfy the definition of a qualified rollover contribution in section 408A(e) (i.e., it must satisfy the requirements for a rollover contribution as defined in section 408(d)(3), except that the one-rollover-per-year limitation in section 408(d)(3)(B) does not apply).

(b) An amount can be converted by any of three methods—

(1) An amount distributed from a traditional IRA is contributed (rolled over) to a Roth IRA within the 60-day period described in section 408(d)(3)(A)(i);

(2) An amount in a traditional IRA is transferred in a trustee-to-trustee transfer from the trustee of the traditional IRA to the trustee of the Roth IRA; or

(3) An amount in a traditional IRA is transferred to a Roth IRA maintained by the same trustee. For purposes of sections 408 and 408A, redesignating a traditional IRA as a Roth IRA is treated as a transfer of the entire account balance from a traditional IRA to a Roth IRA.

(c) Any converted amount is treated as a distribution from the traditional IRA and a qualified rollover contribution to the Roth IRA for purposes of section 408 and section 408A, even if the conversion is accomplished by means of a trustee-to-trustee transfer or a transfer between IRAs of the same trustee.

(d) A transaction that is treated as a failed conversion under section 1.408A-5 A-9(a)(1) is not a conversion.

Q-2 What are the modified AGI limitation and joint filing requirements for conversions?

A-2. (a) An individual with modified AGI in excess of $100,000 for a taxable year is not permitted to convert an amount to a Roth IRA during that taxable year. This $100,000 limitation applies to the taxable year that the funds are paid from the traditional IRA, rather than the year they are contributed to the Roth IRA.

(b) If the individual is married, he or she is permitted to convert an amount to a Roth IRA during a taxable year only if the individual and the individual's spouse file a joint return for the taxable year that the funds are paid from the traditional IRA. In this case, the modified AGI subject to the $100,000 limit is the modified AGI derived from the joint return using the couple's combined income. The only exception to this joint filing requirement is for an individual who has lived apart from his or her spouse for the entire taxable year. If the married individual has lived apart from his or her spouse for the entire taxable year, then such individual can treat himself or herself as not married for purposes of this paragraph, file a separate return and be subject to the $100,000 limit on his or her separate modified AGI. In all other cases, a married individual filing a separate return is not permitted to convert an amount to a Roth IRA, regardless of the individual's modified AGI.

Q-3 Is a remedy available to an individual who makes a failed conversion?

A-3. (a) Yes. See section 1.408A-5 for rules permitting a failed conversion amount to be recharacterized as a contribution to a traditional IRA. If the requirements in section 1.408A-5 are satisfied, the failed conversion amount will be treated as having been contributed to the traditional IRA and not to the Roth IRA.

(b) If the contribution is not recharacterized in accordance with section 1.408A-5, the contribution will be treated as a regular contribution to the Roth IRA and, thus, an excess contribution subject to the excise tax under section 4973 to the extent that it exceeds the individual's regular contribution limit. This is the result regardless of which of the three methods described in A-1(b) of this section applies to this transaction. Additionally, the distribution from the traditional IRA will not be eligible for the 4-year spread and will be subject to the additional tax under section 72(t) (unless an exception under that section applies).

Q-4 Do any special rules apply to a conversion of an amount in an individual's SEP IRA or SIMPLE IRA to a Roth IRA?

A-4. (a) An amount in an individual's SEP IRA can be converted to a Roth IRA on the same terms as an amount in any other traditional IRA.

(b) An amount in an individual's SIMPLE IRA can be converted to a Roth IRA on the same terms as a conversion from a traditional IRA, except that an amount distributed from a SIMPLE IRA during the 2-year period described in section 72(t)(6), which begins on the date that the individual first participated in any SIMPLE IRA Plan maintained by the individual's employer, cannot be converted to a Roth IRA. Pursuant to section 408(d)(3)(G), a distribution of an amount from an individual's SIMPLE IRA during this 2-year period is not eligible to be rolled over into an IRA that is not a SIMPLE IRA and thus cannot be a qualified rollover contribution. This 2-year period of section 408(d)(3)(G) applies separately to the contributions of each of an individual's employers maintaining a SIMPLE IRA Plan.

(c) Once an amount in a SEP IRA or SIMPLE IRA has been converted to a Roth IRA, it is treated as a contribution to a Roth IRA for all purposes. Future contributions under the SEP or under the SIMPLE IRA Plan may not be made to the Roth IRA.

Q-5 Can amounts in other kinds of retirement plans be converted to a Roth IRA?

A-5. No. Only amounts in another IRA can be converted to a Roth IRA. For example, amounts in a qualified plan or annuity plan described in section 401(a) or 403(a) cannot be converted directly to a Roth IRA. Also, amounts held in an annuity contract or account described in section 403(b) cannot be converted directly to a Roth IRA.

Q-6 **Can an individual who has attained at least age 70 by the end of a calendar year convert an amount distributed from a traditional IRA during that year to a Roth IRA before receiving his or her required minimum distribution with respect to the traditional IRA for the year of the conversion?**

A-6. (a) No. In order to be eligible for a conversion, an amount first must be eligible to be rolled over. section 408(d)(3) prohibits the rollover of a required minimum distribution. If a minimum distribution is required for a year with respect to an IRA, the first dollars distributed during that year are treated as consisting of the required minimum distribution until an amount equal to the required minimum distribution for that year has been distributed.

(b) As provided in A-1(c) of this section, any amount converted is treated as a distribution from a traditional IRA and a rollover contribution to a Roth IRA and not as a trustee-to-trustee transfer for purposes of section 408 and section 408A. Thus, in a year for which a minimum distribution is required (including the calendar year in which the individual attains age 70), an individual may not convert the assets of an IRA (or any portion of those assets) to a Roth IRA to the extent that the required minimum distribution for the traditional IRA for the year has not been distributed.

(c) If a required minimum distribution is contributed to a Roth IRA, it is treated as having been distributed, subject to the normal rules under section 408(d)(1) and (2), and then contributed as a regular contribution to a Roth IRA. The amount of the required minimum distribution is not a conversion contribution.

Q-7 **What are the tax consequences when an amount is converted to a Roth IRA?**

A-7. (a) Any amount that is converted to a Roth IRA is includible in gross income as a distribution according to the rules of section 408(d)(1) and (2) for the taxable year in which the amount is distributed or transferred from the traditional IRA. Thus, any portion of the distribution or transfer that is treated as a return of basis under section 408(d)(1) and (2) is not includible in gross income as a result of the conversion.

(b) The 10 percent additional tax under section 72(t) generally does not apply to the taxable conversion amount. But see section 1.408A-6 A-5 for circumstances under which the taxable conversion amount would be subject to the additional tax under section 72(t).

(c) Pursuant to section 408A(e), a conversion is not treated as a rollover for purposes of the one-rollover-per-year rule of section 408(d)(3)(B).

Q-8 Is there an exception to the income-inclusion rule described in A-7 of this section for 1998 conversions?

A-8. Yes. In the case of a distribution (including a trustee-to-trustee transfer) from a traditional IRA on or before December 31, 1998, that is converted to a Roth IRA, instead of having the entire taxable conversion amount includible in income in 1998, an individual includes in gross income for 1998 only one quarter of that amount and one quarter of that amount for each of the next 3 years. This 4-year spread also applies if the conversion amount was distributed in 1998 and contributed to the Roth IRA within the 60-day period described in section 408(d)(3)(A)(i), but after December 31, 1998. However, see section 1.408A-6 A-6 for special rules requiring acceleration of inclusion if an amount subject to the 4-year spread is distributed from the Roth IRA before 2001.

Q-9 Is the taxable conversion amount included in income for all purposes?

A-9. Except as provided below, any taxable conversion amount includible in gross income for a year as a result of the conversion (regardless of whether the individual is using a 4-year spread) is included in income for all purposes. Thus, for example, it is counted for purposes of determining the taxable portion of social security payments under section 86 and for purposes of determining the phase-out of the $25,000 exemption under section 469(i) relating to the disallowance of passive activity losses from rental real estate activities. However, as provided in section 1.408A-3 A-5, the taxable conversion amount (and any resulting change in other elements of adjusted gross income) is disregarded for purposes of determining modified AGI for section 408A.

Q-10 Can an individual who makes a 1998 conversion elect not to have the 4-year spread apply and instead have the full taxable conversion amount includible in gross income for 1998?

A-10. Yes. Instead of having the taxable conversion amount for a 1998 conversion included over 4 years as provided under A-8 of this section, an individual can elect to include the full taxable conversion amount in income for 1998. The election is made on Form 8606 and cannot be made or changed after the due date (including extensions) for filing the 1998 Federal income tax return.

Q-11 What happens when an individual who is using the 4-year spread dies, files separately, or divorces before the full taxable conversion amount has been included in gross income?

A-11. (a) If an individual who is using the 4-year spread described in A-8 of this section dies before the full taxable conversion amount has been included in gross income, then the remainder must be included in the individual's gross income for the taxable year that includes the date of death.

(b) However, if the sole beneficiary of all the decedent's Roth IRAs is the decedent's spouse, then the spouse can elect to continue the 4-year spread. Thus, the spouse can elect to include in gross income the same amount that the decedent would have included in each of the remaining years of the 4-year period. Where the spouse makes such an election, the amount includible under the 4-year spread for the taxable year that includes the date of the decedent's death remains includible in the decedent's gross income and is reported on the decedent's final Federal income tax return. The election is made on either Form 8606 or Form 1040, in accordance with the instructions to the applicable form, for the taxable year that includes the decedent's date of death and cannot be changed after the due date (including extensions) for filing the Federal income tax return for the spouse's taxable year that includes the decedent's date of death.

(c) If a Roth IRA owner who is using the 4-year spread and who was married in 1998 subsequently files separately or divorces before the full taxable conversion amount has been included in gross income, the remainder of the taxable conversion amount must be included in the Roth IRA owner's gross income over the remaining years in the 4-year period (unless accelerated because of distribution or death).

Q-12 Can an individual convert a traditional IRA to a Roth IRA if he or she is receiving substantially equal periodic payments within the meaning of section 72(t)(2)(A)(iv) from that traditional IRA?

A-12. Yes. Not only is the conversion amount itself not subject to the early distribution tax under section 72(t), but the conversion amount is also not treated as a distribution for purposes of determining whether a modification within the meaning of section 72(t)(4)(A) has occurred. Distributions from the Roth IRA that are part of the original series of substantially equal periodic payments will be nonqualified distributions from the Roth IRA until they meet the requirements for being a qualified distribution, described in section 1.408A-6 A-1(b). The additional 10-percent tax under section 72(t) will not apply to the extent that these nonqualified distributions are part of a series of substantially equal periodic payments. Nevertheless, to the extent that such distributions are allocable to a 1998 conversion contribution with respect to which the 4-year spread for the resultant income inclusion applies (see A-8 of this section) and are received during 1998, 1999, or 2000, the special acceleration rules of section 1.408A-6 A-6 apply. However, if the original series of substantially equal periodic payments does not continue to be distributed in substantially equal periodic payments from the Roth IRA after the conversion, the series of payments will have been modified and, if this modification occurs within 5 years of the first payment or prior to the individual becoming disabled or attaining age 59, the taxpayer will be subject to the recapture tax of section 72(t)(4)(A).

Q-13 Can a 1997 distribution from a traditional IRA be converted to a Roth IRA in 1998?

A-13. No. An amount distributed from a traditional IRA in 1997 that is contributed to a Roth IRA in 1998 would not be a conversion contribution. See A-3 of this section regarding the remedy for a failed conversion.

[**Author's Note.** The following new Q&A 14 was added by Temporary Regulations section 1.408A-4T, T.D. 9220 (Aug. 22, 2005). The regulations were modified and finalized in T.D. 9418, 73 FR 43860-43863 (July 29, 2008), revising Q-14 and A-14 and removing Temporary Treasury Regulations Section 1.408A-4T).]

Q-14 What is the amount that is treated as a distribution, for purposes of determining income inclusion, when a conversion involves an annuity contract?

A-14. (a) *In general*—(1) *Distribution of Fair Market Value Upon Conversion.* Notwithstanding § 1.408-4(e), when part or all of a traditional IRA that is an individual retirement annuity described in section 408(b) is converted to a Roth IRA, for purposes of determining the amount includible in gross income as a distribution under § 1.408A-4, A-7, the amount that is treated as distributed is the fair market value of the annuity contract on the date the annuity contract is converted. Similarly, when a traditional IRA that is an individual retirement account described in section 408(a) holds an annuity contract as an account asset and the traditional IRA is converted to a Roth IRA, for purposes of determining the amount includible in gross income as a distribution under § 1.408A-4, A-7, the amount that is treated as distributed with respect to the annuity contract is the fair market value of the annuity contract on the date that the annuity contract is distributed or treated as distributed from the traditional IRA. The rules in this A-14 also apply to conversions from SIMPLE IRAs.

(2) *Annuity contract surrendered.* Paragraph (a)(1) of this paragraph A-14 does not apply to a conversion of a traditional IRA to the extent the conversion is accomplished by the complete surrender of an annuity contract for its cash value and the reinvestment of the cash proceeds in a Roth IRA, but only if the surrender extinguishes all benefits and other characteristics of the contract. In such a case, the cash from the surrendered contract is the amount reinvested in the Roth IRA.

(3) *Definitions.* The definitions set forth in § 1.408A-8 apply for purposes of this paragraph A-14.

(b) *Determination of fair market value*—(1) *Overview*—(i) *Use of alternative methods.* This paragraph (b) sets forth methods which may be used to determine the fair market value of an individual retirement annuity for purposes of paragraph (a)(1) of this paragraph A-14. However, if, because of the unusual nature of the contract, the value determined under one of these methods does not reflect the full value of the contract, that method may not be used.

(ii) *Additional guidance.* Additional guidance regarding the fair market value of an individual retirement annuity, including formulas to be used for determining fair market value, may be issued by the Commissioner in revenue rulings, notices, or other guidance published in the Internal Revenue Bulletin (see § 601.601(d)(2)(ii)(b)).

(2) *Gift tax method*—(i) *Cost of contract or comparable contract.* If with respect to an annuity, there is a comparable contract issued by the company which sold the annuity, the fair market value of the annuity may be established by the price of the comparable contract. If the conversion occurs soon after the annuity was sold, the comparable contract may be the annuity itself, and thus, the fair market value of the annuity may be established through the sale of the particular contract by the company (that is, the actual premiums paid for such contract).

(ii) *Use of reserves where no comparable contract available.* If, with respect to an annuity, there is no comparable contract available in order to make the comparison described in paragraph (b)(2)(i) of this paragraph A-14, the fair market value may be established through an approximation that is based on the interpolated terminal reserve at the date of the conversion, plus the proportionate part of the gross premium last paid before the date of the conversion which covers the period extending beyond that date.

(3) *Accumulation method.* As an alternative to the gift tax method described in paragraph (b)(2) of this paragraph A-14, this paragraph (b)(3) provides a method that may be used for an annuity contract which has not been annuitized. The fair market value of such an annuity contract is permitted to be determined using the methodology provided in § 1.401(a)(9)-6, A-12, with the following modifications:

(i) All front-end loads and other non-recurring charges assessed in the twelve months immediately preceding the conversion must be added to the account value.

(ii) Future distributions are not to be assumed in the determination of the actuarial present value of additional benefits.

(iii) The exclusions provided under § 1.401(a)(9)-6, A-12(c)(1) and (c)(2), are not to be taken into account.

(c) *Effective/applicability date.* The provisions of this paragraph A-14 are applicable to any conversion in which an annuity contract is distributed or treated as distributed from a traditional IRA on or after August 19, 2005. However, for annuity contracts distributed or treated as distributed from a traditional IRA on or before December 31, 2008, taxpayers may instead apply the valuation methods in § 1.408A-4T (as it appeared in the April 1, 2008, edition of 26 CFR part 1) and Revenue Procedure 2006-13 (2006-1 CB 315) (See § 601.601(d)(2)(ii)(b)).

Treasury Regulations Section 1.408A-5
Recharacterized Contributions
(T.D. 8816, 64 FR 5597-5611 (Feb. 4, 1999), revised by
T.D. 9056, 68 FR 23586-23590 (May 5, 2003))

This section sets forth the following questions and answers that provide rules regarding recharacterizing IRA contributions:

Q-1 Can an IRA owner recharacterize certain contributions (i.e., treat a contribution made to one type of IRA as made to a different type of IRA) for a taxable year?

A-1. (a) Yes. In accordance with section 408A(d)(6), except as otherwise provided in this section, if an individual makes a contribution to an IRA (the FIRST IRA) for a taxable year and then transfers the contribution (or a portion of the contribution) in a trustee-to-trustee transfer from the trustee of the FIRST IRA to the trustee of another IRA (the SECOND IRA), the individual can elect to treat the contribution as having been made to the SECOND IRA, instead of to the FIRST IRA, for Federal tax purposes. A transfer between the FIRST IRA and the SECOND IRA will not fail to be a trustee-to-trustee transfer merely because both IRAs are maintained by the same trustee. For purposes of section 408A(d)(6), redesignating the FIRST IRA as the SECOND IRA will be treated as a transfer of the entire account balance from the FIRST IRA to the SECOND IRA.

(b) This recharacterization election can be made only if the trustee-to-trustee transfer from the FIRST IRA to the SECOND IRA is made on or before the due date (including extensions) for filing the individual's Federal income tax return for the taxable year for which the contribution was made to the FIRST IRA. For purposes of this section, a conversion that is accomplished through a rollover of a distribution from a traditional IRA in a taxable year that, 60 days after the distribution (as described in section 408(d)(3)(A)(i)), is contributed to a Roth IRA in the next taxable year is treated as a contribution for the earlier taxable year.

Q-2 What is the proper treatment of the net income attributable to the amount of a contribution that is being recharacterized?

A-2. (a) The net income attributable to the amount of a contribution that is being recharacterized must be transferred to the SECOND IRA along with the contribution.

(b) If the amount of the contribution being recharacterized was contributed to a separate IRA and no distributions or additional contributions have been made from or to that IRA at any time, then the contribution is recharacterized by the trustee of the FIRST IRA transferring the entire account balance of the FIRST IRA to the trustee of the SECOND IRA. In this case, the net income (or loss) attributable to the contribution being recharacterized is the difference between the amount of the original contribution and the amount transferred.

(c) If paragraph (b) of this A-2 does not apply, then, for purposes of determining net income attributable to IRA contributions, the net income attributable to the amount of a contribution is determined by allocating to the contribution a pro-rata portion of the earnings on the assets in the IRA during the period the IRA held the contribution. This attributable net income is calculated by using the following formula:

$$\text{Net Income} = \text{Contribution} \times \frac{(\text{Adjusted Closing Balance} - \text{Adjusted Opening Balance})}{\text{Adjusted Opening Balance}}$$

(2) For purposes of this paragraph (c), the following definitions apply—

(i) The term adjusted opening balance means the fair market value of the IRA at the beginning of the computation period plus the amount of any contributions or transfers (including the contribution that is being recharacterized pursuant to section 408A(d)(6) and any other recharacterizations) made to the IRA during the computation period.

(ii) The term adjusted closing balance means the fair market value of the IRA at the end of the computation period plus the amount of any distributions or transfers (including contributions returned pursuant to section 408(d)(4) and recharacterizations of contributions pursuant to section 408A(d)(6)) made from the IRA during the computation period.

(iii) The term computation period means the period beginning immediately prior to the time the particular contribution being recharacterized is made to the IRA and ending immediately prior to the recharacterizing transfer of the contribution. If a series of regular contributions was made to the IRA, and consecutive contributions in that series are being recharacterized, the computation period begins immediately prior to the time the first of the regular contributions being recharacterized was made.

(3) When an IRA asset is not normally valued on a daily basis, the fair market value of the asset at the beginning of the computation period is deemed to be the most recent, regularly determined, fair market value of the asset, determined as of a date that coincides with or precedes the first day of the computation period. In addition, solely for purposes of this paragraph (c), notwithstanding A-3 of this section, recharacterized contributions are taken into account for the period they are actually held in a particular IRA.

(4) In the case of an individual with multiple IRAs, the net income calculation is performed only on the IRA containing the particular contribution to be recharacterized, and that IRA is the IRA from which the recharacterizing transfer must be made.

(5) In the case of multiple contributions made to an IRA for a particular year that are eligible for recharacterization, the IRA owner can choose (by date and by dollar amount, not by specific assets acquired with those dollars) which contribution, or portion thereof, is to be recharacterized.

(6) The following examples illustrate the net income calculation under section 408A(d)(6) and this paragraph:

Example 1. (i) On March 1, 2004, when her Roth IRA is worth $80,000, Taxpayer A makes a $160,000 conversion contribution to the Roth IRA. Subsequently, Taxpayer A discovers that she was ineligible to make a Roth conversion contribution in 2004 and so she requests that the $160,000 be recharacterized to a traditional IRA pursuant to section 408A(d)(6). Pursuant to this request, on March 1, 2005, when the IRA is worth $225,000, the Roth IRA trustee transfers to a traditional IRA the $160,000 plus allocable net income. No other contributions have been made to the Roth IRA and no distributions have been made.

(ii) The adjusted opening balance is $240,000 [$80,000 +$160,000] and the adjusted closing balance is $225,000. Thus the net income allocable to the $160,000 is – $10,000 [$160,000 × ($225,000 – $240,000)/$240,000]. Therefore, in order to recharacterize the March 1, 2004, $160,000 conversion contribution on March 1, 2005, the Roth IRA trustee must transfer from Taxpayer A's Roth IRA to her traditional IRA $150,000 [$160,000 – $10,000].

Example 2. (i) On April 1, 2004, when her traditional IRA is worth $100,000, Taxpayer B converts the entire amount, consisting of 100 shares of stock in ABC Corp. and 100 shares of stock in XYZ Corp., by transferring the shares to a Roth IRA. At the time of the conversion, the 100 shares of stock in ABC Corp. are worth $50,000 and the 100 shares of stock in XYZ Corp. are also worth $50,000. Taxpayer B decides that she would like to recharacterize the ABC Corp. shares back to a traditional IRA. However, B may choose only by dollar amount the contribution or portion thereof that is to be recharacterized. On the date of transfer, November 1, 2004, the 100 shares of stock in ABC Corp. are worth $40,000 and the 100 shares of stock in XYZ Corp. are worth $70,000. No other contributions have been made to the Roth IRA and no distributions have been made.

(ii) If B requests that $50,000 (which was the value of the ABC Corp. shares at the time of conversion) be recharacterized, the net income allocable to the $50,000 is $5,000 [$50,000 × ($110,000 – $100,000) / $100,000]. Therefore, in order to recharacterize $50,000 of the April 1, 2004, conversion contribution on November 1, 2004, the Roth IRA trustee must transfer from Taxpayer B's Roth IRA to a traditional IRA assets with a value of $55,000 [$50,000 + $5,000].

(iii) If, on the other hand, B requests that $40,000 (which was the value of the ABC Corp. shares on November 1) be recharacterized, the net income allocable to the $40,000 is $4,000 [$40,000 × ($110,000 – $100,000)/ $100,000]. Therefore, in order to recharacterize $40,000 of the April 1, 2004, conversion contribution on November 1, 2004, the Roth IRA trustee must transfer from Taxpayer B's Roth IRA to a traditional IRA assets with a value of $44,000 [$40,000 + $4,000].

(iv) Regardless of the amount of the contribution recharacterized, the determination of that amount (or of the net income allocable thereto) is not affected by whether the recharacterization is accomplished by the transfer of shares of ABC Corp. or of shares of XYZ Corp.

(7) This paragraph (c) applies for purposes of determining net income attributable to IRA contributions, made on or after January 1, 2004. For purposes of determining net income attributable to IRA contributions made before January 1, 2004, see paragraph (c) of this A-2 of section 1.408A-5 (as it appeared in the April 1, 2003, edition of 26 CFR part 1).

Q-3 **What is the effect of recharacterizing a contribution made to the FIRST IRA as a contribution made to the SECOND IRA?**

A-3. The contribution that is being recharacterized as a contribution to the SECOND IRA is treated as having been originally contributed to the SECOND IRA on the same date and (in the case of a regular contribution) for the same taxable year that the contribution was made to the FIRST IRA. Thus, for example, no deduction would be allowed for a contribution to the FIRST IRA, and any net income transferred with the recharacterized contribution is treated as earned in the SECOND IRA, and not the FIRST IRA.

Q-4 **Can an amount contributed to an IRA in a tax-free transfer be recharacterized under A-1 of this section?**

A-4. No. If an amount is contributed to the FIRST IRA in a tax-free transfer, the amount cannot be recharacterized as a contribution to the SECOND IRA under A-1 of this section. However, if an amount is erroneously rolled over or transferred from a traditional IRA to a SIMPLE IRA, the contribution can subsequently be recharacterized as a contribution to another traditional IRA.

Q-5 **Can an amount contributed by an employer under a SIMPLE IRA Plan or a SEP be recharacterized under A-1 of this section?**

A-5. No. Employer contributions (including elective deferrals) under a SIMPLE IRA Plan or a SEP cannot be recharacterized as contributions to another IRA under A-1 of this section. However, an amount converted from a SEP IRA or SIMPLE IRA to a Roth IRA may be recharacterized under A-1 of this section as a contribution to a SEP IRA or SIMPLE IRA, including the original SEP IRA or SIMPLE IRA.

Q-6 **How does a taxpayer make the election to recharacterize a contribution to an IRA for a taxable year?**

A-6. (a) An individual makes the election described in this section by notifying, on or before the date of the transfer, both the trustee of the FIRST IRA and the trustee of the SECOND IRA, that the individual has elected to treat the contribution as having been made to the SECOND IRA, instead of the FIRST IRA, for Federal tax purposes. The notification of the election must include the following information: the type and amount of the contribution to the FIRST IRA that is to be recharacterized; the date on which the contribution was made to the FIRST IRA and the year for which it was made; a direction to the trustee of the FIRST IRA to transfer, in a trustee-to-trustee transfer, the amount of the contribution and net income allocable to the contribution to the trustee of the SECOND IRA; and the name of the trustee of the FIRST IRA and the trustee of the SECOND IRA and any additional information needed to make the transfer.

(b) The election and the trustee-to-trustee transfer must occur on or before the due date (including extensions) for filing the individual's Federal income tax return for the taxable year for which the recharacterized contribution was made to the FIRST IRA, and the election cannot be revoked after the transfer. An individual who makes this election must report the recharacterization, and must treat the contribution as having been made to the SECOND IRA, instead of the FIRST IRA, on the individual's Federal income tax return for the taxable year described in the preceding sentence in accordance with the applicable Federal tax forms and instructions.

(c) The election to recharacterize a contribution described in this A-6 may be made on behalf of a deceased IRA owner by his or her executor, administrator, or other person responsible for filing the final Federal income tax return of the decedent under section 6012(b)(1).

Q-7 **If an amount is initially contributed to an IRA for a taxable year, then is moved (with net income attributable to the contribution) in a tax-free transfer to another IRA (the FIRST IRA for purposes of A-1 of this section), can the tax-free transfer be disregarded, so that the initial contribution that is transferred from the FIRST IRA to the SECOND IRA is treated as a recharacterization of that initial contribution?**

A-7. Yes. In applying section 408A(d)(6), tax-free transfers between IRAs are disregarded. Thus, if a contribution to an IRA for a year is followed by one or more tax-free transfers between IRAs prior to the recharacterization, then for purposes of section 408A(d)(6), the contribution is treated as if it remained in the initial IRA. Consequently, an individual may elect to recharacterize an initial contribution made to the initial IRA that was involved in a series of tax-free transfers by making a trustee-to-trustee transfer from the last IRA in the series to the SECOND IRA. In this case the contribution to the SECOND IRA is treated as made on the same date (and for the same taxable year) as the date the contribution being recharacterized was made to the initial IRA.

Q-8 **If a contribution is recharacterized, is the recharacterization treated as a rollover for purposes of the one-rollover-per-year limitation of section 408(d)(3)(B)?**

A-8. No, recharacterizing a contribution under A-1 of this section is never treated as a rollover for purposes of the one-rollover-per-year limitation of section 408(d)(3)(B), even if the contribution would have been treated as a rollover contribution by the SECOND IRA if it had been made directly to the

SECOND IRA, rather than as a result of a recharacterization of a contribution to the FIRST IRA.

Q-9 **If an IRA owner converts an amount from a traditional IRA to a Roth IRA and then transfers that amount back to a traditional IRA in a recharacterization, may the IRA owner subsequently reconvert that amount from the traditional IRA to a Roth IRA?**

A-9. (a)(1) Except as otherwise provided in paragraph (b) of this A-9, an IRA owner who converts an amount from a traditional IRA to a Roth IRA during any taxable year and then transfers that amount back to a traditional IRA by means of a recharacterization may not reconvert that amount from the traditional IRA to a Roth IRA before the beginning of the taxable year following the taxable year in which the amount was converted to a Roth IRA or, if later, the end of the 30-day period beginning on the day on which the IRA owner transfers the amount from the Roth IRA back to a traditional IRA by means of a recharacterization (regardless of whether the recharacterization occurs during the taxable year in which the amount was converted to a Roth IRA or the following taxable year). Thus, any attempted reconversion of an amount prior to the time permitted under this paragraph (a)(1) is a failed conversion of that amount. However, see section 1.408A-4 A-3 for a remedy available to an individual who makes a failed conversion.

(2) For purposes of paragraph (a)(1) of this A-9, a failed conversion of an amount resulting from a failure to satisfy the requirements of section 1.408A-4 A-1(a) is treated as a conversion in determining whether an IRA owner has previously converted that amount.

(b)(1) An IRA owner who converts an amount from a traditional IRA to a Roth IRA during taxable year 1998 and then transfers that amount back to a traditional IRA by means of a recharacterization may reconvert that amount once (but no more than once) on or after November 1, 1998 and on or before December 31, 1998; the IRA owner may also reconvert that amount once (but no more than once) during 1999. The rule set forth in the preceding sentence applies without regard to whether the IRA owner's initial conversion or recharacterization of the amount occurred before, on, or after November 1, 1998. An IRA owner who converts an amount from a traditional IRA to a Roth IRA during taxable year 1999 that has not been converted previously and then transfers that amount back to a traditional IRA by means of a recharacterization may reconvert that amount once (but no more than once) on or before December 31, 1999. For purposes of this paragraph (b)(1), a failed conversion of an amount resulting from a failure to satisfy the requirements of section 1.408A-4 A-1(a) is not treated as a conversion in determining whether an IRA owner has previously converted that amount.

(2) A reconversion by an IRA owner during 1998 or 1999 for which the IRA owner is not eligible under paragraph (b)(1) of this A-9 will be deemed an excess reconversion (rather than a failed conversion) and will not change

the IRA owner's taxable conversion amount. Instead, the excess reconversion and the last preceding recharacterization will not be taken into account for purposes of determining the IRA owner's taxable conversion amount, and the IRA owner's taxable conversion amount will be based on the last reconversion that was not an excess reconversion (unless, after the excess reconversion, the amount is transferred back to a traditional IRA by means of a recharacterization). An excess reconversion will otherwise be treated as a valid reconversion.

(3) For purposes of this paragraph (b), any reconversion that an IRA owner made before November 1, 1998 will not be treated as an excess reconversion and will not be taken into account in determining whether any later reconversion is an excess reconversion.

(c) In determining the portion of any amount held in a Roth IRA or a traditional IRA that an IRA owner may not reconvert under this A-9, any amount previously converted (or reconverted) is adjusted for subsequent net income thereon.

Q-10   Are there examples to illustrate the rules in this section?

The rules in this section are illustrated by the following examples:

A-10. **Example 1.** In 1998, Individual C converts the entire amount in his traditional IRA to a Roth IRA. Individual C thereafter determines that his modified AGI for 1998 exceeded $100,000 so that he was ineligible to have made a conversion in that year. Accordingly, prior to the due date (plus extensions) for filing the individual's Federal income tax return for 1998, he decides to recharacterize the conversion contribution. He instructs the trustee of the Roth IRA (FIRST IRA) to transfer in a trustee-to-trustee transfer the amount of the contribution, plus net income, to the trustee of a new traditional IRA (SECOND IRA). The individual notifies the trustee of the FIRST IRA and the trustee of the SECOND IRA that he is recharacterizing his IRA contribution (and provides the other information described in A-6 of this section). On the individual's Federal income tax return for 1998, he treats the original amount of the conversion as having been contributed to the SECOND IRA and not the Roth IRA. As a result, for Federal tax purposes, the contribution is treated as having been made to the SECOND IRA and not to the Roth IRA. The result would be the same if the conversion amount had been transferred in a tax-free transfer to another Roth IRA prior to the recharacterization.

Example 2. In 1998, an individual makes a $2,000 regular contribution for 1998 to his traditional IRA (FIRST IRA). Prior to the due date (plus extensions) for filing the individual's Federal income tax return for 1998, he decides that he would prefer to contribute to a Roth IRA instead. The individual instructs the trustee of the FIRST IRA to transfer in a trustee-to-trustee transfer the amount of the contribution, plus attributable net income, to the trustee of a Roth IRA (SECOND IRA). The individual notifies the trustee of the FIRST IRA and the trustee of the SECOND IRA that he is recharacterizing his $2,000 contribution for 1998 (and provides the other information described in A-6 of this section). On the individual's Federal income tax return for 1998, he treats the $2,000 as having been contributed to the Roth IRA for 1998 and not to the traditional IRA. As a result, for Federal tax purposes, the contribution is treated as having been made to the Roth IRA for 1998 and not to the traditional IRA. The result would be the same if the conversion amount had been transferred in a tax-free transfer to another traditional IRA prior to the recharacterization.

Example 3. The facts are the same as in Example 2, except that the $2,000 regular contribution is initially made to a Roth IRA and the recharacterizing transfer is made to a traditional IRA. On the individual's Federal income tax return for 1998, he treats the $2,000 as having been contributed to the traditional IRA for 1998 and not the Roth IRA. As a result, for Federal tax purposes, the contribution is treated as having been made to the traditional IRA for 1998 and not the Roth IRA. The result would be the same if the contribution had been transferred in a tax-free transfer to another Roth IRA prior to the recharacterization, except that the only Roth IRA trustee the individual must notify is the one actually making the recharacterization transfer.

Example 4. In 1998, an individual receives a distribution from traditional IRA 1 and contributes the entire amount to traditional IRA 2 in a rollover contribution described in section 408(d)(3). In this case, the individual cannot elect to recharacterize the contribution by transferring the contribution amount, plus net income, to a Roth IRA, because an amount contributed to an IRA in a tax-free transfer cannot be recharacterized. However, the individual may convert (other than by recharacterization) the amount in traditional IRA 2 to a Roth IRA at any time, provided the requirements of section 1.408A-4 A-1 are satisfied.

Treasury Regulations section 1.408A-6 Distributions (T.D. 8816, 64 FR 5597-5611 (Feb. 4, 1999))

This section sets forth the following questions and answers that provide rules regarding distributions from Roth IRAs:

Q-1 How are distributions from Roth IRAs taxed?

A-1. (a) The taxability of a distribution from a Roth IRA generally depends on whether or not the distribution is a qualified distribution. This A-1 provides rules for qualified distributions and certain other nontaxable distributions. A-4 of this section provides rules for the taxability of distributions that are not qualified distributions.

(b) A distribution from a Roth IRA is not includible in the owner's gross income if it is a qualified distribution or to the extent that it is a return of the owner's contributions to the Roth IRA (determined in accordance with A-8 of this section). A qualified distribution is one that is both—

Made after a 5-taxable-year period (defined in A-2 of this section); and

Made on or after the date on which the owner attains age 59½, made to a beneficiary or the estate of the owner on or after the date of the owner's death, attributable to the owner's being disabled within the meaning of section 72(m)(7), or to which section 72(t)(2)(F) applies (exception for first-time home purchase).

(c) An amount distributed from a Roth IRA will not be included in gross income to the extent it is rolled over to another Roth IRA on a tax-free basis under the rules of sections 408(d)(3) and 408A(e).

(d) Contributions that are returned to the Roth IRA owner in accordance with section 408(d)(4) (corrective distributions) are not includible in gross income, but any net income required to be distributed under section 408(d)(4) together with the contributions is includible in gross income for the taxable year in which the contributions were made.

Q-2 When does the 5-taxable-year period described in A-1 of this section (relating to qualified distributions) begin and end?

A-2. The 5-taxable-year period described in A-1 of this section begins on the first day of the individual's taxable year for which the first regular contribution is made to any Roth IRA of the individual or, if earlier, the first day of the individual's taxable year in which the first conversion contribution is made to any Roth IRA of the individual. The 5-taxable-year period ends on the last day of the individual's fifth consecutive taxable year beginning with the taxable year described in the preceding sentence. For example, if an individual whose taxable year is the calendar year makes a first-time regular Roth IRA contribution any time between January 1, 1998, and April 15, 1999, for 1998, the 5-taxable-year period begins on January 1, 1998. Thus, each Roth IRA owner has only one 5-taxable-year period described in A-1 of this section for all the Roth IRAs of which he or she is the owner. Further, because of the requirement of the 5-taxable-year period, no qualified distributions can occur before taxable years beginning in 2003. For purposes of this A-2, the amount of any contribution distributed as a corrective distribution under A-1(d) of this section is treated as if it was never contributed.

Q-3 If a distribution is made to an individual who is the sole beneficiary of his or her deceased spouse's Roth IRA and the individual is treating the Roth IRA as his or her own, can the distribution be a qualified distribution based on being made to a beneficiary on or after the owner's death?

A-3. No. If a distribution is made to an individual who is the sole beneficiary of his or her deceased spouse's Roth IRA and the individual is treating the Roth IRA as his or her own, then, in accordance with section 1.408A-2 A-4, the distribution is treated as coming from the individual's own Roth IRA and not the deceased spouse's Roth IRA. Therefore, for purposes of determining whether the distribution is a qualified distribution, it is not treated as made to a beneficiary on or after the owner's death.

Q-4 How is a distribution from a Roth IRA taxed if it is not a qualified distribution?

A-4. A distribution that is not a qualified distribution, and is neither contributed to another Roth IRA in a qualified rollover contribution nor constitutes a corrective distribution, is includible in the owner's gross income to the extent that the amount of the distribution, when added to the amount of all prior distributions from the owner's Roth IRAs (whether or not they were qualified distributions) and reduced by the amount of those prior distributions previously includible in gross income, exceeds the owner's contributions to all his or her Roth IRAs. For purposes of this A-4, any amount distributed as a corrective distribution is treated as if it was never contributed.

Q-5 Will the additional tax under 72(t) apply to the amount of a distribution that is not a qualified distribution?

A-5. (a) The 10-percent additional tax under section 72(t) will apply (unless the distribution is excepted under section 72(t)) to any distribution from a Roth IRA includible in gross income.

(b) The 10-percent additional tax under section 72(t) also applies to a non-qualified distribution, even if it is not then includible in gross income, to the extent it is allocable to a conversion contribution, if the distribution is made within the 5-taxable-year period beginning with the first day of the individual's taxable year in which the conversion contribution was made. The 5-taxable-year period ends on the last day of the individual's fifth consecutive taxable year beginning with the taxable year described in the preceding sentence. For purposes of applying the tax, only the amount of the conversion contribution includible in gross income as a result of the conversion is taken into account. The exceptions under section 72(t) also apply to such a distribution.

(c) The 5-taxable-year period described in this A-5 for purposes of determining whether section 72(t) applies to a distribution allocable to a conversion contribution is separately determined for each conversion contribution, and need not be the same as the 5-taxable-year period used for purposes of determining whether a distribution is a qualified distribution under A-1(b) of this section. For example, if a calendar-year taxpayer who received a distribution from a traditional IRA on December 31, 1998, makes a conversion contribution by contributing the distributed amount to a Roth IRA on February 25, 1999 in a qualifying rollover contribution and makes a regular contribution for 1998 on the same date, the 5-taxable-year period for purposes of this A-5 begins on January 1, 1999, while the 5-taxable-year period for purposes of A-1(b) of this section begins on January 1, 1998.

Q-6   Is there a special rule for taxing distributions allocable to a 1998 conversion?

A-6. Yes. In the case of a distribution from a Roth IRA in 1998, 1999 or 2000 of amounts allocable to a 1998 conversion with respect to which the 4-year spread for the resultant income inclusion applies (see section 1.408A-4 A-8), any income deferred as a result of the election to years after the year of the distribution is accelerated so that it is includible in gross income in the year of the distribution up to the amount of the distribution allocable to the 1998 conversion (determined under A-8 of this section). This amount is in addition to the amount otherwise includible in the owner's gross income for that taxable year as a result of the conversion. However, this rule will not require the inclusion of any amount to the extent it exceeds the total amount of income required to be included over the 4-year period. The acceleration of income inclusion described in this A-6 applies in the case of a surviving spouse who elects to continue the 4-year spread in accordance with section 1.408A-4 A-11(b).

Q-7   Is the 5-taxable-year period described in A-1 of this section redetermined when a Roth IRA owner dies?

A-7. (a) No. The beginning of the 5-taxable-year period described in A-1 of this section is not redetermined when the Roth IRA owner dies. Thus, in determining the 5-taxable-year period, the period the Roth IRA is held in the name of a beneficiary, or in the name of a surviving spouse who treats the decedent's Roth IRA as his or her own, includes the period it was held by the decedent.

(b) The 5-taxable-year period for a Roth IRA held by an individual as a beneficiary of a deceased Roth IRA owner is determined independently of the 5-taxable-year period for the beneficiary's own Roth IRA. However, if a surviving spouse treats the Roth IRA as his or her own, the 5-taxable-year period with respect to any of the surviving spouse's Roth IRAs (including the one that the surviving spouse treats as his or her own) ends at the earlier of the end of either the 5-taxable-year period for the decedent or the 5-taxable-year period applicable to the spouse's own Roth IRAs.

Q-8   How is it determined whether an amount distributed from a Roth IRA is allocated to regular contributions, conversion contributions, or earnings?

A-8. (a) Any amount distributed from an individual's Roth IRA is treated as made in the following order (determined as of the end of a taxable year and exhausting each category before moving to the following category)—

(1) From regular contributions;

(2) From conversion contributions, on a first-in-first-out basis; and

(3) From earnings.

(b) To the extent a distribution is treated as made from a particular conversion contribution, it is treated as made first from the portion, if any, that was includible in gross income as a result of the conversion.

Q-9 Are there special rules for determining the source of distributions under A-8 of this section?

A-9. Yes. For purposes of determining the source of distributions, the following rules apply:

(a) All distributions from all an individual's Roth IRAs made during a taxable year are aggregated.

(b) All regular contributions made for the same taxable year to all the individual's Roth IRAs are aggregated and added to the undistributed total regular contributions for prior taxable years. Regular contributions for a taxable year include contributions made in the following taxable year that are identified as made for the taxable year in accordance with section 1.408A-3 A-2. For example, a regular contribution made in 1999 for 1998 is aggregated with the contributions made in 1998 for 1998.

(c) All conversion contributions received during the same taxable year by all the individual's Roth IRAs are aggregated. Notwithstanding the preceding sentence, all conversion contributions made by an individual during 1999 that were distributed from a traditional IRA in 1998 and with respect to which the 4-year spread applies are treated for purposes of A-8(b) of this section as contributed to the individual's Roth IRAs prior to any other conversion contributions made by the individual during 1999.

(d) A distribution from an individual's Roth IRA that is rolled over to another Roth IRA of the individual in accordance with section 408A(e) is disregarded for purposes of determining the amount of both contributions and distributions.

(e) Any amount distributed as a corrective distribution (including net income), as described in A-1(d) of this section, is disregarded in determining the amount of contributions, earnings, and distributions.

(f) If an individual recharacterizes a contribution made to a traditional IRA (FIRST IRA) by transferring the contribution to a Roth IRA (SECOND IRA) in accordance with section 1.408A-5, then, pursuant to section 1.408A-5 A-3, the contribution to the Roth IRA is taken into account for the same taxable year for which it would have been taken into account if the contribution had originally been made to the Roth IRA and had never been contributed to the traditional IRA. Thus, the contribution to the Roth IRA is treated as contributed to the Roth IRA on the same date and for the same taxable year that the contribution was made to the traditional IRA.

(g) If an individual recharacterizes a regular or conversion contribution made to a Roth IRA (FIRST IRA) by transferring the contribution to a traditional IRA (SECOND IRA) in accordance with section 1.408A-5, then pursuant to section

1.408A-5 A-3, the contribution to the Roth IRA and the recharacterizing transfer are disregarded in determining the amount of both contributions and distributions for the taxable year with respect to which the original contribution was made to the Roth IRA.

(h) Pursuant to section 1.408A-5 A-3, the effect of income or loss (determined in accordance with section 1.408A-5 A-2) occurring after the contribution to the FIRST IRA is disregarded in determining the amounts described in paragraphs (f) and (g) of this A-9. Thus, for purposes of paragraphs (f) and (g), the amount of the contribution is determined based on the original contribution.

Q-10 Are there examples to illustrate the ordering rules described in A-8 and A-9 of this section?

A-10. Yes. The following examples illustrate these ordering rules:

Example 1. In 1998, individual B converts $80,000 in his traditional IRA to a Roth IRA. B has a basis of $20,000 in the conversion amount and so must include the remaining $60,000 in gross income. He decides to spread the $60,000 income by including $15,000 in each of the 4 years 1998-2001, under the rules of section 1.408A-4 A-8. B also makes a regular contribution of $2,000 in 1998. If a distribution of $2,000 is made to B anytime in 1998, it will be treated as made entirely from the regular contributions, so there will be no Federal income tax consequences as a result of the distribution.

Example 2. The facts are the same as in Example 1, except that the distribution made in 1998 is $5,000. The distribution is treated as made from $2,000 of regular contributions and $3,000 of conversion contributions that were includible in gross income. As a result, B must include $18,000 in gross income for 1998: $3,000 as a result of the acceleration of amounts that otherwise would have been included in later years under the 4-year-spread rule and $15,000 includible under the regular 4-year-spread rule. In addition, because the $3,000 is allocable to a conversion made within the previous 5 taxable years, the 10-percent additional tax under section 72(t) would apply to this $3,000 distribution for 1998, unless an exception applies. Under the 4-year-spread rule, B would now include in gross income $15,000 for 1999 and 2000, but only $12,000 for 2001, because of the accelerated inclusion of the $3,000 distribution.

Example 3. The facts are the same as in Example 1, except that B makes an additional $2,000 regular contribution in 1999 and he does not take a distribution in 1998. In 1999, the entire balance in the account, $90,000 ($84,000 of contributions and $6,000 of earnings), is distributed to B. The distribution is treated as made from $4,000 of regular contributions, $60,000 of conversion contributions that were includible in gross income, $20,000 of conversion contributions that were not includible in gross income, and $6,000 of earnings. Because a distribution has been made within the 4-year-spread period, B must accelerate the income inclusion under the 4-year-spread rule and must include in gross income the $45,000 remaining under the 4-year-spread rule in addition to the $6,000 of earnings. Because $60,000 of the distribution is allocable to a conversion made within the previous 5 taxable years, it is subject to the 10-percent additional tax under section 72(t) as if it were includible in gross income for 1999, unless an exception applies. The $6,000 allocable to earnings would be subject to the tax under section 72(t), unless an exception applies. Under the 4-year-spread rule, no amount would be includible in gross income for 2000 or 2001 because the entire amount of the conversion that was includible in gross income has already been included.

Example 4. The facts are the same as in Example 1, except that B also makes a $2,000 regular contribution in each year 1999 through 2002 and he does not take a distribution in 1998. A distribution of $85,000 is made to B in 2002. The distribution is treated as made from the $10,000 of regular contributions (the total regular contributions made in the years 1998–2002), $60,000 of conversion contributions that were includible in gross income, and $15,000 of conversion contributions that were not includible in gross income. As a result, no amount of the distribution is includible in gross income; however, because the distribution is allocable to a conversion made within the previous 5 years, the $60,000 is subject to the 10-percent additional tax under section 72(t) as if it were includible in gross income for 2002, unless an exception applies.

Example 5. The facts are the same as in Example 4, except no distribution occurs in 2002. In 2003, the entire balance in the account, $170,000 ($90,000 of contributions and $80,000 of earnings), is distributed to B. The distribution is treated as made from $10,000 of regular contributions, $60,000 of conversion contributions that were includible in gross income, $20,000 of conversion contributions that were not includible in gross income, and $80,000 of earnings. As a result, for 2003, B must include in gross income the $80,000 allocable to earnings, unless the distribution is a qualified distribution; and if it is not a qualified distribution, the $80,000 would be subject to the 10-percent additional tax under section 72(t), unless an exception applies.

Example 6. Individual C converts $20,000 to a Roth IRA in 1998 and $15,000 (in which amount C had a basis of $2,000) to another Roth IRA in 1999. No other contributions are made. In 2003, a $30,000 distribution, that is not a qualified distribution, is made to C. The distribution is treated as made from $20,000 of the 1998 conversion contribution and $10,000 of the 1999 conversion contribution that was includible in gross income. As a result, for 2003, no amount is includible in gross income; however, because $10,000 is allocable to a conversion contribution made within the previous 5 taxable years, that amount is subject to the 10-percent additional tax under section 72(t) as if the amount were includible in gross income for 2003, unless an exception applies. The result would be the same whichever of C's Roth IRAs made the distribution.

Example 7. The facts are the same as in Example 6, except that the distribution is a qualified distribution. The result is the same as in Example 6, except that no amount would be subject to the 10-percent additional tax under section 72(t), because, to be a qualified distribution, the distribution must be made on or after the date on which the owner attains age 59½, made to a beneficiary or the estate of the owner on or after the date of the owner's death, attributable to the owner's being disabled within the meaning of section 72(m)(7), or to which section 72(t)(2)(F) applies (exception for a first-time home purchase). Under section 72(t)(2), each of these conditions is also an exception to the tax under section 72(t).

Example 8. Individual D makes a $2,000 regular contribution to a traditional IRA on January 1, 1999, for 1998. On April 15, 1999, when the $2,000 has increased to $2,500, D recharacterizes the contribution by transferring the $2,500 to a Roth IRA (pursuant to section 1.408A-5 A-1). In this case, D's regular contribution to the Roth IRA for 1998 is $2,000. The $500 of earnings is not treated as a contribution to the Roth IRA. The results would be the same if the $2,000 had decreased to $1,500 prior to the recharacterization.

Example 9. In December 1998, individual E receives a distribution from his traditional IRA of $300,000 and in January 1999 he contributes the $300,000 to a Roth IRA as a conversion contribution. In April 1999, when the $300,000 has increased to $350,000, E recharacterizes the conversion contribution by transferring the $350,000 to a traditional IRA. In this case, E's conversion contribution for 1998 is $0, because the $300,000 conversion contribution and the earnings of $50,000 are disregarded. The results would be the same if the $300,000 had decreased to $250,000 prior to the recharacterization. Further, since the conversion is disregarded, the $300,000 is not includible in gross income in 1998.

Q-11   **If the owner of a Roth IRA dies prior to the end of the 5-taxable-year period described in A-1 of this section (relating to qualified distributions) or prior to the end of the 5-taxable-year period described in A-5 of this section (relating to conversions), how are different types of contributions in the Roth IRA allocated to multiple beneficiaries?**

A-11. Each type of contribution is allocated to each beneficiary on a pro-rata basis. Thus, for example, if a Roth IRA owner dies in 1999, when the Roth IRA contains a regular contribution of $2,000, a conversion contribution of $6,000 and earnings of $1,000, and the owner leaves his Roth IRA equally to four children, each child will receive one quarter of each type of contribution. Pursuant to the ordering rules in A-8 of this section, an immediate distribution of $2,000 to one of the children will be deemed to consist of $500 of regular contributions and $1,500 of conversion contributions. A beneficiary's inherited Roth IRA may not be aggregated with any other Roth IRA maintained by such beneficiary (except for other Roth IRAs the beneficiary inherited from the same decedent), unless the beneficiary, as the spouse of the decedent and sole beneficiary of the Roth IRA, elects to treat the Roth IRA as his or her own (see A-7 and A-14 of this section).

Q-12   How do the withholding rules under section 3405 apply to Roth IRAs?

A-12. Distributions from a Roth IRA are distributions from an individual retirement plan for purposes of section 3405 and thus are designated distributions unless one of the exceptions in section 3405(e)(1) applies. Pursuant to section 3405(a) and (b), nonperiodic distributions from a Roth IRA are subject to 10-percent withholding by the payor and periodic payments are subject to withholding as if the payments were wages. However, an individual can elect to have no amount withheld in accordance with section 3405(a)(2) and (b)(2).

Q-13   Do the withholding rules under section 3405 apply to conversions?

A-13. Yes. A conversion by any method described in section 1.408A-4 A-1 is considered a designated distribution subject to section 3405. However, a conversion occurring in 1998 by means of a trustee-to-trustee transfer of an amount from a traditional IRA to a Roth IRA established with the same or a different trustee is not required to be treated as a designated distribution for purposes of section 3405. Consequently, no withholding is required with respect to such a conversion (without regard to whether or not the individual elected to have no withholding).

Q-14   What minimum distribution rules apply to a Roth IRA?

A-14. (a) No minimum distributions are required to be made from a Roth IRA under section 408(a)(6) and (b)(3) (which generally incorporate the provisions of section 401(a)(9)) while the owner is alive. The post-death minimum distribution rules under section 401(a)(9)(B) that apply to traditional IRAs, with the exception of the at-least-as-rapidly rule described in section 401(a)(9) (B)(i), also apply to Roth IRAs.

(b) The minimum distribution rules apply to the Roth IRA as though the Roth IRA owner died before his or her required beginning date. Thus, generally, the entire interest in the Roth IRA must be distributed by the end of the fifth calendar year after the year of the owner's death unless the interest is payable to a designated beneficiary over a period not greater than that beneficiary's life expectancy and distribution commences before the end of the calendar year following the year of death. If the sole beneficiary is the decedent's spouse, such spouse may delay distributions until the decedent would have attained age 70 or may treat the Roth IRA as his or her own.

(c) Distributions to a beneficiary that are not qualified distributions will be includible in the beneficiary's gross income according to the rules in A-4 of this section.

Q-15   Does section 401(a)(9) apply separately to Roth IRAs and individual retirement plans that are not Roth IRAs?

A-15. Yes. An individual required to receive minimum distributions from his or her own traditional or SIMPLE IRA cannot choose to take the amount of the minimum distributions from any Roth IRA. Similarly, an individual required to receive minimum distributions from a Roth IRA cannot choose to take the amount of the minimum distributions from a traditional or SIMPLE IRA. In addition, an individual required to receive minimum distributions as a beneficiary under a Roth IRA can only satisfy the minimum distributions for one Roth IRA by distributing from another Roth IRA if the Roth IRAs were inherited from the same decedent.

Q-16 How is the basis of property distributed from a Roth IRA determined for purposes of a subsequent disposition?

A-16. The basis of property distributed from a Roth IRA is its fair market value (FMV) on the date of distribution, whether or not the distribution is a qualified distribution. Thus, for example, if a distribution consists of a share of stock in XYZ Corp. with an FMV of $40.00 on the date of distribution, for purposes of determining gain or loss on the subsequent sale of the share of XYZ Corp. stock, it has a basis of $40.00.

Q-17 What is the effect of distributing an amount from a Roth IRA and contributing it to another type of retirement plan other than a Roth IRA?

A-17. Any amount distributed from a Roth IRA and contributed to another type of retirement plan (other than a Roth IRA) is treated as a distribution from the Roth IRA that is neither a rollover contribution for purposes of section 408(d)(3) nor a qualified rollover contribution within the meaning of section 408A(e) to the other type of retirement plan. This treatment also applies to any amount transferred from a Roth IRA to any other type of retirement plan unless the transfer is a recharacterization described in section 1.408A-5.

Q-18 Can an amount be transferred directly from an education IRA to a Roth IRA (or distributed from an education IRA and rolled over to a Roth IRA)?

A-18. No amount may be transferred directly from an education IRA to a Roth IRA. A transfer of funds (or distribution and rollover) from an education IRA to a Roth IRA constitutes a distribution from the education IRA and a regular contribution to the Roth IRA (rather than a qualified rollover contribution to the Roth IRA).

Q-19 What are the Federal income tax consequences of a Roth IRA owner transferring his or her Roth IRA to another individual by gift?

A-19. A Roth IRA owner's transfer of his or her Roth IRA to another individual by gift constitutes an assignment of the owner's rights under the Roth IRA. At the time of the gift, the assets of the Roth IRA are deemed to be distributed to the owner and, accordingly, are treated as no longer held in a Roth IRA. In the case of any such gift of a Roth IRA made prior to October 1, 1998, if the entire interest in the Roth IRA is reconveyed to the Roth IRA owner prior to January 1, 1999, the Internal Revenue Service will treat the gift and reconveyance as never having occurred for estate tax, gift tax, and generation-skipping tax purposes and for purposes of this A-19.

Treasury Regulations Section 1.408A-7
Reporting (T.D. 8816, 64 FR 5597-5611 (Feb. 4, 1999))

This section sets forth the following questions and answers that relate to the reporting requirements applicable to Roth IRAs:

Q-1   What reporting requirements apply to Roth IRAs?

A-1. Generally, the reporting requirements applicable to IRAs other than Roth IRAs also apply to Roth IRAs, except that, pursuant to section 408A(d)(3)(D), the trustee of a Roth IRA must include on Forms 1099-R and 5498 additional information as described in the instructions thereto. Any conversion of amounts from an IRA other than a Roth IRA to a Roth IRA is treated as a distribution for which a Form 1099-R must be filed by the trustee maintaining the non-Roth IRA. In addition, the owner of such IRAs must report the conversion by completing Form 8606. In the case of a recharacterization described in section 1.408A-5 A-1, IRA owners must report such transactions in the manner prescribed in the instructions to the applicable Federal tax forms.

Q-2   Can a trustee rely on reasonable representations of a Roth IRA contributor or distributee for purposes of fulfilling reporting obligations?

A-2. A trustee maintaining a Roth IRA is permitted to rely on reasonable representations of a Roth IRA contributor or distributee for purposes of fulfilling reporting obligations.

Treasury Regulations Section 1.408A-8
Definitions (T.D. 8816, 64 FR 5597-5611 (Feb. 4, 1999))

This section sets forth the following question and answer that provides definitions of terms used in the provisions of sections 1.408A-1 through 1.408A-7 and this section:

Q-1 Are there any special definitions that govern in applying the provisions of sections 1.408A-1 through 1.408A-7 and this section?

A-1. Yes, the following definitions govern in applying the provisions of sections 1.408A-1 through 1.408A-7 and this section. Unless the context indicates otherwise, the use of a particular term excludes the use of the other terms.

(a) Different types of IRAs—

(1) IRA. Sections 408(a) and (b), respectively, describe an individual retirement account and an individual retirement annuity. The term IRA means an IRA described in either section 408(a) or (b), including each IRA described in paragraphs (a)(2) through (5) of this A-1. However, the term IRA does not include an education IRA described in section 530.

(2) Traditional IRA. The term traditional IRA means an individual retirement account or individual retirement annuity described in section 408(a) or (b), respectively. This term includes a SEP IRA but does not include a SIMPLE IRA or a Roth IRA.

(3) SEP IRA. section 408(k) describes a simplified employee pension (SEP) as an employer-sponsored plan under which an employer can make contributions to IRAs established for its employees. The term SEP IRA means an IRA that receives contributions made under a SEP. The term SEP includes a salary reduction SEP (SARSEP) described in section 408(k)(6).

(4) SIMPLE IRA. section 408(p) describes a SIMPLE IRA Plan as an employer-sponsored plan under which an employer can make contributions to SIMPLE IRAs established for its employees. The term SIMPLE IRA means an IRA to which the only contributions that can be made are contributions under a SIMPLE IRA Plan or rollovers or transfers from another SIMPLE IRA.

(5) Roth IRA. The term Roth IRA means an IRA that meets the requirements of section 408A.

(b) Other defined terms or phrases—

(1) 4-year spread. The term 4-year spread is described in section 1.408A-4 A-8.

(2) Conversion. The term conversion means a transaction satisfying the requirements of section 1.408A-4 A-1.

(3) Conversion amount or conversion contribution. The term conversion amount or conversion contribution is the amount of a distribution and contribution with respect to which a conversion described in section 1.408A-4 A-1 is made.

(4) Failed conversion. The term failed conversion means a transaction in which an individual contributes to a Roth IRA an amount transferred or distributed from a traditional IRA or SIMPLE IRA (including a transfer by

redesignation) in a transaction that does not constitute a conversion under section 1.408A-4 A-1.

(5) Modified AGI. The term modified AGI is defined in section 1.408A-3 A-5.

(6) Recharacterization. The term recharacterization means a transaction described in section 1.408A-5 A-1.

(7) Recharacterized amount or recharacterized contribution. The term recharacterized amount or recharacterized contribution means an amount or contribution treated as contributed to an IRA other than the one to which it was originally contributed pursuant to a recharacterization described in section 1.408A-5 A-1.

(8) Taxable conversion amount. The term taxable conversion amount means the portion of a conversion amount includible in income on account of a conversion, determined under the rules of section 408(d)(1) and (2).

(9) Tax-free transfer. The term tax-free transfer means a tax-free rollover described in section 402(c), 402(e)(6), 403(a)(4), 403(a)(5), 403(b)(8), 403(b)(10) or 408(d)(3), or a tax-free trustee-to-trustee transfer.

(10) Treat an IRA as his or her own. The phrase treat an IRA as his or her own means to treat an IRA for which a surviving spouse is the sole beneficiary as his or her own IRA after the death of the IRA owner in accordance with the terms of the IRA instrument or in the manner provided in the regulations under section 408(a)(6) or (b)(3).

(11) Trustee. The term trustee includes a custodian or issuer (in the case of an annuity) of an IRA (except where the context clearly indicates otherwise).

Treasury Regulations Section 1.408A-9
Effective Date (T.D. 8816, 64 FR 5597-5611 (Feb. 4, 1999))

This section contains the following question and answer providing the effective date of sections 1.408A-1 through 1.408A-8:

Q-1 To what taxable years do sections 1.408A-1 through 1.408A-8 apply?

A-1. Sections 1.408A-1 through 1.408A-8 apply to taxable years beginning on or after January 1, 1998.

Treasury Regulations Section 1.408A-10
Coordination Between Designated Roth Accounts
and Roth IRAs (T.D. 9324, 72 FR 21103-21116 (Apr. 30, 2007))

Q-1. Can an eligible rollover distribution, within the meaning of section 402(c)(4), from a designated Roth account, as defined in A-1 of § 1.402A-1, be rolled over to a Roth IRA?

A-1. Yes. An eligible rollover distribution, within the meaning of section 402(c)(4), from a designated Roth account may be rolled over to a Roth IRA. For purposes of this section, a designated Roth account means a designated Roth account as defined in A-1 of § 1.402A-1.

Q-2. Can an eligible rollover distribution from a designated Roth account be rolled over to a Roth IRA even if the distributee is not otherwise eligible to make regular or conversion contributions to a Roth IRA?

A-2. Yes. An individual may establish a Roth IRA and roll over an eligible rollover distribution from a designated Roth account to that Roth IRA even if such individual is not eligible to make regular contributions or conversion contributions (as described in section 408A(c)(2) and (d)(3), respectively) because of the modified adjusted gross income limits in section 408A(b)(3).

Q-3. For purposes of the ordering rules on distributions from Roth IRAs, what portion of a distribution from a rollover contribution from a designated Roth account is treated as contributions?

A-3. (a) Under section 408A(d)(4), distributions from Roth IRAs are deemed to consist first of regular contributions, then of conversion contributions, and finally, of earnings. For purposes of section 408A(d)(4), the amount of a rollover contribution that is treated as a regular contribution is the portion of the distribution that is treated as investment in the contract under A-6 of § 1.402A-1, and the remainder of the rollover contribution is treated as earnings. Thus, the entire amount of any qualified distribution from a designated Roth account that is rolled over into a Roth IRA is treated as a regular contribution to the Roth IRA. Accordingly, a subsequent distribution from the Roth IRA in the amount of that rollover contribution is not includible in gross income under the rules of A-8 of § 1.408A-6.

(b) If the entire account balance of a designated Roth account is distributed to an employee and only a portion of the distribution is rolled over to a Roth IRA within the 60-day period described in section 402(c)(3), and at the time of the distribution, the investment in the contract exceeds the balance in the designated Roth account, the portion of investment in the contract that exceeds the amount used to determine the taxable amount of the distribution is treated as a regular contribution for purposes of section 408A(d)(4).

Q-4. In the case of a rollover from a designated Roth account to a Roth IRA, when does the 5-taxable-year period (described in section 408A(d)(2)(B) and A-1 of § 1.408A-6) for determining qualified distributions from a Roth IRA begin?

A-4. (a) The 5-taxable-year period for determining a qualified distribution from a Roth IRA (described in section 408A(d)(2)(B) and A-1 of § 1.408A-6) begins with the earlier of the taxable year described in A-2 of § 1.408A-6 or the taxable year in which a rollover contribution from a designated Roth account is made to a Roth IRA. The 5-taxable-year period described in this A-4 and the 5-taxable-year period of participation described in A-4 of § 1.402A-1 are determined independently.

(b) The following examples illustrate the application of this A-4:

Example 1. Employee D began making designated Roth contributions under his employer's 401(k) plan in 2006. Employee D, who is over age 59½, takes a distribution from D's designated Roth account in 2008, prior to the end of the 5-taxable-year period of participation used to determine qualified distributions from a designated Roth account. The distribution is an eligible rollover distribution and D rolls it over in accordance with sections 402(c) and 402A(c)(3) to D's Roth IRA, which was established in 2003. Any subsequent distribution from the Roth IRA of the amount rolled in, plus earnings thereon, would not be includible in gross income (because it would be a qualified distribution within the meaning of section 408A(d)(2)).

Example 2. The facts are the same as in *Example 1,* except that the Roth IRA is D's first Roth IRA and is established with the rollover in 2008, which is the only contribution made to the Roth IRA. If a distribution is made from the Roth IRA prior to the end of the 5-taxable-year period used to determine qualified distributions from a Roth IRA (which begins in 2008, the year of the rollover which established the Roth IRA) the distribution would not be a qualified distribution within the meaning of section 408A(d)(2), and any amount of the distribution that exceeded the portion of the rollover contribution that consisted of investment in the contract is includible in D's gross income.

Example 3. The facts are the same as in *Example 2,* except that the distribution from the designated Roth account and the rollover to the Roth IRA occur in 2011 (after the end of the 5-taxable-year period of participation used to determine qualified distributions from a designated Roth account). If a distribution is made from the Roth IRA prior to the expiration of the 5-taxable-year period used to determine qualified distributions from a Roth IRA, the distribution would not be a qualified distribution within the meaning of section 408A(d)(2), and any amount of the distribution that exceeded the amount rolled in is includible in D's gross income.

Q-5. Can amounts distributed from a Roth IRA be rolled over to a designated Roth account as defined in A-1 of § 1.402A-1?

A-5. No. Amounts distributed from a Roth IRA may be rolled over or transferred only to another Roth IRA and are not permitted to be rolled over to a designated Roth account under a section 401(a) or section 403(b) plan. The same rule applies even if all the amounts in the Roth IRA are attributable to a rollover distribution from a designated Roth account in a plan.

Q-6. When is this § 1.408A-10 applicable?

A-6. The rules of this § 1.408A-10 apply for taxable years beginning on or after January 1, 2006. [Reg. § 1.408A-10.]

Appendix E

Revenue Procedures, Announcements, and Notices

Author's Note: The Internal Revenue Bulletin (IRB) is the authoritative instrument for announcing all substantive rulings of the IRS necessary to promote a uniform application of tax law. Copies of the IRB, as well as Federal tax forms and publications, can be found on the Internet at *http:// www.irs.gov/app/picklist/list/internalRevenueBulletins.html*.

Revenue Procedure 2006-13, 2006-3 I.R.B. 315 (January 17, 2006)

[**Summary:** Non-Roth IRA annuity conversion safe harbors. The IRS will allow the fair market value of an annuity contract that has not yet been annuitized to be determined using the approach described in Treasury Regulations Section 1.401(a)(9)-6, Q&A-12, with three modifications. Those modifications include that (1) all nonrecurring charges (including front-end loads) assessed in the 12 months preceding conversion must be added to the account value; (2) no future distributions are assumed in determining the actuarial present value of additional benefits; and (3) the exclusions described in Treasury Regulations Section 1.401(a)(9)-6, A-12, are disregarded. A simplified safe harbor for pre-2006 Roth IRA conversions is also provided. For Roth IRA conversions where the annuity contract has not yet been annuitized and the contract was distributed (or treated as distributed) before January 1, 2006, only the first of the three modifications (see above) is applied to the calculation.]

Author's Note: Final Treasury Regulations Section 1.408A-4, Q&A 14 (T.D. 9814, 73 Fed. Reg. 43860-43863) concerning the valuation of a non-Roth annuity contract that is converted to a Roth IRA was released in July 2008. The regulations are reproduced in Appendix D.

SECTION 1. PURPOSE

This revenue procedure provides safe harbor methods that are permitted to be used in determining the fair market value of an annuity contract for purposes of determining the amount includible in gross income as a result of the conversion of a traditional IRA to a Roth IRA, as described in Q&A-14 of § 1.408A-4T of the temporary regulations. The safe harbor method provided in Section 3 of this revenue procedure is available to determine the fair market value of an annuity contract that has not yet been annuitized with respect to any Roth IRA conversion described in A-14 of § 1.408A-4T until further guidance is issued. The simplified safe harbor method provided in Section 4 of this revenue procedure is available where such a conversion occurs before January 1, 2006.

SECTION 2. BACKGROUND

Under § 408(d) of the Code and A-7 of § 1.408A-4 of the regulations, any amount that is converted from a traditional IRA to a Roth IRA is includible in gross income as a distribution for the taxable year in which the amount is distributed or transferred from the traditional IRA. In the case of a conversion involving property, the conversion amount generally is the fair market value of the property on the date of distribution or the date the property is treated as distributed from the traditional IRA. Under A-1 of § 1.408A-7, any amount converted from a traditional IRA to a Roth IRA is treated as a distribution for which a Form 1099-R must be filed by the trustee maintaining the traditional IRA.

Temporary regulations under § 408A regarding the valuation of annuity contracts upon conversion of a traditional IRA were published in the Federal Register on August 22, 2005 (T.D. 9220, 2005-39 I.R.B. 596 [70 FR 48868]). Section 1.408A-4T, A-14 of the temporary regulations states that, when a traditional individual retirement annuity is converted to a Roth IRA, the amount that is treated as distributed is the fair market value of the annuity contract on the date the annuity contract is converted. Similarly, when a traditional individual retirement account holds an annuity contract as an account asset and the account is converted to a Roth IRA, the amount that is treated as distributed with respect to the annuity contract is the fair market value of the annuity contract on the date the annuity contract is distributed or treated as distributed from the traditional IRA.

A-14 of § 1.408A-4T does not apply to a conversion of a traditional IRA where the conversion is accomplished by the complete surrender of an annuity contract for its cash value and the reinvestment of the cash proceeds in a Roth IRA, but only if the surrender extinguishes all benefits and other characteristics of the contract. A-14 of § 1.408A-4T does not apply in that circumstance because the contract is not being converted. Instead, the cash from the surrendered contract is reinvested in the Roth IRA.

A-14 of § 1.408A-4T also provides rules for determining the fair market value of an annuity contract in the case of a conversion. These rules vary depending on certain factors, including whether the conversion occurs soon after the contract was sold, whether there has been a material change in market conditions, and whether future premiums are to be paid. A-14 of § 1.408A-4T applies to any conversion where an annuity contract is distributed or treated as distributed from a traditional IRA on or after August 19, 2005. As indicated in the preamble to the temporary regulations, no implication is intended concerning whether or not a rule adopted in the regulations is applicable law for earlier conversions.

The temporary regulations also provide authority for the Commissioner to issue additional guidance regarding the fair market value of an annuity contract, including formulas to be used in determining fair market value. The Service and Treasury requested and received comments regarding this anticipated guidance. Commentators indicated that a more specific methodology for valuing the annuity contracts is needed and noted that they are currently implementing the method under A-12 of § 1.401(a)(9)-6 of the regulations for valuing annuity contracts that have not yet been annuitized.

Under A-12 of § 1.401(a)(9)-6, an employee's entire interest under an annuity contract that has not yet been annuitized (which is used to determine the employee's required minimum distribution) is the sum of the following: (1) the dollar amount credited to the employee or beneficiary under the contract (which may not be reduced to reflect any surrender charges under the contract) and (2) the actuarial present value of any additional benefits (such as survivor benefits in excess of the account balance, any guaranteed minimum benefits, and any charges that are expected to be refunded, rebated or otherwise reversed at a later date) that will be provided under the contract.

For this purpose, the actuarial present value of any additional benefits is to be determined using reasonable actuarial assumptions, including reasonable assumptions as to future distributions, and without regard to an individual's health. However, paragraph (c)(1) of A-12 of § 1.401(a)(9)-6 provides that the actuarial present value of the additional benefits may be disregarded if: (1) the sum of the dollar amount credited to the employee or beneficiary under the contract and the actuarial present value of the additional benefits is no more than 120 percent of the dollar amount credited to the employee or beneficiary under the contract and (2) the additional benefits satisfy certain other requirements. Also, paragraph (c)(2) of A-12 of § 1.401(a)(9)-6 provides that the actuarial value of the right to receive a final payment upon death that does not exceed the excess of the premiums paid less the amount of prior distributions may also be disregarded if it is the only additional benefit under the contract. Because some benefits may be disregarded, the methodology of A-12 of § 1.401(a)(9)-6 does not always reflect the full value of all of the benefits under the contract.

SECTION 3. SAFE HARBOR METHOD FOR ROTH IRA CONVERSIONS

The Service and Treasury recognize that it may be difficult to determine the fair market value of an annuity contract under the temporary regulations. Moreover, the Service and Treasury believe it is appropriate to permit the use of a modified version of the methodology applied under A-12 of § 1.401(a)(9)-6 as a safe harbor method to be used in determining the fair market value of such an annuity contract. Accordingly, this revenue procedure provides that, until further guidance is issued, for purposes of determining the amount includible in gross income as a result of the conversion of a traditional IRA to a Roth IRA as described in A-14 of § 1.408A-4T, the fair market value of an annuity contract that has not yet been annuitized is permitted to be determined using the methodology provided in A-12 of § 1.401(a)(9)-6 with the following modifications:

1. All front-end loads and other non-recurring charges assessed in the twelve months immediately preceding the conversion must be added to the account value.

2. Future distributions are not to be assumed in the determination of the actuarial present value of additional benefits.

3. The exclusions provided under paragraphs (c)(1) and (c)(2) of A-12 of § 1.401(a)(9)-6 are not to be taken into account.

SECTION 4. SIMPLIFIED SAFE HARBOR METHOD FOR PRE-2006 ROTH IRA CONVERSIONS

The Service and Treasury recognize that Forms 1099-R must soon be issued for Roth IRA conversions occurring in 2005. Accordingly, this section 4 provides that, in the case of a Roth IRA conversion where an annuity contract that has not yet been annuitized is distributed or treated as distributed before January 1, 2006, for purposes of determining the amount includible in gross income as a result of the conversion of a traditional IRA to a Roth IRA as described in A-14 of § 1.408A-4T, the fair market value of the contract is permitted to be determined using the methodology provided in A-12 of § 1.401(a)(9)-6 except that all front-end loads and other non-recurring charges assessed in the twelve months immediately preceding the conversion must be added to the account value.

DRAFTING INFORMATION * * *

Notice 2007-7, Section IX, 2007-5 I.R.B. 395 (January 29, 2007)

[**Summary:** Code Section 408(d)(8) is applicable to distributions made in taxable years 2006 through 2009. Under Code Section 408(d)(8), generally, if a distribution from an IRA owned by an individual after the individual has attained age 70½ is made directly by the trustee to certain organizations, the distribution is excluded from gross income. A distribution that is eligible for this exclusion is called a qualified charitable distribution. Roth IRAs are permitted to make qualified charitable contributions.]

* * *

IX. Section 1201 OF THE PPA '06

Q-34. **Is there an overall limit on the amount that may be excluded from gross income for qualified charitable distributions that are made in a year?**

A-34. Yes. The income exclusion for qualified charitable distributions only applies to the extent that the aggregate amount of qualified charitable distributions made during any taxable year with respect to an IRA owner does not exceed $100,000. Thus, if an IRA owner maintains multiple IRAs in a taxable year, and qualified charitable distributions are made from more than one of these IRAs, the maximum total amount that may be excluded for that year by the IRA owner is $100,000. For married individuals filing a joint return, the limit is $100,000 per individual IRA owner.

Q-35. **Is the exclusion for qualified charitable distributions available for a distribution made to any organization eligible to receive charitable contributions that are deductible by the donor for income tax purposes?**

A-35. No. Qualified charitable distributions may be made to an organization described in § 170(b)(1)(A), other than supporting organizations described in § 509(a)(3) or donor advised funds that are described in § 4966(d)(2).

Q-36. **Is the exclusion for qualified charitable distributions available for distributions from any type of IRA?**

A-36. Generally, the exclusion for qualified charitable distributions is available for distributions from any type of IRA (including a Roth IRA described in § 408A and a deemed IRA described in § 408(q)) that is neither an ongoing SEP IRA described in § 408(k) nor an ongoing SIMPLE IRA described in § 408(p). For this purpose, a SEP IRA or a SIMPLE IRA is treated as ongoing if it is maintained under an employer arrangement under which an employer contribution is made for the plan year ending with or within the IRA owner's taxable year in which the charitable contributions would be made.

Q-37. **Is the exclusion for qualified charitable distributions available for distributions from an IRA maintained for a beneficiary if the beneficiary has attained age 70½ before the distribution is made?**

A-37. Yes. The exclusion from gross income for qualified charitable distributions is available for distributions from an IRA maintained for the benefit of a beneficiary after the death of the IRA owner if the beneficiary has attained age 70½ before the distribution is made.

Q-38. **If a 2006 distribution satisfies all the requirements under § 408(d)(8), but it was made before August 17, 2006 (the date PPA '06 was enacted), is the amount distributed excludable as a qualified charitable distribution?**

A-38. Yes. Section 408(d)(8) is applicable to distributions made at any time in 2006. Thus, a distribution made in 2006 that satisfies the requirements under § 408(d)(8) is a qualified charitable distribution even if it was made before August 17, 2006.

Q-39. **Is the amount of a qualified charitable distribution deductible as a charitable contribution under § 170?**

A-39. No. For purposes of determining the amount of charitable contributions that may be deducted under § 170, qualified charitable distributions which are excluded from income under § 408(d)(8) are not taken into account. However, qualified charitable distributions must still satisfy the requirements to be deductible charitable contributions under § 170 (other than the percentage limits of § 170(b)), including the substantiation requirements under § 170(f)(8).

Q-40. **Is a qualified charitable distribution subject to withholding under § 3405?**

A-40. No. A qualified charitable distribution is not subject to withholding under § 3405 because an IRA owner that requests such a distribution is deemed to have elected out of withholding under § 3405(a)(2). For purposes of determining whether a distribution requested by an IRA satisfies the requirements under § 408(d)(8), the IRA trustee, custodian, or issuer may rely upon reasonable representations made by the IRA owner.

Q-41. **Is a check from an IRA made payable to a charitable organization described in § 408(d)(8) and delivered by the IRA owner to the charitable organization a direct payment to such organization?**

A-41. Yes. If a check from an IRA is made payable to a charitable organization described in § 408(d)(8) and delivered by the IRA owner to the charitable organization, the payment to the charitable organization will be considered a direct payment by the IRA trustee to the charitable organization for purposes of § 408(d)(8)(B)(i).

Q-42. **Will a qualified charitable distribution be taken into account in determining whether the required minimum distribution requirements of §§ 408(a)(6), 408(b)(3), and 408A(c)(5) have been satisfied?**

A-42. Yes. The amount distributed in a qualified charitable distribution is an amount distributed from the IRA for purposes of §§ 408(a)(6), 408(b)(3), and 408A(c)(5).

Q-43. What are the tax consequences of a direct payment of an amount from an IRA to a charity where the transaction is intended to satisfy the requirements of § 408(d)(8) but fails to do so?

A-43. If an amount intended to be a qualified charitable distribution is paid to a charitable organization but fails to satisfy the requirements of § 408(d)(8), the amount paid is treated as (1) a distribution from the IRA to the IRA owner that is includible in gross income under the rules of § 408 or § 408A, as applicable; and (2) a contribution from the IRA owner to the charitable organization that is subject to the rules under § 170 (including the percentage limits of § 170(b)).

Q-44. Will a distribution made directly by the trustee to a § 170(b)(1)(A) organization (as permitted by § 408(d)(8)(B)(i)) be treated as a receipt by the IRA owner under § 4975(d)(9)?

A-44. Yes. The Department of Labor, which has interpretive jurisdiction with respect to § 4975(d), has advised Treasury and the IRS that a distribution made by an IRA trustee directly to a § 170(b)(1)(A) organization (as permitted by § 408(d)(8)(B)(i)) will be treated as a receipt by the IRA owner under § 4975(d)(9), and thus would not constitute a prohibited transaction. This would be true even if the individual for whose benefit the IRA is maintained had an outstanding pledge to the receiving charitable organization.

* * *

Notice 2006-44, 2006-20 I.R.B. 889 (April 24, 2006)

[**Summary:** The IRS has provided a sample plan amendment for sponsors, practitioners, and employers who want to provide for designated Roth contributions in their Code Section 401 plans. Code Section 402A provides for the treatment of elective Roth deferrals as designated Roth contributions effective for tax years beginning on or after January 1, 2006. Revenue Procedure 2005-66, I.R.B. 2005-37, 509 (Section 5.05(3)), requires plan sponsors to comply with the requirement to timely adopt a discretionary amendment by the end of the plan year in which the amendment is effective. The sample amendment is intended to help plan sponsors meet this requirement.]

I. Purpose

This notice provides a sample plan amendment for sponsors, practitioners, and employers (plan sponsors) who want to provide for designated Roth contributions in their § 401(k) plans. The sample amendment will help those plan sponsors comply with the requirement to timely adopt a discretionary amendment by the end of the plan year in which the amendment is effective, as set forth in section 5.05(3) of Rev. Proc. 2005-66, 2005-37 I.R.B. 509.

II. Background

Section 402A was added to the Code by section 617 of the Economic Growth and Tax Relief Reconciliation Act of 2001, Pub. L. 107-16 (EGTRRA) to provide for the treatment of elective deferrals as designated Roth contributions, effective for taxable years beginning on or after January 1, 2006. Amendments to the final regulations under §§ 401(k) and 401(m) relating to designated Roth contributions were published in the *Federal Register* on January 3, 2006 (71 F.R. 6).

III. Sample Plan Amendment

In General. A sample plan amendment is provided in the Appendix that individual plan sponsors and sponsors of pre-approved plans can adopt or use in drafting individualized plan amendments. Because the amendment in the Appendix is a sample amendment plan sponsors are not required to adopt the amendment verbatim. In fact, it may be necessary for plan sponsors to modify the sample amendment to conform to their plan's terms. In addition, some plan sponsors may need to revise the sample amendment to conform the amendment to the administration of the plan. An issue not addressed in the sample amendment is the extent to which an employee can elect that a distribution (other than a corrective distribution of excess distributions) is to be made from either the designated Roth account or any other account of the employee under the plan. A plan sponsor is permitted to (and may find it necessary to conform the amendment to the plan's operation) revise the amendment in the Appendix (including the default provisions of the amendment) to address this issue.

Time and Manner of Adoption. Plan sponsors who want to provide for designated Roth contributions in their § 401(k) plans must adopt a discretionary amendment as provided in Notice 2005-95, 2005-51 I.R.B. 1172. The deadline to adopt a discretionary amendment is the end of the plan year in which the amendment is effective, as set forth in section 5.05(3) of Rev. Proc. 2005-66. The timely adoption of the amendment must be evidenced by a written document that is signed and dated by the employer (including an adopting employer of a pre-approved plan).

Maintaining the Pre-approved Status of a Pre-approved Plan. The Service will not treat the adoption of the sample plan amendment provided in the Appendix or an individualized plan amendment that reflects the qualification requirements of the regulations under §§ 401(k) and 401(m) relating to designated Roth contributions as affecting the pre-approved status of a master and prototype (M&P) or volume submitter plan. That is, such amendment to an M&P plan that is adopted by an employer will not cause the plan to fail to be an M&P plan. Similarly, such amendment to a volume submitter plan that is adopted by an employer will not cause the plan to fail to be a volume submitter plan. In either case, the amendment will not result in the loss of reliance on a favorable opinion, advisory, or determination letter. In the case where the amendment causes the plan to fail to satisfy § 401(a), the plan will not be disqualified if a remedial amendment that corrects the failure is adopted before the end of the remedial amendment period.

Format of the Sample Amendment. The format of the sample plan amendment generally follows the design of pre-approved plans, including all M&P plans, that employ a "basic plan document" and an "adoption agreement." Thus, the sample plan amendment includes language designed for inclusion in a basic plan document and language designed for inclusion in an adoption agreement to allow the employer to indicate whether, or when, the corresponding basic plan document provision will be effective in the employer's plan and to select among options related to the application of the basic plan document provision. Sponsors of plans that do not use an adoption agreement should modify the format of the amendment to incorporate the appropriate adoption agreement options in the terms of the amendment. In such case, the "notes" in the adoption agreement portion of the sample amendment should not be included in the amendment that will be signed and dated by the employer. Designated Roth contributions are referred to as Roth elective deferrals and designated Roth accounts are referred to as Roth elective deferral accounts in the sample amendment in the Appendix.

DRAFTING INFORMATION * * *

Appendix

Sample Plan Amendment

Article ___. ROTH ELECTIVE DEFERRALS

Section 1. General Application

1.1 This article will apply to contributions beginning with the effective date specified in the adoption agreement but in no event before the first day of the first taxable year beginning on or after January 1, 2006.

1.2 As of the effective date under section 1.1, the plan will accept Roth elective deferrals made on behalf of participants. A participant's Roth elective deferrals will be allocated to a separate account maintained for such deferrals as described in section 2.

1.3 Unless specifically stated otherwise, Roth elective deferrals will be treated as elective deferrals for all purposes under the plan.

Section 2. Separate Accounting

2.1 Contributions and withdrawals of Roth elective deferrals will be credited and debited to the Roth elective deferral account maintained for each participant.

2.2 The plan will maintain a record of the amount of Roth elective deferrals in each participant's account.

2.3 Gains, losses, and other credits or charges must be separately allocated on a reasonable and consistent basis to each participant's Roth elective deferral account and the participant's other accounts under the plan.

2.4 No contributions other than Roth elective deferrals and properly attributable earnings will be credited to each participant's Roth elective deferral account.

Section 3. Direct Rollovers

3.1 Notwithstanding section ____, a direct rollover of a distribution from a Roth elective deferral account under the plan will only be made to another Roth elective deferral account under an applicable retirement plan described in § 402A(e)(1) or to a Roth IRA described in § 408A, and only to the extent the rollover is permitted under the rules of § 402(c).

3.2 Notwithstanding section ____, unless otherwise provided by the employer in the adoption agreement, the plan will accept a rollover contribution to a Roth elective deferral account only if it is a direct rollover from another Roth elective deferral account under an applicable retirement plan described in § 402A(e)(1) and only to the extent the rollover is permitted under the rules of § 402(c).

3.3 The plan will not provide for a direct rollover (including an automatic rollover) for distributions from a participant's Roth elective deferral account if the amount of the distributions that are eligible rollover distributions are reasonably expected to total less than $200 during a year. In addition, any distribution from a participant's Roth elective deferral account is not taken into account in determining whether distributions from a participant's other accounts are reasonably expected to total less than $200 during a year. However, eligible rollover distributions from a participant's Roth elective deferral account are taken into account in determining whether the total amount of the participant's account balances under the plan exceeds $1,000 for purposes of mandatory distributions from the plan.

3.4 The provisions of the plan that allow a participant to elect a direct rollover of only a portion of an eligible rollover distribution but only if the amount rolled over is at least $500 is applied by treating any amount distributed from the participant's Roth elective deferral account as a separate distribution from any amount distributed from the participant's other accounts in the plan, even if the amounts are distributed at the same time.

Section 4. Correction of Excess Contributions

4.1 In the case of a distribution of excess contributions, a highly compensated employee may designate the extent to which the excess amount is composed of pre-tax elective deferrals and Roth elective deferrals but only to the extent such types of deferrals were made for the year.

4.2 If the highly compensated employee does not designate which type of elective deferrals are to be distributed, the plan will distribute pre-tax elective deferrals first.

Section 5. Definition

5.1 Roth Elective Deferrals. A Roth elective deferral is an elective deferral that is:

(a) Designated irrevocably by the participant at the time of the cash or deferred election as a Roth elective deferral that is being made in lieu of all or a portion of the pre-tax elective deferrals the participant is otherwise eligible to make under the plan; and

(b) Treated by the employer as includible in the participant's income at the time the participant would have received that amount in cash if the participant had not made a cash or deferred election.

(Adoption Agreement Provisions)

Article _____, Roth Elective Deferrals: (Check and complete, if applicable.)

_____shall apply to contributions after January 1, 2006.

_____shall apply to contributions after _____. (Enter a date later than January 1, 2006.)

(Note: If neither option is chosen, the amendment will not be effective even if the amendment is signed and dated.)

Section _____, Direct Rollovers: (Check, if applicable.)

The plan:

_____will not accept a direct rollover from another Roth elective deferral account under an applicable retirement plan as described in § 402A(e)(1).

(Note: The default position is that the plan will accept a direct rollover of Roth elective deferrals from another Roth elective deferral account. The default position will apply unless this option is checked.)

_____

Employer's signature and date

Announcement 2008-44, 2008-20 I.R.B. 892 (May 19, 2008)

IRS ANNOUNCES TAX, PENALTY RELIEF FOR WITHDRAWAL OF STIMULUS PAYMENT AMOUNTS FROM IRAS.

[**Summary:** The IRS will provide tax and penalty relief for individuals whose economic stimulus payments are directly deposited to, and later withdrawn from, an IRA, Roth IRA, or similar tax-favored account.]

This announcement provides that individuals who have payments made by direct deposit under the Economic Stimulus Act of 2008, P.L. No. 110-185, to their IRAs or certain other accounts afforded special tax benefits under the Internal Revenue Code may remove the payments without incurring any adverse tax consequences.

Internal Revenue Code (Code) § 6428, as amended by § 101 of the Economic Stimulus Act of 2008, provides for payments to be made to eligible individuals in an amount determined under rules contained in § 6428. These payments are generally known as "Economic Stimulus Payments." Taxpayers who indicated on their 2007 federal income tax return that refund amounts should be directly deposited into one account specified on the return will have their Economic Stimulus Payment directly deposited to that same account. The account specified by the taxpayer could be a checking or saving account, or an account that is given favorable tax treatment under the Code, such as an IRA, a health savings account (HSA), an Archer MSA, a Coverdell education savings account (CESA), or a qualified tuition program account (QTP or section 529 program). Distributions from these tax-favored accounts are subject to rules and restrictions specified in the Code. The Economic Stimulus Payment for a taxpayer who elected to directly deposit his or her 2007 refund into more than one account, however, will be sent as a check and will not be directly deposited into any of the taxpayer's accounts.

An individual may withdraw from a tax-favored account an amount less than or equal to the amount of the Economic Stimulus Payment directly deposited into such account, notwithstanding any restrictions in the Code. To the extent that the withdrawal is made no later than the time for filing the taxpayer's income tax return for 2008, plus extensions (or in the case of a CESA, the later of May 31, 2009, or the time for filing the taxpayer's income tax return for 2008, plus extensions), the amount withdrawn is treated as neither contributed to nor distributed from the account. Thus, the amount withdrawn will not be subject to regular federal income tax nor to any additional tax or penalty under the Code.

The Service recognizes that financial institutions may not be able to distinguish these contributions and distributions from others that may occur. Therefore the financial institution receiving the direct deposit of the Economic Stimulus Payment and making the distribution should report the deposit and distribution in the usual manner. Taxpayers who choose to withdraw their Economic Stimulus Payments will receive instructions in their Form 1040 package that will allow them to report the distribution on their individual income tax return in a manner that shows that the amount withdrawn is not subject to taxes or penalties.

Announcement 2007-55, 2007-1 I.R.B. 1384 (June 4, 2007)

[**Summary:** Sponsors of prototype Roth IRAs who wish to accept rollover contributions from designated Roth accounts under Code Section 402A must amend their prototype Roth IRA documents to reflect that the Roth IRA permits the rollover contributions. An eligible rollover distribution from a designated Roth account established under the program can be rolled over only to another designated Roth account or to a Roth IRA.]

This announcement provides that sponsors of prototype Roth IRAs who wish to accept rollover contributions from designated Roth accounts described in § 402A of the Internal Revenue Code must amend their prototype Roth IRA documents to reflect that the Roth IRA permits these rollover contributions.

Internal Revenue Code § 402A, added by section 617 of the Economic Growth and Tax Relief Reconciliation Act of 2001 ("EGTRRA"), Pub. L. 107-16, authorizes employers to offer, beginning in 2006, a qualified Roth contribution program as part of a § 401(k) plan or a § 403(b) plan. An eligible rollover distribution from a designated Roth account established under the program can be rolled over only to another designated Roth account or to a Roth IRA. Rev. Proc. 2002-10, 2002-1 C.B. 401, provided guidance on amending IRAs and IRA-based plans to reflect changes to the Code made by EGTRRA, but the guidance did not address qualified Roth contribution programs. Consequently, currently approved prototype Roth IRAs generally do not contain language permitting the acceptance of rollovers from designated Roth accounts.

Sponsors of prototype Roth IRAs may now wish to amend their documents to provide for the acceptance of rollovers from designated Roth accounts. In order for a Roth IRA that is intended to be a prototype Roth IRA to accept an eligible rollover contribution from a designated Roth account prior to an amendment permitting such rollovers, the prototype Roth IRA document must be amended and adopted no later than December 31, 2007, in accordance with procedures acceptable under Rev. Proc. 2002-10. Thus, if a prototype Roth IRA accepts a rollover from a designated Roth account prior to the date of amendment, the mere acceptance of such rollover contribution will not affect the Roth IRA's prototype status provided the adoption of the amendment is timely. No application to the Service is required for continued reliance on an Opinion Letter. The model Roth IRAs (Forms 5305-R, 5305-RA and 5305-RB) already contain language permitting the acceptance of rollovers from designated Roth accounts, thus, users of such forms do not need to amend their IRA document to permit such rollovers.

The Roth IRA Listing of Required Modifications ("LRMs"), including acceptable designated Roth account rollover language, is available on the Service's Web Site at www.irs.gov. (Search for "LRMs".) These LRMs have also been updated to reflect other recent law changes, such as section 833(c) of the Pension Protection Act of 2006, P.L. 109-280, relating to inflation adjustments to the modified adjusted gross income limits that are used to determine the amount of Roth IRA contributions.

Notice 2008-30, 2008-12 I.R.B. 638 (March 24, 2008)

[**Summary:** Many of the provisions of the PPA concerning distributions that were effective beginning in 2007 or earlier were addressed in Notice 2007-7 (2007-5 I.R.B. 395). This guidance addresses provisions of the PPA on rollover conversions from eligible retirement plans to Roth individual retirement accounts. Additional nonRoth guidance was also provided.]

I. PURPOSE AND BACKGROUND

This notice provides guidance in the form of questions and answers with respect to certain distribution-related provisions of the Pension Protection Act of 2006, P.L. 109-280 ("PPA '06"), that are effective in 2008. This notice also provides, in Part V, guidance on amending plans to require that distribution of excess deferrals includes earnings from the end of the taxable year to the date of distribution ("gap-period" earnings).

The sections of PPA '06 addressed in this notice are § 824 (relating to roll-overs from eligible retirement plans to Roth IRAs), § 1004 (relating to additional survivor annuity options), and § 302 (relating to interest rate assumptions for lump sum distributions). Notice 2007-7, 2007-5 I.R.B. 395, provides guidance with respect to certain provisions of PPA '06 that are primarily related to distri-butions and that were effective beginning in 2007 or earlier.

II. SECTION 824 OF PPA '06

Prior to amendment by PPA '06, § 408A of the Code provided that a Roth IRA could only accept a rollover contribution of amounts distributed from another Roth IRA, from a nonRoth IRA (i.e., a traditional or SIMPLE IRA) or from a des-ignated Roth account described in § 402A. These rollover contributions to Roth IRAs are called "qualified rollover contributions." A qualified rollover contribu-tion from a nonRoth IRA to a Roth IRA is called a "conversion." An individual who rolls over an amount from a nonRoth IRA to a Roth IRA must include in gross income any portion of the conversion amount that would be includible in gross income if the amount were distributed without being rolled over. For dis-tributions before 2010, a conversion contribution is permitted only if the IRA owner's adjusted gross income does not exceed certain limits.

Section 824 of PPA '06 amended the definition of qualified rollover contribu-tion in § 408A of the Code to include additional plans. Under this expansion, in addition to the rollovers described in the preceding paragraph, a Roth IRA can accept rollovers from other eligible retirement plans (as defined in § 402(c)(8)(B)). The amendments made by § 824 of PPA '06 are effective for dis-tributions made after December 31, 2007.

Q-1. Can distributions from a qualified plan described in § 401(a) be rolled over to a Roth IRA?

A-1. Yes. The rollover can be made through a direct rollover from the plan to the Roth IRA or an amount can be distributed from the plan and contributed (rolled over) to the Roth IRA within 60 days. In either case, the amount rolled over must be an eligible rollover distribution (as defined in § 402(c)(4)) and, pursuant to § 408A(d)(3)(A), there is included in gross income any amount that would be includible if the distribution were not rolled over. In addition, for tax-able years beginning before January 1, 2010, an individual can not make a quali-fied rollover contribution from an eligible retirement plan other than a Roth IRA if, for the year the eligible rollover distribution is made, he or she has modified adjusted gross income ("MAGI") exceeding $100,000 or is married and files a separate return.

Q-2. Can distributions from other types of retirement plans be rolled over to a Roth IRA?

A-2. Subject to the limitations described in the final sentence of A-1 of this notice, the new definition of qualified rollover contribution in § 408A(e) includes distributions from annuity plans described in § 403(a) and (b) and from eligible governmental plans under § 457(b).

Q-3. Does the additional tax under § 72(t) apply to a qualified rollover contribution from an eligible retirement plan other than a Roth IRA?

A-3. No. Pursuant to § 408A(d)(3)(A)(ii), the additional tax under § 72(t) does not apply to rollovers from an eligible retirement plan other than a Roth IRA. However, as with conversions, if a taxable amount rolled into a Roth IRA from an eligible retirement plan other than a Roth IRA is distributed within 5 years, § 72(t) applies to such distribution as if it were includible in gross income. *See* § 408A(d)(3)(F).

Q-4. Under § 401(a)(31)(A), must a plan permit a distributee of an eligible rollover distribution to elect a direct rollover to a Roth IRA?

A-4. Yes. Section 401(a)(31) requires that a plan follow a distributee's election to have an eligible rollover distribution paid in a direct rollover to an eligible retirement plan specified by the distributee. Section 1.401(a)(31)-1 of the Income Tax Regulations provides rules for direct rollovers, including exceptions for small amounts and multiple distributions.

Q-5. Is the plan administrator responsible for assuring the distributee is eligible to make a rollover to a Roth IRA?

A-5. No, the plan administrator is not responsible for assuring the distributee is eligible to make a rollover to a Roth IRA. However, a distributee that is ineligible to make a rollover to a Roth IRA may recharacterize the contribution pursuant to § 408A(d)(6).

Q-6. What are the withholding requirements for an eligible rollover distribution that is rolled over to a Roth IRA?

A-6. An eligible rollover distribution paid to an employee or the employee's spouse is subject to 20% mandatory withholding under § 3405(c). Pursuant to § 3405(c)(2), an eligible rollover distribution that a distributee elects, under § 401(a)(31)(A), to have paid directly to an eligible retirement plan (including a Roth IRA) is not subject to mandatory withholding, even if the distribution is includible in gross income. Also, a distribution that is directly rolled over to a Roth IRA by a nonspouse beneficiary pursuant to § 402(c)(11) (see Q&A-7 of this notice) is not subject to mandatory withholding. However, a distributee and a plan administrator or payor are permitted to enter into a voluntary withholding agreement with respect to an eligible rollover distribution that is directly rolled over from an eligible retirement plan to a Roth IRA. See section 3402(p) and the regulations thereunder for rules relating to voluntary withholding.

Q-7. Can beneficiaries make qualified rollover contributions to Roth IRAs?

A-7. Yes. In the case of a distribution from an eligible retirement plan other than a Roth IRA, the MAGI and filing status of the beneficiary are used to determine eligibility to make a qualified rollover contribution to a Roth IRA. Pursuant to § 402(c)(11), a plan may but is not required to permit rollovers by nonspouse beneficiaries and a rollover by a nonspouse beneficiary must be made by a direct trustee-to-trustee transfer. A nonspouse beneficiary that is ineligible to make a qualified rollover contribution to a Roth IRA may recharacterize the contribution pursuant to § 408A(d)(6). A surviving spouse who makes a rollover to a Roth IRA may elect either to treat the Roth IRA as his or her own or to establish the Roth IRA in the name of the decedent with the surviving spouse as the beneficiary. (*See* Notice 2007-7, Q&A-13, for a rule on how to title a beneficiary IRA.) A nonspouse beneficiary cannot elect to treat the Roth IRA as his or her own. (*See* Notice 2007-7, Part V.)

In the case of a rollover where the beneficiary does not treat the Roth IRA as his or her own, required minimum distributions from the Roth IRA are determined in accordance with Notice 2007-7, Q&As-17, -18 and -19.

III. SECTION 1004 OF PPA '06

Section 401(a)(11) of the Code applies to defined benefit plans and to certain defined contribution plans that are subject to the funding standards of § 412 or that do not satisfy certain other requirements to be exempt from § 401 (a)(11). * * *

IV. SECTION 302 OF PPA '06

Section 417(e)(3) of the Code provides rules for the determination of the present value of plan benefits for purposes of § 417(e). * * *

V. GAP-PERIOD EARNINGS

The final regulations under § 402(g), published in the Federal Register (72 FR 21103) on April 30, 2007, provide that the gap-period earnings must be included with the distribution of excess deferrals to the extent the employee is or would be credited with an allocable gain or loss on those excess deferrals for the gap period, if the total amount were to be distributed. * * *

DRAFTING INFORMATION * * *

Notice 2004-8, 2004-4 I.R.B. 333 (January 26, 2004)

[**Summary:** The IRS has identified certain abusive Roth IRA transactions as tax avoidance transactions and listed transactions subject to the disclosure, list-maintenance, and registration requirements of Code Sections 6011, 6111, and 6112. The notice describes situations where individuals shift income into their Roth IRAs by transferring property from a pre-existing business into a Roth IRA for less than fair market value to avoid the Code Section 408A contribution limits. The Service indicated that it may challenge the transactions on several grounds, recharacterize the transactions for tax purposes, and assert that they give rise to prohibited transactions under section 408A(e)(2)(A).]

The Internal Revenue Service and the Treasury Department are aware of a type of transaction, described below, that taxpayers are using to avoid the limitations on contributions to Roth IRAs. This notice alerts taxpayers and their representatives that these transactions are tax avoidance transactions and identifies these transactions, as well as substantially similar transactions, as listed transactions for purposes of § 1.6011-4(b)(2) of the Income Tax Regulations and §§ 301.6111-2(b)(2) and 301.6112-1(b)(2) of the Procedure and Administration Regulations. This notice also alerts parties involved with these transactions of certain responsibilities that may arise from their involvement with these transactions.

Background

Section 408A was added to the Internal Revenue Code by section 302 of the Taxpayer Relief Act of 1997, Pub. L. 105-34, 105th Cong., 1st Sess. 40 (1997). This section created Roth IRAs as a new type of nondeductible individual retirement arrangement (IRA). The maximum annual contribution to Roth IRAs is the same maximum amount that would be allowable as a deduction under § 219 with respect to the individual for the taxable year over the aggregate amount of contributions for that taxable year to all other IRAs. Neither the contributions to a Roth IRA nor the earnings on those contributions are subject to tax on distribution, if distributed as a qualified distribution described in § 408A(d)(2).

A contribution to a Roth IRA above the statutory limits generates a 6-percent excise tax described in § 4973. The excise tax is imposed each year until the excess contribution is eliminated.

Facts

In general, these transactions involve the following parties: (1) an individual (the Taxpayer) who owns a pre-existing business such as a corporation or a sole proprietorship (the Business), (2) a Roth IRA within the meaning of § 408A that is maintained for the Taxpayer, and (3) a corporation (the Roth IRA Corporation), substantially all the shares of which are owned or acquired by the Roth IRA. The Business and the Roth IRA Corporation enter into transactions as described below. The acquisition of shares, the transactions or both are not fairly valued and thus have the effect of shifting value into the Roth IRA.

Examples include transactions in which the Roth IRA Corporation acquires property, such as accounts receivable, from the Business for less than fair market value, contributions of property, including intangible property, by a person other than the Roth IRA, without a commensurate receipt of stock ownership, or any other arrangement between the Roth IRA Corporation and the Taxpayer, a related party described in § 267(b) or 707(b), or the Business that has the effect of transferring value to the Roth IRA Corporation comparable to a contribution to the Roth IRA.

Analysis

The transactions described in this notice have been designed to avoid the statutory limits on contributions to a Roth IRA contained in § 408A. Because the Taxpayer controls the Business and is the beneficial owner of substantially all of the Roth IRA Corporation, the Taxpayer is in the position to shift value from the Business to the Roth IRA Corporation. The Service intends to challenge the purported tax benefits claimed for these arrangements on a number of grounds.

In challenging the purported tax benefits, the Service will, in appropriate cases, assert that the substance of the transaction is that the amount of the value shifted from the Business to the Roth IRA Corporation is a payment to the Taxpayer, followed by a contribution by the Taxpayer to the Roth IRA and a contribution by the Roth IRA to the Roth IRA Corporation. In such cases, the Service will deny or reduce the deduction to the Business; may require the Business, if the Business is a corporation, to recognize gain on the transfer under § 311(b); and may require inclusion of the payment in the income of the Taxpayer (for example, as a taxable dividend if the Business is a C corporation). *See* Sammons v. United States, 433 F.2d 728 (5th Cir. 1970); Worcester v. Commissioner, 370 F.2d 713 (1st Cir. 1966).

Depending on the facts of the specific case, the Service may apply § 482 to allocate income from the Roth IRA Corporation to the Taxpayer, Business, or other entities under the control of the Taxpayer. Section 482 provides the Secretary with authority to allocate gross income, deductions, credits or allowances among persons owned or controlled directly or indirectly by the same interests, if such allocation is necessary to prevent evasion of taxes or clearly to reflect income. The § 482 regulations provide that the standard to be applied is that of a person dealing at arm's length with an uncontrolled person. *See generally* § 1.482-1(b) of the Income Tax Regulations. To the extent that the consideration paid or received in transactions between the Business and the Roth IRA Corporation is not in accordance with the arm's length standard, the Service may apply § 482 as necessary to prevent evasion of taxes or clearly to reflect income. In the event of a § 482 allocation between the Roth IRA Corporation and the Business or other parties, correlative allocations and other conforming adjustments would be made pursuant to § 1.482-1(g). *Also see* Rev. Rul. 78-83, 1978-1 C.B. 79.

In addition to any other tax consequences that may be present, the amount treated as a contribution as described above is subject to the excise tax described in § 4973 to the extent that it is an excess contribution within the meaning of § 4973(f). This is an annual tax that is imposed until the excess amount is eliminated.

Moreover, under § 408(e)(2)(A), the Service may take the position in appropriate cases that the transaction gives rise to one or more prohibited transactions between a Roth IRA and a disqualified person described in § 4975(e)(2). For example, the Department of Labor[1] has advised the Service that, to the extent that the Roth IRA Corporation constitutes a plan asset under the Department of Labor's plan asset regulation (29 C.F.R. § 2510.3-101), the provision of services by the Roth IRA Corporation to the Taxpayer's Business (which is a disqualified person with respect to the Roth IRA under § 4975(e)(2)) would constitute a prohibited transaction under § 4975(c)(1)(C).[2] Further, the Department of Labor has advised the Service that, if a transaction between a disqualified person and the Roth IRA would be a prohibited transaction, then a transaction between that disqualified person and the Roth IRA Corporation would be a prohibited transaction if the Roth IRA may, by itself, require the Roth IRA Corporation to enter into the transaction.[3]

Listed Transactions

The following transactions are identified as "listed transactions" for purposes of §§ 1.6011-4(b)(2), 301.6111-2(b)(2) and 301.6112-1(b)(2) effective December 31, 2003, the date this document is released to the public: arrangements in which an individual, related persons described in § 267(b) or 707(b), or a business controlled by such individual or related persons, engage in one or more transactions with a corporation, including contributions of property to such corporation, substantially all the shares of which are owned by one or more Roth IRAs maintained for the benefit of the individual, related persons described in § 267(b)(1), or both. The transactions are listed transactions with respect to the individuals for whom the Roth IRAs are maintained, the business (if not a sole proprietorship) that is a party to the transaction, and the corporation substantially all the shares of which are owned by the Roth IRAs. Independent of their classification as "listed transactions," these transactions may already be subject to the disclosure requirements of § 6011 (§ 1.6011-4), the tax shelter registration

---

[1] Under section 102 of Reorganization Plan No. 4 of 1978 (43 FR 47713), the Secretary of Labor has interpretive jurisdiction over § 4975 of the Internal Revenue Code.

[2] For the Roth IRA Corporation to be considered as holding plan assets under the Department of Labor's plan asset regulation, the Roth IRA's investment in the Roth IRA Corporation must be an equity interest, the Roth IRA Corporation's securities must not be publicly-offered securities, and the Roth IRA's investment in the Roth IRA Corporation must be significant. 29 C.F.R. §§ 2510.3-101(a)(2), 2510.3-101(b)(1), 2510.3-101(b)(2), and 2510.3-101(f). Although the Roth IRA Corporation would not be treated as holding plan assets if the Roth IRA Corporation constituted an operating company within the meaning of 29 C.F.R. § 2510.3-101(c), given the context of the examples described in this notice, it is unlikely that the RothIRA Corporation would qualify as an operating company.

[3] See 29 C.F.R. § 2509.75-2(c).

requirements of § 6111 (§§ 301.6111-1T and 301.6111-2), or the list maintenance requirements of § 6112 (§ 301.6112-1).

Substantially similar transactions include transactions that attempt to use a
single structure with the intent of achieving the same or substantially same tax
effect for multiple taxpayers. For example, if the Roth IRA Corporation is owned
by multiple taxpayers' Roth IRAs, a substantially similar transaction occurs
whenever that Roth IRA Corporation enters into a transaction with a business of
any of the taxpayers if distributions from the Roth IRA Corporation are made to
that taxpayer's Roth IRA based on the purported business transactions done
with that taxpayer's business or otherwise based on the value shifted from that
taxpayer's business to the Roth IRA Corporation.

Persons required to register these tax shelters under § 6111 who have failed
to do so may be subject to the penalty under § 6707(a). Persons required to
maintain lists of investors under § 6112 who have fail to do so (or who fail to
provide such lists when requested by the Service) may be subject to the penalty
under § 6708(a). In addition, the Service may impose penalties on participants
in this transaction or substantially similar transactions, including the accuracy-
related penalty under § 6662, and as applicable, persons who participate in the
reporting of this transaction or substantially similar transactions, including the
return preparer penalty under § 6694, the promoter penalty under § 6700, and
the aiding and abetting penalty under § 6701.

The Service and the Treasury recognize that some taxpayers may have filed
tax returns taking the position that they were entitled to the purported tax benefits of the type of transaction described in this notice. These taxpayers should
consult with a tax advisor to ensure that their transactions are disclosed properly and to take appropriate corrective action.

Drafting Information * * * *

Appendix F

Pension and Welfare Benefits Administration (PWBA) Opinion Letter

PWBA Opinion Letter 98-03A (March 6, 1998)

[Summary: The exemption permitting registered broker-dealers to provide reduced-fee or no-cost services applies to Roth IRAs.]

Dear * * *

This is in response to your letter of December 31, 1997, in which you request guidance regarding whether a Roth IRA as defined in Section 408A of the Internal Revenue Code of 1986 (the Code), will be considered an IRA for purposes of Prohibited Transaction Exemption (PTE) 97-11 (62 FR 5855, February 7, 1997).

Section 302(a) of the Taxpayer Relief Act of 1997 (Pub. L. 105-34, title III, Sec. 302(a), August 5, 1997, 111 Stat. 788) created a new IRA, called the Roth IRA, by adding Section 408A to the Code.

You represent that your members and clients will begin offering Roth IRAs beginning in 1998. You further state that you are concerned that the prohibited transaction provisions in the Employee Retirement Income Security Act of 1974 (ERISA) may restrict certain common industry practices or transactions which involve the operation of Roth IRAs. Although these transactions have been the subject of prohibited transaction class exemptions involving (traditional) IRAs, you note that without guidance from the Department of Labor (the Department), it is unclear that such relief would extend to Roth IRAs. Specifically, you have inquired about the availability of relief under PTE 97-11 with respect to Roth IRAs.

PTE 97-11 permits the receipt of services at reduced or no cost by an individual for whose benefit an IRA or if self-employed, a Keogh Plan is established or maintained or by members of his or her family, from a broker-dealer registered under the Securities Exchange Act of 1934 pursuant to an arrangement in which the account value of, or the fees incurred for services provided to, the IRA or Keogh Plan is taken into account for purposes of determining eligibility to receive such services, provided that the conditions of the exemption are met. The term "IRA" is defined in section III(b) of PTE 97-11 as:

an individual retirement account described in section 408(a) of the Code. For purposes of this exemption, the term IRA shall not include an IRA which is an employee retirement benefit plan covered by Title I of ERISA, except for a Simplified Employee Pension (SEP) described in section 408(k) of the Code or a Simple Retirement Account described in section 408(p) of the Code which provides participants with the unrestricted authority to transfer their balances to IRAs or Simple Retirement Accounts sponsored by different financial institutions.

Section 408A(a) of the Code provides that, except as provided in this section, a Roth IRA shall be treated for purposes of this title in the same manner as an individual retirement plan. Section 408A(b) of the Code provides that for purposes of this title, the term "Roth IRA" means an individual retirement plan (as defined in Section 7701(a)(37)) which is designated (in such manner as the Secretary may prescribe) at the time of the establishment of the plan as a Roth IRA. Such designation shall be made in such manner as the Secretary may prescribe.[1]

Section 7701(a)(37) of the Code defines the term "individual retirement plan" to mean: (A) an individual retirement account described in Section 408(a), and (B) an individual retirement annuity described in Section 408(b) of the Code.

It is the opinion of the Department that a Roth IRA which satisfies the definition of an individual retirement plan in Section 7701(a)(37) of the Code is an "individual retirement account" described in Section 408(a) of the Code for purposes of the definition of the term "IRA" contained in III(b) of PTE 97-11. Therefore, a Roth IRA, as described above, which is not an employee benefit plan covered by Title I of ERISA (except for certain SEPs and Simple Retirement Accounts described in Sections 408(k) and 408(p) of the Code, respectively) would be covered by the relief provided in PTE 97-11, if all the conditions therein are met.

This letter constitutes an advisory opinion under ERISA Procedure 76-1. Section 10 of the Procedure explains the effect of an advisory opinion.

Sincerely,

Ivan L. Strasfeld
Director
Office of Exemption Determinations

---

[1]No regulations have been promulgated to date.

Appendix G

Lists of Required Modifications
and Information Packages (LRMs)

Roth IRA List of Required Modifications and Information Package (Dated: May 2007)

(For use with prototype Roth IRAs intending to satisfy the requirements of Code sections 408A and 408(a) or (b).)

This information package contains samples of provisions that have been found to satisfy certain specific requirements of the Internal Revenue Code as amended through the Tax Relief and Health Care Act of 2006 (Pub. L. No. 109-432) Such language may or may not be acceptable in specific Roth IRAs, depending on the context.

Part A, provisions 1–12, applies to Roth individual retirement accounts under Code sections 408A and 408(a). Part B, provisions 13–21, applies to Roth individual retirement annuities under sections 408A and 408(b). Changes from the May 2006 LRM package are underlined.

PART A. ACCOUNTS—Roth trust or custodial accounts under Code sections 408A, 408(a) and 408(h).

(1) Statement of Requirement: The Roth IRA is organized and operated for the exclusive benefit of the individual, Code sections 408A and 408(a). Sample Language:

> The account is established for the exclusive benefit of the individual or his or her beneficiaries.

(2) Statement of Requirement: Maximum permissible annual contribution and restrictions on kinds of contributions, Code sections 219(b), 219(f)(1), 408(d)(3)(G), 408(p)(1)(B), 408(p)(2)(A)(iv), 408A(c), 408A(d)(6) and 408A(e) and Regulations sections 1.219-1(c)(1) and 1.408A-3, -4 and -5. Sample Language:

> *(a) Maximum permissible amount.* Except in the case of a qualified rollover contribution or a recharacterization (as defined in *(f)* below), no contribution will be accepted unless it is in cash and the total of such contributions to all the individual's Roth IRAs for a taxable year does not exceed *applicable amount (as defined in (b) below)*, or the individual's compensation (as defined in *(h)* below), if less, for that taxable year. The contribution described in the previous sentence that may not exceed the lesser of *the applicable amount* or the individual's compensation is referred to as a "regular contribution." However, notwithstanding the dollar limits on contributions, an individual may make a repayment of a qualified reservist distribution described in Code § 72(t)(2)(G) during the 2-year period beginning on the day after the end of the active duty period or by August 17, 2008, if later. A "qualified rollover contribution" is a rollover contribution of a distribution from an IRA that meets the requirements of Code § 408(d)(3), except the one-rollover-per-year rule of § 408(d)(3)(B) does not apply if the rollover contribution is from an IRA other than a Roth IRA (a "nonRoth IRA"). For taxable years beginning after 2005, a qualified rollover contribution includes a rollover from a designated Roth account described in Code § 402A; and for taxable years beginning after 2007, a qualified rollover contribution also includes a rollover from an eligible retirement plan described in § 402(c)(8)(B). Contributions may be limited under *(c)* through *(e)* below.

> *(b) Applicable Amount.* The applicable amount is determined under (i) or (ii) below:

> (i) If the individual is under age 50, the applicable amount is $3,000 for any taxable year beginning in 2002 through 2004, $4,000 for any taxable year beginning in 2005 through 2007 and $5,000 for any taxable year beginning in 2008 and years thereafter. After 2008, the $5,000 amount will be adjusted by the Secretary of the Treasury for cost-of-living increases under Code § 219(b)(5)(D). Such adjustments will be in multiples of $500.

> (ii) If the individual is 50 or older, the applicable amount under paragraph (i) above is increased by $500 for any taxable year beginning in 2002 through 2005 and by $1,000 for any taxable year beginning in 2006 and years thereafter.

(iii) If the individual was a participant in a § 401(k) plan of a certain employer in bankruptcy described in Code § 219(b)(5)(C), then the applicable amount under paragraph (i) above is increased by $3,000 for taxable years beginning after 2006 and before 2010 only. An individual who makes contributions under this paragraph (iii) may not also make contributions under paragraph (ii).

(c) Regular Contribution Limit. If (i) and/or (ii) below apply, the maximum regular contribution that can be made to all the individual's Roth IRAs for a taxable year is the smaller amount determined under (i) or (ii).

(i) The maximum regular contribution is phased out ratably between certain levels of modified adjusted gross income ("modified AGI," defined in *(g)* below) in accordance with the following table:

Filing Status	Full Contribution	Phase-out Range	No Contribution
		Modified AGI	
Single or Head of Household	$95,000 or less	Between $95,000 and $110,000	$110,000 or more
Joint Return or Qualifying Widow(er)	$150,000 or less	Between $150,000 and $160,000	$160,000 or more
Married—Separate Return	$0	Between $0 and $10,000	$10,000 or more

If the individual's modified AGI for a taxable year is in the phase-out range, the maximum regular contribution determined under this table for that taxable year is rounded up to the next multiple of $10 and is not reduced below $200. After 2006, the dollar amounts above will be adjusted by the Secretary of the Treasury for cost-of-living increases under Code § 408A(c)(3). Such adjustments will be in multiples of $1,000.

(ii) If the individual makes regular contributions to both Roth and non-Roth IRAs for a taxable year, the maximum regular contribution that can be made to all the individual's Roth IRAs for that taxable year is reduced by the regular contributions made to the individual's nonRoth IRAs for the taxable year.

(d) Qualified Rollover Contribution Limit. A rollover from an eligible retirement plan other than a Roth IRA or a designated Roth account cannot be made to this IRA if, for the year the amount is distributed from the other plan, (i) the individual is married and files a separate return, (ii) the individual is not married and has modified AGI in excess of $100,000 or (iii) the individual is married and together the individual and the individual's spouse have modified AGI in excess of $100,000. For purposes of the preceding sentence, a husband and wife are not treated as married for a taxable year if they have lived apart at all times during that taxable year and file separate returns for the

taxable year. For taxable years beginning after 2009, the limits in this paragraph (d) do not apply to qualified rollover contributions.

(e) SIMPLE IRA Limits. No contributions will be accepted under a SIMPLE IRA Plan established by any employer pursuant to section 408(p). Also, no transfer or rollover of funds attributable to contributions made by a particular employer under its SIMPLE IRA Plan will be accepted from a SIMPLE IRA, that is, an IRA used in conjunction with a SIMPLE IRA Plan, prior to the expiration of the 2-year period beginning on the date the individual first participated in that employer's SIMPLE IRA Plan.

(f) Recharacterization. A regular contribution to a nonRoth IRA may be recharacterized pursuant to the rules in section 1.408A-5 of the proposed regulations as a regular contribution to this IRA, subject to the limits in *(c)* above.

(g) Modified AGI. For purposes of *(c)* and *(d)* above, an individual's modified AGI for a taxable year is defined in section 408A(c)(3)(C)(i) and does not include any amount included in adjusted gross income as a result of a rollover from an eligible retirement plan other than a Roth IRA (a "conversion").

(h) Compensation. For purposes of (a) above, compensation is defined as wages, salaries, professional fees, or other amounts derived from or received for personal services actually rendered (including, but not limited to commissions paid salesmen, compensation for services on the basis of a percentage of profits, commissions on insurance premiums, tips, and bonuses) and includes earned income, as defined in section 401(c)(2) (reduced by the deduction the self employed individual takes for contributions made to a self-employed retirement plan). For purposes of this definition, section 401(c)(2) shall be applied as if the term trade or business for purposes of section 1402 included service described in subsection (c)(6). Compensation does not include amounts derived from or received as earnings or profits from property (including but not limited to interest and dividends) or amounts not includible in gross income. Compensation also does not include any amount received as a pension or annuity or as deferred compensation. The term "compensation" shall include any amount includible in the individual's gross income under section 71 with respect to a divorce or separation instrument described in subparagraph (A) of section 71(b)(2). In the case of a married individual filing a joint return, the greater compensation of his or her spouse is treated as his or her own compensation, but only to the extent that such spouse's compensation is not being used for purposes of the spouse making a contribution to a Roth IRA or a nondeductible contribution to a nonRoth IRA.

(3) Statement of Requirement: An investment in collectibles will be treated as a distribution, Code section 408(m). Sample Language:

> If the trust acquires collectibles within the meaning of Code section 408(m) after December 31, 1981, trust assets will be treated as a distribution in an amount equal to the cost of such collectibles.

(**Note to reviewer:** This provision is not required if the arrangement precludes any investments that could be construed as collectibles. Code section 408(m)(3) provides an exception to this rule for certain coins and precious metals.)

(4) Statement of Requirement: Prohibition against investment in life insurance, Code section 408(a)(3). Sample Language:

No part of the trust funds will be invested in life insurance contracts.

(5) Statement of Requirement: Distributions before death are not required, Code section 408A(c)(5). Sample Language:

No amount is required to be distributed prior to the death of the individual for whose benefit the account was originally established.

(6) Statement of Requirement: Distribution upon death, Code sections 408A(c)(5) and 408(a)(6) and Regulations sections 1.408A-6 and 1.408-8. Sample Language:

(a) Notwithstanding any provision of this IRA to the contrary, the distribution of the individual's interest in the account shall be made in accordance with the requirements of Code section 408(a)(6), as modified by section 408A(c)(5), and the regulations thereunder, the provisions of which are herein incorporated by reference. If distributions are made from an annuity contract purchased from an insurance company, distributions thereunder must satisfy the requirements of § 1.401(a)(9)-6 of the Income Tax Regulations (taking into account Code section 408A(c)(5)), rather than the distribution rules in paragraphs (b), (c) and (d) below.

(b) Upon the death of the individual, his or her entire interest will be distributed at least as rapidly as follows:

(i) If the designated beneficiary is someone other than the individual's surviving spouse, the entire interest will be distributed, starting by the end of the calendar year following the calendar year of the individual's death, over the remaining life expectancy of the designated beneficiary, with such life expectancy determined using the age of the beneficiary as of his or her birthday in the year following the year of the individual's death, or, if elected, in accordance with paragraph (b)(iii) below.

(ii) If the individual's sole designated beneficiary is the individual's surviving spouse, the entire interest will be distributed, starting by the end of the calendar year following the calendar year of the individual's death (or by the end of the calendar year in which the individual would have attained age 70$\frac{1}{2}$, if later), over such spouse's life, or, if elected, in accordance with paragraph (b)(iii) below. If the surviving spouse dies before distributions are required to begin, the remaining interest will be distributed, starting by the end of the calendar year following the calendar year of the spouse's death, over the spouse's designated beneficiary's remaining life expectancy determined using such beneficiary's age as of his or her birthday in the year following the death of the spouse, or, if elected, will be distributed in accordance with paragraph (b)(iii) below. If the surviving spouse dies after distributions are required to begin, any remaining interest will be distributed over the spouse's remaining life expectancy determined using the spouse's age as of his or her birthday in the year of the spouse's death.

(iii) If there is no designated beneficiary, or if applicable by operation of paragraph (b)(i) or (b)(ii) above, the entire interest will be distributed by the end of the calendar year containing the fifth anniversary of the individual's death (or of the spouse's death in the case of the surviving spouse's death before distributions are required to begin under paragraph (b)(ii) above).

(iv) The amount to be distributed each year under paragraph (b)(i) or (ii) is the quotient obtained by dividing the value of the IRA as of the end of the preceding year by the remaining life expectancy specified in such paragraph. Life expectancy is determined using the Single Life Table in Q&A-1 of section 1.401(a)(9)-9 of the Income Tax Regulations. If distributions are being made to a surviving spouse as the sole designated beneficiary, such spouse's remaining life expectancy for a year is the number in the Single Life Table corresponding to such spouse's age in the year. In all other cases, remaining life expectancy for a year is the number in the Single Life Table corresponding to the beneficiary's age in the year specified in paragraph (b)(i) or (ii) and reduced by 1 for each subsequent year.

(c) The "value" of the IRA includes the amount of any outstanding rollover, transfer and recharacterization under Q&As-7 and -8 of section 1.408-8 of the Income Tax Regulations.

(d) If the sole designated beneficiary is the individual's surviving spouse, the spouse may elect to treat the IRA as his or her own IRA. This election will be deemed to have been made if such surviving spouse makes a contribution to the IRA or fails to take required distributions as a beneficiary.

(7) Statement of Requirement: Individual's interest must be nonforfeitable, Code section 408(a)(4). Sample Language:

The interest of an individual in the balance in his or her account is nonforfeitable at all times.

(8) Statement of Requirement: Prohibition against commingling of assets, Code section 408(a)(5). Sample Language:

The assets of the trust will not be commingled with other property except in a common trust fund or common investment fund.

(9) Statement of Requirement: Separate accounting for the interest of each individual under a Roth IRA established by an employer or employee association, Regulations section 1.408-2(c)(3) and Regulations section 1.408A-2. Sample Language:

Separate records will be maintained for the interest of each individual.

(**Note to reviewer:** The above provision is required only in Roth IRAs that are sponsored by the employer or employee association.)

(10) Statement of Requirement: Annual reports by trustees, Code sections 408(i) and 408A(d)(3)(D) and Regulations sections 1.408-5 and 1.408-8. Sample Language:

> The trustee of a Roth individual retirement account shall furnish annual calendar-year reports concerning the status of the account *and such information concerning required minimum distributions as is prescribed by the Commissioner of Internal Revenue.*

(11) Statement of Requirement: Substitution of non-bank trustee or custodian, Regulations section 1.408-2(e)(6)(v). Sample Language:

> The non-bank trustee or custodian shall substitute another trustee or custodian if the non-bank trustee or custodian receives notice from the Commissioner of Internal Revenue that such substitution is required because it has failed to comply with the requirements of Regulations section 1.408-2(e).

(**Note to reviewer:** This provision is required only in IRA accounts that are sponsored by non-bank trustees or custodians.)

(12) [Reserved]

PART B. ANNUITIES—Roth annuities under Code sections 408A and 408(b).

(13) Statement of Requirement: The Roth IRA is organized and operated for the exclusive benefit of the individual, Code sections 408A and 408(b). Sample Language:

> The contract is established for the exclusive benefit of the individual or his or her beneficiaries.

(14) Statement of Requirement: Maximum permissible annual contribution and restrictions on kinds of contributions, Code sections 219(b), 219(f)(1), 408(d)(3)(G), 408(p)(1)(B), 408(p)(2)(A)(iv), 408A(c), 408A(d)(6) and 408A(e) and Regulations sections 1.219-1(c)(1) and 1.408A-3, -4 and -5. Sample Language:

> *(a) Maximum Permissible Amount.* Except in the case of a qualified rollover contribution or a recharacterization (as defined in *(f)* below), no contribution will be accepted unless it is in cash and the total of such contributions to all the individual's Roth IRAs for a taxable year does not exceed *the applicable amount (as defined in (b) below),* or the individual's compensation (as defined in *(h)* below), if less, for that taxable year. The contribution described in the previous sentence that may not exceed the lesser of *the*

applicable amount or the individual's compensation is referred to as a "regular contribution." However, notwithstanding the dollar limits on contributions, an individual may make a repayment of a qualified reservist distribution described in Code § 72(t)(2)(G) during the 2-year period beginning on the day after the end of the active duty period or by August 17, 2008, if later. A "qualified rollover contribution" is a rollover contribution of a distribution from an IRA that meets the requirements of section 408(d)(3) of the Internal Revenue Code, except the one-rollover-per-year rule of section 408(d)(3)(B) does not apply if the rollover contribution is from an IRA other than a Roth IRA (a "nonRoth IRA"). For taxable years beginning after 2005, a qualified rollover contribution includes a rollover from a designated Roth account described in Code § 402A; and for taxable years beginning after 2007, a qualified rollover contribution also includes rollover from an eligible retirement plan described in § 402(c)(8)(B). Contributions may be limited under *(c)* through *(e)* below.

(b) Applicable Amount. The applicable amount is determined under (i) or (ii) below:

(i) If the individual is under age 50, the applicable amount is $3,000 for any taxable year beginning in the 2002 through 2004, $4,000 for any taxable year beginning in 2005 through 2007 and $5,000 for any taxable year beginning in 2008 and years thereafter. After 2008, the $5,000 amount will be adjusted by the Secretary of the Treasury for cost-of-living increases under Code § 219(b)(5)(D). Such adjustments will be in multiples of $500.

(ii) If the individual is 50 or older, the applicable amount under paragraph (i) above is increased by $500 for any taxable year beginning in 2002 through 2005 and by $1,000 for any taxable year beginning in 2006 and years thereafter.

(iii) If the individual was a participant in a § 401(k) plan of a certain employer in bankruptcy described in Code § 219(b)(5)(C), then the applicable amount under paragraph (i) above is increased by $3,000 for taxable years beginning after 2006 and before 2010 only. An individual who makes contributions under this paragraph (iii) may not also make contributions under paragraph (ii).

(c) Regular Contribution Limit. If (i) and/or (ii) below apply, the maximum regular contribution that can be made to all the individual's Roth IRAs for a taxable year is the smaller amount determined under (i) or (ii).

(i) The maximum regular contribution is phased out ratably between certain levels of modified adjusted gross income ("modified AGI," defined in *(g)* below) in accordance with the following table:

Filing Status	Full Contribution	Phase-out Range	No Contribution
		Modified AGI	
Single or Head of Household	$95,000 or less	Between $95,000 and $110,000	$110,000 or more
Joint Return or Qualifying Widow(er)	$150,000 or less	Between $150,000 and $160,000	$160,000 or more
Married— Separate Return	$0	Between $0 and $10,000	$10,000 or more

If the individual's modified AGI for a taxable year is in the phaseout range, the maximum regular contribution determined under this table for that taxable year is rounded up to the next multiple of $10 and is not reduced below $200. After 2006, the dollar amounts above will be adjusted by the Secretary of the Treasury for cost-of-living increases under Code § 408A(c)(3). Such adjustments will be in multiples of $1,000.

(ii) If the individual makes regular contributions to both Roth and non-Roth IRAs for a taxable year, the maximum regular contribution that can be made to all the individual's Roth IRAs for that taxable year is reduced by the regular contributions made to the individual's nonRoth IRAs for the taxable year.

(d) Qualified Rollover Contribution Limit. A rollover from an eligible retirement plan other than a Roth IRA or a designated Roth account cannot be made to this IRA if, for the year the amount is distributed from the other plan, (i) the individual is married and files a separate return, (ii) the individual is not married and has modified AGI in excess of $100,000 or (iii) the individual is married and together the individual and the individual's spouse have modified AGI in excess of $100,000. For purposes of the preceding sentence, a husband and wife are not treated as married for a taxable year if they have lived apart at all times during that taxable year and file separate returns for the taxable year. For taxable years beginning after 2009, the limits in this paragraph (d) do not apply to qualified rollover contributions.

(e) SIMPLE IRA Limits. No contributions will be accepted under a SIMPLE IRA Plan established by any employer pursuant to section 408(p). Also, no transfer or rollover of funds attributable to contributions made by a particular employer under its SIMPLE IRA plan will be accepted from a SIMPLE IRA, that is, an IRA used in conjunction with a SIMPLE IRA plan, prior to the expiration of the 2-year period beginning on the date the individual first participated in that employer's SIMPLE IRA plan.

(f) Recharacterization. A regular contribution to a nonRoth IRA may be recharacterized pursuant to the rules in section 1.408A-5 of the regulations as a regular contribution to this IRA, subject to the limits in (b) above.

(g) Modified AGI. For purposes of (c) and (d) above, an individual's modified AGI for a taxable year is defined in section 408A(c)(3)(C)(i) and does not include any amount included in adjusted gross income as a result of a rollover from <u>an eligible retirement plan other than a Roth IRA</u> (a "conversion").

(h) Compensation. For purposes of (a) above, compensation is defined as wages, salaries, professional fees, or other amounts derived from or received for personal services actually rendered (including, but not limited to commissions paid salesmen, compensation for services on the basis of a percentage of profits, commissions on insurance premiums, tips, and bonuses) and includes earned income, as defined in section 401(c)(2) (reduced by the deduction the self employed individual takes for contributions made to a self-employed retirement plan). For purposes of this definition, section 401(c)(2) shall be applied as if the term trade or business for purposes of section 1402 included service described in subsection (c)(6). Compensation does not include amounts derived from or received as earnings or profits from property (including but not limited to interest and dividends) or amounts not includible in gross income. Compensation also does not include any amount received as a pension or annuity or as deferred compensation. The term "compensation" shall include any amount includible in the individual's gross income under section 71 with respect to a divorce or separation instrument described in subparagraph (A) of section 71(b)(2). In the case of a married individual filing a joint return, the greater compensation of his or her spouse is treated as his or her own compensation, but only to the extent that such spouse's compensation is not being used for purposes of the spouse making a contribution to a Roth IRA or a nondeductible contribution to a nonRoth IRA.

(15) Statement of Requirement: Distributions before death are not required, Code section 408A(c)(5). Sample Language:

No amount is required to be distributed prior to the death of the individual for whose benefit the contract was originally established.

(16) Statement of Requirement: Distribution upon death, Code sections 408A(a)(6) and 408(c)(5) and Regulations sections 1.408-8 and 1.408A-6. Sample Language:

(a) Notwithstanding any provision of this IRA to the contrary, the distribution of the individual's interest in the IRA shall be made in accordance with the requirements of Code section 408(b)(3), as modified by section 408A(c)(5), and the regulations thereunder, the provisions of which are herein incorporated by reference. If distributions are not made in the form of an annuity on an irrevocable basis (except for acceleration), the distribution of the interest in the IRA (as determined under section _____) must satisfy the requirements of Code section 408(a)(6), as modified by section 408(c)(5), and the regulations thereunder, rather than the distribution rules in paragraphs (b), (c), (d) and (e) below.

Note to reviewer: The blank should contain a reference that corresponds to LRM #16(c).)

(b) Upon the death of the individual, his or her entire interest will be distributed at least as rapidly as follows:

(i) If the designated beneficiary is someone other than the individual's surviving spouse, the entire interest will be distributed, starting by the end of the calendar year following the calendar year of the individual's death, over the remaining life expectancy of the designated beneficiary, with such life expectancy determined using the age of the beneficiary as of his or her birthday in the year following the year of the individual's death, or, if elected, in accordance with paragraph (b)(iii) below.

(ii) If the individual's sole designated beneficiary is the individual's surviving spouse, the entire interest will be distributed, starting by the end of the calendar year following the calendar year of the individual's death (or by the end of the calendar year in which the individual would have attained age $70\frac{1}{2}$, if later), over such spouse's life, or, if elected, in accordance with paragraph (b)(iii) below. If the surviving spouse dies before required distributions commence to him or her, the remaining interest will be distributed, starting by the end of the calendar year following the calendar year of the spouse's death, over the spouse's designated beneficiary's remaining life expectancy determined using such beneficiary's age as of his or her birthday in the year following the death of the spouse, or, if elected, will be distributed in accordance with paragraph (b)(iii) below. If the surviving spouse dies after required distributions commence to him or her, any remaining interest will continue to be distributed under the contract option chosen.

(iii) If there is no designated beneficiary, or if applicable by operation of paragraph (b)(i) or (b)(ii) above, the entire interest will be distributed by the end of the calendar year containing the fifth anniversary of the individual's death (or of the spouse's death in the case of the surviving spouse's death before distributions are required to begin under paragraph (b)(ii) above).

(iv) Life expectancy is determined using the Single Life Table in Q&A-1 of section 1.401(a)(9)-9 of the Income Tax Regulations. If distributions are being made to a surviving spouse as the sole designated beneficiary, such spouse's remaining life expectancy for a year is the number in the Single Life Table corresponding to such spouse's age in the year. In all other cases, remaining life expectancy for a year is the number in the Single Life Table corresponding to the beneficiary's age in the year specified in paragraph (b)(i) or (ii) and reduced by 1 for each subsequent year.

(c) The "interest" in the IRA includes the amount of any outstanding rollover, transfer and recharacterization under Q&As-7 and -8 of section 1.408-8 of the Income Tax Regulations and the actuarial value of any other benefits provided under the IRA, such as guaranteed death benefits.

(d) For purposes of paragraph (b)(ii) above, required distributions are considered to commence on the date distributions are required to begin to the surviving spouse under such paragraph. However, if distributions start prior to the applicable date in the preceding sentence, on an irrevocable basis (except for acceleration) under an annuity contract meeting the requirements of section 1.401(a)(9)-6T of the Income Tax Regulations, then required distributions are considered to commence on the annuity starting date.

(e) If the sole designated beneficiary is the individual's surviving spouse, the spouse may elect to treat the IRA as his or her own IRA. This election will be deemed to have been made if such surviving spouse makes a contribution to the IRA or fails to take required distributions as a beneficiary.

(17) Statement of Requirement: Participant's interest must be nonforfeitable, Code section 408(b)(4). Sample Language:

The interest of the individual is nonforfeitable.

(18) Statement of Requirement: Contract is nontransferable by the owner, Code section 408(b)(1). Sample Language:

This contract is nontransferable by the individual.

(19) Statement of Requirement: Application of refund premiums, Code section 408(b)(2). Sample Language:

Any refund of premiums (other than those attributable to excess contributions) will be applied, before the close of the calendar year following the year of the refund, toward the payment of future premiums or the purchase of additional benefits.

(**Note to reviewer:** Language that meets the requirements of this provision must be included in annuities that provide for participation in dividends.)

(20) Statement of Requirement: Contract may not require fixed premiums; however, the sample language below does not violate this requirement, Code section 408(b)(2) and Proposed Regulations section 1.408-3(f). Sample Language:

If the premium payments are interrupted, the contract will be reinstated at any date prior to maturity upon payment of a premium to the insurance company, and the minimum premium amount for reinstatement shall be _____ (not to exceed $50), however, the insurance company may at its option either accept additional future payments or terminate the contract by payment in cash of the then present value of the paid up benefit if no premiums have been received for two full consecutive policy years and the paid up annuity benefit at maturity would be less than $20 per month.

(21) Statement of Requirement: Annual reports by trustees or issuers, sections 408(i) and 408A(d)(3)(D) and Regulations sections 1.408-5 and 1.408-8. Sample Language:

The issuer of a Roth individual retirement annuity shall furnish annual calendar year reports concerning the status of the annuity *and such information concerning required minimum distributions as is prescribed by the Commissioner of Internal Revenue.*

Cash or Deferred Arrangement (CODA) List of Required Modifications and Information Package (Dated: January 2006)

Editor's Note: Specific mention of Roth 401(k) include the following items:

(For use with master or prototype (M&P) plans intending to satisfy the requirements of Code §§ 401(k) and 401(m).)

This information package contains samples of plan provisions that satisfy certain specific requirements of the Internal Revenue Code, as amended through the Working Families Tax Relief Act of 2004 (P.L. 108-311). Such language may or may not be acceptable in specific plans, depending on the context. Note that these CODA LRMs assume the plan will permit catch-up contributions (defined in Code § 414(v)) for participants age 50 and over and, after 2005, Roth Elective Deferrals (defined in § 402A).

These LRMs reflect the final regulations under Code §§ 401(k) and 401(m) that were published in the Federal Register on December 29, 2004 (and on January 3, 2006, in the case of Roth Elective Deferrals). These final regulations apply to plan years beginning after 2005; however, a plan is permitted to apply the final regulations in plan years ending after December 29, 2004, provided the plan applies all the rules in the final regulations as of such earlier date. Where applicable, these LRMs use the later effective date. If the earlier effective date is desired, the plan must so state.

These LRMs do not reflect changes to the Code made by the Gulf Opportunity Zone Act of 2005, P.L. 109-135.

* * *

(III) ELECTIVE DEFERRAL ELECTIONS (Code §§ 401(k), 402A and 414(v) and Regs. § 1.401(k)-1(e) and (f))

Statement of Requirement: The Plan must provide a means by which an employee who is eligible to participate in the CODA may elect to have the Employer make payments either (1) as contributions to a trust under the Plan on behalf of the employee in accordance with a cash or deferred election, or (2) to the employee directly in cash. Such an employee, if age 50 or over by the end of his or her taxable year, must also be permitted to make Catch-up Contributions as defined in Code § 414(v). In addition, in the case of Roth Elective Deferrals (after 2005), participants must be able to designate some or all of their Elective Deferrals as Roth Elective Deferrals, which must be maintained in a separate account.

The Plan must specify a reasonable period at least once each Plan Year during which a participant may elect to commence Elective Deferrals. Such election may not be made retroactively. A participant's election to commence Elective Deferrals must remain in effect until modified or terminated.

The Plan must also specify a reasonable period at least once each Plan Year during which a participant may elect to terminate an election or to modify the amount, type (Roth or Pre-tax) or frequency of his or her Elective Deferrals.

A plan that provides for automatic enrollment, whereby a stated amount is automatically withheld from a participant's salary and contributed to the plan as an Elective Deferral (either Roth, Pre-tax or a combination of both, as specified in the plan) unless he or she affirmatively elects a different amount (including no amount) or type of Elective Deferral, must provide the participant with an effective opportunity to elect a different amount (including no amount) and type.

Sample Plan Language:

An employee eligible to make Elective Deferrals under the Plan may submit a deferral election to the Plan administrator at any time, specifying the amount (in whole dollars or whole percentages) and type (either Roth, Pre-tax or a specific combination) of Elective Deferrals to be withheld from each wage payment. Such election will be effective for the first pay period beginning after 5 business days from receipt of the election, unless a later pay period is specified by the employee. An employee's election will remain in effect until superseded by another election. Elective Deferrals contributed to the Plan as one type, either Roth or Pre-tax, may not later be reclassified as the other type.

A participant's Roth Elective Deferrals will be deposited in the participant's Roth Elective Deferral account in the Plan. No contributions other than Roth Elective Deferrals and properly attributable earnings will be credited to each participant's Roth Elective Deferral account, and gains, losses and other credits or charges will be allocated on a reasonable and consistent basis to such account.

The Plan will maintain a record of the amount of Roth Elective Deferrals in each participant's Roth Elective Deferral account.

[**Note to reviewer:** See LRM V for definition of Elective Deferrals.]

* * *

(V) DISTRIBUTION OF EXCESS ELECTIVE DEFERRALS (Code §§ 401(a)(30), 402(g) and 402A and Regs. § 1.402(g)-1)

Statement of Requirement: A mechanism must be provided by which a participant may notify or be deemed to notify the Plan administrator of Excess Elective Deferrals and upon such notice, but prior to April 15 of the year following the year in which the deferrals were made, the Excess Elective Deferrals and any earnings thereon will be distributed. Deemed notification occurs if Excess Elective Deferrals arise solely from Elective Deferrals made under this Plan or any other plan, contract or arrangement of the Employer.

Sample Plan Language:

A participant may assign to this Plan any Excess Elective Deferrals made during a taxable year of the participant by notifying the Plan administrator on or before the date specified in the adoption agreement of the amount of the Excess Elective Deferrals to be assigned to the Plan. A participant is deemed to notify the Plan administrator of any Excess Elective Deferrals that arise by taking into account only those Elective Deferrals made to this Plan and any other plan, contract or arrangement of the Employer.

Notwithstanding any other provision of the Plan, Excess Elective Deferrals, plus any income and minus any loss allocable thereto, shall be distributed no later than April 15 to any participant to whose account Excess Elective Deferrals were assigned for the preceding year and who claims Excess Elective Deferrals for such taxable year or calendar year. For years beginning after 2005, distribution of Excess Elective Deferrals for a year shall be made first from the participant's Pre-tax Elective Deferral account, to the extent Pre-tax Elective Deferrals were made for the year, unless the participant specifies otherwise.

[**Note to reviewer:** For years beginning after 2005, if both Pretax Elective Deferrals and Roth Elective Deferrals were made for the year, the Plan may specify that distribution of Excess Elective Deferrals will consist of a participant's Pre-tax Elective Deferrals, Roth Elective Deferrals or a combination of both, to the extent such type of Elective Deferrals was made for the year.]

Determination of income or loss: Excess Elective Deferrals shall be adjusted for any income or loss up to the date of distribution. The income or loss allocable to Excess Elective Deferrals is the sum of: (1) income or loss allocable to the participant's Elective Deferral account for the taxable year multiplied by a fraction, the numerator of which is such participant's Excess Elective Deferrals for the year and the denominator is the participant's account balance attributable to Elective Deferrals without regard to any income or loss occurring during such taxable year; and (2) 10 percent of the amount determined under (1) multiplied by the number of whole calendar months between the end of the participant's taxable year and the date of distribution, counting the month of distribution if distribution occurs after the 15th of such month.

[**Note to reviewer:** A plan may use any reasonable method for computing the income or loss allocable to Excess Elective Deferrals, provided such method is used consistently for all participants and for all corrective distributions under the plan for the plan year, and is used by the plan for allocating income or loss to participants' accounts. For taxable years beginning before January 1, 2006, income or loss allocable to the period between the end of the taxable year and the date of distribution could be disregarded in determining income or loss on Excess Elective Deferrals for such years.]

Definitions:

1. "Elective Deferrals" shall mean any employer contributions made to the Plan at the election of the participant in lieu of cash compensation. With respect to any taxable year, a participant's Elective Deferrals is the sum of all employer contributions made on behalf of such participant pursuant to an election to defer

under any qualified cash or deferred arrangement ("CODA") described in Code § 401(k), any salary reduction simplified employee pension described in § 408(k)(6), any SIMPLE IRA plan described in § 408(p) and any plan described under § 501(c)(18), and any employer contributions made on behalf of a participant for the purchase of an annuity contract under § 403(b) pursuant to a salary reduction agreement. For years beginning after 2005, the term "Elective Deferrals" includes Pretax Elective Deferrals and Roth Elective Deferrals. Pre-tax Elective Deferrals are a participant's Elective Deferrals that are not includible in the participant's gross income at the time deferred. Elective Deferrals shall not include any deferrals properly distributed as excess annual additions.

2. "Roth Elective Deferrals" are a participant's Elective Deferrals that are includible in the participant's gross income at the time deferred and have been irrevocably designated as Roth Elective Deferrals by the participant in his or her deferral election.

3. "Excess Elective Deferrals" shall mean those Elective Deferrals of a participant that either (1) are made during the participant's taxable year and exceed the dollar limitation under Code § 402(g) (including, if applicable, the dollar limitation on Catch-up Contributions defined in § 414(v)) for such year; or (2) are made during a calendar year and exceed the dollar limitation under Code § 402(g) (including, if applicable, the dollar limitation on Catch-up Contributions defined in § 414(v)) for the participant's taxable year beginning in such calendar year, counting only Elective Deferrals made under this Plan and any other plan, contract or arrangement maintained by the Employer.

Sample Adoption Agreement Language:

Participants who claim Excess Elective Deferrals for the preceding taxable year must submit their claims in writing to the Plan administrator by [ ][SPECIFY A DATE BEFORE APRIL 15].

* * *

(VII) DISTRIBUTION OF EXCESS CONTRIBUTIONS (Code §§ 401(k)(8) and 4979 and Regs. § 1.401(k)-2(b))

Statement of Requirement: Excess Contributions for a Plan Year, plus any income and minus any loss allocable thereto, must be distributed no later than 12 months after such Plan Year. For plan years beginning after 2005, if both Pre-tax Elective Deferrals and Roth Elective Deferrals were made for the year, the Plan may specify that distribution of Excess Contributions will consist of a participant's Pre-tax Elective Deferrals, Roth Elective Deferrals or a combination of both, to the extent such type of Elective Deferrals was made for the year. If such excess amounts are distributed more than 2 months after the last day of the Plan Year in which such excess amounts arose, then Code § 4979 imposes a 10-percent excise tax on the Employer with respect to such amounts.

Sample Plan Language:

Notwithstanding any other provision of the Plan, Excess Contributions, plus any income and minus any loss allocable thereto, shall be distributed no later than 12 months after a Plan Year to participants to whose accounts such Excess Contributions were allocated for such Plan Year, except to the extent such Excess Contributions are classified as Catch-up Contributions. Excess Contributions are allocated to the Highly Compensated Employees with the largest amounts of employer contributions taken into account in calculating the ADP test for the year in which the excess arose, beginning with the Highly Compensated Employee with the largest amount of such employer contributions and continuing in descending order until all the Excess Contributions have been allocated. To the extent a Highly Compensated Employee has not reached his or her Catch-up Contribution limit under the Plan, Excess Contributions allocated to such Highly Compensated Employee are Catch-up Contributions and will not be treated as Excess Contributions. If such excess amounts (other than Catch-up Contributions) are distributed more than 2 months after the last day of the Plan Year in which such excess amounts arose, a 10 percent excise tax will be imposed on the employer maintaining the Plan with respect to such amounts.

Excess Contributions shall be treated as annual additions under the Plan even if distributed.

Determination of Income or Loss: Excess Contributions shall be adjusted for any income or loss up to the date of distribution. The income or loss allocable to Excess Contributions allocated to each participant is the sum of: (1) income or loss allocable to the participant's Elective Deferral account (and, if applicable, the Qualified Nonelective Contribution account or the Qualified Matching Contribution account or both) for the Plan Year multiplied by a fraction, the numerator of which is such participant's Excess Contributions for the year and the denominator is the participant's account balance attributable to Elective Deferrals (and Qualified Nonelective Contributions or Qualified Matching Contributions, or both, if any of such contributions are included in the ADP test) without regard to any income or loss occurring during such Plan Year; and (2) 10 percent of the amount determined under (1) multiplied by the number of whole calendar months between the end of the Plan Year and the date of distribution, counting the month of distribution if distribution occurs after the 15th of such month.

[**Note to reviewer:** A Plan may use any reasonable method for computing the income or loss allocable to Excess Contributions, provided such method is used consistently for all participants and for all corrective distributions under the Plan for the Plan Year, and is used by the Plan for allocating income or loss to participants' accounts. For Plan Years beginning before 2006, income or loss allocable to the period between the end of the Plan Year and the date of distribution could be disregarded in determining income or loss on Excess Contributions for such years.]

Accounting for Excess Contributions: Excess Contributions allocated to a participant shall be distributed from the participant's Elective Deferral account and Qualified Matching Contribution account (if applicable) in proportion to the participant's Elective Deferrals and Qualified Matching Contributions (to the extent used in the ADP test) for the Plan Year. For Plan Years beginning after 2005, distribution of Elective Deferrals that are Excess Contributions shall be made from the participant's Pre-tax Elective Deferral account before the participant's Roth Elective Deferral account, to the extent Pre-tax Elective Deferrals were made for the year, unless the participant specifies otherwise. Excess Contributions shall be distributed from the participant's Qualified Nonelective Contribution account only to the extent that the Excess Contributions exceed the amount of Excess Contributions in the participant's Elective Deferral account and Qualified Matching Contribution account.

Definition:

"Excess Contributions" shall mean, with respect to any Plan Year, the excess of:

1. The aggregate amount of employer contributions actually taken into account in computing the ADP of Highly Compensated Employees for such Plan Year, over

2. The maximum amount of such contributions permitted by the ADP test (determined by hypothetically reducing contributions made on behalf of Highly Compensated Employees in order of the ADPs, beginning with the highest of such percentages).

* * *

(XII) LIMITATIONS ON EMPLOYEE AND MATCHING CONTRIBUTIONS (Code §§ 401(a)(4) and 401(m) and Regs. § 1.401(m)-2) (Generally required in all plans where Matching Contributions are provided for—unless the Plan is designed to be a 401(k) SIMPLE plan or a Safe Harbor CODA— or if Employee Contributions are permitted under the Plan.)

Statement of Requirement: Employee Contributions and Matching Contributions must meet the nondiscrimination requirements of Code § 401(a)(4), and the Actual Contribution Percentage ("ACP") test of § 401(m). If Employee Contributions (including any Elective Deferrals recharacterized as Employee Contributions) or Matching Contributions are made in conjunction with a CODA, then the ACP test is in addition to the ADP test under § 401(k). Qualified Matching Contributions and Qualified Non-elective Contributions used to satisfy the ADP test may not be used to satisfy the ACP test.

Sample Plan Language:

<u>Prior Year Testing</u>

The Actual Contribution Percentage ("ACP") for a Plan Year for participants who are Highly Compensated Employees for each Plan Year and the prior year's ACP for participants who were Nonhighly Compensated Employees for the prior Plan Year must satisfy one of the following tests:

1. The ACP for a Plan Year for participants who are Highly Compensated Employees for the Plan Year shall not exceed the prior year's ACP for participants who were Non-highly Compensated Employees for the prior Plan Year multiplied by 1.25; or

2. The ACP for a Plan Year for participants who are Highly Compensated Employees for the Plan Year shall not exceed the prior year's ACP for participants who were Non-highly Compensated Employees for the prior Plan Year multiplied by 2, provided that the ACP for participants who are Highly Compensated Employees does not exceed the ACP for participants who were Non-highly Compensated Employees in the prior Plan Year by more than 2 percentage points.

For the first Plan Year this Plan permits any participant to make Employee Contributions, provides for Matching Contributions or both, and this is not a successor plan, for purposes of the foregoing tests, the prior year's Non-highly Compensated Employees' ACP shall be 3 percent unless the Employer has elected in the adoption agreement to use the Plan Year's ACP for these participants.

<u>Current Year Testing</u>

If elected by the Employer in the adoption agreement, the ACP tests in 1 and 2, above, will be applied by comparing the current Plan Year's ACP for participants who are Highly Compensated Employees for each Plan Year with the current Plan Year's ACP for participants who are Non-highly Compensated Employees. Once made, the Employer can elect Prior Year Testing for a Plan Year only if the Plan has used Current Year Testing for each of the preceding 5 Plan Years (or if lesser, the number of Plan Years the Plan has been in existence) or if, as a result of a merger or acquisition described in Code § 410(b)(6)(C)(i), the Employer maintains both a plan using Prior Year Testing and a plan using Current Year Testing and the change is made within the transition period described in § 410(b)(6)(C)(ii).

Special Rules:

1. A participant is a Highly Compensated Employee for a particular Plan Year if he or she meets the definition of a Highly Compensated Employee in effect for that Plan Year. Similarly, a participant is a Non-highly Compensated Employee for a particular Plan Year if he or she does not meet the definition of a Highly Compensated Employee in effect for that Plan Year.

2. Multiple Use (Before 2002): If one or more Highly Compensated Employees participate in both a CODA and a plan subject to the ACP test maintained by the Employer and the sum of the ADP and ACP of those Highly Compensated Employees subject to either or both tests exceeds the Aggregate Limit, then for Plan Years beginning before 2002 the ACP of those Highly Compensated Employees who also participate in a CODA will be reduced in the manner described in section [ ] of the Plan so that the limit is not exceeded. The amount by which each Highly Compensated Employee's Contribution Percentage Amounts is reduced shall be treated as an Excess Aggregate Contribution. The ADP and ACP of the Highly Compensated Employees are determined after any corrections required to meet the ADP and ACP tests and are deemed to be the maximum permitted under such tests for the Plan Year. Multiple use does not occur if either the ADP or the ACP of the Highly Compensated Employees does not exceed 1.25 multiplied by the ADP and ACP, respectively, of the Non-highly Compensated Employees. Restrictions on multiple use do not apply for Plan Years beginning after 2001.

[**Note to Reviewer:** The blank should contain the section of the Plan that references the ACP correction method.]

3. For purposes of this section, the Contribution Percentage for any participant who is a Highly Compensated Employee and who is eligible to have Contribution Percentage Amounts allocated to his or her account under two or more plans described in Code § 401(a), or arrangements described in Code § 401(k) that are maintained by the Employer, shall be determined as if the total of such Contribution Percentage Amounts was made under each plan and arrangement. If a Highly Compensated Employee participates in two or more such plans or arrangements that have different plan years, all Contribution Percentage Amounts made during the Plan Year under all such plans and arrangements shall be aggregated. For plan years beginning before 2006, all such plans and arrangements ending with or within the same calendar year shall be treated as a single plan or arrangement. Notwithstanding the foregoing, certain plans shall be treated as separate if mandatorily disaggregated under regulations under Code § 401(m).

4. In the event that this Plan satisfies the requirements of Code §§ 401(m), 401(a)(4) or 410(b) only if aggregated with one or more other plans, or if one or more other plans satisfy the requirements of such sections of the Code only if aggregated with this Plan, then this section shall be applied by determining the ACP of employees as if all such plans were a single plan. If more than 10 percent of the Employer's Non-highly Compensated Employees are involved in a plan coverage change as defined in Regulations § 1.401(m)-2(c)(4), then any adjustments to the Nonhighly Compensated Employees' ADP for the prior year will be made in accordance with such Regulations, unless the Employer has elected in the adoption agreement to use the Current Year Testing method. Plans may be aggregated in order to satisfy Code § 401(m) only if they have the same Plan Year and use the same ACP testing method.

5. For purposes of the ACP test, Employee Contributions are considered to have been made in the Plan Year in which contributed to the trust. Matching

Contributions and Qualified Nonelective Contributions will be considered made for a Plan Year if made no later than the end of the 12-month period beginning on the day after the close of the Plan Year.

Definitions:

1. "Aggregate Limit," for Plan Years beginning before 2002 only, shall mean the sum of (i) 125 percent of the greater of the ADP of the Non-highly Compensated Employees for the prior Plan Year or the ACP of Non-highly Compensated Employees under the plan subject to Code § 401(m) for the Plan Year beginning with or within the prior Plan Year of the CODA and (ii) the lesser of 200 percent or 2 plus the lesser of such ADP or ACP. "Lesser" is substituted for "greater" in "(i)," above, and "greater" is substituted for "lesser" after "2 plus the" in "(ii)" if it would result in a larger Aggregate Limit. If the Employer has elected in the adoption agreement to use the Current Year Testing method, then, in calculating the Aggregate Limit for a particular Plan Year, the Non-highly Compensated Employees' ADP and ACP for that Plan Year, instead of for the prior Plan Year, is used.

2. "Actual Contribution Percentage" ("ACP") shall mean, for a specified group of participants (either Highly Compensated Employees or Non-highly Compensated Employees) for a Plan Year, the average of the Contribution Percentages of the Eligible Participants in the group.

3. "Contribution Percentage" shall mean the ratio (expressed as a percentage) of the participant's Contribution Percentage Amounts to the participant's Compensation for the Plan Year.

4. "Contribution Percentage Amounts" shall mean the sum of the Employee Contributions, Matching Contributions, and Qualified Matching Contributions (to the extent not taken into account for purposes of the ADP test) made under the Plan on behalf of the participant for the Plan Year. Such Contribution Percentage Amounts shall not include Matching Contributions that are forfeited either to correct Excess Aggregate Contributions or because the contributions to which they relate are Excess Deferrals, Excess Contributions, or Excess Aggregate Contributions. If so elected in the adoption agreement the Employer may include Qualified Nonelective Contributions in the Contribution Percentage Amounts. The Employer also may elect to use Elective Deferrals in the Contribution Percentage Amounts so long as the ADP test is met before the Elective Deferrals are used in the ACP test and continues to be met following the exclusion of those Elective Deferrals that are used to meet the ACP test.

5. "Eligible Participant" shall mean any employee who is eligible to make an Employee Contribution, or an Elective Deferral (if the Employer takes such contributions into account in the calculation of the Contribution Percentage), or to receive a Matching Contribution (including forfeitures) or a Qualified Matching Contribution. If an Employee Contribution is required as a condition of participation in the Plan, any employee who would be a participant in the Plan if such employee made such a contribution shall be treated as an eligible participant on behalf of whom no Employee Contributions are made.

6. "Employee Contribution" shall mean any contribution (other than Roth Elective Deferrals) made to the Plan by or on behalf of a participant that is included in the participant's gross income in the year in which made and that is maintained under a separate account to which earnings and losses are allocated.

7. "Matching Contribution" shall mean an employer contribution made to this or any other defined contribution plan on behalf of a participant on account of an Employee Contribution made by such participant, or on account of a participant's Elective Deferral, under a plan maintained by the Employer.

Sample Adoption Agreement Language:

If this is not a successor plan, then, if checked [ ], for the first Plan Year this Plan permits any participant to make Employee Contributions, provides for Matching Contributions or both, the ACP used in the ACP test for participants who are Nonhighly Compensated Employees shall be such first Plan Year's ACP.

(Do not check this box if the Employer has elected in the adoption agreement to use the Current Year Testing method.)

[ ] If checked, this Plan is using the Current Year Testing method for purposes of the ADP and ACP tests. (This box cannot be "unchecked" for a Plan Year unless (1) the Plan has used Current Year Testing for each of the preceding 5 Plan Years (or if lesser, the number of Plan Years the Plan has been in existence) or (2) if, as a result of a merger or acquisition described in Code § 410(b)(6)(C)(i), the Employer maintains both a plan using Prior Year Testing and a plan using Current Year Testing and the change is made within the transition period described in § 410(b)(6)(C)(ii).)

[**Note to reviewer:** An M&P plan may use different testing methods for the ADP and ACP tests provided the Plan doesn't permit (1) recharacterization of Excess Contributions, (2) Elective Deferrals to be used in the ACP test or (3) Qualified Matching Contributions to be used in the ADP test.]

(XIII) DISTRIBUTION OF EXCESS AGGREGATE CONTRIBUTIONS (Code §§ 401(m)(6) and 4979 and Regs. § 1.401(m)-2(b))

Statement of Requirement: Excess Aggregate Contributions for a Plan Year must be distributed no later than 12 months after such Plan Year. However, any excess amounts distributed more than 2 months after the last day of the Plan Year in which such excess amounts arose will be subject to a 10-percent excise tax under Code § 4979. This tax is imposed on the Employer with respect to such amounts.

Sample Plan Language:

Notwithstanding any other provision of the Plan, Excess Aggregate Contributions, plus any income and minus any loss allocable thereto, shall be forfeited, if forfeitable, or if not forfeitable, distributed no later than 12 months after a Plan Year to participants to whose accounts such Excess Aggregate Contributions were allocated for such Plan Year. Excess Aggregate Contributions are allocated to the Highly Compensated Employees with the largest Contribution Percentage Amounts taken into account in calculating the ACP test for the year in which the excess arose, beginning with the Highly Compensated Employee with the largest amount of such Contribution Percentage Amounts and continuing in descending order until all the Excess Aggregate Contributions have been allocated. If such Excess Aggregate Contributions are distributed more than 2 months after the last day of the Plan Year in which such excess amounts arose, a 10 percent excise tax will be imposed on the employer maintaining the Plan with respect to those amounts. Excess Aggregate Contributions shall be treated as annual additions under the Plan even if distributed.

Determination of Income or Loss: Excess Aggregate Contributions shall be adjusted for any income or loss up to the date of distribution. The income or loss allocable to Excess Aggregate Contributions allocated to each participant is the sum of: (1) income or loss allocable to the participant's Employee Contribution account, Matching Contribution account, Qualified Matching Contribution Account (if any, and if all amounts therein are not used in the ADP test) and, if applicable, Qualified Nonelective Contribution account and Elective Deferral account for the Plan Year multiplied by a fraction, the numerator of which is such participant's Excess Aggregate Contributions for the year and the denominator is the participant's account balance(s) attributable to Contribution Percentage Amounts without regard to any income or loss occurring during such Plan Year; and (2) 10 percent of the amount determined under (1) multiplied by the number of whole calendar months between the end of the Plan Year and the date of distribution, counting the month of distribution if distribution occurs after the 15th of such month.

[**Note to reviewer:** The Plan may use any reasonable method for computing the income or loss allocable to Excess Aggregate Contributions, provided that such method is used consistently for all participants and for all corrective distributions under the Plan for the Plan Year, and is used by the Plan for allocating income or loss to participants' accounts. For Plan Years beginning before 2006, income or loss allocable to the period between the end of the Plan Year and the date of distribution could be disregarded in determining income or loss on Excess Aggregate Contributions for such years.]

Forfeitures of Excess Aggregate Contributions: Forfeitures of Excess Aggregate Contributions may either be reallocated to the accounts of Non-highly Compensated Employees or applied to reduce employer contributions, as elected by the Employer in section [ ] of the adoption agreement.

Accounting for Excess Aggregate Contributions: Excess Aggregate Contributions allocated to a participant shall be forfeited, if forfeitable or distributed on a pro-rata basis from the participant's Employee Contribution account, Matching Contribution account, and Qualified Matching Contribution account (and, if applicable, the participant's Qualified Nonelective Contribution account or Elective Deferral account, or both). For Plan Years beginning after 2005, distribution of Elective Deferrals that are Excess Aggregate Contributions shall be made from the participant's Pre-tax Elective Deferral account before the participant's Roth

Elective Deferral account, to the extent Pre-tax Elective Deferrals were made for the year, unless the participant specifies otherwise.

Definitions:

1. "Excess Aggregate Contributions" shall mean, with respect to any Plan Year, the excess of:

a. The aggregate Contribution Percentage Amounts taken into account in computing the numerator of the Contribution Percentage actually made on behalf of Highly Compensated Employees for such Plan Year, over

b. The maximum Contribution Percentage Amounts permitted by the ACP test (determined by hypothetically reducing contributions made on behalf of Highly Compensated Employees in order of their Contribution Percentages beginning with the highest of such percentages).

Such determination shall be made after first determining Excess Elective Deferrals pursuant to section [ ] of the Plan and then determining Excess Contributions pursuant to section [ ] of the Plan.

Sample Adoption Agreement Language:

In computing the Actual Contribution Percentage, the Employer shall take into account, and include as Contribution Percentage Amounts:

[ ] a. Elective Deferrals

[ ] b. Qualified Nonelective Contributions under the Plan or any other plan of the Employer.

The amount of Qualified Nonelective Contributions that are made under section [ ] of the Plan and taken into account as Contribution Percentage Amounts for purposes of calculating the Actual Contribution Percentage shall be:

[ ] a. All such Qualified Nonelective Contributions.

[ ] b. Such Qualified Nonelective Contributions that are needed to meet the Actual Contribution Percentage test stated in section [ ] of the Plan. (Box b can only be checked if the Employer has elected in the adoption agreement to use the Current Year Testing method.)

The amount of Elective Deferrals made under section [ ] of the Plan and taken into account as Contribution Percentage Amounts for purposes of calculating the Actual Contribution Percentage shall be:

[ ] a. All such Elective Deferrals.

[ ] b. Such Elective Deferrals that are needed to meet the Actual Contribution Percentage test stated in section [ ] of the Plan. (Box b can only be checked if the Employer has elected in the adoption agreement to use the Current Year Testing method.)

Forfeitures of Excess Aggregate Contributions shall be:

[ ] a. Applied to reduce employer contributions for the Plan Year in which the excess arose, but allocated as in b, below, to the extent the excess exceeds employer contributions or the Employer has already contributed for such Plan Year.

[ ] b. Allocated, after all other forfeitures under the Plan, to the Matching Contribution account of each Non-highly Compensated Employee who made Elective Deferrals or Employee Contributions in the ratio that each such employee's Compensation for the Plan Year bears to the total Compensation of all such employees for such Plan Year. For Plan Years Beginning after 2005, such forfeitures shall be allocated to each Non-highly Compensated Employee in the ratio that each such employee's Elective Deferrals for the Plan Year bears to the total Elective Deferrals of all such employees for such Plan Year.

[**Note to reviewer:** Forfeitures cannot be used as Qualified Nonelective Contributions, Qualified Matching Contributions or Elective Deferrals. For Plan Years beginning after 2005, matching formulas, other than those above, such as flat-dollar or ones that target matches at lower paid Non-highly Compensated Employees, must satisfy additional requirements specified in Regulations § 1.401(m)-2(a)(5).]

* * *

(XV) NONFORFEITABILITY AND VESTING (Code §§ 401(k)(2)(C), 401(m)(4)(C)(ii), 411(a)(1) and 411(a)(3)(G)) Statement of Requirement: An employee's right to his or her accrued benefit derived from Employee Contributions and Elective Deferrals made pursuant to his or her election must be nonforfeitable. Qualified Nonelective Contributions and Qualified Matching Contributions must be nonforfeitable when made.

Sample Plan Language:

The participant's accrued benefit derived from Elective Deferrals, Qualified Nonelective Contributions, Employee Contributions, and Qualified Matching Contributions is nonforfeitable. Separate accounts for Elective Deferrals other than Roth Elective Deferrals, Roth Elective Deferrals, Qualified Nonelective Contributions, Employee Contributions, Matching Contributions, and Qualified Matching Contributions will be maintained for each participant. Each account will be credited with the applicable contributions and earnings thereon. Matching Contributions (including Qualified Matching Contributions) must be forfeited if the contributions to which they relate are Excess Deferrals (unless the Excess Deferrals are for nonhighly compensated employees), Excess Contributions, or Excess Aggregate Contributions.

(XVI) DISTRIBUTION LIMITATIONS (Code § 401(k)(2)(B) and Regs. § 1.401(k)-1(d))

Statement of Requirement: Elective Deferrals, Qualified Nonelective Contributions, and Qualified Matching Contributions, and income allocable to each, must comply with the distribution limitations under Code § 401(k)(2)(B) and Regulations § 1.401(k)-1(d).

Sample Plan Language:

A participant's Elective Deferrals, Qualified Nonelective Contributions, and Qualified Matching Contributions, and income allocable to each are not distributable earlier than upon the participant's severance from employment (separation from service, for Plan Years beginning before 2002), death, or disability.

[**Note to Reviewer:** The following distributable events may be included in either the basic plan document or as elective provisions in the adoption agreement.]

Such amounts may also be distributed upon:

1. Termination of the Plan without the Employer maintaining another defined contribution plan (other than an employee stock ownership plan as defined in Code § 4975(e)(7) or 409(a), a simplified employee pension plan as defined in § 408(k), a SIMPLE IRA plan as defined in § 408(p), a plan or contract described in § 403(b) or a plan described in § 457(b) or (f)) at any time during the period beginning on the date of plan termination and ending 12 months after all assets have been distributed from the Plan. Such a distribution must be made in a lump sum.

2. The attainment of age 59½ in the case of a profit-sharing plan.

3. The hardship of the participant as described in section [ ].

[**Note to Reviewer:** The blank should contain the section of the Plan that corresponds to LRM XVII.]

For Plan Years beginning before 2002, such amounts could also be distributed upon:

4. The disposition by a corporation to an unrelated corporation of substantially all of the assets (within the meaning of Code § 409(d)(2)) used in a trade or business of such corporation if such corporation continues to maintain the Plan after the disposition, but only with respect to employees who continue employment with the corporation acquiring such assets. Such a distribution must be made in a lump sum.

5. The disposition by a corporation to an unrelated entity of such corporation's interest in a subsidiary (within the meaning of Code § 409(d)(3)) if such corporation continues to maintain the Plan, but only with respect to employees who continue employment with such subsidiary. Such a distribution must be made in a lump sum.

All distributions that may be made pursuant to one or more of the foregoing distributable events are subject to the spousal and participant consent requirements (if applicable) contained in Code §§ 401(a)(11) and 417.

[**Note to Reviewer:** Roth Elective Deferral accounts are permitted for years beginning after 2005, and distributions from such accounts (other than corrective distributions) are not includible in the participant's gross income if made after 5 years and after the participant's death, disability, or age 59½. Earnings on corrective distributions of Roth Elective Deferrals are includible in gross income the same as earnings on corrective distributions of Pre-tax Elective Deferrals.]

(XVII) HARDSHIP DISTRIBUTIONS (Code § 401(k)(2)(B), Regs. § 1.401(k)-1(d)(3) and Rev. Proc. 2005-16, § 6.03(15))

[**Note to Reviewer:** A profit-sharing plan may permit distribution of Elective Deferrals (but not earnings thereon, nor of Qualified Nonelective Contributions and Qualified Matching Contributions) on account of financial hardship only under the deeming rules contained in the regulations under Code § 401(k). However, the Plan may provide that amounts eligible for such distribution include earnings on Elective Deferrals and the amount credited to the participant's Qualified Matching Contributions and Qualified Nonelective Contributions accounts as of December 31, 1988, or, if later, the end of the last Plan Year ending before July 1, 1989.]

Sample Plan Language:

Distribution of Elective Deferrals (and any earnings credited to a participant's Elective Deferral account as of the later of December 31, 1988, and the end of the last Plan Year ending before July 1, 1989) may be made to a participant in the event of hardship. A hardship distribution may only be made on account of an immediate and heavy financial need of the employee and where the distribution is necessary to satisfy the immediate and heavy financial need. Hardship distributions are subject to the spousal consent requirements contained in Code §§ 401(a)(11) and 417, if applicable.

Special Rules:

1. The following are the only financial needs considered immediate and heavy: expenses incurred or necessary for medical care, described in Code § 213(d), of the employee, the employee's spouse or dependents; the purchase (excluding mortgage payments) of a principal residence for the employee; payment of tuition and related educational fees for the next 12 months of post-secondary education for the employee, the employee's spouse, children or dependents; payments necessary to prevent the eviction of the employee from, or a foreclosure on the mortgage of, the employee's principal residence; payments for funeral or burial expenses for the employee's deceased parent, spouse, child or dependent; and expenses to repair damage to the employee's principal residence that would qualify for a casualty loss deduction under Code § 165. (determined without regard to whether the loss exceeds 10 percent of adjusted

gross income). The last two needs (funeral expenses and home repair) only apply to Plan Years beginning after 2005.

2. A distribution will be considered as necessary to satisfy an immediate and heavy financial need of the employee only if:

a. The distribution is not in excess of the amount of the immediate and heavy financial need (including amounts necessary to pay any federal, state or local income taxes or penalties reasonably anticipated to result from the distribution);

b. The employee has obtained all distributions, other than hardship distributions, and all nontaxable loans under all plans maintained by the Employer; and

c. All plans maintained by the Employer provide that the employee's Elective Deferrals (and Employee Contributions) will be suspended for 6 months (12 months, for hardship distributions before 2002) after the receipt of the hardship distribution.

3. In addition, for hardship distributions before 2002, all plans maintained by the Employer must provide that the employee may not make Elective Deferrals for the employee's taxable year immediately following the taxable year of the hardship distribution in excess of the applicable limit under Code § 402(g) for such taxable year less the amount of such employee's Elective Deferrals for the taxable year of the hardship distribution.

* * *

Appendix H

Employee Benefit Limits

Marjorie Martin
Aon Consulting

Many of the dollar thresholds used in limiting the level of benefits available through tax-advantaged programs are adjusted to reflect changes in the consumer price index (CPI) relative to the base period used for each limit. The limit for a particular year is adjusted based on the cumulative increase through the third quarter of the preceding calendar year. The adjusted limits are then rounded down to the nearest multiplier specified for the particular limit. The limits for 2009, for example, are based on the CPI factors through the third quarter of 2008. The Economic Growth and Tax Relief Reconciliation Act of 2001 (EGTRRA) overrides many of the pre-EGTRRA CPI adjustments with specific increases over a five-year period before CPI increases restart for items with fixed increments. The following table reflects these fixed limits.

Indexing of Employee Benefit Limits

	Calendar Year				
Purpose	*2005*	*2006*	*2007*	*2008*	*2009*
Base 402(g) deferral limit	$ 14,000	$ 15,000	$ 15,500	$ 15,500	$ 16,500
457 limit	$ 14,000	$ 15,000	$ 15,500	$ 15,500	$ 16,500
401(k)/403(b)/457/ SARSEP,[1] catch-up deferrals	$ 4,000	$ 5,000	$ 5,000	$ 5,000	$ 5,500
SIMPLE limit	$ 10,000	$ 10,000	$ 10,500	$ 10,500	$ 11,500
SIMPLE catch-up deferrals	$ 2,000	$ 2,500	$ 2,500	$ 2,500	$ 2,500
IRA/Roth-IRA limit	$ 4,000	$ 4,000	$ 4,000	$ 5,000	$ 5,000
IRA/Roth-IRA catch-up contributions	$ 500	$ 1,000	$ 1,000	$ 1,000	$ 1,000
DB[2] maximum benefit	$170,000	$175,000	$180,000	$185,000	$195,000
DC[3] maximum addition	$ 42,000	$ 44,000	$ 45,000	$ 46,000	$ 49,000
HCE compensation[4]	$ 95,000	$100,000	$100,000	$105,000	$110,000

| Purpose | Calendar Year | | | | |
	2005	2006	2007	2008	2009
Key Employee:					
Officer[5]	$135,000	$140,000	$145,000	$150,000	$160,000
1% Owners	$150,000	$150,000	$150,000	$150,000	$150,000
Compensation[6]	$210,000	$220,000	$225,000	$230,000	$245,000
SEP threshold	$ 450	$ 450	$ 500	$ 500	$ 550
ESOP (5-year distribution factor)	$170,000	$175,000	$180,000	$185,000	$195,000
ESOP (account balance)	$850,000	$885,000	$915,000	$935,000	$985,000
Taxable wage base[7]	$ 90,000	$ 94,200	$ 97,500	$102,000	$106,800
SECA tax for self-employed individuals, combined rate	15.3%	15.3%	15.3%	15.3%	15.3%
Old-age, survivors, and disability insurance tax rate	12.4%	12.4%	12.4%	12.4%	12.4%
Hospital insurance (Medicare)	2.9%	2.9%	2.9%	2.9%	2.9%
Social Security tax for employees and employers,	7.65%	7.65%	7.65%	7.65%	7.65%
Combined rate old-age, survivors, and disability insurance tax rate	6.20%	6.20%	6.20%	6.20%	6.20%
Hospital insurance (Medicare)	1.45%	1.45%	1.45%	1.45%	1.45%

Source: Marjorie Martin, Aon Consulting, Inc., Somerset, NJ. Prepared June 7, 2009.

[1] This number represents the catch-up limit available under Code Section 414(v). Code Sections 457(b)(3) and 402(g)(7) provide separate catch-up rules that must also be considered in an appropriate situation.

[2] Defined Benefit limit applies to limitation years ending in indicated year.

[3] Defined Contribution limit applies to limitation years ending in indicated year.

[4] Compensation during the plan year beginning in the indicated year identifies Highly Compensated Employees for the following plan year.

[5] Generally, compensation during the determination year ending in the indicated year identifies Key Employees for the following plan year.

[6] Compensation limit applies to plan years beginning in indicated year. Annual compensation limits for certain eligible participants in governmental plans that followed Code Section 401(a)(17) limits (with indexing) on July 1, 1993 are: $360,000 for 2009; $345,000 for 2008, $335,000 for 2007, $325,000 for 2006, and $315,000 for 2005.

[7] Calculation differs from CPI description provided above.

Internal Revenue Code

[References are to question numbers.]

I.R.C. §

Treasury Regulations

[References are to question numbers.]

Revenue Procedures and Revenue Rulings

[References are to question numbers.]

Letter Rulings

[References are to question numbers.]

Notices and Announcements

[References are to question numbers.]

Notices

87-16	4:34, 4:36
88-38	5:7
89-25	4:22, 4:34, 4:36
97-26	2:18
97-50	2:18
98-49	1:31, 3:69
99-41	2:18
2000-39	2:26, 2:31
2001-42	10:4
2001-61	2:14
2002-27	1:3, 9:62, 9:64
2002-62	2:18
2003-3	1:3
2004-8	2:4
2004-83	2:18
2006-44	2:46, 10:4
2007-7	6:8, 8:3, 9:2, 9:3
2007-7, Q&A-17	3:59, 3:60
2007-7, Q&A-18	3:59, 3:60
2007-7, Q&A-19	3:59, 3:60
2008-30	1:3, 3:1, 3:12, 3:30, 3:50, 3:52, 3:53, 3:55, 6:8

Notices

2008-30, Q&A-2	3:64
2008-30, Q&A-3	3:61
2008-30, Q&A-5	3:58
2008-30, Q&A-6	3:62
2008-30, Q&A-7	3:58–3:60
2008-102	2:1
2009-9	5:1, 5:12, 7:14

Announcements

91-179	9:27
93-8	1:32
97-122	1:13, 1:20, 1:22
99-2	1:17, 2:48
99-57	3:38, 3:71
99-104	3:38, 3:71
2001-106	2:36
2002-49	1:30
2005-80	2:4
2007-55	1:30
2008-44	4:22

Employee Retirement Income Security Act

[References are to question numbers.]

Economic Growth and Tax Relief Reconciliation Act

[References are to question numbers.]

Department of Labor Regulations and Advisory Opinions

[References are to question numbers.]

Code of Federal Regulations

[References are to question numbers.]

Pension Protection Act

[References are to question numbers.]

United States Code

[References are to question numbers.]

Table of Cases

[References are to question numbers.]

C

D

E

R

S

Index

[References are to question numbers.]

E

W

Z